FRANCESCO CAROTTA
Jesus was Caesar

FRANCESCO CAROTTA

Jesus was Caesar

On the Julian Origin of Christianity

AN INVESTIGATIVE REPORT

translated by
Tommie Hendriks
Joseph Horvath
Manfred Junghardt
Ed Young

with a foreword
by Fotis Kavoukopoulos
and an afterword
by Erika Simon

2005 ASPEKT

Revised version of the German original

Original title: War Jesus Caesar?
© Francesco Carotta, Kirchzarten, Germany
© 1999 Wilhelm Goldmann Verlag, München
Verlagsgruppe Bertelsmann GmbH
© 2005 Uitgeverij Aspekt b.v.
Amersfoortsestraat 27, 3769 AD Soesterberg, The Netherlands
info@uitgeverijaspekt.nl / http://www.uitgeverijaspekt.nl
Bibliography, Glossary and Chronology: Tommie Hendriks
Cover design: © Peter Koch
Flap photograph: © Tommie Hendriks
Setting and layout: Die Kontraster, Freiburg, Germany
Print: Krips b.v., Meppel, The Netherlands

Expert assessment archaeology: Erika Simon, Ph.D.
Expert assessment linguistics: Fotis Kavoukopoulos, Ph.D.
Expert assessment theology: Gert Lüderitz, epigraphist

ISBN: 90-5911-396-9

All rights reserved. No part of this publication may be reproduced
in any form or by any means without the written permission of the publisher.

For
Margarete

Publications

This work was preceded by four publications on the subject, where the thesis was first formulated and a further elaboration was announced:

1. *BellaMadonna/Memoria 2089*, Cam Ed.: Almanac of the Kore Verlag, Freiburg i.Br. 1988, ISBN 3-926023-75-9. 'Madonna mia' (p.9-15), Cam.
2. Cover story in the *Stadtzeitung* (City Newspaper) of Freiburg i.Br. n 4, April 1989: 'Jesses! Madonnenerscheinung in der Wiehre' (Jesus, my goodness! Apparition of the Madonna in the Wiehre), (Magazin: p.22-24) Cam & Blumenteig.
3. *BellaMadonna/Memoria 2090*, Cam Ed.: Almanac of the Kore Verlag, Freiburg i.Br. 1989, ISBN 3-926023-76-7. 'Caesars Kreuzigung—Das Evangelium nach Kleopatra' (Caesar's crucifixion—The Gospel according to Cleopatra), (p.I-IX), Cam.
4. *die tageszeitung*, Berlin, Monday, December 23, 1991: 'Jesus Christus, Caesar incognito' (Jesus Christ, Caesar incognito), (whole last page, 'die Wahrheit' (The Truth): p.20), Cam.

After the publication of the Dutch edition an article on the study described in this book was published in the specialist journal *Quaderni di Storia*:

- *Quaderni di Storia*, Edizioni Dedalo, Bari, n° 57, gennaio-giugno 2003, 'Il Cesare incognito – da Divo Giulio a Gesù', Francesco Carotta. (Palchetto: p. 357-375). ISSN 0391-6936 88-220-2557-1.

Contents

	Foreword by Fotis Kavoukopoulos	9
	Introit	11
I	Prima Vista	31
II	Vitae Parallelae	47
III	Crux	59
	Excursus – Re-Orientation	125
IV	Words and Wonders	169
V	Synoptic Comparison	213
	Final Observations – History	325
	Afterword by Erika Simon	357
	Notes	359
	Chronology	475
	Glossary	482
	Literature	490
	Illustrations	506
	Maps	510
	Acknowledgements	512

Fotis Kavoukopoulos

Foreword

Reading Francesco Carotta's book has fascinated me, as would a novel, leading the mind of the reader step by step to the solution of an obscure intrigue. This voyage was like a liberating and exhilarating breath of fresh air which progressively swept away prejudices and received ideas. But if this push towards my illumination succeeded—even beyond the author's contribution to any number of methodological presuppositions concerning philology, social psychology, ethnology and the connection of political history with theology—it was because he had had the audacity to attack the words themselves of the Gospels in order to map out their hidden side: not simply their history but especially the irresistible dynamics of their dislocation.

This is not to say that Saussure had not prepared me, in theory, for this shock. The linguist who had worked extensively on anagrams and who had warned well about what can happen to a tradition in the course of its transmission, writes in one of his notes: 'Imagining that a legend commences with a meaning, has still the same meaning since its first inception, or even to imagine that it cannot have had any meaning at all, is an operation beyond my comprehension.'

It is the opposite of what the savants have done with the texts originating from oral traditions by superposing on the logic and economy of the oral productions their identitary vision of the edition of written texts. It is the case for the Homeric oral tradition where the entirely natural variations in every oral recitation by every bard, are traced back to a single invariable text that is supposed authentic. According to the working hypothesis of the book, that is also the case for a Hellenistic text coming from a certain manuscript tradition, like the Gospel of Mark, whose Latin origin would be incompatible with the idea of a text transmitted once and for all by the deity. Actually, here philology and theology find their common limits and point of departure: the truth of meaning, be it that of the order of mythology or of religious revelation can only be guaranteed in the closed universe of a controlled scripture. Scripta manent …

The presentation of Mr. Carotta has the advantage of recognizing the major importance of dislocations and slips from one form to another and from one meaning to another in the transmission of an ancient oral or written text. The fault that was opened due to technical failings of the means of oral transmission, has allowed, e.g. in the dynastic courts of Ionia of the eighth century BC, the appropriation of ancient Mycenaean oral poetry and from it the making of those Homeric poems that glorify the ancestors of the princes and even the colonization of Ionia; the failings in the transmission of manuscripts would have allowed certain dominant groups in the orient at the time of the Imperium Romanum *to make the cult of Caesar a Judaizing and Hellenizing religion.*

Now Mr. Carotta demonstrates that this process can only take place upon a background of puns, lapses and misapprehensions mixed together. It is the same process that creates the argots of particular social groups but also our own idiolects and which, more widely, makes the languages evolve over the course of time. From this point of view etymology (which means 'true origin') is just the search for conscious or unconscious mistakes occurring with the speakers that have primarily altered the form and/or meaning of the words. On the basis of this book, one can ask oneself whether it would not also be interesting, instead of going backwards towards whatever origin of the words, to illustrate the processes of their deformation and reshaping which are carried out by the speakers again and again as time goes by.

In any case, Carotta's book, while it presents itself as a research into the 'true' Gospels, produces before our eyes a series of puns and misunderstandings, the genitors of another text, a text far away from its origin (as seen by the output). This last one, however, has arisen from a 'false' conviction that by demolishing its philological supports nullified its theological essence. Now, after the reconstructions of the author, one observes, that even there (or particularly there?) where, as with Mark, it can be a matter of transition from one language to another and not only from one epoch to another, the roads taken by the authors and copyists remain those of the evolution of all speaking; that the life of spoken language creeps in between the words of the text and furnishes them with a completely new meaning and poses a completely new series of questions to the exegetes.

Introit

This is a research report. However, it is written so that it can be easily understood by the interested layperson.

The impetus for this study was an article published in 1959 by R. Herbig, entitled 'Neue Studien zur Ikonographie des Gaius Iulius Caesar.' It was apparent from this article that the preserved images of Caesar did not correspond to the mental image we hold of him. The triggering factor for the book in hand was the sight of Caesar's portrait in the Torlonia Museum (cf. ill. 8, 10, 12, 17) and Erika Simon's comment that it might be the head of the statue that Antonius had placed on the Rostra after the assassination of Caesar. It bore the inscription 'Parenti optime merito—to the most meritorious parent', in order to awaken feelings of both pity and revenge in the observer. In function and expression the Torlonia head resembled the sorrowful face of Christ in the Pietà and since Pietà representations are typical for Jesus Christ but not for Julius Caesar, the question arose as to whether the later Jesus borrowed other elements from the earlier Caesar.

Asked about this, theologians said it was not surprising since even emperor Vespasianus was reported to have healed the blind and crippled, exactly as described in the stories about Jesus. Such things were simply expected from the emperor's charisma. Curious because of this, the author started investigating.

As a linguist and computer scientist he felt himself addressed professionally. Because he soon noticed that both curricula vitae, that of Caesar and that of Jesus, ran parallel. He also found that the names of people and places hardly differentiate in either report: Gallia *and* Galilaea, Corfinium *and* Cafarnaum, Junius *and* Judas, Màrìa *and* Marìa, Nicomedes of Bithynia *and* Nicodemus of Bethania, Pontifex Lepidus *and* Pontius Pilatus, *etc. In addition, he noticed that other names, dissimilar to each other, seemed to be translations: the* Caecilii *as the blind, the* Claudii *as the lame,* Metellus *as mutilated, the man with a withered hand. And those conquered by Caesar are found again, as those healed by Jesus. And those besieged by Caesar are possessed in the Jesus story—whereby it was noticed that 'besieged' and 'possessed' are both 'ob-*

sessus' in Latin. Even the respective figures close to them correspond with each other. For example, Caesar's precursor and opponent, the great Pompeius, was beheaded and his head presented in a dish, and the very same thing happens to John the Baptist.

There are differences to be ascertained. Both were murdered; Caesar, however, was stabbed while Jesus was crucified—but with a stab wound in his side. A Cassius Longinus *gave Caesar the deadly stab with a dagger, while Jesus was stabbed with a lance on the cross—but also by a* Longinus! *(This* Longinus *became a saint, and his feast day is on March 15—the same date as the ides of March, on which Caesar was murdered by the homonymous* Longinus*). Caesar's corpse was burned unlike Jesus', but it was shown to the people as a wax figure hanging on a cross-shaped tropaeum. And* cremo *in Latin means 'to cremate', but the similar sounding Greek word* kremô *means 'to hang', 'to crucify'.*

So, in the history of Caesar and Jesus, people and places have the same names. But even more important is the fact that these names appear in the same order. And this also applies to famous citations. Often verbatim:

Caesar: *'Who is not on any side, is on my side.'* Jesus: *'Who is not against us, he is for us.'*

Caesar: *'I am not King, I am Caesar.'* About Jesus: *'We have no king but Caesar.'*

Caesar: *'The best death is a sudden death.'* Jesus: *'What you will do (i.e. lead me to death) do quickly.'*

Caesar: *'Oh, have I saved them, that they may destroy me?'* About Jesus: *'He saved others, himself he cannot save.'*

Sometimes with a small, discreet shift of meaning:

Caesar: *'Alea iacta esto—Cast the die.'* Jesus: *'Cast out, fisher'* whereby the Greek word *'(h)aleeis',* fisher, *instead of the Latin word* 'alea', die, *is used.*

Caesar: *'Veni vidi vici—I came, I saw, I conquered.'* And in the Jesus story the blind man, who has been healed, says: *'I came, washed and saw,'* whereby *'enipsa',* I washed, *replaces* 'enikisa', *I conquered.*

In addition it turned out that contradictions in the Gospels became understandable if they were traced back to the Caesar sources. The Galilean 'Sea' for example, which is made up of fresh water and is thus not a 'sea', is named correctly however, because it is originally the 'Gallic Sea', a part of the Adriatic.

Finally, all the symbols of Christianity are anticipated in the cult of Divus Iulius, the posthumously deified Caesar: the titles (God, Son of God, the Almighty, the Merciful, the Savior or Redeemer, etc.); the Mother of God; the cross in all its variations; the crucified one; the face *on the Pietà; the crown of thorns; the long hair; the beard, the loincloth; the rod; the halo; the star of Bethlehem; the resurrection; the ascension, etc.*

Thus, recognizing they were actually one and the same story became unavoidable. To anticipate the result: Jesus proves to be Divus Iulius, the deified Caesar, passed down in tradition.

This discovery is not completely new. In the 50's the German theologian Ethelbert Stauffer noted that the Easter liturgy did not follow the Gospel narrative, but the funeral ritual of Caesar. Unfortunately, only his early work 'Christ and the Caesars' was translated into English, not his later 'Jerusalem and Rome' which stated things more clearly. What is new is the proof presented in this study that the entire Gospel is a mutated history of the Roman Civil War, from the Rubicon to the assassination and burial of Caesar, i.e. from the Jordan to the 'capture' and the 'crucifixion' of Jesus. The basis of the Marcan Gospel is to be looked for in the Historiae *of Asinius Pollio. His* Historiae *are lost to us, but were used by Appianus and Plutarchus, sometimes copied word for word, allowing for a comparison with the Gospel of Mark.*

In our study—which lasted more than ten years because the author was an entrepreneur in information systems and a publisher during that time, and could conduct research only in his spare time—we have often taken direct routes, detours, and even wrong turns because of general assumptions that proved to be misleading. For example, the communis opinio *that Jesus never wrote anything and that the Gospels were preached for a long time before anyone wrote them down. This latter assumption led to the idea that there was a grapevine form of communication which proved to be incorrect. The mistakes and distortions in the passing down occurred in the copying and translation process, in the written much more than the oral transmission. Some of these direct routes and detours can still be recognized in the text of this book. That should not irritate readers, but allow them to follow the study as it develops. While reading it should be taken into consideration that some hypotheses have been refined and reformulated during the course of the research.*

In order to not reinvent the wheel, the results of others were drawn upon where possible and appropriate. Naïve or bigoted readers who take interpolations of classical texts by ecclesiastical hand seriously, such as the so-called Testimonium Flavianum *or the supposed mention of Christ in Tacitus or Suetonius, and unwittingly—or against one's better judgement—accept them as pure fact, have come to the wrong place: for we will not fight nor defend windmills. But supposedly progressive people who think that the Gospels are only fabricated fairy tales will also learn otherwise. The Gospels, even if naively distorted and disguised, are true history just as the Church has always maintained. We ask the reader to read with an open mind, or to simply not read it at all.*

The results of this investigation are not a matter of debate anyway, and being objective facts cannot be argued away. Just as the earth does not stop rotating on its axis simply because the Church had such trouble getting along with Galileo or because we continue to speak romantically of sunsets, Jesus does not stop being Divus Iulius simply because obscurantists today, once again, do not want it to be true, or because believers continue to habitually name him so in prayer, as non-believers do in curses.

The reader might ask why the disclosure presented here has not spread like wildfire if it is valid, or why the whole world is not talking about it. This has been and is discussed, among other places on our website (www.carotta.de/forum.html). Mainly two reasons have been supposed.

The first is that hardly anyone dares to stand up for a theory they do not feel competent in. Nowadays there is such specialization of knowledge that it is difficult to find anyone who possesses equal knowledge of both Caesar and Jesus, and is at the same time familiar with all the historical, archeological, text-critical, philological, linguistic and methodological questions involved, and who is also trained in logic and well versed in Latin as well as Greek or Aramaic, etc. All honest scholars reach a point where they say: as far as my area of expertise is concerned the information is correct, but I cannot speak for the other areas involved. This, of course, allows the dishonest the opportunity to appear as if they know better and claim that everything rests on shaky foundations, giving overly cautious decision makers on historical and religious questions in the media an excuse for not touching that hot potato themselves, but leaving it to others.

The second reason is that this discovery requires a paradigm shift: away from geocentricity towards heliocentricity, away from the supposed centrality of the so-called Holy Land, back to that which today is easily forgotten—the Roman Empire. There are many things preventing this 'conversion'. One would have to admit that Christianity was already subject to deception early on, and that the history of the deceptions which were successively carried out ad maiorem Dei gloriam, *i.e. in the interest of each consecutive ruler, did not start with the fictitious Donation of Constantine, but much earlier, from the very beginning. Then it must be admitted that a successful antique dealer who understood supply and demand palmed relics off on Helena, mother of Constantine; that the Crusades were undertaken to liberate a holy grave that was never in Jerusalem, while at the same time the real grave in Rome was destroyed as a heathen relic; that Caesar is honored incognito in churches, temples and mosques throughout the entire world, and that the controversial dictator shapes the residual religious-moral backbone of the* Oikoumene, *i.e. our global community. That's a bit much! It is understandable that some people hope that chalice passes them by, and there are again priests, this time priests of the media, who refuse to look through Galileo's telescope.*

A third reason could be given. The basic approach of this research is in the spirit of the Enlightenment. It is part of a long chain that goes from Laurentius Valla, (exposure of the Donation of Constantine as a forgery) via Voltaire, (If God created Man in His own image, Man has more than reciprocated), to Bruno Bauer, (the original Gospel writer is found in Roman Hellenism). But paradoxically it concedes that the Church is right, which has always maintained that the Gospels describe a true story. Moving the events from Rome to Jerusalem is less a falsification than if the whole story were fabricated. As a result this disclosure threatens to alienate its natural allies who now say they have not fought ecclesiastical obscurantism for centuries in order to reap the emperor as God! We had almost succeeded in presenting Jesus as pure myth and now he returns historically real, yes, even as an actual person. Over our dead bodies! (By which it is meant ours, not theirs!)

This research is in accordance with the Protestant demand for free inquiry and critical examination of the Scriptures, a demand to which we owe, among other things, the search for the historical Jesus which admittedly failed, but at the same time laid false or naïve ideas to rest. In the final result, however, it demonstrates that scripture is less reliable than tradition which has retained more of the Divus Iulius Cult and is therefore less adulterated. Even more difficult to accept is the fact that Jesus, alias Divus Iulius, was pontifex maximus *i.e. during his lifetime he assumed the same office as the present Roman pope who is not recognized by Protestants. This might result in the loss of the other inner church allies also. And it will help little to ask them to remember that Caesar, although a Roman himself, waged war against the old Rome expressly to establish a new order.*

That allies could instead arise on the other front is hardly probable, though theoretically possible. The traditionalists are namely at their wit's end and have lately started admitting it. Even Ratzinger, fierce defensor fidei *at the Vatican, recently confessed that the greatest obstacle in spreading the faith today is the fact that the historical existence of Jesus can no longer be made credible. This is understandable, because if due to lack of a historical Jesus, the only concrete thing left is no long-*

er the resurrection, but merely the belief of the early Christian community in the resurrection, what happens to Easter then? And how can an empty grave have any meaning when he who should lie there never existed? The death and resurrection of God which took place in this world are reduced to sheer symbols and are in danger of being eliminated from the world—along with the Church. But now, with Jesus as Divus Iulius, as the deified Caesar, no one can claim any longer that he did not historically exist, because no mortal or immortal had a more real and tangible historical presence. Believers would finally have a reason to rejoice, even to triumph. But, just as a man cannot make a horse drink the water he has led him to, we cannot force people to be happy with this. And the anxiety accompanying the exposure of this historical deception will be felt more deeply by the most well-meaning, orthodox people. So from this camp too, the unexpected allies will be no multitude.

A fourth reason lies finally in the fact that like with every solution to a mystery, this one also has a disappointing effect. The end of delusion also means the end of illusion. The charm of myth is gone, the fairy tale has been dreamt, waking up is sobering—it would be nice to dream awhile longer. Dracula is no longer intriguing when one knows that he really was Prince Vlad Tepes Draculea. The hieroglyphics were much more interesting before Champollion, when allegorical meanings could be attached to them in salons. Galileo is not as much fun as Von Däniken. Thus, while the archeologist and devout Catholic Erika Simon did not hesitate to write the afterword to this book and to stand by it with her good name, self-named protectors of the fabulating orthodoxy did not want 'to take the people's Jesus away from them' (literally quoted from a statement by the religion department of a television station that vetoed a documentary about this research) especially when they themselves thrive on it, sometimes fabulously. Yet this is the most beautiful of all fairy tales that Caesar, removed from the world, posthumously and incognito could dwell in our religious dreams, a true incubo *of the world*.

* * *

Formulating the assertion—Jesus was Caesar—might seem strange. This has less to do with the claim itself than with our images of Caesar and Jesus. These images, as those of the most important personalities of the world's Pantheon, were always more shaped by myth than reality and even today they depend more on the zeitgeist than on objective knowledge. In our minds Caesar is a hardcore Roman commander (who would associate him with his proverbial clemency, his compassion for the enemy?) whereas Jesus is supposed to be a peaceful wandering preacher—his 'I did not come to bring peace, but the sword' is meanwhile more often falsely attributed to the prophet Mohammed.

Yearning for a peaceful world led to a polarized distortion of both images. They became such self-evident truths that no one ever questions them.

One hardly knows Caesar from school, but from historical films and comics. He is apparently accused of being the father of all dictators. Since he cannot be classified as 'a Hitler', or 'a Stalin', attempts are made to blank him out, at least: A short history of antiquity recently published in Germany not only devoted no chapter to him, but not even a paragraph; he was mentioned only in passing beside Cicero. No biography of Caesar published after WWII tells of his funeral: they all end with his assassination so that both author and reader can give in to the unrestrained frenzy of the supposed tyrannicide and do not get in the embarrassing situation of having to mention or even more to explain the fact that the people revolted against his assassins and achieved his apotheosis. But whether or not a person's funeral belongs with their life story would be a good question. So one leaves him unburied rather than contend with the demon of his resurrection. Caesar commander, Caesar dictator: yes; Caesar pontifex maximus, *Caesar son of Venus, Caesar himself God: no.*

It is much the same with Jesus, and even so just the opposite. No one knows him anymore either. Who reads the Gospel nowadays? Yearnings for the original Church and early Christianity only allow for idealized images of him, oleographs, pure and innocent, in opposition to the Christian one corrupted in history. Even more so since textual criticism and the search for the historical Jesus has questioned his existence for centuries, so that everyone can form their own unrestrained image of Jesus. If he never existed then he could have been anything, and even more so, can become anything. Exorcist, resistance fighter, labor activist, national hero, feminist, gay, black, Jew—he can and must be everything and anything. But just not a dictator and not a Roman! He cannot come from the empire of evil, much less have founded it! Although everyone knows that Christianity spread within the borders of the Roman Empire, under Romans, and that the head of Christianity is today still seated in Rome.

Thus our own more or less unconscious images form the main hindrance to formulating the question: Was Jesus Caesar? We will see that targets and actuals differ considerably in this balance sheet also. Jesus and Caesar have more similarities than imaginable. It was not pure chance that both of them conquered the world in sandals.

The second thing that must be known is that this is not a debate about questions of religion, but merely of the history of religion—more precisely: about the archaeology of religion. The discussion is not about belief in Jesus, but only who the historical Jesus was.

Now the believing Christian as well as the unbelieving atheist might be of the opinion that it is obvious who Jesus was or was not, in whom they do/do not believe: the miracle worker, barefoot prophet from Galilee, who under Pontius Pilate was put to death under uncertain circumstances in Jerusalem and whose followers believe he rose from the dead.

Unfortunately, it is not that simple, because while Christianity is a factor that screams for the historical existence of its auctor, it is also a fact that no classical historian knew Jesus. He is only impeccably documented in the Gospels (the 'historical references' given are too late and doubtful). That is why even the existence of Jesus became a subject of faith, not only his resurrection and teachings. That is the historical mystery, the true messianic secret of Jesus that to date has found no rational solution.

We suggest a change of scene, and abandon the opposing ditches in which the two enemy parties remain entrenched. We simply assume, as in mathematics, that the problem is solved and so we examine under what conditions that is the case. If both are correct, that Jesus Christ had to exist historically for Christianity to come into being, but at the same time the thaumaturgic itinerant preacher from Galilee could never have existed otherwise classical historians would have made timely reports of it, then the only possibility is that Jesus existed somewhere else and was later resettled in Galilee.

By a remarkable coincidence, 100 years before the supposed birth of Jesus another god-man was born, Gaius Julius Caesar, a righteous man, who was also murdered and elevated to the Gods after his death. Then a resettlement actually did take place, namely that of his veterans who were recruited in Gallia and resettled throughout the entire Empire, among other places in Galilaea, in the territory of King Herodes who was allied with the Romans.

Since the life story of both of these god-men, Jesus and Divus Iulius, show such amazing parallels (listing them is the purpose of this book), we are forced to recognize them as one and the same story, one that has been mutated and delocalized in the process of tradition and translation. In the same way a faithful Brazilian today would say that Saint Francis was not born in Assisi (Umbria), but in Assis (Rio Grande do Sul) or that St. George killed the dragon in Bahia, that he even came from that city, the liberator of Corfinium coming from Gallia became *the exorcist of Cafarnaum coming from Galilee: Julius Caesar became Jesus Christ. Just as St. Francis wandered from Assisi to Assis as soon as Europeans resettled in the Americas, Divus Iulius of Gallia wandered to Galilee as the legionaries recruited in Gallia settled as veterans in Galilaea. The linguistic shift, here Italian and Portuguese (Assisi > Assis), there Latin and Greek (Gallia > Galilaia; Corfinium > Cafarnaum) helped to make the imported God and/or saint a native. Stories wander and are revised to fit in, then and now: the Christ child in the manger in Brazil is in some places a small native and in others a little black infant just as the Seven Samurai became cowboys in the American remake of the film. Resettlement resets stories.*

The third thing that should be known, which preoccupies the nonreaders more than the readers, is where the journey goes: What are the consequences?

There is no reason to panic here either. The journey goes nowhere, there are no consequences—for now. The believer will continue to believe in his Jesus, and say to himself that it does not matter to him who the historical Jesus was, even if it must be Caesar, the main thing is, he did exist. The nonbeliever will be happy that there is proof that Jesus never existed and accept that he was Caesar, the main thing is, he never existed. Both will have to revise their image of Caesar, but that will pain them little, because one gets it almost exclusively from Hollywood or Asterix nowadays, (and that is plainly not the historical Caesar). The bomb under Christianity which is either feared or evoked will not ignite—at least not yet.

In the long term a change in consciousness will occur, however. Nothing is as before. One listens differently to Bach's St. Matthews Passion when one knows it is really played for the divine Caesar. Easter is experienced differently when one knows that it is the death and resurrection of the historical Divus Iulius being celebrated. Caesar's De Bello Civili *is read differently when it is known that this book is the personally written Gospel of Jesus Christ. The four Gospels are read differently also, when we know that the first version came from God himself, who personally wrote history, but the second version was written by men who wrote history as they comprehended it, and the last version was written simply by jackasses who were faithful, but copied again and again according to their understanding and misunderstanding. Under these conditions it is not possible to rely solely on scripture or faith, neither* sola fide *nor* sola scriptura *helps. But now it is possible to distance ourselves from all those unspeakable conciliar disputes and schisms of belief which poisoned history and divided people when we know that the disputes were among jackasses who long since did not know of what and of whom they spoke and that in these quarrels blind orthodox believers sent one-eyed heretics, one after another, into the desert.*

It will have a crucial effect to know again, and know definitely, that Jesus was a Roman and not a Jew as the Jews have generally always claimed. They did not know and persistently denied this man, who supposedly came from their people. Thus the charge that the Jews were the murderers of God is finally cleared out of the way, since Caesar was murdered by the 'Junii' and not the 'Jews'. At the same time the idea that Jesus descended from the Jewish people can also be dismissed— which just might desacralize the relationship with them and deliver them from the tragic situation of eternal persecution and/or eternal claim for reparation.

Church fathers who have been stamped as heretics will be belatedly rehabilitated, such as Marcion—who said the God of the New Testament, the God of love and salvation has nothing to do with the old one, the God of righteousness and revenge, who maintained that the Gospels and the letters of Paul were forged by Judaists—or as Tatianus who testified that the genealogy of Jesus was fictitiously added in order to make him a descendant of David. The cult of the emperor, recognized more and more as the forerunner of Christianity, must be studied with different eyes. Above all we will understand those who say opposition between the Old and the New Covenants is an oriental metaphor for the old Rome of the and the new Rome of Caesar; between the old order, righteous but exploiting, and the new order, liberating and promoting brotherly love; or as poets have observed, between ROMA and its mirror image AMOR.

The relationship to religion will change. If one knows that religion is the form in which an empire survives its fall, can a religion still be regarded as something private? If baptism represents, not only symbolically but also historically, the recruiting of legionaries for Christ—i.e. in reality the pledge of allegiance taken to the Julian emperor—should we be surprised by fundamentalism? What kind of tolerance might be expected then except the mercy of the victor? If one knows that the cult of Divus Iulius represents the origin of Christianity, is the longed for early Christianity to be seen in it? If Islam or possibly even Buddhism (see final chapter) are only other forms of the same primary cult, may we cherish the hope of returning to the historical unity of all believers once again? And if we know that Caesar, although God's Son and even God himself (or maybe for that very reason), personally did not believe in life after death, will it be possible that believers and non-believers meet in him?

***

This English edition, revised and with added material, appears in spring 2005, shortly after the third Dutch edition. The first Dutch edition appeared in November 2002, three years after the original German edition, thanks to the engagement of Tommie Hendriks, experimental psychologist who initiated the translation sua sponte *and Jan van Friesland, television programming director who made sure this research became known and thus led the way to having the book published.*

Like the Dutch translation, this English one also originates from the initiative of readers who were of the opinion that this text absolutely should be available to those who don't know German. I personally would have preferred a Latin translation, however since English currently happens to be the most globally understood language as our translators argued, I did not wish to resist further, and so complied with their desire after all and did my part to assist them.

Now some of them prefer British English, the others American English. Therefore a middle course was sought to satisfy all, but it possibly leaves everyone unhappy in the end. And I don't know whether by doing this we have contributed to a desirable English koine *or have done it a disservice. Hopefully the reader will be mesmerized by the content so much that he condones the style changing from chapter to chapter and even sometimes within a chapter, depending on the translating hand.*

I thank Manfred Junghardt, a German surgeon living in the Caribbean, who took the initiative and started the translation process together with Tommie Hendriks, experimental psychologist from Utrecht, at the same time translator of the Dutch edition. In the course of time others joined: Joseph Horvath, an American who grew up in Germany, psychologist; Ed Young in Hawaii, an American computer technician and writer.

Each did their best to make this translation easy to read and at the same time true to the original. I thank them not least for the patience they had with a pedantic author and incorrigible Latinist who would rather see the English language maltreated than carry out adjustments.

The process of translation with six initially unpracticed persons (in addition to the four named above there were two more who also took part—we express our thanks to them—but have opted out), and from them all hardly one was perfectly bilingual, proved to be extremely awkward and demanding, but also amusing and instructive. To name but two examples: One of us mistook Paul's 'Cilicia' for 'Sicilia'; another 'Aramaic' for 'Armenian', by which we demonstrated that we, too, are perfectly capable of making confusions and the delocalizations to accompany them. It was no different for reviewers: One of them once rendered 'Scipio' as 'Scorpio' and 'Hortensius' as 'Horrensius'. If we did not have modern e-mail's fast correction and control possibilities at our disposal, and if the erroneous texts had simply been copied manually and sent into the world like two thousand years ago, to even be used as the basis for further translations into other languages or for back-translations, we would then be in the same fine mess that we amazingly find was the case with the Evangelists.

And so, arriving at the end of the process we are all more experienced and the wiser, and we can smile about our situation and feel a little like Evangelists ourselves. At any rate, in translating and writing we, too, have tried to serve the truth and God.

May readers enjoy the book and may the reading of it be fruitful for all: donum bonae frugi.

But enough said: Let us rather let the translators have a word themselves—including the one who is working on a Spanish version.

Saturday, July 13, 2002 (Caesar's birthday 2102nd) — revised 2005.

***

When someone is interested in history, he cannot avoid the phenomenon of religion. And I am interested in history. I had to realize that the moving and formative forces exerted by the different religions were very important for the development of history. Whole societies or parts of them rose or faded away as a result of religious movements. But where have the displaced rulers gone—how did gods and goddesses come into being? Where are their archetypes?

There were and there are too many of them, each carrying the respective features of the culture that revered them. Why is this so? The polytheistic division of labor was brought to an end by monotheism. The river-god of the early farmer then became the one and only God of a society or even of several peoples. After its complete development monotheism tied the Jewish people together. For whom was it useful then to invent a son of God, a duplication of God, which appears as a logical contradiction to me? At this point the author starts and shows with all his analytical tools of the trade how a living and adored God of those times—Caesar—became the Son of God, the Christ.

The reading of this book fascinated me, because of its detailed analysis of the historical situation, which too often also became a religious statement, because it met the political will and usefulness.

And if it was very stimulating for me to understand and classify religious-historical relationships, why should this pleasure be withheld from English readers?

This was the most important point to me for participating in the translation.

Manfred Junghardt—Waren/Müritz

***

The milieu of my childhood was not marked by a strong religious zeal. Now and then my father would put such fervor into perspective. If you started to answer a question of his with 'I believe', he could at times interrupt you by saying with a smile, 'Believing is what you do in church, my son. Here, you have to know for sure.' By the time I went to high school much of my youthful interest in what happened on Sundays in church had faded. During Mass I kept myself busy by rehearsing the Latin texts in my missal and comparing them with their Dutch counterparts. I still know the Lord's Prayer by heart: Pater noster qui es in caelis…

Not long thereafter I must have come to the understanding that the Gospel presents us with quite a lot of physical impossibilities, such as walking on water and raising the dead. The introduction to the so-called arguments for the existence of the Supreme Being strengthened this understanding. The peculiar idea that the Gospel had been written under the influence of an active agent from the transcendent world—on God's orders so to speak—expressed a logic you could not easily argue with and you preferred to stay in line with the brilliant savant Laplace, who, after explaining the complete astronomy to Napoleon, answered the emperor's remark that God was not mentioned in his treatise with 'Sire, I do not need that hypothesis.' His countryman Voltaire did not need it either and said so roguishly: 'If God made us in his image, we have certainly returned the compliment.' Indeed, the concept of God as a product of the human mind is a widespread notion in our Western world. God resides in our grey matter, but that reason by itself does not make it less real to a great many people.

My scepticism on the historical reality of the Gospel story increased even more when I learned that the oldest manuscripts of the complete Gospel date from centuries after the actual events. In addition there is the capital fact that there are more differences among the Gospel manuscripts than there are words in the New Testament. And these differences can be quite substantial: Only two of the four Evangelists present a genealogy of Jesus, which, however, differ completely from one another in that hardly any names of the long list of Jesus' so-called ancestors provided by Matthew (1:1-17) correspond to those given by Luke (3:23-38) and in addition to this there are numerous differences in name between the manuscripts of one and the same Evangelist.

So apart from unreality the Gospel story is also marked by uncertainty and unreliability. But the greatest problem for me was to accept that the events as told by the Gospel should have triggered a world religion. It simply did not look possible to me that a barefooted preacher, sprung from the religious fundamentalism of a nomadic people once hardened in the desert, could have lit the brush fire of Christianity. For that matter, the actions of Jesus seemed to me too accidental and too implausible, his doctrine too indistinct, his words too vague and too soft. And what of the manner of his death? Well, in those days that was not sensational either. No, the words credo quia absurdum *were wasted on me. While around me Jesus sometimes was simply smoothed out as a pure, unrecoverable legend, or was at other times dissolved in a mythical mist or transformed into a sheer literary character, I was left with an enormous problem: it became increasingly clear to me that a historically satisfying explanation for the origin and early development of Chris-*

tianity had never been given. Where, for heaven's sake, is that world-shattering event, that Flood in biblical terms, the earth-shaking Sept. 11th, to use a recent image? Where is that devastating event that made it possible to redefine the abnormal, the fantastic and the physically impossible, as normal? A religious drive or need surely is a necessary condition for the genesis of a particular religion. However, it is absolutely not a sufficient condition for the genesis of a world religion. Consequently I was left with the enigma of the origin of Christianity and the paradoxical historicity of its instigator.

In my student days the problem faded into the background. I became totally absorbed in the scientific world of experimental psychology where I specialized in learning and perception. For many a year I worked at the university and took part in fundamental research in the difficult field of human olfaction. Yet, I never lost interest in historical problems. Then, in December 1999, I struck upon the German investigative report 'Was Jesus Caesar?' At first I held it to be a strange joke, but after reading the whole intriguing report I found myself in silent wonder. Had I really found the solution to the Christian enigma?

In order to avoid being taken for a ride I decided to reread the book. This time with the relevant primary literature close at hand. So I read the study meticulously a second time with the writings of Appianus, Dio Cassius, Plutarchus, Suetonius and others within reach. No matter how I tried I could not find improper or wrong use of the sources or any other mistake in the author's analysis of the parallel biographies of the two most famous men living at the start of our Western calendar. Which in itself is of course not sufficient proof of the theory that the worship of Divus Iulius—the deified Caesar—mutated within a period of some 7 generations to the cult of early Christianity. Proof of that is found in hundreds of systematic similarities between the two lives, the explanatory power of the theory as compared to the usual one, and an overwhelming amount of circumstantial evidence with regard to almost every aspect of the Christian church. Never in history had there been such great opportunity to watch the genesis of a god. Not just the genesis of some arbitrary god, but the genesis of our own personal God, who appeared to be successful for two thousand years.

I considered the findings of this German study to be so important for a world-wide and sophisticated discussion on the origins of Christianity and Islam that I felt obliged to deliver a Dutch translation and contribute to the present English version.

The inscription on Caesar's first cult statue ran PARENTI PATRIAE – usually translated as 'to the Father of the Country'. As I once was during *my childhood years, I am again on my knees in church, comparing the texts in my missal. And I read: 'Our Father who art in heaven...' and I now realize that he is neither a man nor a woman.* PARENS *is father and mother in one. Never did our god let half of humanity down.*

Tommie Hendriks—Utrecht

* * *

'Jesus Never Really Existed'. *This was the headline of an interview in* die tageszeitung (taz), *an established alternative German daily newspaper, published in the spring of 2001. The overline asked: 'Was Jesus actually Caesar, Mr. Carotta?' Now, the* taz *is known and popular with its readers for satirical headlines especially on the front page and fantastic stories which mostly appear on the last page that is titled 'the truth'. This interview, however, took up the whole of page three, it was not the issue of April 1st and seemed absolutely serious. Fascinated by the idea, I read the text several times and although—or perhaps because—as a former altar boy I felt familiar enough with the Gospel to know that Jesus could not possibly have been Caesar, nevertheless, from the reasons the interviewed man gave I had a feeling that there was some truth in it. Immediately I ordered the book and read it three times from cover to cover in the following weeks, marvelling more and more, seeing more connections each time, and soon becoming convinced that no matter how outrageous the mutation seemed it was actually true: Jesus, i.e. the historically transmitted Divus Iulius, did exist after all and still exists incognito. The latter I comprehended only later.*

It was the most informative and thrilling nonfiction work I had ever read, and it was written wittily and well at that. Had anybody told me before that I would study with such enthusiasm a book about the historical Jesus of all people, whom I long ago had banished as a pesky fairy-tale told by wet-nurses and priests, or even would intensively occupy myself with the subject, I would have laughed at them. But now, being happy with this rare find I recommended it to all my friends and with that I, in turn, came across disconcertment, fright and sometimes laughter. Wondering about the implications of this epochal discovery and the consequences it might entail I wrote a congratulations and thank-you letter to the author from which a lively, very interesting and instructive correspondence evolved. In the course of which a temporary dispute arose: With all his knowledge and ability I considered him a cleric in disguise—a misconception and confusion as I understood gradually—whereas he called me a militant atheist who willfully hurt other's religious feelings, which regrettably did occur sometimes. The preoccupation with the origin of Christianity, caused by the reading of this book, which does not require a credo quia absurdum *gave me more calm and a better understanding of religion and faith. And just as it is healing for the individual to confront his or her own past and make it conscious, the collective might also achieve a similar beneficial effect by learning the historical truth about its civilization and religion, and resolving the historical trauma.*

When the author offered me the opportunity to participate in the English translation, which, amazingly, had still not appeared by early 2003, I gladly accepted, honored by the chance to contribute to the international publication of this unique work. It was a laborious task, annoying at times due to the multitude of mistakes made in the cooperation of translators with different cultural and linguistic backgrounds, but also an enriching experience and fun, because the translation process conveyed a vivid idea and amusing practical examples of how some of those corruptions took place that produced the Gospels as we know them.

Joseph Horvath—Konstanz

* * *

It was through the Internet that I first encountered the author's historical discovery and mentions of his book. I was doing my own research for a book about ancient Roman/Jewish relations, and had somehow stumbled on this unique bombshell of an idea: that the stories of Jesus Christ had their origin in the history of Julius Caesar. At first skeptical, the more I read of this new line of research, the more convinced I became, and the more amazed.

I set my project to the side, and delved into studying Julius Caesar and the century or two of Roman history after his death more closely, while I waited impatiently for the English version of this intriguing book to be published. This was not a large setback to my own work at all. The origins of Christianity still fell within the domain of my subject matter since there is no doubt that Christianity results from a Roman and Jewish interaction. (Although in the light of this new information, I now would need to reassess many of my previous thoughts on the subject!) So I studied and found much to support what I knew of this extraordinary discovery, but the constant apple of my eye, so to speak, was to get a copy of this book and read it.

October 2003 rolled around, and still no English version was available. In frustration, I began to correspond with the author directly, and I attempted to convince him of my sympathetic interest in his ideas, and my great desire to read his book. He proved to be a friendly and engaging e-mailer, and I made every effort to be the same. One thing led to another, and he offered me a place on the translation team, which I accepted with no hesitation.

It has been many months since then, and I have never regretted my decision. Participating in the very involved process of translating a detailed work of scholarship has been educational, and it's been both greatly enjoyable and a privilege to deal closely with such intelligent, well-informed individuals who are enthusiastically interested in religion, history, and language, and are unafraid of new and challenging ideas. It has also been eerily ironic to watch a book being translated, seeing in action the problems and issues involved in it, when the book itself deals so very keenly with the process of translation, and with the mind-boggling misunderstandings that can result because of those very same problems. But most of all it has been exciting to take part in a project the subject matter of which is both close to me and my interests, and which will also be very important to many others who read this amazing book.

My lifelong fascination with history and religion certainly included Christianity, simply because it is my own religion and I have always felt an undeniable inner demand to know the full truth behind it. Having been raised as a Protestant, with a wife who is Catholic, and having decided to send our daughter to a Catholic school, the questions raised by the author's research are of some significance to me. But far from making me 'lose faith' or disdain Christianity, the surprising effect has been a deepening of my interest in and respect for Catholicism. Walking into a Catholic church for me now, is like walking into my backyard knowing that a much loved shade tree is actually a species long thought to be extinct; or it is like walking into a large time machine, perhaps a little error-prone, that is still capable of bringing a fascinating part of the distant past into the present moment. It is like looking at something you have known all your life, and yet only now seeing it for the first time with clarity, and only now fully realizing how dearly fond you are of it, how much importance and relevance and power it still has, and, joyfully, how much more it could yet become and achieve, if only, if only...

Yes, this book will be disturbing because so much turns out to be so wrong. Jesus, Christianity, Julius Caesar, Roman history, the Jewishness of Christianity, all these and more, are not at all what or who we thought they were. For example the standard perceptions of Julius Caesar, his cult, and their historical importance are incorrect and must be reexamined and something wholly unexpected resurrected in their place. He was, and is, far more important than we had ever thought. The mind reels at trying to grasp the extent of it. We cannot avoid the fact that the western world will never be the same; Christianity may even face its biggest crisis. But in crises there is opportunity. It will be up to us to find and preserve the meaning here, to steer a safe course and redefine our civilization and religion using this new and more accurate information. Perhaps if we navigate with care, if we have learned what is worth learning, we will make sure that the new definitions will include justice, love, generosity and forgiveness, just as Caesar—Jesus would want us to.

Ed Young—Honolulu

* * *

At the beginning of 2003, I was working on the preparation of a Passion Play, the 'St. Mark Passion', which I—as a Catholic priest of a Spanish village, Rascafría—have staged together with the young people and the children of the village since 1995. Although we faithfully followed the text, each year we researched many historical sources to ascertain the context and to represent it more accurately on stage. During an Internet search to learn more about the historical context and discover whether anyone else was doing something similar, I came upon the website www.carotta.de. To my astonishment, the Passion and the whole Gospel had a truly Roman context, and they do lead back to Julius Caesar.

Immediately I contacted the author. He answered all the questions I asked him with the absolute honesty of a philologist and historian. Everything that he sent to me I had checked by experts who remained pensive, perplexed, and although they told me that it was a new theory that was hard to prove, they could not prove to me that it was false. So I became engrossed in the investigation, changed the whole context of the St. Mark Passion, which after all was neither Jewish nor Essenian, but Roman, and for the first time I directed a Passion Play knowing that it was not the true story but a rewritten one.

Year after year, the alterations we had made were explained to the young people. After this performance I showed them the complete investigation and told them that the next Passion we present will be the historical, not the literary one. They agreed to that.

Now we are working on the recovery of the original 'Passio' while at the same time we are translating 'Jesus was Caesar' into Spanish. With the help and philological as well as historical advice of the author, the 'Passio' will soon be published, and with the help of the young people also staged.

Pedro García González—Madrid

I

Prima Vista

1. Denarius of L. Aemilius Buca (44 BC): CAESAR DICT(ator) PERPETVO

This is how Caesar is supposed to have looked[1] before his murder: weakened by fatigue but somehow spiritualized because of it, nearly transfigured. Here is a man of vision, of willpower and—with subtle irony—also a man of *clementia*. Already he has entered into another realm of existence. The legend on the coin reads *dictator perpetuo*, but what we are shown is *Divus Iulius*.

The dictator was the first Roman to whom the Senate granted the right to have his image minted on coins, and it happened only a few weeks before his death. In the view of the attitudes of the time this constituted a superhuman honor. While Caesar posed for him, the minter must have felt the god in his presence.

Now famous, a marble bust from Tusculum (cf.ill. 1./2./3.) has been identified as that of Caesar[2] by the typical saddle of the crown accentuated by the bold forehead, the angular jawline, the 'vulturine' neck, and—last but not least—by the ironic lines of the mouth. Here is the same vision and will, but the *clementia* is more concealed by a stronger sense of irony. One can see the ruler of the world advancing, and sense there is a claiming of ownership, and an inaccessibility. Before us is the Caesar of *veni vidi vici*.

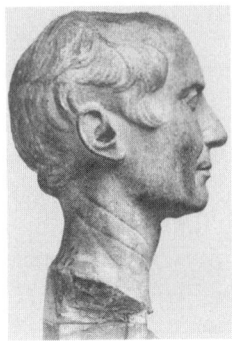  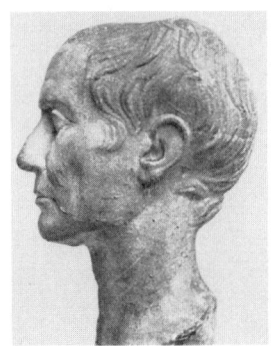

2./3./4. Tusculum head

In fact, this head could have been fashioned up to two years before the above coins were struck, because in the time between 46 and 44 BC a number of statues were consecrated to Caesar in Italy.³

In this case too, the sculptor for whom Caesar posed was obviously not unimpressed.

This marble head itself became a model for later statues during the time of the emperors, as can be seen here by its juxtaposition with the colossal head in the Farnese collection:

5. Tusculum head   6. Farnese head in Naples

Moreover, this head from Tusculum has given rise to a conjecture regarding another head in the Torlonia museum, which fascinates the researchers and leaves them divided: namely, is this his real face, or the face that met the expectations of the time? The features are the same except for the direction of the eyebrows, but the expression is completely different. This head seems to have had some influence on the later statues of Caesar, ones in which the Clementia was accentuated as it is with the head in the Vatican. For comparison, below we have set the head in the Torlonia museum between the Tusculum and the Vatican heads:

7. Tusculum head   8. Torlonia head   9. Head in Vatican

We can easily see that the latter two heads were made after the death of Caesar, as piety has restored his hair and his head shape conforms to an ideal.

But how long after Caesar's death did this take place? We know that the head in the Vatican originates from the Augustan period, but for the Torlonia head the facts are still contested. Some assign this particular specimen to the Claudian period, but they do not rule out a connection with a contemporary genesis.[4] Others think that it is an original, made shortly after Caesar's death.

Now, whether it be original or a copy of an original, the hypothesis has been proposed that this kindly face, deeply etched by suffering, yet of such strong willed countenance—an expression quite singular in the iconography of Caesar—belonged to the statue erected by Marcus Antonius on the Rostra after Caesar's murder. According to a letter of Cicero[5] it bore the legend: PARENTI OPTIME MERITO. It was to awaken feelings of both pity and revenge in the observer.[6]

If true, we would thus be standing before the Pietà of Caesar.

The question of whether Caesar himself had acted as a model to the sculptor is not rendered superfluous by the fact that he was already dead. Because at his funeral a wax figure had been made of him precisely for this occasion and placed on the Rostra by Marcus Antonius.[7] Possibly a mold of the face of the deceased Caesar had been taken for this event, and was employed again later when the statues were made. The fact that the lines are those of Caesar, but not the expression, could in-

10. Caesar's Pietà?

dicate that it was a death mask of the deceased. It follows, too, that the shape of the head would be different because the mold would only have been taken of the face.

Then it would indeed be Caesar's Pietà.[8]

In any event, it is a fact that a statue of Caesar had already been placed on the Rostra during his lifetime, for all the ancient writers substantiate it. It was part of the honors granted him after the battle of Munda, his final victory over the Pompeians. Cassius Dio even speaks of two statues:

> 'And they also set up two statues of him on the Rostra, one representing him as the Savior of the citizens and the other as the Deliverer of the city from siege, both wearing the customary wreaths for those achievements.'[9]

Laurel

One wreath was the *corona civica*—the 'citizen's crown'—made from oak leaves: those who were saved owed this to the one who had saved them. The other wreath was the *corona obsidionalis*—the 'siege crown'—braided of the grass growing in the fields where the besieged had been surrounded. This wreath was presented to the field general who had freed them.[10]

When Antonius, in early October 44, ordered the erection of the statue that we are now interested in, the other statues that had previously stood on the Rostra had already been toppled and destroyed in the disturbances after Caesar's death.[11] The one rededicated by Antonius would have replaced one of these, and to replace the second statue one was probably set up on Octavianus' column.[12] We have to imagine the above-mentioned pietà head crowned with one of these two wreaths, either of oak leaves or grass. These statues of Caesar wearing the oak crown were not only in Rome but were to be found throughout the whole empire. This was because, by dint of ancient custom, each individual saved by Caesar owed him a wreath of oak leaves. And in the course of that murderous worldwide civil war, was there anyone he had not saved? He had saved his own followers from being massacred by the enemy, on the battlefield he had spared the defeated enemy and protected them from falling victim to the rage of blind wrath or revenge. He defended them personally and even physically. Indeed, he even saved them politically by restoring them to their positions and ranks.

A corresponding decree by the Senate helped to convince the ungrateful. The inscriptions on the pediments of the numerous statues dedicated to Caesar that have survived, especially in the East, bear titles not only such as *pontifex maximus, dictator or consul,* but also *sôtêr, euergetês, patrôn, theos*—savior, benefactor, patron, god, etc.[13]

Unfortunately, the statues that belonged to these pediments have not been preserved—except for one head, found in Thasos and exhibited in the local museum.[14] It is heavily damaged and weather-beaten, but the features must have been very approximate at best, even when it was first made. In the East they were not accustomed to the same realism as in Rome. And, for images of a god, the features do not have to be realistic, but rather conform to an ideal model.

11. Head with oak wreath in Thasos

The oak wreath etched into the marble is plain to see, and it is also reminiscent of later depictions of emperors such as Augustus or Vespasianus.

But engraving the oak wreath into the marble was not the original custom. Originally he who was saved was responsible for ensuring that his savior was always provided with a wreath of fresh leaves. And the savior really wore it. Because of the zeal of his followers,[15] Caesar's statue in Rome would certainly not have lacked fresh wreaths.

If a weatherproof wreath were needed, one of metal would be provided. Indeed, if we look at the Torlonia head in profile especially towards the back of the neck, we plainly see a raised arch where the wreath would have sat:

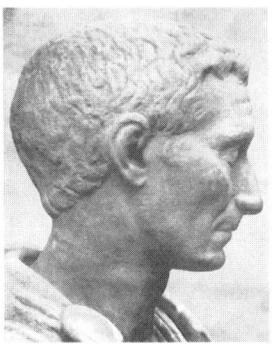

12. Torlonia head

Now what did the pietà look like with an oak wreath? With which oak wreath was it crowned and from which oak?

The shape was in fact not uniform, nor even was the way in which it was worn, as is demonstrated by the statues and coins of later emperors decorated with such wreaths. And the wreath on Caesar's head depicted on coins is never an oak wreath, but rather a triumphal wreath—the so-called laurel[16] or more precisely a golden copy based on an Etruscan design, the *corona aurea*.[17]

To Caesar, the oak wreath was the more sacred one. He earned his first as a young man serving in combat during the conquest of Mytilene. And if the confirmed partisan of Sulla, M. Minucius Thermus—the governor of Asia for whom Caesar served as a military officer—awarded the *corona civica* to the nephew of Marius who had been prosecuted by Sulla, then it is very probable that Caesar had earned it indeed, having physically saved the lives of Roman citizens in battle.[18]

This finally opened up the political career of Caesar, who had been under proscription until then, hunted by pursuers and not allowed to exercise his office as *flamen Dialis* (high priest of Jupiter). But his career was to remain ever controversial and contentious. After his victory over Pompeius and the Senatorial party at Pharsalos in 48, he ordered that his oak wreath should finally appear on coins, but it was not placed on his head, but on that of Venus, his divine ancestress.[19]

13./14. Denarii of Caesar, 48 BC; *Rev.:* Venus with oak wreath, l. number: .LII

On the reverse of these denarii we see a tropaeum with Gallic weapons, along with an axe (ill. 13.) or a prisoner (14.). Beneath the tropaeum, or with it in a cross formation, is his name: CAESAR. The message was clear: he had freed all Romans from the ancestral threat of the Gauls, so now all Roman citizens owed their lives to him. But doubly indebted were those who, instead of being grateful, had tried to rob him and his legionaries of their triumph and the rewards due them for their grueling nine-year long campaign. His enemies had wanted the war, but now, defeated, they had to rely on his grace and consider themselves lucky that *Venus Genetrix*, mother Venus, was nevertheless still so peace loving and merciful.

And just to make it clear who it was symbolized by the head of Venus, he had added his age, LII – 52, on the other side precisely where Cupid appeared in the same series.[20] A new era had begun,[21] and all of the people could now start celebrating the birthday of their savior, and of their *parens*, who had given them the gift of life. But it is well known how they carried out their duty: they waited a long time until the opportunity finally arose—and they murdered him.

And then the oak wreath promptly migrated to another head—that of Brutus. Interestingly, the depiction of this oak wreath with its totally different meaning in the year 42 has been passed down to us in near perfect condition. That is because this murderer of Caesar immortalized his deed on a gold coin:[22]

15. Aureus of Brutus; both Bruti with an oak wreath

On one side is depicted the ancient Brutus who had driven the last kings out of town (509 BC), on the other side he himself—the new Brutus—who, emulating his ancestor, had freed the city and the world of the new king Caesar. Hence the reasoning for the oak wreaths: both Bruti had saved every single citizen from tyranny, even from death, because a life by Caesar's grace was the death of a free citizen—at least in Brutus' thinking.

And nobody knew this better than he himself, for he was exactly in that situation. Although ever favoured and protected by Caesar (there were rumors that this occurred for his mother Servilia's sake, and the talk of the town was that he even was Caesar's son), Brutus fought on the side of his uncle Cato in the civil war against Caesar. Then, among the defeated at Pharsalos, he was pardoned by Caesar and even taken into his circle of friends and assisted in a further career. Now the prodigal son had murdered such a tyrant.

His gold coins propagated the idea that he, Brutus, was the true savior of the citizens, not Caesar. Accordingly, his coins bore the same wreath as had Venus on Caesar's coins, and as the statue of Caesar did in Rome and throughout the empire.

Isolated, Brutus' wreath looks like this:

16. Brutus' *corona* – isolated

It seems to be made out of *quercus ilex* with its small and pointed leaves. We are still in the pre-Augustan period, and so this wreath too, like that of Caesar's Venus, has a graceful, Hellenistic look.

If we set it upon the Torlonia head with the help of computer graphics we obtain this result:

17. Caesar's Pietà with *corona quercea*

The Torlonia head now looks very much like an image of Jesus with his crown of thorns.

Unfortunately it is not possible for us to repeat the same visual experiment with the other wreath, the one of grass which adorned the second statue that was erected on the Rostra (see above), because no definite representations of the *corona obsidionalis* have been passed down to us.[23] The name, *corona graminea*, suggests that the grass wreath was very probably made from couch grass, because the name *graminea* means couch grass both in the Romance languages and in botanical terminology. And a wreath made of Mediterranean couch grass would awaken associations with a crown of thorns for sure.[24]

Caesar's iconography seems to anticipate a motif central to that of the Christ: in the representation of the suffering and tortured man who overcomes his own death, who by passing through death becomes God.

A cult statue

The resemblance between Caesar's grass wreath and Jesus' crown of thorns may be a coincidence:[25] who did not wear wreaths in classical antiquity! But the fact that a statue of Caesar may have had the appearance of a pietà, before which, if it were positioned in a church each little old lady would make the sign of the cross, makes one ponder.

Moreover, the inscription on the base—PARENTI OPTIME MERITO, 'to the most meritorious parent'—reads like a replica of that found on the temple of Jupiter—(D)IOVI(PATRI) OPTIMO MAXIMO, 'to the Father God (Jupiter) best and greatest' and which is still to be seen on our churches in the abbreviated form DOM (DEO OPTIMO MAXIMO), 'to the best, highest God'.

On the other hand, the acronym POM could be read as PONTIFICI OPTIMO MAXIMO: which only seems to be an understatement. Because the office and dignity of *pontifex maximus* had been Caesar's sheet anchor and was a decisive source of power during the beginning phase of the civil war.

With the conclusion of his prolonged Gallic proconsulate at the end of the year 50 BC, Caesar no longer held Republican office. His candidature in absentia for the consulate of 49 BC was impeded by the hostility of the Senatorial party and the about-face of Pompeius. He divided the Senate with the clever offer to lay down his command if Pompeius did the same. By doing this he made it possible for his opponents to declare him an enemy of the state only if they violated the intercession rights of the tribunes who advocated for him and for the peace.

It was exactly this issue that brought him into the arena as *pontifex maximus*, because the tribunes of the people were sacrosanct, and there was a grave historical precedent. In 133 BC it was just such a people's tribune, Tiberius Gracchus, who had lost his life as a consequence of the violation of the tribune's power of *intercessio* or 'veto'. Another tribune, M. Octavius, bribed by the landed gentry of the Senate, hindered the approval of a people-friendly land law by using his power of *intercessio* and was subsequently removed from office by the people's assembly on Tiberius' order. The people indeed had the right to remove a tribune of the people from office if he misused his *intercessio* power with the aim of betraying his party. Nevertheless, at the next best opportunity, when Tiberius stood for re-election as a tribune of the people, the then *pontifex maximus* Scipio Nasica blamed him for violating the constitution. He called for a lynch mob and led the pack of senators who slew Tiberius and 300 of his followers on the Capitol hill and threw their bodies into the Tiber. This mass murder was never expiated. On the contrary, ten years later it was repeated on Tiberius' brother Gaius and 3000 of his followers in an even more bloody manner.

This massacre of a tribune of the people—with the blessings of a *pontifex maximus*—had been the spark that 80 years earlier ignited the civil wars which were a murderous struggle for control of the land. So, remembering the fate of the Gracchi, the tribunes of the people for 50 and 49, Curio and Antonius, fled under threat to their lives to find Caesar in Ravenna on the other side of the Rubicon, awaiting the result of the negotiations. He too, like Tiberius in days of yore, was impeded in his re-election because of an alleged violation of the constitution, but this time he was the *pontifex maximus*. This time it was not an Optimate but a Populare who now held the authority to intervene in the dead-end political stalemate as the highest priest and custodian of the constitution. This time, with his loyal army, tested in battle, he had the power to do so, and as his veterans were awaiting their dues in the form of land allotments, it was even his duty to do so. Caesar realized that the sacred dignity of the *pontifex maximus* would be decisive, just as it had been in the time of Tiberius and M. Octavius, only this time under reverse conditions. So he dared to throw the dice over the Rubicon. The fortunate result of that venture made a god out of the *pontifex maximus*.

The first of all his coins, the denarius that he had struck while possibly still in Gallia Cisalpina, shows the theological dimension which the political and military conflict had from the beginning.

Contrary to what we would expect, the elephant was depicted on the reverse, rather than the obverse side of the coin. One can realize this by the fact that the name CAESAR is always found on the reverse of all the other coins,[26] likewise the theme—the victory over Gaul. The 'dragon' which the elephant is stamping on is a *carnyx,* a typical Gallic horn; 'Caesar' was said to mean elephant in the Punic language,[27] and perhaps Caesar was called that by the Gauls, who had come to know the elephant through Hannibal. This latter had invaded Italy at that time not only with his elephants, but with his Gallic allies as well.

20. Caesar's first Denarius, 49/8 BC

Caesar presented himself on his coin as the one who had finally defeated the Gauls. However, he had recruited in Gaul, his best legionaries were Gauls, his cavalry Germans. So inevitably he was seen as a new Hannibal, who invaded Italy at the head of a Gallic army. Now, at the beginning of the civil war, this apparently suited him very well: it raised the level of deterrence.[28]

But the most interesting aspect of this first—programmatic—coin of Caesar is what is missing: the head of a god. Not his Venus, not Jupiter, nor the Saturn of the Pompeians are to be found on the obverse as tradition would have demanded, but rather the insignia of the highest priest. Here, by this means, the *pontifex maximus* takes the place of a god. This undoubtedly suited the Epicurean Caesar because the *pontifex maximus* was literally 'godless'. Each *flamen* had his own god, the *flamen Dialis* Jupiter, the *flamen Martialis* Mars, the *flamen Quirinalis*

Romulus Quirinus, the *sacerdos Vestalis* Vesta, etc. Only the *pontifex maximus* had none, and that was why he had the power to supervise *pontifices, flamines* and *vestals*—to stand in the place of each and all of them—and if necessary chastise them as well. He who was godless was the highest priest of all the gods and of the Deity in general. With Caesar this godless priest took the place of God.

Consequently, it was in the inscriptions on the statues dedicated to him in Ionia after the victory of Pharsalos where he was first entitled *pontifex maximus*. The additional titles of *dictator* or *consul, sôtêr,* savior, or *euergetês,* benefactor, may or may not have appeared. *Pontifex maximus,* in Greek *archiereus,* or respectively *archiereus megistos,*[29] always appeared right up front. And on the rare occasions when it did not appear, it was substituted with *theos*[30]—god—the Greek translation of the Latin *divus*—which Caesar had chosen for himself instead of *deus*— an antiquated variant which was closer to *Dieus,* the old name of *Jupiter* or more respectively *Zeus*. Sometimes the inscription read *theos epiphanês,* the 'appearing God, coming to light', which accentuated the proximity to Jupiter's sphere. And thus the *pontifex maximus* became *divus*.

There was no problem with this in Ionia, where the people were used to greeting and praying to their Hellenistic rulers as gods. As Alexander had risen to the status of Amon-Zeus, so too were the succeeding houses of the Diadochs considered dynasties of gods. Now a Roman had taken their place: the new ruler was the new god. Not an epigone, but rather a new Alexander: as he had been identified with Zeus, so now was Caesar with Jupiter—change within continuity.

Yet in Rome, the city that took pride in murdering kings as tyrants and driving them out—beginning with Romulus and Tarquinius—Caesar was murdered as being just such a one. So the title *divus* was suspended as well. But even the murderers of the tyrant could not prevent the funeral of the *pontifex maximus,* which the *furor populi* transformed into his apotheosis. This inspired Antonius with the hope that his *Divus Iulius*—who had been *flamen Dialis* from the time of his youth—could soon be raised to become a new Jupiter. Soon. But for the moment, in the face of the Senatorial support for Caesar's murderers, not the least of which was Cicero's, the allusion had to suffice.[31]

In order to give the statue and its inscription telic force, Antonius put the word *parenti* at the beginning. This was a direct reference to the title *parens patriae*—parent of the native city, (pro)creator of the empire— which was finally conferred on Caesar and also appeared on his latest coins. With that title, the *patres* had finally acknowledged their own *parens,* and obligated themselves to protect with their lives the life of the one who had saved them. In response, Caesar had dismissed his Spanish bodyguard—and then his enemies murdered him. Because they had not been successful in damning Caesar as a tyrant, the title *parens* only waited in a state of abeyance, eventually offering the leverage to expose Caesar's murderers as parricides. This would kindle the hatred of the people against them, along with the wrath of the furies. There was no escape. This was very clear to Cicero.[32]

Cicero had been given the title *pater patriae* because he had ordered the Catilinarians to be executed without trial, making him the spiritual mentor of those *patres* who had now killed Caesar. When he wrote to Cassius that the choice of this word *parenti* not only made them all assassins, but parricides as well, Cicero was still playing things down, because it in fact even made them matricides. By selecting the word *parens,* 'parent, parturient, procreator', instead of *pater,* 'father', the martyred son became fused with the mother Venus. So not only was the putative fatherhood of the ruler referred to, but also the primary, creative parenthood that Caesar's acts had manifested, for he had not only governed the empire, he had created it first. It was into this empire that he had led his veterans, settling them in the rural cities that he had established: Horace calls him *pater urbium*—father of the cities.[33] Appearing on the colonial coins throughout the whole empire were the words: *parens,* parent, *conditor,* founder, or simply *creator.*[34]

For his veterans he was father and mother, and between the two, more mother than father, for they knew his love for them, his indulgence and his care. In this sense the word *parenti* on Antonius' statue was directed at the *pietas,* the filial love of the veterans. *Optime meritus:* the one who had merited the most, whose *emeriti,* as his discharged soldiers, they were. Now, if those who called themselves *optimates,* considering themselves to be the very best, murdered the *optime meritus,* then what on earth could his *emeriti*—his veterans—expect from them? What might happen to the promised land allotments? Did not Brutus want to use the public purse to compensate the landed gentry—who considered the state acres as their own—so that they could buy back the allotments of the veterans? Were the veterans to become landless once more?

So, there was only one hope left to the large numbers of veterans in the city, waiting for the confirmation of their land grants: to be led into war against the murderers of their 'parent', their creator, so that they might exact cruel revenge on them and elevate Caesar to the highest god, the heavenly guarantor of his and their empire on earth—*Divus Iulius,* their god—who was, for them, more of a *Venus Genetrix* than a *Jupiter*.

And so they were more than receptive to the plans of Antonius, whose word carried authoritative weight with them. He had been the right arm of Caesar, and by the time of the erection of the above mentioned statue, he was not only consul but the designated *flamen Divi Iulii,* the predestined high priest of the new god. Even if one assumes that he was not inaugurated yet,[35] he was nevertheless appointed *flamen* to Caesar whilst Caesar was still living.[36]

Therefore the statue erected by Antonius on the Rostra was not only political propaganda, but the first cult statue of the new empire's god. If it was the column mentioned by Suetonius that served as its pediment—and the first word of the inscription, *parenti,* lends itself to this assumption—then it was the object of a real cult.

> 'Later the people erected on the Forum a massive column of Numidian marble, nearly twenty feet high, with the inscription PARENTI PATRIAE, "to the parent of the fatherland". And for a long time afterwards they used to offer sacrifices at the foot of this, make vows there and settle disputes by oaths taken in Caesar's name.'[37]

Precisely because the statue remained without an official character, but rather had only a partisan one, it was all the more effectively designed. As is known, it did not fail to have the desired effect. The coalition against Caesar's enemies successfully formed: Cicero was murdered in 43, and Brutus and Cassius, being defeated in 42 in Philippi, killed themselves. Caesar could finally be consecrated as *Divus Iulius,* and thus his improvised apotheosis—which had been enforced at his funeral by the people, enraged at his assassination—was later legitimized. He had been victorious over death and achieved his elevation to the gods posthumously. The 'evil spirit' that the dead Caesar turned into for his assassins—appearing to Brutus again in Philippi and forcing Cassius to kill himself with the same dagger he used against Caesar—was raised to the heavens as a god, like a new Romulus Quirinus.[38] Caesar's statue of 44 demanded just that.

The inscription on the Base

Different than those in Ionia, the inscription here is Latin. But we can easily imagine how it would have sounded to the ears of Greek-speaking Romans, and there were many of them. At this time they made up more than half of the empire's population, especially in the capital.[39] Not only officers, entrepreneurs, technicians, merchants, publicans, scholars, pedagogues, physicians, lawyers, priests, actors etc., but there were also the Greek-speaking veterans themselves, those from the East and those from the West who participated in the Eastern campaigns.

It should be observed that linguistically, *parens*, 'parent' or 'father' and *creator*, in the sense of 'founder' especially a 'founder of cities', is called *ktistês* by the Greeks, while *optimus* is usually rendered *aristos*—both translations are well documented, additionally on Roman imperial coins in the East. Conversely, the words *meritus*, 'meritorious', as well as *bonus*, 'good'—whereby *optimus*, 'the best', is an intensification—can in this sense be appropriately translated by the Greek word *chrêstos*, a word whose classical pronunciation was already becoming replaced by the late Hellenistic *christos*, which is still used today.[40] Hence, on the base of the first cult-statue of the new god Caesar, the Greek speaking people read that the divine founder of the empire was *optime meritus* which meant for them *chrêstos*, respectively *christos*. This would not surprise them, because they were used to addressing their deceased on epitaphs with *chrêste*,[41] 'good'. For Caesar the word fit perfectly, because he was 'good': proven by his much acclaimed clemency. Indeed, the defeated Pompeius had called upon his followers to reconcile themselves to the stronger Caesar because he would be well-disposed and 'good': *chrêstos*.[42]

Parens, optimus, meritus—ktistês, aristos, chrêstos. Three words, each of them (the last one is very telling) resembling in appearance and pronunciation that of another word, *christos*, 'anointed', which later emerged as the title of Jesus.[43] The possibility of confusing *chrêstos* with *christos* was so easy and natural, that the spelling with an 'ê' instead of an 'i' is still to be found in some writings of the Classics (for example Tacitus' *chrestiani* which was changed to *christiani*, or Suetonius' *chresto* as well, interpreted by some as *Christus*) and also in the New Testament in various places.

But this happened later, in another context. For the moment, nobody would have gained anything by a possible confusion of *chrêstos*, 'meritorious', with *christos*, 'anointed', nor would they have taken offence, because both high priests and kings were anointed, and Caesar had been both at once—the first in very fact, the second by reputation. Moreover, as chance would have it, *christos* also looks like an abbreviation of *archiereus megistos*, the Greek form of *pontifex maximus*, the first earthly title of their God.

Christos indeed looks like a contraction of *archiereus megistos*, no farther removed from each other as e.g. *Köln* from *Colonia*, *Lyon* from *Lugdunum*, *Zaragoza* from *Caesaraugusta*, *Bizerte* from *Hippo Diarrhytus* or *priest* from *presbyteros*. The letters surviving the contraction are here visually demonstrated by capitals:[44]

*ar*CHI*e*R*eus meg*ISTOS > CH*ie*RISTOS > CHRISTOS.

Furthermore, the word *christos* regularly is found abbreviated in Christian writings, sometimes with both first initials of *XPICTOC*, X and P, written one over the other in form of a monogram. And this is not so far away from the initials of *pontifex maximus*, P and M: ₽ respectively ☧.

If the approximate resemblance of *christos* with *ktistês*, *aristos* or *chrêstos* is purely coincidental, *christos* is not at all an accidental contractional form of *archiereus megistos* but an inherent one. If the title was used in prayer—and that can be inferred from the fact that this appellation ranks first on all the base inscriptions of his votive statues—then this long title would inevitably have contracted by its perpetual formulaic repetition.

All this makes one wonder: Caesar's statue not only looked like a pietà, but the inscription on the base also evoked the Christ.

Is this air of familiarity, that we have detected in the iconography and the titles of Caesar and Jesus respectively, merely coincidental or does it indicate a relationship of dependence?

As Caesar was born exactly a century before Christ and the above-mentioned statues and inscriptions on the bases are from the year 48 respectively 44 before Christ, then a dependent relationship can only point in one direction: Christ would not only have been born after Caesar, but also created after him.

In order to examine this, we need to place Caesar's history and the Gospel side by side and see if further resemblances occur, and if so, whether they indicate mere borrowing or infer real filiation.

New ground is being broken. We will begin—so we can avoid becoming quickly lost in the details—by scanning the terrain from a bird's eye view, detecting the rough outlines at first, and then in the second phase we will dig into the texts for further proof.

We have selected a task that is accomplishable. Just as there are different Gospels preserved for us, so there are also different histories of Caesar. We can choose as our strategy a comparative analysis. This method has an additional advantage. If aerial photos reveal that the two shapes do not show the same contours—are not congruent—we would already have come to a result, even if a negative one. There is no need to project.

And because we do not have to approach this reductively, there is no need to engage in the ticklish methodological questions involved in the search for the historical Jesus either, at least not initially. We can come straight to the point.

II

VITAE PARALLELAE

Both Caesar and Jesus start their rising careers in neighboring states in the north: Gallia and Galilee.

Both have to cross a fateful river: the Rubicon and the Jordan. Once across the rivers, they both come across a patron/rival: Pompeius and John the Baptist, and their first followers: Antonius and Curio on the one hand and Peter and Andrew on the other.

Both are continually on the move, finally arriving at the capital, Rome and Jerusalem, where they at first triumph, yet subsequently undergo their passion.

Both have good relationships with women and have a special relationship with one particular woman, Caesar with Cleopatra and Jesus with Magdalene.

Both have encounters at night, Caesar with Nicomedes, Jesus with Nicodemus.

Both of them are great orators and of the highest nobility, descendant of Aeneas and son of David, yet nevertheless both are self-made men. Both struggle hard and ultimately triumph, hence each has a 'triumphal entry': Caesar on horseback and Jesus on a donkey.

Both have an affinity to ordinary people—and both run afoul of the highest authorities: Caesar with the Senate, Jesus with the Sanhedrin.

Both are contentious characters, but show praiseworthy clemency as well: the *clementia Caesaris* and Jesus' Love-thy-enemy.

Both have a traitor: Brutus and Judas. And an assassin who at first gets away: the other Brutus and Barabbas. And one who washes his hands of it: Lepidus and Pilate.

Both are accused of making themselves kings: King of the Romans and King of the Jews. Both are dressed in red royal robes and wear a crown on their heads: a laurel wreath and a crown of thorns.

Both get killed: Caesar is stabbed with daggers, Jesus is crucified, but with a stab wound in his side.

Both die on the same respective dates of the year: Caesar on the Ides (15th) of March, Jesus on the 15th of Nisan.

Both are deified posthumously: as Divus Iulius and as Jesus Christ.

Both leave behind priests: Marcus Antonius and Peter. Both have a posthumous heir: Gaius Octavianus adopted by Caesar's Last Will and Testament and John the disciple whom Jesus adopts while on the cross ('Woman, behold thy son!').

Now, there is one thing that stands out as being strikingly incongruous: Caesar was a commander, while Jesus was a thaumaturge.

However, in his funeral oration for Caesar, Antonius depicted all of Caesar's many great achievements as miracles.[45] These miracles of Caesar included the survival of a storm at sea[46] and even the raising of the dead: for the people took it to be a miracle that Caesar brought the honors of Marius 'back from Hades into the city' after many long years of Sulla's dictatorship.[47]

In turn, some of Jesus' miracles concern the banishing of demons, which indeed represents the absolute, theological form of warfare.

The picture we usually have in mind is of Caesar waging merciless war,[48] in stark contrast with Jesus preaching of love and bringing the Kingdom of God, which we assume to be one of peace, love and unity. This is in spite of the well-known passage:

> 'Think not that I am come to send peace on earth; I came not to send peace, but a sword. For I am come to set a man at variance against his father, and the daughter against her mother, and the daughter-in-law against her mother-in-law. And a man's foes shall be they of his own household'.[49]

And Jesus continues by praising those who take his people in and give them victuals. Clearly, these are civil war conditions. Thus Jesus brings about the Kingdom of God explicitly through civil war—even if he did not desire to use such means—exactly as Caesar himself did.

In turn, the *clementia Caesaris* is scarcely mentioned, if it is not completely ignored, even though Caesar meant it to be an important political statement:

> 'Let this be the new policy of victory that we arm ourselves with mercifulness and liberality.'[50]

This political program of love-your-enemies was carried out so consistently, that he perished[51]—like Jesus.

Even the limitations to their *clementia* are the same: Caesar forgave all his enemies—except the repeat offenders who mocked his *clementia*;[52] Jesus forgave all sinners—except those who sinned against the Holy Spirit.[53]

Thus the main features of the picture seem to fit. Let us now have a closer look at the people who surround Caesar and Jesus in order to see if there are any more parallels.

First approach

Pompeius, for example, is beheaded and his head is presented in a bowl to the person who supposedly wanted him killed—exactly what the Gospels tell us happened to John the Baptist.

Antonius negotiates with Caesar's assassins, dines with them and dissembles; Peter is recognized at the enemies' campfire and denies Jesus.

Caesar's lover Cleopatra, later Antonius' lover and mother of their children, is finally humiliated at Octavianus' feet—Magdalene, who talks to Jesus about love and announces Jesus' resurrection to Peter, washes the Lord's feet with her tears.

Caesar's uncle Marius, banished but brought back from Hades, lived with his wife Iulia and with Martha, a fortune teller; Jesus' uncle Lazarus, resurrected from the dead, lived with his sister Mary and with a woman called Martha, who foretells his resurrection.

Now we shall move on to the few properties we mentioned above.

The victory of Caesar was sealed by a palm tree sprouting from the floor of a temple. While the people were giving him an ecstatic ovation, hailing him king, they waved olive branches. Jesus, too, was hailed as a king, and still today olive branches are waved on Palm Sunday. His horse is a donkey, which is a strange steed for a king, for the animal is no faster than a man on foot. But the horse of Caesar must also have been quite strange, for the equestrian statue of Caesar on the Forum Iulium had human feet.

We imagine the crown on Caesar's head to be a laurel wreath: the triumphal wreath. Those statues of Divus Iulius that depict him as Soter, Savior, Redeemer, have wreaths of oak leaves or of grass, however, resembling both in form and meaning the crown of thorns worn by Jesus the Savior[54]—as we have seen. Jesus, in turn, is crowned with a laurel wreath by a legionary as depicted on a sarcophagus dating from 340/370 AD, on which the oldest known image of the Passion can be seen (fig. 116, p. 387).[55]

Let us now examine the locations, starting with the few names mentioned so far.

The rise of Caesar begins in Gaul, that of Jesus in Galilee. Caesar, coming from Gallia (Gaul), crosses the Rubicon and arrives in Corfinium; Jesus, coming from Galilaea (Galilee), crosses the Jordan and arrives in Capernaum (also Caphernaum). Gallia and Galilee are the respective neighboring countries in the north. Both have to cross boundary rivers: the Rubicon separated Gallia from Italia, whereas the Jordan actually separated Galilee from the Decapolis and the Gaulanitis, but the Evangelists write as if Judaea were located immediately on the other side of the river. Corfinium and Capernaum respectively are the first cities in which they arrive. The stormy seas that are crossed by Caesar and Jesus also act as borders: across the Ionian Sea lies Ionia, as Greece was and is called in the Orient;[56] across the Sea of Galilee again lie Decapolis and the Gaulanitis, but for the Evangelist it is again Judaea.

The same attributes and properties (from now on all called 'requisites', for short) appear within the same structures. The resemblance of the names is astonishing too: *Gallia* and *Galilaea, Corfinium* and *Caphernaum, Italia* or *Ionia* on the one hand and *Judaea* on the other.

Considering the resemblance of the names and the similarity of the requisites, a sequence emerges: Gallia + boundary river + Corfinium ≈ Galilaea + boundary river + Caphernaum. Now, if we try to extend this sequence, we find that Caesar expels the commander of the enemy occupying the town of Corfinium; Jesus expels the unclean spirit of a possessed man. The English words occupied and possessed both have the same Latin equivalent: *obsessus*.

For Jesus it was also about power and struggle, 'for he was teaching by proxy' as Luther translates the passage of Mark; 'for he taught them as one that had authority' in the King James Version. Taking the sentence literally it becomes still clearer:

'for he instructed them as the one who had power'.[57]

The hostile spirit also sees him that way:

'Let us alone; what have we to do with thee, Jesus of Nazareth? Art thou come to destroy us?'[58]

Therefore the sequence can be extended: Gallia + boundary river + Corfinium + occupying commander + expulsion = Galilee + boundary river + Caphernaum + possessed man + expulsion.

When comparing Caesar and Jesus we ascertain the existence of similar requisites within analogous structures and sequences.

As far as names are concerned, it is easy to list the people around Caesar and then find their corresponding representatives in the story of Jesus. Keeping to the few people and places mentioned so far:

The Characters and their Actors

        Caesar : Jesus
      Pompeius : John (the Baptist)
      Antonius : Simon (Peter)
        Curio : Andrew
      Cleopatra : Mary Magdalene
     Nicomedes : Nicodemus
   (Decimus) Brutus : Judas
   (Marcus) Brutus : Barabbas
       Lepidus : Pilate
Octavianus (Augustus) : John (the beloved disciple)
Marius (+ Iulia and Martha) : Lazarus (+ Mary and Martha)
      The Senate : The Sanhedrin
         Gaul : Galilee
       Rubicon : Jordan
      Corfinium : Caphernaum
        Rome : Jerusalem
       Italy/Ionia : Judaea

It is conspicuous that some are identical—*Martha* = *Martha*—or might be held to be. The wife of *Marius* could certainly be named *Maria (Mary)*, all the more likely by non-Romans.[59] Their different function—wife resp. concubine versus sister—is thus relativized that the sisters are 'loved'.[60]

Other names are similar: *Gallia* ≈ *Galilee*, *Corfinium* ≈ *Caphernaum* (which in the Latin manuscripts is written *Cafarnaum*), *Ionia* ≈ *Judaea*. The first two are within the framework of the usual metathesis of the liquidae ('l' and 'r').[61] In the last we observe that *Ionia* and *Iudaea* are quite similar in Greek script: *ΙΩΝΙΑ* ≈ *ΙΟΥΔΑΙΑ*. In the decisive letter—*N* versus *Δ*—there is only a deviation in the direction of the third line. That, coincidentally, Italy is not written very differently—*ITAΛIA* ≈ *IOYΔAIA*—could explain the confusion in the Gospel wherein Judaea is located on the other side of the Jordan as well as on the other side of the Sea of Gennesaret.

Lepidus and *Pilatus* (Pilate) are quite close in appearance too, as *Pilatus* looks like a syllabic metathesis of *Lepidus*: *Lepidus* > *Piledus* > *Pilatus*.[62] Idem for *Nicomedes* and *Nicodemus*.

The difference between *Brutus* and *Barabbas* is somewhat greater, but is not unbridgeable: Comparing the semantically relevant sound alone—Barabbas is a semitic name and in those languages only the consonants and consonanced vocals are of semantic relevance—we have *BRVT* versus *BRAB*. Moreover the meaning of Barabbas is understood to be 'Bar-Abbas', 'son of the father', and when Caesar was being stabbed he exclaimed to Brutus : 'You too, my son?' So the term 'son of the father' is appropriate for Brutus.

All the other parallel names seem to be different from each other: *Brutus ≠ Judas, Rome ≠ Jerusalem* etc.

But with a second look there are analogies to be detected here too.

The full name of *Brutus*, the traitor, was *Decimus Iunius Brutus*. *Iunius* can be rendered in Greek as *Iunas*, just as the Latin *Lucius* became the Greek *Lukas*.[63] Now, *Iunas* is very close to *Judas*, comparable to the above *Ionia = Judaea*, especially in Greek lettering: *IOYNAC ≈ IOYΔAC*. The only difference is the third line of *N* and *Δ*. *Decimus*, for its part, means 'the tenth', so *Decimus Iunius* could be understood as 'Junas the Tenth'. And the name of the traitor in Mark is 'Judas, one of the twelve'.[64]

Marius too, as an 'outlawed'—*latro* in Latin—is acoustically and visually not far removed from *Lazarus*.[65]

In *Johannes* (the disciple *John*), it seems that the article had been added: Octavianus Augustus, called the young, and in this respect, the new Caesar, in Latin *iuuenis*, Greek *(h)o neos (Kaisar)*,[66] soon becomes aurally and visually *Johannes: iuuenis > Johannes, (h)o neos > Johannes*.[67]

John (the Baptist) could have been written *Gnaios* instead of *neos*: (the) *Gnaeus* (Pompeius), *(h)o Gnaios* (Pompeios); or in the sources the more common nickname *Magnus*, which, if the '*M-*' is ignored, resembles *Gnaeus: (M)agnus ≈ Gnaeus*. Both are easily heard and read as *Johannes: (M)agnus* respectively *Gnaeus > Johannes, (h)o Gnaios > Johannes*.[68]

Curio however, does not come close to *Andreas (Andrew)* tonally, but it does so in meaning as if *Curio* originated from *uir*, Latin for 'man'[69] just as *Andreas* stems from the Greek *anêr, andros* also meaning 'man'. The same goes for *senate* and *sanhedrin*, which simply means *council*, not only in Rome and Jerusalem.[70]

And *Mary Magdalene—Maria of Magdala*, i.e. 'Maria of the tower'[71]—matches *Cleopatra* in sense. As Caesar's mistress she could be regarded as a *Iulia* and as a *Iulia* she could then be a *Maria* (see above).[72] Distinct from all the other *Mary's*, in her case the name *Maria of the tower* would not be wrong at all, because the tower in which she met her death became the most famous tower of all. Barricaded in this tower, she resisted Octavianus till the bitter end.[73]

The resemblance that *Antonius* has with *Simon (Petrus)* has somewhat more color. Interestingly, in most cases *Petrus* is called *Simon* and *Simon* appears in the accusative form, with the ending '*-a*', as when he appears for the first time in Mark: '...he saw Simon...'[74]—Σίμωνα, *Simona*. But this looks like Antonius, read from right to left:

ANTONIVS <l> SVINOTNA > CYINΩTNA > CIMΩNA

—heterographic: like a foreign Aramaic word in Greek.[75]

In regards to the names of other places, the *Rubicon* doesn't sound anything like the *Jordan,* and with respect to meaning—if the *Rubicon* is understood as *Red river*—it could only be connected with the Red Sea. But this is wide of the mark. It so happened that after crossing the Rubicon, Caesar also had to cross the river *Aternus* on the border of the city, before he was able to set upon Corfinium. The name *Aternus* could be connected to the *Jordan:* leaving aside the initial sound iota—which frequently occurs in the Semitic languages (like *Johannes, Joseph* etc.)— *(I)ordanes* looks like a metathesis[76] of *Aternus* with an exchange of the related sounds 't' and 'd':

Aternus > Artenus > Iordanes.

It just so happens that the Rubicon flows into the Adriatic between Ravenna and Senigallia, and thus into the Gallic sea, which structurally and linguistically corresponds to the 'Sea of Galilee'—what the Evangelist conspicuously calls the Lake of Gennesaret—through which the Jordan flows. Finally, in pursuing Pompeius after the Rubicon and the Aternus, Caesar had to cross the Ionian sea—the position of which relative to the Rubicon and the Aternus resembles the relative position of the Red Sea to the Jordan. In addition there is a certain coincidental literal resemblance between the *(mare) Ionium* und *Iordanes*.

With regard to *Rome* and *Jerusalem* it is not necessary to be too concerned about the differences in name. The name of Rome is hardly mentioned in the ancient sources: it is usually just referred to as 'the city'. For example, in the citation above from Plutarchus, where it is reported that the people saw it as a miracle that after the long years of Sulla's dictatorship Caesar had brought the honors of Marius back from Hades 'into the city': *eis tên polin*. The city being referred to in any given instance depended on the context.[77] But if the name Rome is mentioned explicitly, like in the phrase *eis Rômên* '(in)to Rome', which occurs frequently, *(H)ierousalêm* (Jerusalem) is not so far removed *(EICPΩMHN ≈ IEPOYCAΛHM)*. The other variant of the name *(H)ierosolyma*, even contains the letters of *Roma* in sequence: *(H)ieROsolyMA*.

Concerning the meaning, we note the following:

Hiero means holy. So *Hierosolyma* is the *holy Solyma*. But *Solyma* (or *Salem*)[78] is thought to mean peace.[79] So *Hierosolyma* signifies nothing other than the *holy city of peace*. But de facto this was really only Rome, the city that had secured the peace of the world: the *Pax Augusta* was proclaimed *urbi et orbi* in the year 17 BC and the temple of Janus was closed. In order to commemorate this event Augustus had ordered the building of a monument—the *ara pacis,* the Altar of Peace. Now *(H)ieru-salem* reflects *ara pacis*—in the first section by the sound, in the second by the meaning:[80] *ara > (h)ieru; pacis > salem.*

So we have gone through the short list of names mentioned at the beginning of our chapter. We have established that persons and places occurring in the stories of Caesar and Jesus bear names that are either very close aurally or visually, or they look like the translation of each other.

The Names of the Lord

As is well known, the *nomina sacra* are reflected in the writings of the Gospel by abbreviations—usually the first and last letter—so we cannot compare the original name, but only that which has been passed down to us. Concerning the abbreviation for Jesus—*IêsuS > IS*—it is worth noting that *IuliuS* would be abbreviated the same.[81]

When comparing the complete names that have been passed down to us, we can establish other interesting things as well.

It is widely accepted that *Jesus* is the Greek form of the name *Jeshua,* respectively *Joshua* or *Jehoshua*—which literally means 'Jahweh helps' or 'Jahweh saves', analogously 'Godhelp'. If this is the case, then *Jesus* can be seen as the translation of the Greek *sôtêr*—'savior', 'redeemer'—respectively *euergetês*—'optime meritus', 'benefactor'—all titles of honor for Caesar,[82] just as they often appear in the literature and are documented as inscriptions on the bases of the statues dedicated to him in the East after Pharsalos.

This is reason enough to have a more precise look at the inscriptions of the other statues consecrated to Caesar in Ionia. Were there perhaps already parallels to Jesus' titles?

This is a typical dedication to be found on the Ionian islands:
The people (worship) Gaius Iulius Gaius' Son Caesar, Pontifex Maximus and Imperator, [for the second (time) Consul and Dictator], Savior and Benefactor [of all Greeks].[83]
Over on the mainland in Ephesus, the then capital of the multi-ethnic province of Asia, he is even hailed as 'God from God' and 'universal Savior of mankind':

'The cities in Asia and the communities and nations (worship) Gaius Iulius Gaius' Son Caesar, Pontifex Maximus and Imperator, (for) second (time) Consul, (the) appearing God (coming) from Ares and Aphrodite (from Mars and Venus), the common Savior of the whole of mankind...'[84]

These are all titles that we are familiar with being applied to Jesus. Starting from the last:

Savior of all the Greeks—or even *the whole of mankind*—reminds us of our *Savior*, for *sôtêr* is the same as *servator* or *salvator*.

Benefactor is not much different in meaning than our *merciful Lord*.

The appearing God, coming from Ares (Mars) and Aphrodite (Venus)—this also seems familiar to us: *Son of God and the Holy Virgin, God incarnate*.[85]

Imperator, Consul, Dictator—we know this from Christology and the litanies, this is our *Almighty*, the *Pantokrator* of the Greeks.[86]

As we have seen, *pontifex maximus* in its Greek form *archiereus megistos* contains *Christos* as a possible contraction.[87]

We even find resemblances in the names:

Caesar, Greek *Kaisar*, is not far removed from *Nazara*, the oldest version of *Nazareth*, especially in the accusative—*Kaisara*.[88]

Gaius' Son, or *Son of Gaius*, is embarrassingly redolent of *Son of Man*.[89]

And finally—*Gaius Iulius*, like *archiereus megistos*, is a further candidate for an abbreviation that could lead to *Jesus*: *GAIuS iUliuS > IÊSUS*.[90]

Summarized—Caesar's inscriptions on his earliest cult statues in Ionia would be, in Christian interpretation:

To Jesus, Son of Man, Nazarene, to Christ and the Almighty [Pantokrator,][91] *Son of God and God incarnate, merciful Lord and Savior of all mankind*.

These titles are well known. But it is most astonishing, that even the translational variants of the names and titles are just as well known.

Jesus, for example, is not only the possible abbreviation of *Gaius Iulius*, but coincidentally also of *Divus Iulius (DIuUS iUliuS) > Jesus* and *Divi Filius (DIuUS filiUS > Jesus)*.[92]

From the beginning *Kaisar* (Greek for Caesar) was equated with *kyrios* (Lord) because of the resemblance in sound.[93] It is not documented that Caesar called himself *dominus*, although he did remain seated like a lord when he was approached by a delegation of senators at the temple of Venus, whereas the cruciform depiction on the reverse of his coins evokes the dominion over the four cardinal points, the *dominus terrarum*. It is known that Augustus did not want to be called

Lord, which only serves to demonstrate that he indeed was. This form of address became normal for the later emperors. Interestingly enough, Jesus also is addressed rather by 'master' than by 'Lord', and he is only entitled 'Lord' in the later Gospels.[94] So *kyrios*, which regularly appears in the manuscripts as *nomen sacrum* in the abbreviated form *KC*, could have sneaked in for *Kaisar*—or *Kaisar Sebastos*, Greek for *Caesar Augustus*—which absolutely can be covered by the same token,[95] at a time and place where the address 'Lord' for the Kaisar was no longer as scandalous as it was at the time of Caesar.

The ancient name for dictator was *magister populi*,[96] which was preserved in the form of address: *magister*. Jesus is addressed in just this way: *didaskale*, master—or in translation, *rabbi*.[97] As if the words *dictator* and *magister* were taken in their specific scholarly meaning.[98] That Jesus' dictations are orders really is proved by the passage in Mark among others where the word *didaskôn* occurs: 'for he taught them as one that had authority.'[99] So here *rabbi* can stand in for *magister* as the form of address for *dictator*.

This polysemy of the names and titles lets us infer that there are doublets and crossovers of wording,[100] but exactly this would explain the variety of names, titles and forms of address for Jesus.

Our déjà vu experience continues: we realize to our surprise that Caesar's titles on the bases of the statues dedicated to him anticipate those of Christ—in toto as well as word by word. The differences can be explained by regular abbreviations—like in *Gaius Iulius* > *Jesus* or *archiereus megistos* > *christos*—or by a naive translation—like in *son of Gaius* > *Son of man* or *dictator* > *rabbi*—or by simple mistakes in writing—*Kaisar* > *Kyrios* and *Kaisara* > *Nazara*.

These are typical aberrations and alterations that occur in the development of a tradition, in which oral transmission[101] via various languages as well as the written actions of redactors and copyists are entangled in each other. Textual criticism has demonstrated that this has also been the case with the Gospels.

The mistakes in writing are not unusual and the other anomalies also remain within the bounds of what is usual in transitions between languages: the sound and lettering is preserved, or the meaning is, or a combination of both. This is a well known mechanism which occurs not only in folk etymologies and bowdlerization[102] but also in official scholarly translations, as for example in the translation of Latin terms into Greek, the second official language of the empire.[103]

Because we have not yet carried out a comparison based on the context, we still do not know whether mistakes or folk etymologies actually were involved. This is the reason why we are left with different hypotheses standing side by side, which are possibly mutually exclusive and can only be thought of within processes of oral or written tradition. For example, whether *Johannes* might have evolved from the Latin *iuvenis* or the Greek *(h)o neos,* or from *(M)agnus, Gnaeus* or *(h)o Gnaios.*

It must be observed by now that both phenomena may lead to a delocalization,[104] so that the imagined scenery accompanying the story can make a transition from Rome to Jerusalem. When we hear 'Sanhedrin', we think of Jerusalem rather than Rome, although it is known that 'Sanhedrin' means 'Senate'. And if we normally associate Caesar with Romans, it does not necessarily mean that the scene is located in the city of Rome: all the authorities empire-wide at that time were Romans. Is it the city of Rome or the world of Rome? *urbs* or *orbis?*

However cursory our study of the parallels has been so far, the observed resemblances between the names of persons and places concerning Caesar and Jesus are so regular that a closer examination is advisable to see if the Vita Caesaris could have been the exemplar for the Gospels.

Firstly we need to ask a crucial question, for if it cannot be answered all other questions are rendered superfluous:

Where is the cross in the Caesar story?

III

CRUX

We have shown some similarities and parallels between Caesar and Jesus. There are just as many to be found when we compare the narratives of their respective passions.

Both Caesar and Jesus were murdered. In both cases their elimination was of no gain to the murderers: Brutus died and so did Judas; Caesar had a successor, Jesus resurrected; Caesar was elevated to the gods, Jesus ascended into heaven.

The main discrepancy lies in the fact that Caesar was stabbed and Jesus crucified. At this point the parallels seem to come to an end.

So let us have a closer look at this essential difference.

Firstly, to get our bearings, we will recall the structure of their respective passion narratives.

The structure of the passion

Concerning Caesar we have (a) the conspiracy, (b) the assassination, (c) the posthumous trial, (d) the cremation, (e) the conflict about his heritage, (f) the succession.

Concerning Jesus we have (a) the conspiracy, (b) the capture, (c) the trial, (d) the crucifixion, (e) the burial, (f) the resurrection.

A structural correspondence is plain to see. The main discrepancy is that Caesar was murdered at the attack, whereas Jesus was merely captured. All the other differences are the result of this: regarding their trials, the only difference is that one is already dead whilst the other one is still alive. Whether we are dealing with funeral or crucifixion depends on whether Jesus was still alive or not at the time. Conflict about the inheritance on the one hand and the burial of Jesus' body on the other only seem to be different: in both cases it is about the *corpus*. Succession or resurrection, it is about the Empire—whether on earth or in heaven.

A posthumous trial?

The first question we have to deal with is whether Jesus was still alive at his trial.

It is striking that Jesus says nothing more after his capture.

'But he held his peace, and answered nothing.'[105]

And when he does finally speak, what does he say?

'Thou sayest it.'[106]

Which again means nothing: the other one says it, not he himself.

It is not necessary to take Jesus' last words into consideration: they are an invention in some phase or other of the tradition. This is something all scholars agree on. Namely, that it was a common literary topos in antiquity to put last words into the mouth of anyone famous who was dying. Indeed, Mark, and after him Matthew, have the famous 'My God, my God, why hast thou forsaken me?'; Luke has instead: 'Father, into thy hands I commend my spirit'; John, showing little respect, has him settle his last Will and Testament—'Woman, behold thy son! ... Behold thy mother'—then toast to it—'I thirst'—and to set the seal on it—'It is finished'.[107] Everybody has put something different into his mouth: this proves that he said nothing, otherwise there would only be one version.[107]

The same can be applied to his conversation with those who were crucified along with him. Mark merely reports that they reviled him and offers no further elaboration. The conversation only starts with the later Evangelists.

Conclusion: Jesus is silent after his capture. He, the fearless individualist, acting alone against everybody from the beginning—he who had come not to bring peace but the sword—should suddenly become speechless? Here, the gifted orator with whom the word was from the beginning, and who had something eloquent and incisive to say on every occasion, whether it were Sermons on the Mount or parables, is now dead silent at his trial, the crucial moment when he finally has a stage? We immediately think of the apology of Socrates, the other famous orator who was unjustly condemned. This silence of Jesus is inexplicable—that is why there is such an extensive literature about it.

Was his trial conducted posthumously? Was he already dead?

The following sentence of Mark is also quite strange:

'...and they bring him unto the place Golgotha, which is, being interpreted, The place of a skull.'[108]

Here Mark says *pherousin,* 'they carried him', and not, as one would expect, 'they led him'. We hesitate because, here, where according to the traditional story Jesus should still be alive, he is 'carried' to the place of a skull. Was he not capable of going by himself? We note that just before this, Simon the Cyrenian had been forced to take Jesus' cross and carry it. So he must have been unable to do it himself. Of course this debility is usually attributed to the earlier flagellation that he had endured. But the fact is, if Mark is to be taken literally, he not only did not carry his cross, he even had to be carried himself.

If we take an objective look at the corpse of Jesus, we have to observe that it bears a very unusual feature for someone who was crucified, namely a stab-wound in the side, and one so open and fresh that blood ran out of it. Very peculiar indeed, so much so that John, who quotes this detail, feels himself obliged to provide us with an explanation for the inexplicable:

'But when they came to Jesus ... one of the soldiers with a spear pierced his side, and forthwith came there out blood and water.'[109]

And because it was apparently unheard of, John fiercely swears that it is true:

'And he that saw it bare record, and his record is true: and he knoweth that he saith true, that ye might believe.'[110]

And because still no one believes him John explains why he should be believed:

'For these things were done, that the scripture should be fulfilled... (Zach. 12:10): "They shall look on him whom they pierced."'[111]

Critical biblical critics smirk here and say that the passage obviously has been invented to ensure that the prophecy is fulfilled: and they are right, but only partly.

Here we are dealing with a so-called midrash, a very formalized method for interpreting something inexplicable. The idea is that everything must already be present in the *biblia iudaica;* if an unusual event takes place and one has to justify it, then at least one passage has to be found in the Jewish books that can serve as a *vaticinium ex eventu,* a prophecy after the event. Some Gospel critics even deem the events in the Gospel text *eventus ex vaticiniis,* which would mean they are entirely invented on the basis of the prophecies. They thus misjudge intention and mechanism of the midrash. For, one sees immediately that the unexplainable must already be present so that the corresponding passage can be sought, otherwise simply any passage could be sought to justify anything. But the Gospels do not contain just anything but something definite, and very precisely defined at that.

Thus we conclude that the passage in John is probably interpolated—the other Evangelists know nothing about it—however the reason to search for a corresponding passage was pre-existent: they had stabbed him. That we may regard as a certainty.

An indirect proof that John is speaking the truth here is brought to us by an apocryphon, which means a scripture not accepted into the canon, the so-called Gospel of Nicodemus, also known as the Acts of Pilate. There it is said that the soldier who perforated his side with a lance was named Longinus.[112] Theologians speculate here that the name Longinus may have been invented: because lance in Greek is lonchê, the soldier was consequently named Longinus: in this they break the rules of the art. For 'Longinus' is a proper name, 'lance' a common term; the one rare and personal, the other one universally known. Experts speak of a *lectio difficilior* and a *lectio facilior*—by this they mean that in the process of tradition the easier word can replace the more difficult one: never the other way round. Thus Longinus is certain, and the pointed weapon was associated with his name and so became a lance. But the pointed weapon could have been of a different kind.

From where did John take the stab in the chest of Jesus? It can only have happened at his capture, where there was a violent engagement and the naked sword was drawn:

'...and kissed him. And they laid their hands on him, and took him. And one of them that stood by drew a sword, and smote a servant of the high priest, and cut off his ear.'[113]

We are accustomed to hearing sword used here and not dagger, because in the King James Version it was translated this way. But Mark does not say sword, but *machaira,* which primarily means knife, then dagger, or at most a short sword—like, for example, the Roman *gladius*.

That murderers were involved in the so-called arrest of Jesus is revealed by Mark's choice of words in the next verse:

'And Jesus answered and said unto them, Are ye come out, as against a thief, with swords and with staves to take me?'[114]

Luther translates: '...as against a murderer'. We can be confident that a gang went wild with daggers and other weapons, and indeed so wild that they wounded each other in the face. The arrest of Jesus seems to have been more murderous than it looks at first glance. Due to the fact that Jesus does not speak a word after the arrest and is later depicted with an open chest-wound, untypical for a crucified one, it is reasonable to assume that he was murdered at this point and that his so-called arrest was actually his capture, his entrapment, and—as Mark's choice of words indicates—his assassination.

John could have easily borrowed the stab in the side of Jesus from here and have made use of it at the descent from the cross.

So while we are at it, let us have a quick look at the parallel passage in the assassination of Caesar. The supposition that the Caesar source could have been used as a model for Mark is substantiated by the following detail, mentioned by Appianus:

'Many of the attackers wounded each other, whilst they stabbed with the daggers.'[115]

If we leave the servant in Mark's account of the capture of Jesus out of consideration for a moment[116] and understand that the High Priest himself was the target of the stabbing, then Mark's report superbly summarizes the attack on Caesar, *pontifex maximus*, High Priest.

And who stabbed him?—Longinus—C. *Cassius Longinus*:

'Cassius stabbed into the face…'[117]

—says Appianus; and Suetonius:

'Of all the many stab wounds, according to the judgement of Antistius, his personal physician, only one was mortal, namely the second, which he took in his chest.'[118]

A posthumous crucifixion?

Well, the logical conclusion of this would be that the crucifixion of Jesus was actually his funeral, and therefore, either the crucifixion did not take place at all, or if it did, it too was posthumous.

But it is written that he was crucified, that Simon of Cyrene carried his cross and that there was a sign hanging over this cross. So we will have to investigate how the Evangelists, the writers of the Gospels, depict the crucifixion, the cross and the sign. Let us start with this last one.

The sign

Mark writes: 'And the superscription of his accusation was written over, THE KING OF THE JEWS'; Luke: 'And a superscription also was written over him in letters of Greek, and Latin, and Hebrew, THIS IS THE KING OF THE JEWS'; Matthew: 'And set up over his head his accusation written, THIS IS JESUS THE KING OF THE JEWS'; John: 'And Pilate wrote a title, and put it on the cross. And the writing was, JESUS OF NAZARETH THE KING OF THE JEWS'.[119]

Here we have cited the four Gospels in the supposed order of their genesis: the oldest is thought to be Mark (the so-called Protoevangelium); then follow Luke and Matthew, which show a lot of conformity to Mark (that is why they are called Synoptics), but in contrast to Mark they present in places some 'unpublished material' (the famous source

Q and the *Sondergut*, special material); John is supposed to be the latest of them all, but he belongs to a tradition different from the other three.

It is striking that the further away in time the Evangelist is from the events being reported, the more he has to say when it should be the other way around. Let us follow the thread from the other direction.

John has added the epithet Nazoraean (meaning from Nazareth), the cross and Pilate; Luke has added (in some manuscripts) that it was written in letters of Greek, and Latin, and Hebrew; Matthew for his part has added the name Jesus and that the sign was positioned above his head. And what was it that Mark added to his exemplar? After the word 'king', should he not have appended the words 'of the Jews'? So we have to conclude that originally there was only the accusation of being king, which had been written (wherever).

But the case is no different with Caesar.[120] It is well-known that he was murdered because it was assumed he was striving for regality.[121]

The inscription over Jesus' head in Mark was: *(h)o basileus tôn Ioudaiôn*, 'the King of the Jews'.

But Iulius is written in Greek *IOYΛIOC*—*Ioulios*, in the accusative *IOYΛION*—*Ioulion*, (the temple) of Iulius is named *IOYΛIEION (HPΩON)*—*Ioulieion (hêrôon)*—which both visually resemble *IOYΔAIΩN*—*Ioudaiôn*—because of the resemblance of D and L ($\Delta \approx \Lambda$) in the graphic. *Basileus* did not always mean king, in Greek it could frequently indicate the Latin *imperator,* as also *basileia* could indicate *imperium*.[122]

'King of the Jews' and 'Imperator Iulius', or 'Imperator (from the house) of the Iulians' are confusable in Greek.

The cross

Was the inscription on the cross at all? Where did the cross stand?

It is only explicitly mentioned as being in the hands of Simon of Cyrene:

> 'And they compel one Simon a Cyrenian, who passed by, coming out of the country, the father of Alexander and Rufus, to bear his cross.'[123]

The King James Version lingers in our ears: '...to bear his cross.' But Mark says *arêi*: '...*to take up his cross, lift it.*'[124] This is strange. According to Mark, Simon did not bear the cross in Jesus' place but rather lifted it up, erected it. Did Jesus ever come in contact with that cross?

Crucified?

Let us look at the development of the sentence that tells us Jesus was crucified:

Mark: 'And when they had crucified him, they parted his garments, casting lots upon them,...'
Matthew: 'And they crucified him, and parted his garments, casting lots...'
Luke: '...there they crucified him...'
John: 'Where they crucified him...'[125]

It is striking that John and Luke first emphasize that he was crucified; Matthew and Mark speak of the parted garments and about the casting of lots. We learn that he was crucified because it happened just at the moment that they were parting the garments and casting the lots: incidentally, as it were.

The crucifixion seems to have graduated from a side issue to the central issue. And even after this metamorphosis, the speech is only about the act of the crucifixion itself, not about a cross: a verb rather than a substantive.

If we have a closer look at this verb, it turns out that *staurô* does not mean crucify, but to put up posts or slats or a palisade, or more precisely to fence in. Namely, the origin of the verb is *stauros,* which means stake, post, slat, and especially in the plural: palisade. First the Christians used the verb in the sense of 'to put up a post', then the post was interpreted as a stake and later on as a torture stake—a cross. So, 'put up stakes or posts' became 'lift to the cross', whereby in the mind, due to the iconography, the image of 'nailed to the cross' developed. [126]

Above we have utilized the 'Christian' translation of Mark's sentence:

'And when they had crucified him, they parted his garments, casting lots upon them...'

But a Greek of the first century would not have understood the sentence in this way, either not at all, or if so, rather in this sense:

'...and when they were putting up stakes, posts or slats or a palisade around him, they parted the garments, and cast valuable pieces on it...'

—because the Greek word for lot—*klêros*—originally means all that is received as an allotment, especially an inheritance, an heirloom.

A strange sentence. It rather seems to describe the erection of a funeral pyre and the ritual casting of gifts for the dead on it than the erection of a cross.

The preceding sentence of Mark is even stranger:

> 'And they gave him to drink wine mingled with myrrh: but he received it not.'[127]

This sentence does not say anything. We are informed that Jesus has not taken anything: a piece of non-news. It is inexplicable why this sentence should be here at all. Obviously, the other Evangelists could not interpret it either and started, each after his own manner, to make a 'reasonable' reorganization of the existing requisites.

Matthew, who likes to search through the Jewish scriptures, found the psalm (69:21): 'They gave me also gall for my meat; and in my thirst they gave me vinegar to drink.' And he promptly rewrote it:

> 'They gave him vinegar to drink mingled with gall: and when he had tasted thereof, he would not drink.'[128]

Some of the manuscripts refer to wine instead of vinegar. But it is assumed that the original word was vinegar and not wine, as otherwise Matthew would not have found it in the psalm. And because he found vinegar, the gall replaced the myrrh. Probably, Mark often used the word wine instead of vinegar—through the intermediate word *oxys oinos* 'sour, vinegary wine'—because of the resemblance of the words and because myrrh was added to the wine, not to vinegar. But for the others, vinegar held its position. Therefore the myrrh had to fade out, only to pop up again in another place.

In fact, Luke simply left out the myrrh: the soldiers only offer vinegar to Jesus.

> 'And the soldiers also mocked him, coming to him, and offering him vinegar...'[129]

He does not tell us if Jesus took it or not.

He makes the women bring the myrrh to the grave, interestingly enough not in the form of myrrh—*myrrha, MYPPA*—but instead as ointment—*myra, MYPA*:

> '...and [they] beheld the sepulchre, and how his body was laid. And they returned, and prepared spices and ointments;'[130]

At this point in Mark's account he only speaks of 'aromatics', *arômata*. It looks as though Luke combined it because of the resemblance of the names *arômata* and *myra*.[131]

John lets this sentence disappear completely from this particular place where it explains nothing—because myrrh was not ingested but used externally, resulting in Mark and Matthew being forced to say: '...he would not drink'—and moves it backwards to places where it makes more sense. He separates the vinegar from the myrrh: he has vinegar being offered to Jesus, together with hyssop, and he takes it:

'...and they filled a sponge with vinegar, and put it upon hyssop, and put it to his mouth. When Jesus therefore had received the vinegar...'¹³²

John has the myrrh being brought, not by the women, but by Nicodemus when Jesus' corpse is collected: '...and brought a mixture of myrrh and aloes, about an hundred pound weight.' Why the aloes are suddenly added to the myrrh is explained as follows: '...with the spices, as the manner of the Jews is to bury.'¹³³

After we have reviewed the four canonical Gospels, it is certain that the original requisites are the following: *MYPPA* or *MYPA*—*myrrha* or *myra*, 'myrrh' or 'ointment', *OΞY(ς)*—*oxy(s)*, 'sour' (vine) and *OYK* respectively *OYN EΛABEN*—*ouk/oun elaben*, 'did not take' respectively 'did take'.

Now, if we wanted to decide between these alternatives, we would have to give the first requisite *myra* priority over *myrrha*, because Mark does not say *myrrh*, but *esmyrnismenon*, i.e. actually 'anointed', but in Mark it still has the sense of 'myrrhed, with a little bit of myrrh'.¹³⁴

In the second and third requisite there is a resemblance in the lettering between *oxy* 'sour' and *ouk/oun* 'not/but'. Because Mark does not have 'oxy' anymore, his 'ouk' would appear to be the residuum of it. And as 'ouk' is unstable—it is not by chance that John replaces it with 'oun'—only 'oxy' and 'elaben' can be regarded as valid.

This means that we are only left with the requisites: *MYP(A) / OΞY / EΛABEN*—*myr(a) / oxy / elaben*.

Thus we arrive at the following conclusion: Abstracting from the popular translations and taking them literally, the two verses in which Mark tells us that Jesus was crucified only attest:

'*myr(a) / oxy / elaben*. And when they were putting up stakes, posts or slats or a palisade around him, they parted the garments, casting valuable pieces on it...'

Above we have noticed that the second verse of Mark seems to describe the erection of a funeral pyre and the ritual deposit of gifts for the dead.

If now the words of the first verse are read from the same viewpoint as in the second, it is conspicuous that *MYPA*—*myra*—is nearly identical in lettering to *ΠYPA*—*pyra*—meaning 'pyre', and that *MYP*—*myr*—can be confused with *ΠYP*—*pyr*—'fire' (think of e.g. 'pyre', pile to be burned, 'pyromaniac', incendiary, 'pyrotechnic', fireworks, or 'pyrite', firestone). *OΞY*—*oxy*—also means 'sour', but originally 'sharp'—and together with verbs of movement or action it takes on the meaning of 'quickly'. Now, if we combine *oxy* and *elaben*, it takes on the sense of: 'was promptly', 'took quickly', 'grasped the opportunity'.

Both verses of Mark can now produce a coherent meaning:

'...and while the pyre caught fire, they quickly assembled stakes, posts, slats and palisades, placed them around it, tore up their garments and threw valuable pieces on it...'

It would be sufficient, if a copyist had confused ΠΥΡΑ ≈ ΜΥΡ(Ρ)Α, *pyra* and *myrrha,* encouraged by the fact that in a Jewish funeral myrrh is used but no fire, to finally render 'pyre' as 'myrrh'. Then follows the confusion of the one *oxy,* 'quickly/sharp', with the other meaning 'sour'—and already we are attending a completely different funeral: instead of stake, pyre and cremation we have crucifixion and inhumation.

And since we find ourselves already there, let us take a closer look at Caesar's funeral using three versions. The first is Appianus:

«There they collected together pieces of wood and benches, of which there were many in the Forum, and anything else they could find of that sort, for a funeral pyre, throwing upon it the adornments of the procession, some of which were very costly. Some of them cast their own wreaths upon it and many military awards.»[135]

Plutarchus:

«...and they hauled benches, barriers and tables from the place and heaped them around the corpse...»[136]

Suetonius:

'...and immediately the throng of bystanders heaped on it dry branches and the judges' chairs with the court benches and whatever else came to hand and could serve as an offering. Then the flute players and actors pulled off their robes which they had taken from the equipment of his triumphs and put on for the occasion, tore them apart and flung them into the flames, likewise the veterans of the legions threw the arms with which they had adorned themselves for the funeral. Many of the matrons similarly offered up the jewels which they wore together with their children's lockets and purple-fringed tunics.'[137]

It is easy to detect that the passage from Mark is an abridgment of Caesar's funeral. The same requisites are present in both. The defining difference only exists in our minds. It is we who know that Caesar was burned and Jesus was crucified. But in the cited sentences and the original text, the required details are the same. The difference in interpretation is brought and applied by us.

In the same way, if in the next sentence the Caesar sources say that the pile was set alight, it is necessary to know beforehand that the corpse was burned. Because, as it often happens, so here too the Greek word may have totally different meanings. Which one is right depends on the context. Appianus:

'Then they set it and all the people waited by the funeral pile throughout the night.'[138]

The translators add after 'they set it' 'afire', because they know what it is about, so in order that we—not being used to Greek mental gymnastics and acrobatics—do not loose the thread. The Greek does not add anything at all, he relies on the understanding and the knowledge of the reader: after all, he is a Greek like himself. But what happens if the reader a hundred years later has a different knowledge and a different understanding, lives in another country where Greek is a foreign language, finds himself in another political context wherein the text is possibly used for other purposes and where the listeners have different interests? Here we find ourselves wandering along the edge of a precipice: one can sense the abyss. But back to the text again.

The primary meaning of the word *exêpsan* is not even 'set afire', but actually 'set on'. Plutarchus chose the version *hyphêpsan*: 'to set on from underneath'. We can see what can become of it. There is something set on (from underneath). If this something is a fire, it burns; if it is a sign, then it is nailed on; or if it is even a man, then he is hanging on the cross.[139]

From this examination we can conclude that while Jesus' crucifixion is not necessarily a crucifixion at all, it actually replicates the cremation of Caesar.

Coincidence or system?

Of course, all of this is still speculation and circumstantial evidence. But now the text itself gives us the opportunity to ascertain whether the parallels between Caesar and Jesus are coincidental or systematic. We merely have to check if, for example, the following or preceding sentences contain the same requisites in both sources. If this can be shown to be the case, then one cannot speak of coincidence anymore.

The preceding sentence in Appianus:
>'...but the people returned to Caesar's bier and they bore him to the Capitol...'[140]

And in Mark:
>'...And they bring him unto the place Golgotha, which is, being interpreted, The place of a skull.'[141]

It is striking that both sources in the Greek language use the same verb *'pherô'*: 'bear', 'carry', 'bring'. In Jesus' case we would have expected the word 'led', for he still was alive. This expectation is so strong that it has been correspondingly corrected in some manuscripts.[142]

Even more striking is that the place has the same name: Capitol. In Mark, of course, it is translated: the place of a skull. The Romans derived *Capitolium* from *caput*. The tale is that an Etruscan king, *Olus* (i.e. *Aulus Vulcentanus*) was killed and buried there, and that the Capitoline temple and hill received its name after his skull was later found: 'the head of Olus'—*caput Oli*—*Capitolium*.[143]

That Golgotha is the translation of place of skull and not vice versa is evident in Luke, who only has 'the place of skull' and says that the place was 'called' this way (and not translated), as well as in John, who says explicitly that the place was 'said' the 'place of a skull', which 'means' Golgotha in Hebrew.[144]

The wording 'place of skull' used by Mark—*Kraniou Topos*—seems a little stiff in the Greek, and Luke has replaced it by the more graceful *ton topon tôn Kraniôn*. Therefore the more original version of Mark—*Kraniou Topos*—was not an appellation, but the name itself. Strangely enough it represents not only the translation of *Capitolium*, but also its alteration: *Capi > Kraniou; tolium > Topos*—with the same first letter and confusable lettering of the second part, especially in the accusative: TOLIVM > TOΠON (the erroneous separation of *Capitolium* is inevitable because, unlike Latin, no Greek word can end with a 't'.)

Let us have a look at the same passage in Suetonius, where, associated with the igniting of the funeral pyre, other requisites are mentioned—this passage immediately precedes the one by Suetonius cited above. The irrelevant part is in parenthesis:

> '[...and while some were urging that it be burned in the temple of Jupiter Capitoline, and others in the *Curia* of Pompeius,] suddenly two unknown men, girt with swords and brandishing a pair of javelins, with blazing wax tapers set fire to it.'[145]

Where are the requisites in Mark?

> 'And with him they crucify two thieves; the one on his right hand, and the other on his left.'[146]

We already know that 'set fire to' has become 'crucify'; and here is the confirmation. The only bemusing thing is that in Suetonius it was they who lit the fire, whereas in Mark they are being crucified: in the one case an active, in the other, a passive role. But he who understands Greek knows that besides active and passive there is also the famous/infamous medium, so that one and the same form can mean both 'to set on / to crucify' and 'be set on / be crucified' it depends on how it is perceived and how one wants to see it.

The two guys girt with swords and brandishing a pair of javelins are explained simply as thieves. In fact, it was dangerous burning a body in the Forum, on the *via sacra,* directly in front of the house of the *Pontifex maximus* and the old *Regia,* in the midst all the temples: the regular funeral pyre for Caesar had been erected on the *Campus Martius,* the Field of Mars—as it had been for his daughter.[147] Only after Caesar's being taken up among the gods, was it possible to reinterpret this sacrilegious act—burning his body in this most holy place—as his apotheosis, his ascension to heaven.

As these guys had two javelins in their hands, apparently one in the right and one in the left, and because they again were two, they themselves wound up on crosses—one to his right and one to his left.

Here too the requisites are the same: two anonyms / wrongdoers / the right and the left hand / to set fire to (to crucify).

However, there are many more requisites in Suetonius and Appianus than we have seen in Mark so far: the 'two javelins' for example; or above, when the people throw a lot of different things on Caesar's funeral pyre: the crowd, the Forum, the flute-players, the actors, the triumphal garments, the long-serving soldiers, the legion, the weapons, the wreaths, the military decorations, the jewelry, the matrons, the golden lockets, the purple-fringed tunics, the children, the wearing of apparel and taking it off, the throwing upon, the sacrifice and offerings, the last respects.

What has Mark made of all this?

'And the soldiers led him away into the hall, called Praetorium; and they called together the whole band. And they clothed him with purple, and platted a crown of thorns, and put it about his head, And began to salute him, Hail, King of the Jews! And they smote him on the head with a reed, and did spit upon him, and bowing their knees worshipped him. And when they had mocked him, they took off the purple from him, and put his own clothes on him, and led him out to crucify him.'[148]

We recognize many of the requisites at once, even if Mark has rearranged them masterfully: the soldiers, the Legion (the whole band), the Forum (hall, or more precisely, Praetorium), the triumphal garment / purple-fringed tunic (purple), the greeting to Caesar at his last triumph *ave rex* (rendered literally: Hail, King), the actors (the mockery by the soldiers), the last respects (the worshipping), the donning of apparel, the disrobing, the throwing upon, (clothe, unclothe, reclothe).

Other requisites are more hidden, however: the flute-players—*tibicines*—now smite with a reed. Flute, in Latin *tibia,* 'hollow cylindrical bone', is correctly rendered in Greek as *kalamos,* 'reed' (in both languages the instrument is named after the material), the second part of *tibi-cines, -cines,* is derived instead from the Latin *cano,* 'sing', 'play' from the nearer sounding Greek *kinô,* 'move'; the verb ruled by *tibicines* is *inicere,* which not only means 'throw above', but sometimes 'smite on': so both verbs fuse and the 'flute-players' become those who 'smite with the reed'. The weapons and the wreaths of the soldiers are braided together to a crown of thorns: the weapons mentioned are the 'spears' (borne by the two strangers)—in Latin *iaculum,* in Greek *akontion; stephanos* 'wreath' was the next word; but *akanthinos stephanos* means wreath of thorns: out of 'spear' and 'wreath' we get a 'pointed wreath', a 'wreath of thorns', a 'crown of thorns'. Consequently 'throw upon' here becomes 'put on'—'put on the head'. The 'matrons' together with 'the children' *goneus, gonê* are generally mistaken as *gony* 'knee' and that is why the soldiers fall down on their knees. Finally the 'lockets' on the necks of the children, being hollow in order to contain the heraldic amulet of the family, are named in Latin *bullae,* literally 'bubbles': misunderstood as 'bubbles of saliva', they become 'spit in the face'.

So there is nothing missing. No word has been taken away or added. The same words were only taken in another meaning, which made a reorganisation of the story necessary in order for it to make sense again—but of course it becomes a different one. The interpretation changes, but the requisites—even though transformed—continue to exist.

In addition, this passage gives us the opportunity to prove the resistibility of the requisites. We have just seen how two different requisites in the Caesar story—the triumphal garment of the actors and the children's purple-fringed tunics—compete with each other to represent the purple in which the soldiers in Mark's story array Jesus. This means that one of the requisites in the Caesar sources has not been used. It hovers in the ether, wandering around, waiting for the opportunity to be put to a 'sensible' use elsewhere. It is easy to detect whether it is the triumphal garment of the actors or the children's purple-fringed tunics: the purple and the wreath belong together with the triumphal garment, whereas the children's tunics only have a purple fringe. So the still unused requisite is the children's tunics. What is it called in Latin? Simply *praetexta*—literally 'pre-woven'. The meaning was that something additional was woven at the front: in the case of the togas of officials and senators it was the well-known purple border; in the case of the children it would have been a tunic with purple borders as well, like we still see today with our choristers of the Catholic churches, sometimes even with floral patterns. This term 'pre-woven tunic' has not been used by Mark at all: we have to wait for it to turn up in another place. As we have seen, Matthew and Luke depend much on Mark, so it is better to seek it in John. We find it right away:

'Then the soldiers, when they had crucified Jesus, took his garments, and made four parts, to every soldier a part; and also his coat: now the coat was without seam, woven from the top throughout.'[149]

The King James Bible says *coat* for *tunic*. John says *chitôn*, i.e. exactly the same, even etymologically, as the Latin *tunica*. *Praetexta*, 'pre-woven' is understood as 'woven before, not sewn' and indeed 'from the top throughout' like the purple borders of the Romans as well.

The following sentence by Appianus (we already know the beginning):

'[Then they set alight the pyre] and all the people waited there throughout the night.'[150]

And in Mark as read in the Bezae Cantabrigiensis (**D**):

'And it was the third hour, and they watched over him.'[151]

Luke:

'And the people stood beholding.' ... 'And it was about the sixth hour, and there was a darkness over all the earth until the ninth hour.'[152]

Here too, we can observe the congruence of requisites—the people keeping vigil, the darkness. In regards to the amount of time involved, it is obvious by the variety offered that they were later suggestions by the Evangelists. As a matter of fact, the Greek *hôra* can mean any arbitrary period of time, from the seasons right down to the hour, whether it be day or night. The 'third hour' of Mark could quite well be 'the third night-watch'.

Before we continue comparing the whole Gospel with the entire *Vita Caesaris*, a brief interim assessment seems appropriate. Here we have seen that the *Vita Caesaris* and the story of Jesus, looked at from an arbitrary point, be it forwards or backwards, when comparing the oldest sources, in the original text, not only exhibit the same requisites, but in the same order, and in some passages they even show the exact same sequences. And if the requisites differ from each other, it is because another translation was made, but any resulting abnormalities still remain within the bounds of normal folk-etymologies and the mistakes of copyists.

Because such parallels are too inherent to be attributed to literary topoi and even more so because Caesar's biography is history and not literature—there is only one interpretation left: the Gospel is a Greek version of the *Vita Caesaris* although an anomalous one. It looks as if the fact that Matthew (in particular), by infusing the text with so many citations from the Jewish Bible, adulterated the picture to such an extent that the most Roman story of all—which had belonged to the whole empire and its peoples—could emerge as a Jewish one.

We now want to test this concretized hypothesis by returning to the question we asked initially: Where is the cross in the Caesar story?

We have seen that in all likelihood Jesus was not crucified whilst alive, and perhaps not even at all. Then, we observed that his crucifixion shows a high structural conformity with Caesar's cremation. Now, in the case of Jesus, the cross cannot be ignored. We are not inclined to think that Mark has simply fantasized the cross on the basis of a martyr's stake due to the presence of all the court benches, judges' seats and palisades. This would contradict his painfully meticulous treatment of the requisites, even if his result has fallen wide of the mark. If the Gospel is the hidden *Vita Caesaris,* then a dominant role must have been played by a requisite, that by its nature would have predestined it to be mistaken for a cross in a changed environment, and indeed, it would have to have been connected with Caesar's funeral, even if it was a cremation.

Hence, let us follow the procedure of Caesar's funeral with more attention, with special concern for the imagery used there. What we will behold is an unusual tropaeum with an unexpected image of Caesar attached to it, and we will hear the voice of an unsettling face of Caesar.

The new images of Caesar

As was usual at the funeral of a distinguished Roman, so here too the wax figure of Caesar was to be carried in front of the bier and then placed on the Rostra, so that during the funeral oration the people could see him as he had been in life.

But Caesar's wax statue could not be adorned in full robes as was the usual custom: it would have been dressed with the triumphal robe which was none other than the red robe of the ancient kings,[153] the one that had made his murderers see red and decide to carry out their assault on the tyrant. Now at this time Brutus and Cassius were still in the city. They had managed to receive amnesty for themselves and buy the neutrality of several veterans with the promise to compensate expropriated landlords from the state treasury so they could buy their properties back. Marcus Antonius, friend and relative of the deceased and moreover holder of the office of consul and designated *flamen Divi Iulii*—High priest of Divus Iulius, the new god that Caesar was to become after his death—had to consider himself lucky to still be alive, and that Caesar's estates had not been auctioned, that his acts had not been repealed, and that the Liberators who had at first planned to drag the corpse of the tyrant through the streets and throw it into the Tiber had instead complied with the insistence of Caesar's father-in-law Piso that the Pontifex Maximus should be lain to rest with the customary honors.

In the midst of this stalemate, Antonius had the momentous idea of fashioning Caesar's wax-figure in such a way that the people would see him as he had lain after the murder—with the blood-stained toga displaying all the rents of the daggers on his martyred body, and with his arms spread out just as he had fallen. Indeed nobody had seen him there where he had fallen because they all ran for their lives after the assault—both friend and foe. Antonius, who had remained outside, fled first. But from the house tops where the people had barricaded themselves, they could see Caesar's injured face and his arms hanging out of both sides of the litter as three of his servants carried the body home through Rome's narrow alleys to his wife Calpurnia.[154]

As this wax figure would not have been visible if it had lain flat on the bier, Antonius ordered it hung on the cross-like tropaeum where, as tradition required, the insignia of victory were affixed. This created an ironic, provocative, unbearable tropaeum, where the image of the victor himself was hung in the midst of the trophies of war. The wax figure was still clad in his passion garment, and the tropaeum was constructed in such a way that it could be rotated so that everybody could clearly see it.

When Piso brought Caesar's body into the Forum, it was placed on the bier on the Rostra[155] so that the tropaeum stood at the head of the funeral bier—a golden ciborium after the fashion of the temple of Venus Genetrix, wherein lay the son of the goddess on a bed of ivory adorned with gold and purple, like the new Osiris on the womb of Isis.[156]

For the funeral obsequies a death mask of Caesar had also been made, as was the custom, so that the deceased himself could address the funeral guests by means of a masked actor who imitated his voice and gestures. This was sometimes done with some levity, but on this occasion with gallows humor and deadly earnest.

Both wax-images, the figure hanging on the tropaeum and the mask worn by the actor, were the main requisites of Antonius' staging of Caesar's funeral liturgy. And he employed them dramatically.[157]

> 'During the performance verses were sung which would evoke emotions of compassion and indignation, such as the line from Pacuvius' *"Contest for the Arms of Achilles"*:
> "*Men servasse, ut essent qui me perderent?*—What, did I save these men that they might murder me!"
> —and others with a similar sentiment from Atilius' Electra.'[158]
> 'The people could endure it no longer. It seemed to them monstrous that all the murderers who, with the single exception of Decimus

Brutus, had been made prisoners while belonging to the faction of Pompeius, and who, instead of being punished, had been advanced by Caesar to the magistracies of Rome and to the command of provinces and armies, should have conspired against him, and that Decimus—who had betrayed him and lured him to the trap—should have been deemed by him worthy for adoption as his son.'[159]

With the reading of the will the atmosphere changed completely, because the supposed tyrant now proved himself a benefactor, bequeathing a remarkable amount to each individual Roman, in addition to leaving the Roman people his famous gardens on the banks of the Tiber. They slowly began to regret that they had been in favor of the amnesty. And from the enormous crowd of people flocked together there arose the increasingly loud sounds of lamentation and misery, and all those who were armored beat their weapons together.

In this situation it is easy to imagine which verses of the Electra the people chanted like a choir: namely those that served as *improperia,* as lamentations over the ingratitude of the murderers.

'And now under the earth the immortal reigns.'

'So that he emerge from the depths of the grave, / gracious, a saviour in the face of the enemy.'

'And that you hear it, Nemesis of the recently deceased.'

'The curses achieve their aim./ Alive are those who lay beneath the ground! / The murderous blow redounds on the head of the murderer, / led by those once murdered.'

'...as for the father I must wreak vengeance on his assassins.'[160]

This was the time for Antonius' funeral oratory. But:

'Instead of the usual Laudatio, Antonius ordered a herald to read aloud the decree of the Senate which awarded all divine and human honours to Caesar, furthermore the oath of loyalty in which they had all pledged themselves to his personal safety. Antonius added very few words of comment.'[161]

He only commented on what the herald read out:

'At each resolution, Antonius turned his face and his hand towards Caesar's body illustrating his discourse by his action. To each appellation he added a brief remark full of grief and indignation. As, for example, where the decree spoke of the father of the fatherland, he added "This is a testimony to his clemency!" and again where he was made "sacred and inviolable" and "everyone was to be held unharmed who should seek refuge with him"—"Nobody", said Antonius, "who found refuge with him was harmed, but he, whom you declared sacred and inviolable, was killed, although he did not extort these honours from you as a tyrant, and did not even ask for them."'[162]

'Whereupon the people, like the chorus in a play, mourned with him in the most sorrowful manner, and from sorrow became filled again with anger.'[163]

'...somewhere in the midst of these lamentations Caesar himself seemed to be speaking, recounting by name his enemies on whom he had conferred benefits, and of the murderers themselves exclaiming, as it were in amazement: "*Men servasse, ut essent qui me perderent?*—Ah, did I save them that they might murder me?"'[164]

And the herald read all the decisions of honor and oaths of allegiance; Antonius indicated what they had made of that by pointing again and again towards the murdered man; Caesar's voice resounded from behind the death mask; the people answered with a fitting strophe from the *Electra*. And thus the indignation increased.

When the herald read aloud the oaths wherein all obliged themselves to protect Caesar and his person with all their power, and wherein all had sworn that he who did not come to his aid in the case of a conspiracy should be condemned to death, Antonius lifted his hand toward the Capitol and cried 'Father Jupiter, I am prepared to help him as I have vowed, but because the other senators have preferred an amnesty, I pray that they will bring us blessings.' The senators were alarmed and hoped that Antonius would retract the accusations and threats; but Antonius distracted: 'It seems to me, fellow-citizens, that what has come to pass is not the work of men but of an evil spirit'. So he blamed it on the devil—and conjured him up at the same time.

'After these words he gathered up his garments like one inspired by God, girded himself so that he might have the free use of his hands, took his position in front of the bier as in a play, bending down to it and rising again, and first hymned him again as a celestial deity, raising his hands to heaven in order to testify to his divine origin.'[165]

Finally Antonius went to the tropaeum, where the symbols of Caesar's victories were attached and in rapid and fluent speech counted out his wars, the battles, the victories, the spoils, extolling each exploit as miraculous and all the time exclaiming 'Thou alone hast come forth unvanquished from all the battles thou hast fought. Thou alone hast avenged thy country of the outrage brought upon it three hundred years ago, bringing to their knees those savage Gallic tribes, the only ones ever to have broken into and burned the city of Rome.' He counted out all the titles the people had awarded Caesar, conscious that no other man could equal his merits:

> 'Therefore for the gods he was appointed Pontifex Maximus, for us Consul, for the soldiers Imperator, and for the enemy Dictator. But why do I tell you all this when in one phrase alone you called him Pater Patriae?'[166]

And here Antonius lowered his voice from its high pitch to a sorrowful tone, and mourned and wept as for a friend who had suffered unjustly:[167]

> 'Yet this father, this Pontifex Maximus, this inviolable being, this hero and god, is dead, alas ... murdered right here within the walls as the result of a plot—he who safely led an army into Britain; ambushed in this city—he who had enlarged its Pomerium; murdered in the Senate house—he who had reared another such edifice at his own expense; unarmed—the brave warrior; naked—the promoter of peace; the judge—near the tribunals; the magistrate—at the seat of government; at the hands of citizens—he who none of the enemy had been able to kill even when he fell into the sea; at the hands of his comrades—he who had so often shown mercy to them! Of what avail, O Caesar, was your humanity, of what avail your inviolability, of what avail the laws? Nay, though you enacted many laws that men might not be killed by their personal foes, yet how mercilessly you yourself were slain by your friends! ... And now you lie dead in the Forum through which you often led the triumph crowned. Wounded to death you have been cast down upon the Rostra from which you often addressed the people. Woe for the blood-bespattered locks of grey, alas for the rent robe, which you donned, it seems, only to be slain in it!'[168]

And with his spear he lifted the garment hanging on the tropaeum and shook it aloft, rent by the dagger blows and red with the blood of the Imperator. With this movement he exposed the Simulacrum hanging on the tropaeum and rotated it in all directions by means of a turn-table.[169] And thus was Caesar's martyred body suddenly revealed for all to see—like Christ on the cross.

The pitiful sight did not fail to have its effect. Blinded by wrath, the people rose up and hunted for Caesar's murderers who were long gone, but they tore to pieces one whom they did find—a certain Helvius Cinna who was a good friend of Caesar but who had the great misfortune of bearing the same name as another Cinna who had made a speech against the deceased.

> 'Without hearing any explanation about the identical names, they rent him to pieces in an act of savagery: no part of the body could be found for the funeral!'[170]

His head, however, was speared on a lance and paraded about.[171]

Now the furious crowd returned to the bier and took hold of it. Here, one wanted to take it to the place where he had met his death—the Curia of Pompeius—which they desired to reduce to cinders. There, another tried to convey it up to the Capitol for cremation as something consecrated in order to give him a place amongst the gods. The priests blocked their way because of the risk of fire. It went to and fro. The crowd raged. The soldiers intervened and the consuls had some of the more audacious men thrown down from the Capitoline rock.[172] So the people placed the bier back in the Forum at the site where the ancient Roman house of the Kings and the house of the Pontifex Maximus stood.

'...all of a sudden two strangers appeared, girdled with swords and with two spears in their hands and ignited the bier with wax-torches!'[173]

'...and immediately the spectators assisted the blaze by heaping on it dry branches and the judges' chairs and the court benches and whatever else came to hand. Thereupon the musicians and the professional mourners, who had walked in the funeral train wearing the robes that he himself had worn at his four triumphs, tore these in pieces and flung them onto the flames—to which veterans who had assisted at his triumphs added the arms that they had borne. Many women in the audience similarly sacrificed their jewellery together with their children's breast-plaques and purple-fringed tunics.'[174]

Now the most daring stormed up to the houses of the murderers with torches and tried to set them on fire, but the neighbors hindered them because of their fear of a blaze and finally they persuaded them to forgo the arson. Meanwhile the people kept vigil at the funeral pyre and even stayed for some time more:

'Public grief was enhanced by crowds of foreigners lamenting after the fashion of their own countries, especially Jews who came flocking to the Forum for several nights in succession.'[175]

'The crowd established an altar on the place where the pyre had been—Caesar's emancipees already had collected his bones and buried them in the family crypt—and wanted to sacrifice then and there and offer gifts to Caesar as to a god. However, the consuls threw down the altar and punished some of those who showed their dissatisfaction.'[176]

So says Dio. And the parallel conclusion by Appianus:

'There an altar was first erected, but now there stands the temple of Caesar himself, as he was deemed worthy of divine honors. For Octavianus, his son by adoption and who took the name of Caesar, followed in his footsteps in political matters, greatly strengthened the government that was founded by Caesar and which remains to this day,[177] decreed divine honors to his father.'[178]

Caesar a prototype of Jesus?

All events related to Caesar's death were so dramatic—with treason, murder, and subsequent apotheosis—that the Passion story of the god incarnate becomes the centerpiece of each vita of Divus Julius. That is why a biography of Caesar, especially an ancient one always reads like a hagiography and leaves an impression of sacredness. So for example it could be said:

'...the panegyric Emperor-biography, composed by Nicolas of Damascus, Chancellor and Historian of Herodes' palace in the years 23-21 BC, reads in part like a Gospel-text.'[179]

This is not limited to the pro-Caesarean authors nor does it rely on subjective impressions. That the Christian Easter-liturgy follows the ritual of Caesar's funeral like a script has already attracted attention:

'The funeral ritual for Divus Iulius [is] a unique passion-liturgy ... this celebration is one of the most essential events of history contemporaneous with the New Testament.'[180]

This is all the more striking as one would expect that the Easter-liturgy would follow the Gospel and not the funeral ritual of Caesar. Some details and requisites are not grounded in the Gospel Passion-story, but they find their counterpart in Caesar's funeral. Think for example of the unveiling of the cross, accompanied by the chant:

'Here is the cross of torture on which the salvation of the world hung.'[181]

It corresponds to the action of removing Caesar's toga on the tropaeum and to the content of the words of Antonius. Think of the ensuing *improperia,* the lamentations of the crucified one over the ingratitude of the people of Israel which are sung in the Catholic liturgy of the Good Friday Mass. They conform to Antonius' demonstrated repetitive example: the reading out of each of the benefactions conferred on his people which are counter-pointed by the lamentations over the murder of God. Consider the beginning:

'My people, what did I do to you? How did I offend? Answer me. I led you out of Egypt, you lead your savior to the cross.'[182]

It sounds like the words spoken through Caesar's death-mask: 'Ah, did I save them, that they should murder me?' Only that here the liberation from the threat of the Gauls is spoken of, there it is the liberation from the hand of Egyptian oppression, and, instead of the lines from Pacuvius and the Electra, one seems to hear those verses from the Bible with a parallel meaning, which would have been recited by the Jews who, as Suetonius tells us, kept a long vigil at Caesar's funeral pyre and sung 'songs of lament'—'according to their custom'.[183]

Think of the adoration of the cross, of the procession behind the cross, and finally of the renewing of baptismal vows. There is also the Easter-fire on Holy Saturday. While the congregation waits in the dark church for the Easter Light, the priest ignites a small pile of wood, a little pyre outside, on which the Easter candle is lit.[184] The correspondence with the funeral pile and Caesar's apotheosis is striking, even in the re-enactment: the believers carry the fire into the night, as once the fire-brands were carried to the houses of Caesar's murderers, whereas the holy water sprinkled and distributed in the church recalls the corresponding extinguishing of the fires. The Easter-communion itself—where nothing is permitted to remain—evinces an unsettling symmetry with the total annihilation of Caesar's intimate, Cinna.

There even appears to be another corresponding custom preserved by the people independent of the ecclesiastical hierarchy. When the triumvirate finally managed to gain the upper-hand over the murderers of Caesar, they decreed that the Ides of March—which the murderers had celebrated on their coins as the day of liberation from the tyrant—be damned as *dies parricidii*, 'the day of parricide'. Further, they converted the venue of the murder, Pompeius' Curia, into a latrine, so that everyone had the opportunity to express their greater or lesser opinion of the self-styled Liberators.[185] The Catholic farmers in Germany, at least those from within the *limes,* seem to have conserved this practice until today, because they regard the celebration of Good Friday as a provocation, and on that day they vent their displeasure by spreading compost and manure on their fields.

A chronological Re-Orientation?

Now, as is well-known, Caesar is a century more ancient than Jesus (born exactly 100 years before the official birth of Christ) and he died still 76 years before Jesus (Caesar 44 BC, Jesus traditionally 33 AD). So four to five generations lie between them.

Thus the cult of Divus Iulius is older than that of Jesus, and in the face of change, liturgy tends to be conservative. We can rule out the notion that the similarities between the two rituals can be attributable to their both drawing upon collective oriental examples,[186] because Caesar's ritual was improvised—it had to be—due to the context in which it fell. So it is more logical to consider the unconventional but nevertheless possible alternative, namely, that Divus Iulius could have been the prototype for Jesus.

And our texts even offer some circumstantial evidence for this assumption.

A praetexta?

In the reconstruction of Caesar's funeral, Appianus was our main source with Suetonius serving as a guideline. Appianus is more elaborate, but his offerings have a repetitive character. These repetitions give rise to the supposition that he employed not only the *Historiae* of Asinius Pollio as a schema,[187] but used literary sources as well.[188] We can point to the funeral oration of Antonius as a possibility, which was published according to custom, or even a praetexta *Iulius Caesar*[189] which developed from it—a drama—written with classic Roman gravity. In fact, Appianus' account reads like the libretto of a play, where the repetitions seem to arise from the arrangement of the different roles in sequences.

It is true that a praetexta *Iulius Caesar* has not been passed down to us, but it is quite probable that Antonius' funeral oration was published.[190] And because Antonius, when giving his funeral oration, had the herald recite the decrees that honored Caesar while he himself only commented on them, and also selected the verses from the Electra and set the tone for the people's chorus, then the text of his funeral oration must have had the character of a libretto. As *flamen Divi Iulii,* who on the basis of the honor decrees was beholden (like all the other priests) to liturgically celebrate Caesar's victories annually, he would not have neglected to celebrate Caesar's funeral, which precisely because of its staging and oratory could amount to his apotheosis. Had Appianus attended Passion-plays designed to honor Divus Julius? The immediacy that characterizes his account invites such a conclusion.

In light of this situation, it gives cause for thought that the tradition of the Passion play has been preserved right up to the present day—for which Appianus' account could have served as an excellent exemplar.

Was it the original one?

In any case, in the sequence of Marcion, who saw Jesus on the cross as a mere *phantasma* (cf. TERT. *adv. Marc.* 4.42), and Nestorius, the Koran also rejects the notion that Jesus was crucified and it says, that 'a very similar figure appeared to them' or more precisely 'was shown' (Sure 4.157). Hence it confirms that the idea of Jesus' crucifixion was a later and contested one (as late as 325 AD, the Council of Nicaea in its creed, the *Symbolum Nicaenum,* does not say anything about crucifixion or Pilate). It even sounds as if it developed from a stage-setting that displayed Caesar's wax-figure on the cruciform tropaeum. Was it the Passion play of the original Easter ritual? In actuality, Jesus is scarcely depicted dying on the cross throughout the whole of the first millennium (cf. also note 157 p. 384).

A delocalization?

In perusing the above cited historical texts, especially in the Greek original, it is striking that the sole reason we know that the whole scene occurred in Rome is because—we just happen to know it. The name itself is not mentioned: it is referred to as 'the city'. It could be any city. The fact that Romans are involved does not locate the scene: at this time all the officials in the empire were Romans. Also the Senate is often called Synedrion,[191] so that we easily could imagine it to be in Jerusalem, all the more post festum, when only the mourning Jews remained at the reliquies. (cf. p. 79).

Caesar too, is barely mentioned by name:[192] we hear of the one 'killed', the 'murdered', the 'martyred', of the 'dead', the 'corpse', the 'body' and the 'bier', rarely of the 'autocrat', the 'dictator', the 'king', or the 'tyrant'; but rather we hear of the 'high priest', 'son of God', of 'God'; or of the 'saviour', the 'father', and if we do hear of him, then it is just 'him'. It could easily be assumed that another person is being spoken of—Jesus.

The personae surrounding him play well-known roles too: there is a follower who betrays him, and a murderer who gets an amnesty; there is somebody who bears his cross, someone who demands his body, and somebody who proclaims his apotheosis.

The requisites also seem to be familiar: the cross-shaped tropaeum, the wax-figure on the cross, the spear, the passion-garment, the *improperia*, the Easter fire, the empty tomb, the stone that has rolled over. And—we even have the Via Dolorosa and the Pietà:

'A little later, three slaves, who were nearby, placed the body on a litter and carried it home through the Forum. The wounds on the face and the arms hanging down were visible on both sides, as the curtain had been drawn back. There was no one who refrained from tears at the sight of him who for a long time had been revered as a god. Much weeping and lamentation accompanied them from either side, from mourners on the roofs, in the streets, and in the vestibules. When they approached his house, a far greater wailing met their ears, for his wife rushed out with a number of women and servants, calling on her husband and bewailing her lot in that she had in vain counselled him not to go out on that day. But he had suffered a fate far worse than she had feared.'[193]

All the participants in the Roman drama were incidentally old acquaintances of the Jews, who remained conspicuously long at Caesar's cremation site. Because they all had also made an appearance in Jerusalem: Caesar's adversary Pompeius had conquered the city and the temple in 63. It is no coincidence that Cicero (*Att.* 2.9.1) mocked him as *noster Hierosolymarius*, 'our Jerusalemite'—with a play on words on 'Marius', Caesar's uncle. Pompeius had brought the rebellious Aristobulos as a captive to Rome. After Crassus' defeat against the Parthians in 53/52, Cassius Longinus had been able to hold Syria and renegade Judaea only with brute force, in the process he had had Pitholaos, who had defected and led the rebellion after Aristobulos, executed—i.e. probably crucified. At the beginning of the civil war Caesar had freed Aristobulos and sent him back to Jerusalem—without success, because some Pompeians poisoned him. For a long time the burial of his body was denied until Antonius later sent it, embalmed in honey, to the Jews to bury it in the royal tombs (cf. note 183).

Now all these Jerusalemite protagonists cast similar, appropriate respective roles in Rome also:

Pompeius was dead already, but it was in front of his statue, which incidentally Caesar had had re-erected, where Caesar was murdered. Thus Pompeius had his revenge, but also showed himself to be ungrateful posthumously.

Cassius Longinus had raged and murdered again. And the exposition of Caesar's body as a wax simulacrum on the cruciform tropaeum had to have even more so called to mind the execution of Pitholaos by the hand of the same Longinus, as well as all the other crucified ones of Judaea.

And Antonius repeated the same act of piety on Caesar that he once had shown to Aristobulos: again he has the dead one buried anyway, against the resistance of the Pompeians. This time he does not have the martyred body embalmed in honey, but, appropriate for the cremation, duplicated and affixed to the cruciform tropaeum not least to the shame of Longinus.

Now all these players, well-known to the Jews, also appeared in a drama which happened during their most important holiday: Passover.

An accidental coincidence of the calendar?

For although Caesar had reformed the calendar one year earlier, switching over from the old-Roman one which had become a mess, to the solar one, called the Julian after him—which actually made the concurrence of the Roman Ides on the 15th of March, now reckoned according to the sun, with the Jewish Passover, still reckoned according to the moon, on the 15th of Nizan a rarity—it just so happened that in 44 BC the 15th of March, of all days, was a full moon day: that is to say that on Caesar's Ides of March it was Passover at the same time (cf. note 183).

Due to an even less probable coincidence, Caesar's funeral on the 20th of March fell on a Sunday, of all days, so that Caesar's funeral which was perceived as his resurrection occured on the same day of the week as the resurrection of Jesus.

The simultaneous occurence of both 'coincidences', that there is a full moon on the 15th of March and the 20th is a Sunday, happens once every 532 years! (cf. note 183).

There is enough here to justify our looking for other evidence indicating that the cross of Jesus originated from Caesar's tropaeum.

Let us first address the context.

The Crucifixion of Caesar

One of the more famous anecdotes concerning Caesar tells of when he fell into the hands of pirates during his youth. It happened near the island of Pharmakussa, on the Ionian coast between Miletus and Halicarnassus. Caesar wanted to go to Rhodes to hear the lectures of Apollonius Molo, the most eloquent teacher of that time. Pirates were greatly feared because they did not handle their victims with kid gloves, even killing or throwing overboard the more obstinate. The pirates that captured him only wanted twenty talents ransom which insulted Caesar because, as he advised them, he was worth at least fifty. He sent his companions into the surrounding area to raise this hefty sum and spent almost forty days alone with the pirates during which time he complained when they disturbed his sleep, gambled and competed in fighting with them and read aloud poems and speeches. Since they were not enthusiastic Caesar called them uneducated barbarians and promised and swore to hang them soon. All this delighted their hearts and they thought they had hooked the most hilarious of patrons. So when he paid them the fifty talents ransom they readily let him go. When he reached shore he manned some ships, set out to sea, and surprised the pirates still anchored on the island. He captured most of them and had them crucified as he had sworn under oath to do, which they had taken to be his joking. But because he abhorred cruelty even in revenge, he had them strangled first so that they would not suffer.[194]

By the way, we should note that the Church, of all institutions, followed suit in this leniency in punishment and was always anxious to have heretics strangled before they were burnt at the stake. But back to our theme.

We see that from the start of his career Caesar was associated with crucifixion, but not in the same way as Crassus and Pompeius who defeated the Spartacus slave rebellion and lined the streets with the crucified rebels. For Caesar himself had fallen into the hands of those pirates who had furnished Spartacus' fleet, and had risked being speared or drowned by them with scorn and derision.

The terminology does not allow enough differentiation to know whether Plutarchus says that Caesar had the pirates crucified or impaled, and says that when Caesar spoke the threat he said he would have them *kremân*, 'hung by the neck,' 'hung', or 'strung up'.[195] When Caesar carries out the threat Plutarchus says that he *anestaurôsen* them, he had them 'impaled', 'speared'. Suetonius remains vague at first and says generally that 'he had them executed' *(supplicio adfecit)*, and then becomes more precise by saying literally that he had them 'fixed, stuck to the cross' *(cruci suffixit)*. Strictly speaking, it cannot be decided from Suetonius either whether it is about a *crux punica*, i.e. *acuta*, a 'punic' or 'sharp' crucifixion, which was an impalement. For the Roman pronounced the penalty; the executioner carried it out according to the custom of the country or his own taste.[196]

Assuming it was a crucifixion similar to popular iconography, with the arms outstretched and nails in the hands and feet, we see that Plutarchus used *stauros* as root for his verb *anestaurôsen*, 'he speared'. *Stauros* means primarily 'stake', in this case in the sense of a 'martyr's stake' and is used as the translation for *crux*. Thus, here we would have, independent of Christian literature, an equation *stauros* = *crux*, 'martyr's stake' = 'cross', and in fact one referring to Caesar, not to Jesus. The other verb that Plutarchus uses, however—*kremô*, 'hang by the neck', 'hang', 'string up'—is so very similar to the Latin *cremo*, 'burn, cremate', that the cremated Caesar could become the 'crucified one'.

Be that as it may, one must assume that at Caesar's funeral the tropaeum that Antonius raised with Caesar's simulacrum hanging on it was seen by people who remembered his pirate-crucifixion, and regarded this as a crucifixion committed by robbers on a Roman. Thus the assassins of Caesar must have been regarded as common criminals: an unbearable exchange of roles crying out for revenge.

It is therefore understandable why, when the tropaeum with Caesar's wax effigy nailed to it was displayed, the people seized the first Cinna that they met, tore him apart, stuck his head on a pole and carried it around: *occidit caputque eius praefixum hastae circumtulit*, says Suetonius. We see here how this *praefixum hastae*, which is normally translated with 'fixed on a lance', but could as well be rendered as 'hefted to a stake'—the original meaning of *hasta* is 'pole', thin 'stake', only later via 'shaft' did it come to mean 'lance'—joins that *suffixum cruci*, 'nailed to a martyr's stake' we came across with the pirates. Since Helvius Cinna co-suffered the martyr death of Caesar—lat. *cruciatus*—because of a mix up of names, the carrying around of Cinna's *hasta* with his head on it can, under changed conditions, be perceived as co-carrying Caesar's martyr stake, i.e. the cross of Jesus. Thus *cruciatus* becomes *crucifixus*, the martyr death becomes the crucified one and *Helvius Cinna* confused with *Cornelius Cinna* becomes one of the two crucified with him.

The tragedy within the tragedy

The decisive impetus for perceiving Caesar's *cruciatus* as crucifixion was given by the repetition of Caesar's assassination carried out on his successor and namesake *Gaius Caesar*, i.e. Caligula.

This time, too, the main ringleader was a *Cassius (Chaerea)*, and that it was meant as a repetition of the 'tyrannicide' of the other Gaius Caesar is clarified not least by the watchword chosen by the murderers, which they shouted while stabbing with the daggers: *Repete!*—'once more' (cf. SUET. *Cal.* 58).

This second act of the assassination of *Gaius Caesar* took place during a mime play that was written by a *Catullus* (coincidentally also a namesake of Caesar's bosom foe, the poet *Catullus*) and named after an infamous brigand: *Laureolus*—'small laurel'. From Flavius Josephus we learn that in this mime play 'the bandit chief was nailed to the cross', and this had been consciously chosen as the background scene for the 'spectacle of the tyrannicide' performed on Caligula (Jos. *A.J.* 19.1.13 [§94]).

This, too, was no coincidence. Because it had been Caesar who had particularly supported the mime plays and himself had maintained mimes. And then a mime had also performed at his funeral, as we saw, imitating gesture and voice of the deceased and speaking, as if from beyond, the famous verse of Pacuvius: 'Alas, did I save these men that they might murder me?'

Now *Gaius Caesar* had been murdered as a tyrant again, during a mime play, in which a bandit chief was crucified. It was inevitable that this would rub off on the later depictions of Caesar's funeral—whether in Passion plays or in the liturgy. As a result, the exposition of his body as wax figure had to be perceived as crucifixion and mockery from the time of Caligula's death.

Speaking of repercussions, let it be mentioned briefly here that the execution of Vitellius by followers of Vespasian might have molded the image of Jesus' *Via Dolorosa* also. SUET. *Vit.* 17: 'They dragged him to the Forum with his arms bound behind his back, a rope around his neck, with rent garments and half-naked. All along the *Via Sacra* he endured the grossest abuses by deeds and words…'.

The image of the flagellation of Jesus, which accompanies the crucifixion, however, was co-influenced by the manner of execution of Antigonus which Cassius Dio described as outrageous. Antigonus was flagellated and crucified in Jerusalem—by the hand of the same Antonius who performed Caesar's funeral (cf. note 183).

But Caesar had himself already experienced a flagellation of sorts. His political enemies had a man flagellated in order to challenge and insult Caesar by demonstrating that the Roman citizenship rights he had granted to the man would not be honored (cf. p. 310).

Suppression by Decree?

What may have contributed to perceiving Caesar's *cruciatus* as crucifixion, might have its roots in the original charter from the time of the Divus Iulius Cult.

The day of Caesar's assassination, the Ides of March, was declared *dies parricidii*, the day of parricide, the *dies ater, nefastus*, the black day, the abominable day. Any recognition of the day and the deed was forbidden, because this would have led to its celebration by the anti-Caesar side also. The place of the assassination was even made into a latrine and thus the deed itself was presented as filth. The obvious consequence was the detachment of day and place from the memory of Caesar and the worship of the Divus Iulius. In a religious sense, the stabbing took place on no day and in no place, never and nowhere, i.e. it was rendered undone. The resurrection of Divus Iulius, rung-in with the people's revolt at his funeral and completed by the victory over his assassins in Philippi, undid his death even more in retrospect, all the more since with Octavianus the new, younger Caesar, *Divi Filius*, existed, live and in the flesh. There was no death and no murder anymore. That which remained alive was the memory of the Passion, of the *cruciatus*, which naturally had to be relocated, while the expositio, the presentation of Caesar's martyred body in the form of an exposed wax figure hanging on a tropaeum, had to be reinterpreted as a crucifixion (ill. 115 in note 157). That means that the first impetus to the reinterpretation of Caesar's stabbing as the crucifixion of Jesus was the inherent necessity and inner logic of the Divus Iulius Cult. The mistakes of copyists and translators, who made *cruciatus crucifixio, cremo kremô* and the dagger of the conjuror *Longinus* the spear of the soldier *Longinus,* are not the result of their stupidity, but are their creative attempts to bring the history of the Passion in accord with the political and theological necessity of undoing the stabbing of Caesar.

An important point in the *lex templi*—the law that decreed the building of the Divi Iulii Temple on the place of Caesar's cremation in the Forum Romanum initiating the worship of the new God throughout the entire empire—was the ban placed on the Gens Iulia from thenceforth carrying along images of the dead Caesar in the funeral processions of his family members. (In funeral processions it was the custom to carry the image of the newly deceased in front of the procession; from the family mausoleum the images of the dead family members came to meet him halfway, to welcome him, and to accompany him to the family grave). The reason was that, from that point on, he was no longer to be considered as a dead person—as his murderers, Cicero *imprimis,* would have wanted it—but as a living god, as the people demanded and Octavian decreed it. This ban had an iconographic effect and resulted in his image as Divus Iulius no longer having the facial features of Caesar (see ill. 48, 92, 98). This means that the uncoupling of Divus Iulius from Caesar was deliberate and desired from the beginning. So that the God—who, unlike the man from whom he emerged like a butterfly from a caterpillar, was never born and never died but always was, is and will be, eternally—having discarded everything human, is received, perfectly celestial, amongst the Gods.

The tropaeum

As we have seen, Caesar's couch was placed in a gilded shrine modeled after the temple of Venus Genetrix, and at its head stood the tropaeum, shrouded in the robe he wore when he was murdered. Overlapping the sources led to the conjecture that the wax simulacrum of Caesar hung on the tropaeum to portray him as he had fallen after being stabbed, at first covered with his blood stained robe.

The tropaeum was supposed to be a victory column, and in this case it was a complex one, because Caesar had celebrated four triumphs and an ovation. As we touched on in the first chapter, the coins celebrating Caesar's victory over Gaul document what a simple tropaeum looked like.

21. Caesar Denarius, ca. 46 BC.

One can see that the connection to Venus was there from the outset: Venus Genetrix is on the front of the coin, the tropaeum on the back. At Caesar's funeral the tropaeum was at the head of a small Venus temple which served his couch as a ciborium, as it were. On the coin, Venus has a young Cupid/Iulus nearby, and in the small Venus temple the great descendent of Venus and Iulus, imbedded as if in her lap, lay Gaius Iulius.

An idea of how the tropaeum might have stood at Caesar's casket is given by a coin that a mint master, C. Coelius Caldus, minted for his homonymous grandfather, who was honored with the title of imperator and victory columns because of his military successes in Spain in the year 50 BC. There is a figure lying on a lectisternium—no doubt grandfather Coelius Caldus—with a tropaeum at each end. Since the coin was minted only six years before Caesar's death, it demonstrates how Caesar's tropaeum might have stood towards his couch in the miniature-temple of Venus. The back of the coin:

22. Caldus Denarius

We have to ignore the one tropaeum, allow the lectisternium to take the form of a small Venus temple and think of poles for carrying the bier.

The idea that not the bier was carried, but rather that the dead man himself carried his own 'cross', is conveyed through two circumstances.

First: next to the Rostra stood the *volcanal,* the archaic altar of Vulcan, in *lapis niger,* black marble: According to tradition, Romulus had been murdered there by the senators. Thus the new Romulus, Caesar, was laid out directly beside the place where the old Romulus had suffered the same fate. Caesar's body was finally cremated at the other end of the Forum within sight of the temple of Jupiter Stator on the *Via Sacra,* that Romulus according to tradition had dedicated to the highest god at the location where the Latins, fleeing from the Sabines, had finally come to a halt. One of the statues in Rome that according to ancient sources portrayed Romulus carrying the tropaeum, must have stood there honoring the city's founder—it cannot be thought otherwise.[197] During the entire funeral ceremony the mourners not only had before them Caesar's tropaeum on which hung the wax simulacrum covered with his bloody, torn toga, but also a statue of Romulus portraying the first king carrying into the city—at that time on foot—the first tropaeum for the very first Roman triumph. Images of Romulus statues can be seen on coins of later emperors as well as on wall paintings and house fronts in Pompeii. Romulus is portrayed as Mars and Mars as Romulus,—except that the god is naked. For a better idea of this we depict a Mars coin:

23. Romulus; 24. Romulus on wall paintings in Pompeii; 25. Mars

We see here how the tropaeum in archaic times was shouldered and carried by the triumphator himself along the *Via Sacra.*

The tropaeum looks tiny and feather light in these pictures as it is carried by Romulus or Mars without a hint of difficulty on his left shoulder like a travel bag or almost as if playing it like a fiddle. In reality it looked much different. Plutarchus has given us a description of the very impressive triumph of Romulus which might have also been a description of the man-sized Romulus statues. After the rape of the Sabine women, Romulus won a first victory against the king of Caenina, Acro, who, without waiting for support from the other Sabines, immediately had gone into battle against the Latins. Romulus smote Acro in duel combat and had to fulfill a vow: he had sworn that if he won, he would himself carry the armor and weapons of his enemy to Jupiter and dedicate them to him.

'Romulus thought about how to best fulfill the oath to Jupiter and at the same time offer the citizens a pleasing drama. He had a mighty oak tree which stood by the camp felled and formed into a tropaeum upon which he had the whole suit of armor of Acro orderly mounted and fastened. He himself girded his clothing and wreathed his head with laurel, his mane flowing. He heaved the tropaeum and held it up straight, supporting it with his right shoulder, and proceeded intoning the song of victory in which the armed soldiers following him joined in while the citizens welcomed them with joy and wonder. This procession was the beginning and model for later triumphs and the tropaeum was dedicated to Jupiter Feretrius. Romans say ferire for "smite" and Romulus had prayed that he might smite and overthrow the man.'[198]

The tropaeum was thus carved out of an oak and Acro's suit of armor was attached to it: so it was no less an act of strength to carry the tropaeum than it was to kill Acro. It was not by chance that all the triumphators after Romulus made their entrance in a chariot.

Nevertheless, or for this very reason, it seems that Romulus—by carrying his heavy tropaeum on the *Via Sacra* himself, and whose statue stood around the corner forming the quasi-background for the funeral of the new Romulus, Caesar—had set the stage for Jesus to carry his own heavy cross on the *Via Dolorosa*.

Secondly: Caesar's tropaeum—which stood at the head of his funerary couch within the model of the Venus temple, and which held not only the spoils of his victories but also his blood-sprayed garment which Antonius allowed to flutter in the wind, and which, as we have seen, very likely held the wax effigy—infuriated the people as it hung in front of them with the herald reading salutations and oaths. What happened to the tropaeum as Caesar's bier was carried away from the Rostra and, swaying ever so slightly, reached the other end of the Forum where it was suddenly ignited and burned upon the improvised pyre made up of chairs, benches palisades? Did the herald who served as ministrant for Antonius raise the tropaeum as Romulus once had and carry it in Caesar's place, behind or in front of his bier and in place of the victory song did he recite the verses of Pacuvius: 'Alas, did I save these men that they might murder me?' Was the herald Caesar's Simon of Kyrene?[199] And what did he do with the tropaeum when the bier was suddenly ignited and the people quickly gathered material to burn on the improvised pyre? Did he place the tropaeum back at the head of the funerary couch, as earlier on the Rostra? Did the tropaeum burn with it, as the cross still does today during the Easter Fire? Did the wax figure help to make the fire burn brightly, so that the soul of the deceased ascended into heaven and the pyre of the great dead became the apotheosis of the new god? Did the people light their torches on the burning wax figure and run with them to the houses of Caesar's assassins to set them ablaze just as believers today light their candles from the Easter candle which itself is ignited on the little pyre in front of the church on Easter Saturday? Did the passion robe that Caesar wore and which was also burned, inspire the musicians and actors to tear their own festive clothes from their bodies and throw them in the flames? Did the decorated weapons of those defeated by Caesar, for example Vercingetorix, which certainly hung on the tropaeum and then melted in the fire, induce Caesar's legionaries to throw their parade arms onto it, inspire the matrons to throw their jewelry as well as the lockets and the pre-woven tunics of their children?

In any case, the assumption that the cross of Jesus is derived from Caesar's tropaeum explains peculiarities found not only in the Gospels, but also in the Easter liturgy—both Orthodox and Catholic—including the popular Passion plays.

One objection that can be raised is that a Roman tropaeum does not necessarily resemble a cross: first of all because only the spoils of the enemies were hung on the tropaeum, not the enemy themselves; Secondly because it is T-shaped, not †-shaped.

This objection provides the opportunity to offer an explanation that might lead to a better understanding of the cross. It was most commonly rebellious slaves who were nailed to the cross—if we follow Tacitus, initially even exclusively rebellious slaves.[200] Slaves were the conquered whose dishonorable conduct in war did not earn them the right to become citizens after their defeat, as was usual Roman practice. It was this practice that distinguished the empire and made it great.[201] Slaves could earn freedom in military service or community service so that they or their children could become Roman citizens. If however, they chose rebellion instead, they were considered to be relapsed and incorrigible. While as defeated people they were required to watch the weapons of their leaders being nailed to the tropaeum, now after their slave rebellion was put down, they were themselves nailed to it as relapsed offenders: the cross was the tropaeum of the recidivists.

The reference to the form is in itself also not an argument, because as we have seen, not only the tropaeum, but also the cross was classically symbolized by a T instead of with a †. Technically they were called *crux commissa*, 'Antonius' cross' (as if by chance Antonius appears again) and *crux immissa*, 'Latin' or 'Passion cross'. In Christian iconography one often finds T-shaped depictions.[202]

The Tropaea of the Pompeians and Caesar's Cross

Perhaps what decisively triggered Caesar's victory column to be perceived as his own martyr's stake was the use of the tropaeum motif in the anti-Caesarean propaganda of the Pompeians.

Anxious for reconciliation, Caesar only celebrated victories against non-Roman enemies, as we saw after Pharsalos, when he made the pacification of Gaul the motif of his coins and not the victory over Pompeius. In contrast, Metellus Scipio, who gathered the rest of the Pompeian forces in Africa, put a tropaeum on an imperatorial denarius of 47 that could only have portrayed a defeated Roman:

26. Scipio Denarius, ca. 47 BC.

The Spanish round shield leads to the assumption[203] that the weapons portrayed belonged to Sertorius the Roman rebel who, between 80 and 77, gained a victory against Caecilius Metellus, Scipio's adoptive father, and Pompeius in Spain. After an indecisive battle he was betrayed and deceitfully murdered so that Metellus and Pompeius had been able to triumph in Rome. Scipio wanted to thus warn Caesar, who the Pompeians saw as a new Sertorius, that in spite of his victory in Pharsalos the last word had yet to be spoken. The minting in Africa added force to the threat because it was there that Caesar's legate Curio had been defeated and killed by the ally of the Pompeians, the Numidian king, Iuba.

It helped neither Metellus Scipio, who was defeated in Africa, nor the sons of Pompeius who were later defeated in Spain: but in the end, the very men pardoned by Caesar still managed to murder him, just as Sertorius had been before. And so it would follow that at Caesar's funeral the sight of his wax simulacrum hanging on the tropaeum must have made his victory column appear as the martyr stake with which the Pompeians had threatened him. Hence the rage of the people: they would not allow Caesar's funeral to become the triumph of the conspirators! His cross had to be overcome and restored as a sign of victory.

It is unnecessary to point out how this anticipates the ambivalent nature of the Christian cross, which is at the same time a symbol both of martyrdom and of the ultimate victory, beyond death.

When Brutus had the presumption to eternize the murder of Caesar as an act of liberation on his coins and at the same time have himself acclaimed imperator for insignificant victories against the Bessians in Thrace—which only served to consolidate his base of power against the Triumvirs—and then dared to imitate Caesar's coin mintage precisely by using the tropaeum motif, it meant that his whole coin propaganda, which fit so well with that of the old Pompeians, had to have been perceived as an illustration of the Passion narrative of Caesar.

27. Denarius for Pompeius, 54 BC; 28./29./30. Denarii for/of Brutus, 42 BC.

From left to right we have: the denarius minted by Faustus Cornelius Sulla, the son of the dictator Sulla, in honor of his father-in-law Pompeius around 54 BC. The three tropaea allude to the three triumphs of Pompeius over Europe, Asia and Africa; one denarius of Brutus' legate Costa and one of Brutus himself, both of which show the acclamation as imperator after the victory over the Bessians; the denarius minted in Greece by Pletorius Cestianus, an officer of Brutus, with *pilleus* (liberty cap), two daggers and dating—EID(ibus) MAR(tiis), 'on the Ides of March'.

Seen through 'Christian' eyes, the coin on the far left depicts the one crucified flanked by two other crucified men, then we have the crucified alone, and then with Mary and John weeping before the cross.

This arrangement shows how the portrayal of the Ides of March can become a general symbol of Golgotha. The daggers would be those crucified with him, and the liberty cap Golgotha itself, with the missing cross in the middle added in the mind's eye because of its constant presence on the other coins and how it leads one to imagine a view after the deposition from the cross.

When taken separately, however, the less educated people may have associated this portrayal of the liberty cap and daggers with the commonly held image of the Jews. The liberty cap also belonged to the freedman, who clung to it with his shaved head because without it he would fall into bondage again, and the Jews mostly achieved Roman citizenship by manumission. Moreover, the *pilleus* was the cap worn during the Saturnalia and the Jews were considered to be worshippers of Saturnus because of their observance of the Sabbath. The dagger, the *sica,* was in a way an attribute of the Jew: he is portrayed in Gothic cathedrals as *sicarius,* the man with a dagger. The denarius of Iunius Brutus, the *sicarius* of Caesar, could be seen as being a piece of silver of Judas Iscariot, especially since another 'son' of Caesar, Antipatros, the commandant of the Jews whom Caesar had adopted in gratitude for his help in Alexandria, also had sided with the murderers after the Ides of March and supported Cassius, later to perish with them (cf. note 183).

It cannot be denied that it was only with and since Caesar and only among his followers that the tropaeum was perceived as a cross, while for the Pompeians it had always remained a tropaeum. It is easy to recognize this by comparing the development of the motif in the respective mintings.

As can be seen here, Pompeian mint masters never stressed the cross shape of the tropaeum. On the denarius minted for Pompeius the three tropaea are so close together that any naïve beholder might perceive them as three small soldiers. Additionally, during the conflict with Caesar, as the desperate Pompeians began reproducing his coin propaganda and imitating his motifs, the tropaeum did become more cross-like. However, the effect was diluted by a vertical placement of the requisites and the lettering, and by leaving the center empty.

This Pompeian *horror crucis* can be marvelled at most clearly on Brutus' coins. The assassin of Caesar went the farthest in imitating his presumptive father: he not only adopted single motifs, but entire compositions. For comparison, we place the copy—imperatorial coinage of Brutus in Greece in 42 on the right—next to the original minting of Caesar's during his last Spanish campaign in 46 BC. The respective basic graphic patterns are shown laterally.

It is amazing how Brutus manages to frame the clear, and one could think almost unavoidable, cross shape of Caesar's composition with typical vertical Pompeian stokes, thus enclosing the cross motif in a sort

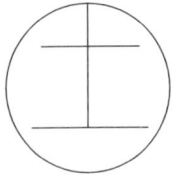   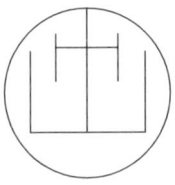

31./32. Caesar Denarius, ca. 46 BC, and one of Brutus, 42 BC.

of 'box' (compare ill. 26 to 29 to see the constancy of this Pompeian 'box'). It is as if the senatorial ethos found its expression by avoiding the focal point, but otherwise chose a form as unobtrusive as possible and collegially framed.

Caesar's attitude was completely different.

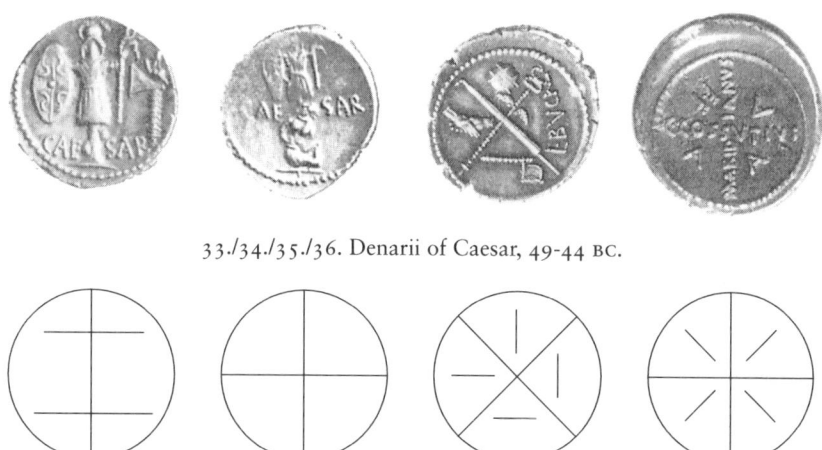

33./34./35./36. Denarii of Caesar, 49-44 BC.

The transition in his coinage from a tropaeum in the beginning to a more and more plain and stylized cross is obvious.

The conqueror of Gaul seems to have been influenced by the Celtic cross. He then varied the motif and expressed it more and more clearly. Using the tropaeum with a prisoner set underneath as the starting point he added his interrupted signature CAE_SAR to help portray a more distinct Celtic cross; later he replaced the memorial of victory with the signs of peace: a winged caduceus and crosswisely arranged fasces without the axe; finally he abstained from any kind of concrete representation and resorted to pure lines, with the name of his moneyer running along them—in this case COSSVTIVS MARIDIANVS. In the last two examples the opportunity arose to fill in the angles—the second coin from the right uses the name of the moneyer (here L. BVCA) with more symbols of a peaceful state order: axe (justice), crossed hands (*concordia civium*, harmony of citizens), globe (*oikoumene*, world order); the last coin has the Latin abbreviation for moneyer: AAAFF, A(ere) A(rgento) A(uro) F(lando) F(erundio). Thus the Celtic cross of Caesar developed into an oriental sun cross, from a four-rayed to an eight-rayed one. Whether or not this hinted at his calendar reform where he changed from lunar to solar reckoning is open to speculation.

His adoptive son Octavianus, who entitled himself DIVI (IVLII) FIL-IVS after Caesar's consecration, took up this motif in a twofold respect: one time starting from a Celtic cross (ill. 34) which he varied in multiple ways, another time as a further development of the solar cross (ill. 36) which he used as the basic pattern for the *sidus Iulium*, Caesar's comet. As an example of the first we show the reverse sides of a double series of three:

Pictured in the upper series are the goddess Pax with the cornucopia and laurel twigs, Venus playing with the weapons of Mars, and winged Victoria with a laurel wreath and a palm leaf; the lower series shows the corresponding postures of Octavianus as he speaks to his troops, gives the signal to attack and as victor puts his foot on the globe.[204] Five out of six coins show the cross motif: all with a martial theme. The sole exception is Pax. The cross of the son is more martial than that of the father and attends his own aggrandizement.

37. Octavianus' Denarii, before 31 BC. Print: CAESAR_DIVI·F(ilius)

Naked on a columna rostrata, as a herm of Jupiter with lightning underfoot or behind his head: In the cross he makes himself Jupiter.

38./39./40. Denarii of Octavianus, before 31 BC.
(the first two display only the back of the respective coin).

Sun, Moon and Stars

After marching through Syria and vanquishing Pharnaces[205] Caesar seems to have had his eye on the East, not only the Egyptian East, but also the formerly Assyrian East. This was all the more evident when he began planning the campaign against the Parthians during the first months of the year 44. At any rate, the well-known attempt to bestow royal dignity upon Caesar was connected to a prophecy according to which only a king would be able to defeat the Parthians.[206] On Caesar's coins, this growing interest in the East found its expression not only in the orientalizing of his sun cross, but also in the symbolic usage of the moon and star which appears in his imperatorial minting.

41./42. Imperial Denarii of Caesar

Thus Caesar combined all the oriental attributes of cosmic world domination on himself.

In Rome the symbols of the moon and stars were already connected to the Sabines (depicted is a denarius of Augustus' mintmaster P. Petronius Turpilianus, who alluded to his Sabine origin in his motifs).

This might have been because the Sabines, seen from Rome, were located in the near, even if Italian East—which did not change anything about the reference to the east. But the fact that the astral symbolism was associated with the Sabines made this a conciliatory gesture by Caesar, since the Sabines were the people whom the Latins, under Romulus, had robbed of their women and in the ensuing battle had badly harried the Latins, even occupying the Capitol. But finally, with the help of the women, they reconciled with the Latins and co-settled in Rome—the re-

43. Denarius of Augustus, Moneyer P. Petronius Turpilianus

sult were the Romans. The message to the Orientals was: As happened once with the Sabines, so you too can now become new Romans like the Gauls in the West.

The star that Caesar used, of course, had to be interpreted as a Venus-star, for Venus was equated with Astarte, whom the Assyrians already symbolized by her star. This was represented with not only six, but sometimes eight points, so that in the Assyrian configuration of cosmic world domination with sun, moon and star of Astarte, the latter was not graphically distinct from the solar depiction. This is easily seen in the following example of the sun god, Shamash,[207] here next to a sun rising from the head of the Egyptian pharaoh.

44. (a, b) The son is rising from the head of the Pharaoh. Detail: sun wheel.
45. (a, b, c) Shamash; details; sun wheel resp. moon, sun and star of Astarte.

Thus the eight-rayed sun cross in the last of Caesar's coins introduced a further development towards the eight pointed star, which became fully evolved in the picture of Caesar's comet, the *sidus Iulium*, after his death. Augustus had a comet placed on the heads of all statues of Caesar, because the people believed that the comet that appeared during the games honoring the dead Caesar was really his soul which had ascended to heaven. It looked like the following:

Sun, Moon and Stars

46./47./48. Denarii of Augustus; 49.(a, b) Denarius of Lentulus

On the left we have two representations of the sidus Iulium, on the right we see how the comet stood on the head of the statues of Caesar, and how Augustus places the comet on the head of Divus Iulius who is holding a Victoria in his hand.

The development went from eight points to six points plus the script of the name. How this happened is made clear by the above side-by-side sequence of the coins: It is obvious that the moneyer of the second Divus-Iulius-star did not consider the fact that the script of the name DIVVS IVLIVS, which was on the top and bottom of the first coin, once displaced to the middle, takes the space of a double jag and should have been left out completely because of the limited space. In more elegant representations it will have consistently dropped out and this might have led to the six pointed star plus the script of the name, which in turn is assumed as the intermediate stage of both six pointed stars on the heads of the statues.

This six-pointed star with the script of the name DIVVS IVLIVS shows a remarkably similar structure to the Christogram, which was so named because in it the beginning letters of the Greek *XPICTOC Christos*, *X* 'chi' and *P* 'rho', can be recognized.

50./51. *Sidus Iulium* and *Christusmonogram* (coin of Magnentius)

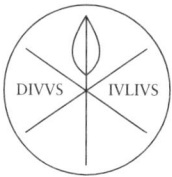 

The alpha and omega in the Christogram replaces the DIVVS IVLIVS in Caesar's comet. The Ω strikingly resembles a VV which in connection with the surrounding Latin text—here SALVS·DD·NN·AVG·ET·CAES, 'the well-being (salvation) of our Lords Augusti and Caesars' reminds of the U (v) found numerously in DIVVS IVLIVS. In addition the graphic of the ω looks like an upside down M—easily recognized in the enlargement of the plate pictured below from whose bottom the Christogram is taken. This is a find from late antiquity, from Tomi on the Black Sea.[208] Around the foot of the plate runs a text in Latin, but in graecizing characters, saying that the plate is a 'reproduction of an old object belonging to our most honorable Bishop Paternus':

'† EX ANTIQVIS RENOVATVM EST PER PATERNVM REVERENTISS·EPISC· NOSTRVM AMEN †'

52. (a, b) Detail of the Christogram on the Paternus plate

The word PATERNVM inscribed in the lower part of the of the orbital inscription demonstrates how closely the upside down M resembles ω. If the ω is perceived as an M read circularly than A and M would be the beginning letters of *Archiereus Megistos,* Greek for *pontifex maximus,* which we suppose might have been shortened into *Christos.* That would be coherent with the perception of the entire Christogram as chi-rho, as X and P written on top of each other, the beginning letters of *XPICTOC Christos.*

Another hint that the Christogram originates from the *sidus Iulium* is found in their functions, which are identical. Caesar's comet was regarded by the people as the soul of Caesar which had risen to heaven— the Christogram on our gravestones symbolizes the soul of the dead which has risen to heaven, or, as the priest explains it to the mourners, it represents the hope of resurrection in Christ. Ergo, we are back to the beginning.

The Habitus of Divus Iulius

If we study the denarius of Lentulus (ill. 49 = 53) carefully, we see that Divus Iulius points to Jesus in regard to habitus as well.

The practice of putting the *sidus Iulium* on Caesar's statues is generally considered to have started in the year 12 BC.[209] Since the temple of Divus Iulius was consecrated in 29 BC, then its cult statue might have been the model for this coin.

53.(a, b) Denarius of Lentulus: Augustus crowns Divus Iulius with the comet

He is crowned—probably with an oak wreath—and wears his comet on his head. We have already mentioned Caesar's oak wreath as model for the crown of thorns worn by Jesus, and Caesar's comet as the origin of the Christogram and aureole. The only thing left to point out is that the aureole of Jesus is not a simple flat disk, but structured with rays or jags as the *sidus Iulium* (see ill. 46–50), albeit in recent iconography the number of points has become smaller, with a tendency to four, so that the cross is accentuated.[210] The torso (see ill. 60a) is naked. The muscle cuirass possibly worn here, suspected by the epaulettes, stresses the nakedness more than conceals it. The loincloth—in this example the *paludamentum* of the commander—only visually differentiates itself from the 'Hüftmanteltypus', the '(military) cloak type', the 'sagum type', (see below ill. 59c) used in Hellenistic times for heroic portrayals. This is exactly the way Jesus is portrayed with naked torso, whether at his baptism, crucifixion or resurrection; his loincloth—sometimes shorter, sometimes longer—is also tied at the side so that its style completely reflects that of Divus Iulius (cf ill. 53b and 54).

53.b: Divus Iulius; 54.a: Resurrection; 54.b: Salvator Mundi;

The staff that Divus Iulius holds in his left hand is generally thought to be a lance, but if it is one, then its tip would be towards the rear, or in front, pointed downwards—for even the cult statues of the war god Mars hold it in that position[211]—and it would accordingly have been perceived as a commander's staff. Jesus also carries such a staff on occasion, with or without additional decoration (a little flag, little cross, etc.), in depictions of his resurrection, sometimes combined with a cross standing on the globe, similar to the figure that Divus Iulius is holding in his right hand (see ill. 53 b, 54 a and 54 b).

55.(a, b) Lentulus Denarius; 56. (a,b) Augustus Denarius

The small statue in his right hand is usually interpreted as being winged Victoria standing on the globe: the symbol of world domination, to the right would be two small wings (or a wing and a palm of victory), to the left her outstretched right arm would hold a wreath. It is most certainly a globe under her feet, because it was a central motif used by Caesar (see ill. 35). Augustus often portrayed Victoria in this way, too (see ill. 37 c). In reality, however, the tiny figure on the globe held by Divus Iulius looks somewhat strange for a Victoria: the typical flounces on the lower back of her dress are missing, and the position is emphatically cross-shaped, with the orthogonal right arm, while the wreath is nowhere to be seen. In the similarly sized Victoria in the Augustus coin pictured above (ill. 40 = 56), the flounces are evident. She does not stand on a globe, but directly on the hand of Augustus. Her dress flutters behind her; The arm is longer and bent upwards, and there is a hint of a wreath (see also ill. 37 c).

As crowning Victory, she would have been very inappropriate in the hands of Divus Iulius, this Victoria Nike, because whom should she crown? Caesar consistently placed the crowning Victory in the hand of Venus (ill. 84, 109 below): he was the one to be crowned, as he is here. If he held Victoria with the wreath in her hand himself then someone else would be the triumphator—which would diminish his unlimited rule and majesty, and this was impossible during his lifetime, unbearable after being made god. Augustus on the other hand, was strategically incompetent and had to thank others for his military victories—

Hirtius for Mutina, Antonius for Philippi, Agrippa for the next (Perusia, Naulochos, Actium, the Cantabrians), Tiberius for the later—and thus Victoria handing the victory wreath makes sense: she stands on his hand as she stands on Venus' hand on the Caesar coins (ill. 84 and 109).[212] In any case her wings tilt downwards and seem to suggest that the Victoria of Augustus lands on earth while if the figure on the Divus Iulius coin has wings they point upwards and indicate movement towards heaven. It is questionable however if both of the lines pointing upwards from the right (from viewer's position) are actually wings (or a wing and a palm of victory), because if the tiny figure is actually Victoria she could have been portrayed *en face*—both other figures, Divus Iulius and Augustus, are also *en face*—so that their wings might actually be horizontal arms. Then both of the other lines in the upper right would not be wings, but something else. But what? Illustrations of Victoria from that time have been preserved and they show her carrying a tropaeum instead of a wreath and *en face*.[213]

Victoria on the globe: 57. with tropaeum; 58. with wreath and palm

Is Divus Iulius holding a Victoria who in turn carries a tropaeum in her hand? It is possible. Since a tropaeum was something big, at least as big as the figure that carried it and the victory wreath was small, Victoria would have disappeared behind the tropaeum she carried and formed a sort of cross—as seen on the antefix on the left.

It is noticeable that Victoria is portrayed as a woman with bosom and wide-hipped—in spite of the rough features easily recognizable on the Augustus coin—while the tiny figure in the right hand of Divus Iulius seems more manly, with a wide thorax and small hips. (ill. 55b) Since the right outstretched arm is shorter than Augustus' Victoria and stands on one foot, the figure itself looks more like a tropaeum than Victoria carrying a tropaeum or wreath.[214]

Luckily we have the possibility of verifying the special composition of Caesars' 'Victory on the globe'. Namely, it is found twice in rather large format in the preserved Julian-Claudian plastic—once on the cuirassed statue of Cherchel and also on that of the Prima Porta Augustus. Each is in a different but prominent place.

On the breastplate of the cuirassed statue unearthed in the former Iuba residence in northern Africa, Iol-Caesarea, (today Cherchel), there is a scene similar to the one on the Lentulus denarius and which possibly originates from an even older pattern. Because the head and any inscription is missing, the statue is difficult to classify. The range of possibility extends from Augustus to Nero, and even further to Hadrian. All but one of the figures pictured have been positively identified, and belong to the theological-political program of Octavianus after Philippi:

   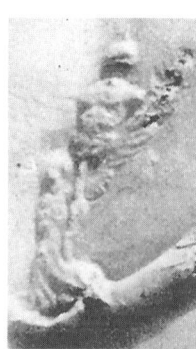

59. (a, b, c, d) Breastplate Statue from Iol-Caesarea (Cherchel)

Mars is recognizable as a planet god in the top middle section of the breastplate (ill. 59 b). Underneath him to the left is Amor, and in front of him towards the middle is Venus with the weapons of Mars, clearly making a reference to the Iulians. To the very right is the winged Victory who is crowning a young man in front of her with a wreath, the *corona civica*, the oak wreath: the crowned one must be a ruler from the house of the Iulians. But which one? Researchers argue this question: Was it Divus Iulius himself or Gaius Caesar?[215] No matter what the answer, the young, heroic man (ill. 59c) displays a habitus akin to that of Divus Iulius on the Lentulus denarius: a similarly draped military cloak (sagum), the same pose, the same oak wreath—still held, of course, by Victoria, but in the same manner as Augustus holds the *sidum Iulium* on the coin of Lentulus; the fact that the *sidus Iulium* is missing might indicate a design pattern extant before the year 12 BC or be traced to the damaged head, as the missing rod might be traced to the left hand that has broken off. The tiny figure, however, which the crowned one holds in his right hand—analog to Divus Iulius in the Lentulus denarius—is more recognizable here (ill. 59d). It was so important that the sculptor placed it exactly in the middle of the breastplate on the *linea alba*. It is a tropaeum that is either held by a Victoria molded in delicate relief from which only the lower part of the dress and a wing would be visible,[216] or standing apart, decorated with a palm leaf. In the latter case the tropaeum would be leaning against the trunk of the palm to the left, which might be interpreted as the one that had sprouted from the floor of the temple of Tralleis[217] at the time of the victory of Pharsalos.

Did the cult statue of Divus Iulius hold a similar tropaeum in its hand? Can the pattern of the cult statue of Divus Iulius be detected here on the breastplate at Cherchel—independent of whether the young hero portrayed is the idealized Divus Iulius or a prince of the Iulian-Claudian ruling house posed to look like him? At least the first question can be answered with yes.

For on another breastplate—namely the Prima Porta statue, today in the Vatican—which is definitely from the time of Augustus (in this case the statue's head is preserved), a similar tropaeum can be seen below the right shoulder blade.[218]

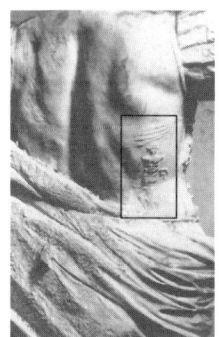

60. (a, b, c) Breastplate Statue from Prima Porta; 61. Miniature tropaeum

A tip of a wing is clearly identifiable above the tropaeum (ill. 60c) which implies that such a wing would have to be assumed on the tiny figure in the hand of Divus Iulius. This does not answer the question as to whether an entire Victoria is holding a tropaeum, or if only a Victoria wing was hung on the tropaeum that was decorated with a palm of Victory.

Neither the Cherchel breastplate nor the Prima Porta, which each depict the tropaeum, are originals, but are rather reproductions *en miniature,* as it can actually be seen in a bronze in Berlin-Charlotteburg[219] (ill. 61). If you add the missing helmet, place it on a globe and decorate it with the palm of Victoria and then shrink it to the size of a denarius, what you will have is a figure similar to that which Divus Iulius holds in his hand on the Lentulus denarius.

Seen through Christian eyes, this is the same cross on the globe that Christ holds in his hand, especially as the infant Jesus—the small chubby cheeked little Jesus, swirling and fluttering around the Madonna just as Cupid does around Venus—the baby Jesus so breast-fixated that it seems he knew that Caesar had made her the greatest goddess, *Venus Genetrix,* the child-bearing Venus. The globe with the cross on it which he suddenly and surprisingly holds in his outstretched hand is a tropaeum: not a martyr's stake, but his sign of victory.

Interestingly enough, when the first Christian motifs on Roman imperial coins turn up, the same variations as with the above tropaea are seen: the tropaeum becomes a cross, sometimes standing on the globe sometimes not, sometimes held by Victoria, sometimes between two figures (as on the Cherchel cuirass between Venus and the crowned one); At times it is called *salus mundi,* salvation of the world, at others it is encircled with a wreath:

62. Decentius; 63. Anthemius; 64. Eudocia, 65. Olybrius, 66. Augustulus

What this means is that already on a cuirass from Iulian-Claudian times, and not only from the time of Constantine onwards, a 'cross' was engraved in the middle of the chest and that the cult statue of Divus Iulius held a similar one in its hand. The later *in hoc signo vinces* of Constantine—the flaming cross, the sign by which he would conquer—did not simply fall out of the sky.

Asked differently: Was the cult statue of Divus Iulius never 'found' because it was already present in every church?

The Resurrection of Divus Iulius

There is a Buca denarius that needs to be mentioned. It is unanimously dated in the year 44, the year of Caesar's death and obviously portrays the resurrection of Caesar or at least its paradigm.

67. Buca denarius, 44 BC – Caesar' pyre—the resurrection of Divus Iulius

Many commentators insist on seeing this as the depiction of Sulla's dream. According to Plutarchus, in 82 BC Athena or Bellona appeared to Sulla before his march on Rome and gave him thunderbolts as a sign of future victory over his enemies. This interpretation causes considerable difficulties[220] because, first of all, it is hard to imagine how Caesar's moneyer Buca could have managed to conceive, let alone mint, a pro-Sullan and therefore—despite the *clementia Caesaris*—an anti-Caesarean coin in the year 44; Secondly, not only is there an absence of military atmosphere (there are no weapons to be seen, not even in the habitus of the goddess, which in Sulla's case should have been warlike) the most important element is missing in the Buca portrayal: the thunderbolts. Instead, the goddess wears a veil and crescent on her head and holds torches in her hands. The person lying in front of the Victoria with a palm branch, and apparently supported by her, is about to sit up again, but his head remains tilted back as if he were dead. He lies on an untypical funeral couch looking like a flaming pyre, that has just been set afire by the one torch held downward while the other one points at the sky. One cannot help but interpret this as a picture of Caesar, who, just as his body is being cremated (torches, fire beneath the couch), is about to sit up, being carried away to the gods and prevailing posthumously. The saga of Selene and Endymion would have been the prototype, with the diademed Venus head on the front of the coin and the fact that Caesar's corpse was actually laid out inside a model of the Venus temple only emphasizing such an association. We would thus have here before us, referring to Divus Iulius, the first portrayal of the resurrection, which at the same time is reminiscent of a Pietà group. This explains why in Christian iconography both of these motifs exist next to the Ascension—although very distinctive from it.

68. Caesars pyre; 69. Good Friday procession figures

In terms of the Pietà it should be noted that no counterpart of it can be found in the Gospel, whereas it does appear with Caesar: 'In the night before his murder Caesar suffered an attack of faintness, his wife, however, saw him streaming with blood in a dream...' (APP. *BC* 2.115.480).

70. Pietà: Calpurnia's dream

Christophorus and other symbols

The portrayal of the central motif of the Julians can also be read in a 'Christian' way: the son of Venus, Aeneas, flees from Troia, and at the same time manages to carry his father, Anchises, on his shoulders and take the palladium with him—thus saving the descendants of Anchises as well as the Trojan claim to rule Asia by getting them over to Latium.

71. Caesar denarius, ca. 47 BC.

This was an allusion to Caesar's brilliant withdrawal from Dyrrhachium, which the Pompians interpreted as fleeing and used as propaganda against him. Their interpretation, however, was a misjudgement that was to lead to their defeat at Pharsalos and the strengthening of Caesar's power. The recourse to the Aeneas myth elevated the contingent into the sphere of the eternal and presented the rule of *Iulius*—and later of all *Iulii*—as ordained by God.

Through 'Christian' eyes it seems to foreshadow the St. Christopher motif. The fact that Anchises is older, while Christophor carries the Christ child on his shoulder should not be irritating. Here Anchises is in the position of progenitor for his descendants, especially for the last born—it is no coincidence that he will undergo a doubling in later illustrations: instead of the *palladium*, Aeneas will take the young Ascanius-Iulus by the hand.

Thus we have tracked down almost all the main symbols found later in Christianity. We have shown only a few examples of parallel Christian iconography because it would inundate the framework of this publication to mention all of them. It would be easy to show, for example, how the Caesar coins with the head of Venus on the front—with or without Cupid—and tropaeum or cross motif on the back (ill. 13, 14 and 21), became the model for the medallions popular with the people that show the Madonna—with or without a child—on one side and a cross on the other.

The motifs using sun, moon and stars (ill. 41–43), and especially the comet (ill. 46–49), are omnipresent with the Christ child or Madonna, and not only at Christmastime.

Moon and stars are also found in Islam, as well as a preference for the graphism of the script seen on the denarius of Cossutius Maridianus (ill. 36). The question might even be asked as to whether or not the six-pointed Jewish star was modeled on Caesar's. After all, the rebellion of Bar Kochba, the 'son of the star', put down by Hadrian, only occurred in 132-135 AD. Did Bar Kochba enroll the blessing of Caesar's comet for himself?

Individual Caesar motifs that hardly play a role in Christianity are found again in political symbolism or in other religions—like the elephant, symbol of Caesar's name (ill. 20), which in France still is the symbol of the king, whereas in Buddhism it plays an important role in the genealogy of Buddha—or underwent a pseudo-religious recycling. For example the Triskelis, symbol of the three-sided island of Sicily, fought over in the civil war, was changed into a cross in the usual way by Caesar's moneyer—in this case a kind of swastika:

On the left is its portrayal on a denarius of the consuls of 49 BC, Cornelius Lentulus and Claudius Marcellus, who together with Pompeius instigated the civil war and then left Italy: the triskele, surrounded by a

72. Lentulus and Marcellus denarius; 73. Allienus denarius

garland of corn and a Medusa face, has three legs. On the right, on a denarius of Allienus, who governed Sicily for Caesar in 47: Trinacrus, god of Sicily holds the triskele in his hand. Together with the arm and visually extended by Trinacrus' foot standing on the bow of a ship it certainly forms the impression of a swastika, a sun wheel.

Not to be forgotten in this connection is of course, the five pointed star of Mars, which has until recently shone brightly in the political heavens as a red star and is still found on some flags. This, too, found its prototype in Caesar's comet. Stuck on the head of statues of Caesar, the six-pointed form loses the bottom jag almost completely so that a five pointed straddle-legged star remains visible (see ill. 48 and 49b). Regarding its connection with Mars, consider that the Octavianus who set the *sidus Iulium* on the heads of Caesar statues was the same one who also had the temple of *Mars Ultor*, the 'Avenging Mars,' built instead of the Clementia-temple promised to Caesar and that the Ephesus inscription mentioned in the previous chapter addressed Caesar not only as the son of Venus, but also as the son of Mars. His star might then be perceived as the star of Venus as well as Mars.

The para-religious ideological-political utilization of these symbols—the swastika and the five pointed star—in such recent history, is an indication of how long a shadow Caesar's symbolism has thrown and continues to throw.

Caesar's Saints

In the previous chapter we were able to establish that the characters playing important roles around Caesar find their actors in the disciples and adversaries of Jesus. We can also say that within the iconography observed on coins, the pictorial motifs and the symbolism also correspond to each other.

Let us begin with Pompeius, the former partner and later adversary of Caesar's—who has his counterpart in John the Baptist. He was portrayed as Neptune, because of his command of the seas and coasts, as well as his victory over pirates. It is known that he enjoyed this role.

Navigare necesse, vivere non necesse, 'To navigate is necessary, to live is not'—was his motto.

74./75. Denarii of Nassidius and of Sextus Pompeius, 38 BC.

These two coins, one of the Pompeian Nassidius, the other of Pompeius' son Sextus, were minted after the initial victory over Octavianus in the sea battle near Cumae in 38 BC. In competition with Octavianus—who, by the aggrandizement of his adopted father Caesar to *Divus Iulius*, himself became the son of god—Sextus portrayed his father Pompeius as Neptune. On the left Pompeius is identified as the sea god by name: NEPTVNI, and with a trident and dolphin. On the right even his facial features have been replaced with the stereotypical features of the god, bringing him closer to resembling the John the Baptist of Christian iconography.

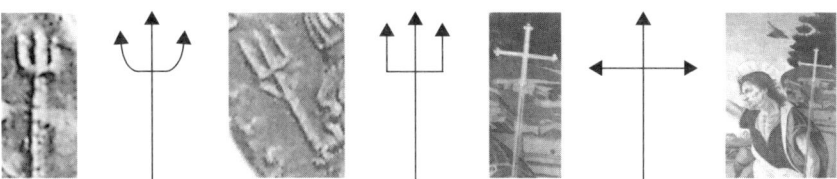

76. Development from the trident of Pompeius/Neptune to staff of John the Baptist

John does not hold a trident, but a staff which ends on the top in a sort cross. Nevertheless this 'cross' is unusual because the three open arms seem to have three points on them like a trident so that the staff of the Baptist develops from the trident of Neptune as soon as the outer points are shortened and formed without angles.

Pompeius' own name—MAGNVS—which he bears on most coins, has a conspicuous counterpart in that *AGNVS* which appears on the banderole that the Baptist carries beneath his trident. On it are written the words he spoke, according to Jn. 1:29, when he saw Jesus: 'Behold the Lamb of God, which taketh away the sin of the world.' Often only the first words are rendered in Latin, *ECCE AGNVS (DEI)* which is not far from the usual coin inscription CN·MAGNVS (IMP). *AGNVS* has often been written wrong: *ANGNVS, AGNIVS*, etc., as if the elimination of the beginning letter '*M*' generated an additional similar letter in the inner part of the word. Even the Greek word that here stands for lamb, *O AMNOC,* seems similar to *MAGNVS* and in addition contains the missing '*M*' from *AGNVS*.

This 'lamb', which appears in the Gospel of John suddenly and inexplicably (the other Evangelists know nothing about it), develops its own dynamic in the Baptist iconography. It later appears not only as a word on the banderole, but portrayed as an actual lamb, so that it becomes the attribute of the Baptist—which is inconsistent with the word of the Gospel, because there it is Jesus who is called the lamb.

The other attributes of Pompeius/Neptune used by Pompeius or his sons—such as the dolphin under Pompeius' head on the first coin, or the ship on the reverse—were not constant and were challenged by the Triumvirs. The dolphin, for example, an attribute of his ancestral mother Venus, was often used by Octavianus, Caesar's adoptive son, in his own iconography. The same goes for the ship, which after the successful crossing of the Ionian Sea during the civil war against Pompeius, became a standard motif in Antonius' widespread coinage. Here we have a glass pendant with a portrait of Octavianus with *rostrum,* (bow of a ship) and dolphin, as well as a coin of Antonius with the galleys.

77. Glass pendant with likeness of Octavianus; 78. Dupondius of Antonius

Thus both of these motifs are found not with the Baptist, but with the saints, who correspond to Octavianus and Antonius: the dolphin with Jesus himself[221] as the Son of God, and the ship with Simon Peter. However, other secondary motifs of Pompeius/Neptune can well be found in the Baptist. Compare how the water (of the Jordan), in which a crab is often pictured[222] finds its match in the crab on the denarius of Cassius,[223] as well as in the form of the sea victory tropaeum which combines figureheads, bows and the heads of Scylla and Charybdis, as seen on the coin of Sextus Pompeius pictured above (ill. 75); or in the waves, which wander from the beard of Neptune to the shaggy fur of the Baptist; finally the star above Pompeius' ship (see ill. 74) which as *sidus Iulium* was in steady hands, but might have contributed to the aureole of the Baptist (we should note here that all saints whose counterparts in the Caesar story display a star or sun in their iconography had an aureole very early in Christian iconography, even before these became a general attribute of all saints).

The reason why the ship finally adhered to Antonius/Simon Peter and not Octavianus/Son of god/John would be explained by the fact that after Caesar's death Antonius was mockingly referred to as 'Charonit'. He had gathered all of Caesar's files and notes and kept them under lock and key but edited them as and when required to make his own decisions appear to be derived from them. Hence his derisive nickname 'Charonit' as if by night he crossed the river Styx in Charon's ferry to confer with Caesar's soul.[224] This fact probably contributed to the ship of Antonius finally becoming the barque of Peter in Christian imagination.

Completely dressed in priestly robes as *augur* and *imperator* at the same time—in spite of the unsuccessful war against the Parthians—Antonius appears on a denarius of 38 or 37 BC. The shining Sol as the sun deity on the reverse might, beside the claim to power in the old Seleucidian realm, have some connection with Divus Iulius, who had been the legitimate world ruler after the time of Pompeius. Antonius, of course, was Caesar's *flamen* and with the mitre on his head and the lituus in his hand he seems like a bishop—the majestic posture and the sacral context placing him somewhere between oriental ruler and god-king: as pope *ante litteram*.

77. Antonius' denarius, 38-37 BC.

Like the pope he also has the tiara, namely the Armenian one which he had appropriated in 36 BC:

81. Denarius of Antonius, 36 BC, Rev.; 82. Papal Emblem

What is noticeable here is the crosswise arrangement of the bow and arrow which graphically resembles Caesar's Buca denarius of February, 44 BC (ill. 35) and represents the transition to the papal coat of arms—whereby the bow and arrow were transformed into keys possibly because Antonius kept Caesar's files under lock and key.

After Caesar's assassination Antonius had himself portrayed *capite velato* and unshaven whereby the veiled head characterized him as a celebrating priest, the beard made him a mourner: Antonius as Caesar's mortician. This is emphasized by the noticeable imitation to both of Caesar's last coins (we have already shown the reverse of one of them, in ill. 36) where he had also been portrayed *capite velato*.[225]

Denarii of Caesar: 83. (Maridianus); 84. (Macer); March 44 BC.

85./86. Antonius' and Caesar's denarii (Macer); after the Ides of March

The reverse with the desultor, a circus rider with a victory wreath and palm behind it, refer to the games during the Parilia which fell on April 21st, the anniversary of the founding of Rome by Romulus on which now Caesar's victory in Munda was celebrated too. It was probably planned to glorify Caesar as the new founder of the city, as *parens patriae*. But after he was murdered as Romulus had been, the reverse of the coin with the horses galloping to heaven and the *desultor*, must have been seen as a portrayal of his ascension. For the ascension of Romulus was portrayed in a similar way, and, as if by chance, the oldest known illustration of Christ's ascension was too, which is located in the mausoleum of the Iulii in the necropolis beneath St. Peter's in Rome (ill. 87 and 88).[226]

Since an almost identical stamp was used by the same moneyer for a contemporaneous minting that depicted the temple promised to the *clementia Caesaris* at that time[227] Antonius here figures as high priest

 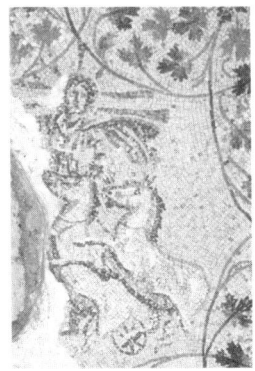

87. Altar of Augustus, Back: Ascension (Romulus? Divus Iulius?)
88. Necropolis under St. Peter's, Rome: The triumphing Christ

of Caesar's apotheosis. It is striking that the veil, both on Caesar (ill. 83 and 84) and on Antonius (ill. 85), can be mistaken for long wavy hair by non-initiated people, especially if there is already the thought of the unkempt beard of Antonius. So, we would have here not only the origin of Simon Peter's outward-appearance with long hair and bushy beard, but also of the long hair of Jesus.

As to Jesus' beard, the following can be observed: As the adopted son and successor to Caesar, Octavianus represented the genuinely resurrected man, and quickly had himself portrayed as a mourning, unshaven youth. The reverse sides of these mintages are specifically designed—one with pontifical instruments, the other depicting the temple actually built for Caesar—to compete with the denarii of Antonius.

90./91. Denarii of Octavianus, 37-36 BC.

Here we might find the origin and explanation for the downy beard of Jesus, who as a thirty year old man should have a full beard: it might come from that of the still young Octavianus.

Octavianus' greatest trump in this power struggle with Antonius for the political inheritance of Caesar was the inherited name of his adoptive father. On what is perhaps his first coin, an aureus from 43 BC, after his appointment as consul and before forming the triumvirate with Antonius and Lepidus, Octavianus strives for identification with Caesar so much that he might be confused with him:

92. Aureus of Octavianus, ca. 43 BC.

On the basis of the picture it would be difficult to decide who is Caesar and who is Octavianus—Caesar is on the right, recognizable by the wreath and folds on his neck. Even the inscriptions allow only the initiated to recognize it. Left: CAESAR·COS·PONT·AVG·; right: CAESAR·DICT·PERP·PON·MAX·. Which translates: 'Caesar, consul, pontifex, augur'—thus Octavianus—resp. 'Caesar, dictator for life, pontifex maximus'—Caesar.

Antonius, as Caesar's former companion, a consul and designated *flamen Divi Iulii,* claimed to have prior rights. He countered with a similar denarius on which he takes Octavianus' place—thus Caesar's facial expression conforms to that of Antonius:

93. Denarius of Antonius, ca. 43 BC.

—along with strengthening his solidarity with Lepidus, who succeeded Caesar as *pontifex maximus.* This resulted in both high priests already forming the sacerdotal duumvirate which Octavianus would need to form the triumvirate:

94. Denarius of Antonius and Lepidus, ca. 43 BC.

There are no portraits on these coins, only the regalia of each official position: those of the *augur* Antonius on the left, and those of the *pontifex maximus*, Lepidus, on the right. The names are inscribed with the same addition, *imperator:* M·ANTON·IMP·; M·LEPID·IMP·. Thus both names seem to be a double name: *Antonius Lepidus*. Put more specifically: *Lepidus* appears to be the cognomen of *Antonius*. For he remained the dominant man as clearly shown by the aurei edited after the ensuing formation of the triumvirate. Two coins of this same series: on the one Antonius and Lepidus, on the other Antonius and 'Caesar', i.e. Octavianus. He is on both:

95./96. Aurei of the triumviri, Antonius with Lepidus, Antonius with Octavianus, 42 BC.

The origin of the surname Peter, given to Simon, might be found in this configuration: *Lepidus* possibly understood as if it were derived from *lapis, lapidis*, 'stone', which is also the meaning of Petrus; Additionally, the primacy of Simon Peter in the Roman Church, who as the vicar of Christ has kept the function of *flamen Divi Iulii*, and as *summus pontifex* still holds the office of *pontifex maximus*.

Another parallel to be found is the conflicting appearance of the new Caesar who is first before and then against Antonius, and this finds its twin in the appearance of the resurrected Christ to the disbelieving Simon and the twelve, because the resurrected Christ first appeared to Mary Magdalene, who we assume corresponds to Cleopatra, and who then ran to Peter (Jn. 20:1-2). So it is not insignificant to know that there are also coins depicting Antonius and Cleopatra together.

97. Denarius of Antonius and Cleopatra, 32 BC.

Could these be the original portraits of Simon Peter and Mary Magdalene?

Before concluding our tour d'horizon of heathen-Christian portraits, we should take a final look at the physiognomy of Octavianus, so we might draw certain conclusions about the appearance of Divus Iulius.

98. Sesterce of Octavianus 40 BC; 99. Denarius of Augustus (Gaius?) 17 BC.

On the left we see how Octavianus presented himself in 40 BC, as the son of Caesar who had just been declared god; on the right in 17 BC how he portrayed his oldest grandchild, Gaius born 20 BC at the adoption of his grandchildren.[228]

By overlapping both portraits on the left, with the wreath of DIVOS IVLIVS and the longer hair and beginning beard of DIVI FILIVS, we have an acceptable Renaissance picture of Jesus. Even the age fits well, because Augustus had the deified Iulius presented ageless, in the best years of manhood—as illustrations 48 and 92 confirm. The childlike face on the right, with the candelabra and the cruciform arrangement of the reverse, might make a good Christ child.

In fact, the Christ child has other attributes of Augustus as well. Researchers have known this for a long time and commentators have vulgarized it. There is the ox, donkey and lamb, for example. The ox, because Octavianus was born at the foot of the Palatine *ad capita bubula*, in a city district referred to as 'by the ox heads'.[229] This finds its expression in the Christian manger at the foot of the palace (= Palatine), because the manger is near the head of the ox in the stable. The donkey because the meeting with a donkey herder named *Eutychus,* 'good-luck child', with his little donkey named *Nikon,* 'victor', had prophesied to Octavianus the victory at Actium. Octavianus placed an iron statue of them in the temple built after the victory[230]—Jesus still rides on a donkey in some Spanish churches, and a donkey is found next to the ox in the manger. The lamb which was often portrayed as Capricorn,[231] the zodiacal sign of Octavianus, also appears in the manger, but for reasons of decency it appears as a testicleless little sheep or as the Lamb of God.[232]

Obviously, all of these motifs were mandatory, because Octavianus had inherited them from his adoptive father Caesar. The ox symbolized the founder of cities because it was used in the ritual plowing of the furrow for the city walls, and Caesar had founded many colonies, and Octavianus had still to carry out the already existing plans for many others. The donkey, because Caesar's legate and historian Asinius Pollio—the name meaning 'ass' colt'—suspecting that the war against Cleopatra was actually a civil one against Antonius, made it necessary for Octavianus to contrast that pacifist one with his own victorious 'ass'. And the lamb, not only because Caesar himself had become the 'lamb of god' owing to the date of his assassination, the Ides of March being when a one-year-old lamb—*ovis Idulis*—was offered as sacrifice to Jupiter, so that his murder took on a ritual character; but also because Caesar had established the new collegium of the *luperci Iulii* and Antonius had offered him the fateful diadem just during the Lupercalia, which was used as pretext for his assassination and thus Caesar himself became the immolated *lupercus, lupae hircus*, 'the she-wolf's ram', which was essential for Octavianus to equal and neutralize.

Except for the donkey, we find all of the Caesarean-Augustan animal motifs in the representation of mother earth (or Saturnia Tellus or Italia)[233] on the Ara Pacis, with which earlier pictures of the Venus Genetrix were overlaid (cf. ill. 100, p. 121).

101. Ara Pacis, Detail: Saturnia Tellus (Mother Earth, Italia, Pax?)

That is the Madonna of the manger. There are two children here instead of one because of the Roman twins, Gaius and Lucius, as well as the east and west. This would not present a problem for Christian eyes, for the second child would be John, visiting his cousin the baby Jesus.[234] The same eyes would see the figure on the left as an angel, and in the head of the sea monster on the right we might sense the laughing donkey placed next to Joseph—thus completing the manger scene.

The Trinity of Divi Filius

Finally, we should call attention to the fact that on the coin of 12 BC which depicts Augustus placing the *sidus Iulium* on Caesar's statue (see ill. 49), he himself stands next to *Divus Iulius* and is the taller one, crowned with a wreath and holding the *clipeus virtutis,* the 'shield of virtue', so that the impression of an inversion arises, as if God the Father is decorating God the Son and not the other way around. Octavianus Caesar Augustus: Son of God, Christ Child and God the Father.

Octavianus first partly replaced the Capitoline Trias—Jupiter-Juno-Minerva—with Mars Ultor-Venus-Divus Iulius and satisfied himself with his role as the Son of God. Later when he had finally gained the first real victory of his own, namely winning back the military standards lost by Crassus to the Parthians through diplomatic channels, he substituted Saturn for Mars Ultor (ill. 103 and 104) and Tellus/Mother Earth for Venus—as documented, among other places, on the Prima Porta Statue and the Ara Pacis (see ill. 101).

102. Trias from Carthago: Venus, Mars and young heros (Divus Iulius?); Heavenly god: 103. Cherchel, Detail: Mars; 104. Prima Porta, Detail: Saturn

After he had, in the meantime, dedicated himself to Apollo and Diana—the Apollo aspect of Christ (sun) and the Diana aspect of the Madonna (moon) has often been emphasized and is undisputed—and then managed to advance himself to the position of God the Father, equal to Jupiter, Octavianus furthermore had his own genius placed between the two lares (in the Lararia), especially revered by the plebs, as a triad at all crossroads.

105. Lararium. Back, painted: Genius of the *pater familias* between lares

By doing this, Augustus compiled his own trinity—*Divus Iulius, Divi Filius* and *Genius Augusti*—which partly replaced the more original triad, *Venus, Divus Iulius* and *Anima Caesaris,* in the imagination of the people, but never superseded it.

It is highly significant that for both of these Augustan constellations, counterparts are again found in Christianity:
- The existence of a theologically correct trinity: Father, Son and Holy Spirit, while the people persist, at least in Romanized countries, in preferring the close 'Mother of God' to the distant 'God the Father'.
- The iconographical trinity, which has, however, especially in icon painting, three almost identical figures relating to each other, reminds us of the genius of Augustus placed between the lares.

A trinity was indispensable. Because the fateful triumvirate had been too powerful and had buried the old order, it was then necessary to invent a redeeming counterpart, to which the thanks for this new order could be given: a trinity that, not by chance, determined the end point of Christian theology.

Excursus

Re-Orientation

Before delving into the details of a comparison of Caesar and Jesus it is appropriate to discuss whether Caesar was a true god, or a would-be god à la Caligula or Nero. For if he was not a true god, then any dependency Jesus might have upon him would be only incidental and unimportant. Conversely, we have to examine whether Jesus was a real person or not. For if he was a real man, any possible parallels in this case, too, would just be incidental, and could be seen in the same light as those one may establish between Caesar and Alexander or even Napoleon.

As it is not essential to read the arguments in this excursus before reading the next chapter, the initiated or busy reader may choose to skip to the summary at the end of this excursus for the moment, in order to not lose the thread and possibly return to the subject matter dealt with here later.

Was Divus Iulius a true God?

Divus Iulius was not a secondary god, but was made equivalent to the highest God, Jupiter,[235] and became the God of the whole Roman Empire.

A reading of the sources leaves us in no doubt. Already, the decisions of the Senate intended to honor Caesar after Munda, the last battle in Spain at which the last Pompeians were definitively defeated, were extraordinary and well outside the norm of Roman custom:

'Then Caesar hastened to Rome. Victor of all civil wars he was feared and celebrated like no one before him; therefore all kinds of exaggerated honors were created and bestowed upon him, even superhuman ones: offerings, celebrations, sacrifices and statues in all temples and public places in each of the provinces, for every community and for all the kings allied with Rome. The inscriptions of the statues were various; on some of them he wore an oak wreath as the savior of the native country, because according to an old custom those who had been saved used to decorate whoever was responsible for their salvation with it. He was proclaimed 'Father of the Country' and elected dictator for life as well as consul for ten years. His person was pronounced sacred and inviolable and it was decreed that he could dispatch his official functions from a throne of ivory and gold; furthermore, he always should offer sacrifices in the triumphal robe, the city annually had to celebrate the days of his victories; priests and priestesses had to offer public prayers for him every five years and the administrators had to swear an oath immediately after being appointed not to resist any command of Caesar. To honor his birth the month Quintilis was renamed Iulius (July), furthermore, numerous temples were to be built to him as a god, inter alia one for him together with the personified Clementia (leniency, grace) hand in hand. So much was he feared as ruler and so strongly was he beseeched to bestow his mildness and grace unto them. There were even some who wanted to proclaim him king, until he learnt of it and forbade it under dire threat as the very idea was despised by their ancestors as a sacrilege. He dismissed his Praetorian bodyguard who had served him since their war days, and appeared in public alone with the usual servants ... He also pardoned his enemies and promoted many of those who had borne arms against him.'[236]

These honors which were decreed during his lifetime began to be enacted more or less straightaway, but came into full effect after his death, specifically when the members of the triumvirate conclusively defeated the assassins of Caesar. All the honors not only retained their spirit but became something more: the violence that was done to him, and the refusal of the people to accept his murder, served to guarantee his honor, title, and cult, forever. *Dictator perpetuo* meant thenceforth not only for his lifetime but for eternity. Even the fact that he did not want to become a king in this world only helped to gain him the kingdom in the other world. In the same manner as the earlier Osiris, Minos and Zeus, he was now granted not only jurisdiction in the world to come, but even jurisdiction over the present world from that other world:

'Later the people erected a massive pillar, crafted from Numidic marble and almost twenty feet high, bearing the inscription PARENTI PATRIAE 'to the parent of the fatherland'. And persisted to sacrifice there for a long time, swear oaths and to settle law suits by an oath in his name.'[237]

Furthermore, the site was made inviolable and served as a refuge for all those who were being persecuted, because everybody was given the right of asylum there. And this was the case not just in Rome, but across the whole Empire and in allied countries, in every place where a pillar or a statue of Divus Iulius stood.

This pillar in the Forum was situated right where the body of Caesar had been burned. This is the site where Octavianus built the first temple to his adoptive father, and this temple then served as the model for all the others, called *caesarea,* which were built throughout the Empire and beyond.

The cult of Divus Iulius expanded in the East as well as in the West, and systematically so after the peace of Brundisium and the division of the Empire under Antonius, Octavianus and Lepidus. All three had an interest in promoting it. Antonius as *flamen Divi Iulii,* as high priest of the God Iulius, Octavianus even as *Divi Filius,* as son of God.[238] Finally Lepidus, successor to Caesar in the service as *pontifex maximus,* cared for the religious bonds in Africa. The practice of the cult not only served the respective interests of each member of the triumvirate, but represented the religious expression of the unity of the Empire.

Later, when Octavianus eliminated Antonius and promoted himself to Augustus, he built *augustea* instead of *caesarea* which incorporated many aspects of the original *caesarea.*[239] So the cult of the Divi Filius was fused with that of Divus Iulius.

There is archeological evidence that indeed the cult permeated the whole Empire and, as one would expect, was practiced most zealously in the places where the presence of Caesar had been more prominent: for example in Gallia, especially in the Cisalpina, the Narbonensis, in Alexandria, and in Antiochia. In the front line, of course, stood the colonies of his veterans, scattered through the whole Empire. And also in the towns where the members of the triumvirate had been most active: e.g. Philippi, Perusia, Ephesos etc.[240]

The cult had its deepest roots there, where the most zealous of the *socii et amici populi romani* had to protect the border of the Empire, Herodes the Great: in Caesarea, Samaria, Galilee, Decapolis, Gaulanitis, Koilesyria. Herodes, himself Iulius by name, because his father Antipatros had been adopted by Caesar in gratitude for his help in the Alexandrian war, was designated King of Judaea by the members of the triumvirate, although, or perhaps because, he was not a Jew (his father was an Idumaean, his mother an Arabic princess, a Nabataean). In order to protect the interests of Rome against the nationalists of the area and against the Parthians, Antonius, then later Augustus, placed numerous Roman legions at his disposal. When the veterans were discharged, he raised up colonies after Caesar's example, from which he recruited the offspring. In the center of these colonies stood, of course, the temple of Divus Iulius: the *caesareum.* It was not by chance that he renamed his capital, the former Tower of Strato, Caesarea, as well as renaming Samaria Sebaste, Greek for Augustea. We also find a town in Herodes' territory called Iulias—later renamed by Augustus to Livias—a Caesarea Philippi, an Agrippias and, under his successors, a Tiberias. Whereas in Jerusalem the defence tower was called Antonia. When Herodes died, even from his deathbed still defending the Roman eagles on the Jewish temple against religious fanatics, his army and even part of his bodyguard consisted of Thracian and Gaulish legionaries as well as Germanic equestrians. These were people who themselves or their fathers had served under Caesar or Antonius, and who surely recognized no other God but this very Divus Iulius.[241]

Under the emperors who succeeded Augustus, the cult of Divus Iulius was further cultivated, interestingly enough, this mostly occurred during the times when the emperor cult met the most resistance. Under Tiberius e.g., who did not want to be worshipped himself, or after Caligula, who made himself a god while still living, and was murdered and condemned to the *damnatio memoriae*. Even Vespasianus, himself an atheist, systematically renewed and propagated the cult of Divus Iulius after the murder of Nero and the extinction of the Iulian-Claudian line. Significantly, Vespasianus was proclaimed emperor exactly where Herodes had reigned: in Judaea.

The cult of Caesar was a fact, definitively established. For, as Suetonius said, he had been numbered among the gods not only because of the proclamation of a decision, but also because of the conviction of the people. So his cult was less the predecessor of the emperor cult than it was a refuge for its opponents.[242]

Question: Whatever has happened to this cult?

Spolia and Legacies

The cult of Divus Iulius, together with that of his filiation Divi Filius, disappeared suddenly with the advent of Christianity. What is particularly interesting is the fact that the *caesarea* and *augustea* became the first Christian churches, and consequently the statues of Jesus replaced the statues of Divus Iulius and Divi Filius respectively. The other well-known early Christian churches took the place of the erstwhile temples of the various Mother goddesses—above all the temples of Venus—which were especially sacred to the Julian clan and now came to serve as churches to the Virgin.

A vivid picture of this greets the visitor to Rome today. The numerous churches to be seen in and around the Forum, as excavation has made clear, were built on the foundations of the ancient temples. Elsewhere the story is the same. The visitor to the Orient will soon realize that the first Christian basilicas had previously been heathen temples, while the later basilicas reused the so-called spolia from their ruins as building materials. Ancient temples destroyed by earthquakes provided the materials for the construction of new basilicas, and the combination of different styled columns, pilasters and capitals still clearly testifies to this today. Later, as a consequence of the withdrawal of the Romans from the Eastern Empire and the spread of Islam, the process involving a change in meaning repeated itself. By adding a prayer niche to their southern sides, the surviving basilicas were converted to mosques, and new mosques were built from the spolia of the basilicas that did not survive.

The structures were retained as one religion transitioned to the next. As in Roman times Jupiter was superimposed upon Baal or Hadad (e.g. in Baalbek), and Venus upon Astarte or Atargatis, so we find that the later basilicas and churches to Mary replace—and are even in the same place as—the basilicas built after the model of the Aemilia and Iulia basilicas, respectively the Venus and Artemis temples.

The same principle that applies to God and the Mother of God also seems to apply to the saints. Where we would expect to find Roman sacred sites or memorials to the conquerors of the East—Pompeius and Agrippa—we instead find churches consecrated to John the Baptist and St. George. Even Islam, which introduced absolute monotheism, has not completely erased all the traces of the former veneration of saints. The head of John the Baptist is still venerated in the mosque of Damascus today, while the cult of St. George has not only survived in the churches that remain there, but still enjoys universal reverence amongst the Moslem population also.

Now John the Baptist exhibits structural similarities to Pompeius: a proximity to and rivalry with Jesus, respectively Caesar, and both were beheaded. St. George, for his part, has structural similarities to Agrippa—dragon slayer corresponds to crocodile slayer, i.e. conqueror of Egypt. (Here also we observe that *George* is the Greek translation of *Agrippa,* as a synonym for *agricola*—farmer—from *ge-ôrgos*, 'earthworker').

Euhemerus and the Aftermath

The founders of empires in antiquity were wont to become gods, e.g. before Caesar, Alexander became Amon-Zeus, and the ancients knew, at least since the time of Euhemerus, that Uranus, Cronos and Zeus had previously been earthly rulers who were posthumously elevated to godhead, and that was because they had been *euergetai* and *sôtêres*—benefactors and saviors. So Osiris had been an ancient Pharaoh, Attis a Phrygian pastoral chieftain, Adonis a Canaanite ruler of hunters, Demeter an Aegean peasant priestess-queen, Mithra a Persian prince. This idea was indeed labeled as atheist, but nevertheless it provided the groundwork for the cult of the ruler, which was first adopted by the Hellenistic dynasties, then later became a rule with the Roman emperors.[243] By performing the appropriate deeds and actions, they could be elevated to the gods posthumously. It was only the attempt to make themselves gods in their own lifetime, as was the case with Demetrios Poliorketes or Caligula, that was severely frowned upon, often ended badly, and usually led to the *damnatio memoriae*—the damnation of the memory. This was true in most cases. For certain founders of empires, such as Alexander and to an extent Caesar and Augustus, were partly granted something that was denied to their imitators—to be deified during their lifetimes and to ascend into heaven even more so after their deaths. But again: this was only partly true, because even the empire founders were not deified in their own country, but rather on the fringes of their respective empires. Alexander was deified in Egypt as Amon, Caesar firstly in Asia Minor as *soter* and *theos*, Augustus in the provinces, hidden behind the cult of the Dea Roma or his own Genius. But in Macedonia, the ancestral homeland of Alexander and hence that of his Diadochi, there was never a ruler cult, and in Rome there was no cult of Augustus during his lifetime.

So whether he is locally absent on the fringe of the empire, or temporally absent because he has since passed away, God is world ruler only *in absentia*. God is the long shadow of the world ruler.

From the Euhemeristic point of view it appears to be the case, at least in regard to the founders of empires, that their cults outlive even the fall of the empires that they established. As Zeus had been a former ruler, he remained a god when his empire had gone to ground.

This appears to be the case not only for the mythological gods, as Christianity itself is no exception. It is clear to us, even if unconsciously, that Christianity is the form in which the Roman Empire has survived its fall. This applies at least to the Roman Catholic Church. Not only is the Pope still the *pontifex maximus* of our time, but he also has the full power of that office. Even the boundaries of his sovereignty appear to have been bequeathed to him by the Romans. It is well known that at the time of the Reformation in Germany the dividing line ran conspicuously along the ancient Roman Limes: on this side the Catholics, on that side the Protestants, just as it once was the Romans on this side, and the barbarians on the other. It can similarly be observed that the dividing line between the Catholic and Orthodox churches runs along the boundary line between the Eastern and Western Roman Empires—whereby the Bosnian and Albanian Moslems represent the rearguard of the Turkish armies that marched in during the Middle Ages.

In summary, it can generally be said that religion is the form in which an empire survives its own fall.

The disappearance of the cult of Divus Iulius would therefore be unique in history, contrary to all experience in both mythological and historical time, Christian as well as non-Christian.

Now the question arises: Has the cult of Divus Iulius disappeared, or have its spolia been taken over by Christianity?

A vita Divi Iulii…

The cult was omnipresent for centuries. Not only was it *ubiquitous* because Divus Iulius was *synnaos* with all the other godheads—meaning his statue was to be found in all temples and not just in his own—but it also was *sempitern*, because the cult was intended to exist forever. We read again the already quoted decree of the Senate after Munda:

'…the city should annually celebrate the days of his victories'.

Think of what this meant: because his victories had been innumerable, there was enough cause to celebrate the entire year. That requires a liturgy, wherein the ritual celebration of his victories was the centerpiece.

Admired in his lifetime, after his death, Caesar's victories were simply regarded as miracles performed by a God—as the speech of Antonius at Caesar's funeral makes clear:

> '(Antonius) hymned him again as a celestial deity, raising his hands to heaven in order to testify to his divine origin. At the same time he enumerated with rapid speech all his wars, battles, victories and all the nations he had brought under the nation's sway, and the spoils he had sent home. Each exploit was depicted by Antonius as a miracle.'[244]

That means: the liturgical celebration of the victories of the new God became the acclamation of his miracles. So if a *vita Divi Iulii* was written for liturgical use (and would a planned and organized worldwide cult be thinkable without a liturgical text?) it would have borne the features of a hagiography with life, death and miracles: *vita mors miracula*.

And lo and behold: the Gospel of Mark is of the genre of a Hellenistic vita of a ruler, in the ancient terminology 'a historical monograph about a famous man (a hero or god)'.[245]

Question: Which famous man in those days was both a hero and a god as well, long enough before Mark so that this 'historical monograph' could become a Gospel story, but recent enough that his memory would still be alive in the people—who else but Caesar?

...or a Caesar legend?

Is it at all possible that elements of Caesar could find their way into the Gospel? When were the Gospels written?

The Gospels and the other texts of the New Testament were written at the end of the first century of our era (usual dating: between 70 and 100 AD). The churches try to date them 20 to 30 years earlier to accommodate the possibility that at least the oldest Gospel, that of Mark, was written by eyewitnesses. So there are at least five and maybe even eight generations between Caesar's death (44 BC) and the redaction of the Gospels. Time enough—for a legend to form.

Caesar's fame among all people is spoken of repeatedly in all sources—similar to Alexander's, whose legend, originating from oral tradition, was written as a novel and it varied in many languages. But no romance about Caesar has come down to us. Was Caesar's legend never written down? Or was it, but in such a mutilated form that after many successive translations the source is no longer recognizable, similar to how uncertain we are of which historical figure is hidden behind the Siegfried of the German legend? Could parts of Caesar's legend be woven into other legends? Could this have happened with the Gospels?

In fact, the Gospel of Mark looks like an Alexander romance to the eyes of specialists:

> 'In more than just one respect the Alexander romance is possibly the closest analogy to the Gospel. Not only the traditions and the redactional history, but also the techniques of composition and rhetoric—and language and style—show a lot of analogies. Furthermore the content, the manner of the working over of the sources and generally the form of depiction all show great resemblances. So the Alexander romance might be the closest parallel to the genre of the Gospel.'[246]

But the Gospel according to Mark is not an Alexander romance. So whose romance is it? Who existed three centuries after Alexander that could be compared to Alexander if not Caesar? Is Mark's Gospel a Caesar romance?

Was Mark written in Latin?

According to the tradition, Mark's Gospel was written in Rome in Latin, twelve years after the resurrection of the Lord.[247]

Detailed examinations of the oldest manuscripts—especially the bilingual Latin/Greek—have shown that with Mark the Greek text in fact is dependent on the Latin.[248] And there is still more: the deviations between the readings in the Greek manuscripts are explained best if they are seen as different versions of translation of the Latin text. [249] Also the fact that the Church Fathers—demonstrably Clement, Irenaeus and Justin—cite the Latin Mark, which they translate ad hoc into Greek, speaks for the priority of the Latin version.

Thus, the findings of modern textual research compel us to take the old tradition about Mark seriously: the road leads to Rome.

And how is it with the 'twelve years after the resurrection of the Lord'? Twelve years after Caesar's murder and apotheosis, Asinius Pollio started to write his *Historiae,* the first time Caesar's history was taken down, and it was used by later historians like Appianus and Plutarchus as a model.

Coincidence?

Roman spolia in the Christian Gospel

It has been observed for some time now that the Gospels contain miraculous healings that appear to be simplified reports of those Vespasianus had performed in Egypt, where according to Tacitus the emperor healed a blind man and a man with a withered hand:

> 'Throughout the month when Vespasianus was waiting for the summer winds and a secure sea, many miracles occurred that revealed the grace of heaven and the inclination of the gods toward Vespasianus. A man of Alexandria known for his blindness bent his knee before him and asked, sighing, for his blindness to be healed—he did this in the name of the god Serapis, who was especially honored by this superstitious people. And so he prayed to the monarch, that he should be gracious unto him and smear his saliva on his eyes and eyelids. Another—who had a bad hand—asked the emperor in the name of the same god to touch it with the sole of his foot. At first Vespasianus laughed and refused. But when they pressed upon him, he feared to be seen as arrogant; at the same time their entreaties and the calls of the flatterers gave him hope. At last he demanded a medical report declaring if such a blindness and suchlike paralysis could

be healed by human help. The physicians said a variety of things: the blind man had not lost his sight completely and it would return if the obstacle was removed. The other had contorted limbs: by the use of healing balms he could become whole again. Perhaps the state of affairs would move the gods, and he—the monarch—would serve as a tool of the Godhead. And finally if the healing were to be successful, the fame would be his, and if not, mockery would befall the two unfortunates. Upon this he was convinced that he would be lucky and that afterwards the people would trust him with everything, so Vespasianus carried out the act with a friendly demeanor before the eyes of the crowd standing by. Immediately the hand was usable again and the blind man could see the daylight anew. Both cases are still remembered by eyewitnesses today, and they have no reason to lie.'[250]

Moreover the Gospel contains the core of a speech, reported by Plutarchus, in which Tiberius Gracchus bemoaned that the appropriation of public land by the aristocrats had rendered the farmers landless and the poorest of people.

Speech of Tiberius Gracchus:

'The wild beasts of Italy have their holes and their hiding places but the men who fight and die for Italy enjoy only the light and the air. Homeless, they roam restlessly with wife and child. Our rulers lie when they call on the soldiers to fight for the graves and shrines of their ancestors. Because none of these Romans can point to a paternal altar or an ancestral tomb. But rather, they fought and died to bring wealth and luxury to others. They are called masters of the world and they have not a single clod of earth that is their own.'[251]

Matthew:

'And Jesus saith unto him, The foxes have holes, and the birds of the air have their nests, but the Son of man hath not where to lay his head.'[252]

Between Tiberius Gracchus and Vespasianus, the *termini post quem* and *ante quem,* lived Caesar and Augustus.

Question: Could it be that there are anecdotes in the Gospels which were taken from Divus Iulius, and respectively Divi Filius, and then attributed to Jesus? Are not Caesar and Augustus more important than Tiberius Gracchus and Vespasianus? Was it not Caesar who brought the political program of the Gracchi to realization (not by chance does Appianus, imitating Asinius Pollio, begin his history of the Roman civil war with the Gracchi)? Is he not the founder of the Empire? Would there even have been a Vespasianus without him?

Was Caesar consciously faded out of the picture?

Until today no one has done a systematic search for traces of Caesar in the Gospel. There is a long tradition of such neglect.

Even the Church Fathers, who have so much to say about the Roman emperors, are strikingly silent about Caesar. Was the greatest of them all, the founder of the Empire, not worth a word or did other texts already speak of him, and if so, which ones? Were they afraid to even mention in passing this man who became a god? He, whose proverbial *clementia* matched the gentleness of Jesus. He, whose martyr's death anticipated the passion of Jesus, and whose resurrection first—in the form of the vengeful ghost of Philippi—visited a just punishment upon his murderers, then later—in the figure of the son of god, Augustus—brought eternal peace, the kingdom of heaven on earth? Was the cult of Divus Iulius—the deified Caesar—a stumbling block to the Church Fathers just as the cult of the emperor had been, or was it unbearable to them that the cult of Divus Iulius, the divine founder of the Empire, was so remote and contrary to the respective all-too-human emperors, in the same manner as the later Jesus cult? Did they fail to recognize that the Easter liturgy follows the ritual of Caesar's funeral like a script, or was it precisely this that they wanted to keep secret? Did they not notice that some of the *Vitae Caesaris* read like a Gospel text, or did they want to hush up the competition?

And yet it is written: 'Render unto Caesar the things which are Caesar's!'

In spite of—or rather due to—this denial, Caesar appears to stay bound up with Jesus in the collective subconscious as if he were his alter ego. Here, the well-known anecdote concerning the 'Caesar-like' Napoleon is significant. When the emperor discussed Christianity with Wieland in October 1808 at Weimar, he whispered in his ear that it was a great question—that of whether Jesus Christ had lived at all. He received this answer:

> 'I am aware, Majesty, that there were some unsound people who have doubted it, but it seems to me as foolish as to doubt that Julius Caesar lived—or that your Majesty lives today.'[253]

It is as if, no sooner had a resurrected Caesar like Napoleon appeared, that it dawned on the scholars that this presence was somehow also a proof for the existence of Jesus Christ. Strange.

Sermo castrensis

There is another indication that leads, if not directly to Caesar himself, at least to his legionaries. The Gospels, especially that of Mark, are full of Latinisms:

Outside of proper names like *Kaisar* (from *Caesar*), *Iulius*, *Lucius*, *Paulus*, *Titus* or ethnic and sectarian appellations like *Herodiani*, *Christiani* being borrowed from Latin, there are also others: *legio* 'legion', *centurio*, *praetorium*, *custodia* 'watch', *census* 'tax', *colonia*, *speculator* 'spy, scout', *sicarius* (from *sica*, 'knife') 'assassin', *titlus* (from *titulus*, 'title') 'inscription', 'sign', *fragellium* (from *flagellum*) 'flail', 'whip', 'lash', *reda* 'travelling car' (a Celtic loanword), *membrana* 'thin skin', 'parchment', *denarius* 'a ten', *quadrans* 'quarter, i.e. smallest coin', *libra* 'balance', 'pound', *milion* (as singular to *milia [passuum]*) 'mile', *modius* 'bushel', *sextarius* 'sextain', 'pint', *semicinctium* 'apron', *sudarium* 'handkerchief', etc. Sometimes Mark even explains Greek terms by Latin ones: for example, that two *leptà* 'mites' are one *quadrans* or that *aulê* 'court', 'courtyard', 'farmstead' are to be understand as *praetorium*.[254]

The fact that the Latinisms are most numerous in the oldest Gospel, and their frequency declines in the later ones, led to the hypothesis that a Latin original of the Gospel might exist.[255] Until today the original has still not been found, and the hypothesis still waits for its discovery.

In the meantime attention has been drawn to the fact that Mark's Latinisms belong, one and all, to the jargon of the legionaries, indeed, so much so that we may speak of a *sermo castrensis*.[256]

Also, because the same Mark writes a vulgar Greek without the use of the later Hebraisms and Septuagintisms of Matthew and Luke, and uses popular Aramaisms instead, the track leads us to the Roman veterans in Syria, either to those of the Colonia Iulia of Heliopolis (Baalbek) or to those who were settled by Herodes in Caesarea, Galilaea, Samaria and Decapolis. Namely, they were the ones who had originally spoken the Latin of the legionaries, and were settled in rural areas where they inter-married with the local population that still spoke Aramaic, whereas the official language of the Empire was Greek by this time.[257]

Curiously enough, the originally Gallic word *reda*, 'travelling car' also belongs to the Latinisms of the New Testament. But the Roman army in the East and those of Herodes as well were demonstrably formed for the most part by Gallic legionaries—who surely did not come without their *redae*.

Question: Has the oral 'special material' incorporated into the Gospels been picked up from the descendents of the Roman veterans in the Orient? If so, then they had much knowledge to share about their God—about Divus Iulius. For through him, with him and in him they became the Lords of the world. They would not have wasted words on any one of the many Jesuses they had crucified.

Second question: Was the Gospel perhaps the cult book of Divus Iulius, which was read aloud to the veterans in the temple of their God, in the *caesareum?* Originally in Latin, was this text later, when the only Latin that the subsequent generation understood was the jargon of the camp and the language of command, gradually translated into Greek, the language of the people of the Eastern Empire?

This is what the further phraseological Latinisms occurring in the Greek Mark indicate. For example: *rhapismasin auton elabon* for *verberibus eum acceperunt,* 'received him with strokes' for 'hit him'; *symboulion poiein* for *consilium facere,* 'make council' for 'hold council' respectively 'pass a resolution'; *to ikanon poiein* for *satisfacere,* 'do enough' for 'give satisfaction', 'satisfy'.

The impression given is that it was translated from the Latin into Greek bit by bit, word-for-word wherever possible, and still often left incomplete.

Membrana: a thin skin or a parchment codex?

It may seem logical that *membrana*, in the sense of 'thin skin', belonged to the jargon of the legionary, like *sudarium,* 'handkerchief' for example, or *semicinctium,* 'apron'. But in the relevant citation of the New Testament, *membrana* is used in the second sense of the word, namely as a synonym for 'parchment'. The apostle Paul writes in his second letter to Timotheus:

'The cloak that I left at Troas with Carpus, when thou comest, bring with thee, and the books, but especially the parchments.'[258]

Here the King James Bible uses 'parchment', which is called *membranae,* 'thin skins', in the Greek original—a striking use of a Latin borrowed word. It has been proven that parchment rolls are not meant here, for which the Greek word *diphtherai* would have been available. Rather this neologism indicates a technical innovation of the Romans: the *codex,* what we today call a book. The name *membranae* indicates that these are parchment codices, not the kind made of papyrus.[259]

At first the Romans had stitched the codices together from papyrus. Parchment was never popular in Rome. In classical times the Romans almost exclusively used papyrus for their scrolls. It was not till it became scarce during the occupation of Egypt by Antiochus Epiphanes (170-168 BC), that they, nolens volens, had to resort to a replacement for papyrus: the furs from Pergamon, parchment. When papyrus became available again, the Romans had meanwhile discovered an advantage of the parchment: it was washable and hence capable of being written on again. This advantage however, only became useful with the discovery of the codex in the second half of the first century BC. So alongside the papyrus codices, the actual *libri*, appeared the parchment codices, the *membranae*, partly as notebooks and partly as pocketbooks. Because they were almost indestructible and thus well fitted for travelling they were popular with the poets, who were often 'On the Road'.[260]

It is known that the introduction of the codex, the book, goes back to Caesar, who frequently had to introduce technical reforms during his varied military expeditions. Apparently the *volumina*, the scrolls, were too voluminous and impractical for him. Expressed in the computer terminology of today: the book had the advantage over the scroll, because it changed information stored in sequential form to a paginated form, allowing random access, which was no small advantage in war when overview and swiftness are decisive. Naturally, this could not escape the notice of Caesar, who was ever obsessed with celerity: he simply systematically introduced the codex. Being the revolutionary that he was, it seems he even derived some pleasure from sending his letters to the ultra-conservative Senate folded and bound, instead of using the traditional method of scrolls in capsules.

> 'There are still letters from him to the Senate, and it seems that he was the first to use the form of a notebook with pages, whilst earlier the consuls and the military leaders always send transversally written papyrus scrolls.'[261]

In the Roman civil war the codex, the book, so it seems, became the symbol of the Caesarean revolution, while the volume, the scroll, signified the Senatorial reactionaries.

In any case, the triumph of the codex over the volume, the book over the scroll, developed in tandem with the growth and consolidation of the imperial order, a process in which the imperial chancellery and the military administration played an important, if not decisive role. And the process was a long one. As the papyrus findings show, during the first two centuries after Christ the scrolls still outnumbered the codices. It was not till the third century that the relationship was on a par. From the time of Constantine on, the relationship changed in favor of the book, and from the sixth century the scroll disappears.[262]

This was the case with pagan scriptures. Christian scriptures on the other hand, were written on codices from the beginning. Indeed, they were written only on codices, in stark contrast to the Jewish texts, which continued to be written on scrolls. The early Christians seem to have had a holy dread of scrolls, a kind of *horror voluminis*, because when they were forced to write on scrolls in times of papyrus shortage, they wrote on the inconvenient uneven rear side of the scrolls, remarkably enough even if the front side was unused![263]

This conduct of the Christians is well known. The book was so typical for the Christian that in iconography the man with the book could stand for the Christian, and the Christian became the epitome of 'the man of the book'. This is not an insignificant circumstance to which we owe the saving of the ancient legacies preserved by the monks and their tireless copying work throughout the entire Middle Ages.

However, this original fixation of the Christians on the book remains a mystery. Because the reasons for favoring the book over the scroll existed equally for all. Non-Christians had problems accepting the book, most of all the Jews, who held the scroll in a place of honor for a particularly long period of time, and who still use it in their liturgy today. So, why just the Christians?

This question remains unanswered until today.[264]

In light of our investigation, the suspicion arises that the early Christians may simply have felt obligated to continue an existing Roman practice. Was not Paul the Jew the one who said of himself: 'I am a Roman citizen!'?

Most pointedly, the Christians could have been bound to the custom of the *castra*, the Roman military camp. Just as the later *claustrum*, the cloister, seems to be copied from the *castrum*, a 'fortified post'—not only in name but also in its form and structure—so too could the Christian preference, if not to say the unconditional inclination toward the book, originate from the Roman, the imperatorial, and in the last instance, Caesarean tradition.

To put it differently, the solution to the mystery of why the Christians always wrote on codices and never on scrolls, could be the following: they followed the example of the apostle Paul who had written on *membranae*. But whose example did Paul follow? Maybe that of Jesus? Was it Jesus who wrote in books? Was he the inventor of the book—he, of whom it is said that he left behind nothing written?

But we know whose example Paul followed: the example of the inventor of the codex: Gaius Iulius Caesar—Divus Iulius.

Was Divus Iulius Jesus?

Is Jesus a historical figure?[265]

The theoretical possibility that elements of Divus Iulius were substantially absorbed by the Jesus story is plausible only if Jesus is not an undisputed independent historical figure. So, what really is the situation with the historicity of Jesus?

Jesus is only found in Christian literature, and not in the historical records. This alone gave rise to early doubts. The critical examination of Christian literature has furthermore shown that the geographical and chronological framework, as well as the speeches and parables, were for the most part composed by the Evangelists themselves. Much of the remainder was drawn from tradition and their surroundings. Pivotal concepts, like the idea that a man could be the son of God, are alien to the Jewish milieu and must come from the late-Hellenistic, early-imperial world. The true, historical core had shrunk so much that the question was asked if there could have been a process whereby a central idea grew into a story that was not historical at all. Either literarily: i.e. there was no tradition, but simply a writer of the Gospel story—no original Gospel, but only an original Evangelist. Symbolically: the oldest community created for itself in the narratives about Jesus a history meaningful right down to the last detail. Or mythically: the main points of the Gospel tradition were given in mythology and later condensed into history.

Thus we see that already by the nineteenth century the historical existence of Jesus was radically questioned.[266] The result of this was, of course, that in return it was just as passionately confirmed, sometimes even by critical researchers who insist there was a core of historical existence.[267]

Also, with the turn towards a Gnostic-syncretic solution, the assumption that early Christianity had originally been an inner-Jewish phenomenon was increasingly abandoned. From then on, it was doubted that the world phenomenon of Christianity could go back to an illuminated rural Galilaean carpenter, and this led to a radical questioning of Jesus' historical existence.[268]

Meanwhile, the opposing sides of this trench warfare have stabilized along the following lines: That the New Testament can no longer be used as the basis to determine who the historical Jesus was in reality.[269] So it was not the reports that formed the tradition, but the tradition the reports. The texts do not give evidence about Jesus, but only about the Evangelist himself, or at best about his community.

Hence the simple question of whether Jesus lived and who he really was is no longer a matter of knowledge, but of faith.

This agnosticism does allow breathing space for the traditional view, but does nothing to limit fantasy. If it is impossible to write a true biography of Jesus then everybody can write his own. The traditionalists, ready as ever, dust-off their apologetic frescoes and oleographs; all the others invent their own ad hoc Jesus. The modern images of Jesus flourish and multiply on this thriving ground, fertilized by the rotting corpse of the self-admitted failure of 'Historical-Jesus Research'.[270]

There is a simple reason for the failure of the 'Search for the historical Jesus': If the Gospel contains oral tradition, if it, as most scholars assume, was preached long before it was written down, or at any rate is the result of a long editing and copying process, then the solution cannot possibly be found only by attempting to reconstruct this process from the final version backwards.

Here we have to reckon with the effects of the grapevine and folk etymologies, with corruptions and flaky transliterations, incorrect translations, corrupted copies, dictation mistakes, whether originating from misreading or misspelling, from mishearing or slips of the pen. We could imagine errors arising for visual, acoustic or dogmatic reasons, from force of the writer's habits or deliberately formed. It was a babel of languages: Latin, Greek, Aramaic, Syrian, Egyptian/Coptic, as well as Armenian etc. Then there are the dialects. All of this combined with the declining linguistic expertise amongst the copyists and editors. All written by hand, without punctuation, without accents, all capital letters, no spaces between the words, no paragraphs, no chapter divisions, variable spelling, evolving pronunciation,[271] confusing abbreviations,[272] changing sense of the words, different alphabets running to the right or the left with heterographical interposition of foreign words: all invitations to an incorrect reading. On top of this there was frequently a skipping of lines, sometimes a switching of the pages; glosses by different hands which became incorporated into the text through copying; adaptations to parallel passages that resonated more in the ear of the writer. Devastating was the fact that everybody knew that the 'original' he was copying from was itself a copy, into which errors had already crept: providing reason and justification for clever corrections that made the text worse rather than better. And then after everything became sufficiently contradictory, a new editing followed: the creative seized the opportunity and rewrote everything in an 'understandable' manner, adding at this stage some oral tradition and some citations from the Old Testament, in order for it to appear more authentic. To be up-to-date, he also threw in some nice speeches he had heard from the most eloquent itinerant preachers, removed the morally objectionable, the contradictory and the ironic pieces, adapted the locations and edited the connections between loose parts: And a new story was born. Or several: four canonical ones and umpteen apocryphal ones.

Said differently: traduttore traditore; each copy an interpretation with no respect for intellectual property, in sovereign ignorance of copyright laws. After this new editing period when the text was finalized at long last, the 'faithful' handing-down began, which occurred in the first centuries under unfavorable conditions. What this meant for ancient civilization was: an increasing mix of nations and languages, dark times, barbarian invasions, lootings, devastation and decline of the towns, interruptions of the trade routes, separation of the Orient and Occident, libraries destroyed by earthquakes and wars, disappearance of schools and decline of the general education level. For the writers: dependence on the authorities, consideration of the changing patrons, power struggles, excommunications, living in catacombs, autocratic priests, the need to camouflage and the need for recognition, increasing ignorance and presumptuousness. And for the text it meant: dogmatic infringement, mutual accusations of falsification of the texts, book burnings, as well as—with power shifts—enforced deletions and changes to the texts. While in the background we have the constant copying of the copy of the copy, translating of the translation of the translation, brutalization of the text *ad infinitum*. Then came washing day—a return to the original text was called for. But to which one? Probably not to those of the heretics, but to the text approved by the whole Church! Thus there was a collation and balancing of the versions, including the elimination of all special forms, the very forms that might have been the original ones, but that did not matter as long as all heresy was erased! If the need arose, back-translations were relied upon for help,[273] and on such occasions the language was adjusted. And so there came again a new version not universally accepted, that crossed with the former versions in the copying process and gave rise to new brutalizations etc. This is roughly how the texts that have been passed down to us originated, if we believe the researchers.

All this certainly guarantees an inextricable undergrowth.[274] Under these circumstances, it is no surprise that after two hundred years of text-critical study and in spite of a nearly unimaginable expenditure of effort and acute scholarship, the Proto-Gospel still is a variable and the hypothetical second source is still only called Q.

Ultimately, there can be only one way to reach a solution: find the source and compare it to the version at the end of the process of tradi-

CODICVM NOVI TESTAMENTI SPECIMINA

The following two pages show a facsimile of the Codex *D*, *Bezae Cantabrigiensis*. Reproduced is Mark 1:38-2:5. On the left is the Greek text and on the right the corresponding Latin one. Here the following should be observed and noted.
1. All is neatly written in majuscules, i.e. capitals, giving rise to the impression of outstanding legibility at first glance. But the appearance is deceptive because not only are periods, commas and the accents, (which are important for the Greek), missing, but so are the word-spacing, the blanks. Thus the words have to be read out—the potential for incorrect word division is lurking.
2. The Greek text has left marks on the Latin one on the opposite page and vice versa. This not only makes the reading more difficult but—since in the respective text the other language is also visible, as a mirror-image in fact—one is tempted to read from right to left at the same time. In a time when the Aramaic alphabet looked like a Greek one running from right to left, this circumstance strengthened the tendency to read some names in an Aramaic manner.
3. Notes have been written on the margins of the Greek text, in this case there are relatively few, but it is not rare to find real glosses. One can imagine that during the transcription process there might emerge a tendency to include into the text one or another gloss, whichever ones the copyist takes a special liking to.
4. In the Latin text (in the fourteenth line counted from the bottom) one can find the name of the first town into which Jesus went written as *Cafarnaum* and not *Capharnaum* as one would expect if it were a translation from the Greek. This allows for the assumption that the Latin spelling developed autonomously. In our opinion this *Cafarnaum* is a metathesis of *Corfinium*, the first town that Caesar captured after the start of the civil war.
5. In the Greek text one can find an example of a *nomen sacrum*, i.e. an abbreviation of a frequently used sacred name. In the antepenultimate line, from the 9th to the 11th letter, as well as at the end of 6th line counted from the bottom, the name Jesus is abbreviated as *IHC* easily recognizable from the overline. In older manuscripts the same name is abbreviated as *IC*, i.e. just giving the first and the last letter, without the 'h', i.e. 'ê'. It is striking that *IC*, Lat. *IS*, is not only the first and last letter of *IESVS* but also of *IVLIVS*.

See also the glossary entry on *Bezae Cantabrigiensis (ms)*.

ΚΑΤ ΜΑΡΚ

ΕΙϹ ΤΑϹ ΕΝΓΥϹ ΚΩΜΑϹ ΚΑΙ ΕΙϹ ΤΑϹ ΠΟΛΕΙϹ
ΙΝΑ ΚΑΚΕΙ ΚΗΡΥΞΩ ΕΙϹ ΤΟΥΤΟ ΓΑΡ ΕΞΕΛΗΛΥΘΑ
ΚΑΙ ΗΝ ΚΗΡΥϹϹΩΝ ΕΙϹ ΤΑϹ ϹΥΝΑΓΩΓΑϹ ΑΥΤΩΝ
ΕΙϹ ΟΛΗΝ ΤΗΝ ΓΑΛΕΙΛΑΙΑΝ ΚΑΙ ΤΑ ΔΑΙΜΟΝΙΑ ΕΚΒΑΛΛΩ
ΙΗ᾽ ΚΑΙ ΕΡΧΕΤΑΙ ΠΡΟϹ ΑΥΤΟΝ ΛΕΠΡΟϹ ΕΡΩΤΩΝ ΑΥΤΟΝ
ΚΑΙ ΛΕΓΩΝ ΕΑΝ ΘΕΛΕΙϹ ΔΥΝΑϹΑΙ ΜΕ ΚΑΘΑΡΙϹΑΙ
ΚΑΙ ΟΡΓΙϹΘΕΙϹ ΕΚΤΕΙΝΑϹ ΤΗΝ ΧΕΙΡΑ ΑΥΤΟΥ
ΗΨΑΤΟ ΑΥΤΟΥ ΚΑΙ ΛΕΓΕΙ ΑΥΤΩ ΘΕΛΩ ΚΑΘΑΡΙϹΘΗΤΙ
ΚΑΙ ΕΥΘΕΩϹ ΑΠΗΛΘΕΝ ΑΠ ΑΥΤΟΥ Η ΛΕΠΡΑ
ΚΑΙ ΕΚΑΘΑΡΙϹΘΗ ΚΑΙ ΕΝΕΒΡΙϹΑΜΕΝΟϹ ΑΥΤΩ
ΕΥΘΥϹ ΕΖΕΒΑΛΕΝ ΑΥΤΟΝ ΚΑΙ ΛΕΓΕΙ ΑΥΤΩ
ΟΡΑ ΜΗΔΕΝΙ ΕΙΠΗϹ ΑΛΛΑ ΥΠΑΓΕ ΔΕΙΞΟΝ ϹΕΑΥΤΟΝ
ΤΩ ΙΕΡΕΙ ΚΑΙ ΠΡΟϹΕΝΕΝΚΕ ΠΕΡΙ ΤΟΥ ΚΑΘΑΡΙϹΜΟΥ ϹΟΥ
Α ΠΡΟϹΕΤΑΞΕΝ ΜΩΥϹΗϹ ΕΙϹ ΜΑΡΤΥΡΙΟΝ ΑΥΤΟΙϹ
ΙΘ᾽ Ο ΔΕ ΕΞΕΛΘΩΝ ΗΡΞΑΤΟ ΚΗΡΥϹϹΕΙΝ
ΚΑΙ ΔΙΑΦΗΜΕΙΖΕΙΝ ΤΟΝ ΛΟΓΟΝ
ΩϹΤΕ ΜΗΚΕΤΙ ΔΥΝΑϹΘΑΙ ΦΑΝΕΡΩϹ ΕΙϹ ΕΛΘΕΙΝ
ΕΙϹ ΠΟΛΙΝ ΑΛΛ ΕΞΩ ΕΝ ΕΡΗΜΟΙϹ ΤΟΠΟΙϹ ΗΝ
ΚΑΙ ΗΡΧΟΝΤΟ ΠΡΟϹ ΑΥΤΟΝ ΠΑΝΤΟΘΕΝ ΤΕΛΟϹ
Κ᾽ ΚΑΙ ΕΙϹΕΛΘΩΝ ΠΑΛΙΝ ΕΙϹ ΚΑΦΑΡΝΑΟΥΜ
ΔΙ ΗΜΕΡΩΝ ΚΑΙ ΗΚΟΥϹΘΗ ΟΤΙ ΕΝ ΟΙΚΩ ΕϹΤΙΝ
ΚΑΙ ΕΥΘΕΩϹ ϹΥΝΗΧΘΗϹΑΝ ΠΟΛΛΟΙ
ΩϹΤΕ ΜΗΚΕΤΙ ΧΩΡΕΙΝ ΜΗΔΕ ΤΑ ΠΡΟϹ ΤΗΝ ΘΥΡΑΝ
ΚΑΙ ΕΛΑΛΕΙ ΠΡΟϹ ΑΥΤΟΥϹ ΛΟΓΟΝ
ΚΑΙ ΕΡΧΟΝΤΑΙ ΠΡΟϹ ΑΥΤΟΝ ΦΕΡΟΝΤΕϹ ΠΑΡΑΛΥΤΙΚΟ
ΑΙΡΟΜΕΝΟΝ ΥΠΟ ΤΕϹϹΑΡΩΝ ΚΑΙ ΜΗ ΔΥΝΑΜΕΝΟΙ
ΠΡΟϹΕΝΓΕΙϹΑΙ ΔΙ Ο ΤΟΥ ΟΧΛΟΥ
ΑΠΕϹΤΕΓΑϹΑΝ ΤΗΝ ϹΤΕΓΗΝ ΟΠΟΥ ΗΝ Ο ΙΗϹ
ΚΑΙ ΧΑΛΩϹΕΙ ΤΟΝ ΚΡΑΒΑΤΤΟΝ ΟΠΟΥ ΗΝ
Ο ΠΑΡΑΛΥΤΙΚΟϹ ΚΑΤΑΚΕΙΜΕΝΟϹ
ΕΙΔΩΝ ΔΕ Ο ΙΗϹ ΤΗΝ ΠΙϹΤΙΝ ΑΥΤΩΝ
ΛΕΓΕΙ ΤΩ ΠΑΡΑΛΥΤΙΚΩ
ΤΕΚΝΟΝ ΑΦΕΩΝΤΕϹ ϹΟΥ ΑΙ ΑΜΑΡΤΙΑΙ

ἑρμηνηα

τουϲ ἑτερον επιτυχανϲ

sec   marc

INPROXIMAS UICOS ET CIUITATES
UT ET IBI PRAEDICEM AD HOC ENIM UENI
ET ERAT PRAEDICANS IN SYNAGOGIS EORUM
IN TOTAM GALILAEAM ET DAEMONIA EICIENS
ET UENIT AD EUM LEPROSUS DEPRAECANS EUM
ET DICENS SI UOLUERIS POTES ME MUNDARE
ET IRATUS EXTENDIT MANUM SUAM
ET TETIGIT EUM ET AIT ILLI UOLO MUNDARE
ET STATIM DECESSIT AB EO LEPRA
ET MUNDATUS EST ET COMMINATUS EI
STATIM DIMISIT ILLUM ET DICIT EI
UIDE NEMINI DIXERIS SED UADE OSTENDE TE IPSUM
SACERDOTI ET OFFERS PRO EMUNDATIONE TUA
QUAE PRAECEPIT MOYSES IN TESTIMONIUM ILLIS
AD ILLE EGRESSUS COEPIT PRAEDICARE
ET DIFFAMARE SERMONEM
ITA UT NON POSSIT MANIFESTAE INTROIRE
IN CIUITATEM SED FORIS INDE ERTIS LOCIS ERAT
ET CONUENIEBANT AD EUM UNDIQUE
ET ITERUM INTRAUIT IN CAFARNAUM
POST DIES ET AUDITUM EST QUOD IN DOMO ESSET
ET CONFESTIM CONUENERUNT MULTI
UT IAM NON POSSET CAPERE USQUE AD IANUAM
ET LOQUEBATUR ADILLOS UERBUM
ET UENERUNT AD EUM ADFERENTES PARALYTICUM
QUI A QUATTUOR PORTABATUR ET CUM NON POSSENT
ACCEDERE PRAE TURBA
NUDAUERUNT TECTUM UBI ERAT IHS
ET DIMISERUNT GRABATTUM IN QUO ERAT
PARALYTICUS IACENS
CUM UIDISSET AUTEM IHS FIDEM ILLORUM
AIT PARALYTICO
FILI DIMITTUNTUR TIBI PECCATA TUA

CAMBRIDGE, UNIVERSITY BIBL., Nn. 2, 41
(Codex Bezae, D)
fol. 289R: Marc. 1.38 – 2.5 (lat.)
Cf. VOGELS (1929) Tab. 19

tion, namely to our Gospel. Only then can it be determined—on the basis of the obstinate elements, the structures and the requisites, which stand firm in all the reinterpretations and rewritings—whether the source and the mouth are of the same river.

After the war it was hoped that the source of the Gospel would be found in the Qumran scrolls. As it is known, this hope was dashed. There is no trace of Jesus in the Qumran scrolls, only resemblances. What is far more common are the differences: no proclamation of the Kingdom of God, no parables, no turning to the non-Jews, to the weak, poor and deprived of rights, no miracle accounts, no love of the enemy. Jewish resistance fighters yes, but Christians no. And above all: no story, nothing that could have been used as the source of the Gospel.[275]

The uselessness of the Qumran material with regard to the 'Search for the historical Jesus' is of great consequence. The absence of references to Jesus can hardly be interpreted any longer as an accidental failure to find anything, because the site of the find—Chirbet Qumran—probably a fortress like Masada, was destroyed by the Romans most likely in June 68 AD, and until then all kinds of writings from the entire country were taken there to be stored. The silence of these finds harmonizes with that of the historians far too loudly. No matter how charming the digging in Palestine might be, one has to grapple with the hypothesis that Jesus did not live in the Galilean-Judaean region.

And this leads to the alternative: either Jesus did not exist, or one must search for him in a different place.

Discussions of the first possibility—that Jesus never existed—are not new. This basically means we are dealing with fiction. As Voltaire once said: 'If God created Man in His own image, Man has more than reciprocated'. Indeed, the results of the historical-critical research have made the geographical and chronological framework of the Gospel dissolve. But we are then left in an aporia: if Jesus never existed historically, from where did Christianity suddenly appear? And if everything was invented, why would the inventors have chosen to construct so many discrepancies, and so many delicate questions? Why precisely this and not something else? Why did tradition hold fast to these discrepancies? Why has a harmonizing *Diatessaron,* a comfortable blend of all four Gospels, never become generally accepted?

These inherent contradictions lead paradoxically to the fact that at the end of the dismantling, the exegetes find themselves back where they started: with the text. Which also means: with its naivety. They are at the beginning again.[276]

There is only one way out of the loop: to look somewhere else. Not much stands in the way besides our own mental inhibitions. There is little that compels us to locate the whole Gospel story in the region of Galilaea/Judaea/Jerusalem. Geographically, there are only these names; most of the places mentioned in the Gospels are not to be found in reality, for example Mk. 8:10 *Dalmanutha*. And if they can be found, they were not that significant, like *Nazareth*—presented in the Gospel as Galilaea's capital with a big synagogue—when in fact it was less than a village, so much less that indeed: Flavius Josephus never once mentions it.

In respect to the persons mentioned, only two and a half of them are historically documented: Pilate, Herodes and maybe John the Baptist.[277] Not Jesus, not Mary, not the three kings, not Peter, not Lazarus, not Judas, not Barabbas, not Joseph of Arimathea, not Mary Magdalene... Nobody.

We are tempted to look for Jesus outside of the Galilean-Judaean region, in the direction of Rome, not only because of the above mentioned parallels between the Christian liturgy and the Caesar/emperor ritual, and not only because of the fact that Rome was and still is the capital of Christianity, that Gallia and not Galilaea is the oldest daughter of the Church, but also because of clear references that argue against Jerusalem:

– no Gospel was ever written in Aramaic,
– the Greek of the presumably most ancient Gospel in particular, that of Mark, is filled with Latinisms whilst the citations from the Jewish scriptures only emerge in abundance in Matthew.

It is as if the river flowed from Rome towards Jerusalem, not vice versa. In order to explain this anomaly and to still hold the contrary to be true, the exegetes of course have invented a re-Judaization: via Hellenism towards Rome, there and back. But why only the journey to Rome left no trace behind remains an open question.

The possibility that this is a case of delocalization is given by the genesis of the text itself.

We know that folk etymologies and corruptions as they occur in the Gospel—e.g. the camel, *kamêlos*, for which it 'is easier ... to go through the eye of a needle, than for a rich man to enter into the Kingdom of God.' (Mt. 19:24; Mk. 10:25; Lk. 18:25), originally was a *kamilos*, a nautical tow rope, as some manuscripts and the Armenian translation prove—may sometimes lead to delocalizations, to misalignments that accompany the change of scene. It is recognizable also here: with the tow rope we are at sea, with a camel we sail into the desert. And besides, with a scene change, there is no sea change if the camel were the initial word: then the Bedouin would ride a ship of the sea.[278]

The mechanism of these adjustments is clear: that which is known replaces that which is not known. What is known here replaces what is not known here—although it was well known there: where the story comes from. That is what is needed in the sermon. What do I tell bedouins about maritime tow ropes or vice versa mariners about camels?

But what if such deformations also happened with geographical names and those of persons? What if it is true that not only does *kamêlos* stand for *kamilos*, but, for instance, also *Galilea* for *Gallia* or *Pilatus* for *Lepidus*? What if the possessed man in Mark (5:9) was not only originally named *Legion,* but had some legions too? What if the twelve legions Jesus had at his disposal in Matthew (26:53) stood on the earth and not just in heaven?

Is it conceivable that the copyists of the Gospel at that time became victims of the same delusion as did recently the Dominicans of the École Biblique et Archéologique Française, who at first evaluated the findings in the former stronghold Chirbet Qumran: they saw the ruin of a cloister. They identified here a 'refectorium', there a 'scriptorium' and painted the picture of a cloister-like community that led a rigorous, celibate, ascetic and pacifistic life—just like their own. The Dominicans had found themselves![279]

Did something similar occur to the copyists of the Gospels as was experienced by the painters of the icons when they gave the Saints the lineament of their brothers and Christ the face of their Prior?

Did the itinerant preaching and miracle working members of the early Christian communities—with the passage of time and the persistent fine-tuning of the copies of the copies—turn the exemplary fatherly chief commander into one of themselves, a Church Father made in their own image? From the divine founder of the Empire to the proclaimer of the Kingdom of God? Did they gradually convert Divus Iulius, the God of the Roman veteran colonies in the East, into the Jesus of their communities which had found shelter there? Did they become the creators of their creator until they themselves finally became Lords over their Lord?

In summary, we establish that the serious 'Search for the historical Jesus', according to it's own confession, sets aside the question of the historicity of Jesus, or at any rate does not answer it. However, a more simple question can be answered objectively:

Was Jesus a figure of history? Was Jesus the subject of ancient historiography?

Non-Christian sources before 70...

For the time before the Jewish war (66-70 AD) this question is to be answered unambiguously with a no. Independent of the New Testament, no ancient historian mentions *Jesus* before the year 70. The extremely brief and rare passages cited in the past concern a *Chrestos* or certain *christiani* or *chrestiani*: but it is not certain that these actually refer to Christians in today's sense of the word. And, if they do, then the passages only testify that at the time of their origin in the first quarter of the second century their authors only had an indirect and vague conception of the then emerging Christian ideas. Hence, modern research does not consider them as testimonies anymore.[280] Nevertheless we want to discuss them, on the one hand because they are so famous and still wander around, and on the other hand because these examples demonstrate how traditional stereotypes can influence our perception of them, and how the decision for one or another translation of a single word can tilt the entire meaning of the story and steer it in a completely different direction.

In his *Lives of the Caesars,* written at the beginning of the second century, Suetonius reports (according to a common translation) that during the reign of Caesar Claudius (41-54 AD),

'...the Jews, who caused constant turmoil at the instigation of Chrestos, he [Claudius] expelled them from Rome.'[281]

The sentence hardly makes sense. It has been attempted, especially among conservative ranks, to identify this name Chrestos with Christus. However this leads to a chronological difficulty, because Christ had already been crucified under Tiberius. Some critics speculate to the effect that *Chrestos*—in its meaning of 'the good', the 'useful': *chrêstos*—was a common slave name. But this does not lessen the difficulties, because this name did not necessarily enjoy a good reputation with the Jews, and this particular Chrestos is not known from other sources either. The biggest problem, though, is that in order to connect this Chrestos with Christ, one has to assume that Suetonius was mistaken and had confused them. But this means that Suetonius did not know Christ: Suetonius, who of all people was never in want of any background information! Suetonius was born in 70 AD and lived past the year 121. He was unable to write his Caesar-biographies, which include Domitianus, before Domitianus died in 96 AD. This would indicate that at the beginning of the second century, Christ was still so little known that a Suetonius had no notion of him and took him to be a troublemaker named

Chrestos who lived under Claudius in Rome. Hence the identification *Chrestos* = *Christus* causes more problems than it solves.

From a philological point of view, however, *chresto* not only can be the Latin ablative of the Greek *chrêstos,* 'the good (person)', but also that of *chrêston,* 'the good (thing), goods' or of *chrêstês,* which means 'speculator', 'usurer'.[282] Hence the sentence could be translated completely differently, for instance like this:

'...the Jews who practised usury and thereby caused constant turmoil, he [Claudius] expelled them from Rome.'

Which makes sense, especially in the case of Claudius, whose famous decree forbade the Jews from striving to increase their privileges.

Also cited is the so-called persecution of Christians by Nero on the basis of a citation from Tacitus:

After the burning of Rome...

'...despite public aid, despite generous donations by the emperor and expiatory sacrifices to the Gods, the dreadful rumour could not be scotched that the fire was set on orders. And so, Nero, in order to end this rumor, revealed the culprits and imposed the most exquisite punishments on those who were hated for their outrageous acts and who were called by the people *chrestiani*.'[283]

Many have wanted to understand this to mean the Christians. At a later date the hand of a copyist has even inserted an explanation of the word *chrestiani*:

'This name derives from Christ, who was executed by the procurator Pontius Pilatus under the government of Tiberius.'[284]

That this is an interpolation is formally indicated on the one hand by the scholastic nature of the sentence, on the other hand by the fact that *chrestiani* is written with an 'e', but *Christ* with an 'i'. But the logical break in the report is more weighty. That is, the story continues with a very logical consequent conclusion by Nero. Construction speculators were suspected of being behind those who set the fire alight:

'For no one had the courage to check the spread of the fire, because again and again numerous people hindered its extinction with threats, others had openly thrown firebrands and cried aloud that they had a principal standing behind them, whether doing this so they could plunder unrestrainedly, or because they were really ordered to do so.'[285]

In order to not be taken for one of the instigators or one of their accomplices, Nero imposed draconian punishments on the incendiaries and their principals—construction speculators who expected to make a huge profit from the reconstruction. The former were burned alive, the latter torn to pieces by dogs:

'And at first those who confessed were arrested, then on the basis of their testimony a further large circle of people were arrested, and they were found guilty not only of the crime of arson but also of hatred of humanity. And those at death's door suffered mockery: they were wrapped in animal skins and torn to pieces by dogs, or they were (nailed to a cross and destined for the death by fire) burned after day's end as night lights.'[286]

One recognizes by the symmetry of the punishments that Nero has here applied the Talion law: the incendiaries were burned and those torn to pieces by dogs can only have been the speculators, the 'bloodsuckers'. Therefore the word *chrestiani* here can only mean the *chrêstai*, the speculators, as we have seen above in Suetonius' report on Claudius.[287] Then their characterization too does make sense, namely, that they were 'hated by the people because of their outrageous acts'.

The late confusion of those *chrestiani* or *chrêstai*, of the speculators with the Christians, could have arisen because there were possibly Jews amongst the speculators who were punished. This fit the image of the Jews anyhow, all the more so, because at that time the Jewish rebellion was in the air. Hence the lines that immediately follow the above interpolation could refer to Jews, especially to a Jewish mafia of speculators, taken as a *pars pro toto*:

'The fatal superstition, which was at first suppressed, gained ground once more, not only in Judea from where this evil arose, but also in Rome, where all sorts of atrocities and infamies from all the world pour in and find a happy approval.'[288]

Hence these lines could be authentic, as the corresponding short version in Suetonius shows:

'The punishment of death was declared on the *christiani*, a race of humans with a new and objectionable superstition.'[289]

But it is also possible that they belong to the interpolation, because Suetonius is not independent of Tacitus and a prosecution of Jews is not recorded at this time.

Conclusion: If one follows this critique of the passages by Tacitus and Suetonius, then in the historical writings from the time before the Jewish war there is no *Jesus*, no *Christ*, and no *Christians*. And if one does not want to follow it, then it can at least be said objectively that Greek citations are missing, whilst indubitable Latin proofs do not appear until the second century and they concern only *chrestiani* or *christiani*, respectively: *Chrestos* or, barely, *Christus*—with no trace of the name *Jesus*.

...and after 70

Only after the Jewish war, namely with Flavius Josephus, do we find Jesus. However, we find too many of them. The theophoric name which in its full old Hebrew form is Yehoshua—literally meaning 'Jahweh helps' or 'Jahweh saves', in the sense of 'God helps'—was in the usual Greek short form simply understood as 'helper', 'savior',[290] in Latin 'servator', and hence it spread widely, like in Sicily as 'Salvatore' or in Germany as 'Gottfried'. It was of course an early hope that our Jesus would appear amongst the many Jesuses that are put upon the stage by the historian Josephus.

But which one would he be? One of the many Jesuses who were high priests, or Jesus, the leader of the brigands? Jesus was neither the one nor the other. Of the many other Jesuses whose fathers are named, we find a son of Nave, a son of Josedek, of Judas, of Simon, of Phabes, of Josadak, of Gamaliel, of Sapphias, of Gamala, of Thebuthi, of Ananus but no son of Joseph. Only one might fit into the scheme: a Jesus—brother of James. In the last book of the *Jewish Antiquities*, Flavius Josephus mentions that in the year 62, during an interregnum between two prefects, the Sanhedrin in Jerusalem ordered the stoning of a Jacobus (James), 'brother of Jesus, the so-called Christ'.[291]

If the addition of the 'so-called Christ' has not been inserted by a later pious hand—the earliest manuscripts passed down to us are only from the tenth to the fourteenth century—then this Jacobus could be the same one mentioned in the Gospel of Matthew[292] as one of the brothers of Jesus, provided that he would also be the same one we meet in Acts[293] in a leading position in Jerusalem and who is also mentioned by Paul.[294] Then this Jacobus, named the righteous, would be the brother of Jesus, called Christ.

As this chain of evidence relies on too many conditions, it too doesn't help us any more than the Latin testimonies.

The only further proof that can be pointed to is the so-called *Testimonium Flavianum,* the testimony of Flavius (Josephus). In another passage of the same volume, between a report about a Jewish rebellion and its suppression, we find the following text:

'...So this rebellion was suppressed.

[At this time lived Jesus, a wise man, if it is permissible to call him a man at all. For he was the worker of unbelievable deeds and the teacher of the humankind, who received the truth with joy. In this way he attracted many Jews and many Greeks also. He was the Christ. And although Pilatus condemned him to the death on the cross on the inducement of the most distinguished of our people, his former followers did not become unfaithful. Because he appeared living again on the third day as the prophets sent by God had preached so and moreover a thousand other miraculous things of him. And till this very day the Christian people, who name themselves after him, still exist.]

Likewise at this time, still another misfortune befell the Jews…'[295] In all the scientific editions the text is cited in parentheses, because it is generally assumed that it is an interpolation. It is obvious simply in respect to its construction, being that the end of the preceding paragraph finds its logical connection with the beginning of the following: '…So this rebellion was suppressed. / Likewise at this time, still another misfortune befell the Jews.' There is no place in between for the long excursus about Jesus and the Christians.

But this interpolation shows a curious peculiarity: with respect to style it certainly could stem from Josephus himself. Hence, outside of a skillful forgery—perhaps by pupils of Josephus—an interpolation of the author is not excluded either, which appears very plausible in view of the notorious propensity of our Josephus for adventurous variations.

More specifically, Flavius Josephus is well known for the fact that he differs widely from volume to volume, that he often contradicts himself and that he provides sometimes totally different, opaque versions of the same incidents—obviously tailored to the interests of the general political situation, his principal or his addressees. This is particularly conspicuous, because in his different volumes he is for the most part dealing with the same material.

For he is exclusively concerned with Jewish matters. He left behind, outside of a volume on the Jewish war, a work on the Jewish antiquities, an autobiography and an apology for Judaism.

All of it was commissioned by the Flavii—Vespasianus, Titus and Domitianus—whom he served in Rome from the year 70 till past 100 AD. And that was also his curse. For he had been one of the leaders of the Jewish rebellion and had switched sides to Vespasianus under suspicious circumstances,[296] in order to prophesy, allegedly on God's behalf, that Vespasianus was the awaited Messiah from Judaea: that he should become emperor and his son Titus as well. When the incredulous Vespasianus did indeed become emperor shortly afterwards, he granted Josephus his freedom, and from then on he was known as Flavius Josephus. Vespasianus seems to have made him a kind of a minister for Jewish affairs. At the very least, all the volumes of Josephus served the special task of promoting the integration of the Jews who lived in the Roman Empire after the fall of Jerusalem.

It is interesting that the very time Flavius Josephus was active in Rome is also the supposed time of the origin of the Gospel, around 70-100 AD. As the *Testimonium Flavianum,* independent of whether it was inserted by another hand or by the author himself, can be dated at the earliest around the year 100 AD, this passage could be the first historical testimony about Jesus Christ as well as the first evidence of Christian literature influencing the writing of history.

Whichever it may be, *in historiography* Jesus Christ is born around the year 100 AD. The fact is that Josephus in the person of Vespasianus was the godfather of the Messiah of the Roman Empire. No matter whose hand it was that inserted the *Testimonium Flavianum,* it was Josephus' work that brought Jesus Christ into the world. Josephus is the intellectual father of the Roman Messiah and the putative father of Jesus Christ.

Shortly after this the indubitable sources commence, beginning with the letter of the younger Plinius, at the time governor of Bithynia, who asks Traianus how he should deal with the Christians, who merely maintain their superstition but do not evince any active insubordination. Traianus recommends that he not seek out the Christians and only punish them if a report were filed, and even then only if they refuse to pay obeisance to the Roman Gods. Plinius' letter and the answer by Traianus are the official *terminus a quo* of Christianity: 111/112 AD. But Christ emerges in historical writings only indirectly and implicitly, as the *auctor* of Christianity. He does not have a separate existence.

Christian sources

Just as Jesus is said to have left no written records himself, the Christian sources are also indirect.

It is thought that in the authentic letters of Paul[297] parts of an older tradition are quoted: the record of the Last Supper,[298] some words of Jesus, exclamation-like phrases, the so-called kerygmatic formulae.[299] Apart from the Gospels, there is not much further evidence in the New Testament.

Only the Gospels[300] speak explicitly of Jesus, along with the Jesus literature expanding from the second century in varying form and quality. These so-called Agrapha, which include the Apocrypha, i.e. the many Gospels that did not become part of the ecclesiastical canon, produced an after-effect in various places, one of them Islam.

The Gospels tell the *vita* of Jesus, including the *vita mors miracula*—life, death and miracles—and so they are a hagiography. However, they are a *sui generis* hagiography, because they were books for use in the early Church and served for the liturgy, for the sermon, prophecy, instruction, and the solving of controversies, amongst other things. They were meant to explain to the congregations of that time the life and work of Jesus in the light of faith in his resurrection and return, so they were not historiography, but rather theology made from history. In substance, they are mostly compilations of preformed material which had already gone through a complicated development. It is generally assumed that the Gospel was preached for a long period before it was written down. The first problem that presents itself to the researchers is how to differentiate between redaction and tradition, between what has been passed down through writing and what has been passed down orally.

Already this makes the determination of the original text of the autographs a tricky business. As a result, textual criticism is encumbered by theological and dogmatic issues from the outset. In any case the task scarcely seems solvable. The texts that have reached us are, as we saw, not originals but copies of copies of copies. Ancient papyri, able to survive almost exclusively in Egypt because of its climate, provide us with only small parts of the texts. And these textual witnesses correspond with each other in barely half of their words.

The text of the canon can only be traced, with any certainty, back to the middle of the second century. So the actual text of the autographs has not yet been ascertained, because they supposedly originated between 70 and 100 AD, whereas Mark and some of Paul's letters are thought to be some decades earlier. So there is undeniably a gap in the tradition of more than a half century, for Mark and Paul a gap of nearly a whole century. Here total darkness rules. What the textual critic hands to the literary critic is not the autographic text—let alone the original. We are furnished with the text of the canon, however it can only be documented and edited with countless alternative lections. A uniform Greek text has never existed. The ancient Greek translations started from different texts from the outset. But in spite of the new insights, most of the contemporary translations are still based on the so-called *textus receptus,* the one passed down to us most prolifically. However, from the standpoint of the textual critic it is also the worst.

Three of the Gospels—Mark, Matthew and Luke—follow each other mostly in a parallel fashion in respect to text construction and wording; they can be written threefold alongside one another. For this reason their authors are called synoptists. The Gospel of John runs parallel to them only in the Passion narrative, but otherwise consists of long speeches and disputes of Jesus, which often develop from a miracle story. Here John omits a lot of the healing stories, namely those about the possessed, so his text could hardly have been written parallel to the synoptics.

Contrary to the later canon, which places Matthew in the first and the most ancient position,[301] scholarship mostly considers the Gospel of Mark, the shortest, to be also the most ancient. The given dates are between 40 and 60 AD and that is why it is called the protoevangelium; it served as source for both the other synoptics. Matthew and Luke are independent of each other, and both first wrote after the Jewish war that ended in 70 AD. Where either of them, or both of them, correspond with Mark they are obviously using Mark, but where they correspond with each other but not with Mark, they are following a lost logion source ('Q'—theory of the two sources); or, according to another opinion, they are following the oral tradition. In addition they use oral special material (Sondergut). John is independent of the synoptics; if and to what extent he used written sources is a matter of controversy.

In contrast to Mark and John, Matthew and Luke also report a childhood story. But there is a long hiatus from thence to the first public appearance of Jesus, which has given rise to various adventuresome speculations that see the young Jesus heading off to Egypt, India, and even Tibet.

Moreover they both include a genealogy of Jesus which serves the purpose of demonstrating him to be a descendant of David. But they differ fundamentally from each other and were already in early Christian times dismissed as compilations by the so-called heretics, as they are by the modern text critics too.

The geographical and chronological connections, the so-called framework, for which we mostly have to thank the later redactions of Matthew and Luke, vanish completely when extensively examined: they are nothing more than connecting tags of the redaction. The speeches of Jesus prove to be late interpolation and compilation. The material breaks down into small independent units which are mostly undated, colorless, and usually not situated in any known place: words, parables and short logia which are thought to originate from oral tradition.

Many of the independent, single traditions indicate Aramaic and Latin influences, even if they have only been passed down to us in Greek by Hellenistic communities. This is, in any event, true for Mark, whose language is vulgar Greek as we saw above, and larded with Aramaisms and Latinisms. The latter ones are based on the jargon of the legionaries.

Not till the later Matthew and Luke do we see Hebraisms occurring in different forms together with the excising of the Aramaisms and the attempted improvement of Mark's Greek (which also leads to degradations and some impoverishment). Matthew's favorite references to prophecies from the Old Testament turn out to be *vaticinia ex eventu*, as prophecies after the event or as midrashim, explanations of new and objectionable facts on the basis of the old traditional texts: they belong to a later layer and to a time when, in order to convert Jews, they sought to present Jesus as the Messiah foretold by the Jewish prophets.[302] With Luke however, we see the occurrence of Septuagintisms, imitations of the Greek translation of the Jewish scripture, the so-called Septuagint, which was to become the Old Testament of the Christians.

Extensive expert research has shown that, contrary to earlier surmises, none of the Gospels, neither in toto nor in part, was originally written in Aramaic and certainly never in Hebrew. The Greek Gospels passed down to us are not direct translations.[303]

In contrast to canonical opinion which held the Judaizing Matthew to be the most ancient, the Gospels seem to have been originally addressed not to the Jews, but to the Hellenes—and primarily to the less educated at that. In order to explain this anomaly, the hypothesis of a no longer traceable de-Judaization was put forth, a de-Judaization from Jesus to Mark with a subsequent re-Judaization to Matthew and Luke. Then, if this is true, there is hardly enough time from Jesus' death till the redaction of Mark for a complete de-Judaization, even less in fact, because Mark is dated as early as 40 AD as tradition has said for a long time, being 'ten' respectively 'twelve years after the ascension of the Lord'.[304]

Although the general opinion is that the events of Jesus' life are grasped best by the Passion narrative and although Mark is structured biographically,[305] the dominant view is that a reconstruction of the biography of Jesus is no longer a possibility—at least not in Galilaea-Judaea-Palaestina. Hence research into Jesus will by necessity remain research into early Christianity.

From all this it follows that the Gospels are primarily the source for the early Christian Jesus-faith and its history. The Gospel cannot become a source for the historical Jesus until we have differentiated what was original from what has been added. But this is hardly achievable because the original was already selected by and suffused with faith.

And this is the crux of form criticism, which has sought to look behind the known sources to investigate the constructional process of the Gospel traditions in their pre-literary phase, the era before the written recordings by the Evangelists. In this it stands on feet of clay, as it must assume that the factors at work in this process can be reconstructed. So this genre of research must cling to a dogma that states, firstly, this process took place in a circle of non-literary people without a written schema, and secondly, that in such a circle of non-literary people the construction of the material of the tradition leads to a small number of fairly fixed forms which have their own laws with respect to style or form.[306] If this popular milieu was multilingual—and it had to be, for the language of Mark is a vulgar Greek combined with Latinisms and Aramaisms—then the traditions could have come from anywhere and could have undergone all kinds of folk etymological transformations and hybridizations that are no longer retrievable. However, if there was not only an oral tradition but also a written source together with which it became interwoven, then we also should have to reckon with slips of the pen and corruptions. And if we have to also take into account translations, which possibly underwent an earlier transcription from one alphabet to another,[307] along with the concomitant possible misunderstandings and folk etymological deformations, then the form-critical method would completely grasp at nothing.

Accordingly, the results depend greatly upon the diverse assumptions of the researchers,[308] so that here—unlike in textual and literary criticism—it is ultimately always hypothesis against hypothesis, where even subliminal theological quarrels have been fought out.

But the objective observation can be made that the mythological school always distils the historical Jesus down to a myth, whereas parallel to this, especially in the Protestant milieu and even more particularly since the Second World War, the idea of Jesus being a Jew has been emphasized. Their main point: Jesus never existed but he was certainly a Jew.

The redaction-historical method however, thinks itself to be more fruitful, because it depends less on the original assumptions of the researchers. It considers the Evangelists primarily as collectors and transmitters of tradition and looks at the circumstances in the community or 'situation in life', 'setting' *(Sitz im Leben)* where the authors of the Gospels worked on their material. And it differentiates this 'setting' *(Sitz im Leben)*, on the one side from that of the early Christian community *(Urgemeinde)*, on the other from that of Jesus. But because it has only traditional, passed-down conceptions about life in the early Christian community and about the life of Jesus, the dog is chasing its tail again, unfortunately. So this method can only conditionally deliver more or less reliable results, and only in the case of the later Evangelists like Matthew and Luke.

The primary mystery—who was the historical Jesus really?—has not been solved. At least there has been no consensus on any of the answers.

In this respect it is characteristic of the 'Search for the historical Jesus' that the researchers who came to radical results—in the sense that there was barely anything or absolutely nothing left of the historical Jesus—were suspended, even excommunicated. Or they themselves took the initiative and turned their back on the Church, sometimes on Christianity as well, and along with them whole schools. The cases of Bruno Bauer, David Friedrich Strauss, Ernest Renan or Alfred Loisy are well known—only to mention a few. Starting with different political and theoretical motivations we still see the same end result: radical renunciation. Negotiating detours, and each in his own manner, they all came to the conclusion that man was the author of the Gospel.

This mass exodus of critical critics may explain why in the present 'Search for the historical Jesus', despite intensifying doubts, the believers still seem to remain in the majority.

But notwithstanding their tough resistance, in these faithful circles too, the historical Jesus is disappearing more and more. As an example we cite the Catholic 'Introduction to the New Testament' *(Einleitung in das Neue Testament)* by Wikenhauser and Schmid:

'The thesis that the Evangelists were tradents (persons passing down reports) who only added a framework to the material they had collected in order to create a connected scripture—the Gospel—must not be extended to the point of saying that the whole frame of the Gospel is without any historical value. At any rate, about Mark, the most ancient Gospel, it can be said that its frame is partly chronological. That Jesus, after the arrest of his precursor in Galilee, was first active in the environs of Capharnaum, that the first rush of popularity was followed by a decline in enthusiasm and that the resistance of the Jewish spiritual leadership continually grew in intensity, that furthermore Jesus temporarily sought refuge in the north, the pagan Syria, and that he finally went to Jerusalem, where he was captured after some brief activity and condemned to the death on the cross, must be regarded as, on the whole, conforming to historical reality.'[309]

This is not much more than what a Strauss or a Loisy have left us with. As a comparison, here is what, according to Loisy, a historian could still say of Jesus with some certainty:

'He was an itinerant preacher, prophet of a unique oracle. His doctrine, if he had any, was not accepted. With an act of religious inspiration he tried to bring the word of the kingdom to Jerusalem. His presence in the town caused a tumult. He was arrested and condemned by the Roman authorities in summary proceedings, under circumstances which remain unknown to us.'[310]

Very little in fact. And yet even this was denied. Paul-Louis Couchoud brought attention to the fact that the very assumption that a person presented himself as Jahweh within a Jewish milieu and was worshipped as such, not after many generations, but—as rational criticism itself has demonstrated—only a few years after his disgraceful death, means 'knowing nothing about a Jew, or forgetting everything'. Jesus would be the only Jew that the Jews have ever worshipped in almost thirty centuries of religious history.[311]

A resonance of Couchoud's critique of the critical school is also found in *Jesus, Son of Man* by Rudolf Augstein. Like Loisy, he grants Jesus a faded remnant of an historical existence, but adds with Couchoud:

> 'We can almost completely reject the notion that any Jew at this time in Galilee or Judea would have thought himself exclusively to be the Son of God or that he would have passed himself off as such, unless he had gone mad.'[312]

This would mean that either Jesus did not exist or that he was not a Jew.

The first possibility is belied by the existence of Christianity and its sudden emergence throughout the Roman Empire: how could a historical Christianity be imaginable without a historical Jesus, a bush fire without an igniting spark?[313]

The second possibility was indeed examined as well, but always in the immediate environment of the area in question e.g. Leipoldt: *Was the Galilean Jesus a Jew?*[314]—and always with little conviction, without resolution, and consequently drawing little attention.

The fact is that Jesus is the only founder of a world religion whose historical existence is still questioned. This is not the case with Mohammed, nor with the older ones like Romulus or Numa. As we saw with Euhemeros, the ancients did not even question the historical existence of a Hercules or a Zeus. The unhistorical Jesus is an anomaly.

Paul and the so-called heretics

The knowledge, derived from textual and literary criticism, that only the Gospel of Mark was written before the Jewish war and Matthew and Luke later edited it, means that Paul could only have known Mark. So where Paul speaks of a Gospel or quotes from one—if he is referring to one that has been passed down to us and not to his own—he can only have been referring to Mark.[315]

Indeed, the Jesus Christ of Paul is characterized as a Jew as infrequently as is the Christ of Mark.

In his missionary work Paul was not successful among the Jews, while he was very successful with the so-called 'gentiles', i.e. the non-Jews. The towns where he gained a firm footing are without exception

Roman Caesarean colonies—Philippi, Corinth, the cities of Galatia—or centers of worship of Divus Iulius—Ephesus, Colossia, Thessalonica. The leitmotif of his letters is the difference with the Judaists, who try to Judaize those that he had 'evangelized'. He stresses that his Gospel does not come from Jerusalem.[316] He opposes the introduction of circumcision and the observance of the Mosaic law, the so-called 'works of the law' which hold man in bondage. And he does not easily accept that he should hand over the alms collected to Jerusalem: he would rather administer the money himself, and if he indeed had to, then he would only personally hand them over to the 'honored society'.[317]

But we find that those Judaists—simply called Jews by Paul[318]—always come after him: it is not that he tries to sway the Judaized away from the Mosaic law, but that the Judaists try to win Paul's followers over to the Mosaic law. Which means that for Paul's Christians it was the Mosaic law that was new, not liberty from the law: from the very beginning they were free of the Mosaic law and were not freed from it by Paul. It is not until his battling over differences with the Judaists that Paul reveals that he was born a Jew. Until then, even in his missionary work, he was a Roman citizen amongst Roman citizens.[319]

Hence it is not surprising that the so-called heretics, i.e.—those Christians who were a thorn in the side of the developing Judaizing Church, thought along radically Paulinist lines and unanimously opposed the increasing Judaization of Christianity and the Gospel: probably for this reason they were excommunicated.

Marcion, who regarded the cruel and national-egoistic God of the Jews as the opposite of the mankind-saving Christ, did not accept that the Jewish scriptures should become the Old Testament of the Christians. He also rejected the Judaizing additions in the New Testament which were alien to him. He did not recognize large passages of Luke, effectively leaving scarcely more than what appears in Mark, nor did he recognize the pseudo-Pauline epistles.

So Marcion had established the first Christian canon, the first list of the faultless books. In reaction, the anti-Marcionite faction drew up their anti-canon, which only after the victory over Marcion became the general canon of the 'Orthodox'. This means that the canon valid today is not the canon accepted by the entire early Church, but a canon of purpose—one not in general use until the supporters of the first canon were excommunicated. Indeed, this canon is not Judaic through and through.[320] The sequence, however (Matthew erroneously before Mark), the anti-Marcionite prologues, the incorporation of the entire text of Luke (with a re-allocation into the Gospel and the Book of Acts), the admittance of many pseudo-Pauline letters or additions[321] as well as the dubious Apocalypse, after lengthy resistance—all testify to the tendentious orientation of the official canon still regarded as valid today. And this in spite of the fact that modern research generally confirms Marcion's objections—nolens volens, it had to confirm them.

To orient ourselves chronologically: Marcion was excommunicated by the Church in Rome in 144 AD, but his teachings were enormously popular in the East and the West until the fourth century; for a long time his organization resisted systematic persecution by the 'Orthodox'.

Tatianus, also excluded from the Roman community (172 AD), composed a harmony of the Gospels—the so-called *Diatessaron*, a blend 'of the four'—and he translated it into his native language, Syrian. Ostensibly he was excommunicated as an Encratite, 'the austere', as an ascetic and because of his abstinence from flesh, when in fact it was because he had refused to incorporate the Judaizing additions into his harmony of the Gospels. His orthodox fellow countryman Theodoret of Cyrus wrote of him:

> '...who [Tatianus] also wrote the Gospel called 'Through-the-four', by excising the genealogies and everything else that also points to the birth of the Lord from the seed of David according to the flesh. Not only have the followers of Tatianus used this book, but also the devotees of the Apostolic doctrine, because they did not recognize the deception of the composition, but innocently used the book as a convenient compendium. Of myself I have found more than 200 such books, which were held in honor in the communities of our region. I collected them and destroyed them and introduced the Gospels of the Evangelists instead.'

We see that in Syria the Gospels affording Jesus a Jewish genealogy were introduced only later: therefore the older texts had to first be destroyed. So here it was the burning of books that first made Jesus a Jew. In other parts of the Empire it had already happened in the course of the battle against Marcion.

Interestingly, modern textual and literary criticism confirms the fact that the Judaizing genealogies of Matthew and Luke belong to a later layer of redaction. It is also known that many of the letters accredited to Paul have long been recognized as pseudo-Pauline. So research confirms that the early Christian heretics did not seek removal of the Jewish material from the canon, but rather resisted the incorporation of such material.

Hence, resistance to Judaization was mounted not only by the heretics but also by Paul before their time, as well as by many orthodox believers during their time and thereafter, as is apparent from the above citation by Theodoret. This is also proven by the fact that the last book of the New Testament interpreted as anti-Roman—the 'Apocalypse'—was incorporated into the canon only with great difficulty and against centuries of resistance. It is as if the so-called heretics, along with Paul, had tried to conserve the memory of the non-Jewish origins of Roman Christianity.

Jewish sources

A letter which is difficult to date (perhaps shortly after 73 AD—or even second or third century) is that of Mara bar Sarapion to his son. Bar Sarapion was an otherwise unknown Syrian Stoic:

'Or [what did] the Jews [get] from the execution of the wise king, as the empire was taken away from them from that time on? ... The wise king [is however not dead]: because of the new laws he gave'.[322]

A wise king, executed by the Jews and living still. But note here too: no Jesus, no Christ.

The reports in the rabbinic literature are mostly polemic, hence they presuppose Christian literature and, on top of this, they are very vague.[323] For example Jesus is thought to be 'the bastard son of the Roman soldier Pantheras'. It is easy to see that that 'Pantheras' is a metathesis of *parthenos,* Greek 'virgin'. So it could originally have meant: 'the bastard son of Parthenos', i.e. of the *parthenos*—the 'virgin'. What is interesting is what remains: the Roman soldier. The rabbinic tradition seems to be based on a source that retains the memory of a Jesus who was born a Roman and who was the son of a legionary.

Which means that the Jews, the race which Jesus is supposed to descend from—even supposed to descend from the royal House of David—only knew Jesus very late and only from the Christians. And if they did take any notice of him, he was thought to be of Roman origin.

The negative attitude towards Christianity and the denying of Jesus remained constant in Judaism throughout all the centuries until the modern age. Right up to today authoritative Jewish theologians hold Christianity to be a product from the late Hellenistic period, foreign to Judaism.

Another opinion of Jesus did not arise in Judaism until after the Enlightenment. Jesus began to be discovered as a Jew, especially in Zionist circles. This connected with guilt feelings on the Christian side after World War II, especially with protestants who are inclined to Old Testament thinking anyway, and it led to the emphasizing of the Jewishness of Jesus as a reaction against ecclesiastical anti-Judaism.

Admittedly the attempt, especially by the historian Robert Eisler, to demonstrate on the basis of the Qumran findings that early Palestinian Christianity originated in the Qumran movement did not satisfy much else than Christian guilt feelings and the urge for theological reparation. The Qumran scrolls do not contain anything Christian which can be recognized on the basis of their form alone: they are just scrolls and Christians have only written on codices from the very beginning, as was explained above.[324]

So this late and not completely disinterested recognition of Jesus by parts of Jewry cannot undo the fact that the Jews originally did not know Jesus, that they subsequently disqualified him as a Roman bastard and that they otherwise have ignored and denied him throughout the centuries.[325]

Conclusion

Between Divus Iulius and Jesus—these two god-men who emerge at the same historical time in the same cultural and political arena—there exists, for the matter of tradition, a curious complementary asymmetry:

The one, Divus Iulius—an indubitable historical figure—is as God, nonexistent: all writers mention him; but there is no religion, no liturgical texts, no hagiography, no legends.

The other, Jesus—an absolutely doubtful historical figure—is existent only as God: no chronicler mentions him; but there is a religion, even several, and there are liturgical texts, hagiographies and legends.

Either one is abnormal:

It is not normal that the cult of Divus Iulius, the original Roman emperor cult should just vanish into thin air as soon as Christianity emerges. It is not normal that not even one legend of Caesar has passed down to us of a man who inspired his contemporaries no less than did Alexander.

And neither is it normal that Jesus, the *auctor* of Christianity which later became the official cult of the Roman Empire, should suddenly appear and displace Divus Iulius, unnoticed by all the early historians. It is not normal that so many legends of Jesus have passed down to us—legends about a man who inspired the fantasy of his contemporaries so little that a hundred years after his supposed birth a solitary line had yet to appear in the history books.

It must be recognized that the two figures are complementary and that it is only when they are combined that they provide the complete person of a God incarnate: by themselves they are only one-dimensional and amputated.

We will try to track down this asymmetric parallelism, and try to fit together the two figures of Divus Iulius and his *alter ego* Jesus Christ: one on this side and one on the other side of the West-East mirror.

Summary

Divus Iulius

Caesar was God's son from birth: it is well known that the Iulii claimed Venus as their ancestor, through Aeneas and his son Ascanius, whom the Romans also called *Ilus* or *Iulus*. As a youth, he should have been a *flamen Dialis*—the high priest of Jupiter—but he was prevented from attaining this office by political opposition. Instead, he soon after became the highest priest: *pontifex maximus*. And while he was yet living it had been decreed that he—by then ruler of the whole world—should be posthumously numbered amongst the gods: as *Divus Iulius*. Even his murder could not preclude this: his adoptive son Octavianus could quickly call himself *Divi Filius*, 'God's Son'—thereby Caesar became the 'Father God', on a par with Jupiter himself.[326]

Temples were built to him throughout the entire Empire and even beyond: the *caesarea*. On top of this he was to be *synnaos* to all other deities, i.e. his statues had to be placed in each of the other temples—a tolerant monotheistic god.

The liturgy consisted of the celebration of the anniversaries of his victories, which had been appraised, and praised, as miracles. Because he had won more than three hundred of them, and because for the greatest of them more than one day was set aside in thanksgiving, there was something to celebrate virtually every day. His posthumous victory, however, became the greatest celebration; the victory gained over his murderers by his wandering spirit after the Ides of March: treason, passion, funeral, *furor populi*, apotheosis—his Easter.

This worldwide cult disappears, with a conspicuous inconspicuousness—as if swallowed by the earth, just as Christianity appears. Yet not altogether without a trace, because at Easter, which like the Ides of March falls in the springtime, the Christian liturgy follows the ritual of Caesar's funeral.[327] Just as Christianity borrowed much from the cult of the emperor, regardless. The capital of Christendom is still Rome, and Caesar's centre of power her heart.

The cultic books of Divus Iulius have not survived, and we only hear of Caesar through historians. Accordingly, we think of him as a man of history. General, dictator, writer, epicurean, revolutionary—everyone knows this. But as Pontifex Maximus, son of God and God—he is known only to specialists—and even they tend to forget it. Divus Iulius is blanked out.

Jesus

In turn we have Jesus. Historians do not speak of him at all. Nobody knows him. The first mention of him, if it is not an interpolation, is by Flavius Josephus at the end of the first century. The only books we have about Jesus himself are liturgical: the Gospels.[328]

Accordingly, the historical existence of Jesus is still debated today. Because the Gospels are not history books, but are full of preaching and sermonizing, they have been mixed with theology, morality and oral tradition. And indeed, so much so that all attempts to comprehend the historical Jesus behind them regularly fail. They must fail.[329] For if we wish to establish what is true and what is false in the words and deeds of Jesus we are forced to use reductional thinking.

As there are no objective starting points to be found in the work of historians, each researcher sorts the data according to his own taste: the 'Search for the historical Jesus' has become a playing field for all kinds of projection. Due to the fact that in classical antiquity there were as many deified humans as humanized gods, one tendency is to see Jesus as a mythic being like Hercules, Dionysos, Adonis or Osiris. The other tendency is to see him as a man who became a god like Alexander, the Ptolemaeans or the Roman emperors. Even within conservative ranks there is disagreement in relation to the reduction: here the barefooted prophet, the little nabi of Galilea, one amongst so many executed reformers of the world, who just happened to have the luck of being posthumously regarded as the Messiah; there the Word of God, Jahweh himself in all his abstract glory, the pure *forma mentis* to which an earthly destiny gradually accrued. Here a nobody, there: no body.

Speculation is followed by phantasy: Was he an Essene, a Zealot, a collaborator or a nationalist? Was he a revolutionary, a pacifist, a macho man, a feminist, a guru, a therapist? Was he educated in Egypt or India? Do-it-yourself: Jesus for the tinkerer.

And if one, fearing answers, tries to stick to questions, these questions become more and more adventurous: Did he really die on the cross or did he only appear to be dead? Or did someone else die for him, perhaps Simon the Cyrenian? And Barabbas, was he really a murderer or a hero of the people? And wasn't his name Jesus as well? Was he a relative or Jesus himself? And the resurrection, did or did it not happen and how is this to be understood? And who was the favorite disciple, John, Lazarus or maybe even Mary Magdalene? Did he marry Mary Magdalene, and did she escape to the west and have his child?[330]

Question on top of question—and still no historical Jesus.

Complementary asymmetry

Objectively, we can say that Caesar is a historical figure who as a god has vanished without leaving a trace. Jesus, on the other hand, is a god whose historical figure cannot be found.

A striking complementary asymmetry. It is as if we are dealing with the same figure, one that has two faces, like the head of Janus. Could it be that the Gospel is the 'post-Easter' preaching of Divus Iulius of which the 'pre-Easter' historical version can be found in the writings of the ancient authors? That Jesus therefore is Divus Iulius as he is reflected in the East/West mirror? Is Jesus the icon of Caesar? Do the Gospels bear the same relationship to Divus Iulius as the first Christian churches do to the antique temples from which they were built and on whose foundations they stand?

IV

Words and Wonders

In the previous chapter, 'Crux', we determined that Jesus was not crucified, and that a cross had indeed played the main role in Antonius' presentation during the cremation of Caesar: the tropaeum. In that context we also saw that structures, requisites, and names correspond—mutatis mutandis. We have been induced to advance the hypothesis that the Gospels are a vita of Caesar *sui generis*. In spite of amazing parallels this has not been proven as yet.

We thus want to pick up the thread where we left it in Chapter II, 'Vitae Parallae'. There we had established that during the siege of Corfinium Caesar drove out the hostile commander who occupied the city; parallel to that, Jesus drove an unclean spirit out of a possessed person in Capharnaum. Both 'occupied' and 'possessed' are the same in Latin: *obsessus*.

Now we first want to test the parallels we found and see if they yield any constants; with the next siege we must find the next 'possessed'.

The Gerasene Demoniac

A year after crossing the Rubicon and besieging Corfinium, Caesar crossed the turbulent Ionian Sea in winter with just a few ships, and landed near the Ceraunic Cliffs where he dared the unbelievable: even though outnumbered, from the mountains he laid siege to all the troops of Pompeius, who controlled the coast.[331] This was not very successful, as history records it, because Pompeius drew an impenetrable line of defense. Both sides suffered greatly and after months of great exertion and enormous fortification and entrenchment, Caesar finally had to give up his position which had become untenable.

If our parallels hold up, we should soon find Jesus encountering the next 'possessed' person, this time an unbridled one staying on the other side of the stormy sea.

And lo and behold: Jesus and his disciples cross the stormy sea with a number of ships and land in the country of the Gerasenes (or Gergesenes or Gadarenes, depending on the manuscript) just as Caesar did in that of the Ceraunians.³³² There they deal with a 'possessed person' who is 'many' and named 'Legion'. He does not allow himself to be restrained and breaks the chains that bind him, just as Pompeius' legions repeatedly broke the siege of Caesar and his troops.

Here there are also many striking linguistic parallels—*Gerasenes/Ceraunians*³³³—now and then with similar morphological transformations as with *obsessus:* the possessed in the Jesus story remains in the 'tombs', in the *monumenta,* the besieged Pompeius in his entrenchment, in the *munimenta.*³³⁴ Even Matthew's variation (8:28) which speaks of two demoniacs instead of one, finds its counterpart in Caesar and Pompeius who de facto besieged each other.³³⁵

Even the 'swine'—in the Gospels, 'there was there nigh unto the mountains a great herd of swine feeding' (Mk. 5:11)—are also found in Caesar's story with insignificant phonetic variations: 'farm livestock that came from Epirus in abundance...'³³⁶. Here too, two easily mistaken words: *porcus* and *pecus,* swine and farm livestock (which include swine). This surely was an understandable mistake because Caesar's soldiers were suffering from such famine that they ate any animal, and eventually they began to dig for roots like unclean animals; from a root called *chara* they made, besides soup, also bread and ran towards the Pompeians throwing it triumphantly and full of contempt.³³⁷ When Pompeius saw this bread he cried out: 'What kind of beasts must we fight?'³³⁸ *Thêria*—actually means small animals, in the sense of wild unclean animals, beasts. What he meant was, because of the fodder, 'What pigs.' Mk. 5:13: 'And the unclean spirits went out, and entered into the swine'. Into the swine: *choirus*. What appears phonetically and optically as a mix of *chara* and *thêria*.

As with Gaul/Galilee, as well as Corfinium/Capharnaum, similar names and requisites appear within similar structures and sequences. So, we want to see if the parallel sequencing continues.

Jesus walks on the sea

Due to a lack of ships, Caesar was only able to transport approximately half of his troops across the sea. He sent the ships back to Brundisium (modern Brindisi) and commanded Antonius to follow with the rest of the troops and their equipment. Antonius hesitated, however, because of the weather and the cruising enemy fleet. Desperate, Caesar slipped, alone and incognito, onto a small boat during the night to help bring his men across. Using the current of the river which flowed into the sea to his advantage, he wanted to glide across the breakers. However, when in the night the off-shore wind dropped and a strong breeze arose from the sea, the current collided with the sea surge and forced the boat back; the helmsman despaired. At that moment Caesar revealed himself and said: 'Do not fear, you sail Caesar in your boat, and Caesar's luck sails with us!' At first it helped and everyone rowed with double the effort. In the end however, he reluctantly had to give up. Later his men reproached him when they heard what had happened.

This famous anecdote also appears in the Gospels in a slightly different form: Jesus walks upon the sea.

> 'And straightway he constrained his disciples to get into the ship, and to go to the other side before unto Bethsaida, while he sent away the people. And when he had sent them away, he departed into a mountain to pray. And when even was come, the ship was in the midst of the sea, and he alone on the land. And he saw them toiling in rowing; for the wind was contrary unto them: and about the fourth watch of the night he cometh unto them, walking upon the sea, and would have passed by them. But when they saw him walking upon the sea, they supposed it had been a spirit, and cried out: For they all saw him, and were troubled. And immediately he talked with them, and saith unto them, Be of good cheer: it is I; be not afraid. And he went up unto them into the ship; and the wind ceased: and they were sore amazed in themselves beyond measure, and wondered. For they considered not...'[339]

Here too, the names are similar: *Bethsaida/Brentesion*. The same motive: 'while he sent away the people.' The same journey during the night, alone, unknown, in a small barge, the rowing, the wind, the fear, revealing himself, the encouraging words: 'Do not be afraid, it is I'; then the abatement—here of the wind, there of the expedition; and the horror of the clueless men. The only difference: from the sea emerges not the breeze but Jesus himself. Jesus himself?

'...they supposed it had been a spirit'—*phantasma*.

Thus a spirit. And what is the off-shore that which appears in the Caesar story called? *Aura*. And the fresh breeze? *Pneuma*.[340] Two words which not only mean air, but hint of a spirit, especially the second one, *pneuma*.

The only difference in the Caesar and Jesus anecdotes is in the different readings of the words *aura* and *pneuma*. Air or spirit. What remains is that Jesus' spirit walked successfully on water—just as did Caesar's luck!

In Appian's version of Caesar's anecdote he not only speaks of 'Caesar's luck', but also of 'Caesar's demon',[341] which is very close to spirit. In the next paragraph *pneuma* is used again and after that *Postumius*, whom Caesar instructed to secretly cross over in his place and bring the army back. We even find the eponym of the ghost: Caesar's *Postumius* became the *posthumous* Jesus; *Postumius* secretly crossing over the sea became the *phantasma* walking upon the sea.

Finally, even Antonius' hesitation has parallels in the Gospels. Antonius eventually obeys Caesar's repeated calls and ships the rest of the troops and equipment across in an adventurous and dangerous way. Doing so he almost perishes and is forced up to Dalmatia; in the end he fortunately reunites with Caesar. The parallel in the Gospel: the hesitating Peter starting to walk on the water becomes frightened and, beginning to sink, he cries for help until Jesus stretches his hand and catches him: 'O you of little faith, why did you doubt?' (Mt. 14:28-31).

Even the landing place—Dalmatia[342]—could be the same, stranded in a disconnected place:

'And straightway he entered into a ship with his disciples, and came into the parts of Dalmanutha.'[343]

However Dalmanutha does not exist, neither at the Lake of Gennesaret nor anywhere else in the entire region. But *Dalmatia* looks very much like *Dalmanutha*. Even though the context in which Dalmanutha is used is different and behind this name, as we will see, another port is hidden. Dalmatia, which here had become homeless, might have moved into Dalmanutha.

But the remarkable fact here is that by comparing the parallel stories of Jesus' and Caesar's defiance of the stormy sea, we can also explain small and big incongruities of the Gospel text, for which, to date, no rational explanation has been found.

For example, after forcing his disciples to go aboard and before boarding the ship himself, Jesus not only walks on the sea, but meanwhile he also goes up a mountain to pray (Mk. 6:46). The whole scene takes place at the sea, on the shoreline or on the water at the mouth of the river. Jesus leaves the scene and climbs a mountain, but did not really leave the scene, because then suddenly he is on the sea. This incongruity could easily be explained by the fact that *oros*, Greek for 'mountain', very much resembles *ora*, Latin for 'shoreline', respectively *os, oris*, 'mouth (of the river)'.

However, this passage also contains a notorious and even severe case of incongruity within the Gospel. Here Jesus supposedly crossed Lake Gennesaret. Yet the Gospel writers do not speak of a lake, but of the sea. For example, when Jesus calms the storm, 'He speaks to the sea: be still and cease!' To the 'sea': *thalassa*.[344] But here it is about an inland lake, a fresh water lake. Therefore the correct word would be *limnê*,[345] but that is not what is written. Only Luke, who tells a shortened version of the incident, uses *limnê*. There has been no explanation up to today as to why Mark and Matthew systematically and repeatedly use *thalassa*.³⁴⁶

Thalassa only fits in the Caesar story because he crossed over a real sea: the Ionian.

Thus our first test not only highlights the fact that the parallels between Caesar and Jesus are systematic, but also demonstrates that perplexing vocabulary of the Gospel can be explained when traced back to that of the history of Caesar.

However, since the devil is in the details as everyone knows, we now intend to search for well-known details. For instance, the shoe's latchet of John the Baptist, or the argument between the disciples of John and Jesus as to which of the two is really the Christ. As we saw in the beginning, John the Baptist is structurally related to Jesus as Pompeius is to Caesar. Also, Pompeius was Caesar's political godfather, baptizing his career in a sense, before he attacked him and lost. So the latchets of Pompeius' shoes too, should play a role in his argument with Caesar. On the other hand, within the same context there should also be a debate involving him or his disciples as to who is the real 'Christ' that is, if the correspondence of *christos* ≈ *pontifex maximus* we have worked out is correct: who should become *pontifex maximus* in Caesar's place.

The shoe's latchet of John the Baptist

At the beginning of the Gospel of John, John the Baptist says:
> 'He that cometh after me is preferred before me: for he was before me.'³⁴⁷

He repeats this:
> 'He it is, who coming after me is preferred before me, whose shoe's latchet I am not worthy to unloose.'³⁴⁸

The Gospel of Mark combines both:
> 'There cometh one mightier than I after me, the latchet of whose shoes I am not worthy to stoop down and unloose.'³⁴⁹

Thematically the parallel is clear: At the beginning of the civil war as well as at the beginning of the Gospel it was a question of determining who was the first and who was the mightiest; in one story Caesar or Pompeius, in the other Jesus or John. One could speculate about the names, too: on the one hand Pompeius *Magnus*, the 'Great', on the other hand Caesar, the (pontifex) *Maximus*, the 'Greatest', the Highest (Priest).

If we concentrate on the requisites we see that it is about 'coming' and 'going'—the Greek verb *erchomai* can mean either 'coming' or 'going' depending on the point of view—and the fact that he who was in front can suddenly again be behind. It seems to be about fleeing and chasing: as at Pharsalos, where Caesar first fled, chased by Pompeius; later however, the roles were reversed.

We now have to look into the texts and see if Pompeius, on the run after the battle of Pharsalos and being chased by the now stronger Caesar, experiences anything in relation to 'shoes', 'unloosen the latchet', 'stooping down' and 'worthiness'.

The scene is quickly found: After Pompeius fled with Favonius via Larissa to the sea and the two were taken aboard a freighter the following scene took place:

> 'When it was time for supper the master of the ship was preparing everything according to what was available; Favonius noticed that Pompeius began to "take off" his "shoes" himself due to the lack of servants. He "ran to" Pompeius and "helped him with his shoes" as well as by anointing him. And from that time on he continued to give Pompeius such ministry and service as slaves give their masters, even down to the washing of his feet and the preparation of his meals, so that any one who beheld the courtesy and the unfeigned simplicity of that service might have exclaimed: "How well every task 'conforms' to a noble soul".'[350]

The requisites sought are marked: the 'shoes'; 'helping take off' for 'unloosening the latchet'; 'running towards someone and helping to take off shoes' for 'stooping'; 'conforms to' for 'worthiness'. It is obviously the same scene. However, there are more requisites in the Pompeius story than in the John the Baptist story: in the latter story 'service', 'slave', 'master (Lord)', 'dinnertime' or 'preparing the meals' and 'washing the feet' are missing. Where are they? They appear in another, more appropriate place: the Last Supper of the Lord—of Jesus:

> 'He riseth from "supper", and laid aside his garments; and took "a towel, and girded himself". After that he poureth water into a bason, and began "to wash the disciples' feet", and "to wipe them with the towel wherewith he was girded". Then cometh he to Simon Peter: and Peter saith unto him, "Lord", dost thou wash my feet?'[351]

Now we have all the requisites together, the 'supper', the 'Lord' and 'washing of feet', whereby the 'towel' and 'girdle' as slave garments stand for 'slave', and the 'towel wherewith he was girded' which he used 'to wipe their feet' symbolizes the 'service of a slave'.[352]

The second part of the passage on Pompeius has simply wandered to another more useful, more 'Christian' place.

Apart from that, the first part too is not found where expected: it should be after Pharsalos, at the place where in the Gospel story the

Baptist and Jesus have an encounter, and where it is determined who is the Christ (Jn. 3:22-36). We immediately can check whether this was the original place of the Pharsalos story.

Who is the Christ?

In the very first chapter of John's Gospel, the Baptist confesses that he is not the Christ.

> 'And he confessed, and denied not; but confessed, I am not the Christ.'[353]

However, this question—who is the Christ—was explicitly posed only later, in the context of a quarrel started by John's disciples:

> 'Then there arose a question between some of John's disciples and the Jews about purifying ... John answered and said ... Ye yourselves bear me witness, that I said, I am not the Christ...'[354]

If *Christ* stands for *pontifex maximus*—as our hypothesis demands—then the argument in Pharsalos must have not only been about who was the strongest, but specifically who was to be *pontifex maximus*. And indeed, on the evening before Pharsalos, the battle that would decide the highest power in the empire, the most respected followers of Pompeius were arguing about who should afterwards be *pontifex maximus* in Caesar's place. They did not expect Caesar to survive the battle:

> '...some of them even began to argue among themselves as to who would assume Caesar's dignity as *pontifex maximus*.'[355]

Against all expectations Caesar won the battle. Everyone ran to his side and he remained *pontifex maximus*. The power of the great Pompeius evaporated. All that was left for him was his young wife, whom he had just married. He went and saw her in Mitylene, in order to take her with him in his flight:

> 'I see, my husband, that you are lost in sorrow.'

> 'You know only of one lot in my life, Cornelia, the better one that perhaps also deceived you, because its faithfulness to me was unusually prolonged. But we must also suffer this because we are human...'[356]

This philosophical dialogue concerning the abrupt fall of the bridal couple from happiness into sorrow is reflected in the farewell speech of John that otherwise does not make sense about his bride and himself as groom:

> 'He that hath the bride is the bridegroom: but the friend of the bridegroom, which standeth and heareth him, rejoiceth greatly because of the bridegroom's voice: this my joy therefore is fulfilled. He must in-

crease, but I must decrease. He that cometh from above is above all: he that is of the earth is earthly...'[357]

The repeating analogy found between John the Baptist and Pompeius leads us to question whether the conflict between light and darkness stressed at the beginning of John's Gospel belongs in an editorial framework or if it is also borrowed from the history of the Roman civil war.

Light and Darkness

The Gospel of John first presents John the Baptist within a clash between light and darkness:

> 'And the light shineth in darkness; and the darkness comprehended it not.'[358]

The context is the argument between Jesus and the Baptist, or more specifically between their followers, which once more is taken up and stated more precisely in Jn. 3:22.

The theme of the struggle between light and darkness forced itself on Caesar and Pompeius with fateful features the evening before the battle of Pharsalos.

> 'As a light from heaven flew from Caesar's camp to that of Pompeius and went out there, the Pompeians thought it was a sign of glorious triumph over their enemies, while at the same time Caesar predicted he would attack and wipe out the power of Pompeius.'[359]

Pompeius might have won if the darkness had comprehended the light. Now, however, the light shone in the darkness: Caesar won.

So the Evangelist John would have brought the Pharsalos story to the beginning of his Gospel, and in combination with the arming of Pompeius at the start of the civil war, he would already have anticipated the result—Pompeius' defeat at Pharsalos.[360]

The baptism

There can be no Baptist without baptism. The activities of John and Jesus as baptizers correspond to the military mobilizations of Pompeius and Caesar before the outbreak of civil war. The armament of Pompeius had been such a fatal development because in his opinion it was a necessary measure of preparation against a much feared military battle. But in the eyes of Caesar it was an illegal declaration of war against him, the victorious conqueror of the Gauls, who was deserving of triumphal processions. Thus, the arming of Pompeius had provoked Caesar's occupation of Italy and by that it counterphobically resulted in Caesar's seizure of power, which he had feared so much.

Just as Pompeius is reproached for illegal armament, John is reproached for illegitimately baptizing:

'And they asked him, and said unto him, Why baptizest thou then, if thou be not that Christ, nor Elias, neither that prophet?'[361]

And just as Caesar justified his takeover by referring to the illegal levying of troops by Pompeius, so too did Jesus justify his authority by referring to the just as questionable legitimacy of the baptismal activity of John:

'And say unto him, By what authority doest thou these things? and who gave thee this authority to do these things? And Jesus answered and said unto them, I will also ask of you one question, and answer me, and I will tell you by what authority I do these things. The baptism of John, was it from heaven, or of men? answer me.'[362]

One may question how the armament and levying can become baptism. What the commander refers to as armament and levying is, in the eyes of his officers and even more so those of his soldiers: recruitment, inspection and weapon consecration, because that is what they experience.[363]

Well, inspection in Latin is *lustratio*, which actually means 'cleansing', 'lustration', but in military language it stands for 'inspection' because of the acts of ritual cleansing and expiatory sacrifices that accompanied it. Along with the *lustratio*, the inspection of soldiers, went the inspection of weapons, the *armilustrium*, the 'cleansing of weapons' in the sense of 'ceremony of purifying the arms'. The word *lustratio* comes from *luo*, 'to wash' and in the second instance means 'atone', which finds its Greek pendant in the *loutrón*, meaning 'wash', 'bathe,' and comes from the corresponding verb *louô*, also 'to wash', 'to bathe'. In the Christian sense these words became 'baptism', respectively 'baptize.' The transition from 'inspection of soldiers with cleansing of arms' (the Latin *lustratio*) to 'baptism of repentance' (the Greek *loutrón*) came about through the common concepts of 'washing' and 'purifying'. The same meaning is also found in the other Greek word alternatively used for *louô*, *baptizô*, which in the Christian sense is also translated with 'to baptize' (probably because it comes from *baptô*, which means 'to dunk'). Before becoming baptism, *baptisma*, too, simply meant washing: a further excellent literal translation of the Latin word *lustratio*, the inspection. And the fact that baptism was originally seen as the reception into the army of Christ is certainly not contradictory to this idea.

Having read the text through these glasses, Mark henceforth might have seen the classic word for levying, *dilectus*, as *dilutum* or even *dilu-*

vies, diluvium, all words which have to do with washing, watering and rinsing.

Interestingly enough, Mark adds his own explanation to the word *baptisma:* 'baptism of repentance for the remission of sins', *baptisma metanoias eis aphesin (h)amartiôn.*[364] 'Of sins' in Greek is *(h)amartiôn; armorum* in Latin means 'of the arms'. If this *armorum* from an older version was later read as *(h)amartiôn,* the 'remission of sins' would stand for *armilustrium.*[365] Since *aphesis* first means 'release', 'discharge', 'dismissal' and only as a derivative 'remission' we must turn our attention to something else. While Pompeius was arming his soldiers, his new father-in-law Metellus (Scipio) demanded that Caesar dismiss his men. 'Remission of sins' might therefore simply stand for *dimissio armorum.*[366] Since *metanoias,* 'of repentance', looks very similar to *Metellus,* and *baptisma,* 'baptism' is near *postulatio,* 'demand', as well as *kêryssôn,* 'preaching', is not far from *Caesar,* then *kai kêryssôn baptisma metanoias eis aphesin (h)amartiôn* would stand for *a Caesare postulabat Metellus dimissionem armorum.* In English, 'and preaching a baptism of repentance for the remission of sins' would simply stand for 'Metellus demanded from Caesar the dismissal of his army'.

We have now seen that the Gospels of Mark and John find structural parallels in the Vita Caesaris. In the search for the corresponding passages, time and time again, we first looked at the context and then, within the context we sought the requisites.

A third class of clues also took shape: corresponding names. These are sometimes obviously similar—*Gallia* ≈ *Galilee, Corfinium* ≈ *Capharnaum, (h)amartiôn* ≈ *armorum*—sometimes different, as if translated—*lustratio* ≈ *baptisma*—or a functional equivalent: *Christ* versus *pontifex maximus.* This context-based research seems to confirm the parallels we found in the first list of people and their counterparts.

We therefore want to examine the texts more closely in order to more thoroughly test the tangibly emerging hypothesis that the Gospel texts are based on a Caesar source.

Should the Gospel text have found its basis in the history of Caesar's life, then his famous quotations—as well as those not so well known—should be found in the Gospels, too. These quotations should be in the appropriate places within the corresponding context.

We instantaneously think of: *alea iacta est* and *veni vidi vici;* less well-known, but not less typical: *Who is not on any side, is on my side; I am not king, I am Caesar; The best death is the sudden death; Have I saved them, that they may destroy me?!*

Words

Alea iacta est

'The die is cast', or *alea iacta esto,* 'Let the die be cast' as Erasmus rightly corrected, was said by Caesar while still in Gaul, on the Adriatic between Ravenna and Rimini, before crossing the Rubicon. There he saw Antonius and Curio completely distraught, riding towards him in the night from Rome. They had been unable to prevent Pompeius from declaring a state of emergency, a step directed against Caesar.[367] Caesar ventured to cast the die and gained a stroke of luck, for it was he who won the war. He appointed Antonius and Curio to military commands on the spot. The one was to distinguish himself during the crossing of the Ionian Sea, while the other managed to cross the sea to Sicily and from there to Africa.

We noticed that Galilee stands for Gallia, that John the Baptist plays the same role as Pompeius, and that Simon (Peter) has Antonius' role. If these parallels are correct, then just after his baptism by John on the Jordan, we should look for Jesus on the coast of Galilee. We actually do find him on the Sea of Galilee where he encountered Simon and Andreas casting out their nets, because they were fishermen. Jesus said to them: 'Come after me; and I will make you fishermen of men!' (Mk. 1:16-17). Luke tells us that they had worked the entire night and had not caught anything. Simon then cast out his nets as Jesus instructed him and caught such a great number of fish that their nets began to tear. (Lk. 5:5-6)

These are striking similarities, but where is *alea iacta est?* It is only in the Greek text that we can see Caesar's words. (He saw them), 'casting: for they were fishers'—*amphiballontas, êsan gar (h)aleeis*.[368] *Alea,* Latin for die, once understood as *(h)aleeis,* Greek for fishermen, turns over the sentence. *Alea iacta esto,* 'Let the die be cast', becomes 'Fishermen, let (it) be cast'. The cast remains aleatoric still: the fishermen must believe that they will catch something. *(H)aleeis* retains the sound of *alea;* the sense changes to a miraculous catch—or to fishers of men.[369]

For the rest here too, another incongruence in the Gospel texts can be explained. It was never comprehensible why the fishermen in the Gospels were called *(h)aleeis*. This refers to sailors more than fishermen. *(H)aleeis* is derived from *(h)als,* salt. The Sea of Galilee is supposed to be Lake Gennesaret which is the well-known inland lake of the Jordan.

Not a sea. No sea, no sailors, no salt. *(H)aleeis* and 'Sea of Galilee' do not make sense.

In the Caesar text 'sea' makes sense twice. First, the Adriatic Sea is really a sea and secondly, it was really the Gallic Sea. Gallia (Gaul) was also the Cisalpine, what is today Northern Italy.[370]

'Who is not on any side, is on my side'

This was Caesar's answer to Pompeius' declaration *that he will count everyone who does not help the state as an enemy.*[371] By that, Pompeius had meant everyone who remained in Rome while he and his men had declared a state of emergency directed against the invading Caesar—and thereupon left Rome in such a panic that they plundered their own homes, like robbers.

In a similar situation the same words are used. Namely when Jesus is reproached for being the prince of demons who drives out other demons.[372] Then he refers to a strong man who enters the house of another strong man and spoils his house. In Matthew and Luke: *He that is not with me is against me; and he that gathereth not with me scattereth abroad.* In Mark and Luke as Jesus' reply to John: *For he that is not against us is on our part.*[373]

This time it is not only a similar, but an absolutely identical expression, in word and sense, within the same context—the beginning of the civil war—with the same mutual demonization. It looks as if here an almost unchanged source has been reproduced.

Veni vidi vici

'I came, I saw, I conquered': Caesar's pithiest words were also his shortest war report. Thus he reported his extremely swift victory over Pharnakes at the Pontic temple city of Zela (today Zile, in the north eastern part of Asia Minor). The saying was later carried as an inscription in front of the triumphal procession in Rome.

In the sources where the saying appears as a report sent from the Pontic town of Zela it is used not only in the first person, but also in the third by Dio Cassius:

'...he approached the enemy, saw him and conquered.'

'(I) came, saw, conquered.'[374]

Expressions formally corresponding with Caesar's words can be found in two sections of the Gospels. In Mark's text of the healing of a blind man and in John's text of a person born blind, at the temple pool of Siloah.

In the Gospel of John it appears twice: once as a description in the third person just as in the Dio text, and then again from the mouth of a blind person after he has been healed:

'He went his way therefore, and washed, and came seeing.'[375]

'I went and washed, and I received sight.'[376]

In Mark the blind man's utterance is somewhat different:

'I see men as trees, walking.'[377]

Two ('come/go', 'see') of the three elements ('come', 'see', 'conquer') found in the Caesar quotation can also be found in Mark and John. This is especially noticeable in the Greek text because the verb *erchomai (êlthon)* means 'come' and 'go' according to context.[378]

Only in the third element 'wash' versus 'men as trees' do the Gospel writers differentiate from not only Caesar, but also from each other. There is no path in either direction from the verb 'wash' used by John to the phrase 'men as trees' used by Mark. However if they are compared to Caesar's 'conquering' then there is something noticeable:

In Greek 'I washed' and 'I conquered' are acoustically and visually so close to each other that the two can be confused: *enikêsa / enipsa*—pronunciation: 'enikisa / enipsa', graphical image in the manuscripts: ENIKHCA / ENIΨA.

'Men as trees, walking' were seen in the triumphal procession in Rome: the commander with a laurel wreath on his head, the soldiers with every piece of green they could possibly collect, mostly olive branches, the lower the rank the larger the greenery.

So this expression of Caesar may have served as a source for both Gospel writers. The difference in their texts can be attributed to the fact that in Mark's example the quotation is connected with the triumphal procession in Rome—as is the case with Suetonius—while John's source reported in a chronological way and treated the quotation as a report sent from the Pontic town of Zela—as is the case with Plutarchus.

Even the place name continues to exist—*Zela > Siloah*—in almost the exact same pronunciation—*zila > siloa*. The word 'pool/pond' reminds us it was a 'Pontic' city. *Pontos* simply means 'sea'.

But where is the blind man in the Caesar texts? Of course: Pharnakes was blind. In his opposition to Caesar he 'did not see, was conquered and had to go.' And just as Caesar 'drove out'—*expulit*—the defeated Pharnakes, Jesus 'spat'—*exspuit*—in the blind man's eyes.

There is one difference between the Caesar texts and the Gospel passage that still needs to be explained. In the Caesar story the quotation, 'I came, saw and conquered' came from Caesar. In the Gospel it is the blind man who says, 'I went, washed and saw.' How did it come to be interchanged?

Probably because the name *Caesar* was confused with *caecus* 'blind': *Caesar* > *caecus*.

Notice the following: Since Pharnakes is not only conquered and forced out by Caesar but also beaten and murdered by one of his vassals, he is not only *victus*, conquered, but also *caesus*, 'defeated' and 'killed'. Since *caesus* is easy to confuse with *caecus*, 'blind', Pharnakes might have become *caecus* via *caesus*. And since *Caesar* too can be confused with *caesus* the one might have replaced the other.[379]

I am not King, I am Caesar[380]

Caesar's family descended via his father's mother, from the *Marcii Reges*. Following his maternal lineage, he was also a 'King'.[381] He used this word association to humorously play down the cheers of the people who wanted him to be king. As is well known, he was unsuccessful, for his opponents used this as further proof that he still wanted to be made king. Suetonius: 'It was useless.' Plutarchus: 'Great silence followed these words as he gloomily and vexedly walked along.'

There is no historical agreement as to when and where Caesar used this expression. Plutarchus says, 'As Caesar one day returned from Alba'; Appianus, 'on the way home near the city gates'; Suetonius does not name the place or the occasion: 'as the plebs greeted him as king.'[382]

In John's Gospel the sentence is found when Pilate leads Jesus to 'a place that is called the Pavement,' saying to the screaming crowd:

'"Behold, your King!"

The chief priest answered:

"We have no king but Caesar."[383]

Then delivered he him therefore unto them to be crucified.'

In spite of all the uncertainty concerning the location, there is still a similarity in the situation: the road to Alba or the returning home at the city gate on the one hand, 'the Pavement' on the other; screaming crowds in both scenes; being addressed as 'King'; the answer: 'not a King, but Caesar' (our differentiation between Caesar and Emperor does not exist in Greek). Hopelessness and leading away: 'It was useless' and 'he gloomily and vexedly walked along' on the one hand, 'delivered to be crucified' on the other.

The only difference is that Jesus does not say, 'I am not King' as Caesar does. Instead the chief priests say: 'We have no king'. However, this is a difference that makes no difference, because Caesar himself was chief priest, *archiereus, pontifex maximus*.

The best death is the sudden one

'The day before the next session of the Senate Caesar however went to supper at the home of Lepidus. Lepidus was his magister equitum. He took Brutus Albinus with him to drink and as the cup passed he raised the question, "What is the best method to die?" While one expressed this opinion and another that, Caesar himself praised sudden death above all. He thus prophesied his own end and spoke of what was to happen the following day.'[384]

For the next day, Decimus Brutus Albinus was to lead him to where his conspirators would be waiting for him; sudden death would overtake him and his blood would flow.

It is easy to recognize the Last Supper scene from the Gospel.[385] Caesar appears as *dictator* with his *magister equitum,* Grand Master of the Horse, the dictator's second-in-command. In the Gospel the disciples are supposed to go into the city and follow a man carrying a stone jar and wherever he enters, say to the head of the house that the master needs a room for supper. Notice how 'Master'—*didaskalos*—corresponds to *dictator* which in Latin can be misunderstood as schoolmaster. It is not by chance that it became 'Dichter', poet, in German. Lepidus was really head of the house, *oikodespotês*. The word resembles—what a coincidence—a mimicry of *magister equitum,* where *despotês* stands for *magister,* oiko for *equitum,* the first part in sense, the second in sound. Finally, 'stone jar'—*keramos*—is a translation of *Lepidus,* if it is mistakenly derived from *lapis, lapidis*—'stone'—reinforced by the real meaning of *lepidus,* 'pleasing': a pleasing stone jar, a delicate ceramic.

Even the betrayer's name is mentioned: *Decimus* Brutus. In the Gospel texts the betrayer is named as 'one of the twelve.' Decimus means the tenth! Just as *Decimus* was taken to feast with Caesar, so 'one of the twelve' dippeth with Jesus in the dish (Mk. 14:20).

Even the chalice is there, referred to in the Caesar story also as *kylix,* which with him too refers to his blood that is shed: already during that night his wife saw him in a dream, 'covered in much blood'—a premonition of his sacrificial death.[387]

And finally the announcement of imminent death is found in both Caesar and Jesus.

However, one thing seems to be missing in the Gospels, namely the exact comment by Caesar we are looking for: 'the sudden one'. It is not found in the synoptic Gospels. In John, Jesus does say to the traitor:

'That thou doest, do quickly.'[388]

Here is the sentence, even if it is hidden: 'What you do—namely lead me to death—do that quickly'. There it is—the sudden death, in the mouth of Jesus.

Thus we would have found the Caesar quotation we have been looking for in its appropriate context—*[the best death is] the sudden one.*

Men servasse, ut essent qui me perderent

'Have I saved them that they may ruin me?' This verse from Pacuvius' *Contest for the Arms of Achilles,* the leitmotif of the people's lament at Caesar's funeral,[389] was strangely enough said by a mime playing Caesar and acting in combination with Antonius who began the lament while the people answered as the chorus in the tragedy.

During funerals it was the custom to have the deceased himself speak to the mourners in the person of a masked actor who imitated his voice and gestures. Normally this took place with humor and irony, but on this occasion it was with sarcasm and gallows humor:

'...in the middle of the laments Caesar himself seemed to speak of it and to recount all his enemies by name, those he had treated well. And about the assassins themselves he said as if in unbelievable amazement: "Men servasse, ut essent qui me perderent?"—"Have I saved them that they may ruin me?"'[390]

As we know, these words did not miss their mark. The people were outraged and tried to lynch the assassins of Caesar.

The assassins themselves were afraid this would happen and tried to prevent the funeral. They wanted to drag Caesar's body through the streets as the corpse of a tyrant, and then throw it into the Tiber. However, since Caesar was not only *dictator* but also *pontifex maximus,* his father-in-law, Piso, managed to have Caesar buried as such with the help of the consuls.[391]

So the sentence that we were looking for—'Have I saved them, that they may ruin me?'—appeared in the middle of the funeral, in an exchange between Antonius and the chorus in the tragedy, from the mouth of the high priest himself as he is about to be cremated.

Mutatis mutandis we find the same sentence during the crucifixion of Jesus, in the same constellation and in the same mouth:

'Likewise also the chief priests mocking said among themselves with the scribes, He saved others; himself he cannot save.'[392]

What the high priests say in Mark is obviously a translation of the Pacuvius-text, even though the second part has been weakened. We notice that Pacuvius counts as a scribe, while *pontifex maximus* Caesar, an actor himself in the person of his mime in the funeral play directed by Antonius, counts as one of the mocking chief priests.

This is not the first time this has been observed. Another quotation from the high priest Caesar—'I am not King, I am Caesar'—was also placed in the mouth of the chief priests judging Jesus: 'We have no king, but Caesar.' As if exchanging roles with the high priests was the perfect solution in a delicate situation where one cannot or will not put certain words into his mouth.

Our hypothesis that the Gospels are based on a Vita Caesaris is so far confirmed. We now want to find more definite proof. This should establish certainty: either falsification or verification.

Names and Miracles

In order to maintain the parallels between the life of Caesar and the Gospels we had to make certain assumptions. For example, we had to assume that Caesar himself, in his position as *pontifex maximus,* lurks behind the high priests who say, 'We have no king, but Caesar.' We also had to assume that in the sentence, 'I came, I washed, and saw' the blind man was speaking and not Jesus, because *Caesar* was confused with *caecus*. The same applies to the man with the stone jar who does the leading to the head of the household, because *Lepidus* was mistaken for a *lepidus lapis;* or that Jesus in the same scene is called 'master' because the *dictator* Caesar was misunderstood to be 'a dictating schoolmaster', etc.

True, these assumptions are plausible. But as yet they have not been proven unless they truly correspond to a regular 'habit' of the Gospel writers. They can be systematized as: official titles misunderstood as professions (*pontifex maximus* as one of the high priests, *dictator* as schoolmaster, and in the end including even *alea* as fishermen), proper names as generic names (*Pontos* as pond, *Lepidus* as stone jar, *Caesar* as *caecus*), enemies as insane or lame people (*obsessus* as obsessed or *caesus* as *caecus*), who are proper candidates to be healed. From then on miraculous victories are interpreted as victorious miracles.

As can be seen, these word corruptions and bungles correspond not only to the well-known rule of philology that the *lectio facilior* replaces the *difficilior,* but also to the basic tendency of transferring copyists' mistakes as well as to the nature of the oral transmission of information. The sermon is no different than the grapevine: the known replaces the unknown for the individual transmitting information, or, that which the public wishes to hear replaces that which he prefers to conceal.

So we remain within the norm so far. In order to see if this is the rule, or in our case only pure chance, we want to draw some conclusions from the description outlined above and then see if they can be verified in the text.

When an *Asinius Pollio* appears in the Caesar sources, we would have to expect that his name predestines him to metamorphose into an 'ass's colt' in the Gospel. If then, in another well-known Caesar anecdote, someone should pop up with a name that can be misunderstood as an affliction, he, too, must accordingly be healed by Jesus. The Romans liked to use bodily characteristics (*Rufus* the Red-haired, *Lentulus* the Slow, etc.) as names, including many that refer to deformities, such as *Claudius* or *Clodius* the Hobbler or *Caecilius* the Blind. It is fitting that Caesar had conflicts solely with people with such names. In addition to a *Lentulus* there were many *Claudii*, especially a *Clodius*, as well as many *Caecilii*, so that, according to our constants, we must expect to find the healing of several lame and those with gout, as well as various blind people.

Now we will see if all this is accurate.

Asinius Pollio

He was with Caesar at the Rubicon and by his side during the civil war. After Pompeius—Corfinium having surrendered—had left Italy via Brundisium and crossed the sea to Epirus with part of the Senate, and while Caesar was on the verge of marching into Rome, Asinius went to Sicily by Caesar's order to take the island from Cato, the governor appointed by the Pompeians. He accompanied the legate Curio who was to go to Africa from Sicily:

> 'Eventually Asinius Pollio followed Caesar's orders and went to Sicily, which at that time was under Cato's leadership. When Cato asked if he came with an order of the Senate or the people in his pocket to invade a foreign area he received the following answer: "The Lord of Italy delegated this task to me!" Cato contented himself with the reply that he would not offer any resistance out of consideration for his subordinates. He then left for Kerkyra (Corfu) and from Kerkyra to Pompeius. In the meantime Caesar hurried towards Rome...'[393]

Since *Asinius* sounds like the adjective to *asinus*, 'ass', and Pollio like *pôlos* or *pullus*, 'colt', our constant—the assumption that proper names turn into generic names—requires that *Asinius Pollio* appears as *'ass's colt'*, with the requisites belonging to him—two envoys, a legate, verbal arguments, questions of authorization, orders of the Lord, taking over, etc.—creatively organized around the colt.

We do not have to search for long. Just as Asinius Pollio is mentioned immediately before Caesar enters Rome, so we find our ass's colt just before Jesus enters Jerusalem. Here is Mark's version [the most important variations of the other Evangelists have been placed in brackets]:

> 'And when they came nigh to Jerusalem, [unto Bethphage and Bethany, at the mount of Olives, (missing in John)] he sendeth forth two of his disciples, And saith unto them, Go your way into the village over against you: [to the place opposite you (Luke)] and as soon as ye be entered into it, ye shall find a colt tied, [(Matthew) an ass tied, and a colt with her / (John) an ass's colt / a young ass] whereon never man sat; loose him, and bring him. And if any man say unto you, Why do ye this? say ye that the Lord hath need of him; [and straightway he will send him hither (missing in Luke)]. And they went their way, and found the colt tied by the door without in a place where two ways met; and they loose him. And certain of them that stood there said unto them, What do ye, loosing the colt? And they said unto them even as Jesus had commanded: and they let them go.'[394]

Here we find our *Asinius Pollio* again, sometimes only as *Pollio*, 'colt', sometimes with the full name of 'ass's colt' or 'ass with colt'. 'Tied': is this *legatus* understood as *ligatus*, 'legate' as 'ligated'? That makes sense. If Asinius Pollio is an ass's colt then the legate Asinius Pollio can only be a ligated ass's colt. The places are identical: before the entrance into the different capitals. Even the place they come from is there—*Brundisium/Brentesion*. The Gospel writers that actually name the place vary between *Bethphage* and *Bethany* and land not far from *Bethsaida*, which we found in the crossing of the stormy sea, there also in place of *Brentesion*. Sicily as place of the mission remains on the other side of the sea: *katenanti*, 'over against / opposite'[395]—while the name of the 'opposite', *Cato(n)*, the one to be replaced, blatantly echoes: *anti Katônos*, 'in place of Cato'. Both Caesar and Jesus have two envoys. The question of authority appears when Caesar's envoys want to replace the legate of the Senate and is also directed to the disciples of Jesus, 'What do ye, loosing the colt?' The same answer, 'The Lord of Italy delegated this task to me' and 'the Lord hath need of him; and straightway he will send him hither'. The second part of the sentence sounds like Cato giving up the province as well as announcing his withdrawal from Sicily.[396] And the giving in is there, which is also found in the final words, 'and they let them go'.

The name Sicily is missing. Instead there is a fig tree with leaves: 'And seeing a fig tree afar off having leaves, he came, if haply he might find any thing thereon: and when he came to it, he found nothing but leaves.'[397]

'Fig tree': *sykê*, pronounced *siki*. 'Leaves': *phylla*, pronounced *filla*. *Sicilia* is *siki* with *filla*, a 'fig tree with leaves'.

Then a doublet appears. A few verses later the barren fig tree appears again.[398] This doublet too has its counterpart in the Caesar source, because there is a second trip to Sicily: first Asinius then Curio. Observe the sequence:[399] In one text there is Asinius Pollio's mission to Sicily, in the other there is the mission to fetch the ass's colt and there is a fig tree with leaves; here, a brief description of Caesar's entrance into Rome; there a brief description of Jesus' entrance into Jerusalem; here, Curio(n)'s appointment as governor of Sicily with the orders to cross over to Africa, there a second passing beside the fig tree, which is now *xêron*, 'barren'; *xêron* ≈ *Curio(n)* (ΞΗΡΟΝ ≈ ΚΟΥΡΙΟΝ).[400]

Conclusion: As expected, we found *Asinius Pollio* as an 'ass's colt', and as expected the context and requisites are identical except that they are creatively rearranged around the mutated leading actor, and adequately adapted if necessary.

And once again we have an explanation for the differences between the Evangelists! The one says 'colt' only and the other says 'ass's colt' or 'ass with colt' instead, becomes understandable if it is assumed that one found only *Pollio* in his exemplar whereas the other found *Asinius Pollio*.

Caecilii and Claudii

Caecilii, 'blind', and *Claudii*, 'lame.' Many of Caesar's enemies are so named, notably those who had played a decisive part in the outbreak of the civil war.[401] Some were given eyes for hindsight, others got healed legs and a kick in the hindquarters. 'The blind receive their sight, and the lame walk' as the Gospel states (11:5). Jesus healed so many *blind and lame* people that it became his trade mark.

Since *Caecilii* and *Claudii* remain in the shadow of Pompeius, for the most part it is difficult to look for a specific context in which they appear. The blind are partially eliminated for verification because as we have noted others might theoretically belong to this group; for example the *caesi*, soldiers killed in war. Moreover, one or the other *Caecilius*, with the surname *Metellus* must not necessarily become one of the blind, but could become one of the 'mutilated' (as if *Metellus* = *mutilus*).

However, one *Claudius* particularly stands out: *Publius Clodius Pulcher*. The way in which he crosses Caesar, and the way in which Caesar—contrary to all expectations—takes him under his wing so that in the end Clodius becomes one of his political friends, all this is so saliently typical for both Caesar's clementia and his political superiority: ergo the Clodius-anecdote must be found in the Gospels. If not, it would have to be regarded as a falsification of our hypothesis. If we find it with all its requisites, however, the hypothesis can be regarded as verified. We expect to find the Clodius-ancedote as an important story in the healing of a lame person.

Publius Clodius

—at that time still *Claudius,* named *Pulcher,* 'pretty boy', wild and foolhardy, was a friend of Cicero's, and the latter's enthusiastic helper in the suppression of the Catilinarians as well as a ruthless bodyguard. Caesar tried however to give the Catilinarians a fair trial and put his own life in danger in the process. This is the background of the *Bona-Dea*-scandal.

Caesar had already been named *pontifex maximus* and had just been elected *praetor,* the highest judicial official, so he was staying in the city.[402] Thus, in that year the *Bona Dea* festival took place in Caesar's home. Men were excluded from the secret celebrations of this feminine divinity. Clodius was under the nasty suspicion of violating the religious celebration because of Caesar's wife Pompeia. With the help of Pompeia's maids he supposedly dressed as a woman and slipped into the house in order to reach her chambers, but became lost in the house and was discovered.[403] Whether because of Clodius' great popularity, or because he himself was seen as a great seducer of respected women,[404] Caesar did not accuse Clodius. Nevertheless, he had his wife served with divorce papers.

Caesar's political opponents sensed the possibility of ridding themselves of both of them, and so took Clodius to trial for committing a sacrilege. Because of his behavior the priests declared the holy ceremonies invalid, and the most powerful men in the Senate all stepped forward as witnesses against Clodius. They accused him among other evil deeds, of adultery with his own sister, and the husband[406] who was cheated on also testified against him. Even his political friend Cicero testified against him.[407] But Caesar, who was heard as head of the household, spoke in his defence and claimed he had heard nothing of the sort. Asked why he had divorced his wife in spite of hearing nothing, Caesar replied: 'Because members of my household ought not only be free of guilt, but also free of the suspicion of guilt'.[408] Clodius was acquitted: whether out of fear of the people, who were apparently on the side of the sacrilegious Clodius, because of their hatred of the hypocritical self-righteous, or because they were bribed as Cicero claimed, most of the senators withheld their vote by handing in 'voting stones' with unclear letters. Thus Caesar's wife who had implicitly been accused of adultery and sacrilege was also acquitted of any wrong doing.[409]

From that point on, Clodius was considered a political friend of Caesar who made him a people's tribune: in order to make this possible Clodius became a plebeian and changed his patrician name from *Claudius* to *Clodius*. Then he turned against Cicero, accused him of having the Catilinarians executed without due process and actually managed to force him out of the city.

As expected we find the kernel of Clodius's story again as the most famous healing of a lame person, who, as a *one-sided paralytic,* is called a *gout sufferer* in old translations.[410] This time too, we take the more differentiated reading of Mark [and place in brackets the most important variations of the other Gospel writers]:

> '...and it was noised that he was in the house. And straightway many were gathered together, [which were come out of every town (Luke)] insomuch that there was no room to receive them, no, not so much as about the door: and he preached the word unto them. And they [men (Luke)] come unto him, bringing one sick of the palsy, which was borne of four [...brought in a bed a man which was taken with a palsy (Luke) / ...lying on a bed (Matthew)]. And when they could not come nigh unto him for the press, they uncovered the roof where he was: and when they had broken it up, they let down the bed wherein the sick of the palsy lay. When Jesus saw their faith, he said unto the sick of the palsy, Son, thy sins be forgiven thee. But there were certain of the scribes sitting there, and reasoning in their hearts, Why doth this man thus speak blasphemies? Who can forgive sins but God only? And immediately when Jesus perceived in his spirit that they so reasoned within themselves, he said unto them, Why reason ye these things in your hearts? Whether is it easier to say to the sick of the palsy, Thy sins be forgiven thee; or to say, Arise, and take up thy bed, and walk? But that ye may know that the Son of man hath power on earth to forgive sins, (he saith to the sick of the palsy,) I say unto thee, Arise, and take up thy bed, and go thy way into thine house. And immediately he arose, took up the bed, and went forth before them all; insomuch that they were all amazed, and glorified God, saying, We never saw it on this fashion.'[411]

Here again it is the same staging with the same requisites:

It was noised that 'he' was in the house: as the rumour went round about Clodius, so it went round about 'he'—Jesus or the sick of the palsy? There are men who are not in the room, not even outside in front of the door: just as at the *Bona Dea* festival from which men were excluded. The festival, the nightly hustle and bustle, is missing. But Luke says that they came 'out of every town'[412]—*kômê*. And the word *kômos*[413] means festivity, cheerful procession, carousing, night music, noisy, drunk people: as at the *Bona Dea* festival.

Then we have Jesus who preached the word to them just as Caesar had to testify as a witness.[414] The paralytic, 'borne of four, carried by four' to enter the house as Clodius used the maids to gain entrance. 'By four': *hypo tessarôn*—*hypo therapontôn* means 'by the servants'.[415] In the one story a lame person on a bed was brought in by four others and in the other the maids wanted to bring a person to bed: Clodius to the bed of Caesar's wife. But where is the wife? Instead of bringing the lame person to the bed of the woman they rip off the roof: 'of his wife' *uxoris suae*[416]—*exoryxantes* 'ripping open'.[417]

Then Jesus recognizes their belief and forgives the paralytic his sins just as Caesar did not punish the sacrilege at the holy ceremony[418] because he chose to believe the accused, Clodius, his wife and the maids.

The scribes sit and secretly think that Jesus has no right to forgive sins, just as some accused Clodius: *graphê* in Greek means both script and accusation[419] and thus accusers could be seen as scribes. Just as Caesar, as *pontifex maximus,* was reproached for allowing a misdeed to go unpunished, Jesus was reproached for forgiving sins and making himself similar to God.

Both stories have a happy ending: just as Clodius was acquitted of adultery and sacrilege and set free with the help of Caesar, so the paralytic was forgiven his sins and able to take up his bed and return home, to the great horror of his accusers and the amazement of all, because the unbelievable had taken place in religious things.

Note the following: instead of 'go thy way', *peripatei,* some manuscripts have *hypage,* which not only means 'lead away,' 'take away', 'break away' (in a saving sense) it also means 'accuse' and finally also 'to entice (away), to win for oneself'. It seems that in this polysemy we can also find the transition of Clodius to the man who saved him. The words of Jesus to the lame man also point to this transition: 'Son' and the command: 'Arise',—*égeire*—actually, 'wake up, move'.

Here again, we find our most significant 'paralytic', *Clodius,* again in his context. It is obvious, however, that this Clodius anecdote is much longer and that the story of the healing of the lame is insufficient in comparison. Sin is only spoken of in general terms and there is no specific reference to sacrilege. There is no crossing over of Clodius to Caesar's side, no change of Clodius' name nor the ousting of Cicero from the city. Most importantly, the accusation of the woman's adultery, the corrupt judges, the voting stones with illegible letters, the writing of divorcement, etc. are all missing from the story.

However, we need only glance at the Gospel of Mark, before and after the passage of the paralytic, to find the rest of the story: the opening is found in the healing of a leper, the closing in the calling of Levi. It is striking that these three parts have been preserved as a coherent story in Mark. Only the aspect concerning the woman, Jesus and the adulteress, is missing. Excluded in Mark, it became stranded in John—Mark and Matthew retain the writing of divorcement.

The healing of the leper[420] appearing in Mark is, sensibly enough, located directly before the healing of our paralytic, and in its structure it seems to be a summary of the following story and could be seen as a doublet, if a leper had not replaced the paralytic here:

> 'And there came a leper to him, beseeching him, and kneeling down to him, and saying unto him, If thou wilt, thou canst make me clean. And Jesus, moved with compassion [some manuscripts: And he was incensed], put forth his hand, and touched him, and saith unto him, I will; be thou clean. And as soon as he had spoken, immediately the leprosy departed from him, and he was cleansed. And he straitly charged him, and forthwith sent him away; And saith unto him, See thou say nothing to any man: but go thy way, shew thyself to the priest, and offer for thy cleansing those things which Moses commanded, for a testimony unto them. But he went out, and began to publish it much, and to blaze abroad the matter, insomuch that Jesus could no more openly enter into the city, but was without in desert places: and they came to him from every quarter.'

Just as the paralytic is forgiven his sins so here the leper is cleansed. Jesus is moved with compassion or is incensed, without reason, but Caesar has reason to feel resentful towards Clodius. Jesus stretches out his hand and cleanses the leper just as Caesar stretches out his protective hand over Clodius. Noticeable is that Jesus straitly charges the leper, forthwith sends him away and says to him: 'See thou say nothing to any man.' Caesar did the same: he pushed his wife away and Clodius had to deny everything in order to be cleansed. The fact that the paralytic shows himself to the priest also has its pendant: Clodius first justified himself before the *pontifex maximus*⁴²¹ Caesar and then Caesar has to appear as a witness himself.

The interesting point here is that for the priest the cleansing is about what Moses has commanded: *Môsês. Mos:* the 'customs', the 'mores', were what the *pontifex maximus* had to keep watch over.⁴²²

Instead of the story remaining secret, it was made known, here as well as there. Whereby the end of the story is anticipated: he could no more openly enter into the city, but was without in desert places; and they came to him from every quarter. That is exactly what Cicero experienced: Clodius' pushy endeavours forces him into exile, and it did not help that his political friends accompany him a great part of the way.⁴²³

Looking closer, this passage of the Gospel may also have its parallel in Caesar's proconsulship in Gaul, which Clodius helped him achieve and is mentioned by Appianus in the same breath as the expulsion of Cicero.⁴²⁴

Now that we know we are definitely dealing with Clodius, we should look at the names more closely, because here Clodius is not the paralytic but the leper, *lepros*. Clodius was *pollutarum caeremoniarum reus,* 'accused of polluting ceremonies', in a *quaestio de pollutis sacris,* a trial about 'polluted worship.' In the sense of sacrilege. But the sound of *pollutor,* or *pollutarum reus* is closer to *lepros,* 'leper' than *asebês,* 'sacrilegious person', just as *polluta sacra* to *lepra,* the 'leper', especially since this disease is the quintessential 'pollution' in the eyes of the people, while disease in general is seen as God's punishment for personal sin.⁴²⁵

Thus we would have found our sinner again, this time as a leper.

The calling of Levi in Mark immediately follows the healing of the paralytic and corresponds structurally to Clodius joining Caesar after his acquittal. The only difference: he has yet again another name and he has changed his profession: Levi, son of Alphaeus.

'And as he passed by, he saw Levi [Jacob (variant of some manuscripts of the Mark Gospel)] the son of Alphaeus [a publican, named Levi (Luke); a man, named Matthew (Matthew)] sitting at the receipt of custom, and said to him, Follow me. And he arose and followed him. And it came to pass, that, as Jesus sat at meat in his house, many publicans and sinners sat also together with Jesus and his disciples: for there were many, and they followed him. And when the scribes and Pharisees saw him eat with publicans and sinners, they said unto his disciples, How is it that he eateth and drinketh with publicans and sinners? When Jesus heard it, he saith unto them, They that are whole have no need of the physician, but they that are sick: I came not to call the righteous, but sinners.'⁴²⁶

Paragôn, 'as he passed by' as it is normally translated, could also mean 'brought into (court) as witness' and 'enticed, tempted'. That is what Caesar's leniency towards Clodius did. This corresponds to the next words also: 'Follow me!' Which he did, here the publican, i.e. tax collector Levi, there Clodius. And already he is in the splendid company of bon vivants, here the publicans and sinners, who surround Jesus, there the tax farmers, whom Caesar had just exempted from a third of their obligations, and from whom he then borrowed money to finance public shows that were far more lavish in décor and costumes and dazzling gifts than had ever been known before. In the eyes of the outraged senators this represented great sin, because tax-farmers normally did not belong to their class but to the equestrian order.[427] Well, tax-farmer and publican are the same in Latin: *publicanus*.

Here we get a poke in the eye concerning the name. As we know, the full name given to Clodius is *Publius Clodius Pulcher*. In the Gospel his pendant is the 'publican Levi, son of Alphaeus'—*telônês Leui (h)os tou Alphaiou*. If we write the full name of Clodius in capital letters without spaces in the usual manner of the time:

PVBLIVSCLODIVSPVLCHER

It is obvious that if the name is separated incorrectly –

PVBLIVSC LODI VS PVLCHER

—it gets a completely different meaning.

PVBLIVSC can easily be read as *PVBLICVS* and understood as *PVBLICANVS*, 'publican/tax collector'. *LODI* leads to 'Levi'. *VS* is a popular form of the Greek 'son'[428] and resembles *(h)os*, 'the/that (masculine)'. *PVLCHER* sounds as if it were derived from *puls*, 'porridge'[429] in Greek *alphi*.[430] Thus we would have for *VS PVLCHER (h)os tou Alphaiou*, 'that (= the son) of the porridge maker', or 'son of Alphaeus'.

We have seen that in Appianus the name *Clodius* is followed by *Gallia—Cisalpina* and *Ulterior*—of which Caesar became proconsul with the help of Clodius: *Galatia (h)ê entos Alpeôn kai (h)yper Alpeis*, 'Gaul on this side and the other side of the Alps.' Did the *Alps* become *Alphaeus*, did *Cisalpina* become *(h)os (tou) Alphaiou*, 'that of Alphaeus', i.e. 'son of Alphaeus'? Did Mark find his inspiration for the translation of *Pulcher* as 'son of Alphaeus' in the *Alps*?

Altogether we can see that:

Publius Clodius Pulcher > 'publican Levi, son of Alphaeus'.

The variant *Iakôbos*, 'Jacob', as seen in some manuscripts is revealed to be a hebraized version of *Clodius* with the usual Greek article:

(h)o Klodios > Iakôbos

—here the proper name of the 'called one' would be maintained, whereas the variant 'Matthew' (Greek: *Matthaios*) stresses the evil deed: *mataios*—'the sacrilegious one'.

In between we note that tracing the Gospel back to the corresponding Caesar source can explain why the Gospel writers show such variance in what names they use for one and the same person—here Levi, another time Jacob, then Matthew[431]—for which neither the old exegetes nor the modern textual critics have a plausible explanation.

The pendant for the adulterous wife of Caesar is the *pericope of the adulteress;* this pericope is not found in the synoptic Gospels, but exclusively in John.

It may appear improper for us to use this pericope, but it is well known that it only landed in John because it was deleted elsewhere: Where exactly, the textual critics do not know. We can only say that we are lucky to have it at all, for again and again, attempts have been made to remove this 'foreign body' from John, ultimately for so-called purely formal reasons, because it does not fit the style of this particular Evangelist. Augustine delivers the real reason: the leniency Jesus demonstrates towards the adulteress might be misunderstood![432] Even in the bible text used today, it is only referred to in parentheses or with a preceding question mark, meaning it is mentioned with reservation:

> '? And the scribes and Pharisees brought unto him a woman taken in adultery; and when they had set her in the midst, They say unto him, Master, this woman was taken in adultery, in the very act. Now Moses in the law commanded us, that such should be stoned: but what sayest thou? This they said, tempting him, that they might have to accuse him. But Jesus stooped down, and with his finger wrote on the ground, as though he heard them not. So when they continued asking him, he lifted up himself, and said unto them, He that is without sin among you, let him first cast a stone at her. And again he stooped down, and wrote on the ground. And they which heard it, being convicted by their own conscience, went out one by one, beginning at the eldest, even unto the last: and Jesus was left alone, and the woman standing in the midst. When Jesus had lifted up himself, and saw none but the woman, he said unto her, Woman, where are those thine accusers? hath no man condemned thee? She said, No man, Lord. And Jesus said unto her, Neither do I condemn thee: go, and sin no more.'[433]

Here we have the persons and requisites from the Clodius anecdote that were not used yet:

The 'scribes'—whom we already know are the 'accusers' (see above)—and the 'Pharisees'—who represent the 'patricians' in Caesar's version, because his opponents were in their majority *optimates*, 'high society': *pharisaioi / patricii*, PATRICII / ΦAPICAIOI.

The adulteress—the fact that she is not the unfaithful wife of Jesus is of no importance, because Jesus as a cuckold would have been more than the church fathers could handle when you consider that they considered his leniency towards the adulteress a thorn in their collective eye.

Caught in flagrante—both of them.

The trial—with both of them: here the woman is placed 'in the midst'.

The threatened sentence—here stoning, there being hurled from the Tarpeian Rock.

The law, which must be obeyed and which is placed in question, by Jesus and by Caesar—here the law of 'Moses', there the *mos*, the *mores*.

The questioning of Jesus as well as Caesar as competent people and as witnesses—but in both cases only for 'tempting him, that they might have to accuse him.'

For the woman the liberating, biarticulate pronouncement—here 'He that is without sin among you, let him first cast a stone at her', there 'Because members of my household ought not only be free of guilt, but also free of the suspicion of guilt'.

The stones that kill—here the stoning stones, there the voting stones.[434]

The unreadable signs—here when Jesus stoops down and writes with his finger on the earth, there the senators, who also write 'on the earth' because the voting stones on which they made their illegible signs were made of clay. What only seems to be a difference: here the illegible signs are written by '...the one stooping down with his finger' there they are written by the 'sentencing judges': 'stooping down with the finger', *katô kypsas tôi daktylôi—katapsêphisamenoi tôn dikastôn* means 'the sentencing judges'.[436]

None of the accusers are without sin—here the transgressions are unspecified, there the supposed sins of adulterous and bribed senators.

The vote, in the usual sequence—here 'beginning at the eldest', while there, as usual in Rome, the senators vote according to rank.

The acquittal and the refusal to convict—here Jesus's as there Caesar's.

Finally the sending away of the woman—here 'go', there 'repudiation'.

The writing of divorcement is missing here, too. Certainly it is so because otherwise, the woman sent away would then have been revealed as being the wife of Jesus. But since it was a sensitive matter to add words to, or subtract words from the Scripture, we have to expect that the writing of divorcement is to be found somewhere else, for Caesar did divorce Pompeia.[437]

The problematic issue of divorce is found in all of the synoptic Gospels, the writing of divorcement is found in Mark as well as twice in Matthew. In both cases—in opposition to Moses—it is stressed that divorce is admissible only in cases of adultery:

> 'They say unto him, Why did Moses then command to give a writing of divorcement, and to put her away? He saith unto them, Moses because of the hardness of your hearts suffered you to put away your wives: but from the beginning it was not so. And I say unto you, Whosoever shall put away his wife, except it be for fornication, and shall marry another, committeth adultery.'[438]

This corresponds precisely to the case of Caesar, who felt devotedly attached to his previous wife Cornelia and later Calpurnia.[439] While the 'man of principle', Lucullus, accused the woman he divorced of incest with her own brother Clodius; While Mr. Clean, Cicero, wanted to divorce his wife in order to marry the other sister of Clodius, whom people called 'quarter whore' (cheap whore), and whose brother he wanted to dispose of because of the family's reputation; while the vice hunter, Cato, ceded his young wife to a rich old man and then remarried her when she had become a well-to-do widow,[440] there on the other hand was the supposedly immoral Caesar, who only divorced the clumsy Pompeia. He declined to marry rich Cossutia in his youth. He was true to Cornelia in spite of Sulla, whose treacherous assassins followed him. The immoral proved to be more moral than the moral ones—Jesus more Moses than 'Moses', Caesar teaching mores to the moralizers.

Thus we find almost all of the requisites from the Clodius anecdote in the Gospels, spread out in different pericopes, but at least in Mark they form a whole. Only the pericope of the adulteress is separated and has stranded with John. However it remains in another place in some manuscripts: at the end of Luke 21, which begins with *the widow who contributes her mite.*

From Mark, who also used this pericope, we learn that the mite of the widow was a *quadrans,* a Roman 'quarter'. *Quadrantaria,* 'quarter whore' (cheap whore), was the name given to Clodia, Clodius' sister. Her relationship to Cicero—who wanted to marry her, but out of fear of his wife Terentia he spoke out against Clodius—would have been the undoing of her brother if Caesar had not taken him under his wing.

At the end of the Clodius anecdote we want to see how the story of the *quadrantaria* Clodia relates to the one of the poor widow with the mite.

Clodius' sister Clodia was married to Metellus Celer, who died shortly after the Bona Dea trial (59) and even during his lifetime did not stand in the way of Clodia's love affairs. Apart from Cicero, who later paid her back with burning hate and helped to establish her reputation as the most immoral lady in Rome, the merry widow maintained relationships with many men, among others with Caelius Rufus, whom she later accused and who was then defended by Cicero. She became famous, however, as the lover of Catullus, who sang her praises as Lesbia. Plutarchus tells us how she received her nickname:

> 'The latter [Clodia] was called *Quadrantaria,* because one of her lovers had deceived her with a purse of small copper money instead of silver, the smallest copper coin being called a *quadrans* [a quarter of an *as*]. Upon this sister's account, in particular, Clodius's character was attacked.'[441]

Let us compare this quadrans of Clodia with the mite of the widow. This is a word for word translation of the Greek [and in brackets are the word variations as found in most bible translations]:

> 'And he sat down opposite the treasury [collection plate], and watched the multitude putting copper coins [money] into the treasury [collection plate]. Many rich people put in large sums. And a poor widow came, and put in two small copper coins [mite], which make a quadrans [penny, tuppence]. And he called his disciples to him and said to them: Truly I say to you, this poor widow has put in more than all those who are contributing to the treasury [collection plate]. For they all contributed out of their abundance; but she out of her poverty has put in everything she had, her whole living.'[442]

In both cases we deal with small copper coins instead of a great deal of money which the rich have; in both the small copper coin is called quadrans—observe how the Gospel writer hangs on this quadrans although half quadrants were apparently also in circulation at that time: *lepta dyo,* 'halfpenny two' (= 'halfquadrans two'). The difference is in the fact that the *quadrantaria* corresponds to the 'poor widow'. However, it is theoretically not impossible that the words 'poor widow' might have been in the Latin example of Plutarchus, since this reflected Caesar's opinion—compare the expression 'the poor woman' which Caesar used to refer to the 'working and money-making' widow of Cato (see above, note 440). Anyway, it is striking that the second part of 'halfquadrans two'—*lepta dyo*—graphically almost completely resembles that of *Clodia (dyo/dia)*, while the first parts both contain an 'l' (if the text had normally said, without inversion, 'two halfquadrans'—*dyo lepta*—this would not have been the case).

Thus we have finished with our 'paralytics'. To check the checks, or so to say, casting out the nines, we want to see what happened to that other 'blind man', Caesar's unfortunate opponent about whom we wrote that because of his surname *Metellus*, he was a candidate to be seen as a 'mutilated one' (as if *Metellus* = *mutilus*).

Metellus

Metellus was the Pompeian tribune who, shortly after the civil war broke out, tried to stop Caesar from using the public treasury which was kept in the temple of Saturn for the maintenance of his soldiers. It is a famous anecdote exploited as propaganda by Caesar's opponents in order to accuse him of acting illegally.

We must therefore expect to find a parallel in the Gospels where Jesus is blamed for breaking the law by taking something out of the temple for his disciples or taking something from the temple with their help and that a mutilated person intervenes who is properly healed. Since this happened to Caesar at the beginning of the civil war, we must search in the first part of the Gospels.

And lo and behold! Once again we immediately find what we are looking for:[443] The disciples are plucking grain on the Sabbath, David is there who in his need takes the shewbread for himself and his people out of the temple, there is a man with a withered hand who on the Sabbath steps into the middle and is healed. Apparently the Gospel writer not only took our *Metellus* for a *mutilus*, but also confused Saturn with *sata, satorum*—seed, grain—on the one hand and with *Sabbat* on the other, the latter probably because of *Saturni dies—Saturday*.

If we go into detail here, the parallels become so precise that we gain insight into the methods of the Gospel writers. Think of the Caesar anecdote first.

When they heard that Caesar had crossed the Rubicon, the Pompeians and the followers of the Senate party left Rome in such a hurry that they could not take the public treasury and votive offerings with them.[444] After Corfinium was taken and Pompeius had also left Italy, Caesar came to Rome where the citizens, full of joy, replaced their mourning clothes with festive clothes of peace which up till then they were not permitted to wear.[445] For Caesar had confiscated the public treasury remaining in the temple of Saturn instead of taking money from the citizens remaining in Rome as they had feared, and as the Senate party had loudly trumpeted would happen. Since the key could not be found—the consuls had taken it with them—he called for locksmiths and had the bolt torn off and the doors forced open. At that moment the tribune of the people, Metellus, stepped in and wanted to use his right to intercede as tribune and the power of the law to prevent Caesar from taking the money, in particular, the temple treasure. Except in the case of another invasion by the Gauls, nobody was allowed to touch this treasure, which had been stored in the *sanctius aerarium* since the time of Brennus. Caesar commented that he had completely conquered the Gauls and thus freed the city of that curse. He was the commander-in-chief, and not only was the treasure in the temple of Saturn in his power, but so also was Metellus and any other opponents, he could do with them as he desired. As Metellus, supported with some public approval, tried to step in, Caesar became so angry that he threatened Metellus with death and added: 'You know, boy, that it is more difficult for me to say this than to carry it out'. The threat worked and the intimidated Metellus left, and Caesar was given everything he needed for the war, quickly and without difficulty. Then he went to fight Petreius and Afranius in Spain…[446]

Let us now turn to the parallel passage in the Gospel:

'And the disciples of John and of the Pharisees used to fast: and they come and say unto him, Why do the disciples of John and of the Pharisees fast, but thy disciples fast not? And Jesus said unto them, Can the children of the bridechamber fast, while the bridegroom is with them? as long as they have the bridegroom with them, they cannot fast. But the days will come, when the bridegroom shall be taken away from them, and then shall they fast in those days. No man also seweth a piece of new cloth on an old garment: else the new piece that filled it up taketh away from the old, and the rent is made worse. And no man putteth new wine into old bottles: else the new wine doth burst the bottles, and the wine is spilled, and the bottles will be marred: but new wine must be put into new bottles.

And it came to pass, that he went through the corn fields on the sabbath day; and his disciples began, as they went, to pluck the ears of corn. And the Pharisees said unto him, Behold, why do they on the sabbath day that which is not lawful?

And he said unto them, Have ye never read what David did, when he had need, and was an hungred, he, and they that were with him? How he went into the house of God in the days of Abiathar the high priest, and did eat the shewbread, which is not lawful to eat but for the priests, and gave also to them which were with him? And he said unto them, The sabbath was made for man, and not man for the sabbath: Therefore the Son of man is Lord also of the sabbath.

And he entered again into the synagogue; and there was a man there which had a withered hand. And they watched him, whether he would heal him on the sabbath day; that they might accuse him. And he saith unto the man which had the withered hand, Stand forth. And he saith unto them, Is it lawful to do good on the sabbath days, or to do evil? to save life, or to kill? But they held their peace. And when he had looked round about on them with anger, being grieved for the hardness of their hearts, he saith unto the man, Stretch forth thine hand. And he stretched it out: and his hand was restored whole as the other.

And the Pharisees went forth, and straightway took counsel with the Herodians against him, how they might destroy him.'[447]

We now see how the Gospel writer has creatively reorganized all requisites surrounding the main misunderstanding—Saturn. He thus even varies his misunderstanding.

Once *Saturn* is confused with *sata*, which happens easily with the genitive plural *satorum*—and indeed we find the Greek correspondent in the genitive plural: *dia tôn sporimôn*, 'through the seed-fields', which is translated in English 'through the corn fields'—the fantasy of the Gospel writer allows the temple of Saturn its antique function, not to keep the aerarium, the 'public treasury', but to be the holy *horreum,* the last 'silo', the sacrosanct reserve for emergencies. From there on, the disciples of John and the Pharisees (observe how precisely he differentiates between the Pompeians and the other followers of the Senate party), who do not touch these seeds (for they had not been able to take the public treasury with them), are people who fast; the disciples of Jesus, on the other hand, do not fast and pluck the ears of corn (and indeed the soldiers of Caesar took the public treasury). Once placed in this fasting and gorging logic, that other similarly appearing word—*satis,* 'satiated'—did not escape the sharp eyes of the Gospel writer. He begins to circle about the impression of a wedding dinner, confirmed by the never before worn festive clothes, whereby Caesar-Jesus must now function as a bridegroom as long as he is there: for he soon had to go to war again in Spain. Now the Gospel writer had a problem with the old clothes that people had taken off: where should they go? The idea occurred to him to combine this problem with his other problems, because the torn off bolt and the doors broken open were embarrassing to him. He darned this story together with the old garment which tears with the new piece and about a rent that becomes worse. And because not only the bolt but also the doors were there, he varied the story with new wine which bursts the old bottles—after all, man does not celebrate with bread alone.

That is where he lost the thread of the story. When he tries to return to his story he has to start a new one: The soldiers sent into the temple of Saturn are suddenly disciples who go through a seed-field on the Sabbath; they are no longer at the wedding of the bridegroom, but are plucking the ears of corn. You can imagine that they also eat it—and Matthew later says so—but Mark has Jesus talk about David instead, how he went into the house of God during the time of the high priest and not only ate the bread which no one but the priests are allowed to eat but shared with those who were with him. With this Mark actually suggests that Jesus did the same as David, but at the same time he veiled it brilliantly because Jesus only justified the behavior of his disciples: they had plucked some grain, but had not eaten it. That his Lord was a war lord did not need to be said: Lord was enough. Lord, not of the temple treasure, but of the Sabbath: *Saturn, saturni dies, Saturday, sabbat*. And just as the law forbid taking the holy moneys, it was also forbidden to pluck the ears of corn on the holy day. He also elegantly hid *Divus* (Iulius) behind *David*, *chrêmata*, 'the moneys' behind *chreia*, 'the want', the time of 'Brennus' behind that of 'Abiathar' and the *pontifex maximus* behind the 'high priest'. Where is the problem?

Well, the problem is finding the thread again. From the banquet to the cornfield with a detour through the temple. And now? We have to tell the story of attempted intercession by Metellus. Where do we go when we do not know where to go? Obviously into the synagogue. *Synagogue* simply means 'meeting', 'assembly' and there was indeed a crowd of people who met at the temple to see what became of the treasury. There we find our man whom the Lord has 'in his hands' just as he has the *aerarium*, the state funds. And since *Metellus* sounds like *mutilus*, which in Latin means 'mutilated', and because there is also this 'torn open' door of the *aerarium* we prefer to call his hand *exêirêmenê*, 'torn off'. That can be misunderstood in Greek as *exêramenê*,[448] 'dried up', 'withered'—as if it came from *xêron*, 'dry' instead of *airô*, 'tear'— and since Latin *aridum*, 'dry' is similar to *aerarium* we interpret Metellus as: 'man with the withered hand'. Healing a man with a withered hand is much more believable than healing one who had his hand torn off. Of course, nothing is impossible for the Lord, but it is always good to be careful with credibility. And what are we going to do about the intercession? Intercession, what does that mean? To interpose! So let him step in the middle. The lord says so to him: Stand forth! That emphasizes who has something to say here. And the death threat? That is a touchy one: Jesus as murderer in the temple! Let us do it like this: He only said it and did not do it—although the second would have been easier for him. Besides, the temple is that of Saturn: Which has already become the Sabbath. So let him say: 'Is it lawful to do good on the sabbath days, or to do evil? to save life, or to kill?' Then no one has anything negative to say and everyone remains silent—finally even Metellus. The justified anger, however, we leave in, and that he was grieved for the hardness of their hearts. But what happens to our man with the withered hand? He does not touch it and remains whole—he stretches out his hand and is healed. One last thing: The lord returns to war and kills even more. We phrase it differently: Why did he go to war? Because they wanted war. Ergo, we say: 'They held counsel about how to destroy him'. Counsel with whom? With Petreius and Afranius, the legates of Pompeius in Spain? No way: they can be confused with Petrus and Andreas. Instead let's say with Herodes, the murderer of John. You cannot go wrong with that idea.

Even after understanding how the metamorphosis of names can enable us to track down the source of many Gospel miracles, we still must remember that even if there were no real miracles in Caesar's story, there were miraculous signs. Namely, after the victory at Pharsalos and at his death. What happened to these miraculous signs?

Signs and Parables

More than in *miracula*, 'miracles', the Romans believed in *signa*, 'signs', *omina*, 'omens', *prodigia*, 'prodigies', and even maintained separate collegia for sign reading, especially *augures* and *haruspices*: 'bird- and sacrifice seers'. The first observed birds, how they flew and how they ate, the second studied the innards of sacrificed animals, their constitution, and understanding these things to be signs they drew conclusions about the near future and even made *praesagia,* presages. Antonius was proud to be an *augur* and had himself portrayed as such on coins. Octavianus trumped him by taking *augustus* as his last title. Because Caesar as *pontifex maximus* superintended all priestly collegia he knew the job. He did not take sign readers very seriously, least of all the *haruspices*. If the omens were bad he ignored them, even if they predicted his death, with the reasoning that the reader could have laid things out differently if he had wanted. Or, he even made fun of them with the dictum—if for example no heart was found in a sacrificial animal—'a heartless animal, well that is no wonder'. At the same time he tried to weaken their importance because he knew all too well the power of superstition with the people: if the axel of his triumphal wagon broke he continued on his knees and climbed the stairs of the Capitol on them; if he stumbled when arriving in Africa while falling he quick-wittedly opened his arms and said: 'Africa, I have tight hold of you'; and in war he coldly exploited any dejection in the enemy caused by bad omens. But there is not a hint anywhere that he himself was superstitious. He did not believe in life after death either. As an Epicurean he saw death as the end of everything, joy and suffering, as his speech about the Catilinarians shows. Is that the reason he became immortal? Only once did he himself use the word *credo*, 'I believe': but he means 'I think, I suppose'.[449]

The fact that he listed the miraculous signs that accompanied his victory over Pompeius at Pharsalos therefore has special meaning. He never makes mention of the word 'miracle' nor even just the word 'sign'. Strictly speaking there is no sign, none, that predicts his victory. He considers the first and greatest one the fact that simple news of his victory and arrival prevented the legate of Pompeius from plundering the treasure of Artemis of Ephesos; he thus saved the temple treasure once again. He then mentions that the statue of Victoria in the temple of Elis had turned around on the day of his victory; that battle cries, sounds of trumpets and timpani were heard in Antioch in Syria, Ptolomais and Pergamon; and that finally in the temple of Victoria in Tralles where a statue was dedicated to Caesar the people's attention was drawn to a palm that sprouted from between the tiles on the floor and grew to reach the ceiling.[450]

According to ancient understanding these were all signs, but not necessarily special ones; they only bore witness to the tense anticipation with which the cities of Asia awaited the outcome of the world civil war, how fast and with what effect the news of Caesar's victory spread over the world. The fact that he saved the treasures of the temple, that was his character and political way of acting; the fact that the statue of Victoria turned around was only a typical propaganda method used by party members; that the noise of the battle was heard all the way up to and including Syria, well that had to be since so much depended on the outcome, everyone listened eagerly. Only Caesar's victory palm was special, even though it was not an omen either.

Apparently, some found this gap to be painful, for it was filled by the prediction of Gaius Cornelius, a seer from Padua,[451] who prophesied Caesar's victory. On that very day he happened to observe birds and noticed how some birds not only gave information about the battle, but in a certain sense acted it out, and he said to the people standing around:

'The outcome is about to be decided' and as he saw new signs he shouted: 'Caesar, you are victorious!' They were all in consternation and refused to believe the seer's interpretation. The anecdote is found in Dio Cassius as well as in Plutarchus. In the latter only the signs of the palm and the birds are mentioned—and they directly follow each other.[452] Appianus and Suetonius do not mention any signs at all.

That is why we expect to find at most a palm in the Gospels, eventually one accompanied by birds.

Chronologically, Pharsalos follows the Metellus anecdote that we just studied. In between there is only the Spanish campaign, which is important militarily but hardly plays a role in the biographies of Caesar. There is no palm. Shortly after the healing of the man with the withered hand, however, there are two parables dealing with growing plants— the parable of the sower and the parable of the mustard seed—and even birds appear. In the parable of the mustard seed we recognize a number of the requisites we seek:

> 'And he said, Whereunto shall we liken the Kingdom of God? or with what comparison shall we compare it?
>
> It is like a grain of mustard seed, which, when it is sown in the earth, is less than all the seeds that be in the earth: But when it is sown, it groweth up, and becometh greater than all herbs, and shooteth out great branches; so that the fowls of the air may lodge under the shadow of it.'[453]

No palm sprout, but a mustard seed, a small plant that, here too, is first beheld on the ground and then as it grows—as with Caesar's palm; birds are also observed here, in the sky—like the bird show—as well as in the shade—like the palm under the temple roof. If we look at the Greek we see that palm and mustard do not look as different as they do in English: *phoinika* and *sinapi*, ΦΟΙΝΙΚΑ > CINAΠI, or pronounced: *finika* and *sinapi*.[454]

It is questionable, however, whether these are the same birds seen by the seer of Padua, because the entire context is missing. There is neither a battle of the birds, nor any ravens or crows. As we have come to know our Mark he might have easily made *Cornelius* a *cornix*, a 'crow'. Mark does not refer to his birds as *oiônoi*, 'foretelling birds' as Plutarchus does, nor simply as *ornithes* as Dio Cassius. Instead he chooses *peteina*, a word seldom used, which in former days had the form *ptêna* and in fact means 'winged fowls'. Did he choose the unusual word because *peteina* looks more like *phoinika*, 'palm'? Was he unhappy with *sinapi*, because it was not similar enough to *phoinika* and did he place *peteina* on its branches because it sounded more similar?[455]

We have the opportunity to investigate this. The palm sprout complex is not completely finished with the mustard seed. The essential element is missing: The palm sprang from between the tiles on the floor, where no plant can lay roots since there is no earth; it grew to the roof of the temple, where there is no light and where it actually should have withered; and no one sowed it or set it there, it planted itself and grew. That was the wonderful, the miraculous; that is how it showed itself to be a sign.

Conscientious Mark did not miss this and so he added the parable of the sower just before the parable of the mustard seed. He mobilized everything he knew about agriculture and conducted an idyllic, picturesque Sunday sermon for his audience which was apparently a community of farmers.

This was after Pharsalos. Caesar had won—Mark had already reported about his power over evil spirits—and everyone ran to him. He was pursuing Pompeius, who was fleeing to Egypt, and so arrived on the Ionic coast. Now the peoples of the islands and on the continent were to be on his side. As the signs recorded by Caesar indicate, he stopped in Ephesos, the capital of the Roman province of Asia where he received homage from Elis, Antioch, Ptolomais, Pergamon and Tralles. The situation found in Mark is similar:

> 'And he began again to teach by the sea side: and there was gathered unto him a great multitude, so that he entered into a ship, and sat in the sea; and the whole multitude was by the sea on the land.'[456]

Now Mark has a problem: It is not about his words, which Mark easily could repeat, it is also not about his deeds which he could turn into miracles. It is about signs which are being interpreted. He might use the correct Greek word, *sêmeia*, which Plutarchus also used. Mark used it himself in another place where Jesus is asked for signs from heaven (8:11). Whether it was because *parabolai* seemed closer to *prodigia* than *sêmeia*, or because the signs were less important to him than the lesson to be learned, Mark made them into parables:

> 'And he taught them many things by parables, and said unto them in his doctrine.'[457]

In truth it was Mark's own doctrine or a sermon from the last wandering preacher to pass by, but then again it is not completely untrue because it was exactly these signs that Caesar himself enumerated. Now Mark has to somehow find a way to mention the palm—instead he speaks of seeds:

> 'Hearken; Behold, there went out a sower to sow: And it came to pass, as he sowed, some fell by the way side, and the fowls of the air came and devoured it up. And some fell on stony ground, where it

had not much earth; and immediately it sprang up, because it had no depth of earth: But when the sun was up, it was scorched; and because it had no root, it withered away. And some fell among thorns, and the thorns grew up, and choked it, and it yielded no fruit. And other fell on good ground, and did yield fruit that sprang up and increased; and brought forth, some thirty, and some sixty, and some an hundred.'[458]

Here he has almost everything together: the rocky ground without deep soil—like the gaps in the tile floor; the impossibility of growing roots there and that the palm should have withered; that plants without light suffocate—whether under thorns or under the temple roof. And in spite of this they shot up as if on good land. Perhaps not one hundred percent, as on fertile land, but still sixty, or thirty percent. He is missing only one thing here: the palm that grew from the temple floor. Instead he has 'fowls of the air that devour the seeds fallen by the way side'. Again he obviously confused *phoinika*, 'palm' with *peteina*, 'fowls' and as a result mistook *epese*, 'fell' for *ephyse*, 'grew': as the palm sprouted, so something fell for the birds. Now Mark recalls that it was only about a sign:

'And he said unto them, He that hath ears to hear, let him hear.
And when he was alone, they that were about him with the twelve asked of him the parable. And he said unto them, Unto you it is given to know the mystery of the Kingdom of God: but unto them that are without, all these things are done in parables...'[459]

Thus he did not mention Caesar's victory, but at the same time he did, because thus began the Kingdom of God. With Caesar's victory the Kingdom, i.e. the Empire, belonged to him, and at the same time he was God of the Empire. Of all that can be said, one thing is for sure: with Pharsalos a new era was ushered in. The mints in the East, which had earlier dated coins after the era of Seleukos, and later after the era of Pompeius, now counted the years starting from Pharsalos.[460] God's Kingdom held no secrets for those who were in Pharsalos at the time. Those in the Empire 'that are without' only heard about it through the signs. Those who 'had eyes to see', such as the seer, they saw it, and those who could not see only had to listen. However, those who had neither eyes nor ears were members of the opposing party and nothing could help them. Thus Mark found it fitting to add a quotation from Isaiah to the Sunday sermon: that made the whole thing even more believable and stopped evil tongues which claimed to have heard the story differently:

'...that seeing they may see, and not perceive; and hearing they may hear, and not understand; lest at any time they should be converted, and their sins should be forgiven them.'[461]

After placing the signs and the warning Mark also has to explain them. For the signs were only important because they were seen as victory. Since there are no more signs, no wondrous palms and no ominous birds, but only a very ordinary sower, Mark's interpretation can no longer be an explanation of signs, but a simple parable. But to keep an ominous element in the story he makes a secret of it and has Jesus secretly give a banal explanation for a banal story (Mk. 4:13-20). This of course has the additional advantage that when someone accused him of not following tradition and adding new, unbelievable things to the story Mark could say: It was his secret teaching, that is why it has only now become known. That he ordered us to do so:

'And he said unto them, Is a candle brought to be put under a bushel, or under a bed? and not to be set on a candlestick? For there is nothing hid, which shall not be manifested; neither was any thing kept secret, but that it should come abroad.'[462]

By that the Gospel writer has protected himself against accusations of heresy: Marcion sends his compliments. But there was still something left: the palm, it sprouted by itself, without any seed. There the story halts. That has to be prevented, the last tracks must be covered up:

'And he said, So is the Kingdom of God, as if a man should cast seed into the ground; And should sleep, and rise night and day, and the seed should spring and grow up, he knoweth not how. For the earth bringeth forth fruit of herself; first the blade, then the ear, after that the full corn in the ear. But when the fruit is brought forth, immediately he putteth in the sickle, because the harvest is come.'[463]

Now Mark is completely freed from the palm, but he has pointed out something very important: that his victory brought about the Kingdom of God, meaning that veterans were given land, divided in a proper way. To some more was given and to others less, all according to how fertile the land was—still full of thorns and undergrowth, but fertile. And from this land sprang those who listened to him, the children of the children of the veterans. For them the true palm of victory was the piece of land that their fathers had received and they had inherited. They did not pluck dates, but reaped the corn with sickles. Incidentally, they now understood only a little Latin: meanwhile they spoke Greek, like the others in the east, mixed with Aramaic, the dialect of their area and of their mothers. So he spoke as they wanted to hear, of things they understood!

More or less in this way, our Mark, or his ancestor the proto-Mark, probably defended his creative, shoddy work against the superintendence of Rome. He certainly did not listen to any criticism that he had put together his own Jesus but firmly maintained that what he preached was *Divus Iulius,* just as before: the God of the veterans, the God of the forefathers of his Anatolian, Syrian, or Palestinian community. He merely spoke in ways that their descendants—who had not experienced civil wars, who did not know that the Kingdom of God on earth had been born in the labor of civil war and who only connected evil with it—could understand. In their conception, their son of God and God, had not led a civil war, but simply brought peace. He might have had to convince some hardened sinners and he was a bit intense sometimes, but that was all. What he did do was alleviate hunger, and give land to those without. And in doing so he healed the sick, and brought medical help for them. That was the Kingdom of God. And so it should remain.

* * *

Quod erat demonstrandum. Our question as to whether or not the Gospel is based on an original Caesar source has been answered positively by successfully verifying our suppositions. From now on it is no longer a question if this happened, but how.

We started from the prominent words of Caesar and tried to find them in the Gospels. We saw that they can be found there with subtle changes: *'Who is not on any side, is on my side'* was found as *'He that is not against us, is on our part'*; *'I am not King, I am Caesar'* as *'We have no king but Caesar'*; *'The best death is the sudden one'* is *'That thou doest (lead me to death) do quickly'*; *'Have I saved them, that they may ruin me?'* as *'He saved others; himself he cannot save'*. Only in two of the quotations do the subtle changes lead to distortion of the meaning: *'Alea iacta est(o)'* became *'casting: for they were (h)aleeis (fishers)'*; and *'veni vidi vici'* became *'I came, washed and saw'*. The last two quotations were embedded in miracles: *'Casting: for they were fishermen'* later attained in Luke the honorable status of the miraculous draught of fishes; *'I came, washed and saw'* says the healed blind man. Another quotation turned into a complaint about a miracle that failed to materialize: *'He saved others; himself he cannot save'*. But this transformation of words into miracles only happened when the words were spoken in a warlike context: *'Alea iacta est'* at the beginning of the war at the Rubicon; *'veni vidi vici'* announcing victory over Pharnakes; *'Oh, have I saved them that they may ruin me?'* as a dark threat of a posthumously revenging campaign. The main characteristic is: Miraculous victories become victorious miracles. In an analogous way successful sieges are healings of possessed, victories over *Caecilii* and *Claudii* are miraculous healings of blind and lame, the crossing of the stormy sea by the army is a walk on the lake.

We have hinted that this habit of referring to Caesar's victories as miracles began during his own lifetime. Plutarchus reported that the people regarded it as a miracle that he brought the statues of the demonized Marius from Hades into the city and Appianus tells us that Antonius in his funeral oration for Caesar described Caesar's victories as miracles. In this respect the Gospel writers did not do anything new, but only further decorated the legend Caesar was. The deeds of Caesar became the miracles of Jesus.

Just as the miracles developed out of victories, the parables came from the signs that denoted the victories. It would be easy to show how miracles and parables proliferated, how Matthew and Luke fought in the gap opened by Mark and packed and inserted entire cycles of miracles and series of parables. But that has already been done by traditional textual criticism, and here we only need mention it.

As far as language is concerned, we have observed that some parallels between Caesar and Jesus point to misunderstandings of the Caesar source (e.g. *obsessus*: 'possessed' instead of 'besieged'). Logically every besieged in the Caesar texts should correspond to a possessed in the Jesus story: we were able to see that this indeed was the case. Since it seemed that *Caesar* sometimes had been confused with *caecus*, 'blind', *Lepidus* with a 'stone jar', *dictator* with a 'schoolmaster' we investigated if also *Asinius Pollio,* in accordance with the meaning of his name, changed into an *'ass's colt',* and likewise diverse *Caecilii* and *Claudii* into 'blind' and 'lame'. Once again we saw that this was the case: we found the people we sought in the figures we expected. Even more: In the complicated Clodius-anecdote we saw how different articulations were divided among different pericopes which appear very much coherently in Mark. In each of these pericopes the *Clodius* we are looking for appears with another name: as 'the lame' sometimes also called 'gout sufferer', as 'leper', as 'publican Levi, son of Alphaeus', as 'Matthew' or 'Jacob'. With this, altogether, all the variants, surnames and meanings of Clodius are found, either as translation (though vulgarized) or according to sound or writing (though corrupted).

Finally we saw that the same thing happened with *Metellus* who was taken for a *mutilus*, 'mutilated'. Moreover, in the context of his story we were able to recognize which specific confusion led to the pivotal point—here *Saturn* with *seed*—which allowed the entire story to tip so that its reorganization became possible as well as necessary. The misinterpretation of the Latin termini was the condition and basis for the Greek evangelical editing. This was not original, but a new editing.

The number of misinterpretations, which seem to have taken place at the time the Gospel texts developed, may surprise. But they remain within the bounds of what folk etymology can bring about, and only insignificantly exceed that which took place when later Gospel texts were handed down—in the Greek handwritten copies as well as in translations into each of the other languages used in bible tradition beginning with Latin—which is easily seen by glancing at modern textual criticism.[464]

The only thing that is new is our tracing everything back to an original Latin source. However, the presence of Latin in the original Greek text, and especially the many Latinisms in Mark, have long hinted at Latin sources.[465] So far, the extent to which this has been studied is of hardly any consequence, although the hypothesis conforms to the tradition that the Gospel of Mark was written in Latin in Rome (see below).

The result we arrive at—that the Gospel of Mark looks like a rustic-naïve Greek retelling of a Latin vita of Divus Iulius—puts tradition in a new light. Since the misunderstood expressions in the Gospel of John were sometimes Greek—for instance *enikêsa*, 'I conquered', as *enipsa*, 'I washed'—his exemplar might already have been a Greek translation, unless he knew absolutely no Latin instead of only having a poor knowledge of it, like Mark. That might explain why there are so few miracles in John: the *obsessi*, *Caecilii*, *Claudii* or *Metelli* are simply not available to become 'possessed', 'blind', 'lame' or 'cripple'.

In spite of all the differences among the Gospel writers, we were able to see that the passages examined from the Caesar sources and the Gospels can be read parallel over some length. We also noticed that in places where Mark broke down the original coherent story into separate pieces, he nevertheless left the pericopes to a large extent in the original sequencing.

A Caesar-Jesus synoptical comparison is therefore conceivable.

This is what we will systematically dedicate ourselves to in the next chapter.

106. Inscription on the pedestal of a statue in Samos, 46 B.C.

This inscription concerns a dedication to Caesar's wife Calpurnia. According to it her statue once stood on the pedestal shown above. The inscription is important because here the full form of his title is used, *archiereus megistos* which later Emperors managed to enforce. On the pedestal of his own statues from this period the *pontifex maximus* Caesar was simply entitled *archiereus*. Contraction of this full form *archiereus megistos* might have led to *christos*—and we confirmed this idea in the previous chapter by a parallel discussion about the questions 'Who will be pontifex maximus?' and 'Who is the Christ?'.

Thus we have in front of us, on a statue of *Calpurnia*—our *Maria*—the first inscriptional witness for *Christos* (*XPICTOY*, genetive case), though still written in the full form *Archiereus megistos*. The words are recognizable in the third (and partially in the fourth) surviving lines. To help with the understanding we offer this transcription by A.E. Raubitschek (l.c.):

[Ὁ δῆμος Καλπουρνίαν Λευ]-
[κίου Καλπουρνίου Πίσωνος]
[Καισωνίου θυγατέρα, γυναῖ]-
κα δὲ Γαίου Ἰουλίου Καίσαρος,
τοῦ αὐτοκράτορος, τὸ τρίτον
ὑπάτου καὶ <u>ἀρΧιεΡέως μεγIC-
TOY</u>, διὰ τὴν ἐκ τοῦ ἀνδρὸς
αὐτῆς γενομένην περί
[τὴν πόλιν — — — — — —]

[The people (consecrate) Calpurnia, Daughter of Lucius Calpurnius Piso Caesonius, wi]fe of Gaius Iulius Caesar, Dictator, Consul for the third time and Pontifex maximus, because of what her husband did for [the city...].

V

SYNOPTIC COMPARISON

The Gospel according to Mark, considered to be the oldest Gospel, begins grosso modo with the baptism of Jesus on the Jordan and ends with his crucifixion and burial. According to our parallel setting, this would mean that the exemplar for Mark must begin with the crossing of the Rubicon and end with the murder and funeral of Caesar.

This corresponds to the schema of historians for whom the beginning of the civil war constitutes a turning point, while shortly after the Ides of March all reports, biographies as well as chronologies end.[466]

For purposes of determining this more exactly, the following can be noted: before the baptism of Jesus (Mk. 1:9) Mark tells of the work of John as a baptist (Mk. 1:4-5); that would mean that the model for Mark began with Pompeius' levying of troops. Mark's report ends—apart from the false ending 16:9-20[467]—with the rolled-away tombstone and the place of the resurrection. The parallel in Caesar's history is the building of an altar on the place he was cremated, which shortly thereafter was overthrown by the consuls.[468]

Chronologically, Mark's model goes from the 1st of January 49 to the Ides of March 44. Mutatis mutandis Mark contains the material from Book II of the *Civil War* by Appianus, from Book 41 to 44 of *Roman History* by Cassius Dio, and also 28 to 69 of Caesar by Plutarchus and from 30-36 as well as 78-89 of Suetonius' *Divus Iulius*. Caesar's *De bello civili* which also begins on January 1st 49, but ends shortly after the death of Pompeius, covers the beginning of Mark up to shortly after the death of the Baptist (Mk. 6:29).[469]

Both of the other synoptics, Luke and Matthew, contain, as is known, material parallel to Mark which they use as basis and guideline for their Gospels to a differing degree. In addition they use special material (Sondergut) partly in common—the so-called source Q—and partly each has sources of his own. The most noticeable of this special material is the childhood narrative, which is placed before the material borrowed from Mark. There are some added speeches by Jesus, and some also by John (the Baptist), and Matthew includes additional miracles.

John, who is independent of Mark and therefore also independent of Matthew and Luke, nevertheless also begins with the baptismal work of his namesake. To the end of his Gospel, however, he appends beginnings of a story of the resurrected one that is more elaborate than Mark's spurious ending and is probably its model. Furthermore he adds some speeches of his own.

Records of Caesar's childhood have not been preserved and it does not seem to have played an important role, because there are no references to it elsewhere either.[470] But there is plenty about Augustus' childhood in Cassius Dio, who recorded his short childhood history before the deeds of the new Caesar—Octavianus. This, held to be Caesar's own childhood history, would have been moved to the beginning of the Gospels of Matthew and Luke.

This is the same format used by Nicolaus of Damascus in his *Bios Kaisaros*, 'Life of Caesar', commonly translated as *Life of Augustus*.

Nicolaus records the childhood of the young Caesar—Octavianus—up to the murder of Caesar—the Great One—then digresses and writes about the conspiracy against Caesar and his assassination and continues again with the story of the new Caesar—Octavianus. This would explain the conspicious gap found in the story of Jesus' life between his childhood and his public appearance as a grown man.

Thus we would have to look for the model of Jesus' childhood narrative according to Luke and Matthew, as well as the expanded story of the resurrected one in John, within the biography of Augustus. Since this has not been preserved, we need to consult indirect sources.

The assumed Logia of Jesus, the lost collection of sayings, which according to the Two-Source Theory served as the additional source Q for the synoptics (besides the original Mark and oral tradition), could theoretically be sought in a collection of aphorisms of Caesar on the model of the *Dicta collectanea*, composed by himself. In practice one will look in *De bello civili* which contains speeches of Caesar.[471] One will look for them even more closely in the rich anecdotal material Suetonius has treated in chapters 37 to 77 of his Caesar biography mentioned above. It will also be interesting to know whether the speeches rhetorically polished by Cassius Dio possibly provided the material for the speeches found in Matthew and Luke.

The history of Caesar, which we assume to be the exemplar for the Gospels, must have had certain biographical features, because such can be found in Mark, as we have seen. In view of his beginning—1 January 49—we must assume that Mark used an annalistic source, such as Appianus and Plutarchus. For the other synoptics, the same annalistic sources are filled with factually ordered themes and rhetorically decorated speeches as in Cassius Dio. In addition we would expect there was a collection of anecdotes and sayings as in Suetonius, perhaps some things borrowed directly from Caesar's own works, and also from the Vita Augusti, especially from Octavianus' childhood narrative. In principle the same applies to John as to Mark, even if in John's text oral sayings seem to prevail while the ideology is more similar to that of Nicolaus Damascenus.

Mark's source, therefore, is to be found in the *Historiae* of Asinius Pollio. These are lost, but they served as the source for other historians because Asinius was, as we know, an eyewitness to the entire civil war. He was considered to be very critical even towards his Caesar, and being the founder of the first public Roman library—with a Greek and a Latin section—he was very well informed. Asinius Pollio's report is found most accurately in Appianus' *Bellum civile*,[472] and, among the biographers, in Plutarchus, who, however, also used other sources.

An additional source for Luke, Matthew and possibly also John, might be Livius, who was a friend of Augustus, a sympathizer of Pompeius and the Senate. He exhibited a literary bent, but also made translation mistakes, historical discrepancies, and had a lack of expertise in military and political matters. His work, like that of Asinius Pollio, is virtually lost (excerpts have been preserved), but he seems to have been used by Cassius Dio so that an indirect comparison is possible here too.

Then we have Suetonius, whose lack of bias and whose inquisitiveness serves to entertain. With his realism and his fondness for facts, anecdotes, gossip, and the all too human weaknesses, he practiced more hagiography than historiography. In terms of his sources he is an eclectic, but he is considered to be well informed and solid. Since he writes in Latin, he—together with Caesar's own history—is irreplaceable for us, for what Asinius Pollio and Livius write of Caesar is available only indirectly: only in the second hand, and only in Greek.

Velleius Paterculus is also interesting with his very brief Latin outline of Roman history. Other authors only come into question in regards to certain areas.

We can assume that Augustus—with his autobiography and dynastic view of his adoptive father Caesar's history, used as the basis for Nicolaus of Damascus,[473]—is the original source of John. Since Nicolaus Damascenus is preserved only fragmentarily and there is nothing written by Augustus available except for one fragment of his *Commentarii de vita sua*, then we have to rely on indirect comparisons and the sources named above.

All Gospel writers must go back to Asinius Pollio as the primary source, however, because as we have seen all four contain the anecdote of the 'untied' ass, or ass's colt, ergo the 'legate' Asinius Pollio was found in each of their exemplars. Asinius' being sent to Sicily is in Appianus, Plutarchus and Suetonius but not in Cassius Dio. He might already have been missing in Livius, who perhaps left him out to please Octavianus, because Asinius was regarded as an Antonian.

The special material that Matthew and Luke respectively add to Mark might be from Asinius Pollios' *Historiae* as well, but from an earlier time period than the limited, 49-44 BC of the Gospel stories. Thus anecdotes referring to events before 49 would find their places wherever suitable. A similar process could also apply to John.

For the mentioned reason that Asinius Pollio tended to favor Marcus Antonius over Octavianus, he certainly also fits ideologically as the exclusive source of Mark, for whom Peter has a positive role and the competitor in the succession—John, the favored disciple—does not even appear. Because according to our hypothesis Simon Peter corresponds to Marcus Antonius and John to the young Caesar, i.e. Octavianus Augustus.

Peter does well in Mark, and John does well in John.[474] This now opens for us the possibility of associating at least the first and last Gospels, Mark and John, with their respective patrons. The Gospel of *Mark:* according to *Marcus Antonius;* the Gospel of *John:* according to the *young* (Caesar)—Octavianus.[475]

This is confirmed in iconography in which the heraldic animal of Antonius, the lion[476] corresponds to that of Mark, and the eagle of Jupiter which signified Octavian[477] was used for John:

107. Eagle cameo of Augustus / 108. Aureus of Antonius

Pattern of Orientation

In order to offer a better orientation, we have attempted to present our working hypothesis as a stemma.

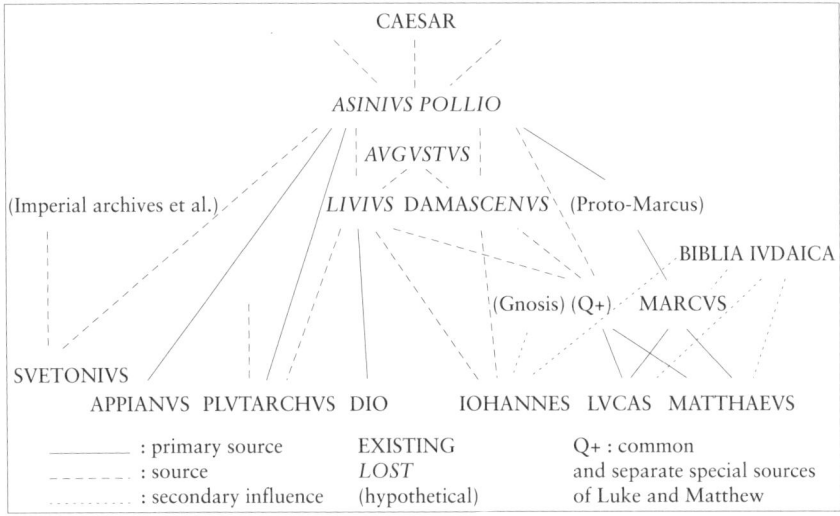

```
─────── : primary source      EXISTING        Q+ : common
- - - - - : source            LOST            and separate special sources
........ : secondary influence (hypothetical)  of Luke and Matthew
```

This must remain in schematic form for reasons of clarity. Other alternative hypotheses, different strengths and layers of influence, intersections, stories of tradition, etc. cannot be included in this visualization.

It is merely a working hypothesis that must be tested first and if necessary can be changed and stated more precisely.

Chronological Shifts

Within this provisionally created framework we can begin to compare Caesar to Jesus part by part. But which passages should be compared?

We cannot simply compare Mark chapter for chapter with Appianus or Plutarchus. Even if we assume that all three are based on Asinius Pollio's *Historiae* we no longer have it, and the same is true for the hypothetical Proto-Mark, who for his part might not have been Asinius Pollio but an in-between source. This was probably in the form of a summary, because Mark is shorter than Appianus' extensive history of the civil war. Mark has no historiographic interest so he leaves out a great deal, similar to Plutarchus' biography. On the other hand, as we have seen, Mark adds material he made up himself.

In addition we must assume that the Gospel writers did not adhere to a strict chronological order. This is a common practice found with ancient writers, who only report the beginning and end chronologically, while in the middle they store everything else, organized thematically, mostly serving as examples of virtues and vices. A good example being Suetonius, Caesar's biographer and even on occasion the otherwise very chronological Plutarchus.⁴⁷⁸ From time to time even historians who are principally annalistic do this, especially when braiding events of the past into the present to explain what is happening. Cassius Dio does this often, and Appianus does it sometimes too. This inevitably leads to chronological uncertainties.

Appianus, for example, reports Publius Clodius' sacrilege, (which took place in 62 BC) only when he writes in an excursus about Clodius' election to the office of people's tribune in the year 59 BC.⁴⁷⁹ Interestingly enough, we also meet Clodius, whom we could locate in Mark as a cripple, leper and tax collector, in a single insertion directly after Capharnaum/Corfinium and before the desecration of the Saturn temple/Sabbath in Rome. As if in Mark's exemplar the plotting tribune Clodius, who in the meantime had been murdered, were remembered when Caesar marches into Rome for the first time in 49. As if Clodius was shown as an example of what had happened to Caesar's political friends in Rome in the meantime, and what would have happened to Curio and Antonius if they had not found refuge in Caesar.

At any rate Bishop Papias of Hierapolis had already warned of Mark around the year 140:

> 'Mark, who was the interpreter of Peter, wrote the words and deeds of the Lord, which he remembered exactly though not in the correct order. Because he had neither heard nor accompanied the Lord, but, as said, later on Peter: This one created his teachings according to need, but did not give an orderly description of the speeches of the Lord. Thus it was not a mistake if Mark wrote things as he remembered them. However he paid attention to one thing: to omit nothing and at the same time not to lie.'⁴⁸⁰

Thus we can assume that the history of Caesar's civil war is completely maintained in the Gospels. But we must also reckon with some displacements in Mark and even more so in the other Gospel writers.

According to our informant, Mark knew the story only from hearsay, and wrote only what he remembered. This memory was, on the one hand his own, and on the other that of other people, whom he may have used as an aid to memory—a method usually applied by historians, and especially popular in reconstructing lost 'holy' texts.⁴⁸¹

If we take Papias at his word then we must assume there was a kind of grapevine effect. This would tally with the assumption of the quest of the historical Jesus which normally supposes the Gospel was preached long before it was written down. Thus it is hypothesized that the compilation of the synoptic Gospels processed general tradition as well as 'oral special material'. In the case of John, the extent to which he used written sources is disputed, and even if he used any at all.⁴⁸²

What sounds even more suspicious is that in Papias' time, when the fixation of scripture had not yet been completed, the general opinion was that Mark had not written the words and deeds of the Lord 'in correct sequence'. This leads to the fearful thought that someone might have felt obliged to restore the 'correct' order. Is the order found in our Mark the one Papias knew or is it one that was 'corrected', because of Papias' comment? This is not a pointless question, because around the time of Papias a dispute erupted between the Marcionites and the anti-Marcionites as to the correct canon.

Especially for us, another comment made by Papias proves thought-provoking: what Mark had heard was Peter's 'teaching according to need'. What this appears to say is that homilies were written down, or copies of notes for homilies. At that time a homily was written, just as they are today, according to a rigid pattern: first a text from the Holy Scripture was chosen to be read, and then a sermon followed that interpreted the text so it would have a practical use in the life of the believer. If Mark has such an origin, then Mark would be to the history of Caesar what the texts of the homily are to the Holy Scripture.

A homily could also contain other citations from the same writing or others fitting the theme. The passages one wanted to reuse were marked, not with a checkmark as is used today ✔, (which is really a 'v' and stands for the Latin *visum* 'seen'), but with a 'Chi-Rho', ☧, being Greek for *chrestos*, 'useful'. These useful parts desired for reuse were premarked in order to be later rearranged in another context. As we have seen, this *chrêstos* was in Hellenistic times pronounced just like *christos*, 'the anointed one', which is also a title of Jesus and for which the same symbol ☧ is used. This is probably a coincidence, but in connection with the comments of Papias it leads to the thought that Christian writings first developed as a 'chrestomathy': a collection of chosen excerpts from scripture for use in the oratorial instruction of preachers. Anyway, as can be proved, this is how the citations from the Jewish scripture became part of the Gospels. We have to see if that later external chrestomathy was preceded by an internal one.

In order to have an idea as to what kind of shifts took place in the Gospels, we can take a glance at the shifts that can be found from one Gospel writer to another.

We have already seen how the myrrh wanders at the crucifixion. With Mark it is mixed with wine, and given to Jesus to drink before the crucifixion.[483] With Luke and John it appears after his death as 'ointments' or mixed with 'aloe' to embalm the body.[484] So we see that the myrrh, which in its original place does not make sense, has wandered to another, more useful, more 'Christian' place.

The fact that the myrrh is still in the right place with Mark and only became incomprehensible, was shown to us in Matthew. The 'myrrh mixed with wine' found in Mark is also in Matthew in the same place and is also given to Jesus to drink, but it is 'wine mixed with bile (or vinegar)'.[485] The myrrh has become bile. That is Matthew's characteristic way of interpreting, his *midrasch*. His method consists of adjusting the problematic passages of the Gospels to the corresponding 'orthodox' passages of Jewish scripture. Because he found in Psalm 69:22:

'They gave me bile to eat and vinegar to drink'

he accordingly rewrote Mark: he might have thought that bile is just as bitter as myrrh. So Matthew first sought the fitting *vaticinium ex eventu* and then *ex vaticinio* adjusted the *eventus*.

Finally, we need to mention on the basis of the same passage how a requisite can proliferate as soon as there is an urge for interpretation. Mark simply states: 'but he did not take it.' Matthew needs an explanation: 'and because he tasted it, he did not want to drink it.' This 'taste it' is new, however it is not a new requisite, but a direct outgrowth of 'not take' within Matthew's interpretation: it is a sub-requisite.

Since with the older Mark the myrrh stands in such an inappropriate place that the younger Matthew, Luke and John changed or moved it, we may assume that it was still in the original place with Mark and only became incomprehensible because it had just recently undergone a metamorphosis—similar to the later one of myrrh in Mark becoming bile in Matthew and ointments in Luke.

We have seen that the myrrh in Mark was generated by a misunderstood word which was different but still similar. We were able to determine that at the root of Mark's *myra* there is Caesar's *pyra*, the funeral pyre erected for the cremation of his body, which takes the same place in the parallel report ($\Pi YPA \approx MYPA$).

On the other hand, the whole block containing the passage in question could have been shifted as we have seen in the example of Clodius—and thus we must always look very closely.

To sum up, we can say that for the purpose of our attempted synopsis we have to rely on the method mentioned in the previous chapter in choosing which passages to compare: first concentrate on the requisites, then on the names and their possible changes, but without being distracted by the changes in meaning, the added sermonizing or the quotations from the Jewish scriptures.

This method will allow us to see the actual extent to which Mark jumbled the order of the texts, and whether this occurred randomly or was dictated by editorial necessity. We just might possibly reproduce the original sequencing of Mark.

MARK

Title

| ACCORDING TO MARCUS (Antonius) | ACCORDING TO MARK (the Evangelist) |

Mark is not the author, but the client, the patron.[486] According to the title this Gospel is based on the version of the Vita Divi Iulii authorized by Marcus Antonius.

Incipit

| The beginning of the Civil War between Gaius Caesar [and Pompeius].[487] | The beginning of the Gospel of Jesus Christ [the son of God].[488] |

Euangelion has obviously replaced *emphyliôn*, 'of the civil wars'. Since the primary meaning of *euangelion* is 'report of victory'—and indeed it was the true good message, which determined the freedom or slavery of the people—and since the civil war ended with the victory of Caesar, it is an understandable substitution.[489] We have seen that the term 'son of God' also applied to Caesar. It is astonishing here, that *(h)yiou theou*, 'son of God' conceals *Pompêiou*: ΠΟΜΠΗΙΟΥ > ΥΙΟΥΘΕΟΥ. This might explain why 'son of God' is missing in some manuscripts.

Pompeius' levying of troops : Baptismal activity of John

| Pompeius was in Rome and armed himself. At the same time Metellus Scipio demanded that Caesar dismiss his soldiers.[490] | John did baptize in the wilderness and preach the baptism of repentance for the remission of sins.[491] |

We have seen that baptism stands for *lustratio*, or for *dilectus*, misunderstood as *dilutum*, and thus for armament and levying; furthermore, that *Caesar* is hidden behind 'preach', *kêryssôn;* behind 'repentence', *metanoias,* we find *Metellus;* and behind 'sins', *(h)amartiôn,* we have *armorum,* 'weapons, army'.

According to the same pattern Rome has here become the desert, or 'desert places' (i.e. the 'wilderness'). *Romae > erêmôi,* 'in Rome' > 'in the desert'.[492]

This we should remember, because this confusion of Rome and desert could be the explanation for why Jesus enters Jerusalem only once in Mark's Gospel, while John enumerates five instances altogether: maybe Mark sent Jesus into the desert the other four times.

Caesar, too, came to Rome five times after the outbreak of the civil war:

—the first time after crossing the Rubicon, via Corfinium (besieging Domitius), Brundisium (chasing Pompeius), and entrance into Rome (dispute at the Saturn temple with Metellus) on the way to Spain (against Petreius and Afranius);

—the second time returning from Spain, on the way to Brundisium (crossing the stormy Ionic Sea), Dyrrachium (Siege of Pompeius), Thessalia (victory of Pharsalos), Egypt (Cleopatra, Alexandrian War), Pontus (Pharnakes, *veni vidi vici*);

—the third time back from Asia Minor, before he went to Africa (Scipio and Cato);

—the fourth time back from Africa (celebration of the four Triumphs) and before he returned to Spain (against the sons of Pompeius);

—the fifth time returning from Spain, as he was murdered before he could march against the Parthians.

We will later examine what Mark makes out of Rome each time, but for the moment we are still at the beginning of the Civil War. Pompeius is in Rome, and therefore for Mark, John is still in the desert. Pompeius will soon leave the city and with him will go the majority of the senatorial party. Does Mark let them leave the desert?

Not at all: He correctly lets the whole world move out of the city and cross the Jordan:

The consuls and the greater part of the Senate fled from the city and urged Pompeius to go out to Italy and mobilize troops. He tried unsuccessfully to recruit the veterans living in Campania and then moved towards Apulia.[493]	And there went out unto him all the land of Judaea, and they of Jerusalem, and were all baptized of him in the river of Jordan, confessing their sins. And John was clothed with camel's hair, and with a girdle of a skin about his loins...[494]

Now he has named Rome 'Jerusalem', Italy is 'Judaean countryside' or 'Jordan', because he 'baptizes' there, he recruits there. That is logically consistent. Thus the veterans settled in the *ager campanus* might have become the 'girdle of a skin', because *zônê dermatinê* evokes *area of the veterans*.[495] This citation taken from the Book of Kings denotes *Elia*, and indicates that these are the veterans settled by *Iulius*.

By referring to this 'girdle of a skin about his loins' Mark probably wanted to anticipate that Magnus/John would soon have to repent for his injustice to Iulius/Elia. He remembered that after his defeat at Pharsalos, Pompeius had to remove his uniform of a commander, don something more fitting for a fugitive, and then flee on the first available horse.[496] With this later robe of rags in mind, Mark might have already taken the hasty, panicky departure with all worldly possession to Campania to be more of a caravan than an army,[497] and therefore turned Campania into a 'camel'—which suggests itself in Greek if you compare the word stems: ΚΑΜΠΑ(νια) > ΚΑΜΗΛ(ος). Since *trechô* means 'walk fast, run, hurry', but *triches* are 'hair', then the 'hurried flight to Campania' could become 'clothed in camel's hair'.[498] Mark seems to have found that appropriate for the repentant John.

Bad omens and appearances in the sky—bloody rain, sweating images of the gods, lightning hitting temples—had accompanied the departure of the senatorial party from Rome and announced the final abolishment of the old system of government and the imminent revolution.[499] The most meaningful of the terrible signs manifested themselves just before Pharsalos. They heralded the defeat of Magnus, i.e. the penance of John. When Pompeius offered sacrifice in the night before the battle, some of the sacrificial animals got away and could not be recaptured...

...and a swarm of honey bees, weak animals, landed on the altar.[500]	...and he did eat locusts and wild honey...[501]

The parallel is evident. To see why, we point to the similarity between 'swarm', *esmos*, and *esthiôn*, 'did eat', between 'settled', *ekathise* and *akridas*, 'locusts' as well as 'honeybees', *melissôn*, and *meli agrion*, 'wild honey'.

The defeat of Pompeius : The witness of John

The next day the bad omens were confirmed during the battle, for the (Pontifex) *Maximus* proved to be stronger than (Pompeius) *Magnus*. We have discussed this passage in a previous chapter:

Defeated by Caesar, Pompeius fled and ordered his servants to go to Caesar. Thus he had to take his shoes off himself, but Favonius did not consider himself too good to help him wash his feet and prepare meals, and so Favonius did readily provide for him these services.[502]	And preached, saying, There cometh one mightier than I after me, the latchet of whose shoes I am not worthy to stoop down and unloose. I indeed have baptized you with water: but he shall baptize you with the Holy Ghost.[503]

Here we just emphasize the similarity between 'service', *(h)ypourgia*, and (h)agion, 'holy', and between *Favonius*, Greek *Phaônios*, and *pneuma*, 'Ghost'—intensified by the fact that *Favonius* is a name for a warm wind, our 'föhn' of the Alps *(Favonius > Faonius > föhn)*, just as *pneu-*

ma primarly means 'breeze', 'wind', and only derivatively 'breath', 'spirit'. The warm wind *Favonius* classically stands for the breath of spring, as for example in the *Pervigilium Veneris* (verse 14) where it appears as *spiritus,* with which Venus pervades and regenerates nature. 'Holy Spirit' would thus stand for 'Favonius's readiness to help'.

What is left to note is that here too, as above in Mk. 1:4, the name *Caesar* is hidden behind *ekêryssen,* 'preached'.

Thus Mark has demonstrated, in anticipation of later events, how John had to expiate his baptismal activity, i.e. how the once great Pompeius had sunk so low, in spite of and because of his enormous armaments. These passages, which should have been told later, after Pharsalos, are instead woven-in here: immediately after the departure from Rome and when Pompeius and the consuls are still in Campania. This did not happen arbitrarily.

Here Mark had a peg on which to hang them. The swarm of bees settling on the sacrificial altar had been able to overlay the rain of blood, and the 'wild' honey, *(meli) agrion,* found its lure in the *ager (campanus),* the Campanian 'acre'.

The Favonius-anecdote and the question as to who was the stronger also had their predecessor there. Pompeius had maintained in the Senate that the number of troops that could be mobilized in Italy was not sufficient to defend Rome against Caesar. Favonius then demanded that Pompeius finally get up and stamp his feet, since he had previously bragged that all he had to do was stamp his foot on the ground in order to fill Italy with his armies. In reality, however, the Italians informed the powerful Pompeius that 'they would abandon him out of fear of one who was even stronger'.[504] This offered Mark the opportunity to take the later passage—in which Pompeius finally fled from the stronger Caesar and where he could no longer stamp his foot, but actually needed help to take off his sandals—and move it forward to this spot. The linguistic peg is probably the similarity between 'stamping' with the foot of Pompeius and 'taking off the sandals' of Favonius: Mark could have his *kypsas,* 'stooping down' (to unloose the latchet of his shoes) from *ktypêsas,* 'stamping' (with the foot on the ground), which helped him mix the two anecdotes with the same actors, Pompeius and Favonius.

So we see that Mark purposefully moves passages, eclipsing weaker ones with more meaningful ones. Since he continues in the same characteristic style, we may assume that at least the original Mark was told in the correct chronological order.

The dream of Gaius : The baptism of Jesus

In the next paragraph Mark turns to Jesus who is in Galilee at the time of his baptism by John—as Gaius Caesar himself was in Gallia at the time of the recruitments of Pompeius:

At the time of Pompeius' armament Caesar had arrived in Gallia Cisalpina and stopped in Ravenna. From there he negotiated with Pompeius who was recruiting in Italy.[505]	And it came to pass in those days, that Jesus came from Nazareth of Galilee, and was baptized of John in Jordan.[506]

We have already seen that *Galilee* must be *Gallia* here. What is amazing is that the Jordan stands for Italy. Since the 'armaments of Pompeius' have already become 'the baptism of John', then 'Italy' where Pompeius recruited must turn into the 'Jordan' where John baptized. The Rubicon, the border to Italy, served as another peg.

Just as amazing is that Mark changes Ravenna to Nazareth. Apparently, he first inverted the order of the syllables—*Ravenna* > *Navera*—and then via *Nazera* landed at *Nazareth*. From Gallia, Ravenna was the last city within Caesar's sphere of power. There at the Rubicon, at the border to Italy, Caesar waited, ready to retaliate with weapons should the Senate decide to take severe measures against the tribunes of the people who were interceding on his behalf, but he hesitated before making an armed invasion of the Roman mother country. And here he had a dream:

They say that in the night before crossing the Rubicon he had a horrible dream. It seemed to him that he slept with his mother in incestuous intercourse.[507]	And straightway coming up out of the water, he saw the heavens opened, and the Spirit like a dove descending upon him: And there came a voice from heaven, saying, Thou art my beloved Son, in whom I am well pleased.[508]

Plutarchus placed the scene before the Rubicon, but Mark has it after Jesus climbs out of the water. This is understandable however, because he has misunderstood the recruitings to be baptisms, and they were already in full swing. The other difference—'dream' not being the same as 'heaven'—is vanishingly small in Greek: 'dream', *onar* > *ouranos*, 'heaven'. The voice from heaven is the vision.

Caesar had had the same dream in Gades (Cádiz)—if it really is two different dreams and not the same one, which he only reflected on again while at the Rubicon. There in Gades he had just seen a statue of Alexander the Great at the temple of Hercules and cried, weary of his own lack of deeds and feeling he had not done anything as remarkable as

Alexander, who at the same age had already subdued the whole world. Then the seers of the nearby Astarte-Temple had come to his help. As a petitioner of the oracle he spent the night in the crypt[509] and there he had the dream that confused him: it seemed to him that he had violated his mother. Hereupon the dream readers gave him great hope. They interpreted the outrageous vision of the dream as an annunciation of his dominance over the entire world, since the mother who had given herself to him in his dream was none other than the earth, who was regarded as the mother of all. Thus report Suetonius and Cassius Dio.[510]

One may wonder what kind of potions the dream interpreters at the temple of Venus Marina in Gades may have given to petitioners of the oracle, in order that they would have clearly interpretable dreams. Being priests of Venus, they probably used aphrodisiacs, mixed in strong sweet wine, 'wet honeys' and even opium (cf. VERG. A. 4.486) and the confusing dream of the normally abstemious Caesar seems to point in that direction. In any case, different from what we, damaged by Freud, might think, here the mother is not Aurelia, who passed away five years before the events at the Rubicon, but Mother Earth.

Incidentally, Caesar's oracle has to be at the Rubicon—which is why Plutarchus put it here. It was essential to make up for an important historical precedent: The older Brutus had at that time been sent to Delphi to question the oracle. When he heard it said that the ruler would be he who would kiss the mother first, he did not hurry home as did his two companions, but threw himself down as soon as he landed in Italy and kissed the earth. The prophecy was fulfilled: Brutus was able to expell the kings and become the first consul. Just as then, when the monarchy was overthrown and replaced by the oligarchy,[511] so now, conversely, with the diminution of the Senate by Caesar's autocratic rule there was again the need for the old oracle to announce the grace of the gods—the difference being that Brutus had at that time thrown himself on the mother earth and kissed her, while now it was the mother herself, who had in the dream given herself to her beloved son and was well pleased in him: a small, but meaningful difference.

Mark, however, primarily understands the 'mother' to be the ancestral mother, Venus. This is clearly recognizable in her attribute, the dove, which of course appears as the crowning Victoria-Nike with wings on the coin, which the *imperator*, the victorious Caesar, had minted. The victory-bringing Victoria is literally portrayed as *Nikê-phoros*: she holds a small Nike, the personification of victory, in her hand. Nike herself holds a laurel wreath in her hand. She is the 'crowning' Nike, in Greek: *peristephês*; however, *peristeros, -a,* means 'dove'.

109. Denarius of Caesar, 44 B.C. *Obv.*: CAESAR·IMP(erator)

Venus' dove also holds a green branch or wreath in its bill at times. It is no coincidence that it resembles the birds mentioned by the seer of Padua announcing the victory of Caesar. Unfortunately it has not been passed down to us what kind of birds they actually were, but he who thought of the son of Venus had to think of Venus' dove.[512]

As we have seen, both Caesar and Pompeius made an offering to Venus on the night before Pharsalos: Caesar vowed that if he won he would build her, the bringer of victory, a temple in Rome; Pompeius dreamt that he had dedicated a temple in Rome to her. Both were fulfilled: the spoils of Pompeius served to decorate the Venus temple built by Caesar.[513] Venus had decided in favor of her beloved son.

Because Mark, as we have seen above, already recalled the prosperous result of the struggle for power (presaged by the dream) and the later victory, he superimposes the eerie dream at the Rubicon in this place also.[514]

Provocation of Caesar : Temptation of Jesus

After Mark has sought heavenly signs, he turns to earthly happenings:

The tribunes of the people fled from Rome and took refuge with Caesar who was in Ravenna and on these tidings marched towards Rimini; their lives threatened by the Senate they rode on a hired cart, dressed up as slaves, at night. In this state he showed them to his legionaries in the morning.[515]	And immediately the Spirit driveth him into the wilderness. And he was there in the wilderness forty days and forty nights, tempted of Satan; and was with the wild beasts; and the angels ministered unto him.[516]

Here we must prepare ourselves for doublets. This time the 'spirit' is not Favonius, but the people's tribunes, probably because of the similarity between *plebs* and *pneuma*. And not only does *Rome*, but also *Ariminum* (Rimini) and in its wake even *Ravenna*, become the 'wilderness', the 'desert': *erêmon*. Similar to the Clodius anecdote where the female servants had become the 'four', so here the 'slaves', *therapontôn*, have become no less than 'forty', *tessarakonta*; 'as slaves during the night' becomes 'forty nights', to which 'the next day (morning)', 'forty days', had to join. The *Senate* is very specifically called *Satan*—due to the sound (simple metathesis) and because of the meaning: The relentless 'adversaries' sat in the Senate. In opposition to this, the *legion* became 'angel', here too because of the sound—*legio(n) > ongile > angeloi* (syllables read backwards as in *Ravenna > Nazareth; legion* is in the singular form; because at first only the XIII Legion was in place)—as well as the meaning: the *legion,* protecting both their commander and the tribunes of the people, becomes the 'ministering angels'. The 'beasts' Jesus found himself with, *thêriôn*, are, however, likely to be the tribunes themselves, on which the mules pulling their cart might have rubbed off, or those that Caesar hitched to his wagon before he himself went to Rimini.[517]

Caesar starts the civil war : Jesus preaches the Gospel

He spoke to the soldiers: Pompeius had defected. Under him, Caesar, they had come to Gaul and pacified it. Under his leadership they had served the state with the greatest success for nine years. In spite of this his mandate had been shortened and Pompeius had received the Empire. Now they should protect the honor and dignity of their commander. The soldiers shouted loudly that they would be true to him and the tribunes.[518]	Now after that John was put in prison, Jesus came into Galilee, preaching the Gospel of the Kingdom of God, And saying, The time is fulfilled, and the Kingdom of God is at hand: repent ye, and believe the Gospel.[519]

In his Commentaries and with the authors who came after him, Caesar made his speech to his soldiers before he crossed the Rubicon. The background for this was that Caesar's mandate in Gaul had been shortened and he was prevented from running in the next consulate elections.[520] The core of the speech dealt with the betrayal of Pompeius who had defected to the Senate party, the proclamation that Caesar and his troops were enemies of the state, as well as the handing over of the supreme command to Pompeius. The pitiful appearance of the exhausted and fleeing tribunes of the people only emphasized the seriousness of the situation.

The parallel between the 'defection' of Pompeius and John's being 'put in prison' becomes more clear when looking at the Greek text of Mark: there *paradothênai* is used and means 'give, hand over, transmit', i.e. 'betray'; however since it can also mean 'entrust' and 'deliver' the translation gets forced towards 'imprison'. Caesar says Pompeius is *deductum ac depravatum: Paradothênai* is not that bad a translation thereof.

We have seen that *evangelion* stands for *emphyliôn*, 'of the civil wars' in the beginning of Mark's Gospel. Here it now stands for the Gallic war, the aim of which in Roman eyes was pacification, but in those of Caesar it also had the purpose of integration into the Empire. Since up to now, behind 'preached', *kêryssôn*, we have always found *Caesar*, here a *Gaius Caesar* in the exemplar will have transformed into *Jesus kêryssôn*, 'Jesus preaching'. We have also seen above that 'of God', *tou theou*, can stand for *Pompêiou*, 'of Pompeius'.

However, 'repentance', *metanoia*, has now and then stood for *Metellus*, but as we have suspected in a previous chapter, it might generally stand for *militum*. Since in this case we have Caesar's speech to his soldiers from his own pen and not from secondary sources, we are fortunate enough to experience Mark's *metanoia* in development.[521]

Caesar says that only after he knew that the soldiers' opinion was for him, did he decide to march to Rimini[522]—which required crossing the Rubicon and opening the civil war: *Cognita militum voluntate*—'having recognized the will of the soldiers'. *Cognita* can in Greek be considered as derived from *gignôskô*, so that one could assume a *gnôtê*; but even *voluntas* in the given sense of 'conviction, disposition, opinion' would also be rendered by a word derived from *gignôskô: gnômê*. Now *metanoia*—actually *metagnoia* or *metagnôsis*—comes also from *gignôskô: meta-gignôskô*, 'to recognize in hindsight', i.e. 'regret' and thus it is also 'repent'. *Meta-gnoia* appears as if it was directly derived from *militum voluntate* (or from *cognita militum voluntate*) by retaining the sound of the first element and translating the second—similar to the way *Castra Regina* became *Regensburg* in German.

Finally, *pistis* not only means 'belief', as translated in the last part of Mark's verse but also and primarily 'loyalty', which is even more noticeable in the corresponding Latin word: *fides*, 'faith, faithfulness'. Thus behind 'Repent ye, and believe the Gospel' is the call to the soldiers to remain faithful to their commander and to the tribunes of the people in the war of vindication which was imminent.

Frontier crossing : At the Sea of Galilee

We can admire Mark's loyalty in the next verse. Like Caesar he does not mention the Rubicon at all. In fact, in his exemplar he found that Caesar had crossed the border between Galilee and Italy, but he makes it a walk by the Sea of Galilee:

Caesar went to Rimini where he met Antonius and Curio. When he reached the Rubicon which forms the border to Italy he paused for a moment directing his eyes at the current. Then he energetically crossed over the river and said: Let the die be cast! After that he swiftly continued his journey, took Ariminum at dawn and advanced beyond.[523]	Now as he walked by the sea of Galilee, he saw Simon and Andrew his brother casting a net into the sea: for they were fishers. And Jesus said unto them, Come ye after me, and I will make you to become fishers of men. And straightway they forsook their nets, and followed him.[524]

Mark hit upon the idea to turn the border with Gaul into the Sea of Galilee because of the river and the current towards which the view is directed. Of course he also knew that on the other bank Capharnaum should appear, which lies at the Lake of Gennesaret; however this seems to have barely played a role here, because he does not say Lake of Gennesaret, but Sea of Galilee, 'by the Sea of Galilee' to be precise. Apparently he confused the 'border', *oros*, with *ora [maris]*, the 'coast', and thus transformed the 'crossing of the Gallic border' into 'a walk by the Galilaean Sea'.

Then he consistently also confused 'die', *alea* with *(h)aleeis*, 'fisher'—as we have seen—so that logically the 'energetic crossing of the river' had to become 'casting (a net) into the sea'. Caught in this fisher logic *Ariminum* in the next sentence was bound to be misunderstood as *hominum*, 'of men', so that 'the capture of Ariminum' wondrously turned into the 'fishing of men'. The fact that directly afterwards Antonius, Curio and the others who had fled to Caesar were made leaders in the army, as we saw in the previous chapter, rubbed off on it.

Now that we have energetically crossed the Rubicon and can follow and admire Mark's copying techniques and his art of re-editing sentence by sentence, it is time that we too, like Caesar, pause and direct our eyes at the current.

By placing the sentences from both textual sources in juxtaposition with each other, we were also able to verify our hypotheses: some were confirmed and some had to be abandoned; some others had to be stated more precisely or revealed more complexity; and doublets have surfaced. If we went even deeper we would probably experience the same once more. The investigation is not at all completed. Moreover, the necessity of clearly demonstrating the transitions from Latin to Greek in English, and making them comprehensible leads to occasional inaccuracies.

All in all, however, we could see that the Markan text is actually a Vita Caesaris, and that Mark relates verse by verse in the same order as the other biographers or the reports about the Roman Civil War. But, he recounts the story as he has understood—or misunderstood—it. His geographical-chronological details—such as 1:9 'he came from Nazareth of Galilee', 1:14 'he came into Galilee', and 1:16 'he walked by the Sea of Galilee'—are not at all, as was presumed, just editorial phrases to patch up pieces of stories. Rather he follows his sources in a well-behaved manner—1:9 'he came to Ravenna in Gallia Citerior', 1:14 'he went to Gaul', 1:16 'he crossed the Gallic border',—which he misunderstands however, and he would rather repeat the same thing three times than omit anything. To that extent, Papias' verdict—that Mark was careful 'not to omit anything and at the same time not to lie'—is confirmed. One can buy that he could not remember any better, because when Mark penned his copy almost a hundred years had passed since the 'Ascension of the Lord'. And while copying he recalled not the Historiae of Asinius Pollio (he apparently had never heard of it and obviously could not even read it correctly in the abridged version), but rather the previous Sunday homily he had in front of him, and from that he transcribed. So, if it was a question of memory then it was one of collective memory: the memories of the community to which he belonged. The grandchildren of the veterans who were settled in Asia, whose mothers and grandmothers were natives, apparently had no connection to Latin any longer, except as *sermo castrensis*, the military language of command and of the barracks. So the text resulting from Mark's copying and editing was considered by them to be a true copy, and is a moving proof of their blind faithfulness.

In this respect we have already reached a conclusion, and therefore it is easier to be realistic. And realistic we must be. In order to present just under one and a half columns of Mark with some clarity, an impressive total of ten pages of text was required, and almost the same number of pages of notes, which would double if the translation of the Latin and Greek quotations were added. We would then have for Mark alone about a thousand pages.

This cannot possibly be the place for such comparisons. With Caesar as our example, we should thus quickly continue our journey so that we can take the strategic points before daybreak. In what follows we will only look by pericope at how Mark has reshaped the history of the civil war into his Gospel. We will not miss much, because we have already extensively discussed a great deal in previous chapters. The parallels worked out there will now serve to help us orient ourselves. Of course we will go into detail where it is necessary.

Siege of Corfinium : The Possessed of Capharnaum

In an earlier chapter we saw that the 'besieged' Domitius in Corfinium became the 'possessed' of Capharnaum due to the double meaning of the Latin *obsessus*. It is noteworthy how Mark uses the name *Domitius*, with which he can do nothing: *Oidamen tis ei*, 'We know thee who thou art' he has the unclean spirit say to the Nazarene:

DOMITIVS ≈ ΟΙΔΑΜΕΝΤΙΣΕΙ

We already know that *Jesus the Nazarene* stands for *Gaius Caesar*. It should be noted however that, since it is frequently found in Mark, the 'unclean spirit' obviously stands for 'Pompeian'. Actually it was obvious: *Anthrôpos en pneumati akathartôi*, 'a man in unclean spirit', namely sounds like *homo in pompeiano exercitu*, 'a man in Pompeius' army'.

Pompeius in Brundisium : The wife's mother with a fever

Pompeius in Brundisium has become *penthera pyressousa*, the wife's mother with a fever (Mk. 1:30-31). Simon had to serve as son-in-law, perhaps because he was to play a special role with the crossing of Caesar's fleet in Brindinsi, more probably however, because Mark thought that *penthera Simonôs* fits with *Brundisium*.

Astonishingly, Pompeius could leave Brundisium, and miraculously the fever left the mother-in-law.

Caesar goes to Rome : Jesus goes into the desert

Here in Mark 1:35 we once again find, as expected, Rome as the 'desert', the 'solitary place', *Romae* as *erêmôi*. This explains why Asinius (ass's colt) or Curio (the withered fig tree) with his unsuccessful campaign have not appeared before now. Since Mark has Jesus enter Rome only once, he had to place the anecdotes of Asinius and Curio before the entrance into Jerusalem. They can be found in Mark 11:1-7 and 11:12-4.

Publius Clodius : Leper, Lame, Levi

As we have seen, the story of Publius Clodius has been divided into different healings and placed as excursus in Mark 1:40-2:17. Since the Clodius stories took place in 62 or 59, and the Civil War only began ten years later in 49, they had to be interpolated somewhere. We assumed that Mark inserted them as a story that was the talk of the town, at the place where Caesar returned to Rome.

Mark might, however, have found another peg to hang it on, namely in the similarity between *Petreius* and *lepros*, 'leper': because afterwards, Caesar moved against Petreius in Spain.

Caesar and the Saturn Temple : Jesus and the Sabbath

As we saw, Mark has treated the taking of the treasury from the temple of Saturn quite elaborately: as a discussion about fasting (*Saturnus* taken for *sata*, 'ears of corn'), and about the Sabbath (*Saturnus* as *Saturni dies*, 'Saturday', as *Sabbath*). Metellus' attempt to intercede became the healing of a withered hand (*Metellus* interpreted as *mutilus*, 'mutilated').

Caesar, Ruler of Italy : Throng of the people

No explanation is necessary. Galilee is Gaul, as usual, Judaea is Italy, and Jerusalem is Rome. Concerning the others—Idumaea, Tyrus, and Sidon—speculation is allowed (Illyria, Tyrrhenum, Sardinia?).

Caesar appoints his legates : Calling of the twelve disciples

Appianus gives two lists. The first contains the names of those designated by Caesar before he departs for Spain to fight against Petreius and Afranius, to 'safeguard Italy, so that Pompeius could never again set foot in the country'. The second list came after his return from Spain, when he 'at his own discretion either sent or replaced governors in all the provinces'. This had become necessary because, among other reasons, Curio had been defeated in Africa and Gaius Antonius in Illyria. In addition, there had been a mutiny in Placentia (Piacenza), which Caesar put down by choosing twelve ringleaders and having them executed. One of the twelve could prove that he was not present at the outbreak of the mutiny, and Caesar therefore had the centurion who accused him executed in his place.[525]

Mark, also, has the calling of the twelve disciples (3:12-19) come first, followed by their being sent forth (6:7-13). He has already assigned them all names the first time around. But already there, he adds the comment that one of them, Judas Iscariot, was to betray him, which reminds us of the treacherous centurion and the question of the substitution is quietly implied. Thus a comparison of both lists of Caesar's legates with Mark's list of the disciples is indicated.

Among those appointed before the campaign in Spain, Appianus mentions: *Aemilius Lepidus* (Rome); *Marcus Antonius* (Italy and the troops stationed there); *Curio* (Sicily, in place of Cato); *Quintus Valerius* (Sardinia); *Gaius Antonius* (Illyria); *Licinius Crassus* (Gallia Cisalpina); in addition *Hortensius* (Admiral of the Ionian Fleet) and *Dolabella* (Admiral of the Tyrrhenic Fleet).

Additionally, after the Spanish campaign the following are mentioned: *Publius Isauricus* (co-consul with Caesar); *Marcus Lepidus* (Spain); *Aulus Albinus* (Sicily); *Sextus Peducaeus* (Sardinia) and *Decimus (Iunius) Brutus* (newly conquered Gaul).

Altogether Appianus has exactly twelve names, in which *Lepidus* appears twice, once as *Aemilius,* once as *Marcus.*

Mark says:

'And he goeth up into a mountain, and calleth unto him whom he would: and they came unto him. And he ordained twelve, [whom he also named apostles] that they should be with him, and that he might send them forth to preach, And to have power to heal sicknesses, and to cast out devils:

[And he ordained the twelve:] And *Simon* he surnamed *Peter;* And *James* the son of *Zebedee,* and *John* the brother of *James;* and he surnamed them *Boanerges,* which is, *The sons of thunder:* And *Andrew,* and *Philip,* and *Bartholomew,* and *Matthew,* and *Thomas,* and *James* the son of *Alphaeus,* and *Thaddaeus,* and *Simon the Canaanite,* And *Judas Iscariot,* which also betrayed him.'[526]

As we see, these twelve correspond to the legates Caesar chose and named himself. That they were appointed instead of the 'Pompeians' can be recognized by the fact that they have 'power to cast out "devils"'.

Once again we meet old friends: *Simon* < *Antonius* (the mirror image of *Antonius,* read as *Simona*); *Petrus* < *Lepidus* (the *Praetor* as *Peter,* in the sequel possibly also *Lepidus* understood as *lapis, lapidis,* as 'stone' and made into *Petrus*—also 'stone'). Here we can watch how *Simon* becomes *Peter.* Appianus says: 'He named Lepidus commandant of the city and Antonius that of Italy.' Mark understood it this way: 'He named Antonius Lepidus' and made it: 'and Simon he surnamed Peter'.[527] The reason might be that from this point in time onwards, Antonius and Lepidus were always paired together, until the death of Caesar and even later in the second triumvirate.

'James (i.e. Jacobus), son of Zebedee' is probably *Marcus Octavius*, a sub-commander of Pompeius, who had been sent to fight Dolabella and had defeated Gaius Antonius in Illyria, thus forcing Caesar to name a successor: OCTAVIVS > OKTABIOC > IAKΩBOC; (for POMPEIVS > ZEBEΔAIOC see below).

Because of his place in the text near Octavius, who defeated him, 'Gaius, the brother of Antonius' could become 'John, the brother of James'. It helped here that *Gaios* is close to *neos*, 'young', so that it can become *John* according to the established pattern. Also, the fact that in Greek 'brother' is not far from 'Antonius' will not have displeased Mark *(ANTΩNION ≈ AΔEΛΦON)*.

Misunderstood as *Tonitruii*[528] both *Antonii* would have become the 'sons of thunder'. However, behind the *Boanerges*, the 'sons of thunder', in Greek *(h)yioi brontês*, there could also stand Brutus, *Decimus Brutus*. Since his cognomen was also *Albinus*, like *Aulus Albinus*, they could both have been apprehended as 'sons of Brutus', *(h)yioi Brontês*, and finally made 'sons of thunder'.[529]

Curio might have become *Andrew* because of the script *(CVRIONEM > ANΔPEAN)* or because of the meaning (*Curio* from *co-vir*, just like *curia* from *co-viria*, and translated with *anêr, andros*)—but it cannot be excluded that the names *Petreius* and *Afranius* might have rubbed off on *Peter* and *Andrew*.

Furthermore, these are clearly identifiable: *Philippus < Lepidus*;[530] *Simon Kananeus < Gaius Antonius (Simon < Antonius, Kananeus < Gaius); Judas < (Decimus) Junius (Brutus); Iscariot < Isauricus.* Thus Mark would have listed *Gaius Antonius* twice, like *Lepidus*, who is also on the list twice; instead he would have made one out of *Judas/Iunius* and *Iscariot/Isauricus*—*Judas Iscariot*—just as he did above with Simon and Peter. Theoretically, *sicarius*, 'treacherous murderer', an epithet minted for another Iunius, Marcus Brutus, could have rubbed off on *Iscariot*. (As a Pompeian, Marcus Brutus is not listed here yet and cannot be since he was only pardoned and readmitted by Caesar after Pharsalos).

There was, however, a *Philippus* among the people's tribunes who in 49 BC interceded for Caesar. Caesar mentions him together with his father, also a *Philippus*,[531] who had married Atia the daughter of Caesar's sister and thus was the stepfather of Octavianus, the later Augustus. Therefore the name *Philippus* might have been in Mark's exemplar, even though it is missing in Appianus.

'Sons of Zebedee' do not appear *expressis verbis* in Mark (only James is the 'son of Zebedee', John is the 'brother of James'; the 'sons of thunder' might therefore only have been aligned with the real 'sons of Zebedee' who appear later (Mk. 10:35-45) and are not necessarily the same. Actually they are *sons of Pompeius*.

As for the other disciples, we may speculate here as we did above, with the names of countries:

There is a third *James* (i.e. *Jacobus*) on Mark's list, 'the son of Alphaeus'. *Clodius* became one of these, as we saw: he would have been posthumously honored here at the same time as *Matthew,* Greek *Matthaios: mataios,* sacrilegious man. Then here too, 'the son of Alphaeus' might come from *Cisalpina,* which in Greek is *(h)ê entos tôn Alpeôn Galatia,* 'Gaul this side of the Alps'. This province was promised to *Licinius Crassus,* and *Crassus* is not very far from *Clodius.* Did *Crassus,* just like the similarly written *Clodius,* become *James* (i.e. *Jacobus*), or did he become *Jacobus* because of his first name *Marcus (Licinius Crassus),* in the way that *Marcus (Octavius)* did?

Thomas might also be an additional doublet of *(An)tonius. Bartholomew* looks like a contraction of *Valerius* and *Dolabella* ('b' was already pronounced like 'v' in Greek at that time); *Ptolemaios Auletes,* who was very well disposed towards Caesar, might be behind *Bartholomew,* whereby 'Bar-Ptolomaeus', 'son of Ptolemaios' reminds us of Ptolemy's daughter *Cleopatra* or of the son of Caesar and Cleopatra, *Caesarion,* whose designated Egyptian dynastic name was also Ptolemaios. Finally, there still remains the possibility that *Bartholomew* derives from *Aristobulos,* whom Caesar had sent to his Palestine homeland along with his legates, to lead a campaign there against Pompeius.[532] *Thaddaeus* might be *Peducaeus,* and in the case that he was called *Judas,* he melted together with *(Decimus) Iunius (Brutus),* like *Isauricus/Iscariot.* But since some writings use the variant *Lebbaeus* for *Thaddaeus,* he would originally have been another doublet of *Lepidus.* For *Matthew* finally, it also suggests itself to see in him that *Matius,* who does not stand on Appianus' list, but to whom his friend Caesar wrote the famous words *'veni, vidi, vici'* from Pontus to Rome. *Matius* fell into disrepute because of his greed, which Plutarchus mentions together with the craziness of Dolabella and Antonius' alcoholism, and therefore he could well be regarded as a *mataios,* one of Caesar's 'sinners' (PLUT. *Caes.* 50, 51). The pseudo-Marius *Amatius* who after Caesar's death erected the first altar at the site of the cremation, could have subsequently slipped into the role of *Matthew* too.

With this final mentioning of uncertain candidates, we have to leave the decision open: perhaps we will find clues during the course of our research to tip the scales in one direction or the other. With these, as well as with the doublets, we can at any rate formulate the question: were they added because Mark simply left out the names of those unimportant legates who remained unknown and replaced them with doublets—or even with other names—in order to maintain the holy number twelve, which was demanded from him by those mutineers destined for execution?

In conclusion, it can be said that Mark has saved all his disciples, none made up, and none left out. Half of the names are clearly recognizable and the other half indicates that they had to be put right. But twelve they are, and Mark has even reproduced correctly that there was an unsound one among them: Caesar's legate in Gallia Ulterior, Decimus *Iunius* Brutus, was to become Caesar's *Judas,* calling for him on the Ides of March to the Senate session, where the daggers of the traitors were waiting for him.

Caesar outside of the city : Jesus is out of his mind

In Rome, Caesar initially spoke to the people outside the city walls, and promised to deliver wheat to them[533]—when Jesus came home the people who had no bread to eat gathered together.[534]

Caesar is 'outside' (of the Pomerium)—Jesus is 'beside' (himself). *Exestê* does not necessarily mean 'out of his mind' but rather 'stood aside, stood out'.

Caesar speaks to the senators : Jesus to the scribes

Caesar also spoke to the senators outside the Pomerium. He opposed the Civil War and tried to induce the senators who had remained in Rome to send envoys to the other senators who had fled to Thessalonica with Pompeius.[535]

In the parallel passage in Mark, Jesus speaks to the scribes who had come from Jerusalem, telling them that Satan cannot drive Satan out, that a kingdom which is divided against itself cannot stand.[536]

Here too *Satan* stands for *Senate,* and since there were two Senates at that time, there are two Satans. In a context of mutual addressing, the *senators* are characterized as *scribes*—which is not surprising, because the form of address for senators was *patres conscripti,* which actually means 'fathers and councilors'. However, because when it is translated word-for-word it means 'fathers and those additionally written in (on the list of the senators)', Mark at one time makes it 'the elders and the scribes', at another time it is 'Pharisees and scribes', or at yet another time '(high) priests and scribes,' and sometimes he even combines them, as in 11:27, 'high priests, scribes, and elders'. He apparently did not see any other possibility for *conscripti* than *grammateis,* 'scribes', while for *patres* he had more possibilities of interpretation: As 'progenitors', as *senatores (patricii),* they were the 'elders'; as 'optimates', *(senatores) patricii,* the 'Pharisees' and as *patres* simply the 'priests'. In Mark's eyes and ears *Pharisaioi* and *presbyteroi* had the added advantage of looking and sounding like *patres*.

It is surprising that here, only 'scribes' appears. It is as if in view of there being two Senates, Mark had divided the *patres conscripti*, having the *patres* move out with Pompeius and leaving the *conscripti* with Caesar.

As usual, the 'unclean spirits' here represent the Pompeians, while the 'Holy Spirit' might be Pompeius himself this time *(Pompeius Magnus* as *to Pneuma to (h)agion?)*, with whom Caesar sought reconciliation, and against whom he at the same time polemized because he had derided Caesar's attempts at peace and had dismissed the sending of ambassadors as a sign of weakness. Thus, the unforgivable 'sin against the Holy Ghost', would be that 'of Pompeius against the desire for peace'.

Beelzebub who 'By the prince of demons he drives out demons' (Mk. 3:22) could be Caesar's father-in-law *Piso* here, who suggested sending envoys to Pompeius:[537] It is not by chance that most manuscripts show the spelling *Beezeboul*.

But nobody wanted to go to Pompeius—the envoys were afraid he could consider them enemies because they had remained in Rome against his directions. Thereupon Caesar decided to move against the Pompeians in Spain.[538] It was then that he spoke the famous words:

'I now go to meet an army without a leader, and when I return I shall meet a leader without an army'.[539]

The same words seem to linger with Mark:

'No man can enter into a strong man's house, and spoil his goods, except he will first bind the strong man; and then he will spoil his house.' (Mk. 3:27).

In this he would have confused 'army', *exercitum*, with *skeue*, '(household) goods', and with *ischyron*, 'strong man', as well as 'leader', *duce*, with *domo*, 'house'.

Against Petreius and Afranius : The true relatives

Petreius, analyzed as *mêtêr sou,* becomes 'thy mother' *(ΠΕΤΡΕΙΟC > MHTHPCOY), Afranius* as *adelphoi sou* becomes 'thy brethren', 'your brothers and sisters' *(AΦPANIOC > AΔΕΛΦΟΙCΟΥ).*

And just like Caesar, who defeated Petreius and Afranius 'outside' in Spain and integrated those of their soldiers who wanted to join into his legions, so likewise Jesus has his mother and brethren stay outside, and declares that those who are around him and do God's will, are his true relatives. Behind 'will', *thelêma, Ilerda,* the place of victory, might be hidden *(ILERDA > LERIDA > (RELIDA) > ΘΕΛHMA).*

With that, Mark has dealt with the Spanish campaign and in doing so has been almost as succinct as Suetonius.

From the beginning of his Gospel up to this point, Mark's reporting of the events from the outbreak of the Civil War to the Spanish campaign has been chronologically correct. The only exceptions were on the one hand the Clodius-excursus, i.e. with Mark the insertion of the healing of the leper and the lame, as well as the calling of Levi (1:40-2:17); on the other hand the relocation of the stories of Asinius and Curio, together with the question of the authority of Jesus, to Mk. 11:1-33.

Starting with the Spanish campaign, Mark begins to considerably jumble the sequence. At this point he should accompany Caesar back from Spain, have him learn en route that he was appointed dictator; have the row with those who mutinied in Placentia—where the twelve are selected; stay in Rome for a short period, and finally make a speech to his soldiers in Brundisium before he crosses the Ionian Sea and begins the siege of Pompeius.

Instead, Mark (4:1-33) inserts the parables which, as we have seen, are a paraphrase of the signs accompanying the victory at Pharsalos and reported to Caesar on the Ionic coast. One can imagine how this came about. Mark simply threw the Ionic Sea and the Ionic Islands in western Greece in one pot with the Ionic Coast and the off-shore islands in the east. Since Greece as a whole was known as Ionia in the Orient he did not notice the mix-up. He even confused it with Italy which he already made into Judaea.

However, it is pointless to explain each time the editorial reasons Mark might have had for his shifts. Maybe the shifts were sometimes due merely to technical circumstances; one knows the theories of mixed-up pages. He possibly wrote his notes first on the blank verso of the papyrus, on whose recto the correct text was written. The codex was made up of four double sheets put together to form four pages respectively. The notebooks consisted of 16 pages. Up to the middle of the codex it was the even numbered pages, and from the middle on it was the odd numbered pages that fell on the smooth front side of the papyrus. Now, if the Gospel text was first written on the rough, reverse side and the sheets were later rebound, then the mess was preprogrammed. There is thus room for fascinating speculation which, however, would be of no value to us at the moment.

Instead of taking Mark's disjointed sequencing, we intend to use the well-established chronology of the Civil War as our basis. With that we can begin to reconstruct the original sequence of Mark's Gospel.

Appointment as Dictator : Confession of Peter

On the way back from Spain Caesar stopped in many communities and heard that the praetor M. Lepidus had put forth a law to establish a dictatorship and that he, Caesar, had been named dictator.[540]

Jesus, too, is on the move, and stops in many different villages with his disciples. *Caesarea Philippi* obviously stands for *Caesar* and *Lepidus*. As *praetor*, Lepidus had Caesar appointed *dictator*. It is *Peter* who says to Jesus: 'Thou art the Christ!' *Peter* is *Lepidus* in the supposed sense as if derived from *lapis, lapidis*, 'rock', in the script and apparently the sound of the word *Peter* also renders *praetor*.

We have seen that *Christ* stands for *archiereus megistos*, i.e. for *pontifex maximus*. Indeed, until that time Caesar had not held any other office except for *pontifex maximus* since the end of his mandate in Gaul. Dictator was his first political municipal magistrate since the outbreak of the Civil War, i.e. from the beginning of the Gospel. Mark obviously made *Christ* into an amalgam of *pontifex maximus* and *dictator*. He has hidden *dictator*—which comes from *dicere*, 'to say': 'he who has the say' — in the reiterated question: 'Whom say ye?' 'Whom do men say that I am?' The wrong answers to these questions conceal the correct names for Caesar: *Elia*, pronounced *Ilia* stands for *Iulius*—via the variant *Ilius*, which emphasizes the descent from Aeneas-Son *Ilus/Ilos*.

Contrary to convention, Lepidus had used the new appellation *dictator* for Caesar immediately, without waiting for the official investiture and inauguration. But Caesar did not want to be a dictator at that time: after only eleven days he gave up the dictatorship and had himself elected consul along with Servilius Isauricus.[541] Jesus is also uncomfortable with the new title he had received from Petrus:

'And he charged them that they should tell no man of him.'[542]

That is the whole secret of the secret of the Messiah: Caesar was appointed *dictator* on the initiative of praetor Lepidus and immediately named as such—and yet he would not have it. Jesus was named *Christ* by Peter—and yet he would not have it: that's the Secret of the Messiah. But just what did he forbid? That they name him Christ? Hardly. The sentence is built differently: 'And he charged them that they should tell no man of him.' What was it no one should 'tell' of him? The text does not 'say': but *dictator* comes from *dicere*, 'say', 'tell'. Mark hid *dictator* behind *dicere*. The Messiah is the *dictator*, Mark's Messiah's secret—a child's puzzle.

Mutiny in Placentia : Rejection in Nazareth

We have already spoken about the mutiny of the two legions in Placentia where in the end the twelve were executed, among them the treasonous centurion.⁵⁴³

The name *Placentia* has become *patrida*, which is rendered as 'own country', 'hometown'. The name Nazareth is not found in Mark. The only reason for why we think we are in Nazareth is that it has been thought that Jesus was called the Nazarene because he came from Nazareth, and because *patrida* is found here (which is translated as 'hometown'): in fact we are in *Placentia*.

The *carpenter* (most of Mark's manuscripts do not contain the words 'son of a carpenter', but 'carpenter') is Caesar himself: the *pontifex*, literally 'bridge builder', became in Greek *tektôn,* and in English 'carpenter'. The remaining part of the title, *Maximus,* is read as *Mari us* and understood as *(h)o (h)yios tês Marias,* 'Mary's Son'—which, by the way, was also a good fit for the nephew of Marius, who was born during the consulate of Marius. Thus *pontifex maximus* became 'carpenter, son of Mary'.

The names of the relatives mentioned here are those of his fallen legates: *Gaius Antonius,* defeated by *Octavius* in Illyria, is the brother of *James* here, as before, while *Octavius* became *Josetos* (apparently the Latin 'C', was interpreted as the Greek sigma lunatum '*C*', i.e. the moon-shaped *sigma,* 's', which is usual in manuscripts: OCTAVIVS > IΩCHTOC). We should keep this in mind because we will see later that another *Octavius, Octavianus,* appears as *Josetos/Joses. Simon* is once more *Antonius,* also as before, and *Judas* is again that *Iunius Brutus* to whom Gaul was subordinated (except for the difference between Cisalpina and Ulterior which has apparently been ignored here).

The punishment Caesar threatened to bring upon the mutineers 'according to the father's law' i.e. the decimation, is dressed up here as 'A prophet is not without honour, but in his own country, and among his own kin, and in his own house.' But he did not have the heart to draw by lot every tenth man from both legions—with 6,000 men in each legion, it would have been 1,200 killed! Instead he took every tenth from the tenth and then once again so as to finally have only twelve ring leaders executed.

'And he could there do no mighty work, save that he laid his hands upon a few sick folk, and healed them.'

The execution of the twelve is bashfully presented as the laying on of hands. It was a healing, inasmuch as after that the soldiers followed him with great enthusiasm to Brundisium, from where he led them across the Ionic against Pompeius. In Mark there is a seamless transition to the sending out of the twelve, sent two by two—just as the mutinous legions are two.

Mark confused three kinds of *missi* with each other, which happened to be twelve in each case: the twelve ring leaders 'sent' to their death; the twelve legates 'delegated' to the provinces; the twelve legions 'commanded' to Brundisium.

By the way, Mark simply skips over the fact that on the way to Brundisium from Placentia, Caesar stopped a second time in Rome by saying:

'And he went round about the villages, teaching.'[544]

This time Mark sent Jesus into the 'villages' instead of the 'desert', and thus out of Rome he made *kômas*, 'villages', not *erêmôi*. To him that seemed more appropriate. It is as if this time he could not find in his exemplar the locative *Romae*, 'in Rome', with the 'e' ending, which he needed at the beginning of *erêmôi*. No 'e' no *erêmôi*, he might have said to himself. If instead he had the accusative *Romam*, 'to Rome', he would first change it into *kômên*, 'village' and because of the context, extend it and use the plural form, *kômas*, 'villages.'

Departure from Brundisium : Sending of the twelve disciples

Reaching Brundisium and having few ships available, Caesar told his troops to leave their luggage, baggage, equipment, and belongings in Italy so that as many men as possible could find space in the ships, unhampered and ready to fight. And not overloaded, the ships would also be more capable of braving the winter weather. It was their goal to surprise the Pompeians, to overtake their positions and to use their provisions. Since they had nothing with them, the soldiers were even more determined to alleviate their need with the abundance of the Pompeians. It worked. Instead of only five legions two additional legions found space on the ships. They crossed in spite of the treacherous wind and overtook Oricum and Apollonia without lifting a sword.[545]

Mark:

'And he called unto him the twelve, and began to send them forth by two and two; and gave them power over unclean spirits; And commanded them that they should take nothing for their journey, save a staff only; no scrip, no bread, no money in their purse: But be shod with sandals; and not put on two coats. And he said unto them, In what place soever ye enter into an house, there abide till ye depart from that place. And whosoever shall not receive you, nor hear you, when ye depart thence, shake off the dust under your feet for a testimony against them. Verily I say unto you, It shall be more tolerable for Sodom and Gomorrha in the day of judgment, than for that city. And they went out, and preached that men should repent. And they cast out many devils, and anointed with oil many that were sick, and healed them.'[546]

'Five and two' seems to have been too complicated for Mark and he made it 'two and two'. The 'be shod' demonstrates how Mark understood *impedimenta*, 'luggage, baggage' or *expediti*, 'unhampered, ready to fight': He recognized *-pedi-* and took it for 'feet'. Thus he understood *impedimenta* as *(h)ypodedemenous* (sandalia), 'shod (with sandals)' and *expediti* as *ek tôn podôn*, as dust shaken 'from the feet'. He mistook 'winter', *cheimôn*, for a *chitôn*, 'tunic'; confused 'to sail across', *perân*, with a *pêran*, sack; and probably changed 'quickly', *rapidus*, into *rabdos*, a 'root' a 'staff'. The 'unclean spirits' are the Pompeians—as always—while *Apollonia* contains the 'oil' with which—*elaiôi*—many 'sick', *arrôstous* (from *Orikos?*) were healed.

It is probable however, that the second part of the Markan pericope starting with 'And he said unto them...' does not belong to the speech in Brundisium, but to a later speech and a later event that was placed here by Mark and editorially mixed.

After the landing in Epirus, Caesar was able to overtake Apollonia and Orikos, but Dyrrhachium, the main camp of Pompeius, did not fall in spite of a long siege. Then after two lost battles Caesar had to give up the siege. His army was suffering from such a terrible famine that an epidemic afflicted his camp. On his way towards Thessalia he reached Apollonia again, and this might have given Mark the peg for this insertion here, in which he grants the first care to the wounded and sick. They were not restored to full health until they came to Gomphoi. This city, as others had, closed its doors to Caesar, assuming that he was fleeing from Pompeius. He made an example of the city and allowed his soldiers to plunder it. They found substantial amounts of food and huge amounts of wine which they drank excessively and continued to drink as they made their way happily forwards. The inebriation, in which especially the Germans distinguished themselves, and who as we know were numerous in Caesars army—particularly in the cavalry—drove the epidemic from their bodies and made new and healthy people of them.[547]

Therefore, it is necessary to read the second half of the Markan pericope quoted above differently also: where the 'disciples', i.e. the 'boys' were not welcomed, 'they 'shook' not only the 'dust from their feet in testimony against them' but left the city in ashes and rubble as an example for others. They not only preached repentance, but let them repent. Two things are curious: the unclean spirits driven out here are not only the Pompeians, but also the epidemic, and the 'healing oil' with which they anointed and cured many sick was the best Greek wine, the miracle-working panacea was an unforgettable collective drunkenness.

This part cannot be stressed enough, because here Mark could see it concretized what people generally thought of Caesar's victories: namely that they were miracles. The wonderful commander became the miraculous thaumaturge (supported by the general belief that Caesar and not Pompeius had been the true therapist of the ailing republic (PLUT. *Caes.* 28)). It was from here that Mark let that thought spread to the neighboring texts and thus all other victories became not only wonders, but also wherever possible, miraculous healings.

Stormy Seas : Quieting of the storm

After his speech, Caesar led his soldiers from the speaker's platform directly to the ships. However, due to the choppy swell on the open sea he had to drop anchor. The wind hampered him so that he himself had to spend the first day of the new year still in Brundisium. In the meantime, two further legions arrived: those who had mutinied and now, nevertheless, had followed him obediently. And Caesar in turn accepted them. Finally the wind died down and the sea became calm and he departed on freighters in wintertime. Caesar's vessels were driven to the Ceraunic Cliffs by the winds, and he sent them back immediately to gather the rest of the troops.[548]

Mark:

'And the same day, when the even was come, he saith unto them, Let us pass over unto the other side. And when they had sent away the multitude, they took him even as he was in the ship. And there were also with him other little ships. And there arose a great storm of wind, and the waves beat into the ship, so that it was now full. And he was in the hinder part of the ship, asleep on a pillow: and they awake him, and say unto him, Master, carest thou not that we perish? And he arose, and rebuked the wind, and said unto the sea, Peace, be still. And the wind ceased, and there was a great calm. And he said unto them, Why are ye so fearful? how is it that ye have no faith? And they feared exceedingly, and said one to another, What manner of man is this, that even the wind and the sea obey him? And they came over unto the other side of the sea, into the country of the

Gadarenes. And when he was come out of the ship, immediately there met him...'⁵⁴⁹

The anecdote is evidently the same. It begins with the embarking, continues with the storm, leads into the landing at the *Ceraunics* or *Gerasenes* and ends with the 'sending back of the ships' or 'meeting him immediately when he was come out of the ship.'

The only thing Mark confused was 'staying in Brundisium' which he changed to 'asleep on a cushion in the back of the ship' confirmed by the fact that in the next anecdote (see below) Caesar also 'threw himself into a corner of the ship like a poor unknown fellow, where he quietly stayed lying' (PLUT. *Caes.* 38). Mark first broke down *Brundisium* into *prymna*, 'back', and, obviously because it seemed too short for him, he again adjusted it into *proskephalaion*, 'cushion'—whereby *katheudôn* was taken as really 'sleeping' and not simply as 'resting'. Then he only needed to move the obedience of the legions to that of the wind and sea—and ready was the stilling of the storm!

Caesar's luck goes with : Jesus walks on the water

We have already dealt in detail with the anecdote regarding Caesar's attempt to travel incognito on a boat back to Brundisium and personally gather the other legions which were late.

We note here that Mark does not report about Antonius' hesitation nor his less than praiseworthy crossing. Only Matthew reports about the hesitating Peter who walks on the water, becomes frightened, begins to sink, and then screams until Jesus catches him (Mt. 14:28-33). The only trace of it remaining in Mark is the landing place of Antonius: *Dalmatia*, which in another place might have rubbed off on *Dalmanoutha* as we have already seen and will yet see.

Siege of Pompeius : Healing of the Possessed

This, too, we have already dealt with—but only half of the story, Mk. 5:1-11. This 'possessed' is named a Gerasene only because Jesus had landed near the territory of the Gerasene, i.e. Caesar at the Ceraunic Cliffs.

As we have seen, it is Pompeius himself who becomes the 'man with the unclean spirit' here. He is 'possessed' because he was 'besieged': the Latin *obsessus* means both. 'No one could restrain him' because he 'continuously broke through the siege', which finally had to be given up. The 'entrenchments', *munimenta*, have been misunderstood as *monumenta*, 'monuments', and thus 'graves'. His name is *Legion* because he has some with him. The 'herd of swine on the hill' could be the 'herd of small animals from Epirus' which served the Caesareans as victuals, but have melted together with the 'army of enemies' due to mutual accusations of being 'animals'.

It should be added here, that the swine could be something else in the next paragraph already. When Caesar was forced to give up the siege after a proper setback, his men begged him to immediately lead them against the enemy to make good the failure, but he did not allow them to do this. Instead he pulled back and lured the Pompeians into an area more advantageous for him, down to the Thessalian plateau, where he defeated them near Pharsalos even though they outnumbered him two to one.[550] Jesus too, is begged by the unclean spirits to send them into the swine, and Jesus gives them leave. And the unclean spirits go out and enter into the swine, and the herd of about two thousand rush down a steep bank into the sea.[551]

Mark, who usually only turns the Pompeians into unclean spirits, this time made Caesar's soldiers also into unclean spirits. Then he believed that he identified *(h)ypechôrei*, 'pulled back' as *choirous*, 'swine', *Thessalia* as *thalassa*, 'sea', *Pharsalos* as *pharagx*, *pharaggos*, 'cleft, chasm, ravine', and thus 'pulling back to Pharsalos in Thessalia' became 'the herd running violently down a steep place into the sea'.[552]

The number 'two thousand', if referring to the strength of the troops, would almost be correct because Caesar had 'twenty two thousand' men: Mark would have simply lost the second part of *dischilioi pros dismyriois*. However, in case this was the relative number—Pompeius had double the number of soldiers that Caesar did—Mark mixed up *diplasioi*, 'double', with *dischilioi*, 'two thousand' (ΔΙΠΛΑCΙΟΙ ≈ ΔΙCΧΙΛΙΟΙ).[553]

The rest of the pericope relates in condensed form the continuing course of the campaign up to the victory of Caesar, the despondency of Pompeius, and his flight:

> 'Pompeius, who from his other wing saw the shattered cavalry fleeing, was out of his mind. He forgot that he was Pompeius the Great. As if a god had stricken him with insanity he went quietly into his tent and sat waiting for that which was to come. As his entire army started to flee and the enemy entered the camp and attacked the defenders he came to his senses and spoke the single thought 'Even into the camp?' He exchanged his commander's clothes for others that would allow him to flee easier and snuck away.'[554]

The parallel report in Mark reads:

> 'And they that fed the swine fled, and told it in the city, and in the country. And they went out to see what it was that was done. And

they come to Jesus, and see him that was possessed with the devil, and had the legion, sitting, and clothed, and in his right mind: and they were afraid. And they that saw it told them how it befell to him that was possessed with the devil, and also concerning the swine. And they began to pray him to depart out of their coasts. And when he was come into the ship, he that had been possessed with the devil prayed him that he might be with him. Howbeit Jesus suffered him not, but saith unto him, Go home to thy friends, and tell them how great things the Lord hath done for thee, and hath had compassion on thee. And he departed, and began to publish in Decapolis how great things Jesus had done for him: and all men did marvel.'[555]

The 'fleeing cavalry' became the 'fleeing swineherders'; the 'storming of the camp' became 'coming into the ship'. Did Mark read 'in the camp', *eis to stratopedon,* here as *eis to ploion,* 'in the ship'? Did he take *stratopedon* not in the sense of 'army camp' and 'army', but as 'fleet' and saw *ploion* in *-pedon?* Did he apprehend 'stormed', *epebainon,* as if it were *embainon(tos),* 'he entered'? Or did the fact that Pompeius came via Larissa to the sea, boarded a boat and fled further via Mitylene to Egypt, influence him? The *Decapolis,* the 'ten cities', where the possessed went, are missing in Plutarchus. But in his parallel passage, Appianus begins mentioning the stations of the flight by naming cities, starting with *Larissa.*

'This they would have' : Second prediction of the passion

As Caesar entered the camp of Pompeius and he saw that even though he had admonished his soldiers to spare the Roman citizens among the enemies, many laid dead on the ground and others were being killed, he said with a sigh: 'They wanted it, they forced me: for I, Gaius Caesar, who has achieved the greatest victories, would have even been sentenced to death if I had dismissed the army.'

Plutarchus reports this, expressly referring to Asinius Pollio, pointing out that Caesar spoke these words in a language other than that in which Asinius had written them. Since Asinius wrote in Latin, Caesar spoke Greek on this occasion, as he did so often when he wanted to be understood by his officers but not his soldiers.[556]

Mark turns this into a prediction of the passion:

'...and he would not that any man should know it. For he taught his disciples, and said unto them, The Son of man is delivered into the hands of men, and they shall kill him; and after that he is killed, he shall rise the third day. But they understood not that saying, and were afraid to ask him.'[557]

What should be stressed here is the fact that Caesar calls himself *Gaius* and not Iulius. Consistently Mark has 'Son of Man': *Gaius* is divided into *Gai us*, 'Son of the Earth, or Son of Man'. That he shall rise the third day is a later addition but not a fabrication: someplace Mark found the ominous *triumvirate* and misunderstood it as *triêmeria*, 'three days'—and placed it fittingly here.

The difference between 'he would have been killed' with Caesar and 'they will kill him' in Jesus is not significant in Greek where the tenses of verbs are not so fixed, but are subject to the aspect.

This prediction of Jesus' passion is counted as the second in the Gospel editions. We have not seen the first yet. It can be found in Mark 8:31-9:1. How does it align with the Caesar story?

There is a hint in this second prediction of the passion which begins:

'And they departed thence, and passed through Galilee.'[558]

It refers us to the beginning of the Gospel before the Jordan or the Rubicon. There, not the second, but the first prediction of the passion of Jesus can be localized, which is given without specification of place and time and in the beginning it sounds like a doublet of the second:

'And he began to teach them, that the Son of man must suffer many things, and be rejected of the elders, and of the chief priests, and scribes, and be killed, and after three days rise again.'[559]

Looking closely we see however, that here 'the elders, the chief priests, and the scribes' are present. We already know that this refers to the address of the senators: *patres conscripti*. We are thus in the Senate and speeches are being held. The continuation is as follows:

'And he spake that saying openly. And Peter took him, and began to rebuke him. But when he had turned about and looked on his disciples, he rebuked Peter, saying, Get thee behind me, Satan: for thou savourest not the things that be of God, but the things that be of men.'[560]

'Satan' stands for the Senate. 'Peter' is Lepidus or Antonius. The threatened Peter who began to rebuke him and who is told, 'Get behind me, Satan!' is Antonius. He had interceded for Caesar, was threatened with his life, and left the Senate, calling on the gods and cursing:

'He stormed out as if possessed, predicted war, murder, proscription, exile, expropriation and all evils that were before them and laid great curses on those who were responsible for these things.'[561]

This prediction of passion addressed to the *Senators/Satan* by Antonius/Peter is turned around by Mark as if it referred to Caesar/Jesus: something else did not fit in with his schema.

When Caesar heard of this, he referred to the threat to the interceding people's tribunes as 'the height of disrespect for all godly and human laws.'⁵⁶² Mark joins in in his way: 'for thou savourest not the things that be of God, but the things that be of men.'

Now that we could locate the first prediction of the passion to the malediction of Antonius as he is chased out of the Senate, we can also align the beginning sentence of the second prediction:

'And they departed thence, and passed through Galilee' is to be understood as: 'And the tribune of the people left the Senate and the city and fled to Caesar in Gaul.'

This also allows us to localize the following speech of Jesus to the people and his disciples. It is the discussion Caesar had with his officers before crossing the Rubicon.

As we know, Caesar hesitated to cross the border river armed, because it meant opening the Civil War. He paused and considered the pros and cons, and conferred with his entourage of friends. He said: 'Not to cross would bring me distress and misfortune, whereas to cross will bring it to all people.' And he asked himself how he would be judged by posterity if he let the weapons decide. But in the end, like a man seized by god, he vigorously crossed over and said: 'Let the die be cast'. And soon he occupied Ariminum and then, as we all know, all other cities and the entire Empire:⁵⁶³

Mark's reproduction:

'And when he had called the people unto him with his disciples also, he said unto them, Whosoever will come after me, let him deny himself, and take up his cross, and follow me. For whosoever will save his life shall lose it; but whosoever shall lose his life for my sake and the Gospel's, the same shall save it. For what shall it profit a man, if he shall gain the whole world, and lose his own soul? Or what shall a man give in exchange for his soul? Whosoever therefore shall be ashamed of me and of my words in this adulterous and sinful generation; of him also shall the Son of man be ashamed, when he cometh in the glory of his Father with the holy angels. And he said unto them, Verily I say unto you, That there be some of them that stand here, which shall not taste of death, till they have seen the Kingdom of God come with power.'⁵⁶⁴

Unlike Caesar, Jesus has no doubts. The alternative has remained, however. Caesar made it clear to his followers that not taking the fatal step would mean their own ruin, to take it would mean civil war. It is the same with Jesus, because as we know now, *evangelion*, 'Gospel', stands for Civil War here. Mark has turned *alea* into *antallagma*, 'ransom', so *Alea iacta est(o)* became: 'to give as ransom'—and to make sense of it he completed: 'Or what shall a man give in exchange for his soul?'

The doubts Caesar had regarding the judgment of those in the future are processed by Mark thus: 'Whosoever therefore shall be ashamed of me and of my words in this adulterous and sinful generation; of him also shall the Son of man be ashamed, when he cometh in the glory of his Father with the holy angels.' The 'angels' are his legions here also.

Feast in the camp of Pompeius : Feeding of the five and four thousand

Before the battle, Caesar had told his soldiers to defiantly tear down the camp walls as they left, to demonstrate to themselves and to the enemy that they had nothing to lose and that they had to take the hostile camp. The soldiers complied with this easily because they were lacking even the most basic necessities in their own camp, while the enemy banquetted in excess.

After taking Pompeius' camp, Caesar quartered himself there just as he had threatened, and he himself ate the food prepared for Pompeius while his army ate that prepared for their enemies.[565] It became a real feast, because the Pompeians had been so sure of success that they had prepared a luxurious meal. Artfully arranged arbors were seen and the tents were laid out with fresh lawn or even garlanded with ivy and myrtles, while the tables were decked with colorful tablecloths and silverware and plentiful cups; the wine was not only poured in the little amphora, as usual, but also in the larger mixing jars where water and wine spritzers would have been expected.[566]

Elements of this anecdote are found in Mark in the feeding of the five thousand and again in the feeding of the four thousand, as well as in the wedding of Cana, of which only John reports. The reason the Gospel writers make a number of separate pericopes regarding this is that the feast in Pompeius' camp was not the only feast of Caesar's 'people'. At the plundering of Gomphoi there had already been an orgy of eating and drinking, as we have seen. And then also, of course, there were the unforgettable *epula*, the public banquets Caesar gave to the people later in Rome while celebrating his triumphs, as well as at the belated festivities honoring his deceased daughter Iulia. And there were the traditional *sportulae*, 'food baskets', with victuals and money. These Caesar gave to the people even more generously than ever before and he established colonies as rewards for the veterans and as the basis of a livelihood for those city dwellers with many children.

The sources speak of several repeated public feasts; of twenty two thousand tables set up across the entire city, even outside on the streets and crossings, all of which were waited on; of six thousand morays, weighing more than two thousand of today's kilos, delivered on credit from a fish breeder named Hirrius, once an enemy of Caesar's; of an amphora (26 l) of Falernum, the best white wine of Italy, for each table of nine guests and in addition a *cadus,* an even larger jar (38 l), not filled with water but with wine from Chios; of a feast that was repeated because someone had complained and said it was too modest and not worthy of the generosity of Caesar—with that other choice wines were mentioned: in addition to Falernum and Chios also Lesbos and Mamertinum; finally it was being said that food was distributed to those that could not be present, not only oil and wheat, but also money—three hundred coins plus one hundred interest on arrears—and what seemed very extraordinary: even meat.[567]

As can be seen, all the elements are gathered here that appear in the feeding of the five thousand (Mk. 6:30-44), the four thousand (Mk. 8:1-9) and the marriage at Cana (Jn. 2:1-11): the silver, or the money (two hundred pieces of silver); the meal outside in the open and in groups and on green grass; the abundance after hunger; the food baskets with the leftover pieces; the bread; the wine; the complaint that it was not enough; the water jars filled with wine.[568]

It should be noted that both of Mark's scenes take place in the 'desert', *erêmôi,* which we know stands for *Romae:* we are thus 'in Rome'. But since there are elements that remind one of the feast in Pompeius' camp—the 'green grass' for example—it is possible Mark might have combined the different anecdotes. Incidentally, the sources do the same, where each author summarizes in his own fashion. Because Jesus boards a boat and travels to Dalmanoutha after feeding the four thousand, just as after the feast in Pompeius' camp Caesar heads for Alexandria by boat, the feeding of the four thousand might originally have had more elements of the feast in Pompeius' camp. Unfortunately, the feeding of the four thousand has been adapted so much to the feeding of the five thousand in successive editions and copies, that it lost any originality. For the same reason we had to deal with the different feasts together.

The 'two fish' or 'many little fish' might have been the morays served by the fish breeder Hirrius during the triumphant feasts of Caesar. Then the number 'two fish' would be right, because officially, except for the repeat dinner, there were two banquets. Since the 'Feasts' were *(h)estiaseis,* but were also called 'sacrifices', *thysiai,* due to the solemnly slaughtered animals, the *ichthyas,* 'the fish', might have crept in as a mixture of *(h)estiaseis* and *thysias.*[569] In this situation the undefined number 'many little fish' would be more apposite.

As far as the quantity of breads is concerned, if Mark confused *prandiis* with *panibus* thus 'feast' with 'bread' then either five or seven is correct, depending on whether the repeated dinner or the meat distribution was counted as extra or not.

The 'wedding at Cana' is the 'feast in honor of Iulia'. Here we once more have the opportunity to observe that John had a different exemplar than Mark who used a Latin one. John's exemplar must have been a Greek one because the Latin form of the name *IVLIA* does not allow for the word *KANA*, but the Greek form *IOYΛIA: IO* can be taken for a *K (IO > IC > K)* as well as *ΛI* as *N (ΛI > N)*:

IOYΛIA

ICYΛIA

KANA (it cannot remain *kyna*: that would mean 'bitch'!)

This explains why Mark does not, and cannot, mention a wedding at Cana, while John does. We will see that he instead makes *Iulia* the daughter of *Iulius*, the daughter of *Jairus*:

IVLIVS > IAIRVS > IAIPOC

We should note here that the prologue to the feeding of the five thousand in Mark 6:31-33, where Jesus calls upon the apostles—

'Come ye yourselves apart into a desert place, and rest a while: for there were many coming and going, and they had no leisure so much as to eat. And they departed into a desert place by ship privately.'

—might refer to the establishment of colonies which Caesar gave to the veterans and city proletariat as a prize for victory and in order to reduce the number of people suffering from hunger in the city. In place of 'establish colonies' there is the picture of 'apostles going off' because in Latin 'establish colonies' is *colonias deducere* literally 'lead colonies away' in the sense of let go away and settle elsewhere. The fact that Mark has them go 'into a desert place' even though they were leaving 'from Rome' might be because the 'deduced' ones were Roman colonies that were founded in far away, and in some cases, actually devastated sites, such as upon the one-hundred year old ruins of the destroyed cities of Carthago and Corinth. Thus he probably mixed up 'from the desert' and 'into the desert'.

Prodigies : Parables

These have been dealt with in great detail in a previous chapter. Here we just bring them to mind because of the sequence of events:

After the victory in Pharsalos, Caesar chased Pompeius to Egypt. He passed the coast of Asia Minor where he heard of the prodigies that had announced or accompanied his victory. As we have seen, these prodigies were paraphrased as parables.

Pompeius to Egypt : End of the Baptist

During his escape, Pompeius took his lovely wife Cornelia aboard in Mytilene. He actually wanted to seek protection with the Parthians but because he did not want his young wife to fall into the hands of licentious barbarians, he decided to go to Egypt and headed for Kasion, a promontory near Pelusium. There his protégé, the thirteen-year-old King Ptolemaios, camped with his regents, court and army in order to prevent his sister/wife Cleopatra—who ruled with him according to the will of their father—from reacquiring, with the help of Syrian Arabs, the throne from which he had expelled her.

Pompeius sent negotiators from the ship to the young king. The king owed him friendship and thanks for help he had given to his father. He conferred with his regents: the governor Achillas; his guardian, treasurer and eunuch Potheinos; and the head of the Gabinians, an old Roman occupation corps that had degenerated into a raw and insubordinate soldiery. The Samian rhetorician Theodotos, the teacher of the young king, was also present. The one group wanted to help Pompeius out of old gratitude, the other feared he could take over the country. Thereupon the rhetorician demanded the head of Pompeius and suggested luring him into an ambush and killing him, thinking this would please Caesar. The rhetorician succeeded in getting his plan accepted. So they sent a detachment commanded by Achillas to Pompeius' ship, among them two Gabinians: a Salvius and a Septimius. The latter, who had once served with Pompeius, addressed him as Emperor and lured him into their boat. As he stood there holding the hand of Philippus, his freedman, they killed him, still in sight of his wife who had remained on the ship. It was the day after his birthday. Then they severed his head and brought it to the rhetorician and Philippus took his headless body and buried it on shore with the help of some Pompeian who happened to be passing by.

When Caesar reached Alexandria three days later, the rhetorician handed him the head of Pompeius on the ship, but Caesar turned away, visibly shaken and when he was handed Pompeius' ring he wept. But he had the evil doers suffer due punishment later.[570]

Mark includes almost all the details in his reproduction:

'And king Herod heard of him; (for his name was spread abroad:) and he said, That John the Baptist was risen from the dead, and therefore mighty works do shew forth themselves in him. Others said, That it is Elias. And others said, That it is a prophet, or as one of the prophets. But when Herod heard thereof, he said, It is John, whom I beheaded: he is risen from the dead.

For Herod himself had sent forth and laid hold upon John, and bound him in prison for Herodias' sake, his brother Philip's wife: for he had married her. For John had said unto Herod, It is not lawful for thee to have thy brother's wife. Therefore Herodias had a quarrel against him, and would have killed him; but she could not: For Herod feared John, knowing that he was a just man and an holy, and observed him; and when he heard him, he did many things, and heard him gladly. And when a convenient day was come, that Herod on his birthday made a supper to his lords, high captains, and chief estates of Galilee; And when the daughter of the said Herodias came in, and danced, and pleased Herod and them that sat with him, the king said unto the damsel, Ask of me whatsoever thou wilt, and I will give it thee. And he sware unto her, Whatsoever thou shalt ask of me, I will give it thee, unto the half of my kingdom. And she went forth, and said unto her mother, What shall I ask? And she said, The head of John the Baptist. And she came in straightway with haste unto the king, and asked, saying, I will that thou give me by and by in a charger the head of John the Baptist. And the king was exceeding sorry; yet for his oath's sake, and for their sakes which sat with him, he would not reject her.

And immediately the king sent an executioner, and commanded his head to be brought: and he went and beheaded him in the prison, And brought his head in a charger, and gave it to the damsel: and the damsel gave it to her mother. And when his disciples heard of it, they came and took up his corpse, and laid it in a tomb.'[571]

The linchpin that makes the entire story switch is the instigator of the death of Pompeius: The *rhetor* becomes *Herod*. All the others follow him: the freed *Philippus* becomes the brother of Herod of the same name and Pompeius' wife *Cornelia* is Herod's wife *Herodias*. The dynastic sibling marriage between Cleopatra and her brother Ptolemaios becomes the forbidden marriage between Herod and the wife of his brother. Pompeius, the supporter of Ptolemaios' father remains of course John, but is characterized as a righteous and holy man. The consultation on the birthday of Pompeius becomes the dinner on Herod's birthday, the *commanders of the Gabinians* become the *lords, high captains, and chief estates of Galilee*. As a Samian, the rhetorician Theodotos, who demanded the head of Pompeius, enjoys a doubling: *(h)o Samios Theodotos* becomes *(orchê)samenês thygatros*, the 'dancing daughter' who requested the head of John. The murderer, *Septimius*, who addressed Pompeius as *imperator* becomes the *spekoulator*, which does not mean 'executioner', but actually 'watcher, spy, or body guard'. The death and beheading of Pompeius 'fleeing', as a 'fugitive'—*phygê*—becomes that of John in 'prison'—*phylakê*. The head that is carried to Theodotos who in turn gives it to Caesar, is now given to the girl who passes it to her mother. It is interesting that the 'daughter' is now called 'damsel', using a conspicuous word: *korasion*—that is close to *Caesar*.

Even what is missing is true: the name of Herodias' daughter, which the Gospel writer does not mention. *Salome* was her name—and it represents a hardly deformed Greek lection of *Salvius*, the other assassin: *CAΛOYI(oc)* ≈ *CAΛΩM(η)*. Mark cannot have the name for the simple reason that he had a Latin exemplar, as we have seen. Only John would have been able to employ it if he had told the anecdote.

The beginning of the Markan pericope—from 'And king Herod heard of him...' to '...It is John, whom I beheaded: he is risen from the dead'—does not so much refer to the rhetorician's fears at Pompeius' arrival in Egypt, as it does to his frustrated hopes when Caesar came and did not value at all what was thought of as a favor, but rather when presented with the horrible gift—'...It is John, whom I beheaded...'—shuddered. Thus Mark has first told about the arrival of Caesar and only then the murder of Pompeius. He thus proves his purely Caesarean point of view.

We note here that behind the name *Elia* that is mentioned here, might be *Iulius*. It is not surprising that we find the official gentile name for Caesar at the place where he succeeds Pompeius in the East.

Caesar in Alexandria : Jesus in Dalmanutha

After Caesar, on his ship lying at anchor in Alexandria, had received Pompeius' signet ring from Theodotos, and with that also gained formal authority over the East which had been dependent on Pompeius, he disembarked, and, as a Roman consul, had his lictors carry before him the fasces, the symbols of office. However, the crowd was incited by Potheinos, and became indignant at the Roman symbols. They cried out that this action diminished the majesty of their king Ptolemaios. But because he insisted on displaying the symbols of Roman authority, repeated tumults came about wherein some soldiers had their weapons taken away, and some were even killed. So he sought refuge in the king's palace and his ship left the port and waited offshore until the following legions arrived in the other ships.[572]

Mark's processing is very true to detail again:
'And straightway he entered into a ship with his disciples, and came into the parts of Dalmanutha. And the Pharisees came forth, and be-

gan to question with him, seeking of him a sign from heaven, tempting him. And he sighed deeply in his spirit, and saith, Why doth this generation seek after a sign? verily I say unto you, There shall no sign be given unto this generation. And he left them, and entering into the ship again departed to the other side.'[573]

Here we have the Dalmanutha on which we thought elsewhere that 'Dalmatia'—the landing site of Antonius/Petrus—might have rubbed off. But in fact *Dalmanoutha* stands for *Alexandria* here. We see most clearly how the mutation occurred if we write the names on top of each other. Since many variants appear in the manuscripts instead of *Dalmanoutha*, for example *Magadan* and *Magdala*, prompting the textual-critics to assume that they have lost the initial letters *'Dal'*, because it was understood as 'of', so we also shall place *Magdala* under Alexandria as well:

A L E X A N D R I A
Δ A Λ M A N O Υ Θ A
   M A Γ Δ A Λ A

This not only means that *Dalmanoutha* stands for *Alexandria*, but we also have to familiarize ourselves with the idea that *Magdalene* does not come from *Magdala*, but from *Alexandria*. This substantiates our initial assumption that Cleopatra stands behind Mary Magdalene.

The Alexandrians rising up against Caesar are here called *Pharisees*. The matter of whether Mark gave them this name because they were followers of *Ptolemy*, or—as he was under age—that of his guardian *Potheinos* who, as we shall see, immediately started to intrigue against Caesar; or simply because Mark called everyone who spoke against Caesar by this name, *Pharisees*, may be put aside for the moment. We will come across it in the next pericope again and then know more.

Anyhow, the 'signs from heaven' are the 'symbols of Rome'. Mark did not understand the *signa* as 'standards' or 'signs of office'—which the Greek word *sêmeia* also denotes—but as 'omens'. Accordingly, 'Roman', *romanus*, became *ouranos*, 'heaven', which surely was not wrong in the imagination of Mark and his community of veterans' descendants. In any case, Mark sticks with the theme: as Caesar did not give up his symbols, so Jesus did not give a sign to the Pharisees. And as Caesar rather had his ship withdraw temporarily until the whole fleet had crossed over, so Jesus 'entering into the ship again departed to the other side.'

Here it should be noted that some modernistic translators of the Bible prefer to refer to Jesus' 'ships' as 'boats', just as they rather call the Galilaean 'sea' a 'lake'. They do this so that their preconception that the theater of action is the Lake of Gennesaret, which is not a sea and has no ships, only boats, remains more credible. They prefer to do violence to the Greek, wherein *ploion* and *thalassa* are regularly used, than to question their own ideas. Now that it has been unquestionably demonstrated that their *Dalmanutha* and their *Magadan*—both of which could never be located on the Lake of Gennesaret—in reality stand for *Alexandria,* they will have to throw some of their ballast overboard nolens volens.

Beware of Potheinos : Beware of the Pharisees

Caesar had planned to settle the differences between the children of the deceased Ptolemaios Auletes, who had formed an alliance with Rome at the time of his consulate and had deposited a copy of his testament there. According to the paternal will, the elder daughter Cleopatra was to become queen together with the underage son Ptolemaios. But Potheinos, who as the guardian of the thirteen-year-old son had him in his grip, but not the strong-willed and intelligent twenty-year-old daughter, did not like that. So he had intrigued against her and chased her away, as we saw.

When she learnt that Caesar was staying in the king's palace, she left her Syrian troops, boarded a barque with a sole companion and managed to get to Caesar undetected under cover of darkness, being carried through the gates of the palace bundled up in bed sheets. She won Caesar's heart by this cunning and courageous idea, and he fully succumbed to her grace and the attraction of interacting with her. So Caesar looked after the cause of Ptolemaios' daughter in a special way and mediated a reconciliation with her brother, which was celebrated with a festive meal.

But this in turn threatened Potheinos' position. In order to engender hatred of Caesar, he told the king's soldiers—to whom he had rationed out mouldy old grain—they should remain quiet and be satisfied, since they were fed on a foreign table. He had the king's table set with wooden crockery and earthenware, and explained that the cutlery of gold and silver had to be delivered to Caesar in payment for an old debt. He said this, even though Caesar had remitted the children of his old partner Ptolemaios half of the amount that their father had owed him.

But Caesar's barber was on the lookout. Suspicious and curious, he left nothing uninvestigated, pricked up his ears everywhere and at the feast he got wind that Potheinos and Achillas were planning an attempt on Caesar. He ordered the hall surrounded and carriers with secret messages were uncovered. Potheinos was gotten rid of; Achillas, to whom

Cleopatra's younger sister Arsinoe fled and later her little brother Ptolemaios as well, initially escaped but was subsequently defeated.

Meanwhile Caesar enjoyed the banquets of Cleopatra, who now reigned alone and gave birth to a son shortly after Caesar had left Egypt: Caesarion.[574]

Mark unravels this story into two pericopes, of which one warns against the leaven of the Pharisees following their demanding of a sign in Dalmanoutha, and the other one deals with the Syro-Phoenicean woman.

Here both pericopes consecutively:

'And from thence he arose, and went into the borders of Tyre and Sidon, and entered into an house, and would have no man know it: but he could not be hid. For a certain woman, whose young daughter had an unclean spirit, heard of him, and came and fell at his feet: The woman was a Greek, a Syro-Phoenician by nation; and she besought him that he would cast forth the evil spirit from her daughter. But Jesus said unto her, Let the children first be filled: for it is not meet to take the children's bread, and to cast [it] unto the dogs. And she answered and said unto him, Yes, Lord: yet the dogs under the table eat of the children's crumbs. And he said unto her, For this saying go thy way; the devil is gone out of thy daughter. And when she was come to her house, she found the devil gone out, and her daughter laid upon the bed.' [575]

Presumably the 'cohorts from Syria', became the 'the borders of Tyrus', from where Caesar expected reinforcement and where Cleopatra had hired soldiers also—*ta (h)oria Tyrou: cohortes > tahoria; Syria > Tyros.* [576]

The 'being hidden' could refer to Caesar, who had barricaded himself in the king's palace, but could also refer to Cleopatra, who came to him by stealth. As Cleopatra was secretly carried to Caesar wrapped in a bedsack, so the woman came to the hidden Jesus and fell down at his feet. *Cleopatra* was not an Egyptian by birth, but a *Hellene*, descended from the Macedonian successors of Alexander—the woman who came to Jesus is characterized explicitly as a *Greek* 'from Syro-Phoenicia'. Mark says *syrophoinis(s)a*, 'Syro-Phoenician', which is amazing, because she was either Greek or Syro-Phoenician. So it is translated with the wisdom of Solomon as 'a Syro-Phoenician by nation'. Strikingly, the Greek writing of *syrophoinisa* relates to the Latin for *Cleopatra* like *Dalmanutha* does to *Alexandria*:

C L E O P A T R A

C Υ P O Φ OI N IC A

Syrophoinisa, furthermore, sounds as if it was a contraction of *Arsinoe* and *Potheinos,* the name of Auletes' other daughter and opponent of her sister Cleopatra combined with that of the younger brother's guardian, who made common cause with her against Caesar. Thus the 'daughter (who) had an unclean spirit' is *Arsinoe* together with *Potheinos,* and a further periphrasis of the same *Syrophoinisa*. Here, little brother *Ptolemaios,* too, has become the 'unclean spirit' along with his guardian *Potheinos*: both have the misfortune to have names that are not so far from *pneuma*, 'spirit', either, like that of *Pompeius*, who was still spooking about. The spirit is the 'devil', of course, because it is hostile, but also 'unclean', because there is an army behind them—here too: *exercitus > akathartos.*

The bread not only stands for the good grain which Caesar commandeered for his soldiers and for the bad grain which was left for those of the king, but also for the gold and silver crockery which was taken from the children for the payment of the debt—whereby Caesar here has the pleasure of becoming *kynaria*, 'dogs'. But he throws out Potheinos because of his evil talk, like Jesus casts out the evil spirit because of his words. And in the end, in both stories a child lies on the bed—when the demon had left.

The second pericope is unnecessarily long:

'Now the disciples had forgotten to take bread, neither had they in the ship with them more than one loaf. And he charged them, saying, Take heed, beware of the leaven of the Pharisees, and of the leaven of Herod. And they reasoned among themselves, saying, It is because we have no bread. And when Jesus knew it, he saith unto them, Why reason ye, because ye have no bread? perceive ye not yet, neither understand? have ye your heart yet hardened? Having eyes, see ye not? and having ears, hear ye not? and do ye not remember? When I brake the five loaves among five thousand, how many baskets full of fragments took ye up? They say unto him, Twelve. And when the seven among four thousand, how many baskets full of fragments took ye up? And they said, Seven. And he said unto them, How is it that ye do not understand?'[577]

As one can see, it contains only two elements:

The mouldy grain, served to the soldiers of the king by Potheinos, becomes the leaven of the Pharisees here. Now we can answer the question that was left open above, of who' the Pharisees represent: it is Potheinos. Interestingly, Herod is mentioned as well, as if in Mark's exemplar the rhetorician Theodotos still had a hand in it.

And then we have the watchful eyes and the attentive ears of Caesar's barber, which become the admonishing questions: 'Having eyes, see ye not? and having ears, hear ye not?'

The rest is Mark's bread kitchen. Only the ending—'How is it that ye do not understand?'—seems to represent an echo of Caesar's failed reconciliation attempt.

Victory over Pharnaces : Healing of a deaf-mute

Caesar left Egypt and passed by Syria and Galatia to Pontus, where Pharnaces had conquered Roman territories, amongst them lesser Armenia, which had been granted to Deiotarus, king of the Galatians. Deiotarus had supported Pompeius, but he had not, so Pharnaces thought Caesar would tolerate his retaking the territories that had once belonged to his father Mithridates the Great. So he left his kingdom at the Cimmerian Bosphorus—today the Crimea—which Pompeius had given him in gratitude for driving his father, who was warring against him, to suicide—and invaded Pontus and Cappadocia over Colchis and lesser Armenia. But as Caesar trusted the faithful Deiotarus rather than the disloyal Pharnaces, he sent Domitius to re-establish Roman rule.

But Pharnaces was able to drive Domitius back, and in his barbaric recklessness he slaughtered the Romans in the territory he occupied, even having not a few of them castrated. But when he learnt that Caesar himself approached and that he had reconciled with Deiotarus and had received troop reinforcements from him, he sent forth emissaries with negotiatory messages, offering him a Golden wreath together with his daughter, and he tried to win him over with the fact that he had not supported Pompeius. In order to misguide him about his plans, Caesar received the first and the second legations in a friendly manner, but at the third he suddenly blamed Pharnaces for having murdered his own father and also for abandoning his benefactor Pompeius—and moreover for having committed an irreparable crime by robbing Roman citizens abroad on business in Pontus of their lives, or even worse, of their procreative capacity. And right away he did battle with him, drove him out of Pontus and completely destroyed his army.

That was the battle of Zela. Caesar was never as proud of a battle as he was of this one. He sent the famous message to Rome, an unsurpassed example of impressive brevity—*veni vidi vici*—and later had it carried before him in the triumph.[578]

We have seen that the Evangelist John made the healing of a congenitally blind man out of it—*veni vidi vici* > *I came, washed myself and saw*—and Mark made it the healing of a blind man—*veni vidi vici* > *I see men as trees walking.* But in John the healing was much more elaborate. We could recognize the name of the Pontic town Zela as 'pond Siloah' as well as 'drive out' (Pharnaces), *expulit,* as *exspuit,* 'spit' (spitting into the blind man's eyes). Mark has brought these elements, the localization and also the *expulit/exspuit,* into a second healing, the healing of a deaf-mute and in doing so duplicated the Pharnaces anecdote. The reason for this division is that in Mark's exemplar, as we saw, the saying occurred in connection with the triumph in Rome, whereas John's source recorded chronologically and interpreted it as a message sent from the Pontic Zela.

So we have to expect a healing spit to play a role in Mark's story of the healing of the deaf-mute, possibly with a threefold alteration of the *veni vidi vici*:

> 'And again, departing from the coasts of Tyre and Sidon, he came unto the sea of Galilee, through the midst of the coasts of Decapolis. And they bring unto him one that was deaf, and had an impediment in his speech; and they beseech him to put his hand upon him. And he took him aside from the multitude, and put his fingers into his ears, and he spit, and touched his tongue; And looking up to heaven, he sighed, and saith unto him, Ephphatha, that is, Be opened. And straightway his ears were opened, and the string of his tongue was loosed, and he spake plain. And he charged them that they should tell no man: but the more he charged them, the more greatly they published it; And they were astonished beyond measure, saying, He hath done all things well: he maketh both the deaf to hear, and the dumb to speak.'579

Tyre might simply stand for *Syria* here and the 'borders of Tyre' point to the fact that Caesar, along with his troops—also here *cohortium > tôn horiôn*—at first landed in Syria. *Sidon* stands for *Zêla* (pronounced *zealer*); the sea of *Galilee* for Pontus perceived as the sea of *Galatia;* and the 'ten cities', the *Decapolis,* could stand for *Deiotarus,* the 'coasts'— *(h)oriôn*—'of the ten cities', however, would reflect not so much his domains than the *cohorts* he put at Caesar's disposal.580 The deaf-mute is of course Pharnaces, who—as one who has been defeated—has to be healed according to the well-tried formula. The name of his infirmity is a surprise however, because for 'deaf-mute' in Greek it should have been sufficient to just use *kôphos,* but Mark instead adds the tautological *mogilalos,* 'having an impediment in speech'. Should *kôphon kai mogilalon* mask 'Cappadocia and Armenia minor'? We would have to compare *kôphon kai* with *Cappadocia,* and *kai mogilalon* with *Armenia minor.* It might be thought that there is no similarity between both of the latter. But after a closer look we determine that the variation remains within the range of Mark's practice.

A R M E N I A M I N O R
Κ ΑΙΜ Ο Γ Ι Λ Α   Λ Ο Ν

To explain the appearance of *-lalon*, 'slurring, speaking', the influence of *kaloumenê*, 'called' could be suspected (cf. Plutarchus': *Armenia (h)ê mikra kaloumenê*, 'Armenia, called the small'). This shift of sense, however, could be based on Caesar's behavior, who at first feigned deafness and muteness to the legations of Pharnaces, in order to misguide them as to his plans.

The glance of the sighing Jesus to 'heaven' might certainly come from the command of the stressed Caesar to restore 'Roman' order: *romanum > ouranon*—as above, but now in the accusative. Whether the *ptysas*, 'spitting', is due to a corruption of *expulit* into *exspuit*, 'drive out' into 'spit', as we saw earlier, or whether Pharnaces' toadyism might have rubbed off on it, is something to talk about. At any rate, the immediately following *hepphatha* very probably simply means *ex Ponto*, 'out of Pontus': 'he drove him out of Pontus', *expulit ex Ponto > exspuit kai: (h)epphatha*, 'he spit and [said]: Be opened'.

Here again we find the threefold measure of the *veni vidi vici*, twice nested in each other and maintained, despite the variations that can be observed from manuscript to manuscript: the one time as 'spit (in the ears), looked (up to heaven) and touched (the tongue)', and the other time as 'sighed, saith, be opened!'. From this it can be inferred that *(h)epphatha*, with its beginning '*e-*', which looks like an augment, covers a more original Greek aorist, which along with 'sighed' and 'saith' formed the threefold measure, and only later was it interpreted as Aramaic. With this we have clear further proof that the Aramaic belongs to the latest layer of redaction.

The order 'to tell no man', the remark 'but the more he charged them, so much the more a great deal they published it' and the 'they were astonished beyond measure' could point to Caesar's pride in the brilliant victory, as well as to its eternal fame, which is based not least on the admired brachylogy, the expression's laconism.

It should be remarked here that not even this time is Galilaea Galilaea. Because when leaving Egypt, Caesar passed from Alexandria to Antiochia by sea and only from there travelled to Galatia overland. Which means he only sailed past Galilaea, and whether he landed in Tyre and Sidon is in question. The report by Dio (*Historiae Romanae* 42.49.2) that Caesar had removed all the votive offerings from the temple of Hercules at Tyre because the citizenry had harbored the fleeing wife and son of Pompeius, arises from Pompeian propaganda, and therefore surely did not appear in Mark's exemplar, as it is also missing with Plutarchus, Appianus and Suetonius.

But Mark shows consistency in the confusion. Here he calls Galatia Galilaea, as he initially called Gallia Galilaea. Now, it is no accident that there is a resemblance in the sound, because in both cases *Galli,* 'Gauls', lived there. The fact that Caesar found his base and backing among the Gauls had its reasons. One might think that the Gauls should have been angry with him because he had conquered Gallia. The contrary is the case: they thought highly of him for recruiting among them. The core of his troops were Gauls, his cavalry Germans—to whom he had even given the horses of Roman knights; Gauls were his colonists, whom he settled all over the Empire,[581] and they also were new senators, appointed by him. The aristocrats derided that he had replaced the Roman toga with Gallic pants, the very admission of those 'semi-barbarians' into the Curia was one of the motives that led to his murder.[582] In fact he did not have anything against Gallic garments, because when his legions were under siege in Germany he made his way to them through hostile territory dressed as a Gaul.[583] That he had taken the Roman temple treasure, which was deposited to finance the defence against any renewed Gallic threat, in order to stamp coins propagandizing the final victory over Gaul (on the coin's pictures), but which were de facto used to pay his Gallic legionaries, who provided him with power over the Roman Senate, made him look definitively like a Gaul in the eyes of the Romans—and even more in the eyes of his Gallic companions. He did not accidentally leave his sword, which had been snatched from him during the battle of Gergovia, hanging in the sacred Gallic site.[584]

So it is only consistent that Mark has made Caesar the 'Galilaean'. If there was something more than just a mere coincidental resemblance of words as the motive, then it was this: Gauls formed the basic stock of the legions that were given to Herodes first by Antonius, then by Octavianus, in order that he could become and remain King of Judaea. Following the Julian example, he later settled them in veteran colonies, particularly in Galilaea, and also in Samaria and Decapolis. Through this, Galilaea became 'Gallic' territory which may have caused Mark to standardize all Gallias and Galatias in his redaction process to Galilaea.

After the victory over Pharnaces, Caesar hurried to Rome, where he started preparations for the war in 'Africa', today called Tunisia, where the rest of the Pompeians had gathered around Scipio and Cato after the defeat at Pharsalos. As we have already seen, Caesar sent his victory-message from Zela in advance—*veni vidi vici*—to Rome.

But Mark cannot possibly send the victory-message right now, because he has changed it into the healing of a blind man—*I see men as trees walking*. So instead he sends the healed 'blind' man, the *caecus*, which we know conceals *Caesar*—and it is not untrue, because immediately after the victory-message Caesar came to Rome himself:

> 'And he sent him away to his house, saying, Neither go into the town [other translations: village]...'.[585]

From this we can see which version of the rendering of the name 'Rome' he decides for: does he send him into the 'desert' or into the 'town [village]'? Here too, as after Placentia, he opts for the second: as if he thought that because of the accusative, movement towards, *kômên*, fits better with *Romam*, but *erêmôi* better with the locative, *Romae*. From this example and those of the preceding cases, it is possible to deduce the following rule: where Mark finds in his exemplar somebody in Rome, like Pompeius at the beginning of the civil war, he makes *erêmôi* from the locative *Romae*—and puts him in the desert; but if someone goes to Rome instead, as Caesar now does after Zela, he makes *kômên* from the accusative *Romam*—and sends him into the village [town] or the villages. This tendency to see Rome as a village or a town is of course thus reinforced, that according to genuine Roman usage one simply used to say *in urbe*, 'in the city', and *ad urbem*, 'to the city', for 'in Rome' and 'to Rome' respectively. The image of the 'desolation (desert, wilderness)', however, was impressed by the civil war during which everything was devastated, not only the country but also the towns, beginning with Rome itself.

The possibility that Pharnaces, being driven out of the Roman territories, may have rubbed off on that sentence 'Do not go into the town [village]!', should thus be regarded as secondary.

Mutiny of the veterans : The evil husbandmen of the vineyard

Caesar hurried to Rome, for in the meantime unrest had built up—amongst the civilian population because credit business had ground to a halt because of the civil war, and amongst the veterans because they wanted to be dismissed and demanded the promised prizes of victory.

The manner in which Caesar dealt with the unrest caused a sensation. Mark renders the restraining of the mutinying veterans as the parable of the evil husbandmen of the vineyard, and the regulation of the credit-business as the answer to the question about the tribute penny. In Mark, both anecdotes also occur in succession.

The mutiny of the veterans had reached a threatening dimension. Most of them stayed in Campania, waiting to advance towards Africa. But there, right before their eyes, they saw the country estates—still owned by the landed gentry—which were to be divided up amongst them, plus the colonies of Pompeius' former veterans settled there in the time of Caesar's consulate. Seeing these prosperous gardens, they did not want to leave for Africa at all anymore. They demanded immediate dismissal and a piece of fertile land which was their right; moreover they expected the payment of the prizes of victory which had been repeatedly promised, but over and over again postponed. The praetor Sallustius, sent to straighten out this affair was almost killed by them. Then they tracked him back to Rome, where he wanted to report to Caesar who was hurriedly making his way there. On the way, amongst others, they killed the two former praetors, the senators Cosconius and Galba, and demanded to speak to Caesar personally. Although his terrorized friends tried to stop him and insisted on sending his bodyguard first, Caesar daringly emerged amongst them and without any announcement went to the Campus Martius, where he then ascended the platform.

The soldiers greeted him as their commander and demanded their dismissal and their land allotments. They did not mention the victory bounties because they thought that he would be under pressure being in need of soldiers for the Africa campaign and hence offer even bigger gifts. Their attempt at extortion did not result in the expected outcome, for he dismissed them on the spot, assigned to them large sections of land in Italy, partly out of the public property and partly bought by himself, where they could settle down as farmers. He also made assurances to pay them the promised amounts—partly at once, and partly with interest in the near future—when he, with the help of other men, would celebrate his triumph. When he then addressed them as *Quirites* instead of the usual *Commilitones*—calling them 'citizens' and not 'fellow-soldiers', which meant that the dismissal had taken effect—they could not bear it anymore and pleaded to be allowed to remain in his service. The soldiers of his favorite legion, the tenth, to whom he made plain his annoyance, even demanded that he cast lots and execute some of the men. So in the face of their bitter remorse Caesar did not want to press the issue any further, reconciled with all his men, and went straight to Africa with those who were willing and still able to fight.

In the opinion of Dio, Caesar was not averse to seeing the most daring of them fall in Africa, for although he was kindly and well-disposed to his soldiers, he disliked anything that smacked of raw and insubordinate soldiery. According to Suetonius, he withheld a third of the booty and allotted land from the ringleaders. Yet Plutarchus records the arousal of bad feelings amongst the conservatives, because in their eyes his treatment of the mutineers was too mild. But in truth it was because he divided their land amongst his men—property that the landed gentry would rather have kept for themselves and their slavery enterprises. It was evident here, that Caesar did not want to deceive his soldiers, as was the usual practice, and that he actually put the program of the Gracchi into effect: he did not grant the veterans a piece of land because they waged war with him, but he had fought war with them so that they would receive their piece of land. That was the unbearable. That's why he gave it to them, not because of, but despite their mutiny.[586]

This time Mark relies on the stylistic device of the parable—similar to his description of the prodigia that accompanied the events of Pharsalos:

'And he began to speak unto them by parables. A certain man planted a vineyard, and set an hedge about it, and digged a place for the winefat, and built a tower, and let it out to husbandmen, and went into a far country. And at the season he sent to the husbandmen a servant, that he might receive from the husbandmen of the fruit of the vineyard. And they caught him, and beat him, and sent him away empty. And again he sent unto them another servant; and at him they cast stones, and wounded him in the head, and sent him away shamefully handled. And again he sent another; and him they killed, and many others; beating some, and killing some. Having yet therefore one son, his wellbeloved, he sent him also last unto them, saying, They will reverence my son. But those husbandmen said among themselves, This is the heir; come, let us kill him, and the inheritance shall be ours. And they took him, and killed him, and cast him out of the vineyard. What shall therefore the lord of the vineyard do? he will come and destroy the husbandmen, and will give the vineyard unto others. And have ye not read this scripture; The stone which the builders rejected is become the head of the corner: (Psalm 118:22-23): This was the Lord's doing, and it is marvellous in our eyes? And they sought to lay hold on him, but feared the people: for they knew that he had spoken the parable against them: and they left him, and went their way.'[587]

This time he has changed Campania to *ampelôna*, 'vineyard'. The 'husbandmen of the vineyard'—who in the Greek text are simply called *geôrgoi*, 'farmers'—are of course the veterans to be settled; obviously the *Vulgate* has preserved a memory of it, for although it constantly calls the husbandmen of the vineyard *agricolae*, corresponding to the Greek *geôrgoi*, at the decisive point 12:9 it uses *coloni*, 'colonists', instead.

The servants who were subsequently sent to the perfidious husbandmen of the vineyard and who were partly beaten and partly killed, are the praetors, of whom some narrowly escaped and others were murdered. The 'beloved son', *(h)yios agapêtos,* is read out of *Cosconius* and *Galba.* The 'heir', *klêronomos,* and 'inheritance', *klêronomia,* both contain the word *klêros,* which means 'lot', standing for the lot which is thrown, as well as for 'everything which is won or inherited', especially 'the lot of land', the 'allotment': In the Caesar-anecdote all three kind of 'lots' appear, the land-lots that he granted the veterans (sometimes from his own property, his 'lot'); and also the lots that the tenth legion wanted to be cast for their decimation.

The 'Lord' of the vineyard is *Caesar,* who is reflected here as *kyrios,* which meets his function well and also imitates his name. The core-sentence in Caesar's speech 'he will fulfil all his promises, when he celebrates his triumph with the help of other men' fades in Mark to 'he will come and destroy the husbandmen, and will give the vineyard unto others'. It also may contain an echo of the punishment the tenth legion demanded as atonement, or the punishment that was in fact executed on the ringleaders in Africa.

The disarming address *quirites,* 'citizens', which ended the mutiny on the spot, is treated specially by Mark: he brings in a psalm, which begins with *(h)o lithos,* meaning 'the stone' but sounds like *quirites.* It also contains the word *kyrios,* which means 'Lord', but sounds like *Caesar;* finally the psalm sings of 'a miracle before our eyes', which was caused by addressing the soldiers with *quirites.* So Mark was surely proud of his smart choice of this quotation.

Then the ending is evident: 'they could not control themselves anymore' becomes: 'And they sought to lay hold on him'. In the last sentence a change of roles takes place: 'he dismissed them and went to Africa' is inverted into 'and they left him, and went their way.'

Interest and repayment : The tribute penny

The credit business had come to a standstill since Caesar had gone to war against Pompeius. The hope of a general remission of debt induced the debtors not to pay back their debts and the creditors to seek compensation by buying on credit themselves.

Caesar rejected the general remission of debt by pointing out that he had the most debts of all—he was even loaned money by his soldiers at the beginning of the civil war—and he wanted to take the responsibility for that: after all, he planned further loans. His financial needs were critical: He needed money to pay the soldiers whom he needed to get at the money—as he superbly described the cycle to the Senate. So in Solomon-like fashion he decided that all interest payments made during the interim period were to go toward paying off the principle, and on the other hand that the value of the goods before the onset of the civil war should be the basis for all further calculations. He established special commissions to make the assessments. With these measures he lowered debt by about a quarter and managed to set business back on track again.[588]

Mark confuses this assessment of debts with an assessment of tax and makes a question of taxation out of it:

> 'And they send unto him certain of the Pharisees and of the Herodians, to catch him in his words. And when they were come, they say unto him, Master, we know that thou art true, and carest for no man: for thou regardest not the person of men, but teachest the way of God in truth: Is it lawful to give tribute to Caesar, or not? Shall we give, or shall we not give? But he, knowing their hypocrisy, said unto them, Why tempt ye me? bring me a penny, that I may see it. And they brought it. And he saith unto them, Whose is this image and superscription? And they said unto him, Caesar's. And Jesus answering said unto them, Render to Caesar the things that are Caesar's, and to God the things that are God's. And they marvelled at him.'[589]

Apparently Mark was mislead by the loan-word *kênsos* (< *census*), which means 'assessment' in Latin, but in Greek took on the meaning 'tax'. So for him, the question of a general remission of debt or of participation in Caesar's state loan becomes the always present—and for those living on the very edge of the Empire the highly explosive—question of 'Should one pay taxes to Caesar or not?' The name *Caesar* (qua emperor) is not covered-up this time. The decision that the value to be paid would be fixed by Caesar's commissions—in Mark's language: So give the creditor what Caesar decrees—becomes: 'render to Caesar the things that are Caesar's'.

The addition of 'and to God the things that are God's' could be accounted for by the fact that in Mark,s exemplar, after all these measures that concerned the credit business and the people, others were cited which aimed to regulate the influence of the aristocracy: on the one hand measures to dissolve all secret societies, which dominated and poisoned political life and preferred to hide behind religious facades and rites of initiation, and on the other hand such measures to increase the significance of the traditional *collegia* of priests and augurs and of the guilds of artists and craftsmen as well.[590] Strangely enough, the full sentence 'Render to Caesar the things that are Caesar's, and to God the things that are God's', still has the structure of Caesar's doctrine of 'the soldiers are needed for money and the money is needed for the soldiers', even if the chiasmus is lost.

The addressing of Caesar as 'master' is correct: at this time Caesar was again *dictator*,[591] for which the address, as we saw, was *magister*, based on the old name for *dictator: magister populi*. Though Mark will have here read *dictator* as *didaskale*, 'master' in the sense of 'schoolmaster', i.e. of *dictator* as 'one who dictates a dictation'. It is as if Mark had stuck to the basic meaning: *dictator* coming from *dicere*, 'to say', as does the derived German word for poet, *Dichter*, the 'sayer'.

Caesar's portrait on the coin is quite topical. Caesar's likeness appears on coins only after the campaign in Africa. But his name was already stamped into the first coin after the outbreak of the civil war, as we saw. The name of the coin, *dênarion*, is also correct, for Caesar had minted mostly silver *denarii*.

At the beginning of the pericope the Pharisees and the Herodians are mentioned. The Pharisees are mostly the Pompeians. In the sources, in Dio for example, it is said that the credit business had been brought to a standstill from when Caesar marched against Pompeius. In this case, by the Pharisees and the Herodians we have to imagine the Pompeians and the Caesareans, who also had different opinions about the question of the repayment of the debts, for the Pompeians belonged mostly to the creditors and the Caesareans to the debtors.

Thus Caesar is also made Herodes here, instead of as usual Jesus only, which is not without an element of humor: Jesus and Herodes as one person. But we already had this representation once before: the head of John was presented to Herodes like that of Pompeius to Caesar.

Cato's death and Caesar's seizure : The healing of the epileptic boy

After the battle of Pharsalos, Cato and Scipio had fled to Africa, today Tunisia, where they had assembled a large force with the help of Juba, King of the Numidians. Cato watched over Utica in the north, where the three hundred men loyal to him and who considered themselves to be the legitimate Senate had gathered as well. These men had left Rome with Pompeius at that time, and till his defeat they had held their sessions in Thessalonike. Scipio, on the other hand, with the more experienced officers—among them Labienus, Petreius and Afranius—had set up camp in Hadrumetum, today Sousse, and kept watch on the coast. They expected Caesar to land on the peninsula in the north-east that juts toward Sicily, as had his unfortunate legate Curio whom he had sent out to Africa at the beginning of the civil war. Then Curio had gotten between the Pompeians in Utica and the Numidians advancing from the south-west—and was annihilated.

Caesar surprised them by landing with few troops in wintertime, south of Scipio's camp. But at first he had difficulties making up for the numerical inferiority of his forces. Once, in an idle moment, his horsemen were sitting down watching an African dancing before them and playing melodically on a flute. All of a sudden their enemies encircled them and threw themselves upon them, killing some of the riders and chasing the others towards the camp. Had Caesar himself not hurried down the rampart to stop their flight, all would have been lost on that day.

Finally, all his ships coming from Sicily were able to meet up with him, and he managed to split Juba's forces by getting the Moorish prince Bocchus to attack Juba's position from the west. Then he put himself in a trap in Thapsos between the lake and the sea so that Scipio and Afranius again split their forces to cut off the northern and southern escape routes. Thus it was possible for Caesar to overrun his opponents Scipio and Afranius in succession, put Juba and his Numidians to flight, and take all their three camps in one day.

Some of the former senators and praetors who escaped the slaughter committed suicide while being captured, because those whom he had pardoned after Pharsalos now no longer held out hope that he would spare them again. And so Petreius and Juba killed each other and Scipio pierced his chest by his own hand and threw himself into the sea. Indeed, Caesar did have unfaithful recidivists executed. But some of them he spared even now. Juba's son—also called Juba—had the best fate. He was indeed paraded along as a captive in Caesar's triumph, but then received the best of educations, which turned the Numidian barbarian into one of the most scholarly Greek speaking Roman historians.

Cato did not himself participate in the battle because he had handed over command to the former consul Scipio, while he himself only commanded the garrison at Utica. Caesar hurried there hoping to find him still alive, and not already dead as had been the case with Pompeius. But when Cato heard of Caesar's victory, he did not flee like most of the others of his circle, but rather pretended to wait faithfully for him, and then committed suicide.

Cato's suicide was not only the expression of haughty pride—as brother of Caesar's beloved Servilia he would have had just as little to fear as Servilia's son Brutus—but it evinced a certain bestiality as well. When his son, whom he embraced in an especially hearty manner before going to sleep, ordered that his sword be removed from the usual place beside his bed, Cato threatened that he could hang himself with his garment, dash his head against the walls, throw himself headfirst from the roof to the ground or kill himself by holding his breath. When the sword was returned to its place, he asked for Plato's work on the soul. But no sooner was he alone than he sliced himself so that his intestines gushed out. The physicians pushed them back in and sewed up the wound. Then he feigned sleep, ripped the dressing with his hands, loosened the suture, tore the wound apart with his nails like a wild animal, drove his fingers into his abdomen and tore his intestines apart till he finally died.

He was some fifty years of age and was esteemed as the most steadfast of all men in maintaining an opinion once formed. However, he determined law, righteousness and morality not on the basis of commonly held sensibilities, but on grounds of lofty philosophical considerations. So judgment of him was divided in life as well as in death. Whilst part of the citizenry of Utica prepared an honorable funeral for him, Caesar in contrast, stated that he begrudged him this death, because Cato also had begrudged Caesar the chance of preserving his life.

So it only remained for Caesar to show his clemency toward Cato's son, whom he pardoned, as well as toward the citizens of Utica, who, unlike the three hundred men of the pseudo-Senate, remained unharmed.

Thus the war in Africa was overshadowed by the suicide of Cato, despite the brilliant victory of Thapsos. On top of this came a rumour that Caesar himself did not participate in the battle at all. Because while he was preparing the army for battle he was overcome by an attack of his disease and lost consciousness. At the first seizure and before he lost consciousness, he let himself be carried up a nearby tower where he waited quietly till it was all over.

Caesar is said to have suffered at least two of these epilepsy-like attacks while performing the duties of office—the first time in Corduba. He tried to prevent any more with a sparse diet, and by enhancing his resistance with long marches and constantly staying in the open air, bare-headed in sun and rain. However the fasting, together with all the fatigue of so many campaigns and years of war conducted at a breathless tempo had its other side: he fell into downright cachexia, which really was conducive to the attacks of feebleness.[592]

Here too, Mark is not interested in the factual events of the war. We will search his story in vain for details of the scene of battle. As usual he turns the victory into a healing. However, since in this case there was one who actually dies—Cato who committed suicide—as well as someone with epilepsy-like attacks—Caesar—he confuses everything and possibly also blends it with the dancing African, the young barbarian Juba and Cato's son, and turns the whole of it into the healing of the epileptic boy.

'And when he came to his disciples, he saw a great multitude about them, and the scribes questioning with them. And straightway all the people, when they beheld him, were greatly amazed, and running to [him] saluted him. And he asked the scribes, What question ye with them? And one of the multitude answered and said, Master, I have brought unto thee my son, which hath a dumb spirit; And wheresoever he taketh him, he teareth him: and he foameth, and gnasheth with his teeth, and pineth away: and I spake to thy disciples that they should cast him out; and they could not. He answereth him, and saith, O faithless generation, how long shall I be with you? how long shall I suffer you? bring him unto me. And they brought him unto him: and when he saw him, straightway the spirit tare him; and he fell on the ground, and wallowed foaming. And he asked his father, How long is it ago since this came unto him? And he said, Of a child. And ofttimes it hath cast him into the fire, and into the waters, to destroy him: but if thou canst do any thing, have compassion on us, and help us. Jesus said unto him, If thou canst believe, all things [are] possible to him that believeth. And straightway the father of the child cried out, and said with tears, Lord, I believe; help thou mine unbelief. When Jesus saw that the people came running together, he rebuked the foul spirit, saying unto him, Thou dumb and deaf spirit, I charge thee, come out of him, and enter no more into him. And the spirit cried, and rent him sore, and came out of him: and he was as one dead; insomuch that many said, He is dead. But Jesus took him by the hand, and lifted him up; and he arose. And when he was come into the house, his disciples asked him privately, Why could not we cast him out? And he said unto them, This kind can come forth by nothing, but by prayer and fasting.'593

We recognize that we are at war with the Senate's party, because the disciples are in conflict with the Pharisees. And as Caesar's legates in Africa were inferior up to this point and could not drive the Pompeians out, so too the disciples are inferior till Jesus' arrival and are unable to drive out the hostile ghost. It is called 'speechless', *alalos*. Who could be meant by this? The young flute playing Berber, who staged the dance with the deadly outcome? Or the young son of the *Berber* King Juba, who from a barbarian, *barbaros*—one who could only stammer Greek—later developed into one of the greatest Greek speaking scholars? Or perhaps Cato's son who is still covertly mentioned here by name. For in the direct address below we see, that the ghost is not only called *alalon*, but also *kôphon*, 'deaf', actually 'deaf-mute'. Did Mark reflect the proper name *Cato(n)* with this neuter *kôphon*?

The seizure of the 'epileptic boy' is depicted twice. Verbs like 'tear' are used, which reminds us of Cato 'tearing out' his intestines, or those like 'pineth away', in Greek *xêrainetai,* which comes from *xêron,* 'dry', which we saw elsewhere reflects *Curio(n).* Whereas, *afrizei,* 'foam' awakens associations with 'Africa', or the dancing 'African'. So we might assume that behind the first seizure was the attack by Caesar, who suddenly appeared in Africa in the winter, and that of the Numidians, who sent a flute playing dancer in advance in order to attack Caesar's horsemen. But the second attack, where the *kôphon* is mentioned, might instead be the episode of *Cato(n)* and his insane act of self immolation. Mark's unification of time, place and action brought both together in his redaction.

We see a confirmation thereof in the fact that Jesus, at the first attack, voices the irreconcilable word of his impatience—'O faithless generation, how long shall I be with you? how long shall I suffer you?'—which cannot introduce a healing, but rather discretely recalls the execution of the faithless recidivists. In the second attack, however, we have a dead man who is not dead yet—as the mortally wounded Cato received treatment—whereas the words of Caesar, who had begrudged Cato his death, now become those that make the dead resurrect. The 'faith' that is involved in the discussion between Jesus and the father of the boy, might here be, as usual, the *fides.* But this time in the sense of *in fidem et potestatem se permittere,* 'surrender in grace or in disgrace'—what Cato did not want to grant Caesar, however much Caesar did not begrudge him his grace: 'If thou canst believe, all things are possible to him that believeth' is a good Markan translation of *in fidem et potestatem se permittere.*

Finally Mark has let Cato's suicide and Caesar's epilepsy-like attack conflate into one. For Caesar's cachexia, which could hardly be healed by self discipline or sparse diet, still lingers in the end of the pericope: 'This kind can come forth by nothing, but by prayer and fasting'. The link between Cato's and Caesar's 'attack' is provided by the question of age: Cato, who dies at fifty, becomes a disease that lasted 'from the childhood on' as if here 'fifty', *pentêkonta,* was understood as *paidiothen,* 'from childhood on'.

The elaborate telling of Caesar's attack can be found in a more fitting place, however—in Gethsemane:

> '...and began to be sore amazed, and to be very heavy; And saith unto them, My soul is exceeding sorrowful unto death: tarry ye here, and watch. And he went forward a little, and fell on the ground, and prayed that, if it were possible, the hour might pass from him.'[594]

There Mark was able to rework Caesar's attack in a 'sensible' and unfortunately also 'all too human' way, as Jesus in fear and trembling before his own death. We will see what occasioned Mark to place it precisely there.

Cato and Anticato : Against the scribes

The polemics about Cato's suicide took on contours of cultural and educational policy. Cicero defended Cato's behavior in a tract wherein he adored his virtue, whereupon Caesar felt obliged to answer with a refutation wherein he praised Cicero's eloquence but denounced Cato's hypocrisy. Both writings, Cicero's 'Cato' and Caesar's 'Anticato', were most eagerly read by the respective party supporters and they polarized readers for centuries. Unfortunately, both writings are lost and we only know parts of their content from secondary literature, mainly through Plutarchus and Appianus (cf. TSCHIEDEL (1981)).

As we have seen earlier, Caesar blamed Cato for, among other things, giving his pregnant wife Marcia to the wealthy and elderly Hortensius, only to remarry her shortly after as a rich widow, thus debasing marriage into a financial transaction out of disdainful greed and using his wife as a profitable loan. Just for camouflage, Cato had worn mourning clothes and did not put up a wreath when attending banquets. No one knows whether he had done this for the deceased Hortensius or for the old order, which from his point of view was threatened by Caesar. In fact, Cato soon appeared everywhere in mourning habit and promptly left to join Pompeius. The inheritance acquired by the rich widow had become his personal war chest.[595]

Mark has probably come across Caesar's polemic against Cato subsequent to the Africa-campaign. It is not by chance that we find the core of the famous polemic again, in typical alteration, after the narrative of the evil husbandmen of the vineyard, i.e. after the mutiny of the veterans:

> 'And he said unto them in his doctrine, Beware of the scribes, which love to go in long clothing, and love salutations in the marketplaces, And the chief seats in the synagogues, and the uppermost rooms at feasts: Which devour widows' houses, and for a pretence make long prayers: these shall receive greater damnation.'[596]

As the grey eminence of the senatorial party, Cato is consequently counted among the 'scribes' here, whom we know are the *conscripti*, from the senators' salutatory address *patres conscripti*. The mourning habit is not emphasized, but indicated at the end, at least as a leathering: 'these shall receive greater damnation.' The long prayers 'made for a pretence' might be an allusion to Cato's endless speeches in the Senate which he delivered to, among other reasons, hinder the opponent's speaking or to delay unpleasant votes. The core-sentence—'Which devour widows' houses'—still clearly renders Caesar's opinion about Cato's marriage policy.

Triumphal processions in Rome : Entry into Jerusalem

Now Caesar returned to Rome and celebrated four triumphs in succession: the Gallic, the Alexandrian, the Pontic and the African—no Pharsalan however, because he did not want to gloat about the victory in a civil war he had been compelled to wage, and he also did not want to insult the memory of Pompeius. On this occasion he fulfilled all his vows and promises, from the distributions to the soldiers and people to the dedication of a temple to his ancestress Venus—nevertheless he erected a beautiful figure of Cleopatra beside the goddess there.[597]

We have already mentioned the triumphs above in connection with other, improvised banquets, such as at the capture of Pompeius' camp at Pharsalos, which in Mark's narration seem to be connected with the banquets on the occasion of the triumphs in Rome. We have also talked about the donations of money, oil, wine and grain as well as the distribution of land to the colonists. The triumphal processions themselves have also been found in Mark already, hidden at the healing of the blind man, as rendition of *veni vidi vici*—*I see men as trees walking*. During the triumph the victors marched past the cheering crowd with a wreath of leaves on their heads.

Mark shows us this cheering crowd at the entrance into Jerusalem, immediately after the anecdote of the loosed ass's colt, where he handled the replacement of Cato by Asinius Pollio in Sicily:

'And they brought the colt to Jesus, and cast their garments on him; and he sat upon him. And many spread their garments in the way: and others cut down branches off the trees, and strawed them in the way. And they that went before, and they that followed, cried, saying, Hosanna; Blessed is he that cometh in the name of the Lord: Blessed be the kingdom of our father David, that cometh in the name of the Lord: Hosanna in the highest. And Jesus entered into Jerusalem, and into the temple.'[598]

It is easy to detect that all the requisites of a Roman triumph appear in slight alteration: the decorated mount, the spread garments, the green branches, the procession, the cry of triumph, the praising of the triumphator and the highest god, Jupiter, the route and the entry into the city and into the temple...

The differences are comparatively small:

There is a donkey instead of a triumphal chariot drawn by four white horses, but at the *ovatio,* the little triumph Caesar received after the last campaign in Spain, the triumphator was mounted, as we saw ('I am not King, I am Caesar'). That this horse later becomes an 'ass's colt' has something to do with *Asinius Pollio.*

'Hosanna' instead of *io triumphe* is owed to the Bible quotation that is brought in here. The Hosanna presumably presented itself to cover the *fescennini,* the rude satirical songs that were sung especially by the soldiers for the triumphator, according to custom. At the Gallic triumph the following was one of the most decent songs to be heard (as Robert Graves translated):

'Home we bring our bald whoremonger,
Romans lock your wives away,
all the bags of gold you lent him
went his Gallic tarts to pay'.[599]

Jupiter, the highest god in whose honor the triumphs were directed, is not missing, because it was in his red garment, chariot and as his personification the triumphator marched past. The name *Jupiter* is analyzed correctly in its components *Diu-Pater* and reflected as 'father David': apparently Mark has used the variant *Div* for *Diu,* which was possibly suggested to him by Caesar's title *Divus* and which forms a better phonetic bridge to 'David'. Strikingly no parallel is drawn between Jupiter (Jove) and Jahweh: Mark does not think in an Old Testamentarian way. The citations from the Jewish Bible do not belong to the ancient layers of tradition.

Jupiter's presence makes it clear that Mark has also woven in the real triumphs of the year 46 and not just the first entry into Rome 49 here. However, the mentioning of Asinius, i.e. the 'foal' at the beginning of the passage and of Jupiter, i.e. 'Father David' at the end, are the only trace of it. We search in vain for the original exemplar for this in the course of the civil war. But interestingly, it is to be found directly before the civil war, where Caesar, coming from beyond the Alps, visits Gallia Cisalpina on the border of Italy to speak with them about the candidature of Antonius for the office of *augur:*

'The arrival of Caesar was greeted by all the cities, Gallic municipalities and Roman colonies as well, with unbelievable displays of honor and love. He had now come there for the first time after his mighty victory over all of Gaul. Nothing was lacking, and whatever they could think of they used to decorate the gates, ways and plazas where Caesar passed by. All the people ran to him with their children, everywhere offerings were made, and the market places and temples were decked out with tables and banquet lounges, as if an overdue triumph were being joyfully celebrated in advance: so great was the generosity of the wealthy and the enthusiasm of the common people'.[600]

This is unambiguously Mark's main source for the entry into Jerusalem. It is clear by the respective beginnings of the next pericope, in Caesar 'after his rapid tour through all of upper-Italy…'—and in Jesus 'and when he had looked round about upon all things…'.[601]

Here we find a second important insight confirmed, which already attracted attention in the Clodius-anecdote: Mark's exemplar contained passages that are chronologically located before the onset of the civil war. We have to reckon with the fact that the restriction to the years 49-44 was one of redaction, not one that was materially predetermined in the source.

The sons of Pompeius : The sons of Zebedee

When the celebrations in Rome had come to an end, Caesar marched off to Spain against the sons of Pompeius. They had recruited an army of amazing magnitude despite their youth, because all of the leading personalities who had been able to save themselves from Africa came to their side, as well as brave peoples like the Spanish and the Celtiberians and slaves whom they promised freedom. Like their father, they had proven themselves able and worthy enough to lead this army and they had already conquered the whole of Baetica and many cities in spite of the presence of Caesar's legates.

At first Caesar did not take them seriously. But then he appeared suddenly, hurrying ahead of his troops, confident that his fame alone would scare the towns that had defected, and also Pompeius' sons. They were not impressed however, trusting in their father's fame and their own strength—which in their eyes measured up to that of Caesar. They even accused the manoeuvring Caesar of cowardice, so that he accepted battle in an unfavorable position on the hillside beneath Munda. Caesar this time, as he had before, made the watchword 'Venus', while Pompeius' sons, fighting for the honor of their unfortunate father, chose 'Pietas' as theirs.

When Caesar saw from a high vantage point how the armies collided and that his troops became frightened and began to relent, he raised his hands to heaven and besought all the gods that so many victories would not be ruined by one defeat. Then he hurriedly made his way to his soldiers, ran through the lines of fighters and shouted out to them asking if they were not ashamed to deliver him into the hands of such boys.

When even this did not change the fearful mood, Caesar snatched a shield from a soldier and shouted to the officers of his staff: 'This will be the end of my life and of your military service!' Then he stormed before the arrays of his soldiers to a distance of ten feet from the enemy. Two hundred lances flew at him, but he was able to avoid some and to catch the others with his shield. Now at last, the tribunes ran in front of him and gave him cover. First the Decumani, the legendary tenth legion, Caesar's *praetoria,* and then the whole army threw themselves on the enemies and finally, towards evening, after the heaviest attack and bravest commitment, managed to overpower them. More than thirty thousand were killed, but Caesar also lost a thousand of his best men. It is reported that he later told friends that he had often fought for victory, but this time for his life.[602]

Out of Pompeius' sons, who claimed the position of power of the 'Magnus' for themselves, Mark makes the sons of Zebedee who want to sit on the right and the left of the Lord's glory.

> 'And James and John, the sons of Zebedee, come unto him, saying, Master, we would that thou shouldest do for us whatsoever we shall desire. And he said unto them, What would ye that I should do for you? They said unto him, Grant unto us that we may sit, one on thy right hand, and the other on thy left hand, in thy glory. But Jesus said unto them, Ye know not what ye ask: can ye drink of the cup that I drink of? and be baptized with the baptism that I am baptized with? And they said unto him, We can. And Jesus said unto them, Ye shall indeed drink of the cup that I drink of; and with the baptism that I am baptized withal shall ye be baptized: But to sit on my right hand and on my left hand is not mine to give; but it shall be given to them for whom it is prepared. And when the ten heard it, they began to be much displeased with James and John. But Jesus called them to him, and saith unto them, Ye know that they which are accounted to rule over the Gentiles exercise lordship over them; and their great ones exercise violence upon them. But so shall it not be among you: but whosoever will be great among you, shall be your minister: And whosoever of you will be the chiefest, shall be servant of all. For even the Son of man came not to be ministered unto, but to minister, and to give his life a ransom for many.'[603]

Here *Pompeius* does not become John as he usually does, but rather 'Zebedee'. That the latter is a doublet of 'the Baptist' is still recognizable by the fact that both sons make the claim to Jesus that they could be 'baptized' like him, where baptism here means, as always, conscription and recruitment. The 'cup' they claim to be able to drink of stands for 'Spain'. This is easy to detect in Greek: 'Spain', *Ibêrian, potêrion,* 'cup'.

Possibly this 'cup', pronounced *potirion,* was also influenced by the Latin *potiri,* meaning 'get hold of' or 'to bring something into one's dominion'—this is what Pompeius' sons did with Spain.

The glory is the fame on which both parties insisted—Caesar on his own and Pompeius' sons on that of their father. The right and the left, where they want to sit and which are mentioned repeatedly, we find in Caesar's case as well: one time as the troops, who run against each other from both sides with different watchwords, then as the hands raised by Caesar begging the gods, and finally as the hands of the boys, into which he does not want to fall.

The 'right' and the 'left', however, have been read into the text by Mark as usual. Probably the 'left' first: because his exemplar mentioned the 'aristocrats', who from Africa had joined Pompeius' sons, and possibly he preferred *ex aristerôn,* 'to the left' over 'of the aristocrats', *ex aristôn.* Then for the sake of symmetry, he interpreted 'the competent ones', 'the skilful ones', the *dexteri*—as 'the right-handed' and transferred them 'to the right'. The signals and watchwords could have helped to bring this about too. Spoken aloud on both sides 'Venus' and 'Pietas', *Aphroditên* and *Eusebeian,* which in the Greek context bear a certain resemblance: mainly to 'to the left', which is rendered one time with *aristerôn,* the other time with *euônymôn.*[604]

The problem of the rulers or the mighty, who lay violent hands on their nations, is concretely realized in the battle situation. The peculiarity of this battle was that the general who was supposed to normally be positioned behind his soldiers, this time went to the front himself, dragging along the tribunes and with the soldiers following behind. Thus the world was turned upside down, the 'lord of the field' (commander) as the 'servant of the field' (soldier), who risks his life and thereby saves his army: a reversal of the usual order that brought victory. This is precisely what is important to Mark, more important than the victory itself: 'And whosoever of you will be the chiefest, shall be servant of all. For even the Son of man came not to be ministered unto, but to minister, and to give his life a ransom for many.' where 'Son of man' stands for *Gai-us,* of course.

As far as Mark's mechanism is concerned, we see here also that he has gleaned the idea of 'ministering' and its parallelism to that of 'giving life' from Caesar's saying to his officers—'This will be the end of my life and also of your military service!'—but the word itself he read into it. There were these 'two hundred spears' thrown at Caesar, and Mark changed 'two hundred', *diakosia,* to *diakonos,* 'servant', and 'spear', *dorata,* to *doulos,* 'servant'. To be consistent he then makes the 'ten feet' of distance from the enemies into 'the Ten', who, without closer definition, revolt against James and John: which is correct, as it was just this ten feet of distance that triggered his men to finally attack the Pompeians. For that he probably just mixed the ten feet of distance with the *Decumani*—the 'teners', the soldiers of the 'tenth' legion, Caesar's *praetoria*—who then had started the fiercest and decisive attack on the Pompeians.

The names 'James' and 'John' present us with the choice of whether John stands for *iuvenis*, 'the youngling', or for *Gnaeus:* we have already considered both possibilities earlier. We can hardly decide it here because, of the two sons of Pompeius, the elder was called *Gnaeus* and the 'younger' *Sextus*. Since neither *Gnaeus* nor *Sextus* show any resemblance to 'James', we have to assume that the name 'Jacob', here next to 'John', has been influenced by another passage where both names appear as a couple, for example in the *Transfiguration of Jesus*, Mark 9:2. We will postpone the solution until the analysis of that pericope.

The name 'Zebedee' is of such a sort that it may have covered an earlier 'Pompeius': POMPEI > ZEBEΔAI(ου). However, he could also have moved to this place—for example together with James—whom we already met as 'Son of Zebedee'.

Let us repeat it here again that Mark does not show any interest in the real events of the war. So one will search in vain for his description of the end of the battle, where Caesar's personal commitment had stopped his wavering and retreating army—but which was decided by the Moorish riders of King Bogud who encircled the Pompeians, and by Labienus' mistake of sending some of the troops to defend the camp, which initiated the general flight of his men. Let alone that he would mention the subsequent romance of Caesar with Bogud's wife Eunoe.

However it can be asked if the later fate of Pompeius' sons does not resonate in Mark's text. The tragic fate of the elder Gnaeus who was killed in flight like his father before him and whose head was brought to Caesar, and that of the more fortunate younger Sextus, who saved himself, recruited troops again and later fought over the Empire for a long period with Caesar's successors Antonius and Octavianus. This is what Jesus' words are reminiscent of, and they sound just as if they are coming from the Baptist's mouth: 'Ye shall indeed drink of the cup that I drink of; and with the baptism that I am baptized withal shall ye be baptized: But to sit on my right hand and on my left hand is not mine to give; but it shall be given to them for whom it is prepared.'

But the most important issue for Mark centered on the service of Gaius as a soldier at the battle front, with his life in peril, which saved Caesar's victory: the first as the last, who in exactly such a way becomes the very first. In order to emphasize this he accepts a change in the sequence of events—and concludes with it.

Caesar Divus Iulius : David's Son and Lord

Victor of all civil wars, Caesar hurried to Rome, now feared and celebrated like no man before him. Faced with his good fortune the Romans bowed their heads and willingly submitted themselves to the yoke. They hoped to find relief under the monarchy and made Caesar an absolute ruler. By decision of the Senate they appointed him as the automatically re-elected consul, dictator for life, the supreme judge of morals. They awarded him the title *Imperator* as first name and *Parens Patriae* as epithet. They placed his statue among those of the kings and his throne in the Orchestra, and gave him the right to wear the red triumphal robe at all times, and to deal with his affairs sitting on a throne of ivory and gold. They declared him sacred and inviolable in his person like a tribune of the people. Thus he had all the prerogatives of an absolute monarch and was more than a king—a title he refused because it had been cursed by the ancestors.

Then they also elevated him in the sacral sphere. He was already High Priest of Jupiter and Pontifex Maximus. Now they even accorded him divine honors: the golden chair in the Curia and before the Tribunal; a chariot of the gods and a litter to bear his statue in the processions during the circus games; his own temples; his own statues next to those of the gods in all temples in Rome, and in each town within the Empire and in those of allies outside the Empire; altars with his own cult and the obligation that priests should celebrate all his victories annually; a seat at the table of the gods; a month of the calendar named after him; and his own board of priests at the Lupercalia. Finally they straight away made him Divus Iulius and provided him, in the person of Marcus Antonius, with his personal high priest, just as for Jupiter. This latter honor was not to be realized until after his death, but it already made him not only god, but also a monotheistic god, an archaic god-king who reigned over the whole world.

The odd thing was that all these honors were given to him by the same Romans who had chased their kings out of the city, and that they did this not only out of fear or to flatter him, but also out of love.

It was a love that he did not disappoint, because he pardoned all who had waged war against him and were still alive, and allowed them to return to Italy unharmed—something nobody else had done before him and it exceeded all human expectations. He even restored them to office and dignity. He returned the dowries to the widows of soldiers killed in battle and gave the orphans their respective share of the fortune. Yes, he even had the statues of Pompeius and Sulla erected again. This gave the true meaning to all the other ways by which he tried to win the love of the people—the games, theater performances, festive meals, donations of grain and the establishing of settlements.

In order to seal this mutual confidence a temple was vowed to Caesar and his clemency. From that time on, contrary to all doubts and misgivings, he dismissed his Spanish bodyguard and trusted in the *sacrosanctitas*, the inviolability of a tribune accorded to him, as well as in the oath of the senators and knights who pledged to protect his life, if necessary, with their own.[605]

Out of this realized god-kingship, Mark makes the question of the highest commandment and the debate about David's Son and Lord:

> 'And one of the scribes came, and having heard them reasoning together, and perceiving that he had answered them well, asked him, Which is the first commandment of all? And Jesus answered him, The first of all the commandments is, Hear, O Israel; The Lord our God is one Lord: And thou shalt love the Lord thy God with all thy heart, and with all thy soul, and with all thy mind, and with all thy strength: this is the first commandment. [Deuteronomy 6:4-5]. And the second is like, namely this, Thou shalt love thy neighbour as thyself. [Leviticus 19:18]. There is none other commandment greater than these. And the scribe said unto him, Well, Master, thou hast said the truth: for there is one God; and there is none other but he: And to love him with all the heart, and with all the understanding, and with all the soul, and with all the strength, and to love his neighbour as himself, is more than all whole burnt offerings and sacrifices. And when Jesus saw that he answered discreetly, he said unto him, Thou art not far from the Kingdom of God. And no man after that durst ask him any question.'[606]

The scribes are the *conscripti*, the senators here also. The one who appears here pars pro toto is the same person who read the decision of honors. We recognize that we are at the end of the civil wars and that Caesar had won, because the argument is seen as finished and Jesus 'had answered well'. It is conceivable that the decision of honors was read by Cicero, who had not actively participated in the civil war. This might be reflected in the fact that this scribe was one of those who only 'had heard' them dispute.

'Our God is one Lord'—this applied now to Caesar, although the reverse order was the original one: Our Lord is one God. This commandment cited from Deuteronomy, requiring unconditional love of the

Lord, sounds like the vow taken by the senators and knights to love Caesar and to protect his life with their own.

The other commandment 'to love his neighbor as himself' covers the Clementia Caesaris, the forgiveness for all his enemies, admittedly without doing justice to the unheard-of quality of this clemency. With Matthew one still finds it as the essence of the new message, of the new morals of the Empire, in clear opposition to the morality of the Old Testament, that every individual and every nation is perfectly capable of:

> 'Ye have heard that it hath been said [Leviticus 19:18], Thou shalt love thy neighbour, and hate thine enemy. But I say unto you, Love your enemies, bless them that curse you, do good to them that hate you, and pray for them which despitefully use you, and persecute you; that ye may be the children of your Father who is in heaven: for he makes his sun rise on the evil and on the good, and sendeth rain on the just and on the unjust.'[607]

Upon this is based not only the life of individuals and peoples, but the living together of different people and races in a world empire. That it is the Roman Empire is made clear by the use of 'in heaven', *en ouranois,* which, as we have seen earlier, conceals *romanus*. The 'Father who is in heaven', is in this case Caesar as *Parens Patriae,* as 'parent of the native city, (pro)creator of the Empire', who as *Divus,* however, moves into the sphere of Jupiter, the weather god who sends rain for all, at his own discretion and yet with fairness at the same time.

By the way, the undeniable fact that Matthew is based on Mark does not necessarily mean that his additions are purely editorial. As can be seen here, this time Matthew's version comes closer to the original Caesar source. He has the phrase, 'love your enemies', which is closer to the *Clementia Caesaris*. How is this possible? Is Matthew based on an older Original Mark, which contained more than Mark? Then the Original Mark would be Matthew, which is absurd. Do Matthew's additions stem from a parallel tradition? If so, from which one? From yet another Q?

Or simply from other Caesar sources? Was Matthew's exemplar also a narrative of Caesar, like the one Asinius Pollio had written down and Mark had creatively re-edited, but with added quotations from other works by Caesar? This can be checked just by considering this example.

This whole problem—old morality versus new morality—was part of Caesar's *Anticato* which he had to write in reply to Cicero's glorification of Cato, circulated in order to do harm to him (see p.82, 197 and 274 as well as notes 189 and 440). These works, *Cato* and *Anticato,* which were frequently read and discussed in antiquity, unfortunately have not been preserved, except for a few quotations. It happens that among them there is one that exactly corresponds to our topic, wherein Caesar accuses the upholder of moral standards of not even having followed the most natural of all commandments, to love thy neighbor, beginning with one's own family:

> Caesar in *Anticatone priore*: '*uno enim excepto, quem alius modi atque omnis natura finxit, suos quisque habet charos.*'
>
> —Caesar writes in the first book of his *Anticato*: 'because except for one, whom nature has created completely different, each one loves his own kin.' (PRISCIANUS 6.36 (GL II 227.2)).

Unfortunately we don't know the literal continuation of it, but as regards contents one can easily imagine it (cf. TSCHIEDEL (1981), p. 105sqq):

'Cato—for this "one"' was definitely Cato, whose singleness had been emphasized by Cicero already (cf. the speech for Murena, 60) and Caesar ironically alludes to that here—this unique upholder of moral standards, was not even able to do what all, humans and animals, do by nature: namely loving their own family. Here Caesar probably alludes to Cato's unloving and opportunistic dealings with his young wife Marcia, whom he had handed over to an old man like a pimp in order to remarry her as a rich widow (see above p. 197), let alone that he could have been able to raise himself to what is necessary in order to end all wars, particularly the civil war, and to secure eternal peace, namely to Clementia: the charity to strangers and even enemies. He was even so obdurate that he has not even allowed me, Caesar, that I pardon him and has committed suicide in order that nobody, especially no enemy, would have the possibility to give that to him which he would not give to anybody, not even his family: mercy.'

This clearly is the original text for the above quotation—the irony being lost, as so often happens.

Thus Matthew's exemplar contained quotations that were missing or abridged in that of Mark, or maybe a more complete Original Mark was available to Matthew. In any case, this passage of Matthew unambiguously shows that originally in the Gospel the matter was not to oppose the Old Testamentary morals with the New Testamentary one of Jesus, but to give a report on how Caesar, in his opposition to the Old Roman morality of somebody like Cato, exemplarily demonstrated how false it was. It was unable to fulfill even natural laws like family loyalty and charity, let alone to even comprehend those that are culturally superior and necessary for the public good, like the concept of Love-thy-enemy. The Evangelist had merely transferred this debate *ad usum Iudaeorum*, for the use of the Jews, delocalized and adapted it, and made it a conflict of Jesus with the old law.

Furthermore, it is conceivable that Mark was intended to be an additional text, a homily corresponding to a text, a Greek embroidery around a Latin fabric, a Gospel to the *vita Divi Iulii*. No one asked for completeness: the text was still known somehow; at least one assumed it was known. Whereas Matthew, who comes later and is anxious for completeness, seems to have here added further material extracted from the text, to the homily of Mark. He has knit the fabric to the embroidery—true to original, of course. Henceforth the *vita Divi Iulii* was superfluous: the Gospels had been born. Mark was now merely a torso—and moved to second place.

So, en passant, we have been able to solve an essential aporia of Gospel exegesis and criticism: why do the later Evangelists know more than the earlier ones? Answer: the earlier ones still knew the story. Mark's knowledge shows through in all that he does not tell.

The following address to Jesus, 'Master', *didaskale*—with Mark, for we are returning to him—stands for *dictator* as usual, but this time it has another, more intensive meaning, because Caesar had been elected dictator for life on this occasion.

The 'burnt offerings' and 'sacrifices' here refer more to the cult established for the new god than to those offerings and sacrifices that accompanied the celebrations for his fifth triumph. The Roman Empire, the *Imperium Populi Romani*, was about to become the *Imperium Divi Iulii*, the 'Kingdom of God.'

The concluding sentence finally—'And no man after that durst ask him any question'—lets the ceremonious end of the civil wars come through. Compare that choice of words with those of Appianus:

'No one dared to contradict him any more.'[608]

Adventus Caesaris : The coming of Christ

Mark 13 is a final chapter, after it the Passion begins. One cannot rule out the possibility that this apocalyptic chapter is the original conclusion of actually all of Mark's Gospel, which could have moved in front of the Passion narrative in order to make room for the false ending 16:9-20. In any case, we find its corresponding counterpart largely in the summary that Appianus gives in *BC* 1.5 as an introduction, and by which he announces the continuation of the civil wars after Caesar's murder.

The peg seems to have been Caesar's building activity. He not only built his new Forum and Temple of Venus but also ordered old buildings, houses and even temples be demolished to make space for them. This lingers at the beginning of Mark's chapter, where a disciple says:

'Master, see what manner of stones and what buildings are here!
—and Jesus answers:

'There shall not be left one stone upon another, that shall not be thrown down.'[609]

In keeping with the known formula, Mark has here too, probably confused *rem (publicam)* with *(h)ieron*—'state' with 'temple'—and then moved on to the collapse of the state and the rekindling of the civil wars after Caesar's murder. He mentions these explicitly when he refers to 'wars and rumors of wars'.[610] The choice of words clearly shows that civil wars and proscriptions are what is meant. Appianus:

'...the chiefs of the factions surrendered their enemies to each other, and for this purpose they did not even spare their friends and brothers, so much did animosity towards rivals overpower the love of kindred.'[611]

Mark:

'Now the brother shall betray the brother to death, and the father the son; and children shall rise up against their parents, and shall cause them to be put to death.'[612]

The 'many' that 'shall come in my name, saying, I am Christ; and shall deceive many',[613] clearly alludes to Antonius, Lepidus and Octavianus who all act in Caesar's name (the latter literally under his name, for he had himself renamed Caesar) and then wage war against each other.[614] As we might expect, the long since familiar names of the apostles—Peter and James and John and Andrew—appear, however 'privately',[615] which hints at the fundamental discord between the men despite their occasional temporary reconciliation.

Even the idea that the civil war will give birth to a new world is predetermined. Mark:

'*Archê ôdínôn taûta*—These are the beginnings of the labor pains' (i.e.: 'the pains of a woman in travail'; KJV: 'of sorrows').[616]

Appianus:

'Such was the ordering of divine Providence to bring into being the universal imperial power of our own day'[617]

Whereby we see the recurrence of the customary blending of the two meanings of *archê*—'beginning' and 'power'.

The famous piece in Mark where he speaks of 'the abomination of desolation' quoted from Daniel 'standing where it ought not', might however mean the proscriptions which no longer should have existed after Caesar's mildness had broken with Sulla's lust for vengeance. But the triumviri did not want to let the murder of the clement Caesar go unpunished. They on their part proscribed the men behind the assassination by means of a publicly posted list, and thus, both justly and illegally, declared many Roman citizens, senators and knights as outlaws, announced large bounties on them, blocked all escape routes, searched all the secret hiding places and the roads leading out of the city, and even the harbors, the marshes and the swamps.[618] This public notification and the merciless fury of the bounty hunters caused panic in those named on the list, and at the same time futile attempts at escape, which Appianus describes in horrific terms. They have lost none of their terror with Mark either. Appianus:

'With the announcement of the lists there were immediate [...] undignified attempts at flight and disguise [...] both in the city and the country. Some men climbed down into wells, others into dirty sewers, others crept into smoke-blackened chimneys or sat dead still under the eves of their roofs which abutted each other. Some indeed had no less fear of their wives and hostile children than they had of the murderers [...]; there were also those who feared their debtors or neighbours who were hoping to seize their properties.'[619]

And Mark:

'But when ye shall see the abomination of desolation, spoken of by Daniel the prophet, standing where it ought not, (let him that readeth understand,) then let them that be in Judaea flee to the mountains: And let him that is on the housetop not go down into the house, neither enter [therein], to take any thing out of his house: And let him that is in the field not turn back again for to take up his garment. But woe to them that are with child, and to them that give suck in those days!'[620]

'Judaea', of course, stands for *Italia,* here too. In the Greek expression for 'abomination of desolation', *to bdelygma tês erêmôseôs,* we again find at its core the familiar Markan equating of *Roma* and *erêmôi,* 'Rome' and 'desert', which is correct, as the proscriptions mainly hit the city-dwellers of Rome, whilst the *bdelygma* is hard to recognize as the Latin *proscription,* presumably because the wording has been overlain by the citation from Daniel (similar to how the 'myrrh' in Matthew became 'gall', due to the quotation, see above).

The conclusion is parallel also. Appianus:

'Of those who were able to escape were some who against all expectations remained alive, who were later honored and rose to office in the city as well as to leading positions in the war, indeed even to triumph'[621].

Mark:

'And except that the Lord had shortened those days, no flesh should be saved: but for the elect's sake, whom he hath chosen, he hath shortened the days.'[622]

The reference to 'many false Christs and false prophets will arise and show signs and wonders'[623] renders the conflicts over the highest priestly offices—Lepidus as *pontifex maximus,* Antonius as *flamen Divi Iulii,* Octavianus as *Divi Iulii filius*—as well as the wars they waged against each other.

Mark's 'foreign body' in the middle of chapter 13—

'But when they shall lead you, and deliver you up, take no thought beforehand what ye shall speak, neither do ye premeditate: but whatsoever shall be given you in that hour, that speak ye.'[624]

—could refer to the interrogations accompanying the proscriptions, but it is possible as well that Mark has come across the primacy of improvisation in Caesar's warfare here:

'Caesar did not take up battle only after previous planning, but every time an opportunity for it arose, often while his troops were still on the march [...].'[625]

This could even have been a peg for Mark on which to hang his recollections of the civil war Caesar had brought to an end, but which had nevertheless flared up again after his death. Caesar's reform of the calendar provided a second peg. It was a reform he undertook while in his role as *pontifex maximus* wherein he transformed the calendar from a lunar to a solar reckoning, a reform that, with only a few minor amendments, is still in effect today. This greatly angered Cicero, who found it unbearable that Caesar was now even giving orders to the heavenly bodies. Though the words that Mark borrowed from Isaiah—

'But in those days, after that tribulation, the sun shall be darkened, and the moon shall not give her light, And the stars of heaven shall fall, and the powers that are in heaven shall be shaken.'[626]

—might have cloaked those of Vergilius (commonly known as Virgil or Vergil), who described how:

'[...] the sun, too, pitied Rome when Caesar died, and hid its shiny face in dim dusky red, and that impious generation feared eternal night; [...] lightning flashed from heaven on high like never before, and terrifying comets blazed down upon the unholy.'[627]

The fig tree, finally, (Mk. 13:28)—*sykê*—whose blooming heralds the coming of summer, reminds us of *Sicily,* which was long fought over between the triumvirate and the last surviving son of Pompeius, and thus for a long time stood in the way of Caesar's adoptive son Octavianus' takeover of power.

The final call of the chapter, 'Watch!', indisputably identifies who is being addressed by Mark's Gospel: the guardians of the Empire, the veterans, who in those days as *evocati* could be called up again—and what in fact the triumviri did.[628]

THE RICH YOUNG MAN AND THE REWARDS OF DISCIPLESHIP 289

Having arrived at this point, we can now have an overview of the whole of Mark's text forward and backward. We have become familiar with his modus operandi and are in a better position to arrange the rest in proper order. Before us lies the Passion narrative, which begins with *The plan of the enemies*[629] and ends with *The resurrection*[630]. We have only a few pericopes left which were not touched upon during our chronological procedure of following the lines of the story of Caesar. Among them are:

The rich young man and The rewards of discipleship

—which turn out to be a Markan rendering[631] of the dispute between Antonius and Octavianus over Caesar's inheritance.[632] One recognizes the problem: Octavianus wanted the money that had been deposited with Antonius, because under the terms of Caesar's will he as the adoptive son was obliged to pay every Roman citizen seventy-five denarii. Since Antonius did not give it to him he sold all of his possessions and even went begging in order to shame Antonius; in this way Octavianus trod in Caesar's footsteps because he was successful in winning over the sympathy of the citizens to his cause and in gaining the loyalty of the veterans who had settled in Campania, and in this way he not only took up the private inheritance of Caesar, but also the political inheritance—the Imperium. Jesus (here Jesus acts as Simon Peter, i.e. Antonius) tells the rich young man (it is the young Caesar, i.e. Octavianus) that he should sell everything he has and give the money to the poor in order to have treasure in heaven (i.e. with the Romans), and to follow him (i.e. Caesar). The disciple is saddened and grieved, whereupon Jesus says that it is easier for a camel to pass thru the eye of a needle than it is for a rich man to enter the Kingdom of God (Here again, like in the first chapter of Mark, we have our 'camel'—which stands for *Campania*). The problem of the eternal life that is to be inherited might have to do with Octavianus' attempt to have Antonius murdered so that he could get at his inheritance. And the problem of leaving behind mother and father might have to do with Octavianus' decision to take up Caesar's inheritance despite the opposition of his mother and stepfather. The word about the first who will become the last, which Peter has to listen to, is what finally happened to Caesar's old comrade-in-arms Antonius: he had to watch a young man leave him far behind. So both these pericopes belong to chapter 13, *The Coming of Christ*. Originally, they both came after the resurrection, but they were probably associated with *The sons of Zebedee*[633] for redactional reasons, and also because the last surviving son of Pompeius also interfered in the dispute over Caesar's inheritance.

The Resurrection of the Dead

—is the question of Caesar's succession and consequently Caesar's legitimate heir. As is known, Calpurnia was childless when he died, and his daughter Julia, whose hand he had given to Pompeius in marriage, had died childless. In Caesar's will, as we shall see later, a posthumous son was named as heir in case one had been born after Caesar's death. We shall also see that it was rumoured that shortly before Caesar's death he had commissioned his friend, the poet Helvius Cinna, to prepare a law that would allow him to marry as many women as he wanted and whichever he wanted in order to ensure issue. This was, of course, aimed at Cleopatra, whose support he needed in the war against the Parthians and whose son would have been made his heir by a legal marriage with her. She, by the way, was Caesar's match in that, having formed a liaison with Pompeius' eldest son before associating with him, she then afterwards attached herself to Antonius, (it is thought that her intermezzo with Cassius had only been a political one), and after his downfall, she tried to do it with Octavianus too, but in vain. This last one made sure that her children were taken from her as unwanted rivals in the succession and inheritance: Caesar's son Caesarion was physically eliminated, and Antonius' children were placed in the care of their stepmother Octavia, Octavianus' sister and former wife of Antonius, whom he had rejected for Cleopatra.

All this leads to the question about the widow's marriage that was put to Jesus by the Sadducees. They posited a woman who had successively married seven brothers who had successively died. The Sadduccees wanted to know whose wife she would be in the resurrection. The answer they received is that God is the God of Jacob—i.e. of Octavianus/Jacobus, who had prevailed as the heir. The closing comment 'He is not the God of the dead, but the God of the living' renders a bonmot of Octavianus, who in Egypt had the sarcophagus of Alexander taken from the crypt and shown to him, adorned it with flowers and a golden crown, but had no interest in seeing the tombs of the Ptolemaeans, saying 'I wanted to see a King, not corpses'.[634]

The blind of Jericho

—*Bartimaeus*, who stood by the wayside crying out and was warned to keep his silence[635] is Artemidorus of Cnidos,[636] who tried to press a scroll warning of the conspiracy into Caesar's hand on his way to the Senate session, and was repeatedly forced back. The names are still easily recognizable—*Artemidorus* > *Bartimaeus*;[637] *Divus* > *Div us* > *son of David*—and the blindness might have to do with the fact that Caesar never got to read the scroll, as if the deity herein had even made him blind to his looming fate, too (this is the same equating, *Caesar = caecus*, that we already came across with *veni, vedi, vici*). Thus this section originally belonged to the Passion account.

Cautions against scandals

The little ones who are not to be offended are Caesar's 'little people' of great deeds who had provided an exemplary, even heroic example.

The 'hand' that you are to 'cut off, if it offends you', calls to mind Caesar's action at the end of the Gallic war when he made an example of those who had scorned his leniency and had again borne arms against him. He had their hands cut off as a deterrent but spared their lives in order to create as many examples for the punishment of rebels as possible (CAES. *Gal.* 8.44). But it is also that of Acilius, who, when his hand was lopped off after grasping the stern of an enemy ship during a sea battle at Massilia (today Marseille), nevertheless leapt aboard and drove off the enemies ahead of him with nothing but the boss of his shield. In this we see that *Massilia* has become *mulos*, the 'millstone', and the sea battle has become the sea into which the millstone is thrown.

The eye that you should pluck out if it offends you is that of Scaeva, who when he was already blinded in one eye, pierced in the hip and shoulder and with no less than 120 spear perforations in his shield, nevertheless maintained his post at the gate of the fort he was committed to guard.

And the 'good salt', *kalon to (h)alas*, that does not loose its savor, and what we should have in ourselves, are people of the same type as the good *Gaius Acilius* and the good *Cassius Scaeva*.[638]

Jairus' daughter and the hemorrhaging woman

—are the same person, namely Julius' daughter Julia who at first had swooned and miscarried when she saw the blood-stained toga of her husband Pompeius who had been slightly wounded during a political rally. Later she died in childbirth and her newborn daughter only survived her by a few days.[639] This tragedy was commonly regarded as the cause for the falling-out between Caesar and Pompeius and thus for the ensuing civil war, because now there was no common heir of Caesar and Pompeius, whose new wife, moreover, belonged to the family of Sulla and with that to the opposing party. The report of Mark[640] corresponds to reality in so far as Caesar's daughter survived her first premature birth, and the baby daughter born later did not (immediately) die. This section, together with the pericopes developed from the story of Publius Clodius *(the healing of the leper, the healing of the lame man and the calling of Levi)*[641], belongs to the time prior to the Rubicon/Jordan, and thus in the time before the start of the civil war and therefore to an episode originally preceding the Gospel, or to an excursus.[642] Also grouped with this is the

Transfiguration of Jesus

—wherein the 'raiment became shining, exceeding white as snow, so as no fuller on earth can white them',[643] could hark back to Caesar's candidature for his brilliant consulate:[644] then the clothes of the *candidate,* which indeed had to be *candid,* would have been taken literally, possibly *candidatus* confused with *consulatus* also. The three disciples, Peter, James and John would this time be the members of the first triumvirate—Pompeius, Crassus, and Caesar himself, who was the youngest in the alliance, both in terms of age and politics—which is also illustrated by the three tabernacles and the triad of Elias, Moses and Jesus. Regarding these names, we are of course already familiar with 'Elias' as the doublet of Iulius, who de facto ran the consulate without a colleague; 'Moses' are the *mores,* the customs, against which the private agreement of the three offended; the 'Son of Man' who must 'suffer many things' and be 'set at nought', is Gaius here too, who won the love of the people and veterans through the agrarian laws, but also drew the hatred of the large property owners, who was blamed for everything at the end of the year and who, for the time being, had no choice but to go to war in Gaul.

The names of the three disciples, however, Peter, James and John, which regularly stand for Antonius, Lepidus and the young Caesar, i.e. Octavianus, open the possibility that the second triumvirate is meant here. There, the tabernacles, as the commander's tents, would fit because the first agreement of the triumvirate took place on a small flat island in the river Lavinius near Mutina (today Modena, in the Po-Valley). There the former enemies met for two days, from morning till evening—within sight of five legions and three hundred men each, whom they had ordered to take positions on the river bank and at the bridges—under the chairmanship of the young Caesar who at the time had just advanced from private citizen to consul. Here too, we have the 'shining exceeding white raiment', in an even more concise sense, because Octavianus had at first recruited his army as a private citizen, and accordingly wore a white toga without the red stripes of the office-holders, but had in the meantime stood as a candidate and become consul, thus encouraging the confusion of *candidatus* and *consulatus* considered above. The tents of the three unfortified camps lined the river banks and the tents of the three generals were clearly visible either on the little island itself or at the bridges because for two days at the end of November nothing was possible without tents. So the three *skênai*, the three 'tents' (Luther's 'huts' or King James' 'tabernacles'), that Peter wants to put up would have found their prototype here; the 'cloud' that overshadowed them, *nephelê*, would stand for the Latin *nebula*, and would then be the 'fog', of the plain of the river Po, which must have been particularly thick around the little river island on that 27th of November 43 BC. The river landscape would have become the mountain by means of the usual confusion of the Latin *ora*, 'shore, bank' with the Greek *oros*, 'mountain'.

As is known, the *proscriptions* against the mandators of Caesar's assassination were also decided there—indicated by Mark at this point as the conflict with the *scribes*. Also Caesar himself was affirmed as *Divus Iulius*—here *Elia*, who 'verily cometh first, and restoreth all things'—so that those murderers of a tyrant became the murderers of God. Hence all the earlier resolutions of the Senate by which Caesar was deified whilst living were confirmed, and new ones were added.

The first was an oath to be sworn on all the measures taken by Caesar, which made them not only binding, but also sacred—with Mark: 'This is my beloved Son: hear him' and there is the usual separation of *Div us* as 'God's son', suggested in particular by the presence of the *Divi filius* (it should be noted, that this custom of those who govern to take an oath on Caesar's records has survived until today in the oath taken on the bible).

The second was the construction of the temple of Divus Iulius and the re-erection of the altar at the site of his funeral pyre, and also the resolution that his statue was to be carried along together with that of Venus in the processions. 'This is my beloved son' thus related to Caesar as the son of Venus, for Antonius hardly acknowledged Octavianus as Divi filius. (Here too, we have the custom of the procession with the Madonna and Jesus, which has been preserved to this day);

The third was that celebrations for future victories would not only be for the victor but for him as well—in Mark this is indirectly found as the resurrection of the dead, the posthumous victory. (And, this custom of giving thanks to Jesus in addition to the victor has survived too);

The fourth was the celebration of his birthday with the wearing of laurel and the staging of festivities—it cannot be located in the text, but the Christmas custom of the fir tree and exchanging of gifts is based on this (in France, Caesar's Gaul, we have an irony of history in that the birthday of the Republic is celebrated on the 14th of July, quite often on the evening before—Caesar's birthday);

The fifth was to declare the day of his murder an abominable day, and to turn the site of his murder into a latrine;

The sixth was the prohibition of carrying his image during the funeral rites of deceased relatives. This is not only preserved in the Easter ritual, in which we have a resurrection that we would not have if Caesar had been numbered among the dead further on, but in Mark it is rendered in detail as 'Elias'—no doubt *Iulius*—who 'verily cometh first, and restoreth all things;' as 'the Son of Man'—no doubt *Gai us*, i.e. Caesar—who 'must suffer many things, and be set at nought', and in the lament 'Elias is indeed come, and they have done unto him whatsoever they listed', and here is where the grounds for the triumvirate's proscriptions becomes noticeable: they thought that since Caesar's clemency had not been rewarded, now severity was advisable.

Before us, however, is the Passion report, the core of which we have already dealt with in the chapter 'Crux', even if from a different perspective.

The plotting of the enemies

—who are still hesitant and in fear of the people,[645] corresponds in the history of Caesar with the conspirators, who were at first fearful and still undecided.[646] The dating is interesting: 'After two days was the feast of the passover.' As if one had misunderstood *idus*, the 'Ides', the middle of the month, as *dies*, 'days': we are still on the Ides of February, the Lupercalia, which herald those of March, Caesar's Easter.

The anointing in Bethany

—in the house of Simon the leper, where 'a woman having an alabaster box of ointment of spikenard very precious; and she brake the box, and poured it on his head'[647]—corresponds to the feast of the Lupercalia, where Antonius, dressed as *lupercus* i.e. almost naked and anointed with oil like an athlete[648], put a king's diadem on the head of Caesar who was sitting on the Rostra. One recognizes the names: Antonius is

Simon as usual, but as *lupercus* he becomes a *lepros*, 'leper'; since he plays a special role here he is doubled: *Antonius* becomes *Bêthania;* the 'platform', the *Rostra* (pl. of *rostrum*), seems to have become an *alabastron*, 'alabaster box', whereas the preciousness of Caesar's 'Golden ivory chair' is found again in the 'ointment of spikenard very precious'. Presumably, this is because Mark's readers associated the conferring of royal dignity not with a diadem, but with anointing; the oil migrated from Antonius' naked body into the hands of the woman via the confusion of 'naked', *gymnos,* with *gynê,* 'woman'—and thus it went onto Caesar's, i.e. Jesus' head. The reason the woman appears is that Antonius, as Lupercus, had to flick the women with a strip of hide, which was desirable because it was regarded as a good omen for the onset of pregnancy and an easy birth. For Caesar, however, Antonius' not exactly smart behavior was his undoing, because although he repeatedly refused the diadem, his opponents nevertheless accused him of wanting to be made king and took it as an opportunity to murder him.[650] With Mark we find, reliably, the expected correspondence: the act of the woman causes displeasure, but Jesus considers it as a pre-anointing for his burial.

The betrayal of Judas Iscariot

—no doubt is the betrayal of Iunius Brutus[651]—we have already seen the correspondence *Iunius > Judas;* generally, Iscariot is associated with *sicarius*, 'assassin'. The money motif in the form of the bribery of Judas appears with Brutus and the persons behind him when they try to win the crowds over with money.[652]

The Last Supper

—is that of Caesar in the house of Lepidus,[653] as seen above.

The prediction of Peter's denial

—is redactionally under the influence of the denial of Peter four pericopes later. At least the end of this pericope—'That this day, even in this night, before the cock crow twice, thou shalt deny me thrice'[654]—must have been moved forward to this position so that it serves as a prophecy. We will see that, chronologically, it belongs behind the *arrest of Jesus* together with the *denial of Peter.*

A prophetic interpretation was in its logical place here already though, with the easily recognizable rest of the pericope, as we will soon see: the protestation of Peter—'If I should die with thee, I will not deny thee in any wise'—alludes to the oath of the senators to protect Caesar's life with their own, or to be his avengers.[655] Because Antonius will later reproach the senators for this at the first parley with the murderers as well as in his funeral speech,[656] the vow is put in Peter's mouth. The oath of the senators caused Caesar to dismiss his body-guard, which made his murder possible: hence, logically, at the beginning of the pericope we see the quotation from Zechariah (13:7): 'I will smite the shepherd and the sheep shall be scattered.' But the murderers came close to being unable to realize their plan, because four days later Caesar wanted to start his campaign against the Parthians, and then he would immediately have been surrounded again by a body-guard.[657] So the planned campaign against the Parthians could be behind Jesus' announcement 'But after that I am risen, I will go before you into Galilee'. Caesar had already sent his legions in advance for this. Galilee could nevertheless stand for Gaul here again as usual, in so far as Caesar planned to cross the Caucasus mountains to the Scythians after the defeat of the Parthians, to then fall on the Germans from behind, and finally move forward to meet up with his army in Gaul.[658] So the 'sheep', *probata,* of the Zechariah citation could have originally been borrowed from an original *Parthi*. Before his departure—in the Senate session in which he was murdered—Caesar was to have been

> 'designated as king because it is written in the books of fate' that the Parthians could only be defeated by a king'.[659]

From this perspective, compare once more Mark's citation from Zechariah:

> 'For it is written, I will smite the shepherd, and the sheep shall be scattered.'[660]

We see how Mark replaces one prophecy with another: apparently at that time the Sibylline books were out of style and the Jewish prophets were in. That it is about Caesar's appointment as a king is still definitely recognizable—besides from the typical parallel of king/shepherd—in that the issue in both cases was taken to be the cause for the greatest and most general offence.[661]

Jesus in Gethsemane

As the most serious example of offence caused by Caesar, the historians give the incident that took place in front of the temple of Venus Genetrix.[662] He was overseeing the plans and the progress of the construction works on his Forum Iulium and remained seated when he received the Consuls, Praetors and the whole Senate who had come to deliver the resolution on the superhuman honors conferred to him. This was taken as an insult to the Senate. It was said that Caesar had tried to stand up but was held back by Cornelius Balbus. Two reasons were put forth: from the opponents, that Balbus had whispered to him: 'Do not forget that you are Caesar and that you may demand to be honored as a higher being' which was in keeping with the intention of the resolutions equating him with Jupiter, but this did not tally with Caesar's answer who sensed flattery compromising his reputation behind them and intimated to the senators that they would better limit the honors instead of increasing them; whereas from Caesar's circle of friends one could hear that he had sensed the onset of one of his fits—Balbus had already had a firm hold on him because of that—and as these were not only accompanied by dizziness but also by epileptic convulsions he would have remained seated in order to have better control of his body until the attack had passed. In any case the senators are said to have turned away despondently. When Caesar realized that his behavior had given his enemies an opportunity they were looking for to use against him, he headed for home, tore his garment from his neck and shouted to his friends that he was ready to offer his throat, and that whoever wanted to should cut it. Nevertheless he asked them to watch over him, but to the question of whether he wanted to be protected by his body-guard again he answered: 'there is nothing more unlucky than to be permanently watched, this is the state of a man in constant fear.' Or according to another version: 'It is better to die once than to constantly await death.' All of this is to be found again in Mark's adaptation:

> 'And they came to a place which was named Gethsemane: and he saith to his disciples, Sit ye here, while I shall pray. And he taketh with him Peter and James and John, and began to be sore amazed, and to be very heavy; And saith unto them, My soul is exceeding sorrowful unto death: tarry ye here, and watch. And he went forward a little, and fell on the ground, and prayed that, if it were possible, the hour might pass from him. And he said, Abba, Father, all things [are] possible unto thee; take away this cup from me: nevertheless not what I will, but what thou wilt.'[663]

If Jesus is Caesar here, the pivotal point would be the following: Caesar asks his friends to watch over him, Jesus says to his disciples: 'tarry ye here, and watch' (Mk. 14:34). The *Forum* would then have been misunderstood as *chôrion* 'court, garden', which then means that Venus as *genetrix* becomes the *Gethsemane* with the advantage that, being interpreted as 'oil press', *capit oleum,* it is one of the possible translations of *Capitolium.*[664] The influence of which is to be assumed here because Caesar had ordered the laurels, wreathed with a diadem, which had been proffered to him at the Rostra or placed on his statue, to be brought there, to Jupiter Optimus Maximus. That this scene takes place in front of a temple would still be recognizable by the fact that Jesus prays. The names of the disciples would be the obligatory Peter, Jacob and John. The request of Balbus to Caesar to remain seated before the senators would still be detectable in the instruction of Jesus to the disciples: 'Sit ye here'. Caesar's imminent and feared fit would be clearly visible in the 'and he began to be sore amazed, and to be very heavy' as well as in the 'fell on the ground, and prayed, if it were possible, the hour might pass from him'. And in the 'my soul is exceeding sorrowful unto death: tarry ye here, and watch' we see Caesar already realizing that he is in imminent mortal danger, his instruction to his friends that they should watch over him, and also his defiant stance that it is better to die once than to be watched for ever. The saying of Balbus 'Do not forget that you are Caesar and that you can demand to be honored as a higher being' is recognizable in the first part of Jesus' utterance—'Abba, Father, all things are possible unto thee': 'the higher being'—probably Jupiter in this context—would be reflected as 'Abba, Father', the second part of *Iuppiter, -piter,* being, exceptionally, etymologically correctly understood as *pater,* and the remaining beginning of the word *Iup-* as its Aramaic double *Abba,* also 'father'. In the 'all things are possible unto thee', both the absolute 'being permitted' spoken by Balbus to Caesar and the power of the *Optimus Maximus* could be sensed. The second part of Jesus' saying 'take away this cup from me: nevertheless not what I will, but what thou wilt' would be Caesar's own words 'that he was ready to offer his throat to whoever might wish to cut it': here *gula* (Gr. *trachêlos*), 'throat', would simply have been mistaken for 'cup' (*kylix,* 'calyx'), which would have led to Mark's *potêrion,* also 'calyx' (cup). But this remains purely hypothetical.

In this case rather than Caesar it could be about Brutus, though, the famous words spoken to him 'you too, my son', being reversed in to 'Abba, Father'. And Brutus had a good scene on the Capitol, which can also be translated with *Gethsemane* as we have seen. The fact is that *Peter* soon reappears, in a central place—however sleeping.[665] *Brutus* had been goaded to ultimately prove himself worthy of the ancient Brutus who had driven out the kings. They did this by writing at night on the statue of the elder Brutus on the Capitol, and also on the Tribunal and the chair where he took his seat as praetor during sessions of the court: 'Brutus you are sleeping!'[666] Parallel to that, we see Jesus, also at night, say to Peter: 'Simon, sleepest thou?' (Here we recognize, of course, how it came about that *Brutus,* too, could become *Petrus,* namely because he was *Praetor*. We also observed this in the case of Lepidus, who as *praetor* had called for Caesar's first dictatorship.)

Another famous sentence spoken by Jesus in this pericope, 'the spirit truly [is] willing, but the flesh [is] weak', is based on Brutus' wife, Porcia, daughter of Cato, who wanted to be let in on the conspiracy. But because Brutus feared that she, out of physical weakness, might let out when tortured, she secretly stabbed herself in the thigh and said: 'You, my husband, though you trust my spirit that it will not betray, you nevertheless are distrustful of my body, and your feeling is but human. But I have found that my body also can keep silence.'[667] But since she, although she was Cato's daughter, had fallen into a faint due to the tension of the day of the attack whilst she waited for news on the outcome, her flesh had still been weak all the same. Whereas Brutus, who did not abandon his plan even though he received the news that his wife had fainted, demonstrated that the will was stronger—thus Mark, despite his slight change to Porcia's saying, stuck to reality. This fainting of the waiting Porcia, who was in fact at first thought to be dead, may have rubbed off on the above verse: 'fell on the ground, and prayed, if it were possible, the hour might pass from him.'[668] However—with the examination of the healing of the epileptic boy (see above)—we already suspected an attack of weakness in Caesar, who suffered from cachexia, to be behind this passage, which is now confirmed by the detailed analysis of the beginning of the pericope.

The following reiteration of the motif of sleep may have to do with the repeated calling to Brutus to finally act. But it can also refer to Calpurnia, whom Caesar, during the night before his murder, observed uttering incomprehensible words and abrupt sighs in deep sleep. She dreamt that she wept for her husband whom she held murdered in her arms. Mark:

> 'and when he returned, he found them asleep again, (for their eyes were heavy) neither wist they what to answer him. [...] behold, the Son of man is betrayed into the hands of sinners.'

Whereby we can detect the name of *Calpurnia* in the 'heavy' eyes, *katabarynomenoi*. Here, as in the whole exit scene, the presence of the traitor Decimus Brutus, who came to get Caesar because he was late due to Calpurnia's fearful excitement, announces itself. He asked if Caesar really did want it reported to the waiting senators that they should go home and return some other time, when Calpurnia has had better dreams. And with this word Brutus grasped his hand and led him away. Mark:

'Sleep on now, and take your rest: it is enough, the hour is come; behold, the Son of man is betrayed into the hands of sinners. Rise up, let us go; lo, he that betrayeth me is at hand.'[669]

Jesus' arrest

—in reality this is his, and hence Caesar's murder.[670] We have already examined it more closely in the chapter 'Crux'. It can be observed how Judas is correctly not called Iscariot, but 'one of the Twelve', here. Indeed, it was not Marcus who called Caesar to the meeting, but *Decimus* Brutus, literally the 'tenth'. That we are in a session of the Senate, and indeed a hostile one, is indicated by the presence of the multitude of 'scribes and elders' in which we again recognize the formula *patres conscripti*. Also 'high priests' is correctly rendered in the plural form, because apart from the *pontifex maximus* Caesar, the sacrificing priests are mentioned.

A sign was also agreed upon with the attack on Caesar: Tillius Cimber went up close to his face and asked for the recall of his exiled brother, whereas others grasped his hands and kissed his chest and head. Then Tillius grabbed his purple toga with both hands and pulled away the garment from his throat and shoulders as if it was the arranged signal for the attack.[671] In Mark this becomes: 'Whomsoever I shall kiss, that same is he; take him, and lead him away safely.'[672]

The mutual injuries of the hasty assailants and the thrust by Cassius at Caesar's face become the strike at the servant of the high priest that results in his ear being cut off whereby 'face' *os, oris*, is misunderstood as 'ear', *auris*.

Caesar's desperate attempt at protecting himself wherein he shouts at the attackers becomes the answer of Jesus who brands those arresting him as murderers. The attack became inescapable due to the agreement that everyone had to strike the victim, which is rendered as: 'but the scriptures must be fulfilled.'

The panicked flight of the murderers out of the Senate house, which becomes a temple in Mark—'I was daily with you in the temple teaching…'—is here as well: 'And they all forsook him, and fled.'

The picture of the youth, dressed only in linen wrapped around his naked body, who followed Jesus 'and the young men laid hold on him: And he left the linen cloth, and fled from them naked'[673] is a composition. On the one hand, we recognize the remnants of the description of the violent fight that Mark has not used yet—Cimber had pulled Caesar's garment from his neck and shoulders, but Caesar had wrenched it back out of his hands, then in turn grabbed the first attacker, Casca, by the hand, spun around and dragged him behind him. But finally, overpowered, he let go of Casca's hand and pulled the toga over his head and abandoned his body to the blows. On the other hand, we can assume that the picture of the murderers was immingled. They had at first wanted to give a speech in the Senate but then, because nobody had remained there, they wrapped their togas like shields around their left arms and ran away.[674] Furthermore there was also Cassius' son at the Forum, who had just reached maturity and celebrated his first donning of the *toga virilis*. He was the one the conspirators had gathered around before the attack.[675] But at the core there are two candidates who might make the youth, namely two late camp-followers of the conspirators: on the one hand Caesar's brother-in-law, the praetor Cornelius Cinna, who appeared unexpectedly in the middle of a crowd of freedom lovers and hirelings who had assembled on the Forum after the attack. He took off his official garment as if to indicate that he would have nothing to do with the gift of a tyrant. On the other hand there was Cornelius Dolabella, a young man of noble birth who was elected by Caesar as his successor for the office of consul for the remaining part of the year. He also appeared in the crowd on the Forum wearing the garment of a consul and nevertheless began to second Cinna's disdain for the murdered Caesar, and he presented himself as an accessory to the conspiracy.[676] With this we have the the young man in double and triple: Cassius' son and Dolabella, as well as the torn away, taken off, renounced and ever fought over garment, the toga of Caesar; those of the murderers and of the young Cassius, and the official garments of Cinna and Dolabella. Both the latter, at the same time, denied their connection with Caesar by this, but soon had to regret it bitterly. Dolabella had to fear for his consulate as he was only 25 and without Caesar's legitimization he was not even of the requisite age. The praetor Cinna, who appeared again in his robes of office at the following pre-dawn sitting of the Senate in the Temple of Tellus, was pelted with stones by the citizens who had not been bought, as well as by Caesar's campaign companions. They even tried to set fire to the building where Cinna sought refuge, and Lepidus barely managed to prevent it. With that we are in the middle of:

The denial of Peter

—particularly as we know that the name *Peter* comes from the *Praetor Lepidus,* whose request for Caesar's first dictatorship became the *confession of Peter* to Christ. Now that—with *Lepidus*—there is a *praetor* again, Mark does not miss the opportunity of contrasting the present denial with the former confession. He feels it is legitimate to do this, because of the maneuvering, even suspicious, behavior of Antonius, who after Caesar's murder operates in close connection with Lepidus and thus in Mark's eyes has definitely fused into *Simon Peter*. Antonius had not joined the conspiracy, which he had gotten wind of from Trebonius. However, he also did not inform Caesar of it, which saved his life—the conspirators abstained from killing him along with Caesar, and contented themselves with engaging him in conversation in front of the Senate-building.[677] On the one hand he wanted to avenge Caesar, but on the other hand he wanted to achieve a positive outcome in the Senate ostensibly for the sake of the peace, but in reality because he feared the Bruti, most of all the traitor Decimus, who had become Caesar's successor in the Cisalpine Gaul and so was in a position to directly threaten Rome with his troops.

All of this contributes to the background for Mark's pericope of Peter's denial. The ambience—the camp fire of the servants where Peter warms himself—is supplied by the circumstances of that dramatic night. Antonius had ordered night-watches and so there were fires burning all over the city.

The color—the repeated crowing of the cock confirming the threefold denial—is provided by the names. The *Tellus*, the 'mother earth', in whose temple the extraordinary pre-dawn session of the Senate took place, which in view of the time of day—the 'fourth night watch', *quarta vigilia*, also called *secundis galliciniis* in popular usage, 'on the second crow of the cock'—is misunderstood as *gallus*, 'cock', so *tellus, telluris* becomes *alektôr*, 'cock', which allows *Cinna's* name to be interpreted as if derived from *cecini*, 'sang, crew'.[678] The cock crowing twice consistently comes from the second *Cinna*, Helvius, Caesar's friend, who, when he heard that Caesar's body was to be cremated in the Forum went to attend the funeral even though he had a fever. When he arrived at the Forum someone in the crowd related his name to a neighbor who had enquired of it, and soon the name was passed from one to the other and quickly the rumor spread that he was that same Cornelius Cinna who had made a contumelious speech against Caesar. Although he denied it and tried to explain the correspondence of the names, the crowd pounced on him and tore him to pieces on the spot. So Helvius Cinna had to pay dearly for the denial of the praetor Cornelius Cinna. Here too, the requisites and names are brought in line according to the reinterpreted story: Caesar's funeral pyre becomes a camp-fire and Cinna's fever becomes 'warming himself' and because he was a friend of the Pontifex Maximus Caesar and was called *Cinna*, he becomes *ancilla*, the 'maid' of the high priest: he is taken to be a *Cornelius* and thus for a *Galilaeus*; and because there were two *Cornelii* (the other Cinna and

Dolabella) he becomes 'one of them', his negating is interpreted as a repeated denial: and naturally *Peter* is blamed for it, because the one doing the denying had been the praetor and so it suggested itself to read *HELVIVS* as ΠΕΤΡΟC also. A modest veil is spread over his bestial dismemberment where not even one piece of his body could be found for the funeral—'And when he thought thereon, he wept.'[679]

Before the high council

The first sentence of this pericope [680]—'And they led Jesus away to the high priest'—of course belongs to the end of *Jesus' arrest,* where we read: 'And they all forsook him, and fled.' The exemplar for both is the report that after Caesar's murder all fled at once and that only three slaves carried the body home on a litter.[681] Because Caesar's residence at the time was the *domus publica,* the house of the *pontifex maximus* at the Forum, Mark's choice of words—'And they led Jesus away to the high priest'—is accurate here, outside of the fact that he was dead already.

'And with him were assembled all the chief priests and the elders and the scribes.'

This could be the extraordinary session of the Senate before daybreak in the temple of Tellus which had been summoned by Antonius, or else the preceding smaller meeting at the opening of Caesar's will in the house of Antonius. In any case, Peter, who this time is Antonius, is logically mentioned immediately:

'And Peter followed him afar off, even into the palace of the high priest: and he sat with the servants, and warmed himself at the fire.'

In spite of the shortened reproduction, all three pieces of information contained here are correct. Antonius, as we saw, had at first been engaged into conversation outside of the building where Caesar was murdered, then he donned the attire of a slave and kept himself hidden. But still during the night in question, he had Caesar's money and symbols of office brought to his house under protection of the night vigils with their flaming torches that he had set up all over the city. He also negotiated with the mediators of the murderers who had withdrawn into the Capitol and arranged the aforesaid Senate sitting. And, so it was said, he finally gave them his son Gaius as a hostage, and that he had entertained Cassius, whereas Lepidus had entertained Brutus. In this respect Antonius also—like Peter—had 'followed him afar off', had been 'even into the palace of the high priest'[682], had 'sat with the servants' and had 'warmed himself at the fire'.

What then follows about the 'witness' which is 'sought for', so that they can 'put him to death' and which gave 'false witness' and which 'agreed not together'—has to be understood from the background of the Senate session, wherein the murderers contradicted each other. When Antonius confronted them with reality they, nolens volens, had to abstain from the idea of declaring Caesar a tyrant and dishonoring his body, because if they had, all his acts would have been quashed and they would have lost all their offices, benefices and provinces. But the report is overlapped by the opening of Caesar's will—the 'witness' upon which all depended: where his private and, as it turned out, political succession—who was 'the Christ, Son of the Blessed'—was settled. Octavianus decided this in his favor when he accepted the heritage and the adoption decreed in the will, which promoted him to being Caesar's posthumous son.

Caesar's testament, which had been deposited with the Vestals, was opened at the request of his father-in-law Lucius Piso and read aloud in the house of Antonius.[683] The 'servants', around whom Peter 'sat' and 'warmed himself at the fire' therefore could quite possibly be the 'keepers of the Vestal fire' with whom the testament was deposited—which also goes better with Mark's *hypêretôn*, which only barely means 'men servants': not by chance does the Vulgate translate it with *ministris* (both the genitive plural of *hypêretôn* as well as the ablative of *ministris*, leave open the matter of whether it indicates male or female). Then the 'palace of the high priest' would not only be the house of Caesar, but the house of Antonius as well. Mark himself makes it clear two pericopes further on (15:16) that *aulê* is not a 'palace' but the *praetorium*, which in the city no doubt is the residence of the highest office holder, who after Caesar's assassination was Antonius as consul in office (the transfer of Caesar's acts and cash-box to Antonius's house was the realization of the *translatio praetorii*). Antonius could be seen as high priest from the Markan theocratic perspective, because the *pontifex maximus* was dead and he being augur and consul had to minister the funeral and the reading of the will (we will see in the pericope following the next, that also Lepidus, as chief of the cavalry and nominated future *pontifex maximus*, will act as high priest).

Antonius and those senators present had had to first decide which testament was legitimate, because in earlier wills Caesar had always designated his son-in-law Pompeius as his heir. Not till the last will did he appoint three heirs, grandsons of his sisters, as substitute for a potential son born posthumously, and as tutors for them he named Antonius and the same Decimus Brutus who was to later murder him. Finally Caesar had taken one of the three substitute heirs, *Gaius Octavius*, into his family and had given him his name (he was now called *Gaius Iulius Caesar Gai filius Octavianus*).[684]

The preliminary determination of the valid will becomes the search for witnesses and the false witnessing in Mark. But in the second attempt, because he understood the 'three heirs', the *tres heredes,* as *treis (h)êmerai,* 'three days', the *testamentum* becomes *ton naon touton,* 'this temple' which instead of 'written by hand' is 'made by hand', whereas 'another', i.e. the new heir Octavius, is not 'taken into the family' but is 'built as a temple' by confusing the two senses of *oikos,* 'family' and 'temple', which causes the ambiguous *poiô,* 'to make' to be misunderstood as 'to build' instead of 'to adopt'.[685]

The fact that it is about the will elucidates the silence of Jesus, who 'answered nothing' when it was his turn to 'witness'—Caesar was dead already. The question of whether he is 'the Christ, Son of the Blessed', however, is directed at the new Caesar, the adopted Gaius Octavius, i.e. Octavianus. And he had an answer: he had not only accepted the heritage and the adoption, but he had from the beginning made the private issue a political one. To the annoyance of his 'tutor', Antonius, he pointedly displayed Caesar's empty chair with a golden wreath, and at his first appearance he had caused a sensation when he stood beside Caesar's statue on the Rostra and swore to the people that 'he would acquire the honors and office of his father' while stretching out his right hand towards the statue: It even froze the blood of Cicero who reports it: 'I do not want to be saved by such a one!'[686] Antonius took it to be an outrageous presumption that a private citizen in Rome could raise the claim that offices could be hereditary. It was even more outrageous than Caesar's concentration of power.

Mark renders Octavianus' speech before the people almost word for word:

> 'Art thou the Christ, the Son of the Blessed? And Jesus said, I am: and ye shall see the Son of man sitting on the right hand of power, and coming in the clouds of heaven.'[687]

'Art thou the Christ?'—provided it is original, because the word 'Christ' is missing at this point in some manuscripts[688]—is to be understood here as 'are you the heir?' here, equating *heres, heredis* with *christos.* The son of the 'blessed' Caesar is Octavianus from the time he accepted the adoption, whose new cognomen *Gai filius,* 'son of man', indicates the fulfillment of the *condicio nominis ferendi,* 'the condition of bearing the name', which was necessary to validate the adoption. Cicero said it clearly: *O puer qui omnia nomini debes*[689], 'O child, who owes everything to name!' The small change: the emerging of 'the clouds of heaven', is accounted for by the citation from Daniel which is superimposed on Octavianus' speech. Antonius' indignation about the outrageous presumption of Octavianus, which escalated into a murderous clash, finds its correspondence in the high priest who 'rent his clothes' and 'condemned him to be guilty of death' because of 'blasphemy'. And thus Mark has also found the knack of coming back to Caesar's body. At the time of the private reading of the testament, it still was undecided whether the body was to be buried at all or be dragged through the city and thrown into the Tiber, and if his property was to be sold by auction and his acts quashed; only the fear of the consul Antonius and the *magister equitum* Lepidus prevented it.[690]

> 'And some began to spit on him, and to cover his face, and to buffet him, and to say unto him, Prophesy: and the servants did strike him with the palms of their hands.'[691]

In view of the mostly lost context, it would be an art in itself to determine exactly how Mark's transformation occurred here. The 'spit on' could be based on Latin *conspuo* which means 'spit together', but it is mostly used in the metaphorical sense of 'to despise and to disdain'. The 'to cover his face' could point to the denied funeral. Behind *prophêteuson*, 'prophesy', could be *proboulos*—a translation of consul—and behind *(h)ypêretai*, erroneously 'servants', Latin *ministri*, we could assume the *magister Lepidus*, whose name would be hidden in *alapis*, Greek *rhapismasin*, the 'servants did strike him'.

But before we leave this pericope we must say a word about that 'Christ', which is equated with 'Son of the Blessed' here, but is not written in all manuscripts. Here *christos* stands for *heres*, 'heir', whereas in all its occurrences so far the explanation that it is a shortened form of *archiereus megistos*, i.e. *pontifex maximus*, has imposed itself. As briefly mentioned before, Octavianus's acceptance of the adoption eclipsed the eventual decision to bury the tyrant Caesar after all, namely as *pontifex maximus*. Hence the word *christos* could originate from an underlying *pontifex maximus* filtering through the overlain text. Besides, the *pontifex maximus* was related to the matters of the inheritance insofar as one of the special honors awarded to Caesar was that his son, in case he were to sire or adopt one, should be designated *pontifex maximus*.[692]

As to the origin and the meaning of the name *Christ*, the Senate session mentioned above could possibly offer an interesting hint. The central decision made was: 'There should be no prosecution of the murder of Caesar, but all his acts and decrees should be confirmed, because this policy is advantageous to the city'. For their own security, the friends of the pardoned murderers had insisted most emphatically on the addition of those last words, whereby Caesar's measures should be upheld not so much for their legal justification but for their usefulness.⁶⁹³ Appianus says *dia chreian*, 'because of the benefit': so now Caesar had official confirmation that he was not the 'righteous', but the 'useful': *chrêstos*. This probably did legitimize Antonius' act of erecting his statue of Caesar with the inscription PARENTI OPTIME MERITO—where *meritus* stands for *chrêstos*. It was a tit-for-tat response. The name *Christos*, provided that it is influenced by *chrêstos*, would be a classic case of the acceptance of an insult which then is defiantly turned to the positive.

Before Pilate

Already recognizable at the beginning of this pericope⁶⁹⁴—

'And straightway in the morning the chief priests held a consultation with the elders and scribes and the whole council [...]'

—the extraordinary pre-dawn Senate session is repeatedly announced here. The most important thing about the debate is reported—that they had argued fruitlessly was already clear in the pericope *Before the high council*. In the second part of the pericope we are told what's what: There it is asked: 'Art thou the King of the Jews?'—i.e. it was about whether Caesar should be seen as a tyrant. If so, Caesar's murderers would have become murderers of a tyrant and thus would have automatically been saved. Because of that the 'chief priests'—here the leaders of the assassins '—'accused him of many things'. But Jesus does not respond; at one time he does say: 'Thou sayest it'. But this is regarded by Mark himself as nothing: 'Answerest thou nothing? [...] But Jesus yet answered nothing'—he was dead already.

Surprisingly, we get to know the result of the session right at the beginning of the pericope:

'[...] and [they] bound Jesus, and carried him away, and delivered him to Pilate.'

This is the execution of the last decision, which provided for the burying of Caesar's body entrusted to his father-in-law Piso. And indeed, we see him later bringing the body to the Forum on the day of the funeral. Here *Lucius Piso* became *Pilatus* and 'bound' in the sense of 'to bandage' refers to the preparation of the body, with 'bandages'.

The anticipation of the handing over to Piso/Pilatus surely has a redactional function, to make it possible for Jesus to be questioned by Pilate and thus make the posthumous trial look like the lawsuit of a living but silent defendant. But Mark had already found a peg in his exemplar. For in it was written that after the Senate session, when everything seemed to have been agreed upon, some senators badgered Piso not to bury Caesar publicly. Piso shouted that they were the true tyrants if they wanted to prevent him from burying the *pontifex maximus* and he demanded a reopening of the session—wherein the aforesaid decision was made.

Behind the astonishment of Pilate, however, at the end of the pericope, could stand the astonishment of Brutus' companions who could not understand why Brutus had tacitly accepted Caesar's public funeral, which later turned out to be a major mistake.

Trial and mockery

During the session a crowd assembled in front of the Senate building. When Dolabella wasted time with an endless speech about his own office, Antonius and Lepidus went outside. Immediately the crowd cried loudly to them but with opposing demands: some demanded punishment for the act, but the majority—for all the hirelings of Brutus were among them also—demanded peace, by which they meant amnesty for the murderers. Upon that, Antonius said that he personally would be in favor of punishment for the murderers and oath breakers, but as consul, the public welfare had to be more important to him than justice. And not only did the majority of the senators recommend amnesty, but so did Caesar himself, who, for the good of the city, had granted life to those citizens he had captured during the civil war; even more: he had allowed each one of his men to spare the life of one man of the opposing party, and thus many escaped free and unharmed, amongst them also Brutus and those who now had planned an assassination and murdered him.[695] This first speech of Antonius to the crowd is retained in Mark almost literally:

> 'Now at that feast he released unto them one prisoner, whomsoever they desired. And there was one named Barabbas, which lay bound with them that had made insurrection with him, who had committed murder in the insurrection. And the multitude crying aloud began to desire him to do as he had ever done unto them.'[696]

After Antonius had given his time and attention to both groups, and after he had increased the tension even more under the guise of reassuring them (thus preparing the way for his coup at Caesar's funeral) he again joined the session that he presided over. Lepidus remained outside, as Master of the Horse he had to secure public order. Now when he was alone without Antonius he at first wept and wailed. Then he tried to appease both groups, who cried louder and louder—the ones: 'revenge for Caesar!'—the others: 'peace to the city!' At this point, he said in a noncommittal manner: 'Which oaths shall secure an endurable peace?' or: 'Caesar, the truly sacrosanct and honorable man, is gone from us, whereas we hesitate to deprive the city of the rest of the men.' When the cry rang out again: 'Then avenge him yourself!', the hirelings, who knew his ambition began to flatter him and offered him Caesar's position as Pontifex Maximus. He did not refuse, but instead said: 'Think of me in this regard later when I appear more worthy!' When the hirelings saw that he took to it, they demanded peace even louder and Lepidus gave in: 'It contradicts religion and law, but in spite of that I will follow your wishes.' After these words he went quickly up into the Senate, where indeed the amnesty for Brutus and the funeral for Caesar were decided. Mark:

> 'But Pilate answered them, saying, Will ye that I release unto you the King of the Jews? For he knew that the chief priests had delivered him for envy. But the chief priests moved the people, that he should rather release Barabbas unto them. And Pilate answered and said again unto them, What will ye then that I shall do unto him whom ye call the King of the Jews? And they cried out again, Crucify him. Then Pilate said unto them, Why, what evil hath he done? And they cried out the more exceedingly, Crucify him. And so Pilate, willing to content the people, released Barabbas unto them, and delivered Jesus, when he had scourged him, to be crucified.'[697]

Mark has rendered these events too, almost unchanged. However Pilate is now no longer Piso, but Lepidus who, acting alone, is no longer in symbiosis with Antonius, that is, (Simon) Peter. With the word 'high priests' he has mixed the hirelings and the *pontifex maximus*. So the resentment over the betrayal of Caesar of those not bribed,[698] mixed with the eagerness of Lepidus for the proffered position of *pontifex maximus*, has become the envy of the high priests who delivered Jesus to Pilate. Out of both demands—'avenge Caesar!' and 'preserve it (peace, i.e. Brutus)!' he has made one: 'Crucify him!'. Possibly, in his Latin exemplar the inherent opposition between 'keep the (sworn oath)' and 'keep the peace' was retained in the cries, which may have been e.g.: 'serva fidem (iuris iurandi)!' and 'serva pacem!', where he inevitably mistook *seruo*, 'to maintain, keep', for *staurô*, 'crucify'. The 'to scourge' at the end indicates in Mark the Latin word *flagello*, which he seems to have confused with *flagito*, 'to demand urgently'—which is in fact what both groups did, especially the hirelings. He may also have confused it with *flagitium*, the 'shameful behavior' of Lepidus and the 'shame' of Brutus' acquittal.

There are some things he did not use, like for example the saying of Lepidus: 'Think of me in this way later when I appear more worthy!', which another Evangelist puts in the mouth of one of the men crucified with Jesus (Luke 23:42: ' remember me when thou comest into thy kingdom'); or the 'weeping and wailing' of Lepidus before the crowd, which by way of confusing *fleo*, 'to weep', *fluo*, 'to flow', and *louô*, 'to wash' may have been the force behind the 'washing of one's hands of it'—the act of Pilate before the people (Mt. 27:24).

The rest of the pericope with the supposed mockery, is the description of Caesar's body as it is carried by Piso (the other 'Pilate') to the Forum (here *praetorion*), and then placed on the bier with the purple garment (idem) and the golden wreath (here the crown of thorns). This has already been extensively dealt with in the chapter 'Crux', together with the following pericope. This is to be added, however:

The idea that Jesus was whipped, was forced upon by the whipping of a respected citizen from Novum Comum, a colony deduced by Caesar. He had been whipped under a pretext by Caesar's enemies in Rome at the start of the civil war in order to demonstrate—since it was illegal to whip Roman citizens—that the Roman civil rights, which Caesar had granted them, did not apply. That whipping, which was carried out with canes, was supposed to cut Caesar to the quick. By doing this, the consul Marcellus had in his rage revealed his true attitude. He declared that the strokes were the mark of the legal status of a stranger, and that the man should take his welts and show them to Caesar (App. *BC* 2.26; Suet. *Jul.* 28.3). The whipping of Jesus and the smiting with a reed on the head, for mockery (Mk. 15:15-19), is reminiscent of the maltreatment the Roman citizen from Novum Comum had to endure in order to hurt and mock Caesar (cf. p. 88).

Crucifixion and death

Here we will only emphasize two points: the last words of Jesus and the women who were present watching from afar.

We have seen how at Caesar's funeral that, according to custom, an actor wearing Caesar's mask and imitating his voice and gestures recited the verse of Pacuvius' *Contest for the arms of Achilles*:

'*Men(e) servasse, ut essent qui me perderent?*—Did I save them that they might murder me?'

—as if Caesar himself were speaking from the beyond. It is the last of Jesus' sayings:

'And at the ninth hour Jesus cried with a loud voice, saying, Eloi, Eloi, lama sabachthani? which is, being interpreted, My God, my God, why hast thou forsaken me?'[699]

Mark has translated the sentence backwards. The last word, *perderent*, which has the meaning of 'to destroy, to ruin' and we thus have translated according to the sense as 'to murder', has been understood by

Mark colloquially as 'to lose'. Hence it has been translated with *enkatelipes*, which is actually correct, because it not only means 'to leave' but also 'to betray', which is what is meant here (he may have thought of *proderent*, 'to hand over, to betray'). Mark has further correctly translated *ut* with *eis* which means 'for what' rather than 'why' (not by chance, the Vulgate also has *ut* here), so that the second part of Mark's sentence, even in the present version, would classically have to be translated 'in order that you betray me' had we not different pictures in our minds. And they originate from the fact that the first part of Pacuvius' verse was not translated into Greek, but read as Aramaic. Mark has at first read *MENE* running from right to left as *ΕΛΙΕΛΙ*, 'o God, o God' (apparently under the influence of manes, 'the manes, the souls of the dead', which were regarded as deified—hence *dii manes*, 'the gods manes'—which was natural in the case of Caesar) but then he has read it again running from left to right as *ΛEMA, SERVASSE* as *ΣABAXΘANI*, as if it were the Aramaic translation of his *perderent*.[700]

With that we may have completely solved this mysterious sentence, around which there has been so much, and so creative, fantasizing.

> 'There were also women looking on afar off: among whom was Mary Magdalene, and Mary the mother of James the less and of Joses, and Salome; (Who also, when he was in Galilee, followed him, and ministered unto him;) and many other women which came up with him unto Jerusalem.'[701]

These women—who are named and whose role as the mothers of sons who are still young is emphasized—who are they? And most of all: what do they want?

It is to be observed that they appear after the 'centurion', who 'stood over against him, saw that he so cried out, and gave up the ghost, he said, Truly this man was the Son of God.'[702] We mentioned in chapter 'Crux' that the young Octavianus, who acted as 'Son of God' by first making his adoptive father a God, might be behind this 'centurion'. Octavianus first acted as 'Son of God', when he made his adoptive father a God. Now that we are somewhat more experienced with the precision in Mark's distortion, we have to realize that the 'centurion' says that a 'man' was the 'Son of God'. So instead, this man could be Octavianus himself, which would mean that the 'centurion' was he who first recognized Octavianus as the 'Son of God' and accepted him as such—even helped him to achieve that status.[703] Naturally that was not Antonius—he acted against such a development with all his power—but Cicero, the most personal enemy of Antonius. And lo and behold: in the Greek text the *'centurion'* is called *kentyriôn* (conspicuously the Latin word is used, which looks and sounds very similar to *Cicero: KIKEPΩN > KENTYPIΩN*). We will see in the next pericope that this 'centurion' further takes on the role of Cicero.

That the women appear at this moment when the struggle over Caesar's succession is being played out will have some meaning. Are they the mothers of Caesar's possible heirs? The provision of the will which stated that secondary heirs were to be considered only if there was no legitimate physical son, had thrown open the door to all the women who either hoped to be pregnant like the wife Calpurnia; or hoped to get their son accepted as legitimate, as happened to the niece Atia, mother of one of the heirs named as substitutes—Gaius Octavius—who was adopted into the family of Caesar, and as happened with Cleopatra, whose son Caesarion was already allowed to bear Caesar's name. She had made him co-ruler with her in Alexandria, where Caesar, so it was rumored, wanted to relocate his capital.[704] Then there was Mucia, mother of Pompeius' children who were waiting for their heritage and now, after Caesar's murder, saw their chance. Also there was Amatius, who held himself forth as a grandson of Marius. In fact, he was not actually called Marius but at least pseudo-Marius. He had erected the first altar at the site of Caesar's cremation and was hence very popular with the people. His mother must have also been a Maria, whether by birth or marriage. Finally there were certainly concubines, among whom were those who had followed Caesar during the Gallic campaign, and who had older rights—it was on everyone's lips that he had had many affairs in Gaul, especially with married women.[705] What we know for sure is that the tribune of the people, Helvius Cinna, whose terrible death we heard about at Caesar's funeral, let it be known that he had formulated a written law—which he had to submit by order of Caesar during his absence—allowing Caesar to marry any woman he wanted, and as many as he wanted, in order to procreate children and thus secure progeny.[706] At least until the arrival of Gaius Octavius, who was still in Apollonia at the time of Caesar's death and who first came to Rome and accepted the adoption some weeks later after he had gathered some forces, the only thing certain was that Antonius was named as one of the tutors of the posthumous heir. Who this would be—and even if there would be one—was yet to be made clear.

Is *Maria Magdalena* (as we saw this is the Markan transcription of *Alexandria*) perhaps *Cleopatra*? Cleopatra was Caesar's mistress like Magdalena was Jesus' 'consort' and 'favourite disciple' whom he 'kissed' (cf. Gospel of Mary; Gospel of Philippus 32, 55). And has *Calpurnia* become *Salome* here *(CALPVRNIA > CAΛΩMH)*? Or has Mark, because of the resemblance of the names in Latin script, confused

Calpurnia with *Cleopatra* and hence called her *Magdalena*? This is conceivable, for Magdalena is named in the first place and the first lady was Calpurnia. In that case Cleopatra would remain Salome. Then we would have to see the connection to *Alexandria* as secondary and ask ourselves if it were not possible that Mark had analyzed *Calpurnia* as *dal purnia*, and then recognized in the second part *pyrgos*, 'tower', which in Aramaic would become *magdala*: 'of the tower', *dal magdala* > *Magdalena*. Is 'Mary, the mother of James the less and of Joses' to be understood as *Atia*, the mother of the young *Gaius Octavius*, represented here as *Joses* and *James*? Are they both called *Maria* because they belonged to the house of the Iulii and because the first and most famous *Iulia*, Caesar's aunt, had been the wife of *Marius*, whilst Caesar himself was regarded as the most famous of the *Marians*? Or is it caused by the indirect influence of the pseudo-Marius Amatius? In any case the name *Maria* is reserved for the *Marians*. Consistently, neither Salome/Cleopatra nor the 'mother of the children of Zebedee'—who is not mentioned by Mark but by Matthew and who is to be understood as the mother of Pompeius' children—is called Maria.

From this view we would have to identify the women, 'Who also, when he was in Galilee, followed him, and ministered unto him, and many other women which came up with him unto Jerusalem' as Caesar's concubines, those who were with him in Gaul and those who had come to Rome with him. Because Mark speaks here of 'many' it can hardly be correct, even of Caesar to whom even more was imputed than was actually the case. So we have to assume that Mark was influenced by the picture of the many matrons of all the peoples who had come with their children to Caesar's funeral.[707]

But this means that here also—as observed previously in the pericope *Before the High Council*—we must reckon with the possibility that the text concerning the problems of Caesar's heritage has overlain an earlier one that was only about Caesar's funeral. This would mean that Caesar's sacred history was at some time re-written backwards, based on the later conflict between Antonius and Octavianus wherein the viewpoint of the latter does not prevail until the end, after Antonius yielded.

Jesus' entombment and resurrection

Here too, Mark has lain two stories over each other. Lying underneath is what ensued immediately at Caesar's cremation site, and on top is what happened when Octavianus arrived in Rome and finally prevailed.

Directly at the cremation site two things had occurred: Caesar's freedmen had collected his bones and had buried them in the family tomb, and the people, probably at the initiative of the pseudo-Marius Amatius, had erected a round altar or more precisely a column at the site where the pyre had been and now wanted to make sacrificial offerings to Caesar as to a god there. In order to pacify the senators however, who were vindictive because of his rebellious funeral speech, Antonius refused to consecrate the altar and had it thrown down with the help of his colleague Dolabella. Using his consular power, he had Amatius killed without trial and he wrought vengeance upon those who expressed displeasure over it. Indeed, there was a man who showed the outraged people the pedestals from which the statues of Caesar were cast down, and also the workshops where they were smashed. The furious crowd immediately turned to incendiarism. Antonius ordered more troops in, killed some, and of those captured, he had the slaves crucified and the free citizens cast down from the Tarpeian rock.[708]

When Octavianus arrived in Rome, these events too made him rage against Antonius. He did not let him rest—he sided with the libelous accusations and the revolt incited against Antonius by Cicero and took part in the war against him in Gaul wherein Antonius suffered a defeat at Mutina—until he finally brought him to the point where he not only agreed to the re-establishment of the altar, but also to the consecration at the site of a temple where Caesar was worshipped as God. At the same time, the family was forbidden to carry his *imago* (a bust portraying the dead) in funeral processions for their deceased ones, in order to underscore the point that he no longer was among the dead, but a living god.[709]

Mark combines both elements and thus follows the example of classic historians like Appianus, who mentions in the same breath the construction of an altar at Caesar's cremation site and the temple later erected by Octavianus.[710]

> 'And now when the even was come, because it was the preparation, that is, the day before the Sabbath, Joseph of Arimathaea, an honourable counsellor, which also waited for the Kingdom of God, came, and went in boldly unto Pilate, and craved the body of Jesus. And Pilate marvelled if he were already dead: and calling unto him the centurion, he asked him whether he had been any while dead. And when he knew it of the centurion, he gave the body to Joseph. And he bought fine linen, and took him down, and wrapped him in the linen, and laid him in a sepulchre which was hewn out of a rock, and rolled a stone unto the door of the sepulchre. And Mary Magdalene and Mary the mother of Joses beheld where he was laid.

And when the Sabbath was past, Mary Magdalene, and Mary the mother of James, and Salome, had bought sweet spices, that they might come and anoint him. And very early in the morning the first day of the week, they came unto the sepulchre at the rising of the sun. And they said among themselves, Who shall roll us away the stone from the door of the sepulchre? And when they looked, they saw that the stone was rolled away: for it was very great. And entering into the sepulchre, they saw a young man sitting on the right side, clothed in a long white garment; and they were affrighted. And he saith unto them, Be not affrighted: Ye seek Jesus of Nazareth, which was crucified: he is risen; he is not here: behold the place where they laid him. But go your way, tell his disciples and Peter that he goeth before you into Galilee: there shall ye see him, as he said unto you. And they went out quickly, and fled from the sepulchre; for they trembled and were amazed: neither said they any thing to any man; for they were afraid.'[711]

In the 'sepulchre' which 'was hewn out of a rock' we recognize the altar—or more precisely—the column of Amatius, because Mark's *mnêma,* respectively *mnêmeion,* is hardly a 'sepulchre', but a 'monument', or 'memorial'. If it is still a 'sepulcher' then it is only in the sense of 'mausoleum'. It was also not necessarily, as the King James translation defines it, 'hewn out of a rock', but *ex petras,* which also means 'made of a single stone block'. With this *lithos,* this marble stone in front of it, we are awkwardly reminded of Amatius' circular 'altar', which after its re-erection was situated in front of the temple of Divus Iulius, and had a twenty foot high column of Numidian marble on it, or beside it, from the beginning.[712] The name of the *pseudo-Marius Amatius* seems to linger in the name of the man who had lain Jesus in the grave, Joseph of Arimathea. Although with this 'honorable counsellor' who asked Pilate for the body of Jesus, Mark may have thought of *Piso*—whom he had already called *Pilate*—who was entrusted (along with Octavianus' mother Atia) with Caesar's funeral,[713] and who in fact brought Caesar's body into the Forum. *Piso* can be sensed behind the name *Joseph of Arimathea* (read backwards as *Osip > Joseph*), and also *Atia,* as a *Julia* was no doubt a *Maria: Piso and Maria Atia > Joseph of Arimathea.* So Mark seems to have accommodated the parts of Caesar's funeral he still had not used, and has led us back to Octavianus by way of his mother Atia, because *Jôsêph* could also stand for *Octauius* (especially in the variant *Jôsêtos,* which pops up again in connection with Maria a few verses later), as soon as one reads the '*c*' of O*c*tauius as Greek '*s*'. The 'centurion', the *centurio,* is *Cicero* as we have already recognized. It is true that he fought so that Octavianus could gain possession of the 'body', because *soma* first and foremost means the material heritage of a person, with substance, values and position, and this is what he wanted from Caesar and what he received. Also the *sindôn* might here be not so much the 'linen', because, as we observed above with Caesar, Cornelius Cinna and Dolabella, but it might rather be the toga in the sense of an official garment and would thus demonstrate the dignity pertaining to it: was it the purple one that Caesar's body wore? Was it the consular toga of Antonius who acted high-handedly against Amatius and neutralized him? Or was it the white one of Octavianus who still held no office and acted by his own initiative, who only later was to wear the praetorian and consular toga?

The 'offerings' of the people—first during the cremation of Caesar's body on which all kinds of precious things were thrown, mostly by the matrons, who even offered jewelry and the collars and the *praetexta*, the 'pre-woven' tunics of their children, then later at Caesar's altar and column, and even the frustrated demand for its consecration—all of it mutates into the women who vainly go to the grave with their aromatics and ointments. There they find the stone rolled away like Amatius' altar; there they find a young man and are affrighted like the crowd was of Antonius; and it is there that the place 'where they laid him' is shown to them—just as the workshop where the toppled statues of Caesar were smashed was shown to the crowd.

From here on however, Mark resorts to other methods. He has the women being asked by the 'young man', the *neaniskos,* who could only be the *puer* Octavianus, and no longer Antonius—because he is 'clothed in a long white garment', i.e. the simple toga of a private citizen—if they are looking for 'Jesus of Nazareth, which was crucified' and 'is risen'. Here he has called himself by his complete new name: *GAIVM CAE-SAREM OCTAVIANVM* > *IHCOYN NAZAPHNON ECTAYPΩMENON.* The young Caesar who suffered because of Antonius is no longer known as Octavianus—which was how Antonius had mocked him—but as the crucified one. He immediately heralds war to Antonius: 'But go your way, tell his disciples and Peter that he goeth before you into Galilee: there shall ye see him, as he said unto you.' Here the defeat in Gaul is heralded. And that the threat was understood as such is shown by the reaction of the women, who turn around and flee from the grave and are found trembling, amazed (or, as Luther translates: horrified) and afraid, which reminds us of Antonius' massacre of the followers of Amatius.

Appearances of the Resurrected One—Ascension

The long ending of Mark's final chapter (Mk. 16:9-20) is regarded as false by the researchers and it in fact represents an inept summary of that which is reported in the other Gospels about the Resurrected One. Hence, acts of Octavianus are to be found here in abbreviated form. The 'two of them' to whom he while on his way reveals himself 'as they walked, and went into the country' are the disciples of Emmaus in Luke; etc.

But the short alternative ending fits seamlessly with the preceding text. It says there, if translated literally, that 'all positions of command were handed over in a short time to those who stood around Peter', but 'then Jesus appeared from the Orient'[714]—which accords well with the state of affairs at the time. Antonius had concentrated all power in himself and in his relatives,[715] by the time Octavianus had arrived from Apollonia and appeared in Rome. Here 'Orient, dawn' *anatolê*, might stand for *Apollonia*—which, coincidentally, is correct insofar as that town was located to the East.[716] The rest of the sentence, where there is talk about 'to send out, to forward', also fits into the picture: the young grand nephew was sent ahead there by Caesar in the expectation of a campaign against the Parthians, who seem to hide behind the word *aphtharton,* 'immortal' here. The *(h)ieron*, which appears in the last part of the sentence, must be the 'temple' built by Octavianus. It could stand for the 'proclamation of eternal salvation', inasmuch as Appianus—in the above mentioned citation (*BC* 2.148), which closes the second book—regarded the construction of the temple of Divus Iulius by the young Caesar as the sign of his assumption of Caesar's power, and thus the symbol and materialization of the form of government that still existed at his time and which had been founded by Caesar: the salutary and eternal Imperium Romanum.[717]

This was probably the ending to the original Mark. But further material, which is chronologically later, has been added. We have seen above that two pericopes—*The rich young man* and *The rewards of discipleship*—represent two aspects of the conflict between Octavianus and Antonius: so they would have had to be placed here, immediately after this so-called short ending.

Then came the reconciliation and the forming of the second triumvirate, which might have been reflected in *the transfiguration of Jesus* (independent of whether the first triumvirate still shows through). Finally came the proscriptions which we saw are traceable in the section on *the Coming of Christ*. The chronological ending of Mark might be the pericope that is usually called *Waiting for the Coming of Christ* (13:33-37) and which ends with the admonishing of his people to: 'Watch!'.

But if this material was not placed behind Caesar's sacred history but rather within it—namely from the Rubicon till his funeral—then it was because there was a massive hurdle to the promotion of Octavianus to Divi Filius. This was the opposition of Antonius. So the story of Octavianus' promotion could only have been incorporated into Mark's exemplar later, after the victory over Antonius and Cleopatra. Even then, however, it had to squeeze itself into the framework which had become traditional already—which it did indeed, to the extent that it overlaid Caesar's story. The Divi Filius had not only sat himself down to the right of Divus Iulius, but even took his chair.

110./111. Denarii of Octavianus and 112. by Platorinus: 42, before 31 and 13 BC.

Numismatic evidence for this systematic occupation of Caesar's official chair can be seen in the successive coinage of Octavianus/Augustus, which displayed the *sella curulis,* Caesar's official chair with his golden wreath, then, as seen, Octavianus on the same *sella* with Victoria in his hand, and finally Agrippa beside Augustus on the official chair, which has become the *bisellium:*[718] the throne of the father; the son sitting on the father's throne; the son of the son sitting to the right of the father.

Now we have passed Mark completely[719] and ought to start on the other Gospels—and actually we could just as well start again with Mark from the beginning.

Our basic suggestion—that the Gospel is the disguised sacred history of Caesar—has been completely confirmed using the example of the oldest Gospel. So now we can calmly abandon the life-boat which up to now we have kept in reserve for our security, namely the idea that only parts of Caesar's vita may have rubbed off on the story of Jesus, and that Jesus would retain an existence of his own, because we did not find anything in Mark that did not have its clear genesis in Caesar's story—however inadequate and in need of revision our analysis may have been so far. The other Evangelists do not add anything essential to Mark's material, and if they do, it can also be found in the life of Caesar as was observed in some places, the last time being with the mother of the children of Zebedee, or another example at the beginning, with the epithet of Asinius Pollio. So the examination of the other Gospels would indeed be interesting, but it would not change the matter.

We could, for example, let the infancy narratives of Octavianus and the Christ child unroll in parallel and discover that *Bethlehem* is *Velitrae* (today Velletri), where Octavianus spent his first years on the estate of his grandparents and where centuries later his *cella,* a tiny room, 'about the size of a pantry' as Suetonius says, was still exhibited.[720] This idea of the tiny pantry combined with the place of his birth—*ad capita bubula,* 'at the head of the oxen', in the area of the Palatine—led to the idea of the 'manger', at the head of the ox at the foot of the palace (Palatine > palace); and that he was born shortly before dawn gave rise to the Holy night.

Jesus' genealogical tree covers the gossip about the ancestry and rank of the family of the Octavii, probably patricians in the time of the Tarquinii and Servius, but then they became plebeians, and this changed only when Divus Iulius reinstated them as patricians (which led to the 'Davidic' origin of Jesus).

The three wise men from the Orient—one of whom is black and who bring gifts of gold, frankincense and myrrh—arise from the gossip exploited by Antonius in his polemics, that Octavianus' grandfather was of African origin and that he had been a banker (gold) in *Thurii* (incense: as if *Thurii* had come from *tus, turis,* 'incense') and had run a shop purveying ointments (myrrh).[721] The idea that they were gift-bringing, genuflecting kings from the Orient is based on Augustus' travel to that region, where the Parthians freely ceded Armenia to him and handed back the battle insignia of Crassus and Antonius, and where even the Indians and Scythians sent memorable delegations to him.[722]

Herod's slaughter of the innocents is not only based on the fact that Herodes indeed ordered children killed, namely his own, which he had from the Hasmonean heir Mariamme, but originally also on Octavianus, because a few months before his birth it was heralded in Rome by a portent that Nature was pregnant with a king for the Roman people. Thereupon frightened the Senate decreed that no male child born that year should be reared; but the men whose wives were pregnant saw to it that the decree was never ratified.[723] As a decree came into force through the process of moulding it into bronze and 'carrying' it, *delatum,* into the 'chamber of bronze', the *aerarium,* then by way of confusion with *granarium,* 'chamber of grain', the picture of the flight of Joseph with Mary and the Christ child to the granary of the Empire, *Egypt,* could have come about.

This picture was obligatory at any rate, because not only did Caesar himself have to flee from Sulla's hired assassins at an early age, but also Livia and her son Tiberius, who was two years old at that time, had to flee from the insidious murderers on the side of Octavianus in 40 BC—the same Octavianus who later was to marry her and adopt her son Tiberius, indeed who himself was to make her the daughter and his own priestess of the nascent Divus Augustus (cf. VELL. PATER. 2.75). They did flee to Sicily and not Egypt, but both countries were the respective granaries lying towards the south, and moreover she took refuge with Sextus Pompeius, who was considered to be the first lover of Cleopatra, even before Caesar. Since barely ten years later the same Octavianus also had the young Caesarion, the son of Caesar and Cleopatra, hunted down and murdered by his henchmen in Egypt, then certain details of Livia's clandestine flight along secret routes, only accompanied by her husband and with the child and future emperor on her arm, could remain memorialized in an abridged and summarizing version as a flight to Egypt. The fact that the Evangelist put the blame for the persecution on Herod probably was for reasons of occultation.

The annunciation and the immaculate conception recount the story of Octavianus' mother Atia, who attended a solemn midnight offering for Apollo whereby her litter was placed in the temple. She fell asleep but suddenly a serpent glided up to her and departed shortly afterwards, and when she awoke she cleansed herself as if after intercourse with her husband. Immediately a mark appeared on her body in the form of a painted serpent which proved to be indelible, and consequently she afterwards abstained from visiting public baths. Nine months later Augustus was born and was therefore regarded as the son of Apollo. The 'maculate' conception naturally had to become an 'immaculate' one for reasons of decency. The serpent of Apollo which glided in had to become the manifesting angel Gabriel (here *draco*, 'serpent', might have been taken as 'dragon' and in the sequel, instead of as devil—which suggests itself—it was taken as *archangelos*, archangel).

The star of Bethlehem, however, is based on Atia's dream, which she had shortly before delivery, that her womb was raised to the stars and that it spread over all heaven and earth. This was naturally combined with the appearance of the *sidus Iulium*, the star of Caesar, the comet that shone throughout the games for the consecrated Divus Iulius that were staged later by the *puer*, the 'child' Octavianus.[724]

The words of *Simeon* in the temple 'for mine eyes have seen thy salvation, which thou hast prepared before the face of all people' are those of *Figulus*, who when he heard the hour of the birth in the Senate declared that the Lord of the world had been born. And the other statement which says that the baby Jesus is the light of the gentiles is the dream of Octavius, Octavianus' father, wherein he saw a vision as if the glorious light of the sun were rising from his wife Atia's lap.⁷²⁵ *Figulus* becomes *Simeon* as if it originated from ficus, 'fig', which is in Greek *sykon*, which led to *Symeôn* by way of *sykeôn*.

Even the disappearance of the Christ-child occurs in the story of Octavianus: one evening he was lain in the cradle by the nurse and the next morning he was not to be found, and only after a long search was he discovered in a lofty tower, lying on the floor facing the rising sun. So Jesus too was lost as a child, the parents thought he was with relatives and other familiar people (corresponding to the nurse) and he was found later only after a long search, in the temple (corresponding with the lofty tower). There the Christ child was conversing with scholars and they were all astounded and startled, and the mother 'guarded everything in her heart', and likewise the little Octavianus, when he began to speak, bade the croaking frogs in the pond to be silent, and they indeed kept silent and still were so at the time of Suetonius, as was told.⁷²⁶ It seems that here the croaking 'frogs', the *ranae,* were taken as *rabbis,* 'scholars'—a very popular image.

So much for our brief contemplation of the respective beginnings of Matthew and Luke. At their endings we can see the apparitions of the resurrected, i.e. the acts of the young Caesar Octavianus on his path to power. The consuls of 43 BC, who marched with the young Caesar to *Mutina* without acknowledging him, became the *Emmaus*-disciples, who did not recognize the risen one. The skeptical *Antonius* becomes the doubting *Thomas;* Octavianus' most vehement opponent, *Sextus Pompeius,* who could only be eliminated after lengthy wars and an erstwhile reconciliation, is understood as 'the sixth ghost' and with the addition of his temporary ally Antonius he becomes the 'seven demons' that Jesus drove out accordingly; *Maria Magdalena* is again here *Cleopatra.* Augustus' secret dinner, of which much was spoken, called *dôdekatheos,* 'of the twelve gods', was where the guests sat at table in the costumes of gods and goddesses and Augustus himself acted as Apollo. The dinner was reproached as a sign of gross insensitivity because there was great famine at the time, and it becomes the appearance of the Risen One to the eleven, who were sitting at the table and whom he admonished because of their 'hardness of heart'.⁷²⁷

But in the middle of their Gospels Matthew and Luke add facts regarding Caesar that either do not appear in Mark or appear in a different manner or in an abbreviated form. So here, for example, one can detect *Brutus* who had switched sides to *Porcius* (Cato), as the prodigal son who joined himself to the *swineherds;* or one can recognize the vain oath of the Pompeians before Pharsalos as the ban on swearing. And we would detect with surprise, that behind Jesus' famous words there are Caesar's laws and ordinances: so behind the *Good Shepherd* who knows his sheep is Caesar's measure to restrict the extension of pasture at the expense of the arable farmland by limiting the use of slaves as shepherds;[728] or we find Caesar's measures to regulate the market—by putting tariffs on imported luxury goods and by rigorous supervision of comestibles[729]—as the cleansing of the temple; and Caesar's general regulation of debt,[730] which we saw earlier in Mark, appears in Matthew as the core sentence in the Lord's prayer 'and forgive us our debts, as we forgive our debtors'. The idea of the *Ave Maria* will be found in the moving and ceremonious funeral speeches for the deceased Iuliae, like for Caesar's wife Cornelia and for Marius' widow:

Amitae meae Iuliae maternum genus ab regibus ortum, paternum cum diis immortalibus conjunctum est [...].[731]

'The family of my aunt Julia is descended by her mother from the kings, and on her father's side is akin to the immortal gods [...]'.

Interestingly, the additional Caesarean material of Matthew and Luke is found with Suetonius, but arranged thematically and not chronologically, so we can deduce that Mark had a purely chronological source at his disposal, whereas Matthew and Luke had access to a thematic one as well. The source of Octavianus' material was probably a similar one, because the information on him is not found in Appianus who arranges things chronologically, but again in Suetonius, namely in the thematic sections, or, in Cassius Dio, but then in an excursus.

On the other hand, our initial hypothesis, which we had taken from established textual criticism, that the deformations firstly arose via folk-etymological processes during the initial oral transmission which then were intensified by corruptions in the written copy-process is not confirmed—*not exactly*. Rather we had to realize that, at least in the case of the names, the deformations are based on original mistakes in the reading of Latin names in Mark. However with the other Evangelists they arose instead in the reading of the Greek ones. Now we would have to start again with Mark from the beginning and there—where we left both hypotheses standing side by side like in the cases of the origins of the name of Maria Magdalena, John the Baptist or of Jacobus (James)—we would have to shed new light in these areas to secure results. But since we cannot rule out, due to the custom of the copyists, that the names in the different Gospels were brought into line with one another—probably those of Mark on the basis of Matthew who was later positioned in front of him in the canon—this could only be established by means of a comparative analysis of the four Evangelists and the written variants. But this would stretch far beyond our framework.

In order to demonstrate what is meant, we take as an example the name *Jakobus*. We have seen that this name always pops up abruptly in Mark without a plausible derivation from Latin. Because this name (Jacobus=James) seldom appears alone but mostly is paired—'James and John', 'James the less and Joses'—it could be a doublet of *Johannes* (John) respectively *Joses,* which originated with the other Evangelists, where their exemplar already had these names in Greek translation and then it was borrowed as a doublet for purposes of uniformity, firstly by Mark and then borrowed from him by the others. This name could be *Octavius,* which in its Latin form would have resulted in *Josetos* and *Joses*—OCTAVIVS > IΩCHTOC (IΩCHC)—but in its Greek form would have led to *Jakobus* (from *Oktabios,* more popular and hence more probable than the scholarly *Oktaouios*: OKTABIOC > IAKΩBOC). Then we would have to check if this fits in all places, and determine where we have to make new classifications. It could turn out that the frequently occurring triad: Peter James John, conceals a more ancient one: Simon Peter Josetos, and that James was added as the second name of the John/Josetos when Simon Peter was held to be one person. This would be a work in itself and not only that: in the end we would have to rewrite this book. Which would be a pity because all the ways, detours and even the wrong tracks are valuable also, for they enabled us to explore the terrain and to exclude easy ways out.

For certain, we do not think that the task of this book is to deliver definitive results for all details. We are rather in the same boat as Columbus, who set out from the West to reach India and inadvertently discovered America. One could not travel to America today using the map he made of the newly discovered islands, and his caravels were not certified by a modern technical association like the Maritime Services Board. But many came after him, found an entire continent and inhabited it. If this one should be the first of many other works to follow, it should already have proved profitable.

What we can survey from this place is, on the one hand, the process that might have led from the sacred history of Divus Iulius to the Gospel, on the other, the historical framework within which it took place. This again will enable us to establish a working hypothesis for the examination of the other books of the New Testament, especially Acts and the Pauline epistles, and to outline a theory on the origin of Christianity and for other related religions as well.

We want to touch on this at the end.

Final Observations

HISTORY

How did the sacred story of Caesar become the Gospel? The answer to this question has not only a technical or historical dimension concerning the handing down of a tradition, but a theopolitical one, as well.

We must be clear on this point first: there was actually no hagiography of Caesar, but rather a *vita Divi Iulii*. Divus Iulius was not the deified Caesar, but a god in his own right: not a deceased god but rather a living god. Because Julius Caesar was the first of the deified Caesars it is easy to be misled by the idea that his cult must have been the prototype for the cult of the Caesars. This is not true, or at least not completely true, although the notion could indeed be construed from the ancient writers. We have already seen how Appianus wrote that, on the model of the deification of Caesar, the later emperors had been afforded the same respect, provided they did not rule tyrannically or bring any great reproach upon themselves. However, the same respect does not mean the same status. This is best recognized when a dynasty comes to an end. We remember the old adage of how Octavianus, when he looked upon the sarcophagus of Alexander and not wanting to see the grave of the Ptolemaeans at all, exclaimed: 'I wanted to see a King, not a row of corpses!' That is the difference between the founder of an empire and its resultant dynasty. The same distinction exists between Caesar and the Roman emperors. And just as Alexander was still a king to Octavianus when the Ptolemaeans had lost the throne of Egypt on the death of Cleopatra, so Divus Iulius was still a god for Vespasianus when the Julio-Claudian line died out with Nero—and it appears that he has survived the demise of the Roman Empire, incognito, as Jesus.

And thus we have to restrict the assertion of the title of this book: 'Jesus was Caesar'. He *was*—as a man. As a God he *is* not: Jesus is Divus Iulius.

Was Jesus a copy? In order to answer this question, we should recall the phenomena we encountered during the course of our examination and try to picture the whole process.

When Caesar died, he had already been declared a Divus by the senators, only to be murdered by the very same men as a tyrant. That his funeral nevertheless became his apotheosis, is due to the skillful tactics and genius of Antonius in acting as a true histrion of God. It was the first Passion Play, where the audience played the chief role, being at once both the chorus of the tragedy and the actors as well. They were driven from the deepest dejection to the highest excitement, burning the corpse of Caesar on the Forum and driving his murderers out of town. This chief role was played by the people and the veterans. Suetonius justly remarks that Divus Iulius was, presumably unlike many others—perhaps unlike all the others—added to the number of the gods *non ore modo decernentium sed et persuasione volgi,* 'not only because of the lip-service of those who decided it, but because of the deepest conviction of the people'. That was the implied tragic dynamic tension of the new cult in its hour of birth, and this has continued until today: the direct relationship between the almighty God incarnate and his people, ready for action, mediated alone by the divine histrion.

Of course the situation became complicated immediately with the appearance of Octavianus and the back peddling of Antonius, who had acted as informal *flamen Divi Iulii*—high priest of the new God—but then refused to recognize Octavianus as *Divi filius,* son of God even if this meant the denial of Divus Iulius himself. So he preemptively destroyed the altar Amatius had set up, and tried to prevent Octavianus from entering upon Caesar's inheritance. The result is well known: With the backing of Cicero, Octavianus aligns himself with the party of the Senate, recruits an army as a private citizen, and marches with them against Antonius. Then, in league with Lepidus, the second triumvirate was established and the proscriptions of the murderers of the tyrant were decreed; they had now become God murderers because of the official elevation of Divus Iulius.

The engine of this development was the people, that is, the plebs and the veterans. It can be observed how each of the actors only held the sympathy of the people and the support of the veterans as long as he was acting, like a long arm of Divus Iulius, according to the way of thinking of the deceased Caesar.

But the *deus ex machina* was Asinius Pollio, Caesar's legate, whom we saw at the Rubicon, in Sicily, in Africa and at Pharsalos. After Caesar's death he fought against Sextus Pompeius in Spain with little success, but managed to come to a settlement with him and then united himself with Antonius. A convicted republican, he loved Caesar above everything else, abhorred the civil war, supervised the distribution of land to the veterans in Gallia Transpadana where he saved the estate in

Mantuanum for Vergilius and was able to achieve the remarkable feat at Brundisium of reconciling the triumvirate who had in the meantime fallen out with each other. While Antonius was in the Orient, Octavianus had bombarded the followers of his brother and his ex-wife Fulvia with lead missiles on which he had ordered the legend DIVVS IVLIVS inscribed, and finally slaughtered 300 of them before the altar of Divus Iulius. Antonius then married Octavianus' sister Octavia and was, at last, formally inaugurated as *flamen Divi Iulii*. The consulate of Asinius Pollio, which sealed the peace and brought the promise of recovery for the depleted state of the farmers, raised great hopes and was celebrated by Vergilius as the return of the *Saturnia regna,* the golden age. In the next year, Asinius led the war against the Parthinians in Illyria (modern Albania), celebrated a triumph and fulfilled the greatest yearning of Caesar, who had not gotten over the fire in the library of Alexandria: With the spoils of war, he built the first public library in the temple of Libertas with a Greek and a Latin wing. This library, even then, took on somewhat of the character of a university, in that he introduced the practice of sponsoring lectures on works that were yet to be published.

In this idyllic time from 40 till 31 BC, all was right in the theological world and in a state of order, or rather, it was partitioned into an orderly triad: The *flamen Divi Iulii* Antonius flourished in the East, experiencing more flops than successes in the war against the Parthians, but as a former *Lupercus Caesaris,* he now took on the status of an incarnation of Dionysus and celebrated Holy Matrimony with Caesar's beloved Cleopatra as the living Isis/Aphrodite. In the West the *Divi filius* Octavianus reigned, in Perusia he raged against Antonius' relatives, took defeats against Sextus Pompeius, whined and plotted revenge—against Antonius and Cleopatra! And in Africa there was the *pontifex maximus* Lepidus, who was forced to make a settlement with Sextus Pompeius (for which he ordered prayer and thanksgiving services). Largely because his wife was the sister of Brutus—which made him suspect in the eyes of the other two—he was neutralized politically, leaving him only with the role of religious head. Behind, together with, and alongside the triumvirate, the three Marias were active: the childless Calpurnia, Atia, the mother of the adopted Octavianus, and Caesarion's mother Cleopatra. A further triad was in the second row: the forgiving sister of Octavianus, Octavia, (ever ready to make sacrifices), Livia, whom Octavianus had married pregnant, and the furious former wife of Antonius, Fulvia.

All these persons—each in their own special way and pursuing their respective varying interests—were involved in politics, which meant, first and foremost: theology. The result of this was that each of them, whether out of zeal or nolens volens, had to actively support the cult of *Divus Iulius,* his mother *Venus* and his *Genius:* by building temples, setting up cult statues, taking care of the liturgy, arranging prayer and thanksgiving services, organizing the cult of the settled veterans, and proselytizing the citizenry. For, he who could garner the most followers could then muster the most legionaries in the next civil war, and would have the largest war chest at his disposal.

To do this, they all required a text. Asinius Pollio furnished the first and most fundamental one: his *Historiae.*

He had concentrated himself entirely on his *recitationes,* his lectures, as a result of seeing that his life's work, the achievement of peace, was threatened by the failed arrangement with Sextus Pompeius and the simmering conflict amongst the triumvirate, which caused a continuous rekindling of civil war, finally leading to Octavianus' campaign against Antonius and Cleopatra—the great war between the Orient and the Occident. He had refused to take interest, or even to side with one or the other. He had told Octavianus that he would rather be part of the spoils of the victor—just for the sake of peace he would rather be faithful to Antonius.

It seems certain that his *Historiae* were the story of the civil wars. They began with the Gracchi and ended with Actium, with the death of Antonius and Cleopatra respectively. His vehement, uncompromising criticism, even against the commentaries of Caesar, as well as the fact that he had been an eyewitness to all the decisive events, gave his text authority. His love for Caesar while also being of republican inclination, combined with his withdrawal from active politics, elevated him above the parties, enabling him to treat Pompeius and even Brutus fairly. That John the Baptist, the evangelic double of Pompeius, is a saint rather than a sinner in spite of everything; that even Brutus not only became Judas and Barabbas, but sometimes could slip into the clothing of Peter and even become a saint as Judas Thaddeus; that Cleopatra can appear as the Syro-Phoenician woman, that she suffers as Magdalene and as a sinner but is nevertheless not condemned, surely all of this is attributable to their respective former standing and their posthumous rehabilitations, but also because it is already prefigured in the first impartial records of Asinius Pollio.

The *Historiae* of Asinius Pollio was surely both the show-piece and the bellwether of his lectures. These literary circles flourished, especially when the civil wars flared up again. They were not merely places of inner exile, into which Cicero allegedly and unavailingly withdrew, but were rather places of intellectual and spiritual resistance. In the public library all the scriptures were stored, read and discussed, even those Octavianus had censored—he went to the extent of withdrawing Caesar's love poems from circulation. The children of Rome's elite studied under Asinius Pollio, the children of the City and Empire, and included, as is well known, were the children of Herodes the Great.[732] While the triumvirate impatiently awaited the filling of positions of power and priesthood, Asinius staked his interest in another aspect of Caesar's soul—that of the scientist and man of letters—and sought after the truth in the library of the Temple of Libertas, the truth which sets you free.

As detected in Mark, the Gospels follow a common source which was also available to Plutarchus, Appianus, Dio Cassius, Suetonius and Velleius—the first two of whom used it almost always, Suetonius selectively and in some places literally, so that we are justified in believing that this source was Asinius Pollio. Because the Gospels are not only history but also texts that were recreated for liturgical use, we can assume that the *Historiae* of Asinius Pollio had a liturgical function too. They were used in the *caesarea,* the temples of Divus Iulius and wherever a cult statue of him was set up, which means—as we saw—in every temple and every city in the Empire and beyond.

The veterans probably had the greatest and most immediate need for it, especially those who had been led into settlements. Because they were strangers to the neighboring tribes, called *pagans*—'villagers'—only the *religio castrensis,* the religion of the army camp, gave them a sense of security. This was portrayed in the cult of their invincible commander-in-chief who was raised to a God, to whom they owed everything, especially the arable land they were allotted. Thus they knew only one God, Divus Iulius. This made them different from all the neighboring villagers who still venerated their local gods. This was also the basis for later conflict between Christianity and Paganism, the religion of the villagers, misleadingly rendered as 'heathens' by our theologians (however, this was not originally incorrect if it referred to the inhabitants of the heath).

Even though the colonies were all appointed by Caesar, he did not have the time to found them all himself. Later his work was continued by the triumvirate, but, practically speaking, mostly by Octavianus, who claimed this task for himself, knowing that the colonies were a safe reservoir for later recruitments. But some colonies were founded by others, even by Caesar's murderers, namely by Brutus in the East. Moreover, there were veterans who followed Antonius into the newly conquered Armenia, those who were stationed with Cleopatra in Egypt and who managed to spend their declining years as villagers in the Nile Delta and in the oasis of Fajum. There were also those who were attached to Herodes, who settled them in his domain in line with the Roman model. So all the veterans had the same God—maybe even those of Brutus who killed Caesar qua tyrant, but allowed him to be buried as Pontifex Maximus—even if they did not have the same *ktistes, creator* or *parens*, the same 'founder', 'creator' or 'father'.

Therefore, for the long winter evenings, for reading to the children, for the liturgy on feast days, for reading to the congregation in the temple and for preaching, they all will have used the same basic text: the *Historiae* of Asinius Pollio which narrated the first civil war from the Rubicon to Caesar's funeral. For all those legionaries settled by Octavianus between the death of Caesar to the deification of Divus Iulius at the time of the second triumvirate, further stories were added; for ones settled later, up to the time of Philippi, more stories will have been added; for the latest of them—like the veterans of the Egyptian campaign who were settled by Agrippa in Nemausus (nowadays Nîmes), even additional stories will have been supplemented up till the time of Actium, the death of Cleopatra, and the victory of their general over the Egyptian crocodile (still the heraldic figure of Nîmes today).

So there was not only one, but several holy books, which were nothing but the subsequent books of Asinius' *Historiae*.

Hence we must reckon not only with the possibility that the other Gospels are based on Asinius, but also that Acts and even the Revelation of John are too.

Then in that case, the Revelation would tell the story of the Egyptian campaign of Octavianus in mystical form. The woman and the dragon would be Cleopatra and her crocodile (representing Egypt), the Antichrist and his prophet would be the *flamen Divi Iulii* Antonius, the decline of Babylon that of Alexandria, the lamb would represent the Capricorn Octavianus who finally becomes the Christ after the victory (absolute heir and—after Lepidus' death—*pontifex maximus* as well), and the millennium is the Imperium Romanum with the new Jerusalem, of course, being Rome.

The Acts initially would tell of the deeds of the apostles, i.e. the legates of Caesar after his demise. Consequently the deeds of Antonius/Simon and his alter ego Lepidus/Peter would be found at first, soon to be joined by Octavianus/John—who surprisingly switch names and roles in the conflict between Peter and Simon, and Peter and Ananias (Cleopatra here being replaced by Saphira). The second part would be the story of the young Caesar, here named the 'small', *paulus*,—totally overlain by the story of *Flavius* Josephus, the Jewish freedman of Vespasianus.

Whereby we would again be with a completely different story. The Evangelist, in this case Luke, displaying interest only with the beginning, has left out the whole story from Octavianus till Nero and concentrates on the new beginning, which commences with Vespasianus, the founder of the Flavian dynasty. But here, surprisingly, he speaks of *Flavius*—sometimes rendering the name as *Saulus*, sometimes as *Paulus*,⁷³³ ΦΛΑΟΥΙΟC > CAOΥΛOC / ΠΑΟΥΛΟC—meaning not Vespasianus, but *Flavius* Josephus.

What is striking about the structural comparison of the second part of Acts with the autobiography of Flavius Josephus is that they are identical in parts. The principal characters in the two works initially persecute their opponents (in Josephus' case those loyal to Rome, in Paul's case the Christians) and both characters later switch to their opponents' camp; both feel torn between living by the Lord and dying meritoriously, both 'have the urge to depart', i.e. to commit suicide, however, both decide 'to remain in the flesh': Josephus to be with Vespasianus, awaiting great glory, i.e. to become emperor, and Paul 'to be with Christ', 'so that your glory be great' (for Flavius Josephus, cf. *BJ* 3.8.1-9, in particular 3.8.5 and 3.8.9, and SUET. *Vesp.* 4 and 5: cf. note 296; for Paul cf. Phil. 1:21-24); both fall from a horse on the road to Damascus; both are in a state of conflict with the central authorities in Jerusalem; both have an argument about the circumcision of non-Jewish followers (in Paul's case with the head of the apostles, *Simon bar Jonas*, in Josephus' case with the head of the rebels, *Simon bar Joras*); both have a supervisor whose name is *Titus* (the son of Vespasianus into whose charge Josephus was delivered, and also the bishop of Paul too, where the Greek word for bishop and supervisor is the same: *episkopos*); both undertake the same journey to Rome, which is interrupted by the same sea storm; both are taken up by a ship coming from Alexandria via Cyrene and both land in Puteoli. Thereafter Flavius Josephus goes to Nero's palace and at this point Acts ends abruptly and incomprehensibly, as if the *damnatio memoriae* (the damnation of the memory) which was imposed on Nero after his murder had forbidden the author from telling us that Josephus/Paulus had received a friendly reception there, especially by the 'God-fearing' Poppaea: It had to be maintained that Paul suffered martyrdom under Nero.

The cause, or connecting point, for grafting the story of Flavius Josephus on to those of Antonius/Octavianus, might have been the resemblance of the names of his opponents to the names given to the actors in the Gospel: In *Galilee* he fought with a *Johannes* about the command; in *Jerusalem* there was a *Simon* (bar Joras) the leader of the insurgents and he supported Johannes; in the meantime he had a wordy quarrel with an *Ananias* as well, etc.

Flavius Josephus, whom we have already met, was initially friendly towards Rome (his journey to Rome and the visit to Nero's house). He was later one of the rebel leaders in the Jewish war (he held a command in Galilaea). After employing a trick to get his comrades to commit suicide he was taken captive and switched to the side of Vespasianus,[734] Nero's general of ordinary lineage whom he declared to be the awaited Messiah. Josephus was imprisoned by him at first, but was soon called to serve in the Jewish war as a double traitor. After the death of Nero, he was praised as the prophet of Vespasianus' assumption of power. So, after the end of the war he was not put in chains like Simon, forced to participate in the triumph and then executed in the Mamertinum. He was instead moved into the palace of Vespasianus, where in the meantime all the temple implements had been collected in a private chapel. From there he sought, via all kinds of propagandistic writings, to win the Romans over to the Jews and their scriptures and—as we now suspect, because if Jesus was Caesar, Flavius Josephus was Paulus—to win the Jews of the diaspora over to his new Messiah.

Vespasianus, for his part, wanted to reanimate and reorganize the cult of Divus Iulius. He had to legitimize his dynasty by pointing to the divine founder of the Empire to whom he was not related, and he had a direct reason for this gratitude. In the aftermath of the war that founder had chosen his party against that of Vitellius when his cult statue at the altar in front of the temple of Divus Iulius swung around of its own accord and oriented itself towards the East.

This might have been the hour of Jesus' birth. On the day of the battle at Pharsalos, the statue of Victoria in the temple of Minerva of Elis had turned from the goddess to face towards the entrance and threshold, and by doing so it heralded, not only Caesar's victory, but his divine elevation as well. In like fashion, the statue of Divus Iulius, now directed to the Orient, not only announced the victory of Vespasianus and the reinvigoration of the Orient, but also the epiphany of the other, Eastern face of the God of the Empire: Divus Iulius could now become Jesus, the figure of Jesus could take over the form of the *statua Divi Iulii ad orientem sponte conversa:* 'turned toward the Orient' or, metaphorically, 'converted'. In this sense the statue of the Divus Iulius was the first *conversa,* the first 'convert'.

When passing this omen down to us, Suetonius in the same breath mentions the prophecy made by the enchained Josephus to Vespasianus—that Vespasianus would soon be emperor and would set him free. This indeed came to pass, and as Vespasianus's minister of propaganda he soon took on the name of Flavius. Flavius Josephus' writings—the *Jewish War,* the *Jewish Antiquities,* as well as his *Autobiography* and his *Apology*—are preserved in scholarly form, and through them he sought to incline the Romans towards the Jews, their history and their scriptures. But where are to be found those other writings his principal had surely expected from him, namely those with the aim of convincing the Jews of the diaspora of his new Messiah in order to integrate them religiously into the Empire? They must have existed, we may suspect, in light of the fact that he mentions his correspondence with Herodes Agrippa and his ongoing verbal and written debates. Has the correspondence of Flavius Josephus in the service of Vespasianus been preserved as Paul's letters? Were the cult and the history of Divus Iulius, under Flavius' supervision, gradually adapted *ad usum iudaeorum?* Were the citations from the classics, which were spread throughout the whole text, replaced with citations from the books of the Jews, in order to convince and convert them? Did the Gospels originate in this fashion? Did Flavius Josephus' followers, after his death, add his vita to those of the formerly great men of the cult of Divus Iulius, so that they could be blended together? Is this how our Book of Acts came into being?

It would not be improbable at all, because researchers, beginning with Bruno Bauer, have long since demonstrated the influence of Flavius Josephus on the final edition of the Gospel. In his vita, we do not fail to find him instructing the learned in the temple while still a child (like Jesus), nor spending years learning with an ascetic clad only in the bark of a tree and cleansing himself with cold water (like John the Baptist), nor the act of 'resurrecting' a crucified relative, whom he bid Titus remove from the cross (just as his namesake *Joseph of Arimathea*—his own name originally being *Joseph bar Matthias*—received from Pilate), and indeed the man in question survived and the two others crucified alongside him died (like Jesus and the two malefactors). Not only is Flavius Josephus, like Paul, a Pharisee with a similar curriculum vitae (see above), but he mentions him even less than he does Jesus. Paul appears in none of his books, not even as an interpolation, which is very conspicuous and it substantiates the opinion expressed above that it is the very same person. Along with other anomalies which repeating here would be superfluous since they are all generally known, this gave rise to the view that the Evangelists must have been very familiar with the life of Josephus and that it greatly influenced their text. In the light of our examination the New Testament proves to be the result of a rubbing off of the *Jôsêpou bíos* on the *vita Divi Iulii* in the process of final editing. Whereby Paul simultaneously proclaims Jesus and conceals him.

The changing of the name *Flavius* into *Saulus* and then into *Paulus* is part of the same mimicry. *Saulus* was intended to retain the Jewish origin, *Paulus* was obligatory because it was the name of the man who built Caesar's first basilica, the famous *Basilica Aemilia: L. Aemilius Lepidus Paul(l)us*, which Plutarchus in Greek simply renders *Paulos* with only one 'l'. (*Caes.* 29.3) This original *Paulus* was the brother (another source says the nephew) of the triumvir *Lepidus,* our *Peter,* and he was also a Saulus who became a Paulus, because only after receiving donations from Caesar (who paid off all his debts and gave him the money for the magnificent reconstruction of the basilica built with the help of one of his ancestors), did he finally cease to oppose him. In 44 BC, as an envoy of the senatorial party he was Saulus again, but by finally becoming Paulus he could escape the proscriptions of the triumvirate, where he was mentioned in the first line. Now, because the single word 'church' characterizes, in all languages, both the building and the institution, so the founder of Jesus' Church had to bear the same name: Paulus, like the man who had built Caesar's first basilica. Caesar's own, the *Basilica Iulia,* which was built in the Forum right in front of it, was finished much later and immediately burnt down—requiring Augustus to rebuild it. As a consequence, the basilica of Paulus became the model for all the other basilicas built in the Empire, the same ones that later became the Christian churches.

But let us return to the origin of the Gospel. If the mutation mentioned above has taken place, then from what our examination has shown so far, the model for it was very likely not a scholarly Greek translation of the *Historiae* of Asinius Pollio, but one that had already been corrupted. Since it must have been one that was informal both in language and in style, as the saying goes: *sacrae scripturae sermo humilis* ('the language of the Holy Scriptures is a humble one') or, if taken literally ('...is one connected with the ground and earthy'), we then must ask ourselves what became of the *Historiae* of Asinius in the hands of our veterans who had settled in the colonies in the interim period?

Along with receiving his land allotment, salary, and rewards for valor, the legionary who had served his time received Roman civil rights, and, what was more important to him, the *ius connubii,* the right to marry a woman of his choice, by which the children nonetheless were Roman citizens and not just limited to receiving the civil rights of their mothers. This gave them the opportunity to either marry their long-time mates who had followed the legions and lived beside the army camps (in the case of more long-term camps, they basically settled themselves permanently), or to marry local women—which was more often the case in the colonies established in more remote regions.

In practice a situation arose wherein the fathers continued to communicate with each other in the *sermo castrensis,* the language of the army camp, i.e. in Latin, while the women at first communicated in the native languages of the respective regions. In the West, Latin triumphed, partly because of the existing relatedness of Celtic and Latin, but mostly because of its greater cultural status; in the East, however, Greek—as the older cultural language and official language of the administration—put up a greater resistance; this was partially true too for Aramaic in the Orient—it had been officially displaced by Greek, but was still spoken as the old language of the Babylonian Empire and lingua franca of the Persian Empire. So in the second, and more particularly in the third generation, a mixed situation arose. Latin was still the military language (and it could be refreshed in the army) but the first cultural language became Greek; the lingua franca was vulgar Greek, which took on a more or less Aramaic character regionally. On top of this there was a difference between town and country, because in the colonies where the veterans had settled and become farmers they spoke their Latin in the country, and their women spoke the vernacular, whereas Greek spread more quickly in the towns built in the centre of the respective regions.[735]

In this situation the holy texts, the *Historiae* of Asinius, were certainly introduced in the Roman colonies at first uniformly and in the original language, and probably remained that way—because everything is contained in the beginning, all the more so especially with religion. But from the third generation onwards a commentary was necessary after the reading of the text. (The older ones amongst us still remember how different or even laborious the experience was when the mass was read in Latin in the Catholic Church.) Therefore the easiest thing for the later generations to do was to make notes. Writing the texts after the manner of Caesar would seem to be the thing to do—this had become the norm in the military administration, the chancellery and probably in Asinius' library as well—so the notes were made not on rolls, but on codices bound like our old books. But the writing material was not paper—which came later from China, nor even parchment (which in those days was only used for washable notebooks except in times of crisis)—but papyrus. It was made out of the water-plant with the identical name, growing only in lower Egypt, that had a marrow soft and poor in fibre. It was separated into fine strips, rectangularly arranged in two layers and then tightly compressed and beaten on a hard base. The ancient Egyptians had written on it with a brush, but the Hellenes with a *kalamos,* 'reed'. For this purpose the surface of the front side was made smooth, whereas on the reverse side the fibres clearly protruded. On this rough and uneven reverse side the ink ran more along the fibres than it did with the stroke, rendering whatever translations, notes and commentaries that were written there difficult to read.

Moreover, because of the mixed linguistic situation and the knowledge of Latin (which deteriorated from generation to generation) initially not everything was translated into Greek (Aramaic was not written, and it was no longer spoken everywhere in the Orient), rather only parts were. We have seen that Mark explains a Greek word like *aulê* by using a Latin one, *praetorium,* so such Latin words were more comprehensible to his congregation until the end, and in the beginnings, this was the case for many more words (we have seen that the same thing happened in the translating of the Jewish bible into Greek, although that process was located in another milieu).

It seems probable that the spelling and characters were not altered in the case of proper names and termini technici, so that there also arose a mixed situation in relation to the alphabets used (it is well known that Latin letters appear occasionally in the Greek text in the surviving ancient bilingual codices of the Gospel). The reading of these reverse-side texts was made even more complicated by the fact that the Latin alphabet corresponded with the old western Greek (which was still in use in some areas), and by the fact that the direction of reading the Greek had been arbitrary over a long period of time, sometimes from left to right and sometimes vice versa, so that if the reader under the influence of Aramaic found the reading of it difficult, he was tempted to try it from right to left, either because of his own habit or because he assumed it from the writer. On top of all this there were the general difficulties we have discussed: all capital letters; no dots and commas; no accents; undefined orthography; a changing pronunciation (itacism or iotacism, 'b' pronounced 'v', and hence the half consonant 'u' written as 'b', and so on). Moreover there were the common mistakes in writing.[736] That was Mark's exemplar.

As long as the priests were members of the community, or in today's language, as long as the clergyman was the former chaplain of the army, there was no great problem. Even the descriptions of the Claudii as lame, the Caecilii as blind, the Metelli as disabled and the Porcii as pigs were part and parcel of the understandable wordplay. The problems originated when priests and writers came from outside, those who hardly knew Latin and had different horizons. For that to happen, one did not have to wait till the time of Vespasianus, who sent out the men of Josephus, to see these problems occur—they were already inevitable since the time of Caesar and Octavianus. For not only were there newly-built colonies, but also *municipia,* especially in the West. These were already existing towns which received Roman civil rights en bloc because of special merits. In the East, in particular, there were Hellenistic towns that had excelled themselves and were granted extra rights accordingly;

concerning the cult of Divus Iulius, it was precisely these towns that distinguished themselves. We indeed saw it was the Ionian towns that commenced practicing the cult after Pharsalos. In towns like Ephesus, Antiochia, Alexandria, Caesarea or even Athens, there would have been, from the very beginning, a need to have a Greek version of the Vita of Divus Iulius. Thus Greek codices could have emerged, or even the first bilingual editions with the scholarly Greek version vis-à-vis the Latin original. Nevertheless, these codices very likely had notes and commentaries on the reverse sides of their pages as well, with an occasional translation in the common language of the Greek people (which was not necessarily the same as the scholarly language of the front page) for the purpose of reading aloud and for homilies. The difference here was that all termini, including the proper names, were already in Greek. That was John's exemplar.

If, then, one of the writers who was accustomed to these Greek-Greek verso-texts, got his hands on another text of the Latin-Greek type, he was tempted to read the remaining Latin words in Greek, for example the *alea,* 'dice', of the Rubicon as *aleeis,* 'fishermen', or Cleopatra as *syrophoinissa,* 'the Syro-Phoenician woman'. And if it was not possible in Greek, then in Aramaic or even in Hebrew, like *Alexandria* as *Dalmanoutha* or *Antonius* backwards as *Simona.*

Thus we are already half way to Mark. After the Jewish war, the finishing touches were provided by the men of Flavius Josephus, and probably under his personal supervision, because he speaks of 'his Gospel'. The final touch was the replacement of the citations from the classics with those from the Jewish scriptures. The biblification was predetermined, the addition of the Jewish Bible as the Old Testament was prepared by Josephus' writing of the *Jewish Antiquities.*

The thing that was still missing—and what brought about the final redaction—was a different point of view. The whole had to be illuminated from the East. Just as the statue of Divus Iulius in Rome had turned itself towards the East, so consequently the Eastern point of view had to flow into the texts.

The logistical base for this was the colonies settled by the divine Iulius respectively the Son of God, Augustus, especially in the east of the Empire. For there occurred a deep break with the next emperor, Tiberius. The stepson of Augustus, himself not a Iulius but a Claudius, did adopt the political heritage, but he did not want to be a princeps towering above the others, but a citizen among citizens (cf. VELL. 74.2): a *primus inter pares.* Consistently, he not only prohibited himself to be called *Dominus,* but particularly to be placed in the succession of the Divi, the 'Gods' (SUET. *Tib.* 26: *Templa, flamines, sacerdotes decerni sibi prohibuit, etiam statuas atque imagines nisi permittente se poni, permisitque ea sola condicione, ne inter simulacra deorum sed inter ornamenta aedium ponerentur. Intercessit et quo minus in acta sua iuraretur ...* – «He forbade the sanctioning of temples, flamens, and priests in his honour, and even statues and busts could only be set up with his permission; and this he gave only on condition that they were not to be placed among the likenesses of the gods, but among the adornments of the temples. Likewise he rejected an oath to be taken ratifying his acts ...».

So he expressly did not want to be *Dominus* nor *Deus*. Though, during the campaign in the north of Germany, at the Elbe, he had already been greeted as such, in fact by an old German who, just to see him, had paddled across the river in a hollowed-out trunk and said: *Sed ego, beneficio et permissu tuo, Caesar, quos ante audiebam, hodie uidi deos ...* – «but I, thanks to you and with your permission, Caesar, have seen the gods today, of which I earlier had only heard ...».

Now the commander Tiberius had rejected all this with his elevation to emperor and not only banned his own cult but also many others. This was felt not least by the Jews, whom he committed to military service, while he even forbade their religion (SUET. *Tib.* 36: *Externas caerimonias, Aegyptios Iudaicosque ritus compescuit, coactis qui superstitione ea tenebantur religiosas uestes cum instrumento omni comburere. Iudaeorum iuuentutem per speciem sacramenti in prouincias grauioris caeli distribuit, reliquos gentis eiusdem uel similia sectantes urbe summouit, sub poena perpetuae seruitutis nisi obtemperassent* – «He abolished foreign cults, especially the Egyptian and the Jewish rites, compelling all who were addicted to such superstitions to burn their religious vestments and all their paraphernalia. Those of the Jews who were of military age he assigned to provinces of less healthy climate, ostensibly to serve in the army; the others of that same nation or of similar beliefs he banished from the city, on pain of slavery for life if they did not obey».)

This, of course, resulted in the young Jews, who had been recruited as legionaries, being settled as veterans later, no doubt together with their comrades-in-arms. And since they were prohibited from practicing their ancestral cult (while a cult of Tiberius was not allowed to arise at all), they certainly indulged in the same *religio castrensis* in the colonies that they knew from the camp—the cult of Divus Iulius.

However, since the other Jews were prohibited from practicing their religion also, and were even expelled from the city of Rome, these, too, went to the same colonies where they met with their own boys, who now as veterans possessed civil rights and due to the *ius connubii* also could easily take a wife from their people. Thus the best prerequisites were created for a certain fusion, not to say a syncretism of Judaism with the cult of Divus Iulius—at least in the background, or underground, according to circumstances. Because the 'late lamented' Caesar had been 'good' (remember: Greek *chrêstos* means both) to the Jews, even more in remembrance, which paints with a golden brush, particularly in comparison with Tiberius' military brutality and his cruelty which increased in old age. And since, by refusing to join them as a living Divus, he let the cult of the old Divi become an orphan, he practically put it up for adoption. It was pre-programmed since the days of Tiberius that at some time a Saulus-Paulus would come, to be well-received especially in the Roman colonies in the east. And so it was only consistent to let, with hindsight, Jesus, the mutated Divus Iulius, die under Tiberius.

And because what Tiberius had begun was continued by Claudius, who, as we saw, also banished the Jews from Rome—for whatever reason (cf. chapter 'Re-Orientation', *Non-Christian sources before 70...* p. 149)—e.g. the Jewish married couple Aquila and Priscilla, who host Paulus in Corinth and employ him as a tent-maker, might rightly be counted among the early Christians.

The center for this mutation, which was to be expected and was laid out well in advance, was the former regions of Herodes the Great and his successors, the tetrarchs, with Palestine as the heartland.

From the beginning there was also a different view, indeed a double one, among the veterans. Herodes the Great had received at least five legions successively, still more after Actium. They belonged to the best of the Caesarean mould: most of them were Gauls, then there were Thracians, and the cavalry were Germans. Their elite formed Herodes' body guard. But they were, and considered themselves to be, Romans, just as they regarded Herodes to be a Roman. Iulius by name, he belonged to the Caesarean gens, if not to the family, thanks to the adoption of his father by Caesar. He had been invested in Rome with the title King of Judea. Together with Antonius and Octavianus, in fact between them, he ascended the stairs to the Capitol, to the temple of Jupiter Optimus Maximus, where stood the statues of the ancient kings and the more recently added statue of the invincible Caesar. The fact that he was not a Roman functionary, but *socius et amicus populi Romani*, a king 'allied to and a friend of the Roman people', in no way made him nor his undertakings any less Roman. It was well known that this status could not be bequeathed, and one need not have been a prophet to suspect that this was the first step towards the tetrarchy becoming a Roman province. It had been no different in Bithynia and Pontus.

This circumstance, however, did not make Herodes' mission any easier, because it diminished his acceptance in his own country. And first of all he had to establish himself as king. His opponents were the heirs of the house of the Hasmonaeans and the pro-Parthian party. With this Roman backing, the legal cards were stacked in his favor against the Parthians, because, with Pompeius' victory over the Seleucids and the actual transfer of Egypt by the Ptolemaean Cleopatra to Caesar, the whole former empire of Alexander had de jure switched over to the Romans. As far as military strength was concerned, there is no doubt that the Parthians' victory over Crassus had to remain an episode. His not being a Jew was apparently not the worst card in his deck against the Hasmonaeans (his mother Cypros was the daughter of a Nabataean sheikh, an Arab; his father was Antipatros, possibly an Idumaean, although Herodes boasted that he was descended from the pioneering returnees from Babylon). First of all because his territory was not inhabited exclusively by Jews, and secondly, the Hasmonaeans themselves were not on the best of terms with the orthodox Jews, because no matter how great the prestige of their most famous representatives, the Maccabaeans, had been, they were still not Davidians. They hardly could be, because the House of David had already been wiped out under the Israelite Princess Athaliah in the ninth century BC. Herodes knew how to use this circumstance for himself. He took advantage of the expectancy of a Messiah, taking the prophecies of the enlightened Essenes seriously—who saw in him the Messiah when he was still a child—and depicted himself as a new David who created a kingdom and built a temple that left those of David in the shade. Of course, he conquered his kingdom using Roman legions, and ordered the Roman eagles to be placed above the gates of the temple, and he even rose from his deathbed to defend their presence there.

On the one hand Herodes was more Roman than the Romans themselves, giving his children Julio-Claudian names—Gaius, Iulius, Marcus, Agrippa, Drusus, Drusilla. We even find an Antonius in his house. In true Roman fashion, he settled the veterans in colonies, especially in Galilaea, Samaria, Gaulanitis, the Decapolis and Paraea. He named the towns in their midst after the gods and divinities of the Julio-Claudian dynasty: Caesarea, Caesarea Philippi, Sebaste, Agrippias, Iulias, Livias, Tiberias... In all these places he himself, as a named Iulius, organized the cult of Divus Iulius (doing the same later for the cult of the Divi Filius and even of the divine women of the dynasty), whose temple he built and whose *archiereus,* high priest, he himself was. At the same time he was the new David, the Messiah, i.e., in the Greek language which he himself used and which alone was authorized in his region, the

Christ. And he was regarded as such for a long time by his followers, as was known to Hieronymus who stated that the Herodians were those who believed that Herodes had been the Christ.737

The veterans, their children and grandchildren (Herodes reigned for a long time) who visited the *caesareum,* the temple of Divus Iulius in their hometown, honored the *pontifex maximus* there—the *archiereus* who had been their God, but whose high priest (also the *archiereus*), was their *ktistes*—the founder of their colony—was Herodes, a Julius himself. Under these circumstances, by the third and fourth generation they would have had difficulty not only in differentiating between *Herodes Iulius* and *Divus Iulius,* but also differentiating between 'relative of the Divus' and 'son of David'. They also would have had trouble distinguishing between one *archiereus* and the other, and between *archiereus* and *christos*—between 'high priest of Divus Iulius' and 'Messiah'.

So the kingdom of Herodes was the region in which this double view of things originated; this fundamental schizophrenia developed in a contested border area that had to be defended with might and main. All that was necessary to change the secondary view to the first was a change of viewpoint, a reorientation. And this happened with the Jewish war, 70 years after Herodes' death. Vespasianus and Titus left behind the legendary tenth legion, Caesar's *praetoria,* in the reconquered temple of Herodes as *praesidium.* After the victory in *Galilaea* against the rebellious Jews, they were also victorious against the rival Vitellius in *Gallia Cisalpina.* They then entered Rome and celebrated the triumph with those legionaries that they had recruited in the colonies settled by Herodes. This gave rise to the first historical blend of *Galilaea* with *Gallia.* Along with their return to Rome came the fulfilment of what had been presaged by the reorientation of the cult statue of Divus Iulius: The legions which had been sent to the East returned with their God—the *pontifex maximus* who had become *Christ,* the *Divus* as *Divus,* as 'son of David', the *Iulius* as *Elia.*

If they bore the temple implements in their hands, they also bore images of this long gruesome war in their heads: the attacks by the rebellious Jews who murdered and pillaged their way into their colonies; the painful resistence; the siege; the long wait for the Roman relief forces and the besieging of the enemy; finally the hard won victory. In their memories was the chameleon-like figure of Josephus: He had gone to Rome to meet Nero and yet was soon active in Galilaea as leader of the insurgents. This Josephus who possibly, secretly, saw himself as a new Messiah, who had fallen from his horse on the road to Damascus, who had salvaged his own life in captivity by pronouncing the modest Vespasianus to be the expected Messiah from Galilaea and Judaea. This Josephus who had betrayed his former brothers-in-arms, who tried to convince them to surrender and was received with stones, who asked Titus to take three crucified insurgents down from their crosses (one indeed survived). This Josephus who came to Rome as Flavius and celebrated the triumph along with the others, whereas the lot of Simon, the leader of his former brothers-in-arms, was to be led in chains in the triumph and later killed in the Mamertinum prison. This was the same Josephus who now from Vespasianus's palace, from his private 'Jewish' chapel, preached his Christ/Messiah to the surviving Jews, and preached to the Romans his idea of the Christ/Messiah.

All these images were so powerful that they could not help but overcome the Herodian ideas which had grown old in the meantime. Nevertheless, these new images also found in the still mighty Herodians their first people and reservoir, even if they had first met with strong resistance. For the Herodians had never been guilty of betrayal, but the 'Flavians' had been twice, so although it is true that they had ended-up on the same side, the old resentments remained. These 'new' Herodians were not only rulers in parts of Herodes' former domain, but had become rulers in others, like in Armenia, which was not coincidentally one of the cradles of the soon-to-emerge Christianity.

Thus was founded the basis for the triumph of the Flavio-Pauline version of the empire-encompassing cult of Divus Iulius. But at the same time, the seed was sown for the future bitter battles with the orthodox believers who were to be branded as heretics: the Neronians, waiting for the return of Nero and the revival of the Julio-Claudian dynasty.

The orthodox Caesareans and Herodians could at least theologically hold the fort against the advancing new redaction of all the holy texts by Josephus' syndicate, as long as the new versions were merely texts of the reverse sides of the pages and they could still refer to the original on the front sides of the pages. But when translations back into Latin were made for the use of the communities in the West, principally in Rome, the original text was displaced. In preserving the bilingual form, the original disappeared. And Marcion could not prevent this. Did he fail in Rome because the Latin retranslations done by the 'Judaizers' among the Paulinists had become accepted as the originals? In any event, after long and bitter struggles the heretics were burned along with their books, and then all memory of the originals vanished as well.

Phobos ekplêssei mnêmên, says Thucydides: 'Terror suppresses the memory.' Is this the reason why we no longer know that Jesus is Divus Iulius? Were the last vestiges of such remembrance incinerated along with the last manuscript, was it one that had the *Historiae* of Asinius

Pollio written on the front sides of its pages? Is this the very reason why the fundamental *Historiae* of Asinius have not been passed down to us?

The question posed above, of whether Jesus is a copy, is now easier to answer. Jesus is Divus Iulius, oriented toward the East. Technically he is not a copy at all: The same hands which turned the cult statue of Divus Iulius to the East wrote the final edition as well—those who turned an adapted, repeatedly copied and glossed version of the civil war's history into the Gospel. Meanwhile there was a copying process in train as well. Based on its outcome, the hand of a creative palace theologian wrote the cult text for the second dynasty.

Jesus is the Divus Iulius of the Flavians: on behalf of a Flavian—Vespasianus; under supervision of a Flavian—Titus; formed by a Flavian—Flavius Josephus alias Paulus; and opposed by a Flavian—Domitianus. His resistance was in vain, for Domitianus was murdered.[738] But that is another story.

The history of early Christianity becomes much more understandable in the light of its origin in the cult of Divus Iulius. The whole succession of councils with the concomitant excommunications of so-called heretics, the debates of Byzantine-like nature in which it was decided who could stay at the emperor's palace and who was to be sent into the desert, suddenly do make sense: If Adam is a translation of Gaius, as we have seen, and if the quintessential Gaius, Caesar, is suspected of loose nocturnal banquets, is it then surprising that the Adamites were suspected of the same? Does it surprise us, then, that the Cainites should have honored Judas Iscariot, if one is aware that Iunius Brutus the sicarius (assassin) not only had followers but himself built colonies and thereby created a lasting base for himself? Why should not the matter of whether Jesus had been merely adopted by the father rather than 'begotten' have been discussed for such a long time if Octavianus also could only become the son of Caesar by adoption? And if Antonius did not accept Octavianus as a complete and full new Caesar, why should not Arius represent the notion of the inferiority of the son to the father in his rejection of the doctrine of consubstantiality?

And if, as we have seen, there were two trinities, the mother Venus, the son Caesar and the anima Caesaris on the one hand; the father Divus Iulius, the Son of God Octavianus Augustus and his Genius on the other hand, why should this not lead to eternal discussions about the true nature of the trinity? If there were two mothers of God, Venus the ancestress of Caesar and Atia, the mother of Octavianus, why then should it not be discussed if Mary was the mother of God or only the mother of the man Jesus? And if there were two Jesuses, the first one Caesar, being both Son of God—of Venus—and also the father of the other Son of God, Octavianus, why should there not have been Christians like the Modalists or the Patripassians, who saw the father himself suffering on the cross and not the son? And if Caesar's death was a sudden one, as he had wished, if he was stabbed and not crucified, why should not the idea of Christ's suffering be rejected by, say, Nestorius—and as a consequence the depiction of Christ suffering on the cross be avoided for nearly a whole millennium? (cf. note 157 p. 384).

If the Judaization of the Gospel was a secondary phenomenon of the time of the second dynasty, why should the Marcionites not deny the identification of the Old Testament God of justice and revenge with the new God of deliverance and mercy? And, in order to pay due regard to details where the devil is hidden, as is well known: Considering that Caesar was notoriously abstinent, it is quite understandable that in the Christian liturgy some water has to be added to the wine to make a true sacramental wine; and why should not those who wanted to be especially faithful to him celebrate the Holy Supper with water rather than wine, like Marcion did? If the resurrection of Lazarus was in fact the rehabilitation of the statues of Marius, and if asylum and the right to settle disputes were to be had at the statues of Caesar, now risen to heaven, why should theurgists not claim that statues of Gods can be brought to life?

And looking at orthodox imagery as well: if the first 'resurrected' Jesus was merged with the figure of the Son of God Octavianus Augustus, why should not the pictures of Jesus show him first as a beardless youth and later give him the waxing beard of a mourner? If the first form in which the divinized Caesar was represented was his empty throne thus rendered by Octavianus, why then should the presence of God in the church be represented in any different manner than by an empty throne, as is the case? Or, looking briefly at symbolism: when Caesar who, as son of the Venus who had sprung from the foam of the sea, served the most expensive fish to the people at his sumptuous banquets, why then should not the fish become his symbol?

We could add much to this: when the axle of his chariot broke and he fell, Caesar continued and climbed the stairs to the Capitol on his knees; the Christian pilgrims have imitated him from that time on. At his landing in Africa he stumbled and opened his arms while falling, saying, 'I hold thee fast Africa!'; The Pope imitates him at the airport of each country he visits. Caesar remained seated when the senators came to him with the declarations of honor before the temple of Venus; the Pope, when newly elected by the conclave, remains seated, whereas all the other cardinals rise. Octavianus had bells attached to the gables of the temples, and they slowly evolved into the bells of our churches. And so on. There is hardly a phenomenon in the history or the customs of the Church whose origin cannot be found in the cult of Divus Iulius and Divi Filius respectively.

2000 years and 100

We reckon our time from the birth of Christ. This calculation was determined by a monk from Scythia minor named Dionysius Exiguus (i.e. Dennis the Little, the Small), who had lived in Rome since 500 AD and died there about 545 AD. In his time he was an acclaimed scholar and, as a translator, he is still recognized today as one of the most important mediators of Greek intellectual culture to the Latin Middle Ages. When he adopted the Alexandrian calculation of the Easter date he introduced the custom of counting time from the birth of Christ and determined that that event took place in the year 754 *ab urbe condita*, 'since the foundation of Rome'. This starting point is obviously too late, because according to it Herodes died in the year 4 before Christ, whereas according to this same starting point Jesus, whose birth troubled Herodes so much that he ordered the slaughter of all the baby boys in Bethlehem, was born in the year 4 to 5 before Christ.

But how could as great a scholar as Dionysius Exiguus make such a gross mistake? And why was this contradictory onset never abandoned? What was the generally accepted, compelling reason to determine year 1 in this way? It is striking that according to Exiguus' reckoning, Caesar was born exactly 100 years before Christ. Was Caesar's birth the compelling reason?

We have seen that a new era began with Pharsalos. The towns in the East, which had until then reckoned time from the Seleucidian era, and later the Pompeian era, began a new reckoning with Pharsalos. But on Caesar's coins, Pharsalos was not indicated by 1, but by the Roman numerals LII = 52, the age of Caesar himself at the time. This reckoning was consecrated with his elevation to Divus Iulius, for it was part of the essential provisions that all priestly colleges had to celebrate his birthday annually, as well as his victories. Which means that everywhere in the Empire and wherever abroad there was a *caesareum* (and they were ubiquitous, even as far as India), there was also an *archiereus*, a priest of Divus Iulius, who maintained a duty list of the celebrated birthdays, days of Pharsalos and Easter days of his almighty God. Dionysius, who was 'little' but not stupid, could not palm off a postponement of 4 to 5 years onto the priests of the Empire (who had in the meantime become Christians and had inherited that duty list together with the *caesarea*), but one of 100 years he could. The round figure would be more readily accepted. If Christ's birth is determined at 754 instead of 654 *ab urbe condita*, the central point was that the figure should end with 54, the same was the case for the duty list after Pharsalos. In this way, the year 1 fell in the consulate of Gaius Caesar, which helped to sell the postponement. For it was not by chance that this planned successor and bearer of the hope of Augustus was named after the great Gaius, and was celebrated like a Christ child and was widely mourned after his tragic early death.

This little shift by Exiguus concealed the big swindle that changed Divus Iulius to Jesus, but only after a fashion. From under the mitre well folded long ears are peeping out.

The consequence is that in the calculation of the new Millennium—which was to have begun in the year 2001—we are off by exactly 100 years. Counting from the birth of the real Christ, aside from the annoying problem of the year 0 (zero), we were then in the year 2101: We had overslept the new millennium for a straight 100 years.

No less interesting is how the above mentioned Dionysius fixed the historical Easter-date, namely on the year 31 AD, which means a round number of 76 years after the introduction of the Julian calendar in 45 BC. This, too, is an even number, because after 76 years an Easter-cycle recurs following the calculations of the Alexandrines, so that with a single table of 76 Easter-dates all the future ones can be determined in advance. Caesar was murdered one year after the introduction of his calendar. Dionysius has Jesus crucified one Easter-cycle later. He not only arranged for Jesus to be born 100 years after Caesar, but he also allowed him to leave the world one Easter-cycle after the introduction of the Julian calendar. For him and his patrons—Pope and patriarchs—the anchoring of the dates of Jesus' birth and death to the respective ones of Caesar was apparently much more important than the chronological inconsistencies, which indeed were caused by it (cf. note 183).

Perspectives

Euhemeros' basic approach—that the gods of today are the good rulers of yesterday—has been confirmed in the case of the greatest and kindest of rulers and gods.

Does this mean that all the parallels that researchers have established between Jesus Christ and Hercules or Dionysus have had their day? Certainly not, but we must realize that they have been filtered and passed down through Caesar and the Caesarean milieu. We will have to take more seriously the fact that it was Caesar who had reintroduced the erstwhile prohibited cult of the Liber Pater (i.e. Dionysius) in Rome, and that Antonius first acted as the Lupercus in Rome, and then later in the East as the new Dionysus, and that he held himself to be a descendant of Hercules. It is true that Antonius had incurred the *damnatio memoriae,* but the emperor Claudius—who was descended from him through his mother Antonia minor—had him rehabilitated. It is, therefore, not astounding that in the time of Claudius and even in the time of Nero and Seneca, Hercules came back into fashion.

As a consequence, we will have to read anew Bruno Bauer, who assigns the 'Proto-Evangelist', the primal writer of the Gospel, to this exact time-period: the area of tension between Seneca and Flavius Josephus. Even if we have now seen that there was a process before the final redaction, and that—just as in physics—nothing was created ex nihilo but things were transformed, we should not exclude the existence of the hand of a final author—in view of the organic construction of Mark with its metrical rhythm.

In regards to future research, the confirmation of the radical thesis of Euhemerus has serious consequences. To put it straight forward: If Jesus was Caesar, if the baby Jesus was not born in the era of Augustus but was Augustus himself, then following the same reasoning, Moses did not flee Egypt with the Hebrews under Pharaoh, but rather he was that Ahmose who drove the Hyksos out of Egypt. If the Gospel tells the story of the Roman civil war through the lens of the Jewish war, then the existence of a real connection between the Hyksos of Ahmose and the Hebrews of Moses is unnecessary, a mere analogy would be sufficient. If the story of the Egyptian plagues were told from the viewpoint of those who had been driven out of Egypt, then in reality it was not the Egyptians who had plagued them, but the Hyksos who had invaded Egypt and were subsequently driven out. As Caesar distributed grain to all suffering from hunger, so the manna of Moses would have been the flour of Ahmose; and as Caesar settled colonies, so Cleopatra later leased out her land in Judaea to Herodes where he again settled colonies of Roman veterans, so the promised land of Moses was the *gê en aphesei* of Ahmose, the land 'awarded, leased, loaned' by the Pharaoh.

Even the fact that the establishment and expansion of Islam benefited from the successive councils, where the different Christian sects had been declared heretics, should be taken more seriously than it is now. Does not the belief in God alone, as opposed to the belief in the Son of God, reflect in the sense of Nestorius' theology the standpoint of Antonius and Cleopatra, who refused to recognize Octavianus as the Son of God? Does not Islam reflect the position of the doubting Thomas, i.e. Antonius? Are the Moslems not only the Christians whom we sent into the desert and who returned with the sabre, but are they not also the legionaries of that Antonius who had already been driven into the desert by Octavianus? Are they not the Syrian Arab forces of that Cleopatra who was not only driven to suicide by Octavianus, but whose child, Caesarion, was also murdered by him? Is this the root cause of the irreconcilable hatred which resists all attempts at oecumenism? Does Islam preserve the disposition of Herodes who was the son of an Idumaean and of the daughter of an Arab sheikh? Are the Moslems the descendants of his Roman veterans and those of the tenth legion, Caesar's *praetoria*, left behind by Titus as the *praesidium* in Herodes' temple? Is this the reason why they call Jerusalem *el-Kuds*—'the sanctuary'—because it is their best rendition of *Aelia Capitolina*, the name given by Hadrian to the newly founded city on the site of the destroyed Jerusalem? Is their God named *Allah*, *al Ilah*, 'the Ilah', for the same reason that *Iulius* became *Elias* in the Gospel? Does the 'dark' 'l' in 'Allah'—the only word in the Arab language that has this—hide a blacked-out sound, or as the phoneticists say, does it 'contain a 'u'', because there is indeed a 'u' there? Did *Ilah* come to be pronounced almost as *Iulah* because of the memory of *Iulius*? Does the famous *la: 'ilá:ha 'illa(: 'a)llá:h(u)*, 'there is no God but God', really only have the 'u' containing 'l' in the second occurrence of the word 'God' because there is an unpronounced 'u' at the end of *a)llá:h(u)*, or rather because 'there is no Divus but Iulius' is still lingering behind it? Do we see preserved in the name *Allah* the true name of Divus Iulius: precisely that *Iulius*, the one and the only, to whom no addition is necessary? Do the Moslems fight for the return to the original religion of Adam, because they have unconsciously retained the remembrance of the equating of *Gaius* with *Adam*, both meaning: 'Son of the earth'? Why does the Mecca-pilgrim wear a white garment, which looks exactly like the Roman *toga exigua* and why does he afterwards receive a Hadschi-hat, which in form and meaning equals the *pileus*, the Roman hat of freedom? Do they perhaps wander to Mecca in order to turn their back to Jerusalem, as once pilgrimage was made to Rome, albeit in another direction? Was there once, where the Kaaba stands today, a Christian sanctuary as some believe? Or maybe an older *caesareum,* respectively a temple of the Dea Roma or of Venus? If Roman temples were also built outside of the Empire all the way to India (see below), what kind of temples would an emperor like *Philippus,* whose name was not *Arabs* by chance, have built in his homeland on the occasion of the Millennial jubilee of Rome? Were the 'heathen things' that Mohamed removed from there in fact Christian, which in comparison to the original Roman seemed so pagan to him? Is it merely accidental that the Shiites, admirers of Ali, the son-in-law of the Prophet and a martyr, who shared the same fate as *Iulius/Ila* and the sound of his name, are to be found in great numbers in the Bekaa plain, there in ancient Coelesyria, where the *Iulii* had left strong praesidia?

Speculation? Fantasy? Or is it the case that Christianity was displaced in the Orient by Islam precisely because the Orientals were too close to the events to be told fairy tales about Divus Iulius by Jews who, from their point of view, had simply wandered in—so consequently they held fast to Divus Iulius and rejected his metamorphosis into Jesus, beginning with the crucifixion which they never accepted? Are we Christians the only fools in history on whom was palmed off the mirror image of our own God and we do not recognize it?

In support of our case we could point out that with his elevation to Godhead, Divus Iulius relinquished his earthly features, so that henceforward he was no longer depicted with the features of Caesar, but rather took on those of an ageless God, susceptible to monopolization by others. Indeed he was depicted on the coins of Antonius with the features of Antonius, on those of Octavianus with those of Octavianus, and on Gaius' statue with the features of Gaius. Sometimes he disappeared altogether: on a coin that displays recto Antonius and verso Octavianus he is only to be recognized in the beards of both mourners; or on the coins of Octavianus he is present *in absentia*—the coin depicting only an empty garlanded throne. From time to time he completely disappeared and was unrecognized, before he returned. So he had the prerequisites to become that *agnostos theos,* the 'unknown God', whose temple Paul had seen in Athens (even if in that specific case it could have been the temple of a ruler who had undergone the *damnatio memoriae*): *Deus absconditus,* as Christ is regarded in mysticism and Allah is always.

From the viewpoint of a radical Euhemerism it is possible to recognize late Caesarean and Augustan aspects in Buddhism too. The name *Bodhisattwa,* which looks like a metathesis of *Sebastos,* Greek for *Au-*

gustus, and sometimes was translated as *Josaphat,* would make us think of our *Josetos,* who as we have seen stood for *Octavius.* And the other name, *Gautama Siddharta* respectively *Gotama Siddhattha,* who is similar to *Octavi(an)us Sebastos.* The sleeping Buddha, like Augustus, who liked to sleep in the open air. The mother *Maia,* whose name is not far removed from *Maria* and *Atia.* The childhood story that tells of how Buddha was conceived laterally from an elephant: we could regard Octavianus as being conceived laterally (being adopted by Caesar), and of course the elephant represented Caesar on his first coin. The prophecy at his birth that the child would be a great king: as was the case with Octavianus. His being the son of a king, like Octavianus was Caesar's adoptive son; his being the prince, like Octavianus becomes the Princeps. The education in the well-guarded palace, just like Octavianus who is born at the foot of the Palatine and who grows up in his father's house in Velitrae. And then, at his first contact with the environment he comes across a beggar, a sick man and a dead man being taken to cremation just like Octavianus, who was himself very ill and who had to become a beggar himself after the cremation of Caesar in order to pay his inheritance to the people. The tree of enlightenment: a fig-tree, symbol of Rome. It is the tree, under which the son sits while his father is ploughing the field: like Octavianus, who was sitting in Rome while father Caesar founded Roman colonies (ploughing in fact was symbolic of founding a city: ploughing the furrow for the town's wall, as demonstrated on the Roman coins of just this period). His argument with a god, who convinces him to become a teacher to save many people: like Octavianus, who was appointed by Caesar via his will and who ultimately had to become the absolute ruler for the welfare of the republic. The struggle for recognition: at first two wandering traders, like the two consuls of Mutina; then the doubting Thomases who cannot be convinced till they learn through suffering, like the other pretenders who had to suffer first before they acknowledged Octavianus; finally the cousin *Devadatta* (literally 'given by god'), who competes with Buddha for power in the religious community and who works toward a schism. He was planning an attack against Buddha but was killed in the attempt: like the cousin Marcus Antonius, *flamen Dialis,* who struggles for power in the Empire; Octavianus had repeatedly planned his murder till he finally drove him to suicide. The long period of peripatetic preaching with the systematic figuration of the life of monks and laymen, like Augustus, whose chief request was the *cura morum,* the supervision of morals of the legionaries and officials as well as the whole of society. Finally death at an advanced age and due to diarrhoea, like Augustus. The syncretism with Apollo, a god with whom Augustus identified himself. The provenance from the western regions, between Bactria and Persia, an area that was the gateway to the West, from where the Parthians as well as a delegation of Indians came to honor Augustus. They built temples to him in the Orient, and in India as well (as seen in the 'Peutinger tables', whose archetype derives from the first half of the fourth century AD). Additionally we observe the pleated style of the garment of the Buddha of Gandhara, resembling the antique art which not by chance originated in the time of Augustus and which was copied throughout the whole Buddhist world; there is also the purple toga of the Tibetan monks of an entirely Roman type, and other peculiarities of the habitus; the puritanism which is strongly redolent of Augustus; various legends connecting Christ with Tibet; the traditional, proven trade from Rome all the way to China, and later the Christian buildings and cave paintings to be found along the silk-road, where Buddhism and Christianity further merged. There is enough here to provoke further pondering.

One might think that the infancy narrative of the Divi Filius Octavianus could not have influenced that of Buddha, simply because Buddha had lived a couple of centuries earlier than Octavianus. It should be taken into consideration here that firstly, the historical existence of Buddha is not substantiated much better than that of Jesus; secondly, that Indian chronology doesn't stand as firm as the occidental one; thirdly, that Octavianus' childhood story, especially the '(Im)maculate Conception' by the mother directly from God, was copied from Alexander's, who had been, both in the east and also in India, promoted to a god and who stands much closer to Buddha temporally; and finally: that great, epoch-making figures, who not coincidentally are elevated to the gods, influence history as well as historiography, and not only history thereafter, but also history preceding them. In Rome, not only had Caesar's elevation to the gods already made it possible to rewrite not only the childhood history of his adoptive son after that of Alexander, but also, for instance, that of his forefather Aeneas whose son *Ilos* was to become *Iulus*, the progenitor of the *Iulii*. The same was re-enacted on the periphery of the Empire, just under different conditions and names. Nothing is impossible with God—and likewise with the god-makers.

And there are the legends, like that of *Siegfried,* who is usually considered to be the saga-like transposition of Arminius but looks very much like *Sertorius,* the Roman rebel who had a prophetic hind and who also was betrayed by a person with one eye. And then there are the fairy tales, the German ones with their seven dwarfs behind the seven mountains, which harks back to the seven hills of Rome—which the Italians also remember with their seven ravens, seven *corvi* (crows), which approximates the seven *colli*, 'hills'. And Snow White with her temporary dying, caused by biting the poisoned apple and by the brush of the poisoned comb of the witch, which seems to be another telling of the fate of Cleopatra, who was bitten by a viper hidden in a basket of figs, but it was also said that in reality she carried the poison about in a hollow hairpin; the spindle, on which Sleeping Beauty stings herself and sleeps for a hundred years till the prince comes, is already present at Cleopatra's death, where it is said that the snake was hidden in a water jar and Cleopatra lured and provoked her with a golden spindle until it appeared suddenly and bit her on the arm: and so was she found by the prince—the *princeps* Octavianus—dead. And Hansel and Gretel, whose full names remind us of Octavianus and Livia (*Johannes* of *Octavianus*, as we have noted; *Margarete*, 'the Pearl', of *Livia*, the 'bluish'), who have to deal with a witch, once again with the hook-nosed Cleopatra, where Hansel displays a bone for a finger, just as Octavianus had an ossified index finger.

After detailed examination of those fields that only appear to be different—religion, legend and fairy tale—it might just turn out that Divus Iulius (with his filiation Divi Filius), apart from forming Christianity, has influenced the formation of other non-Christian monotheisms. And not only this, it might also turn out that he had his legends—no less than did Alexander—which are to be found in our fables and fairy tales.

Could this be the reason why these folk stories and legends have been held in quasi-religious esteem?

If this is the case, then Divus Iulius has cast a shadow longer than we could have hoped for and more uncanny than we could have feared. The deified Iulius would not only have trod the courts of our temples, churches and mosques, but also haunted the yearnings of our youth and the dreams of our childhood—incognito.

What is missing?

Some readers will miss a detailed *table of contents* and an *index*. The running titles might tide over the former; the latter we will try to submit later on our website. Those who are interested will also find an English translation of the introit to the first German edition there.

One may wonder why we have not treated this or that. For example, why not the *genealogies of Jesus*, or the *Sermon on the Mount*? Well, simply because they are not found in Mark. They are a later redactional work of Matthew resp. Luke.

What is conspicuous, however – to touch briefly on this – is not even that the *genealogies of Jesus* are missing with Mark and John, or that Luke gives completely different names than Matthew (not to speak of the numerous variants in the manuscripts), but—as was pointed out not by Voltaire but e.g. his compatriot, the dominican Fr. R.-L. Bruckberger—that with Matthew (1:2-17), noticeably many women appear who actually have no business in a patrilinear line of ancestors and whose questionable chastity hardly corresponds to patriarchal-biblical ideas of marriage. Rather their presence serves to avert the traditional Jewish criticism that Mary did not conceive her son Jesus from her husband. As if Matthew means to say: You see, your *Thamar* (a Canaanite, daugther-in-law of Judas, son of Jacob, who prostituted herself to him), *Rahab* (a whore from Jericho who betrayed her city), *Ruth* (a Moabite and pagan who offered herself to Boaz and forced him to marry her) or the *wife of Uria* the Hittite, (i.e. *Bathsheba,* an adulteress who became the mistress of David who treacherously sent her husband, who had faithfully served him, to death for her (Urias Letter)), were no better in this regard. That is to say, originally Matthew would not draw up a genealogy of Jesus but bring in his usual midrashim, i.e. seek out passages and figures from the scriptures of the Jews that seemed to anticipate the outrageousness found in the new message. But, because it indeed appeared far too scandalous, later hands tried to drown the four females of dubious virtue—non-Jewish, pagan, self-prostituting adulteresses—into a long genealogy so they would be overlooked as much as possible. And because apparently someone still noticed it, Luke changed all names, probably to let the removal of the female names be masked within the exchange of all others. Thus the traces behind Jesus, Mary, Joseph, and the Holy Spirit, that pointed to Augustus and the maculate conception of his mother Atia (not from Octavius, however, but from Apollo) were covered up. Or, in the later generation, those that pointed to Tiberius who was from Livia but not from Augustus. But those unchaste virgins in Jesus' line of ancestors whose names are still to be read with Matthew and who replace their Roman equivalents—e.g. *Acca Larentia, Rhea Silvia, Tanaquil, Ocrisia* or *Cleopatra*—still today rather point to the Roman 'she-wolf' resp. to Caesar's ancestral mother *Venus,* than to patriarchs. And they attest, in a hidden but still undeniable manner, to the late-Hellenistic, Roman, Julian origin of the Gospel—in discourse with the Jews the Christian Jew Matthew may have talked about *Tamar, Rahab, Ruth* and *Bathsheba* as 'our' women, and thus entailing in their wake the incorporation of the Roman *Maria* into the Christian-Jewish amalgam.

The *Sermon on the Mount,* the central sentences of which Luke 6: 20-25 renders—

'Blessed be ye poor: for yours is the kingdom of God. Blessed are ye that hunger now: for ye shall be filled. Blessed are ye that weep now: for ye shall laugh [...] But woe unto you that are rich! for ye have received your consolation. Woe unto you that are full! for ye shall hunger. Woe unto you that laugh now! for ye shall mourn and weep.'

—describes Caesar's political program, who in the spirit of the Gracchi expropriated the big landowners in order to give the land to the impoverished farmers and veterans. Concerning poverty and hungering, one recognizes how he meant it by his speeches in Brundisium or before Pharsalos where he called on his legionaries not to care for baggage and provisions because in the camp of Pompeius there was more than enough to fill all. There it changed abruptly, who had to weep and who had to laugh—in this world: The poor were allotted the best estates of the Roman Empire. The 'poor in spirit', who get their portion only in heaven, are not described as such until after Matthew's fine-tuning (5:1 sqq).

Many another may miss that we did not follow-up on this or that thread. For example, when we noticed that the 15th of March, the day Cassius *Longinus* stabbed Caesar, was made the festive day of the centurion *Longinus* who was promoted to the status of a saint, one may wonder whether this is an isolated case or if there is method behind it.

There is, there is. The feast of *St. Joseph,* e.g., falls on the 19th of March, and this is *Piso*, as we saw, entrusted with the funeral of Caesar. On the 19th of March 44 BC (on *quinquatrus,* the fifth day after the Ides), Piso was busy carpentering the requisites for the funeral of his son-in-law, the *pontifex maximus,* to take place the following day: a litter in the shape of the Venus temple, a tropaeum where the wax effigy had to hang, etc. Therefore, he was not only the father-in-law of the *pontifex* but also his true carpenter and bridge builder for the journey into the beyond: *ponti-fex.* This date, too, emphasizes the fact that Easter, which later became movable, is nothing other than the celebrating of the funeral of Caesar.

But also the old and important Christian festive days fell and still fall, without exception, on the anniversaries of Caesar, on his birth and on his victories—as the resolutions of honor and deification enacted after Munda demanded (cf. p. 125):

«... furthermore ... the city annually had to celebrate the days of his victories ... [and] honor his birth ...»:

Epiphany, on the 6th of January, a great feast before it was downgraded to the day of the Three Kings, was the original Christmas, and coincidentally falls on the date of the *senatus consultum ultimum* (49 BC) that made Caesar the enemy of the state and caused him to cross the Rubicon. Thus it deserves its name: *epiphania,* the 'appearance' of the Lord, since from then on Caesar appeared before Rome in all his glory. But the Three Kings also originate from the Julians albeit from the Divi Filius Augustus and his ancestry—as we could see (cf. p. 319).

Saint Laurence's day, the 10th of August, falls on the day of the victory at Pharsalos (48 BC) and thus explains that this 'holy laurel crowned one' actually represents Caesar as triumphator. *Laurentius* had to appear as an autonomous saint grilled on the gridiron after Jesus' body was no longer understood as burned, but buried, and thus the outstanding feature with Caesar, the cremation, had become orphaned and ownerless. He was also able to absorb other features of Caesar; for instance the book, Caesar's technological invention, which the artists have him carry ostentatiously in his hand (e.g. on the mosaics in Ravenna), or the fact that he had distributed the riches of the church among the poor, as Caesar did in his testament—characteristic features that are bitterly missed with the Jesus of the Gospel and which demanded for a substitute saint.

Caesar's birthday, on July 13th, fell on the last day of the *ludi Apollinares,* the public games in honor of Apollo, which lasted from the 6th until the 13th of July, and so one day was added, the 14th. In this way his feast merged with that of Apollo and since Apollo, among other things, was the god who sent death and ruin on humans and animals, e.g. the plague, Divus Iulius became the good Apollo who averted it and drove it away. The healings from the plague in Christian times are conspicuously connected with this date—as e.g. the Redemptor feast in Venice. There the plague raged for three years (1575-1577) and the city vowed to build a church to the Redemptor, if he brought the plague to a halt—which he did. The epidemic was declared finally defeated on the 13th of July 1577, on Caesar's birthday, but the magnificent *festa del Redentore* is not celebrated on the 13th, but on the third Sunday in July—as if the old command that the day still belonged to the bringer of harm and not to the healer still continued. Similar things could be said about other cities as well, e.g. the feast of *St. Rosalie* in Palermo who also delivered the city from the plague (1624) and whose feast is celebrated in the night of July 14th. Whereby Saint Rosalie joins the list of substitute saints, as the above mentioned Saint Laurence. Where substitute celebration is concerned, the French particularly distinguish themselves, those inhabitants of the same Gaul that Caesar attached to the Roman Empire. In the same night of the *quatorze Julliet* they exuberantly celebrate their *prise de la Bastille*—or so they think. De facto, however, the bastille had by that time stood long since unused, and as far as prisoners to be freed, it is said there was only one bum jailed for disturbance of the peace. It is as if for the French—as well as for the Venetians, the Palermitans, and many others—the date to be celebrated was already a certainty. The date on which one is freed from the plague, be it an epidemic or the *Ancien Régime,* is on Caesar's birthday.

Many another may miss that we do not clearly say where the journey is headed: What is the good of knowing that Jesus was Caesar, resp. is Divus Julius?

We did not want to answer this question and rather leave it to everyone themselves to find out. However, since it is posed over and over again, we want to give two current examples.

At the beginning of his crusade against the 'terrorism' of the Islamic fundamentalists, US President Bush issued the slogan: *You're either with us or with the terrorists.* He did it as a good Christian, believing they were the words of the Lord. After all, they were written in Mt 12:30 and Lk 11:23: *He that is not with me is against me; and he that gathereth not with me scattereth abroad.* By tracing them back to the Caesar sources, we were able to prove that those words were spoken by Pompeius, alias John the Baptist, and that in contrast, Jesus—that is to say Caesar—had actually said the exact opposite, namely: *For he that is not against us is on our part* (Mk 9:40; Lk 9:50) (cf. p. 180). Had the President known this, he might have thought twice about adopting the slogan of a loser, one that makes those who are neutral your enemies and thus leads to isolation. He himself, his country, his allies, and not least the world, could have been spared a painful experience.

Second example: Today, as was once, there is talk of religious wars in which we are entangled, and of religious liberty which should be granted to everyone as his private, inalienable right. With Caesar, however, *religio* hardly means 'religion' in our sense, but either 'superstition' or else—and more frequently—'oath of allegiance'. Are we sure that we should open the floodgates to superstition? And are we sure that an oath of allegiance is a private matter that is none of our business?

* * *

Well, that's it: the book is full and the readers' eyes are tired. For everything else we would like to refer all those who have not had enough yet and still want to know more to our website:

www.carotta.de

Erika Simon

Afterword

The territory in which the new Christian religion spread two thousand years ago can be defined as the Imperium Romanum. *This process met with success because after three centuries the late Roman emperor Constantine the Great made Christianity the official cult of the state. Historical research has always emphasized the tight interconnection between this religion and the Roman world empire. The book at hand ties in with this fact but goes further and reveals new connections which have never been seen that way.*

The author draws parallels between the founder of religion Jesus and Julius Caesar, the Roman, whose name was given to all succeeding emperors. Although Caesar who was assassinated in 44 B.C. was one hundred years older than Jesus, Carotta detects amazing accordances in the reports which circulated about the one and the other in antiquity. The metamorphosis of names in vernacular language – e.g. Gallia could become Galilee – plays an important role in it. Strict etymologists may shake their heads here, but their objections are astray: the circles in which Christianity spread, of course had not studied the subject of linguistics which emerged in the 19th century. The circumstance that the author himself grew up in a milieu with several languages helped him in his analyses.

Contrary to Jesus, Caesar was an army commander but the early propagation of Christian religion occurred to a considerable extent amongst Roman soldiers. Think of the many holy legionaries in the orthodox as well as the catholic church: Theodoros, Mauritius, Valentine and so on. A different question is whether the similarities demonstrated here between Caesar and Jesus can be used to deny the historicity of the latter – something Carotta actually does not do, because he thinks Jesus did exist, just elsewhere and dressed in different clothes than one usually imagines. The problem touches the 'cancellation' of allegedly unhistorical saints like e.g. the Knight George by the catholic church. As if the veneration of a Saint which was practiced over a length of time were not part of history! Moreover, to remain with the Roman church: Al-

though the donation of Constantine turned out to be a forgery, the Papal State based on it has been historical reality through many centuries.

Religion is something deeply historical as well as human. Fundamentalism can only cause damage there. May the book of Francesco Carotta contribute that we remain open to questions concerning early Christianity.

Notes

These notes aspire neither to completeness nor to the naming of the first respective originator of a thought or a theory. Since this work is more a research report than an academic treatise, such aspirations would actually be neither required nor useful. However, should we have violated any rights of primogeniture, this did not happen intentionally and we hereby apologize beforehand, and promise to mend our ways. We also would like to express our gratitude in advance for any references, tips, or clues sent to us.

For abbreviations of collected editions and lexicons, journals and serials, monographs and terms see ZIEGLER & SONTHEIMER (1979). For the Greek authors' names and titles see LIDDELL & SCOTT (1996) and for the Latin ones GLARE (1996).

The Gospel texts translated into English were quoted on the basis of the *King James Version* of 1611. In some cases the *Revised Standard Version* of 1881 and the *New American Bible* of 1970 were relied on. These three translations often differ from each other considerably. Although they all, even the Catholic one, make use of the original languages rather than the Vulgate as a basis for translation, they have the tendency to read the text of the New Testament according to the current interpretation and to amalgamate it with the Old, so that in critical points the newer translations are overtly conflicting with the Greek original text, arbitrarily interpreting e.g. *thalassa*, properly 'sea', as *lake*, *Christos*, 'Christ', as *Messiah*, adapting the orthography of the proper names in the New Testament to those in the Old, e.g. *Elias* to *Elijah*, etc. For this reason we have prefered to use as a basis the King James Version, which is older but more reliable and closer to the *Graeca Veritas*.

I. Prima Vista

1   According to LANGE (1938) this Buca-denarius (collection Mamroth, Berlin-Pankow) represents the definitive Caesar-portrait. The same coin is depicted on the cover of various books, for example in GELZER (^{3}1941) and VANDENBERG (1986). A. ALFÖLDI analyzes in the *Schweizer Münzblätter* 73, 1969, p. 1-7 'the earliest type of denarius by L. Buca with the inscription CAESAR DICTATOR PERPETVO', from which it can be learned that this denarius belongs to one of the earliest types (plate 1, 1-3). Similar features are also found on the Mettius-denarius with CAESAR DICT QVART *(B.M.C. 4135, Crawford 480/2a-b);* since DICT QVART preceded DICT PERPETVO for some time, this Mettius-type would be the more original (cf. A. ALFÖLDI, 'Das wahre Gesicht Caesars', *Antike Kunst* 2, 1959, p. 27 sqq). It can be seen that later dies idealize towards clementia and divus, so that some Buca-denarii (as the denarius depicted here or the one in A. ALFÖLDI, *Schweizer Münzblätter* 73, l.c. plate 1, 3) already show 'Jesus-like' features. For the whole of this iconography cf. R. HERBIG, 'Neue Studien zur Ikonographie des Gaius Iulius Caesar', first published in: *Kölner Jahrbuch für Früh- und Vorgeschichte*, Berlin, ^{4}1959, p. 7 sqq., and again

in: D. RASMUSSEN ed., *Caesar*, Darmstadt 1967, with bibliography and many illustrations.
2   BORDA (1957).
3   VESSBERG (1941), p. 176 sq.
4   So BORDA, l.c.
5   CIC. *Ep. ad fam.* 12.3.
6   Erika SIMON, *Arch. Anz.* 1952, 138 sqq.; *Gymnasium*, 64. Jg., 1957, H.4, p. 295-9.
7   APP. *BC* 2.147
8   The identification of the Torlonia head as a Caesar-portrait was questioned by Paul ZANKER, *Arch. Anz.* 1981, p. 357. He suspects a 'Caesar-Zeitgesicht', a 'time-face of Caesar', i.e. the portrait of an unknown person amongst the leaders of a provincial town, in which 'the effect of the numerous statues to the honor of the divine dictator are reflected'. He thinks that Erika Simon's 'interpretation of it as a pity rousing, posthumous figure, which has found a very positive echo in the newer literature' is based on 'empathy'—and rejects it: 'In spite of great resemblances, mainly in the details of the nose and the mouth, in the accentuated cheek-bones and the structure of the forehead, the head differs clearly in the proportions and the profile from the authentic figures of Caesar of the Turin type (from Tusculum) and the Pisa-Vatican type.'
However, Zanker's opinion 'does not convince' Erika Simon 'nor other colleagues either' with whom she spoke: 'He makes it too easy for himself, because none of his other "time-faces" is penetrated by this energy, none of the others has these typical Caesarean proportions and the accentuated occiput, where the traces of the (metal) wreath have been convincingly demonstrated. And Zanker also uses the term "time-face" (Zeitgesicht), invented by Bernhard Schweitzer, much too broadly' (personal communication). Since both archaeologists use the profile as an argument, we place the Torlonia in the middle between some other, authenticated Caesar-profiles:

   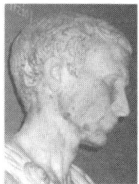 

1. Buca   2. Tusculum   12. Torlonia   18. Uffizi   19. Pisa

Apart from the fact that the typical occiput of Caesar seems to be more accentuated than usual and so the neck has become somewhat thicker to accommodate this, we can find no major differences. That the saddle in the middle of the forehead has been rounded and the hair piously covers the bald front in the heads Torlonia, Uffizi and Pisa marks them all three as posthumous. Only the expression of the Torlonia-face is different, more humble, stressed by the inclination of the head. But the same expression and the same inclination of the head are also found in that of the Palazzo degli Uffizi (as well as in the Vatican-type, see chapter 1 ill. 9).
Anyway, it is not decisive for the economy of our text whether we have here a 'Caesar-face' or a 'Caesar time-face'. That is to say, Zanker bases his examination on the bust of M. Holconius Rufus in Pompeii, who was *Augusti Caesaris sacerdos* according to the inscription on the base, which, in respect of the supposed time of its dedication (between 2/1 BC and 14 AD), still meant *sacerdos Divi Iulii* and *sacerdos Divi Filii* at the same time. Mutatis mutandis the face of the deified Caesar would have

rubbed off on the face of his priest (hardly on the face of the priests of his Son of God Augustus, because Zanker holds Caesar's head in the Torlonia museum to be an 'image of the late republic' as the legend on the illustration explains). In the case of the Torlonia head, one would then have to assume that the features of the deified one have completely transfigured those of his priest. If Zanker were right, we would here be looking at the face of Divus Iulius become independent, instead of 'Caesar's pietà': 'Caesar's transfiguration'. Our starting point would hardly be altered by this.

9   DIO CASS. HR 44.4.5: καὶ ἐπί γε τοῦ βήματος δύο (ἀνδριάντας), τὸν μὲν ὡς τοὺς πολίτας σεσωκότος τὸν δὲ ὡς τὴν πόλιν ἐκ πολιορκίας ἐξῃρημένου, μετὰ τῶν στεφάνων τῶν ἐπὶ τοῖς τοιούτοις νενομισμένων ἱδρύσαντο.
10 GEL. 5.6.11: civica corona appellatur, quam civis civi, a quo in proelio servatus est, testem vitae salutisque perceptae dat. ea fit e fronde quernea; 5.6.8: obsidionalis est, quam ii qui liberati obsidione sunt dant ei duci qui liberavit. ea corona graminea est, observarique solitum ut fieret e gramine, quod in eo loco gnatum esset, intra quem clausi erant qui obsidebantur.
11 APP. BC 3.3.8
12 Cf. WEINSTOCK (1971), p. 365.
13 Details cf. RAUBITSCHEK (1954), p. 65-75; Die Inschriften von Ephesos (The inscriptions of Ephesos), part II, 1979, n° 251.
14 Photography: Deutsches Archäologisches Institut, Rome. Cf. F. CHAMOUX, Fondation Eugène Piot, Monuments et Mémoires 47, 1953, 131 sqq. Tab. 12.
15 Cf. APP. BC 3.3.8-9; CIC. Phil. 1.5.
16 Sometimes also a wreath of myrtle is supposed, cf. L. CESANO, Rendiconti della Pontif. Accad. Rom. Archeol. 23/24, 1947/49, p. 146 sqq., and KRAFT (1969), p. 21 and n. 78: 'könnte man sie auch als Myrtenblätter ansprechen—they could be called myrtle-leaves as well'.
17 That the wreath was called etrusca corona is attested to by TERT. coron. 27, and that the instruments which were used in the triumph are of Etruscan origin by APP. Pun. 66 (cited after LATTE (1960), p. 152). KRAFT (1969), p. 20: 'On the coins Caesar certainly does not wear a natural wreath of laurel or another wreath of green leaves, but an Etruscan corona aurea (after DIO CASS. HR 44.6.3)', an Old Etruscan royal crown, which he distinguishes from the corona aurea of Pompeius (after VELL. 2.4.40). In contrast CRAWFORD (1974), I, p. 488, n. 1 and n° 426.4a, who accepts a 'golden triumphal wreath', but not an 'Old Etruscan royal crown' (he thinks Caesar's golden triumphal wreath is identical to Pompeius' corona aurea). Dio Cassius (HR 44.6.3) speaks of a 'wreath, embroided with gold and decorated with precious jewels'—καὶ τὸν στέφανον τὸν διάλιθον καὶ διάχρυσον.
18 Lucius Cornelius Sulla was the leader of the senate party (the optimates), Gaius Marius of the people's party (the populares). M. Minucius Thermus was an obdurate follower of Sulla who in 88 chased Marius, an uncle of Caesar's, out of Rome. It has not been passed down to us who was saved by Caesar. As at this time only Sullans and optimates held office—and the Marians and populares were either liquidated or had to go into hiding—the person saved by Caesar probably was a political opponent. This could explain his rehabilitation, his later marriage with Pompeia—who was linked to Sulla's family (daughter of Sulla's brother-in-law Q. Pompius Rufus)—and also his political connection with Pompeius, who was a Sullan as well.
19 The sign on the left behind the head of Venus is generally regarded as an ancient form of writing for LII (52) and is interpreted as Caesar's age: born 100 BC, so in 48 BC at Pharsalos he was 52 years old. The female bust is identified as Venus, but by some authors as Pietas. This is explained by the argument that the oak-wreath is not an attribute of Venus, but that it is an act of pietas to save the lives of citizens (for the discussion cf. BATTENBERG, p. 37 sq). On the other hand—Caesar's Venus was not typical: he had not consecrated the temple at the Forum Iulium to Venus gener-

ally but to *Venus Genetrix*. So the relationship between the one saved and the savior was a relation of pietas, because the one saved owed his life to his savior, who was then like father and mother for him. Therefore *Venus* cannot really have attributes of Pietas, whereas *Venus Genetrix* indeed can.

20 Cf. *Crawford* n° 468/1. *Obv.*: Bust of Venus with diadem, with Cupid in the background. *Rev.*: Tropaeum with Gallic arms and carnyces. At the base there is a seated female figure, on the other side a bearded Gaul with hands fastened behind the back. Below the inscription: CAESAR.

21 Indeed the cities of Asia started to date the time after Pharsalos (see below and cf. inter alia LESCHHORN (1993), p. 221 sqq). But apparently for Caesar the year of Pharsalos was not year 1, but the year 52: he reckoned his new era from his year of birth, 100 BC. The reason for this was perhaps that Pharsalos was decisive for the East, as Pompeius had reigned there until then. But for Caesar, the previous year—the Rubicon, Corfinium, Brundisium, Rome—was the year of his assumption of power. Thus he had no uniform time reckoning anyway. His year of birth, however, allowed the connection with Iulus-Aeneas-Venus, the mythical origin from Ilium/Troja (cf. the coin from the same series *Crawford* n° 458, where on the obverse Venus is depicted with a diadem and on the reverse Aeneas carrying the father Anchises on his shoulder and the palladium in his hand), which allowed the connection of Italy with Asia and vice versa. Moreover, by reckoning time from the date of his birth he erased the time of Sulla (and also that of Pompeius) and connected himself directly with the time of Marius.

It is astonishing that, going by this year 52, the Caesarean era is exactly 100 years earlier than the Christian. The dating from Caesar's birth is equivalent to the dating from Christ's birth + 100. Did Dionysius Exiguus, who determined Christ's birth in the 6th century, simply take Caesar's year of birth and add 100 in order to approximately fit this date with Herodes and Pilatus?

22 B.M.C. East 58. Cf. CARSON (1978), vol. I, 269.

23 Whether a *corona graminea* can be recognized on the face-helmet of Battenberge, respectively a *corona obsidionalis* on the Italic-Roman pan of earthenware from Teate, is doubtful. Incidentally, they are completely different in their form of appearance. Cf. KRAFT (1969), p. 16, n. 51.

24 The *corona obsidionalis* was a decoration of higher distinction than the *corona civica*, because it represented not only the rescue of a single citizen but of a whole division or even an army. (FESTUS 193 M. (208 L.): *inter obsidionalem et civicam hoc interesse quod altera singularis salutem signum est, altera diversorum civium servatorum;* PLINIUS 22.8: *quod si civicae honos uno aliquo ac vel humillimo cive servato praeclarus sacerque habetur, quid tandem existimari debet unius virtute servatus universus exercitus?* LIV. 7.37: *secundum consulis donationem legiones gramineam coronam obsidialem, clamore donum approbantes, Decio imponunt.*) Accordingly it was awarded extremely rarely, according to Plinius only seven times in the whole of Roman history (after Caesar only to Augustus, before him to Sulla; PLIN. 22.7-13). It was given to Caesar not only because of a specific event—of which there were more than one, the last time in Munda—but also because he had liberated the city generally from the siege, which means the Oikumene from the opposition party and the spectre of civil war (see above, citation of Dio Cassius, cf. WEINSTOCK (1971), p. 148-152).

It may surprise that the wreath, which represented the highest decoration for the Romans was simply of grass, the lowest of all plants. This came about because the wreaths as well as the plants from whose twigs they were made were consecrated to a particular Godhead. The myrtle, for example, was sacred to Venus (VIRGIL, *Eclog.* 7.62: *Veneri gratissima myrtus*) and so it is not astonishing at all that we find on the head of Caesar, whose ancestress was Venus, a myrtle-wreath (see above). In Greece the laurel was sacred to Apollo, but in Rome to Jupiter, because it is the only tree planted by man that does not get struck by lightning (Jupiter's); so the Triumphator wore it not only for the expiation of the spilt blood of the enemy but as a symbol of restored peace. The oak also was sacred to Jupiter, not least because it serves as a lightning rod and hardly burns and thereby is a protection against lightning. Thus the idea originated that an oak wreath should be awarded to anyone who saved a citizen from a deadly strike. Correspondingly the siege-wreath was made of grass, because the battlefield belonged to the God of the field, Mars, and no other plant symbolizes the field like the grass. Hence the lowest plant meant the highest honor.

It could be that the grass-wreath was originally a sign of capitulation, as the Latin phrase *herbam dare* for 'to surrender' leads us to suspect. So the grass in question has to be a symbol for the surrender of the formerly occupied field either to the victorious enemy or to the liberating ally. Then it would preferably be a strongly rooted grass rather than a long bladed type, especially in the latter case, when the resistance was victorious. It is striking that the term *corona graminea* does not refer to herba, but to *gramen*. Whereas the term *herba* contains the association with blade, this is not essential in the case of *gramen*. So *gramen* seems to be connected rather with the roots than with the blade. Anyway, the botanists speak of *rhizoma graminis* and they mean the rhizome of couch grass or its roots: *graminis* becomes a synonym for couch grass. Also in the Romance languages the word *graminea* became a substantive and it only designates couch grass, as for example the Italian *gramigna*: couch grass and simply weeds. This specialization seems to have started very early, because in classic Latin *gramen* also means weeds.

This fits with the Roman image of Mars, who was the God of war because he was God of the fields and the God of those who cultivated and defended the fields. Accordingly there were two sodalities of Mars-priests: that of the 'arable field brothers' *(Fratres Arvales)*, responsible for the fecundity of the fruits of the land; and the 'leaping fellows' *(Sodales Salii)*, known for their war dances and notorious carousing. The Roman army was an army of farmers and had its origin in the defence of the land. The typical Roman field is not a meadow, but arable lands, so the grass of Mars has to be looked for not in the meadow, but on the acre. And the grass found there is the common couch-grass or quitch, called with different names according to the region (dog-grass, quick-grass, quackgrass, quitch-grass, quake-grass, scutchgrass, twitch-grass, witch-grass, wheatgrass, crepping wheatgrass, devil's-grass, durfa-grass, Durfee-grass, Dutch-grass, Fin's-grass, Chandler's grass): the rapidly growing, indestructible weed, feared by all farmers, which riddles the ground with tough roots and wending runners. It is closely related to wheat, the botanical name is *triticum repens*, 'sudden wheat'. So couch-grass is to wheat as the legionary is to the farmer—not by chance, one would say from the viewpoint of Mars.

The Roman legionary was not just a porridge muncher—as the meat-eating barbarians mocked them—he was an armed farmer. And as such he made use of the spade more often than the sword. His job was fortification. Within hours the camp's fosse was excavated and the wall of the camp was raised. And here suddenly the much hated weed came to the assistance of the legionary: the rapidly spreading couch grass with its strong roots protected the wall from wind and rain.

There is scarcely a grass that can be easily used to braid a wreath, but couch-grass can be used effortlessly—one only has to think of the farmer's saying when they speak of 'wreathes of couch-grass', which they remove from the ground.

The result of our examination is that the *corona graminea* was probably a wreath of couch-grass. The one awarded to Caesar was such a wreath. One of his statues on the Rostra wore the *corona graminea* on the crown. We can imagine it as a wreath of couch-grass—in Latin: a couch-grass-crown.

Those who are familiar with couch can easily imagine how such a wreath may have looked, especially when it was dried up—or if a metal imitation had been made of it to make it weatherproof: the resemblance to Jesus' crown of thorns is striking.

There is still one question left: which field did Caesar's grasswreath come from? Maybe from Ategua, whose defenders he saved in the last Spanish campaign when they were besieged by the Pompeians? Or from Munda, the decisive battle in the same war, where his army faltered and only his personal physical intervention fortified them and finally led to victory?

But Dio Cassius says that he received the grass wreath 'as liberator of the city from the siege' (Dio Cass. HR 44.4.5: τὸν δὲ ὡς τὴν πόλιν ἐκ πολιορκίας ἐξῃρημένου). But the city meant here is neither Ategua nor Munda, but Rome: simply 'the city', together with the Empire, *urbi et orbi*, so to speak, liberated simply from the siege and the enemy, whom it was better not to mention because of the political aim of reconciliation.

For these reasons the grass of Caesar's political siege-wreath will have been from Rome itself, viz., because it had to be the wreath of Mars from the Field of Mars where by tradition the Roman *populus* assembled at arms. Not by chance was this the burial site of Caesar's daughter Julia, where his funeral pyre was initially prepared and where his bones, collected from the ashes, were to be buried.

The crown of thorns on the statues of Jesus in our Catholic churches come from Palestine: they are picked by monks there and prepared in such a manner that they are most identical with the Saviour's real crown of thorns. So the ritual is identical with that of the Roman *corona obsidionalis*: It also has to be made from the grass of the field of deliverance—for Caesar presumably the Campus Martius in Rome. Caesars *corona graminea* and Jesus' crown of thorns differ only as undergrowth from Rome and thorns from Jerusalem do.

25   The other difference between the statues of Caesar and those of Jesus concerns hair length and beard. We noticed a steady increase in hair length for Caesar's statues over time. For he suffered from his baldness, ergo little by little piety gave him back his hair.

With Jesus it is no different. In the early Christian depictions his hair is much shorter than today. The hair grew more and more as the centuries passed, which was furthered by the fact that in ancient times the statues wore genuine human hair which had to be replaced periodically. In most cases the hair was longer than previously, making the statues more life-like (cf. inter alia the tradition about the pilgrimage-cross of Oberried). The same happened with the beard. The early Christian depictions show a beardless Jesus (cf. i.a. ill. 116 p. 387 and 117 p. 388). Not till later, and then only gradually, did he grow a beard, and even then it was always short and unobtrusive. It is interesting that today we still see that on some crucifixes the beard does not cover the face, but only grows under the chin (as on e.g. the above mentioned pilgrim cross of Oberried).

Here it must be remembered that for the Romans, who were very meticulous in matters of body-care, it was a sign of mourning to refrain from cutting the beard and hair. After the military failure at Gergovia Caesar left off shaving his beard till he was able to defeat Vercingetorix. Also Marius—his exiled uncle—did not shave until he was able to return to Rome. Antonius and Augustus did the same until Caesar's murderers were punished and they had themselves depicted on coins in this fashion.

So the depiction of an indication of a beard could have begun with the first wax-statue of the murdered Caesar, which Antonius ordered made and erected in front of the Rostra at the funeral. This would not only have been realistic—as is known the beard apparently continues to grow on a dead body—but would have increased deterrence as well: the bearded murdered one calls for revenge.

26 Cf. BATTENBERG (1980), p. 56.

27 *Historia Augusta*, VER. 2.3; SERV. *Aen.* 1.286 i.a., compare *RE* X 464 sq 'Caesar' is said to have been the Moorish name of the elephant. As it was claimed the Julii with the cognomen Caesar inherited it from an ancestor who had it conferred on him for killing an elephant (in the first Punic war?). It is possible that the elephant was called Caesar by the Gauls as well, because they got to know the animal not through the Greek (Pyrrhus) but through Hannibal. It is said that Caesar, too, had elephants with him in Gaul and that he even used one in Britain at the Thames (POLYAENUS VIII.23.5). Of course there were other explanations of the name 'Caesar': *a caesis oculis*, 'because of the blue eyes' (but Caesar's were black, SUET. *Jul.* 45. The cruel Sulla had blue ones, so the reference to the blue eyes—at least in the name—could have been part of the political discrediting campaign); *a caesaries*, 'because of the hair' (but he was bald, so the explanation could be part of the mockery); finally *a caeso matris utero*, 'born by Caesarean section' (this could be part of the slander that he had raped his fatherland: For the Romans it was the 'mother'land, cf. the anecdotes about the first Brutus, who was the first to kiss the mother (earth); and the dreams reported of Caesar, that he had had incest with his mother). So for Caesar the only useful explanation of his name was the first one—that of the elephant. Moreover it enabled him to stand on equal ground with the opposing Metelli Scipii, who used the elephant as their heraldic animal. His followers certainly appreciated the jibe: at the beginning of the year 49 Metellus Scipio had demanded that Caesar dismiss his troops, whereas Pompeius, on the other hand, was arming. And the other Metellus had tried to stop Caesar from taking the state treasury from the temple of Saturnus. Now Caesar minted his coins from the treasury replete with the elephant and thereby not only took away the state treasury, but also the coat of arms of the proud Metelli.

28 The reverse of his denarius was also aimed at deterrence with the *securis*, the axe of the presiding *pontifex maximus*, in the center. The *securis* was also the axe of the *lictor*, which was used in Republican times for the punishment of decapitation. And it did not look amiable here, adorned as it was with the head of the she-wolf and her biting jaws. To the left we see the other pontifical emblems: the so-called *aspergillum*, the holy water sprinkler which by no accident looks like the *flagellum*, the chastising whip, and also the *simpulum*, the scoop. On the right the *apex*, the pointed hat of the priest. This felt cap with the unmistakable point did not really belong to the attributes of a *pontifex* (who usually acted *capite velato*, with a veiled head) but rather to those of a *flamen*. Caesar had been elected *flamen Dialis*, high priest of Jupiter, whilst still a young man. Sulla had hindered his inauguration, but de jure he held on to the position—at least no-one else took the position as long as he remained alive (that he was not allowed to practise the position certainly suited him afterwards because of the restrictions connected with it: the *flamen Dialis* was not allowed to leave the city or to ride a horse, and he forfeited the post on the death of his wife, the *flaminica*, who therefore was the true holder of it). With the depiction of the apex of the flamen Dialis on his coin, Caesar discreetly suggested two things: that an injustice had been done to him earlier; and the state of emergency decreed against him—and which could only be legitimized by Jupiter—was not blessed by his high priest. So the Pompeians could depict as many Jupiters as they liked on their propaganda coinage (Cf. *Crawford n° 445/1a* and *b, 445/2, 445/3a* and *b, 447/1a, 459, 460/1*), but indeed it was he who was high priest of Jupiter and *pontifex maximus*.

That the sacral titles *pontifex maximus* and *flamen Dialis* were important to Caesar even after his triumphs took place is demonstrated by the denarii *Crawford n° 480/ 19* and *480/20* of the year 44, which show him *capite velato* and wreathed, where the *apex*—which cannot be placed on the head because of the wreath—is depicted behind him. The oak-wreath is indicated here in the title: CAESAR PARENS PATRIAE.

29 Cf. RAUBITSCHEK (1954), p.69, (R) and fig. 5: ἀρχιερέως μεγίστου. *Archiereus megistos* is the tautological but clearer full form (which was employed more by the later emperors—presumably also to make a distinction between him and the local priests of the emperor's cult, who were sometimes called *archiereus* too); *archiereus* is the more elegant and terse short form.

30 Cf. RAUBITSCHEK (1954), p.73: 'The occurrence of the Greek equivalents for Imperator and Pontifex Maximus is indicative of the position occupied by Caesar immediately after his victory at Pharsalos. Only two of the inscriptions (H, I) omit the title "Pontifex Maximus", but they combine with the title "Imperator" the unique designation Θεός.'

31 CIC. *Phil.* 2.110: *Quem is honorem maiorem consecutus erat quam ut haberet pulvinar, simulacrum, fastigium, flaminem? Est ergo flamen, ut Iovi, ut Marti, ut Quirino, sic divo Iulio M. Antonius? Quid igitur cessas? Cur non inaugurari? Sume diem, vide qui te inauguret: conlegae sumus; nemo negabit. O detestabilem hominem, sive quod tyranni sacerdos es sive quod mortui!*

32 Cicero understood the inscription as a direct threat because, as the spiritual father of Caesar's murder, he felt branded as 'parricide'. Cf. *Ep. ad fam.* 12.3.

33 HOR. *Carm.* 3.24; 27.

34 F.e. *CIL* III 3279. AE 1938, 140. DESSAU 6779. GRANT I 266: coin from Corinth with Caesar's head and inter alia the legend CREATOR. The same for Augustus and Agrippa, in: IADER, *CIL* III 2907. 13264. VIVES 3, 10, 25. 11, 27; 36; 39. 12, 41; 42. 10, 26. 11, 39; 40. Cf. VITTINGHOFF (1952), p. 52 and 75. About the divine honours of ἥρως-κτίστης: KAERST (1917), 481sq.

35 According to Plutarchus, *Ant.* 33.1, Antonius was inaugurated after the peace of Brundisium in October 40 BC at the behest of Octavianus.

36 DIO CASS. *HR* 44.6.4; CIC. *Phil.* 2.110.

37 SUET. *Jul.* 85: *postea solidam columnam prope uiginti pedum lapidis Numidici in foro statuit <in>scripsitque parenti patriae. apud eam longo tempore sacrificare, uota suscipere, controuersias quasdam interposito per Caesarem iure iurando distrahere perseuerauit.*

38 This was the perception at that time. The comet that appeared after Caesar's murder received its consecrated meaning after Philippi, as *sidus Iulium*.
Cf. PLUT. *Caes.* 69: Ὁ μέντοι μέγας αὐτοῦ δαίμων, ᾧ παρὰ τὸν βίον ἐχρήσατο, καὶ τελευτήσαντος ἐπηκολούθησε τιμωρὸς τοῦ φόνου, διά τε γῆς πάσης καὶ θαλάττης ἐλαύνων καὶ ἀνιχνεύων ἄχρι τοῦ μηδένα λιπεῖν τῶν ἀπεκτονότων, ἀλλὰ καὶ τοὺς καθ' ὁτιοῦν ἢ χειρὶ τοῦ ἔργου θιγόντας ἢ γνώμῃ μετασχόντας ἐπεξελθεῖν. θαυμασιώτατον δὲ τῶν μὲν ἀνθρωπίνων τὸ περὶ Κάσσιον· ἡττηθεὶς γὰρ ἐν Φιλίπποις, ἐκείνῳ τῷ ξιφιδίῳ διέφθειρεν ἑαυτὸν ᾧ κατὰ Καίσαρος ἐχρήσατο· τῶν δὲ θείων ὅ τε μέγας κομήτης (ἐφάνη γὰρ ἐπὶ νύκτας ἑπτὰ μετὰ τὴν Καίσαρος σφαγὴν διαπρεπής, εἶτ' ἠφανίσθη), καὶ τὸ περὶ τὸν ἥλιον ἀμαύρωμα τῆς αὐγῆς.

39 It is known that about the beginning of the Christian era all educated persons in Rome spoke Greek. Caesar himself was perfectly bilingual, some of his famous sayings like *alea iacta est(o)* are Greek citations ('Ανερρίφθω κύβος, from Menander's *Arrhephoros*, cf. PLUT. *Pomp.* 60.4) and also his last words to Brutus *You too, My son!* he must have spoken in Greek according to Suetonius' reports *(Jul.* 82: Καὶ σὺ τέκνον!). It is less well known that in Rome Greek was the cultural language within living memory and an official one from very early on.

40 The so-called 'itacism', which means that η—'êta'—became 'ita' in pronunciation, with the danger of confusing a whole group of vocals and diphthongs, i. a.: ι, ει, η (η) οι, υ,—'i', 'ei', 'ê', êi', 'oi', 'y'—which then were all spoken 'i' (i. e. 'iota': that's why it is also called 'iotacism'), the same with ε, αι—'e', 'ai'—both 'e', so that not

even ἡμεῖς and ὑμεῖς, i.e. *we* and *you* (respectively *us* and *you*, etc.) could be kept apart. Cf. CHARALAMBAKIS (1984), p.83 7.1.1: Συνέπεσε ἡ προφορά τῶν ι, ει, η (η), οι, υ σέ i.

41 Cf. LÜDERITZ (1994), p.193.
42 PLUT. *Pomp.* 75: τῶν δὲ Μιτυληναίων τὸν Πομπήιον ἀσπασαμένων καὶ παρακαλούντων εἰσελθεῖν εἰς τὴν πόλιν, οὐκ ἠθέλησεν, ἀλλὰ κἀκείνους ἐκέλευσε τῷ κρατοῦντι πείθεσθαι καὶ θαρρεῖν· εὐγνώμονα γὰρ εἶναι Καίσαρα καὶ χρηστόν.
43 As χριστός—*christós* with 'i'—means 'oiled, greased' it was interpreted by the Christians as 'anointed' and was used for the Aramaic 'Messiah' (cf. Jn. 1:41; 4:25, where in both cases Χριστός is added, once as an interpretation, then as a surname).
44 CO*Lo*Nia > KÖLN / LV*gd*VN*um* > LYON / *cae*SARA*u*GV*St*A > ZARAGOZA / *h*IP*p*oDIAR*rh*yTV*s* > BIZERTE / PRES*by*T*er*os > PRIEST—without claiming linguistic accuracy: the phonetic transitions are naturally more complex and depend on the location and the time (for example from the Greek *presbyteros* we have the German *Priester*, the English *priest*, the French *prêtre*, the Italian *prete*, etc.; *Forum Iulii* led as well to *Friuli* as to *Fréjus*, etc.). Aided by the respective special terminologies, we can ponder whether in the transition from *Caesaraugusta* to *Zaragoza* the sounds 'c' or 's' or 'cs' became the initial 'z'—with or without the assimilation of the sibilants. Also, we can ponder whether in the hypothesized transition of *archiereus megistos* to *christos* it was the first or second 'r' that was retained—or a combination of both with or without the metathesis of the liquid—and so on. But this discussion would only complicate the matter at this point in time, all the more so because we still do not know when and where these hypothetical transitions may have happened. So at first it is about taking stock only.

II. Vitae Parallelae

45 APP. *BC* 2.146: [...] ἐν θαύματι αὐτῶν ἕκαστα ποιούμενος.
46 DIO CASS. *HR* 44.44.4. APP. *BC* 2.150.625: Καίσαρι δὲ ἥ τε Ἰόνιος θάλασσα εἶξε, χειμῶνος μέσου πλωτὴ καὶ εὔδιος γενομένη [...]. DIO CASS. *HR* 41.46.3: ἐξέφηνεν ἑαυτὸν καθάπερ ἐκ τούτου καὶ τὸν χειμῶνα παύσων.
47 PLUT. *Caes.* 5: καὶ θαυμάσας ὥσπερ ἐξ Ἅιδου διὰ χρόνων πολλῶν ἀνάγοντα τὰς Μαρίου τιμὰς εἰς τὴν πόλιν.
48 Apparently it is willingly repressed that Caesar was *pontifex maximus* from the beginning of his career, and that he was honored during his lifetime with cultic practices and after his death as a God. Here is just one example representative of many others: in his preface to RASMUSSEN (1967) the editor lists: 'Caesar was a politician and statesman, conqueror, discoverer and general at the same time—and not least an orator and writer of rank [...]'. The *pontifex maximus,* son of Venus and God of the Empire is not mentioned—it is left to specialist studies (cf. inter alia: WLOSOK (1978), PRICE (1984), CLAUSS (1999) or CANCIK/HITZL (Ed.) (2003)).
49 Mt. 10:34-36. Cf. MARTIAL (Poet of the first century AD), *Epigrams*, IX, 72-73:
cum gener atque socer diris concurreret armis
maestaque civili caede maderet humus.
A common school translation recites:
'When Caesar and Pompey each attacked the other
And son killed father and brother his brother.'
http://www.lingua.co.uk/latin1/tour/authors/martial/
It is not a literal translation, having lost the 'dire arms' and the 'mournful earth becoming wet from the civil massacre', but it makes clear that the *gener* and the *socer,* the 'son in law' and the 'father in law', were Pompeius and Caesar fighting one another in a civil, and yes, a domestic war.

If we compare the text of Martial with Mt. 10:34-36 in Latin (Vulgate)—
Nolite arbitrari quia pacem veneri mittere in terram: non veni pacem mittere sed gladium. veni enim separare hominem adversus patrem suum, et filiam adversus matrem suam, et nurum adversus socrum suam: et inimici hominis, domestici eius.
—we see that *gener* and *socer,* 'son in law' and 'father in law', have become *nurus* and *socer,* 'daughter in law' and 'mother in law'. The reason lies in the fact that Matthew is citing Micah 7:6:
'For the son dishonoureth the father, the daughter riseth up against her mother, the daughter in law against her mother in law; a man's enemies are the men of his own house.'
But in Micah there is no reference to a 'sword' or other 'arms', although to 'blood' in Mch 7:2. So Martial's verses are closer to Matthew's passage than Micah's. It is conspicuous that a text like this from Martial was present here, before Matthew himself or later copyists substituted it with the inevitable midrash, in this case a citation of Micah.

50 Letter of Caesar to Oppius and Cornelius, in: CIC. *ad Att.* 9.7 c: *Haec nova sit ratio vincendi, ut misericordia et liberalitate nos muniamus.* STAUFFER (1957), p.20, translates: 'Das muß die neue Siegestaktik und Sicherheitspolitik sein, daß wir Vergebung üben und eine freie und festliche Welt schaffen—This must be the new tactics of victory and security politics that we grant forgiveness and create a free and festive world'. Cf. SUET. *Jul.* 75.

51 This is attested of him by the Church Fathers also—cf. OROSIUS *Hist.* 6.17.1, who says that Julius Caesar perished in the attempt to construct the political world anew, contrary to the example of his predecessors, in the spirit of clemency: *Caesar Roman rediit: ubi dum Reipublicae statum contra exempla maiorum clementer instaurat, auctoribus Bruto et Cassio, conscio etiam plurimo senatu, in curia viginti et tribus vulneribus confossus interiit.'*

52 DIO CASS. *HR* 44.46.5-6: πάντας ὅσοι μὴ καὶ πρότερόν ποτε ἁλόντες ὑπ' αὐτοῦ ἠλέηντο ἀφείς. τὸ μὲν γὰρ τοὺς πολλάκις ἐπιβουλεύοντάς οἱ ἀεὶ περιποιεῖσθαι μωρίαν, οὐ φιλανθρωπίαν ἐνόμιζε [...].

53 Mk. 3:29: ὃς δ' ἂν βλασφημήσῃ εἰς τὸ πνεῦμα τὸ ἅγιον, οὐκ ἔχει ἄφεσιν εἰς τὸν αἰῶνα, ἀλλὰ ἔνοχός ἐστιν αἰωνίου ἁμαρτήματος [...].

54 DIO CASS. *HR* 44.4.5; GEL. 5.6.11.

55 Detail of the passion-sarcophagus in: HINZ (1973-81), I Fig.74. Cf. note 157, ill. 116, second scene from left.

56 Today Greece is still called *Ionia* by the Turks and the Arabs, and the Greeks are still *Ionians.* But also in the West the term is more comprehensive than one thinks. So the *Ionian islands* are less likely to be the eastern ones in front of the *Ionian coastline* of Asia minor like Chios and Samos, but rather the western islands in the *Ionian sea,* the islands in closer proximity to Italy like Corfu, Cephalonia etc.

57 Mk.1:22: ἦν γὰρ διδάσκων αὐτοὺς ὡς ἐξουσίαν ἔχων.

58 Mk.1:24: Τί ἡμῖν καὶ σοί, Ἰησοῦ Ναζαρηνέ; ἦλθες ἀπολέσαι ἡμᾶς;

59 In Rome the woman receives the name of her father's gens, but sometimes even scholars make the mistake of naming her after her husband—so Caesar's wife Pompeia is called 'Iulia' by Appianus (*BC* 2.14). The differing accent, *Mária* and *María* results from the different rules of the Latin and Greek accentuation. Gr. *Mários/María* like *Kýrios/Kyría.*

60 Jn.11:5.

61 For the metathesis of the liquids in the Aramaic cf. Stanislav SEGERT (⁴1990), 3.7.2.5. Like Greek *Herakles* > Latin *Hercules;* German *Riegel* > Czech *lígr.* The variations in the vocals are insignificant, even more so to ears that are familiar with Semitic languages. In the Aramaic—as in the other Semitic languages—only the consonants are semantically relevant. A similar phenomenon exists in the Indo-Europe-

62 For eventual doublets that can be generated from different names, among them especially 'Lepidus' see note 100.
63 Concerning short forms with -âς cf. CHANTRAINE (1933), p. 31 sq.
64 Mk. 14:43: Ἰούδας εἷς τῶν δώδεκα.
65 Cf. the respective meaning of the Italian derivatives: *ladro*—'thief, rogue'—and *lazzarone*—'scoundrel, villain, lout'.
66 Ὁ νέος Καῖσαρ respectively Καῖσαρ ὁ νέος—so Octavianus Augustus is often called to distinguish him from the older (NICOLAUS DAMASCENUS *Vit. Caes.* 14: πρεσβύτερος) or great Caesar (NIC. DAM. *Vit. Caes.* 107: μεγάλος). Cf. i.a.: NIC. DAM. *Vit. Caes.* 14, 16, 17, 32, 36, 37, 51, 107; PLUT. *Brut.* 27.1, *Cic.* 43.6, 44.1 and PLUT. *Ant.* 16.1; APP. *BC* 3.21, 32 and 33. If there was no pressing danger of confusion the ancient historians simply called him *Caesar*—Καῖσαρ.
N.B.: We transcribe here—and from now on—the Greek article ὁ not with 'ho' but with '(h)o' or even 'o',—as well as the other words beginning with *spiritus asper*—because in the late Hellenistic time we are concerned with, the 'h' was not pronounced and was no longer written: the diacritical signs, the accents, the esprits etc. were introduced at a later time. The classical transcription here would give the wrong impression and lead us astray.
67 *Iuuenis* > ὁ νέος > Ἰωάν(ν)ης. There are many examples in the Romance languages of the incorporation of the article into the name—witness the French *Lorient* (< *l'Orient*), *Lancelot* (< *l'Ancelot* < *Anselo* < *Anguselus*), the Italian *Labbadia* (<*l'Abbadia*), etc.
The acoustic transition to Johannes (John) also occurs when the Greek ὁ νέος is omitted and the Latin *iuuenis* is supposed as the starting point. The presence of a 'v' in the Italian form of both words *giovane* and *Giovanni* (and its absence in the popular *Gianni*) would speak for the direct derivation of the name Ἰωάν(ν)ης from the Latin *iuuenis*. A modern example for *young > John* is the football (resp. soccer) player Elber—who was called *il giovane Elber* in Italy 'the young Elber' when he came from Brazil at a young age—and was later called *Giovane* in Germany as well—but with the accent of *Giovànni: Giovàne*, instead of *giόvane*.
68 Because of the weak and aspirant pronunciation of the Greek 'g'—and because of the appearance of the writing.
69 Model: *curia < co-uiria*, meeting of men.
70 NICOLAUS DAMASCENUS (i.a. *Vit. Caes.* XXIII 82) regularly calls the Roman Senate συνέδριον. The distinction between *synedrion*, '(Greek) council' and *synedrium*, 'Jewish council', which is often made in German, is arbitrary. In English the perspicuity of the relation between *senate* and *synedrion* is lost, because the last is rather called *sanhedrin*, using a pseudo-Hebraic word, in fact a late hebraization of an authentic Greek word, composed of *syn*, 'together' and *(h)edra*, 'seat, sitting, session'. The Greek word *synedrion* indicates simply a *council*, i.e. in Rome the *senate*.
71 Aramaic *migdol*, 'tower' respectively 'castle'. Hence the frequency of places with this addition.
72 It is striking that all women who are related to Jesus or who are close to him are called *Maria*.
73 PLUT. *Ant.* 74: αὐτὴ δὲ θήκας ἔχουσα καὶ μνήματα κατεσκευασμένα περιττῶς εἴς τε κάλλος καὶ ὕψος.
74 Mk. 1:16: εἶδεν Σίμωνα.
75 Cf. the reputed relic of the *titulus crucis*, the sign on Jesus' cross, with a text written from right to left, Greek and Latin: BCYNEPAZA(H)N.CI / RSVNIRAZAN.I—for IC.N(H)AZAPENYCB / I.NAZARINVSR, here obviously in imitation of the Jewish

way of writing; the Greek line is a mere Greek transcription of the Latin line rather than a translation, in contrast to all the Greek citations of the Gospels, so that this *titulus crucis* can hardly be considered authentic, even if some devout scholars persist in doing so. Anyway, if authentic, it documents the possibility of writing Greek and even Latin in reversed script in a Jewish context. If not authentic, it documents the inveterate tendency to write Greek and even Latin in reversed script, in order to appear authentic. In fact, in archaic times the Greeks—like the Egyptians and Etruscans—did not always write from the left to the right, but also from right to left. Sometimes they wrote one line to the right and the next line to the left: *boustrophedon*, which means: as oxen reverse during ploughing (cf. the inscription of the Cretan city of Gortyn about its municipal right). It is also assumed that the Septuagint was transcribed in Greek letters first and was then translated with occasional perceptual errors, amongst them the ones due to the misreading of the direction in which various words were to be read (cf. WUTZ (1925). Apart from the Septuagint, transcriptions of Hebrew texts are contained in the writings of Flavius Josephus, Origenes, Eusebius, Epiphanes, Aquila, Symmachus and Theodotion. For the heterographical use of the Aramaic in the Persian cf. SEGERT (⁴1990), 1.7.6. So it is conceivable that a copyist has taken the name *Antonius* to be a reversed, heterographically inserted *Simona* and that he has 'corrected' the supposed mistake.

76 The metathesis, the reordering of sounds, often occurs in transitions between languages, sometimes combined with a wrong etymology. So for example, *wasp*— (from the Latin *vespa*) was in Old English *wæps*, as if it had come from *wefan*—'to weave'—although in this case the etymology could, as an exception, be correct.

77 N.B.: This expression—εἰς τὴν πόλιν, pronunciation: *Is tem bolin*—became *Istambul,* the proper Turkish name for the city of Constantinople. This is similar to the Arab *medina*, which signifies 'city' generally but 'The city' as well.

78 Lxx and PHILO write Σαλήμ, FLAVIUS JOSEPHUS *Ant.J.* 1.180 writes Σολυμᾶ.

79 Paul in Heb. 7:1 sq calls Melchisedek βασιλεὺς Σαλήμ by following Gn. 14:18 and explains it as 'king of peace'. PHILO *leg. all.* 3.79: Μελχισεδὲκ βασιλέα τῆς εἰρήνης—Σαλὴμ τοῦτο γὰρ ἑρμηνεύεται.

80 Similar to the German *Regensburg*, which sounds like 'Castle of Rain', derived from Latin *Castra Regina,* which can be erroneously understood as 'Queen's castle': *castra* > *Burg*, 'castle' (straight translation); *regina* > *Regen*, 'rain' (translation by sound—thus changing the meaning). In fact *Regen*, Lat. *Regina,* is neither the rain nor a queen, but the name of the river flowing there.

81 Older manuscripts—i.a. P. Bodmer II (= P[66])—write *IC* , only more recent ones like the Bezae Cantabrigiensis (= ***D***) write—*IHC*.

82 Cf. i.a. APP. *BC* 2.106: σχήματά τε ἐπεγράφετο ταῖς εἰκόσι ποικίλα, καὶ στέφανος ἐκ δρυὸς ἦν ἐπ' ἐνίαις ὡς σωτῆρι τῆς πατρίδος, ᾧ πάλαι τοὺς ὑπερασπίσαντας ἐγέραιρον οἱ περισωθέντες.

83 Cf. RAUBITSCHEK (1954), p.69, (B), (C), (F), (G), (J), (K), (M), (N), (O): the many similar inscriptions have the following common denominator:
Ο ΔΗΜΟΣ ΓΑΙΟΝ ΙΟΥΛΙΟΝ ΓΑΙΟΥ ΥΙΟΝ ΚΑΙΣΑΡΑ ΤΟΝ ΑΡΧΙΕΡΕΑ ΚΑΙ ΑΥ-ΤΟΚΡΑΤΟΡΑ [ΥΠΑΤΟΝ ΚΑΙ ΔΙΚΤΑΤΟΡΑ ΤΟ ΔΕΥΤΕΡΟΝ] ΣΩΤΗΡΑ ΚΑΙ ΕΥΕΡ-ΓΕΤΗΝ [ΤΩΝ ΕΛΛΗΝΩΝ ΑΠΑΝΤΩΝ]. In square brackets we have the titles that were omitted or were formulated in another manner in one or the other inscription. The accusative indicates that these are not only dedications but in fact are consecrations.

84 *Die Inschriften von Ephesos* (The inscriptions of Ephesos), part II, 1979, N°251: ΑΙ ΠΟΛΕΙΣ ΑΙ ΕΝ ΤΗΙ ΑΣΙΑΙ ΚΑΙ ΟΙ ΔΗΜΟΙ ΚΑΙ ΤΑ ΕΘΝΗ ΓΑΙΟΝ ΙΟΥΛΙΟΝ ΓΑΙΟΥ ΥΙΟΝ ΚΑΙΣΑΡΑ ΤΟΝ ΑΡΧΙΕΡΕΑ ΚΑΙ ΑΥΤΟΚΡΑΤΟΡΑ ΚΑΙ ΤΟ ΔΕΥΤΕ-ΡΟΝ ΥΠΑΤΟΝ ΤΟΝ ΑΠΟ ΑΡΕΩΣ ΚΑΙ ΑΦΡΟΔΕΙΤΗΣ ΘΕΟΝ ΕΠΙΦΑΝΗ ΚΑΙ ΚΟΙ-ΝΟΝ ΤΟΥ ΑΝΘΡΩΠΙΝΟΥ ΒΙΟΥ ΣΩΤΗΡΑ.

85 Like Jesus, Caesar was also «Son of God». Because the Julii were generally considered to be descendants of Venus via Julus and Aeneas and especially he, the favorite son, who had consecrated his victories to her: *Venere prognatus*. Cf. Cic. Ep. *ad fam.* 8.15.2.14; c.VII Id.Mart.49. Linguistically there is to note, that 'Son of God' in Greek can also mean 'Son of the Goddess', because θεός is a commune and also means Goddess, e.g.: ἡ Διὸς θεός, ἡ Ζηνὸς θεός, verbatim 'she the Zeus' God', i.e. the daughter of Zeus; cf. also DIO CASS. *HR* 41.61.4: ἐν τῷ τῆς Νίκης ναῷ [...] καὶ τὴν θεὸν αὐτὴν [...]. Hence υἱὸς θεοῦ (Mk 15:39; Lk 1:35) and thus also υἱὸς τοῦ θεοῦ (passim)—can also mean 'Son of the Goddess'. So Dio Cassius says of Caesar, analogous to the inscription from Ephesos, that he is ἐκ τῆς Ἀφροδίτης (*HR* 44.37.4), descended 'from Aphrodite', while the parallel place in Appianus (*BC* 146) speaks of θεοῦ γενέσεως 'his origin from God' (not 'from the Goddess', although 'from Venus' is meant here). The 'from Ares' in the inscription from Ephesos—instead of the expected 'from Anchises'—originates from the marriage of Mars and Venus, a notion familiar to the Greeks, because it had come to the Romans from them (cf. WISSOWA (²1912) p. 292). Here 'from Ares' alludes politically to Caesar as the new Romulus, who was the son of Mars (cf. also the temple of *Mars Ultor* which was later consecrated to Caesar by his adoptive son Octavianus; the same Augustus was to name his nephew and adoptive son Caius Caesar Ἄρηος υἱός). Possibly it also alludes to the fact that Caesars' father descended on the mothers' side from the *Marcii Reges*, who stemmed from *Ancus Marcius* (cf. SUET. *Jul.* 6.1), with (etymologically correct) derivation of *Marcius* from *Mars*. Caesar had sacrificed to both deities, Mars and his ancestral mother Venus, at midnight before the battle at Pharsalos: APP. *BC* 2.68.281: θυόμενός τε νυκτὸς μέσης τὸν Ἄρη κατεκάλει καὶ τὴν ἑαυτοῦ πρόγονον Ἀφροδίτην [...].
Jesus Son of God can thence stand for *Caius Iulius Venere prognatus*. But since (υἱὸς τῆς) ΑΦΡΟΔΙΤΗΣ is very close to (υἱὸς τοῦ) ΑΝΘΡΩΠΟΥ in tone and appearance of writing, hypothetical mix-ups between 'Son of Man' and 'Son of God' cannot be completely ruled out.
Theós can stand for *divus*. The fact that *theós* can only relatively rarely be found on the pedestals of Ionian statues, even more seldom on the earlier ones (on which instead *archiereus* or *archiereus megistos*, i.e. *pontifex maximus*, is written), is explained thus: that those with *theós* probably came later, in the time after Munda, when the title *divus* was bestowed upon Caesar. Cf. RAUBITSCHEK (1954).

86 In our consecration-inscriptions the Latin title *imperator* is rendered as *autokratôr*. Jesus is called *pantokrator*, the almighty, which sounds like a blend of *imperator* with *autokratôr* or of *hypatos* (consul) with *autokratôr*. But also the *apantôn* of *tôn hellênôn apantôn* could be heard as *panto-*. In the Gospel it is said that Jesus had *exousia*—authority, full power. The classical Latin translation of *exousia* is *potestas* respectively *imperium* (cf. MAGIE 1905, p. 11, 68 and 121). So *exousia* respectively *pantokrator* could represent a collective term for the different political titles of Caesar that were sometimes mentioned together or sometimes alternately: *autokratôr*, *hypatos, diktator—imperator, consul, dictator*.

87 The *nomen sacrum*, the abbreviation for $\overline{XPICTOC}$, $\overline{XP}$, is an anomaly because in most abbreviations, the first and the last letter are the ones preserved—$\overline{ΘEOC}$ > $\overline{ΘC}$, $\overline{IHCOYC}$ > $\overline{IC}$ etc. Thus the normal abbreviation is $\overline{XC}$. So it would be conceivable that the abbreviation $\overline{XP}$ may have replaced the abbreviation for $\overline{KAICAP}$, $\overline{KP}$, through a writing error: K > X.

88 *Jesus Nazarene* is the name and sometimes the address of Jesus. The possessed man of Capernaum in Mark addresses him that way. *Nazarênos*—Ναζαρηνός—is generally understood as 'of Nazareth'. Outside of Mark, sometimes Ναζωραῖος is found instead, but this variation is also interpreted as an adjective to Ναζαρέθ—explicitly so in Matthew 2:23. The Septuagint has Ναζηραῖος. The annotation by BAUER

(^{6}1988), Sp. 1077, that 'the linguistic bridge from Ναζαρέτ to Ναζωραῖος is difficult to construct, and one has to assume that Ναζωραῖος had another meaning before it was connected to Nazaret', something that cannot be emphasized too much. For *Nazareth* there is also the variation *Nazara* which could be older (cf. Lk. 4:16: Καὶ ἦλθεν εἰς Ναζαρά). If we compare in Greek the roots of *Nazarênos* and *Nazareth* with *Caesar*—*NAZAP* ≈ *KAIΣAP*—then the difference appears to be minimal (the differing letters—the inital '*N*' and '*K*'—both consist of three lines: only the beginning and the direction of the last line differ a bit; '*Σ*' and '*Z*' can be confused; '*I*' dissipates easily and it could be held for the commonly appearing dash of the *Z* : '*Ƶ* '. Whereas *Nazara* is close to *Kaisara* (the Greek accusative of Caesar) and also *Nazareth* is close to *Kaisareia* (Greek *Caesarea*: the name of several cities), so *Nazarênos* looks like *Kaisarianos*: *Jesus Nazarene* could stand for *Gaius Iulius Caesar*.

89   Caius Iulius Caesar was 'son of Caius', pronunciation 'Gaius'. Understood as having the meaning of 'son of Gaia', 'son of Mother Earth', the name Gaius stood for the concept of 'man, human' par excellence to the farmers which the Romans were (cf. the vow of marriage of the Roman woman: *Vbi tu Gaius et ego Gaia*—'Where you (will be) man of earth, likewise I (will be), woman of earth'). This is especially the case for Greek ears (In Greek *Caius* is written *Gaios*, like *Gaia*, *gê*, the earth. Cf. γῆ, γᾶ or γαῖα—gê, gâ or gaîa—for 'earth' and in English 'geography'; γαιήϊος—*gaiêios*—'born of the earth, coming from the earth', poetical since Odyssey 7.24; also γηγενής—*gêgenês*—'born of the earth, son of earth, native, autochthon'), and—translated—also for Aramaic ears ('Adam', name of the first man and 'man' in general, is derived from *adamâ*, 'earth, arable land'. According to Gn. 2:7: 'And the Lord God formed man of the dust of the ground [...]'—a play on words; Gn. 5:2: 'Male and female (men) created he them [...] and called their name Adam (man)'— both times 'Adam'. For Christ as 'the new Adam' cf. Rom. 5:14; 1 Cor. 15:45). So *Jesus Son of Man* can stand for *Caius Iulius Cai filius*. However, since both parts of the name (i.e. *Caius Iulius* and *Cai filius*), as demonstrated in the inscriptions, can be easily confused in the Greek—especially when written without a space between the words, as was usual at that time: ΓΑΙΟΝΙΟΥΛΙΟΝ ΓΑΙΟΥΥΙΟΝ, *gaionioulion gaiouuion*—many a *son of man* can also stand for *Caius Iulius*. (The frequent occurrence of *son of man*—82 times in the four Gospels—as well as its use: never as an address, would attest to this.)

90   *Gaius Iulius* as a proper name cannot endure: it is too long. Proper names shrink in usage to a maximum length of two syllables. Johannes becomes Jannis, Jean, Sean, Ian or John, etc. and if officialdom tries to preserve the full form it shrinks just as much in practise—so the German Johannes to Hans for example, or the Italian Giovanni becomes Gianni; of course Johannes can be abbreviated according to the modern trend to Jo but it has to become shorter. The same thing happens to other names with three or more syllables: Margarita becomes Margit or Rita, Joseph can remain (it only has two syllables, but there is in German the option of Sepp), but Giuseppe (three syllables) becomes Beppe, Francesco becomes Franco, Checco, Paco or Franz etc. (but François can remain): always the maximum of two syllables.

The same tendency toward one or two syllables can be observed in the names of towns: Colonia becomes Köln, Confluentes Koblenz, Mogontiacum Mainz, Forum Livii becomes Forlì etc. Gaius Iulius has four syllables. The abbreviations, only *Gaius* or only *Iulius*, rule themselves out because they would lead to confusions. The name has to contract itself. As a comparison *Forum Iulii*, which became *Fréjus*, could help us to understand the process (apparently the vulgar tongue started from the undeclined basic form F*orum Iulius: Forum Iulius* > *Fre-jus*). This shows that the second link of our combination *Iulius* becomes *-ius (-jus)*. The unaccented middle syllable then fades (cf. i.a. POPE (1934): *vigilare* > *veiller; regina* > *reine; nigrum*

> *noir;* legere > *lire,* etc.). So *Gaius Iulius* will have as an intermediate stage *Gais-jus*. The initial soft 'g' becomes 'j', whereas the spirant 's' absorbs the semivowel 'j' of the second link; then the accented vowel in the first link closes itself to 'e' (especially in the case of the Greek *Gaios,* because it is understood as a dialectal version of *gêios*—pronunciation 'ghêios'—Dorean γάιος / Attean γήιος): *Iêsus,* Greek *IH-ΣΟΥΣ*.

Gaius Iulius > *Gais-jus* > *Iêsus* > Ἰησοῦς.

Gaius Julius and *Jesus* can be one and the same name, the one in its elaborate form and the other in the everyday one.

91 The titles in the square brackets correspond in the Christology, besides *basileus* and *kyrios,* to others that are typical for Caesar—*victor, triumphator, imperator,* even *Caesar*—or for Augustus—*dux, custos, princeps* and *Augustus*. Cf. CANCIK (1975), p. 118. That *dictator* is missing in Christology may be based on the fact that the title was prohibited after Caesar's murder. Hence Octavianus took the title *princeps*.

92 At the time when the Gospels originated, which means a century or so after Caesar's death, there were so many Caesars and Julii that it became common to call *Caius Iulius Caesar* rather *Divus Iulius,* 'the divine Julius' (cf. the titles of Suetonius' emperor-biographies). Because *Divus Iulius* was his cult-name it would be conceivable that we should assume *Diuus Iulius* as the starting point for the short name *Jesus* instead of *Gaius Iulius*.

Remarkably—in this case also, the short form would be *Jesus*. The development of the second element would be at first the same: *Iulius* > *-ius (-jus)*. What can become of *Diuus* is illustrated to us by the development of *diu pater* (from an original *dieu pater*) which became *Ju-piter:* the 'd' before 'iu' was eliminated. That this rule was valid also later can be seen in the evolution of *diurnus* which led to the French *jour* and to the Italian *giorno*. So *Diuus* at first becomes *Iuus*. The intermediate stage would be *Iuus-jus*. Then the spirant 's' would absorb the semivowel 'j': *Iuusus*. Finally the accented syllable would lead to a narrowing of the vowel as before—*Iêsus*.

Diuus Iulius > *Iuus-jus* > *Iuusus* > *Iêsus* > Ἰησοῦς.

Moreover, we have to notice here that also Caesar's adoptive son *Octavianus* became *Caius Iulius Caesar Cai filius* by his adoption—and hence he had practically the same name as the father (the cause was the *condicio nominis ferendi:* in order to claim the inheritance C. *Octavius Thurinus* had taken the name of his adoptive father and he was called *Gaius Iulius Caesar Cai filius Octavianus* from then on. The equality of names proved itself to be a political trump. His opponents like Antonius denigrated him as *Octavianus,* sometimes *Thurinus* as well. Today he is called mostly by his later title of honor: *Augustus*. Cf. CANCIK (1975), p. 118). When his adoptive father shortly after was consecrated, the adoptive son was from then on called *Caius Iulius Caesar Divi filius*—'son of God'. But because Caesar was also son of God as descendant of Venus there was practically no possibility of distinguishing them.

Coincidentally we also arrive at the short name *Jesus* when we use *Divi Filius* as the starting point (instead of *Caius Iulius* or *Divus Iulius*). We would namely have to assume *Diuus Filius* as the undeclined basic form (see the above example 'Fréjus'). *Diuus* becomes *Iuus,* as we have seen before, *Filius* to *fius* (disappearance of the unaccentuated syllable). Then the dental fricative 's' would absorb the labiodental fricative 'f': *Iuusus*. And from here on again *Iêsus*.

Diuus Filius > *Iuus-fius* > *Iuusius* > *Iêsus* > Ἰησοῦς.

All Roman roads lead inevitably to Jesus.

We have to reckon with the possibility that Caesar and Octavianus Augustus have competed to generate the name Jesus. Or—expressed differently—we have to be prepared for at least two Jesus-figures.

93 This is documented for *koíranos,* which is close to *kyrios* in both meaning and sound. Cf. the play on words of Areios οὐκ ἀγαθὸν πολυκαισαρίη—'More than one Caesar is not a good thing' (PLUT. *Ant.* 81)—a paraphrase of Odysseus' οὐκ ἀγαθὸν πολυκοιρανίη—'More than one master is not a good thing' (*Iliad* 2.204)—which enticed Augustus to murder Caesarion, the real son of Caesar and Cleopatra.

94 Mark and Matthew speak in only one passage of Jesus as 'the Lord', Ὁ κύριος: Mk. 11:3 = Mt. 21:3. In addition, Mark uses this term only once as a form of address (7:28). Matthew has it several times. Only Luke uses it more often. At the time of Matthew and Luke (between 70 and 100 AD) the term *dominus = kyrios* as a designation of and an address to the emperor had established itself, following Oriental custom.

95 The Greek ΚΑΙΣΑΡ ΣΕΒΑΣΤΟΣ respectively ΚΑΙCΑΡ CΕΒΑCΤΟC for the Latin *CAESAR AVGVSTVS* is the common name of the later emperors, which was abbreviated in different ways in inscriptions and on coins and finally with the simple *K.C.* (cf. VON AULOK (1957-68), nr. 19, coin of Traianus from Amasia in the Pontus). While on the Latin emperors' coins the title *pontifex maximus* was regularly written, mostly abbreviated P. M., on the Greek ones the correspondent *archiereus megistos* is found extremely seldom (if we do not err lastly on a coin of Caligula-Augustus from Crete with the obverse inscription ΓΑΙΟΣ ΚΑΙΣΑΡ ΣΕΒ. ΓΕΡΜ. ΑΡΧ. ΜΕΓ. ΔΗΜ. ΕΞΟΥ ΥΠΑ). This is probably connected with the fact that except for Augustus who could only become *pontifex maximus* i.e. *archiereus megistos* after the death of Lepidus in 12 BC, all other emperors normally took on the title as a rule at their enthronement already, so that at least in the Greek-speaking East *archiereus megistos* was an understood attribute of *Kaisar Sebastos*. This would mean that the title *archiereus megistos* had become ownerless in the East—and could be usurped.

96 Accordingly the *magister equitum,* the Grand Master of the Horse, was his proxy.

97 Cf. Jn. 1:38: 'Rabbi, (which is to say, being interpreted, Master)'. Ῥαββί, ὃ λέγεται μεθερμηνευόμενον Διδάσκαλε. It could also be translated: 'Rabbi—that is master, translated', then ‹Rabbi› would be the translation of ‹Master›.

98 Cf. in English 'dictation', 'to dictate', see also the German 'Dichter' (poet, writer), as well as the address 'Master'. *Rabbi* too is originally an address—'(my) Lord'—which later took on the meaning of *(law-)teacher.*

99 Mk. 1:22: ἦν γὰρ διδάσκων αὐτοὺς ὡς ἐξουσίαν ἔχων [...].

100 We have seen that if sound and meaning fall apart, for the one name Caesar, two can emerge in the Gospel: so Iesus as a possible translation of *servator* or as a result of the wearing off of *Gaius Iulius* respectively *Divus Iulius* or *Divi Filius*. Thus two persons in the Caesar story can stand for one in the Gospel—or vice versa. For example:

Lepidus > Pilatus (preservation of the sound)

Praetor Lepidus > Petrus (the sense of *Lepidus,* misunderstood as *lapis, lapidis,* 'stone'; the sound from *praetor)*

Or vice-versa:

praetor (Lepidus) > Petrus

praetor (Antonius) > Petrus

praetor (Brutus) > Petrus

101 Concerning the *oral transmission* of information, there is the well known experiment: a picture is shown to the first student, who has to describe it to the next one and so on. It is then possible to follow the transformation of the story. If the picture was of a woman in black who undresses in front of a man in white, the result can be that a white man has raped a black woman: Thus a medical examination by a doctor turns into a rape. Provided, of course, that there are racial problems in the

area. The story is totally different at the end but the requisites are the same: woman/black/naked, man/white/power.

In such experiments that examine the spreading of rumors (or of information heard through the grapevine), at first a simplification of the original story is observed, which tends toward the threefold unity of time, place and action like in the old theater. Only later does embellishment take place, the function of which, however, is to explain rationally and credibly that which has become incomprehensible. Therefore requisites, changed by folk etymology, may generate others that fit into the new picture and support the requisites in their new function. In the example mentioned above the discarded garment could be torn suddenly, or a bed or a knife may appear. But above all a great deal can be argued round and round: the interpretation gets the upper hand. Sub-themes will also arise which seek to correct contradictions caused in the main story, etc.

It is virtually impossible to trace a narration found at the delta of an oral river back to its source. But if we have both, the mouth and the (supposed) source, it is easy to determine, by the comparison of the requisites, if one is the source of the other or not. So if 'grapevine' effects did become incorporated in the Gospels, then, in the process of verification of our hypothesis, we first have to pay attention only to the requisites and set the story they are embedded in aside for the moment. In this way a possible filiation may be detected.

102 For an example of a transition through three languages cf. i.a., the medicinal herb *Erythraea* which the Greeks named after the centaur Chiron *Kentaurion*, Latin *centaurium* (cf. PLINIUS, *Nat. hist.* 25.66): misunderstood as *centum aurum* ('hundred gold pieces'), in German/Dutch it went beyond the *Hundertgulden,* 'hundred guilders', to the *Tausendgüldenkraut,* 'thousand guilders herb'. Sometimes transitions are not provable. The Hindi word for ape—*markata*—is found again in *meerkat*: a small long-tailed monkey very fond of climbing (e.g. a southern African mongoose, especially the suricate). A Portuguese mediation, *marcata*, misinterpreted as *mar cata*, 'see cat', seems to be obvious but it is not substantiated (Cf. KLUGE [21] 1975, s.v. *Meerkatze*).

It is particularly in the names of flora and fauna that the folk language is mistaken in determining the origin, inferring the wrong mediator from the sound and then proceeding to a fantastic origin: the *Zizyphus iuiuba,* with its characteristic fruits, the 'red or Chinese dates' is called, according to the botanical name, 'common Jujube' in German, but the thorny shrub or tree of the Jujube, became *Judendorn,* 'thorn of the Jews' in the vernacular. A similar thing happened to the *Helianthus tuberosus,* a root tasting like artichoke which was named after the sunflower *girasole,* 'turning with the sun', by the Italo-Americans, and became *Jerusalem artichoke* in the USA, albeit not an artichoke and not from Jerusalem (communication by Erika Simon).

The role played by a third term as an attraction pole in the mechanism of folk etymology is illustrated by the German *radikal,* 'radical' > *ratzekahl,* 'absolutely bare', influenced by *tabula rasa;* idem with the French *forcené* < *for-senné,* 'out of mind', with the influence of *energumène*. For the incorporation of the article cf. the assistant of Commissaire Moulin in the French TV-criminal series: *Katzmann*, 'cat-man', called *Shalom* (< *chat l'homme*). For the incorporation of other particles cf. the German nickname *Owi* for the smiling Jesus-child in the crib, from the Christmas-song: *Stille Nacht ... Gottes Sohn oh wie lacht / Liebe aus deinem göttlichen Mund / da uns schlägt die rettende Stund, / Christ in deiner Geburt...—Gottes Sohn oh wie lacht,* 'Son of God, O how love laughs from out Thy godly mouth...' > *Gottes Sohn, Owi, lacht,* 'God's Son, Owi, laughs'...: *oh wie,* 'oh, how', was bound together to *Owi,* and taken for the proper name of the Jesus-child.

It is not unusual that animals pop up in folk etymology providing an outlet for the people's respective love or hatred of them.

Elephants never roamed around the London *Elephant and Castle* and one would seek the castle in vain. The name is the legacy of a visit by a Spanish princess, when the common people had to shout out in her language : '*A l'infante de Castilla!*'.

The *Mäuseturm,* 'mice-tower', near Bingen on the river Rhine owes its name not to any *mice* but to the *Maut,* 'toll', that was exacted there: when the memory of the ancient *Maut* was long gone, popular idiom turned the *Maut-tower* into a *Mice-tower* (German *Maus/Mäuse = mouse/mice*).

Buffalo are not to be found in the American city called *Buffalo,* nor any bison, but there is a beautiful river, christened *beau fleuve* by the French, which naturally sounded like *Buffalo* to the ears of the Englishman.

People insist on calling police by animal names in all languages: in Germany they are called *Bullen* (bulls), in French *poulets* (chickens), in England *pigs,* in Italy *poia* and *puia* (buzzard). Different animals, as we see, but they have one thing in common: they always are the animal whose name in the respective languages corresponds most closely to the respective language's word for *police* (*polizia, Polizei,* etc). It does not matter which animal, the main thing is that it is one. And how far removed phonetically the animal's name is from the respective word for *policeman/police* is determined by chance: in the word *Bullen* the hissing end-sound is missing, in the words *pigs* and *puia* the 'l', etc. The main thing being that they are approximately called by their name!

We must not forget that this is not about the development of language in the sense of Indo-European linguistics with its regular sound shifts, but about folk etymologies, folk 'etymolocheats' one could say. This is particularly the case with folk etymologies arising from feelings of awe—the so-called occultatives. We can observe how far removed this can be from the laws of sound shift. This happens if e.g. a Bavarian while cursing conceals his *Sakrament!* (sacrament) behind a *Sack Zement!* (sack of cement), or also when a Venetian covers his *ostia!* (the sacred Host) with *ostrega!* (the humble oyster). We see how sometimes sounds disappear or how they can originate out of necessity, as in this case the 'r', 'z' and 'g'. The main thing is they are hidden, right under our noses!

Folk etymologies can also lead to symbolic reinterpretations. The sausage, e.g., stands for anal or sexual associations in almost all languages, depending on its form and size from *hot dog* to *Negersäckel,* 'black man's pouch', the term for blood-sausage in German rural areas. Almost everywhere—but not in Northern Italy. There, *sausage* is used as a synonym for stupidity: a *salame,* 'salami', is an idiot. The reason is that a big salami is called a *salamon,* which sounds like *Solomon*—the epitome of the wise man. So it is said of anyone who was behind the door when the brains were handed out that he is no 'Solomon', but rather a 'salamon'—a big salami. So salami became a synonym for stupidity—contrary to its namesake. Anyhow the new association also helped to expose some sacerdotal pseudo-wisdom, wrapped in biblical Latin, as brainwashing of the people: an enlightening side effect!

Could this have occurred with us in the same way as in the former times of the Church, when the priest scarcely knew any Latin and the people none, leading to inevitable slips of the pen and the tongue, funny misunderstandings and roguish corruptions: *Hoc est corpus > hocus-pocus. In nomine pax > kannst wechsle, Max?*—'can you change, Max?': originally a play on words between *nomen,* 'name', and *nummus,* 'coin'). Or also on the base of a different language : *Salam aleikum > ich zahl, wenn ich vorbei kum.*—'I'll pay when I come by'.

Is the Gospel the missal of the poor in spirit?

Folk etymologies always occur when vernacular is involved. When, however, scholars cause it one speaks of *Verballhornungen* (erudite corruptions/bastardizations/

transmogrifications). The result is often still more exciting. He who gave his name to this process—of making things worse rather than better by changing the sense whilst intending to correct what was supposedly wrong—was no layman but a scholar, a printer from Lübeck, Germany: Joh. Balhorn the younger. In 1586 he edited the 'Lübische Recht', the law of the city of Lübeck, 'Auffs Newe vbersehen, Corrigiret'. The printer was blamed for the fateful erroneous improvements of the editors. Actually 'one should write 'Verbalhornung' (ver-Balhorn-ung) with only one 'l', but this would present the danger of it being read as 'Verbal-hornung'—and this would be another Verballhornung. For this reason 'Verballhornung' is written with two 'l'"s: is this not itself one: 'Ver-ball-hornung'?

As a matter of fact there are only a few genuine folk etymologies: most of them are scholarly corruptions, that are decreed to be folk etymologies once they are detected in order to preserve them like *forcené* and *Tausendgüldenkraut*.

And there are things that the scholars do not want to admit because of ideological reasons. So the Indo-European philologists with their tribal idea of languages according to the maxim that 'the inheritance goes through the bood', only accept words of consanguinity, and conversely all noble words have to be of consanguinity. So *meerkat* (literally 'sea-cat') is not permitted to originate from the Indian *markata*, and *Arbeit*, 'work', has to be a German word because of the *deutsche Wertarbeit*, 'German quality work'. So it is fabulated that the word *Arbeit* originated from an Indo-Germanic root *orbho-*, which means 'orphaned' and then became the Germanic *arbhêjô*, 'am an orphaned (and hence obliged to heavy work) child'. There's a rub in this explanation: *Arbeit*, 'work', never meant 'child or servant labor', but from the beginning the meaning was 'utilizing nature, agriculture' or even 'hardship' (Cf. KLUGE ^{21}1975, s.v. Arbeit). Further, the word *Arbeit* comes from the south—in the north we already have *Werk, work,* etc. And in the south there is a word that means 'utilizing nature, farming' and 'trouble' as well, which is the medieval Latin *laborat(um)*. Since the initial 'l' sound is often lost in words because it is taken to be the definite article (cf. German *Oleander < lorandum* or Venetian *osmarin < l'osmarin < rosmarin*), we may assume an *aborat* as the intermediate stage which could become, by metathesis of the liquid, *arabot* as the possible basic form for the origin of the Slavic *rabota* (by the loss of the 'a' which was taken to be a Greek article) and the Old High German *arabeit*. But this is not even allowed to be considered: where would we end up?

103 In the bilingual Roman Empire, Greek correspondences were sought for the Latin terms of the official Roman language. In Leipzig in 1905, David Magie published a treatise on the manner of how the Roman festive vocabulary was rendered in Greek, and he identifies three methods which followed each other in the course of the centuries: in the most ancient times by comparison *(comparatio)*—so for example *populus* was rendered as *dêmos*—later, when there were no longer any Greek correspondences, firstly by translation *(interpretatio)*—so for example *censor* became *timêtês*—and finally by adoption, borrowing of the Roman terminology *(transcriptio)*—a process where *dictator* did not become *autokratôr*, but rather *diktatôr* instead (Cf. MAGIE 1905).

But if we take a look at which word succeeds amongst the different possible variants, we find an astonishing fact: for the word *senatus* it is not the classical *boulê* that becomes accepted, nor even *gerousia*, qua meaning the best translation, but (besides *synedrion*) *synklêtos*. For *imperator* (sometimes also for *dictator*) *autokratôr*, 'absolute ruler', was said. For *lictor,* the usher with the lictor-bundles, it was said *liturgos*, 'functionary, servant of the state'. For *Augustus,* the title of the emperor Octavianus and then of his successors too, it was said *Sebastos*, 'revered (Sir)'. If we list all these correspondences, we detect the attempt to choose words that are close in sense as well as in sound. Actually, to preserve the sound, diminutions of sense were tolerated:

senatus > synklêtos / imperator resp. *dictator > autokratôr / lictor > liturgos / Augustus > Sebastos.*

It is seen very clearly with *synklêtos*, which means 'called together, convoked' (and hence more appropriate as the translation of *comitium calatum*) and also with *dictator*, who indeed ruled by himself but did so within the framework of the constitution and so was not *sui iuris*—he was not an 'autocrat'; the same goes for *imperator*, who in his original sense of *victor* was more likely a *nikatôr*, a 'winner'; it also goes for *lictor*, who got his name from *ligo*, the 'bundle' he carried—he was not just a simple 'civil servant'; and it applies to *Augustus,* a name that the Romans took partly from *augeo,* 'to increase, to let it grow' and partly from observation of the flight of birds *(ab avium gustu)*—so it did not stand for a typical 'revered one' at all.

It is striking that the resemblance of sound was always aimed at the ending of the word and only at the beginning of the word if possible.

We rather have to be astonished that in general the other names in the Gospels remain so close to those of Caesar's vita. Seemingly the similarity of sound was more important for the editors of the Gospels than for the magistrates: After all, they had to proselytize; the civil servants did not have to convince anybody.

With respect to Caesar's official titles the Greek terms in comparison to the Latin ones are shown to be similar:

Dictator stays: *diktator; consul* is translated: *hypatos; imperator* is rendered as *autokratôr,* which is not a correct translation. For the word means the same as the Latin *sui iuris*—between 'absolute ruling' and 'plenipotentiary'. Even in the combined meaning of 'unlimited lord and master' *autokratôr* represents *dictator* better than *imperator.* Apparently it was chosen because *autokratôr* is phonetically closer to *imperator*—like the later *sebastos* is closer to *augustus.* A comparable situation is observed between the titles *pontifex maximus* and *archiereus megistos. Arch-iereus* would be enough, because *arch-* already gives the idea of *maximus,* like *iereus* that of *pontifex:* but yet we find in addition also its full form, even if pleonastic, probably because *archiereus megistos* is rhythmically and phonetically close to *pontifex maximus.*

104 The classic example here is the London *Elephant and Castle:* As we have seen above it originates from: 'A l'infante de Castilla!'. This disappoints the tourist who expects to see the castle of a Maharaja and imagines himself in India.

In the Paris Metro one can fantasize being on a railroad trip through Europe: *Anvers, Rennes, Liège, Plaisance, Danube, Crimée, Stalingrad…* or, following Napoleon: *Solferino, Campo-Formio, Wagram, Austerlitz, Le Kremlin-Bicêtre* (the last one is a French corruption of *Winchester*), *Pyramides*—the last one points to Caesar: *Alésia, Rome* etc.

In the US one keeps on coming across doublets of European towns: *Paris, Venice, Amsterdam, Toledo* etc.—without counting the 'New' ones: *New York, New Orleans* etc. In polyglot Switzerland it is even easier to be sent on a journey: thus an American travel guide once counselled caution because all the towns have three names there, a German, a French and an Italian one, for example: *Basel/Bâle/Basilea, Genf/Genève/Ginevra* or … *Luzern/Lausanne/Locarno* (sic!—these three being really three different cities).

In America, names that were originally European have sometimes experienced a second mutation and migration: so it is thought that the people called *Cajun* or *Cajan,* half-bloods in the South of Alabama and Mississippi, received their names from the *Acadian,* descendants of French speaking immigrants from Louisiana who were forcibly resettled.

Stereotype city-names like for example the many called *Heliopolis* or *Nikopolis* caused confusion, especially those which were named after a ruler like *Alexandria, Seleukia, Antiochia, Ptolemais, Caesarea* etc. The greater the ruler's house and duration of the dynasty, the more prevalent the city-name and the greater the confusion, occurring in former times just as it sometimes occurs among modern historians: in which *Antiochia* or in which *Caesarea* did this or that event occur? To which *Alexandria* did Caesar want to relocate the capital of the Empire? The context decides. But what if it is precisely the context that is misleading? Or what if the location itself determines the context? Then an event is suddenly located at another place and the context is fantasized accordingly. Then we find ourselves in a right mess!

Our suspicion is that the Gospels are exactly such a mess. We need to find the original ingredients, and this is only possible if we detect the first delocalization.

III. Crux

105 Mk. 14:61: ὁ δὲ ἐσιώπα καὶ οὐκ ἀπεκρίνατο οὐδέν. Mk. 15:5: ὁ δὲ ᾿Ιησοῦς οὐκέτι οὐδὲν ἀπεκρίθη [...].

106 Mk. 14:62: ὁ δὲ ᾿Ιησοῦς εἶπεν, Σὺ εἶπας ὅτι ἐγώ εἰμι (Θφ pc arm Or); 15:2: ὁ δὲ ἀποκριθεὶς αὐτῷ λέγει, Σὺ λέγεις.

107 Mk. 15:34: Ελωι ελωι λεμα σαβαχθανι; ὅ ἐστιν μεθερμηνευόμενον Ὁ θεός μου ὁ θεός μου, εἰς τί ἐγκατέλιπές με; Mt. 27:46: Ηλι ηλι λεμα σαβαχθανι; τοῦτ' ἔστιν, Θεέ μου θεέ μου, ἱνατί με ἐγκατέλιπες; Lk. 23:46: Πάτερ, εἰς χεῖράς σου παρατίθεμαι τὸ πνεῦμά μου. Jn. 19:26: Γύναι, ἴδε ὁ υἱός σου. 19:27: ῎Ιδε ἡ μήτηρ σου. 19:28: Διψῶ. 19:30: Τετέλεσται.

It should be noted that Caesar's biographers reproduce different traditions of Caesar's last words as well. Appianus (2.117) speaks of Caesar's loud clamor when he was still trying to resist, but that after Brutus' stroke he wrapped himself in his robe and fell to the floor in a dignified posture. Plutarchus (66) agrees with Appianus but knows that initially Caesar shouted to the first attacker Casca in Latin: 'Wicked Casca, what are you doing?' Dio Cassius (44.19) also reports that when they all stabbed at him, Caesar was unable to say or do anything and only wrapped up his face, but that some add, that when Brutus stabbed at him he said the famous: 'You too, my son?' Suetonius also has this dictum, which had come down to him by others. He specifies that Caesar expressed it in Greek, but besides that speaks of Caesar's silence and claims that he only uttered a single sigh. That is to say, with Caesar, as well as with Jesus, the constant factor is the silence with clamor and finally a sigh, while the alleged last words do not appear in all reports, and, when they do, they are not the same.

108 Mk. 15:22: [...] καὶ φέρουσιν αὐτὸν ἐπὶ τὸν Γολγοθᾶν τόπον, ὅ ἐστιν μεθερμηνευόμενον Κρανίου Τόπος.

109 Jn. 19:33-4: ἐπὶ δὲ τὸν ᾿Ιησοῦν ἐλθόντες [...] ἀλλ' εἷς τῶν στρατιωτῶν λόγχῃ αὐτοῦ τὴν πλευρὰν ἔνυξεν, καὶ ἐξῆλθεν εὐθὺς αἷμα καὶ ὕδωρ.

110 Jn. 19:35: καὶ ὁ ἑωρακὼς μεμαρτύρηκεν, καὶ ἀληθινὴ αὐτοῦ ἐστιν ἡ μαρτυρία, καὶ ἐκεῖνος οἶδεν ὅτι ἀληθῆ λέγει, ἵνα καὶ ὑμεῖς πιστεύ[σ]ητε.

111 Jn. 19:36-7: ἐγένετο γὰρ ταῦτα ἵνα ἡ γραφὴ πληρωθῇ, [...] ῎Οψονται εἰς ὃν ἐξεκέντησαν.

112 Acta Pilati XVI, in SCHNEEMELCHER (1990), vol. 1, p. 413.

113 Mk. 14:47: εἷς δέ [τις] τῶν παρεστηκότων σπασάμενος τὴν μάχαιραν ἔπαισεν τὸν δοῦλον τοῦ ἀρχιερέως καὶ ἀφεῖλεν αὐτοῦ τὸ ὠτάριον.

114 Mk. 14:48: καὶ ἀποκριθεὶς ὁ ᾿Ιησοῦς εἶπεν αὐτοῖς, Ὡς ἐπὶ λῃστὴν ἐξήλθατε μετὰ μαχαιρῶν καὶ ξύλων συλλαβεῖν με;

115 App. BC 2.117: πολλοί τε διωθιζόμενοι μετὰ τῶν ξιφῶν ἀλλήλους ἔπληξαν.
116 Servants appear at the attempt on Caesar as well. We will see later in what role; cf. Suet. Jul. 82.
117 App. BC 2.117: καὶ Κάσσιος ἐς τὸ πρόσωπον ἔπληξε.
118 Suet. Jul. 82: Nec in tot vulneribus, ut Antistius medicus existimabat, letale ullum repertum est, nisi quod secundo loco in pectore acceperat.
119 Mk.15:26: καὶ ἦν ἡ ἐπιγραφὴ τῆς αἰτίας αὐτοῦ ἐπιγεγραμμένη, Ὁ βασιλεὺς τῶν Ἰουδαίων. Lk.23:38: ἦν δὲ καὶ ἐπιγραφὴ ἐπ' αὐτῷ, Ὁ βασιλεὺς τῶν Ἰουδαίων οὗτος. Mt.27:37: καὶ ἐπέθηκαν ἐπάνω τῆς κεφαλῆς αὐτοῦ τὴν αἰτίαν αὐτοῦ γεγραμμένην· Οὗτός ἐστιν Ἰησοῦς ὁ βασιλεὺς τῶν Ἰουδαίων. Jn.19:19: ἔγραψεν δὲ καὶ τίτλον ὁ Πιλᾶτος καὶ ἔθηκεν ἐπὶ τοῦ σταυροῦ· ἦν δὲ γεγραμμένον, Ἰησοῦς ὁ Ναζωραῖος ὁ βασιλεὺς τῶν Ἰουδαίων.
120 For the written fixation of the accusation against Caesar cf. Cic. Phil. 2.85-7: [...] adscribi iussit in fastis ad Lupercalia C. Caesari dictatori perpetuo M. Antonium consulem populi iussu regnum detulisse: Caesarem uti noluisse.
Cf. also the writings on the tribunal of Brutus (App. BC 112; Plut. Caes. 62).
121 Cf. i.a. Suet. Jul. 79-80: proximo autem senatu Lucium Cottam quindecimvirum sententiam dicturum, ut, quoniam fatalibus libris contineretur Parthos nisi a rege non posse vinci, Caesar rex appellaretur. quae causa coniuratis maturandi fuit destinata negotia, ne assentiri necesse esset.
122 Cf. Magie (1905), p.62, 68.
123 Mk.15:21: Καὶ ἀγγαρεύουσιν παράγοντά τινα Σίμωνα Κυρηναῖον ἐρχόμενον ἀπ' ἀγροῦ, τὸν πατέρα Ἀλεξάνδρου καὶ Ῥούφου, ἵνα ἄρῃ τὸν σταυρὸν αὐτοῦ.
124 The form ἄρῃ is an active one (conj. aor. 1 a., 3. s.). One could only translate it with 'would carry' if the respective medium: ἄρηται—'he carried for himself, he carried away' were in place here. For airô in contrast to pherô cf. Mk.2:3: καὶ ἔρχονται φέροντες πρὸς αὐτὸν παραλυτικὸν αἰρόμενον ὑπὸ τεσσάρων. Mk.6:8 does not contradict it, because there airô is used in the sense of 'to carry with themselves; to take along'.
125 Mk.15:24: καὶ σταυρώσαντες αὐτὸν διαμερίζονται τὰ ἱμάτια αὐτοῦ, βάλλοντες κλῆρον ἐπ' αὐτὰ [...]; Mt.27:35: σταυρώσαντες δὲ αὐτὸν διεμερίσαντο τὰ ἱμάτια αὐτοῦ, βάλλοντες κλῆρον [...]; Lk.23:33: [...] ἐκεῖ ἐσταύρωσαν αὐτὸν [...]; Jn.19:18: [...] ὅπου αὐτὸν ἐσταύρωσαν [...].
126 'Cross' in the sense of 'to make a cross' is in classic Greek *chiasma* respectively *chiasmos*, 'to order anything cross-shape' *chiazô*. These words are also familiar to us, for example as *chiasma*, the 'crossing over' of chromosomes in biology or as *chiasmus*, 'to put crosswise' in the syntax. The basis was the letter *chi* = X, for the Greeks the genuine symbol of the cross. 'Cross' in the meaning of 'to carry his cross', hence for 'pain' is called *ponos, penthos* or *lypê*. *Stavros*, which as noted above originally meant 'stake', 'slat' or 'palisade', was never associated with the cross in classic times, and even when in the course of the Christianization it took on the meaning 'cross' in the sense of the 'martyr-stake', its symbol was a T and not a †. This originates from the fact that in the Greek word *stavros* the crossing of beams is not constitutive, so little so, that the Christians themselves originally did not translate it with the Latin *crux* either. They should have done that if it had been its back-translation, instead they translated it with *lignum*, 'wood'. This is still preserved in the well known Good Friday formula: *'Ecce lignum crucis, in quo salus mundi pependit'*, which is officially translated as: 'Behold the wood of the cross, on which the salvation of the world was hung', and which could also be translated differently, for example as: 'Here is the wood of torture, wherewith the salvation of the world was paid'. Here it is important however, that it doesn't say *crux* alone, but *lignum crucis*, whereby *stavros* is not rendered by *crux* as one might think but by *lignum*, which means 'wood' in the sense of the substance primarily, thus 'piece of

wood' and in the plural, *ligna*, 'firewood'. And thus we are at Caesar's funeral pile again.

127 Mk. 15:23: [...] καὶ ἐδίδουν αὐτῷ ἐσμυρνισμένον οἶνον· ὃς δὲ οὐκ ἔλαβεν.
128 Mt. 27:34: ἔδωκαν αὐτῷ πιεῖν ὄξος μετὰ χολῆς μεμιγμένον· καὶ γευσάμενος οὐκ ἠθέλησεν πιεῖν.
129 Lk. 23:36: οἱ στρατιῶται προσερχόμενοι, ὄξος προσφέροντες αὐτῷ [...].
130 Lk. 23:55-6: ἐθεάσαντο τὸ μνημεῖον καὶ ὡς ἐτέθη τὸ σῶμα αὐτοῦ, ὑποστρέψασαι δὲ ἡτοίμασαν ἀρώματα καὶ μύρα.
131 It should not be a surprise that 'aromatics' respectively 'aromatics and ointments' is found here: aromatics were used at funerals in both forms to alleviate the cadaverous smell, they were used in cremations to an even greater extent. Besides incense, sometimes whole dolls of cloves were burned as well. Oils and ointments were used for the same purpose and for the preservation of the corpse before the cremation, which sometimes happened many days later, see below.
132 Jn. 19:29-30: σπόγγον οὖν μεστὸν τοῦ ὄξους ὑσσώπῳ περιθέντες προσήνεγκαν αὐτοῦ τῷ στόματι. ὅτε οὖν ἔλαβεν τὸ ὄξος—'Ysop' ὑσσώπῳ or ὑσσῷ—(h)yssôi—looks like a doublet of vinegar ὄξῳ—oxôi—but on the other hand like the anagram of 'Piso', Caesar's father in law, who took charge of the funeral and who brought the body to the Forum.
133 Jn. 19:39-40: [...] φέρων μίγμα σμύρνης καὶ ἀλόης ὡς λίτρας ἑκατόν. ἔλαβον οὖν τὸ σῶμα τοῦ Ἰησοῦ καὶ ἔδησαν αὐτὸ ὀθονίοις μετὰ τῶν ἀρωμάτων, καθὼς ἔθος ἐστὶν τοῖς Ἰουδαίοις ἐνταφιάζειν.
134 This word comes from ΣΜΥΡΝΑ—*smyrna*—variation of ΜΥΡΡΑ—*myrrha*—like for example *smikros* could stand for *mikros*, 'small': The sigma tends to proliferate in Greek. The use of *smyrna* for *myrrha* could be based on the fact that these, like the other oriental aromatics, were imported into Greece through the port of Smyrna, located at the mouth of the Persian royal trade route, which stretched from Susa over Sardes to Ionia. But because with the ΜΥΡΑ—*myra*—of Luke only the part *myr* is common—*esMYRnismenon* (the beginning of the word *es-* can be a prefix in Greek)—so only ΜΥΡ(Α)—*myr(a)*—appears to be certain. For that matter the difference between 'rr' and 'r' in ΜΥΡΡΑ and ΜΥΡΑ is irrelevant, because in the late classical period the double consonants were pronounced like single ones. Cf. CHARALAMBAKIS (1984), Σ. 88 7.1.7· Τά διπλά σύμφωνα (ἄλ-λος, ἄμ-μος) ἄρχισαν νά ἁπλοποιοῦνται στήν προφορά.
135 APP. BC 2.148: [...] καὶ ξύλα αὐτῷ καὶ βάθρα, ὅσα πολλὰ ἦν ἐν ἀγορᾷ, καὶ εἴ τι τοιουτότροπον ἄλλο συνενεγκόντες, καὶ τὴν πομπὴν δαψιλεστάτην οὖσαν ἐπιβαλόντες, στεφάνους τε ἔνιοι παρ' ἑαυτῶν καὶ ἀριστεῖα πολλὰ ἐπιθέντες [...].
136 PLUT. Caes. 68: [...] αὐτῶν τὸ πάθος, ἀλλὰ τῷ μὲν νεκρῷ περισωρεύσαντες ἐξ ἀγορᾶς βάθρα καὶ κιγκλίδας καὶ τραπέζας [...].
137 SUET. Jul. 84: [...] *confestimque circumstantium turba virgulta arida et cum subsellis tribunalia, quicquid praeterea ad donum aderat, congessit. deinde tibicines et scaenici artifices vestem, quam ex triumphorum instrumento ad praesentem usum induerant, detractam sibi atque discissam iniecere flammae et veteranorum militum legionarii arma sua, quibus exculti funus celebrabant; matronae etiam pleraeque ornamenta sua, quae gerebant, et liberorum bullas atque praetextas.*
138 APP. BC 2.148: ἐξῆψαν καὶ τὴν νύκτα πανδημεὶ τῇ πυρᾷ παρέμενον [...].
139 This polysemy of verbs occurs in every language. For example in German when a car 'hält an'—literally 'holds on'—it stops; but if the rain 'hält an'—also literally 'holds on'—it continues; if a law is 'aufgehoben'- literally 'lifted up'—it is 'repealed' and gone, but if milk is 'aufgehoben'—also literally 'lifted up'—it is 'retained' and you still have it; if a synthesis occurs and 'hebt auf'—'lifts up'—thesis and antithesis, it 'resolves' them, although the student of philosophy might ruminate: 'aufgehoben' as in the case with law or milk?

In Greek the polysemy is more extreme: even the most everyday verb, *erchomai*, means 'to come' as well as 'to go'—it depends. The Greeks do not have a problem with that, they even seem to apply their particular verbal gymnastics to other codes. When the foreign driver in Greece unexpectedly sees a street-sign at a crossing with an arrow pointing *down*, he should not search for the entry to a tunnel that leads to the village named on the sign: it simply means the village is located *behind you*; if you want to go there, you have to make a U-turn and go back.

140 APP. BC 2.148: [...] ὁ δὲ δῆμος ἐπὶ τὸ λέχος τοῦ Καίσαρος ἐπανελθὼν ἔφερον αὐτὸ ἐς τὸ Καπιτώλιον [...].

141 Mk. 15:22: [...] καὶ φέρουσιν αὐτὸν ἐπὶ τὸν Γολγοθᾶν τόπον, ὅ ἐστιν μεθερμηνευόμενον Κρανίου Τόπος.

142 αγουσιν Dφ lat—cf. ALAND & NESTLE ([18]1957).

143 ARNOBIUS *Adversus gentes* VI 7; SERVIUS *Aeneid-Commentary* VIII 345; the chronograph of the year 354 specifies that *'caput Oli regis'* was written on the skull in Etruscan letters; cf. also ISIDOR *Origines* XV 2.31.

144 Lk. 23:33: [...] τὸν τόπον τὸν καλούμενον Κρανίον [...]; Jn. 19:17: [...] τὸν λεγόμενον Κρανίου Τόπον, ὃ λέγεται Ἑβραϊστὶ Γολγοθᾶ [...]; Matthew does not contradict this, because both times he says 'called': 27:33: τόπον λεγόμενον Γολγοθᾶ, ὅ ἐστιν Κρανίου Τόπος λεγόμενος [...].

This passage gives us the opportunity to clearly see how ideologically biased the work of latter-day bible translators is. As late as the beginning of the 17th century the King James Version translates Jn. 19:17 (v.s.) verbatim:

'[...] tòn legómenon Kraníou Tópon, (h)ó légetai (H)ebraïstì Golgothá [...]'—'[And he bearing his cross went forth into a place] called *(tòn legómenon)* the place of a skull, which is called *(légetai)* in the Hebrew Golgotha'.

But by now word has got around that *légô* sometimes must also be understood in the sense of 'to mean', which would advise to translate the second 'called'—*légetai*—as 'means'. Accordingly one would have to write (the rest of sentence remaining the same):

'[And he bearing his cross went forth into a place] called *(ton legómenon)* the place of a skull, which means *(légetai)* in the Hebrew Golgotha.'

This, however, apparently is intolerable for the orthodox scholars and actually one has turned up who does not just attenuate the testimony like e.g. the *KJV* but outright distorts it. The *Worldwide English (New Testament) (WE)* plainly reverses the terms and makes it:

'[They took Jesus and led him away. Jesus went out carrying his own cross. They went to a place] that the Jews called Golgotha. That means "the place of the skull bone".'

Thus out of the name's Hebrew translation they make the name itself, and out of the Greek name they make its explanation. Why?—one wonders. The answer is very simple: in order to maintain and reinforce the fiction that the Hebrew name is the original one, and with it to pseudo-scripturally support the delocalization of the whole story from Rome to Jerusalem by an again distorted translation of the Greek text. The thing about it is that they are not even liars: they really believe it is the correct translation. Their ideological glasses sit so firmly on their noses that they do not even notice anymore how they twist the meaning of the text right round. Misrepresentation has become second nature to them. And in order to guard their contorted minds against doubts they distort the letter—without feelings of guilt. After all, the spirit prevails over the letter, doesn't it?

In order to guard against misunderstandings: We do not think that *(h)ó légetai (H)ebraïstì Golgothá* must absolutely denote 'which means in the Hebrew Golgotha'. The established meaning of *légetai* is '(it) is said', like of *legómenon* it is 'the so-called', 'as the saying goes'. *'Tòn legómenon Kraníou Tópon'* could thus be translated as 'according to legend called place of skull'—which leads us back to the saga of the *caput Oli*, 'Skull of Olus', found on the Capitoline hill (cf. text p. 70) and which suggests that the continuation of the sentence *(h)ó légetai (H)ebraïstì Golgothá*, conceals a prior *(h)ó légetai Rômaïstì Kapitôlion*, 'which is called in the Latin Capitolium', representing its bowdlerizing misspelling.

Thus, at the same time it would be shown, though, that our latter-day bible translators still have the 'right' wrong attitude of mind: they are doing nothing else but continuing the concealment of the 'Julian' origin of the Gospel which already occurred in the old manuscripts behind an allegedly 'Judaic' one.

145 SUET. *Jul.* 84: *Quem cum pars in Capitolini Iovis cella cremare, pars in curia Pompei destinaret, repente duo quidam gladiis succincti ac bina iacula gestantes ardentibus cereis succenderunt [...].*

146 Mk. 15:27: Καὶ σὺν αὐτῷ σταυροῦσιν δύο λῃστάς, ἕνα ἐκ δεξιῶν καὶ ἕνα ἐξ εὐωνύμων αὐτοῦ.

147 SUET. *Jul.* 84: *Funere indicto rogus instructus est in martio campo iuxta Iuliae tumulum [...]*. This was independent of the fact that it was part of the honor decrees adopted for Caesar that he should be interred within the Pomerium (cf. DIO CASS. *HR* 44.7.1).

148 Mk. 15:16-20: Οἱ δὲ στρατιῶται ἀπήγαγον αὐτὸν ἔσω τῆς αὐλῆς, ὅ ἐστιν πραιτώριον, καὶ συγκαλοῦσιν ὅλην τὴν σπεῖραν. καὶ ἐνδιδύσκουσιν αὐτὸν πορφύραν καὶ περιτιθέασιν αὐτῷ πλέξαντες ἀκάνθινον στέφανον· καὶ ἤρξαντο ἀσπάζεσθαι αὐτόν, Χαῖρε, βασιλεῦ τῶν Ἰουδαίων· καὶ ἔτυπτον αὐτοῦ τὴν κεφαλὴν καλάμῳ καὶ ἐνέπτυον αὐτῷ καὶ τιθέντες τὰ γόνατα προσεκύνουν αὐτῷ. καὶ ὅτε ἐνέπαιξαν αὐτῷ, ἐξέδυσαν αὐτὸν τὴν πορφύραν καὶ ἐνέδυσαν αὐτὸν τὰ ἱμάτια αὐτοῦ. καὶ ἐξάγουσιν αὐτὸν ἵνα σταυρώσωσιν αὐτόν.

149 Jn. 19:23: Οἱ οὖν στρατιῶται ὅτε ἐσταύρωσαν τὸν Ἰησοῦν, ἔλαβον τὰ ἱμάτια αὐτοῦ καὶ ἐποίησαν τέσσαρα μέρη, ἑκάστῳ στρατιώτῃ μέρος, καὶ τὸν χιτῶνα. ἦν δὲ ὁ χιτὼν ἄρραφος, ἐκ τῶν ἄνωθεν ὑφαντὸς δι᾽ ὅλου.

150 APP. *BC* 2.148: ἐξῆψαν καὶ τὴν νύκτα πανδημεὶ τῇ πυρᾷ παρέμενον [...].

151 Mk. 15:25: ἦν δὲ ὥρα τρίτη καὶ ἐσταύρωσαν (**D**: ἐφύλασσον) αὐτόν. Here the lection of *D* has to be preferred, as *lectio difficilior*. An emendation to 'and they crucified him and watched over him' would not change anything.

152 Lk. 23:35: καὶ εἱστήκει ὁ λαὸς θεωρῶν. 23:44: Καὶ ἦν ἤδη ὡσεὶ ὥρα ἕκτη καὶ σκότος ἐγένετο ἐφ᾽ ὅλην τὴν γῆν ἕως ὥρας ἐνάτης [...].

153 The wax-figure of Augustus at his funeral was clad in the triumphal garb—as later that of Pertinax was as well (cf. DIO CASS. *HR* 56.34.1; 74.4.3). Conversely Traianus was represented at his posthumous Parthian triumph in 117 AD by his imago (cf. *SHA* Hadr. 6.3; J.-C. RICHARD, *REL* 44, 1966, p. 358).

154 Cf. NICOLAUS DAMASCENUS, *Bios Kaisaros*, *FGrH*, ed. F. Jacoby, 26.97: ὁρᾶν δ᾽ ἐνῆν ἔνθεν καὶ ἔνθεν ἀπεσταλμένων τῶν παρακαλυμμάτων, αἰωρουμένας τὰς χεῖρας καί τὰς ἐπὶ τοῦ προσώπου πληγάς.—'as the curtains were drawn back, the dangling arms and the wounds on his face could be seen from both sides.' Cf. also SUET. *Jul.* 82: *Exanimis diffugientibus cunctis aliquandiu iacuit, donec lecticae impositum, dependente brachio, tres seruoli domum rettulerunt.*—'After all had fled he lifelessly lay there for some time until three young slaves placed him in a litter and carried him back home with one arm hanging over the side.'

155 SUET. *Jul.* 84: *pro rostris*—'in front of the Rostra'; APP. *BC* 2.143: ἐπὶ τὰ ἔμβολα—'on the Rostra'.

156 SUET. *Jul.* 84: *[...] et pro rostris aurata aedes ad simulacrum templi Veneris Genetricis collocata; intraque lectus eburneus auro ac purpura stratus et ad caput tropaeum cum ueste, in qua fuerat occisus.*—Cleopatra, who stayed in Rome at that time and whose statue stood in the temple of Venus Genetrix (evidently in her role as incarnation of Isis and hence equated with Venus) apparently co-led the direction.

157 Shakespeare is unfortunately of no help here, because he follows Plutarchus who does not report anything about the ritual of the funeral. Dio's speech of Antonius seems also rhetorically finessed. We reconstruct the situation here mainly from Suetonius and Appianus, who agree with each other; but where Appianus says (*BC* 2.146) that Antonius 'recited many other things', we refer to Dio. We follow partly STAUFFER (1957), p.21-23. But he overlooks that the effigy of wax had to be hanging on the tropaeum, because according to Suetonius (*Jul.* 84, first paragraph: *Funere indicto rogus instructus est in martio campo iuxta Iuliae tumulum et pro rostris aurata aedes ad simulacrum templi Veneris Genetricis collocata; intraque lectus eburneus auro ac purpura stratus et ad caput tropaeum cum ueste, in qua fuerat occisus.*) the toga was hanging there right from the beginning. It must have covered the effigy, as is evident from Appianus (*BC* 2.146: τὸ σῶμα τοῦ Καίσαρος ἐγύμνου καὶ τὴν ἐσθῆτα ἐπὶ κοντοῦ φερομένην ἀνέσειε, λελακισμένην ὑπὸ τῶν πληγῶν καὶ πεφυρμένην αἵματι αὐτοκράτορος.): When Antonius removes the toga, the effigy is exposed. Also the fact that Antonius uses a spear to remove the toga (l. c.), speaks for it unambiguously. With τὸ σῶμα τοῦ Καίσαρος—'the body of Caesar'—Appianus could only mean here the ἀνδρείκελον αὐτοῦ Καίσαρος ἐκ κηροῦ πεποιημένον—'the effigy (literally: the mannequin) of Caesar himself formed from wax' (*BC* 2.147)—because Antonius as priest—apart from being *flamen Diui Iulii* and *lupercus* he was also *augur*—was not allowed to see a corpse (cf. WEINSTOCK 1971, p.354[5], with further proofs); besides—Caesar's body was lying in the death bed as Appianus himself reports: τὸ μὲν γὰρ σῶμα, ὡς ὕπτιον ἐπὶ λέχους, οὐχ ἑωρᾶτο. τὸ δὲ ἀνδρείκελον ἐκ μηχανῆς ἐπεστρέφετο πάντῃ.—'as the body, lying flat on the bier, could not be seen. But the model, with the help of a mechanical device, could be turned in all directions.' This 'mechanical device' could only have been set up in advance, and therefore only at the tropaeum. So the previous sentence of Appianus refers to the erecting of the tropaeum itself, together with the mannequin, or to the heaving of the wax mannequin onto the tropaeum: Ὧδε δὲ αὐτοῖς ἔχουσιν ἤδη καὶ χειρῶν ἐγγὺς οὖσιν ἀνέσχε τις ὑπὲρ τὸ λέχος ἀνδρείκελον αὐτοῦ Καίσαρος ἐκ κηροῦ πεποιημένον· – 'While they were in this temper and already near to violence, somebody raised above the funeral couch a mannequin of Caesar himself made of wax.'

On the relation of *mêchanê* and cross in the liturgy cf. IGNATIUS, *Ephes.* IX, 1: ἀναφερόμενοι εἰς τὰ ὕψη διὰ τῆς μηχανῆς Ἰησοῦ Χριστοῦ, ὅς ἐστιν σταυρός - 'raised above by the *mechane,* the "theatrical machine" of Jesus Christ, which is the cross'. Unless there were several tropaea because, after all, Caesar had celebrated at least

114. *Arma Christi,* The weapons of Christ

four triumphs, or two tropaea, like on the denarius of Caldus, ill. 22, one with the arms of Vercingetorix and one with the wax model of Caesar. This is conceivable insofar as there are two different crosses to be seen in our churches or Ways of the Cross as well: on the one the figure of Christ is attached, on the other the instruments of the crucifixion, what is called *croix des outrages,* 'cross of insults', or *creu dels improperis,* 'cross of improperies', in other languages. In English, like in German, it is not by chance called by the Latin name *Arma Christi,* which stresses its proximity to the Roman tropaeum on which the 'arms' of the succumbing commander were appended as well. Compare ill. 114 with ill. 21 p. 90 and ill. 33 p. 97, i.a.

115. First reconstruction drawing by Pol du Closeau, Nov. 28th, 2002

Based on the descriptions that are preserved by Suetonius (*Jul.* 84.1), Appianus (*BC* 2.146-147), and the parallel tradition, the Utrecht artist Pol du Closeau has tried in a first approximation a drawn reconstruction of the central scene of Caesar's funeral.

The perspective is from the Forum Romanum, from the side of the Basilica Aemilia on the Rostra, the rostrum, where Antonius is just delivering the funeral oration to Caesar. On the left we perceive the gable of the temple of Saturnus and in the background the rocky Capitol with the temples of Jupiter and Iuno. We are in the year 44 BC, so the temple of Vespasianus, which was built later, does not yet exist so we have a clear view of the capitol. The Tabularium which was attached to the Capitol on the end of the Forum remains just outside the section of the picture on the right from this angle.

Caesar's body is laid out in a gilded model of the temple of *Venus Genetrix*. One perceives the frieze with the egg-motif, the symbol of birth *(Genetrix)*, which in Christianity was to become that of reincarnation (Easter eggs). Beneath, the carrying poles can be seen. At head height of this little temple of Venus stands the tropaeum-like device (Suetonius: *tropaeum;* Appianus: *mêchanê*) on which the mannequin made of wax is hanging with the wounds on the body caused by the dagger thrusts. Marcus Antonius is just about to pull away Caesar's gown, the bloodstained toga which first covered the wax figure and the tropaeum, by dint of a lance, and in this way reveals the corpus. In the background the people are crying out, filled with indignation, as can be seen through the bier.

Caesar's wax figure on the tropaeum has outstretched arms not only because on a tropaeum the arms could only be fastened like that (cf. also ill. 61) but because somebody who falls down dead stretches out his arms and because Caesar's body had been seen like that when three servants carried him home with the arms hanging out of the litter on both sides (cf. quotation from Nicolaus Damascenus, p. 83, note 193). For Antonius wanted to show how Caesar had lain there, murdered. But because the body would not have been visible if lying on the Rostra, he had the wax figure produced and erected it—like a tropaeum. Thus Caesar's wax simulacrum which should have depicted him lying, appeared as if it were hanging on a cross.

The tropaeum is made of plain planks instead of round posts here because a wax figure could be affixed better to those. The artist has purposely not drawn any fastenings for the wax figure in this reconstruction. When wax manufacturers were asked about this detail, they said that full-scale representations made of wax can only be held upright by a scaffolding, or a structure. It is known that in antiquity wax figures had a structure made of wood; they were actually wooden figures with a wax outer-layer (cf. MARQUART-MAU (1886), p. 354). The most functional and direct way to fasten such a wooden figure coated with wax to a tropaeum would involve nails through the hands. This would explain why the 'Crucified one' has nails through his hands in spite of the fact that for a real man hanging on the cross, one would best use rope. Anyway, nails would have to be driven through the wrists because if attached to the palms the body weight would tear through the flesh.

As said, this drawing is a first attempt and unfinished: the rents and blood stains on the toga caused by the dagger thrusts are still missing. The drawing was not yet ready when it was shown at the lecture and subsequent discussion in the Lutherse Kerk (Lutheran Church) in Utrecht on Nov. 28th 2002, and also during the telecast 'Buitenhof' in the contribution of Prof. Paul Cliteur Ph.D. on the following Dec. 1st. Both times it caused a sensation. Therefore we want to reproduce it here as incomplete and as effective as it was first shown, with some slight improvements.

It might appear strange because it is not done in an archeologically correct and anatomically perfect late Hellenistic style. It is from the hand of a contemporary artist with his personal style affectionate to popular art. But for that very reason it has an eminently documentary nature, since it brings home to us for the first time how the exposition of Caesar's 'body' during his funeral might have looked, true to the original, according to the sources, but at the same time in an anachronistic, almost naive way so that we can already get a feel for the alienation that the depiction of these scenes was to experience in Christian art in the course of time. As an identikit picture this drawing serves very well: it realizes graphically what the eyewitnesses had seen and makes it possible for us to catch a glimpse of the instant in which the genesis of the 'crucified one' occurred.

This moment was short because as we have seen the sight was unbearable: the people revolted, became enraged, pursued the assassins and burned Caesar's body right there at the Forum. This was interpreted as his resurrection. Accordingly the moment of the re-erecting of the body on the pyre was frozen on Caesar's coins (cf. ill. 67, p. 108) together with the ascension in the apotheosis (cf. ill. 85 and 86, p. 116 as well as ill. 87, p. 117). For the exhibition of Caesar's martyred body had indeed fulfilled its function to incite the people to revolt, but it still belonged to the assassination, i.e. to what one wanted to overcome, to the parricide, the commemoration of which should be wiped out by the execration of the day of murder as *dies parricidii, ater, funestus* (cf. referring to this, p. 88). So it is not astonishing that this image was never shown except for in the liturgy of Passion Week.

A glance at the appearance of the 'crucified one' in Christian art confirms this. In the Christian iconography there are pictures of the 'crucified one' dating only from the 5th century on, and as one who suffers only in the second millennium. Prior to that, the cross appears alone initially as *crux invicta,* as the invincible laureate cross, which the victorious Christ carries like a tropaeum in triumph (compare the way Simon a Cyrenian carries the 'cross' on the late Constantinian passion sarcophagus of 340/370 AD (ill. 116, left) with that of Romulus resp. Mars carrying the tropaeum in ill. 23–25, p. 91. Also notice in the second scene from the left side that the crown of thorns really is a laurel wreath which is held above the head of Christ like in the triumph of the imperator, Christ who is depicted beardless and in toga just as a Roman, the roll in his left hand like the commander's rod; on the right he authoritatively instructs Pilate).

116. Late Constantinian Passion Sarcophagus 340/370 AD, Rome, Vatican

And after 420/430 AD, when the first depictions of the 'crucified' Jesus Christ surface, he doesn't appear as dead man but as one who defies death, victorious, anticipating his resurrection in his posture—like on this ivory relief on the London casket in the British Museum, even emphasized by the anticipated death of Judas by hanging (ill. 117, left). Also note the way Longinus applies his 'lance'-stab to the heart region: like a dagger thrust. And here also, Jesus is beardless, i.e. in Roman symbolism: without mourning—like Divus Iulius.

117. Ivory relief, Italic, 420/430 AD, Crucifiction of Christ, (right) Longinus' thrust into the heart side, (left) Judas' suicide

If one then looks at the development of the picture of the 'crucifixion' through the course of history, two things are detected: firstly the earliest pictures preserved were also popular-naive, and sparsely classical, and secondly there is no effect of gravity at all initially. It was not until the second millennium and then only slowly that gravity becomes apparent in the 'crucified one'—and slowly pulled him down. In former times it was different and in Byzantine resp. Greek Orthodox art it has largely remained that way to date.

Where does this illogical manner of representation stem from? Traditionally two reasons are given: The basis is said to be that originally no one wanted to portray a suffering one but rather one overcoming death-and for that a man in a standing position is better suited. Additionally there must have been a fearfulness of depicting one's own Godman as a crucified one, a fear that allowed cross representations to develop in art only after Theodosius I had abolished the penalty of crucifixion and when the cross no longer triggered negative associations. Meanwhile, one refrains from this earlier prevailing interpretation (the Rabula-Codex and the casket in Sancta Sanctorum in Rome, both from the 5/6th century, indeed show a standing as well as suffering Jesus on the cross), opining that it simply originates from the fact that the Christian artists had no ancient examples of crucified ones available—the crucifixion was sporadically described in texts from classical times, but never portrayed, neither by painters nor by sculptors—and that no pictures nor descriptions of Jesus' crucifixion had been passed down either. These two competing arguments, neither of which are very convincing, point to the helplessness of the circles of experts, who are still struggling for a plausible explanation. The more so as it is obvious that as soon as the man on the cross was perceived to be a crucified one, the artists immediately started to let him hang and fall down more and more. And although the artists in these instances did not have examples either, they knew that somebody who is hanging on a cross just hangs.

118. Box of relics from Palestine, End of the 6th c.; 119. Codex from Syria, 586 AD

120. Carolingian, 9th cent.; 121. 10th cent.; 122. Miniature, 975 AD

123. San Damiano, 12th cent.; 124. Giotto, ca. 1305; 125. Rubens, 1620

This is confirmed by the third century signet stones and gems from the fund of numerous small pilgrim's souvenirs which were produced to satisfy the great demand for them after Helena the mother of Constantine had discovered the pretended 'true' cross of Christ in Jerusalem—at least according to tradition—and brought a part of it to Constantinople and had built a church in Jerusalem, '(To the) Holy Tomb' while Constantine had further memorial buildings erected, all of which attracted more and more pilgrims in the course of time.

Irrespective of whether the signet stone resp. the gem reproduced here is about Christ, Bacchus, Dionysos or somebody else and whether they evolved from a Orphic-Christian syncretism or served for pagan-magic use, they do show that not only the artists of the second millennium but also artists from late Antiquity knew clearly, that one who was crucified has to hang on the cross and not stand up straight. One has to ask oneself whether there was a model for the atypical and unnatural representation of Christ standing on the cross which was the exclusive way of depicting him for a thousand years, a model that counteracted the hanging Christ and demanded that the 'crucified one' was not to hang.

126. Orpheos Bakkikos, signet stone, 3rd cent.; 127. Crucified One, gem, 3rd cent.

The return to Caesar's funeral again explains this paradox: originally it was not the presentation of a crucified one but the *expositio* of a stabbed one lying on the floor who was only erected that all could see him. Thus his arms should not be stretched upwards but rather downwards, or straight out at the most. And this is exactly what can be observed in the antique 'crucifixions'.

The solution to the mystery of the late and anomalous appearance of the 'crucified one' in Christian art would then be easy. The 'crucified one' was at first only shown in the liturgy of the passion of Divus Iulius. This meant, according to tradition during the first centuries, that a wax simulacrum had to be made for it year after year, that was to be burned in the Easter fire. This was very important because it signified the moment of the resurrection, when the people cry out *Christos anesti!* resp. *resurrexit!* Only later, when the Christian aversion to cremation established itself and beginning with Constantine, inhumation became traditional for the emperor as well, could the liturgy be partially adjusted to the texts of the Gospels too. The Easter fire remained in symbolic form, but 'Jesus' was no longer burned in it, and instead of his wax simulacrum only the Easter candle, possibly together with a coburned *Judas* (instead of *Julius*). From then on the simulacrum could also be made of different materials, out of gypsum or carved in wood, and could, for use in the next year, be preserved in the churches, which had been built in the meantime after the acceptation by the emperors. That was more economical too, which was certainly welcome in the meager years that accompanied the triumph of Christianity.

Then it was only a question of time as to when these pictorial representations of the crucified one would occur in art also, for instance at the gates of churches like in Santa Sabina in Rome where it is still visible today. However, since they not only emblematized the suffering of the Christians from the persecutions but also the victory from Constantine's time on, they did not emphasize the suffering, but rather the victorious aspect of the crucified one, for quite some time. It was only after the decay of the Roman Empire and the triumph of the barbarians—and the accompanying subjugation of the free Roman peasants as serfs—that the suffering Christ alone remained as symbol, and of the former victory not even the remembrance remained and if any still did, then it was as a painful one also. The never-ending suffering of the Christians summoned the permanently present and everywhere visualized suffering of Christ. The age of the Crucifixus, of the Crucified one, had dawned. Caesar's tropaeum had finally become Christ's cross.

158 SUET. *Jul.* 84: *Inter ludos cantata sunt quaedam ad miserationem et invidiam caedis eius accomodata, ex Pacuvi Armorum iudicio «Men servasse, ut essent qui me perderent?» et ex Electra Atili ad similem sententiam.*—'Emotions of pity and indignation for Caesar's murder were aroused at the funeral games by singing verses like the line from Pacuvius' play *Contest for the Arms of Achilles*—'What, did I save these men that they might murder me?!'—and others with a similar sentiment from Atilius' *Elektra*.

Pacuvius was a Roman tragedian poet (220-130 BC); the sentence that is cited here is taken from a piece about the Trojan war. Atilius composed an apparently very literal translation of Sophocles' *Elektra* in Latin (cf. STAUFFER 1957).

159 APP. *BC* 2.146.611: οὐκ ἔφερεν ἔτι ὁ δῆμος, ἐν παραλόγῳ ποιούμενος τὸ πάντας αὐτοῦ τοὺς σφαγέας χωρὶς μόνου Δέκμου, αἰχμαλώτους ἐκ τῆς Πομπηίου στάσεως γενομένους, ἀντὶ κολάσεων ἐπὶ ἀρχὰς καὶ ἡγεμονίας ἐθνῶν καὶ στρατοπέδων προαχθέντας ἐπιβουλεῦσαι, Δέκμον δὲ καὶ παῖδα αὐτῷ θετὸν ἀξιωθῆναι γενέσθαι.

160 We follow Ethelbert Stauffer here, cf. STAUFFER (1957), p.21-23: SOPH. *El.* 839 sqq.: καὶ νῦν ὑπὸ γαίας- ΗΛ. Ἔ ἔ, ἰώ. ΧΟ. πάμψυχος ἀνάσσει. 453 sq: αἰτοῦ δὲ προσπίτνουσα γῆθεν εὐμενῆ / ἡμῖν ἀρωγὸν αὐτὸν εἰς ἐχθροὺς μολεῖν. 792: ΗΛ. Ἄκουε, Νέμεσι τοῦ θανόντος ἀρτίως. 1418-21: ΧΟ. Τελοῦσ' ἀραί· ζῶσιν οἱ / γᾶς ὑπαὶ κείμενοι· / παλίρρυτον γὰρ αἷμ' ὑπεξαιροῦσι τῶν / κτανόντων οἱ πάλαι θανόντες. 33 sq: ὅτῳ τρόπῳ πατρὶ / δίκας ἀροίμην τῶν φονευσάντων πάρα.

A resonance of these improperia of March 44 is even found in Cicero in October 44 in his speech against Antonius: *illum interfecerunt, quo erant conservati* (CIC. *Phil.* 2.3.5)—'they have killed the one who had kept them alive'.

161 SUET. *Jul.* 84: *Laudationis loco consul Antonius per praeconem pronuntiauit senatus consultum, quo omnia simul ei diuina atque humana decreuerat, item ius iurandum, quo se cuncti pro salute unius astrinxerant; quibus perpauca a se uerba addidit.*

162 APP. *BC* 2.144.601-3: ἐφ' ἑκάστῳ δὲ τούτων ὁ Ἀντώνιος τὴν ὄψιν καὶ τὴν χεῖρα ἐς τὸ σῶμα τοῦ Καίσαρος ἐπιστρέφων ἐν παραβολῇ τοῦ λόγου τὸ ἔργον ἐπεδείκνυ. ἐπεφθέγγετο δέ πού τι καὶ βραχὺ ἑκάστῳ, μεμιγμένον οἴκτῳ καὶ ἀγανακτήσει, ἔνθα μὲν τὸ ψήφισμα εἴποι "πατέρα πατρίδος," ἐπιλέγων· "τοῦτο ἐπιεικείας ἐστὶ μαρτυρία," ἔνθα δ' ἦν "ἱερὸς καὶ ἄσυλος" καὶ "ἀπαθὴς καὶ ὅστις αὐτῷ καὶ ἕτερος προσφύγοι," "οὐχ ἕτερος," ἔφη, "τῷδε προσφεύγων, ἀλλ' αὐτὸς ὑμῖν ὁ ἄσυλος καὶ ἱερὸς ἀνῄρηται, οὐ βιασάμενος οἷα τύραννος λαβεῖν τάσδε τὰς τιμάς, ἃς οὐδὲ ᾔτησεν.

163 APP. *BC* 2.146.611: ἐφ' οἷς ὁ δῆμος οἷα χορὸς αὐτῷ πενθιμώτατα συνωδύρετο καὶ ἐκ τοῦ πάθους αὖθις ὀργῆς ἐνεπίμπλατο.

164 APP. *BC* 2.146.611 : καί που τῶν θρήνων αὐτὸς ὁ Καῖσαρ ἐδόκει λέγειν, ὅσους εὖ ποιήσειε τῶν ἐχθρῶν ἐξ ὀνόματος, καὶ περὶ τῶν σφαγέων αὐτῶν ἐπέλεγεν ὥσπερ ἐν θαύματι· "ἐμὲ δὲ καὶ τούσδε περισῶσαι τοὺς κτενοῦντάς με, [...]".

165 APP. *BC* 2.146: Τοιάδε εἰπὼν τὴν ἐσθῆτα οἷά τις ἔνθους ἀνεσύρατο, καὶ περιζωσάμενος ἐς τὸ τῶν χειρῶν εὔκολον, τὸ λέχος ὡς ἐπὶ σκηνῆς περιέστη κατακύπτων τε ἐς αὐτὸ καὶ ἀνίσχων, πρῶτα μὲν ὡς θεὸν οὐράνιον ὕμνει καὶ ἐς πίστιν θεοῦ γενέσεως τὰς χεῖρας ἀνέτεινεν [...].

166 DIO CASS. *HR* 44.48: διὰ γὰρ τοῦτο ἀρχιερεὺς μὲν πρὸς τοὺς θεούς, ὕπατος δὲ πρὸς ἡμᾶς, αὐτοκράτωρ δὲ πρὸς τοὺς στρατιώτας, δικτάτωρ δὲ πρὸς τοὺς πολεμίους ἀπεδείχθη. καὶ τί ταῦτ' ἐξαριθμοῦμαι, ὁπότε καὶ πατέρα αὐτὸν ἑνὶ λόγῳ τῆς πατρίδος ἐπεκαλέσατε;

167 APP. *BC* 2.146.609.

168 DIO CASS. *HR* 44.49: ἀλλ' οὗτος ὁ πατήρ, οὗτος ὁ ἀρχιερεὺς ὁ ἄσυλος ὁ ἥρως ὁ θεὸς τέθνηκεν, οἴμοι, τέθνηκεν οὐ νόσῳ βιασθείς, οὐδὲ γήρᾳ μαρανθείς, οὐδὲ ἔξω που ἐν πολέμῳ τινὶ τρωθείς, οὐδὲ ἐκ δαιμονίου τινὸς αὐτομάτως ἁρπασθείς, ἀλλὰ

ἐνταῦθα ἐντὸς τοῦ τείχους ἐπιβουλευθεὶς ὁ καὶ ἐς Βρεττανίαν ἀσφαλῶς στρατεύσας, ἐν τῇ πόλει ἐνεδρευθεὶς ὁ καὶ τὸ πωμήριον αὐτῆς ἐπαυξήσας, ἐν τῷ βουλευτηρίῳ κατασφαγεὶς ὁ καὶ ἴδιον ἄλλο κατασκευάσας, ἄοπλος ὁ εὐπόλεμος, γυμνὸς ὁ εἰρηνοποιός, πρὸς τοῖς δικαστηρίοις ὁ δικαστής, πρὸς ταῖς ἀρχαῖς ὁ ἄρχων, ὑπὸ τῶν πολιτῶν ὃν μηδεὶς τῶν πολεμίων μηδ' ἐς τὴν θάλασσαν ἐκπεσόντα ἀποκτεῖναι ἠδυνήθη, ὑπὸ τῶν ἑταίρων ὁ πολλάκις αὐτοὺς ἐλεήσας. ποῦ δῆτά σοι, Καῖσαρ, ἡ φιλανθρωπία, ποῦ δὲ ἡ ἀσυλία, ποῦ δὲ οἱ νόμοι; ἀλλὰ σὺ μέν, ὅπως μηδ' ὑπὸ τῶν ἐχθρῶν τις φονεύηται, πολλὰ ἐνομοθέτησας, σὲ δὲ οὕτως οἰκτρῶς ἀπέκτειναν οἱ φίλοι, καὶ νῦν ἔν τε τῇ ἀγορᾷ πρόκεισαι ἐσφαγμένος, δι' ἧς πολλάκις ἐπόμπευσας ἐστεφανωμένος, καὶ ἐπὶ τοῦ βήματος ἔρριψαι κατατετρωμένος, ἀφ' οὗ πολλάκις ἐδημηγόρησας. οἴμοι πολιῶν ᾑματωμένων, ὦ στολῆς ἐσπαραγμένης, ἣν ἐπὶ τούτῳ μόνον, ὡς ἔοικεν, ἔλαβες, ἵν' ἐν ταύτῃ σφαγῇς."

169 App. BC 2.146 (cf. note 157): τὸ σῶμα τοῦ Καίσαρος ἐγύμνου καὶ τὴν ἐσθῆτα ἐπὶ κοντοῦ φερομένην ἀνέσειε, λελακισμένην ὑπὸ τῶν πληγῶν καὶ πεφυρμένην αἵματι αὐτοκράτορος. App. BC 2.147.612: Ὧδε δὲ αὐτοῖς ἔχουσιν ἤδη καὶ χειρῶν ἐγγὺς οὖσιν ἀνέσχε τις ὑπὲρ τὸ λέχος ἀνδρείκελον αὐτοῦ Καίσαρος ἐκ κηροῦ πεποιημένον· τὸ μὲν γὰρ σῶμα, ὡς ὕπτιον ἐπὶ λέχους, οὐχ ἑωρᾶτο. τὸ δὲ ἀνδρείκελον ἐκ μηχανῆς ἐπεστρέφετο πάντῃ, καὶ σφαγαὶ τρεῖς καὶ εἴκοσιν ὤφθησαν ἀνά τε τὸ σῶμα πᾶν καὶ ἀνὰ τὸ πρόσωπον θηριωδῶς ἐς αὐτὸν γενόμεναι. Dio Cass. HR 44.35.4 and 44.49.3-4.

170 App. BC 2.147: τήνδε οὖν τὴν ὄψιν ὁ δῆμος οἰκτίστην σφίσι φανεῖσαν οὐκέτι ἐνεγκὼν ἀνῴμωξάν τε καὶ διαζωσάμενοι τὸ βουλευτήριον, ἔνθα ὁ Καῖσαρ ἀνῄρητο, κατέφλεξαν καὶ τοὺς ἀνδροφόνους ἐκφυγόντας πρὸ πολλοῦ περιθέοντες ἐζήτουν, οὕτω δὴ μανιωδῶς ὑπὸ ὀργῆς τε καὶ λύπης, ὥστε τὸν δημαρχοῦντα Κίνναν ἐξ ὁμωνυμίας τοῦ στρατηγοῦ Κίννα, τοῦ δημηγορήσαντος ἐπὶ τῷ Καίσαρι, οὐκ ἀνασχόμενοί τε περὶ τῆς ὁμωνυμίας οὐδ' ἀκοῦσαι, διέσπασαν θηριωδῶς, καὶ οὐδὲν αὐτοῦ μέρος ἐς ταφὴν εὑρέθη.

171 Suet. Jul. 85: caputque eius praefixum hastae circumtulit.
172 Dio Cass. HR 50.3.
173 Suet. Jul. 84: [Quem cum pars in Capitolini Iovis cella cremare, pars in curia Pompei destinaret,] repente duo quidam gladiis succincti ac bina iacula gestantes ardentibus cereis succenderunt [...].
174 Suet. Jul. 84: [...] confestimque circumstantium turba virgulta arida et cum subsellis tribunalia, quicquid praeterea ad donum aderat, congessit. deinde tibicines et scaenici artifices vestem, quam ex triumphorum instrumento ad praesentem usum induerant, detractam sibi atque discissam iniecere flam mae et veteranorum militum legionarii arma sua, quibus exculti funus celebrabant; matronae etiam pleraeque ornamenta sua, quae gerebant, et liberorum bullas atque praetextas.
175 Suet. Jul. 84: In summo publico luctu exterarum gentium multitudo circulatim suo quaeque more lamentata est praecipueque Iudaei, qui etiam noctibus continuis bustum frequentarunt.
176 Dio Cass. HR 44.51.1: βωμὸν δέ τινα ἐν τῷ τῆς πυρᾶς χωρίῳ ἱδρυσάμενοι (τὰ γὰρ ⟨ὀστᾶ⟩ αὐτοῦ οἱ ἐξελεύθεροι προανείλοντο καὶ ἐς τὸ πατρῷον μνημεῖον κατέθεντο) θύειν τε ἐπ' αὐτῷ καὶ κατάρχεσθαι τῷ Καίσαρι ὡς καὶ θεῷ ἐπεχείρουν. οἱ οὖν ὕπατοι ἐκεῖνόν τε ἀνέτρεψαν, καί τινας ἀγανακτήσαντας ἐπὶ τούτῳ ἐκόλασαν, [...].
177 Which is at the time of Appianus.
178 App. BC 2.148: ἔνθα βωμὸς πρῶτος ἐτέθη, νῦν δ' ἐστὶ νεὼς αὐτοῦ Καίσαρος, θείων τιμῶν ἀξιουμένου· ὁ γάρ τοι θετὸς αὐτῷ παῖς Ὀκτάουιος, τό τε ὄνομα ἐς τὸν Καίσαρα μεταβαλὼν καὶ κατ' ἴχνος ἐκείνου τῇ πολιτείᾳ προσιών, τήν τε ἀρχὴν τὴν ἐπικρατοῦσαν ἔτι νῦν, ἐρριζωμένην ὑπ' ἐκείνου, μειζόνως ἐκρατύνατο καὶ τὸν πατέρα τιμῶν ἰσοθέων ἠξίωσεν [...].
179 Stauffer (1957), p.28—where in Bios Kaisaros we read 'Emperor biography', rather than 'Caesar-biography', because Nicolaus Damascenus starts by writing

about the life of the young Caesar—Octavianus Augustus—then inserts an excursus about the elder Caesar, resulting in it becoming a central part of this 'Emperor'-biography.
180 STAUFFER (1957), p. 21.
181 Cf. *Gregorian massbook*, Good Friday: *'Ecce lignum Crucis, in quo salus mundi pependit.'*
182 Cf. *Gregorian massbook*, Good Friday: *'Popule meus, quid feci tibi? Aut in quo contristavi te? Responde mihi. Quia eduxi te de terra Aegypti: parasti Crucem Salvatori tuo [...].'*
183 Suetonius does not say anything about why the Jews were so eager here. Although he is the only one amongst the ancient historians to report the presence of the Jews at Caesar's cremation site, his testimony is generally not doubted by the commentators—there is speculation about their reasons, however.
Some say the reason for the affection of the Jews was Caesar's pro-Jewish policy, since he had granted them many privileges and the right to practice their religion freely. Others say that the Jews were very thankful to Caesar because he had defeated Pompeius, who had conquered Jerusalem and desecrated the temple. They had seen in Caesar the avenging angel—or even the Messiah?
Both arguments seem to suggest themselves, even though they are not without certain contradictions.
The first one—that Caesar had granted a number of privileges and free exercise of religion—is based mainly on Flavius Josephus (Jos. *JA* 14.10.1): Caesar had declared the Jews living in Alexandria as 'fellow citizens of the Alexandrians'—which was not a small thing, because only as such could Egyptians obtain Roman citizenship (cf. PLINIUS, *ep.* X, 6; 7; 10)—and allowed Hyrcanus to keep the office of Jewish high priest because he had come to his help with 1500 men in the Alexandrine war (Jos. *AJ* 14.10.2). In fact, however, according to the same Flavius Josephus, the Idumean Antipater governed Judea at that time, only pro forma on Hyrcanus' order, and it was he who joined Mithridates with 3000 (that is, twice as many) 'foot soldiers of the Jews' (cf. Jos. *BJ* 1.9.3), made a good showing at the capture of Pelusium, was repeatedly wounded during the campaign, and persuaded the Egyptian Jews, who were fighting against Caesar, to change sides (Jos. *JA* 14.8.1). The Idumean Antipater whose wife Kypros, the mother of the later Herod the Great, was a Nabatean sheik's daughter (Jos. *BJ* 1.8.9) apparently also lead the troops of his Nabatean father-in-law along with the cavalrymen of the Nabatean Malchus, whom Caesar had called for help, and who joined Mithridates Pergamenus, who was gathering auxiliary troops from Cilicia and Syria and was advancing by land on his way (*B. Alex.* 1.1 and 26). As reward, Caesar made Antipater a Roman citizen and procurator of all of Judaea after the war.
So he had allowed Hyrcanus to keep the religious office (of Jewish high priest), but had given the political one into the hands of an Idumean and his non-Jewish descendants. However, many among the Jews were glad about this also, the opponents of Hyrcanus as well as those who rejected all Hasmoneans as non-Davidians—e. g. the Pharisees—or were generally opposed to the kingship.
Anyhow, all were glad about Caesar's clemency which they had experienced again, because the Egyptian Jews, especially those from the Onias district in Leontopolis—where since the conquest of Jerusalem by the notorious Antiochos Epiphanes stood a small copy of the Temple of Jerusalem—had fought against Caesar at first and only changed sides after the situation had already tilted in favor of Caesar, and only on massive pressure of Antipater who could produce letters of Hyrcanus on this matter. So they had reason to fear Caesar's revenge. But he tempered justice with mercy this time also.
This could explain why the Jews were especially attached to him from then on.

How grateful they were to him can be recognized by a decree of Augustus whereby he affirmed the regulations of his adoptive father, which Flavius Josephus cites as one of the main records for the privileges granted to Hyrcanus (Jos. AJ 16.6.2[§ 162-165]).

Therein *Caesar Augustus, pontifex maximus (ἀρχιερεύς), tribunicia potestas* permits, with reference to the fact that the nation of the Jews was found to be friendly *(εὐχάριστον – socius et amicus populi Romani?)* not only in his time but especially in the time of his father, the dictator Caesar, as well as due to the agreement of the Roman people: Jews are allowed to pursue their customs according to the 'fatherly' law as at the time of Hyrcanus, the high priest *(ἀρχιερεύς)* of the 'Highest God' *(θεὸς ὕψιστος)*.

It is interesting here that 'fatherly' law means the 'Caesarean' one, the law of the 'father' of Augustus, i.e. Caesar's law (cf. NOETHLICHS p 86). It may be asked whether the confusion with the 'fatherly' law of the Jews, i.e. their father Moses', which suggests itself—incidentally, editors and translators usually blunder into it—was intended by Augustus who, as is generally known, aimed at identification (starting with his own with Caesar, whose name he did not take over by chance). Θεὸς ὕψιστος, 'Highest God' is what Jupiter was called (cf. thereto i.a. A.D. NOCK, «The Guild of Zeus Hypsistos», *Harv. Theol. Rev.* 29, 1936, p. 39-88), an equating that was certainly intended by Augustus, a clear *interpretatio Romana* of *Jahve = Iove*. High priest of the 'Highest God' *(ἀρχιερεύς θεοῦ ὑψίστου)*, anyway, was not only Hyrcanus but also Caesar, who was not only *Pontifex Maximus* but *Flamen Dialis*, too, high priest of Jupiter: And he had appointed Hyrcanus as a smaller duplicate in Jerusalem, as it were. However, the deified Caesar himself was equated with Jupiter also, it is not by chance stated expressly with Cassius Dio *(HR 44,6,4: καὶ τέλος Δία τε αὐτὸν ἄντικρυς ᾽Ιούλιον προσηγόρευσαν)*, so that Caesar appears here not only as father of Augustus but also of Hyrcanus and the Jews themselves, God the Father and Moses at the same time: As new Romulus he analogously was also a new Moses and as new Jupiter a new Jahweh as well. And as Augustus was his adoptive son, it seems here that Hyrcanus together with his God becomes adoptive too—to plagiarize Tertullian, who distinguished *di adoptivi* from *di captivi* (cf. Tertullian, *apol.* 10.5). This, incidentally, is confirmed by the fact that Augustus does not mention Judaea among the provinces nor the allies in his account of his deeds, thus expressing a personal relationship.

Hence, when Antonius lamented that Caesar, of all people, who had freed Rome from the Gallic threat like a new Camillus, had been murdered and all foreigners joined in *suo more*, 'according to their customs' and sang dirges, the Jews will probably have praised him as a new Moses, who had led them out of Egypt again and for whom they now prepared the 'stake': his *stavrós*—by which, at least for the Caesareans among them, was meant not the 'cross', the *lignum crucis*, but the 'flammable wood' for the pyre, as was right and proper for their savior, yes, their father and God (cf. note 157). The lament became an *improperium* addressing those who had joined the murderers thus making themselves co-responsible for his *cruciatus*.

So this fateful hour, on which opinions differed in Rome and the whole Empire, had also divided Jewry: The Caesareans among them—those who did not celebrate with Brutus and Cassius on the Sabbath after Caesar's Passover and would rather be Sabbath desecrators than not mourn for him—had carried out the break with the old law and gone over to the new religion born in that hour: the cult of Divus Iulius which was to become Christianity after the Jewish war.

As for the second assumed reason: the fact that Pompeius, by capturing Jerusalem and storming the Jewish temple, did not make only friends among the Jews cannot be disputed. In the Jewish tradition he was never forgiven for entering into the holy of holies, which was forbidden not only for strangers but even Jews themselves (Jos.

AJ 12.145sq). Still under Traianus when the insurrections broke out in Egypt in 115-117 the Jews exhumed the head of Pompeius from the grove, where Caesar had had it buried, out of revenge for the sacrilege of 63 BC (APP. *BC* 2.90.380). But the fact of the matter is that in the process, Pompeius had entangled himself in inner-Jewish quarrels over the throne, in which the two brothers fighting over regality had made him arbiter, and he then had to support, together with the older one whom he favored, the younger one who was barricading himself in Jerusalem. 'For this calamity of Jerusalem, only the conflict between Hyrcanus and Aristobulus was to blame', Josephus himself realizes (JOS. *AJ* 14.4.5). He also gives great credit to Pompeius for not touching the temple treasure-unlike Crassus later on his unfortunate campaign against the Parthians, who took all the gold with him—and 'behaving as one could expect of his virtue': for he had the sanctuary purified again and appointed Hyrcanus as high priest (JOS. *AJ* 14.4.4). Also, we see that in the following Roman civil war 'the people of the Hebrews and their Arabic neighbors' (APP. *BC* 2.71.294) stood on Pompeius' side: so Pompeius must have come to an arrangement with not a few Jews after the capture of Jerusalem and they with him. That Caesar, inversely, did not only make enemies amongst the Jews by freeing Aristobulus, who had been arrested by Pompeius, cannot be disputed either. Aristobulus was an opponent of Hyrcanus though, who also had his sympathizers. Thus not all Jews will have been furious that the Pompeians poisoned Aristobulus soon afterwards, still in Rome, while in Syria Pompeius' new father in law, Q. Metellus Scipio, had Aristobulos's son decapitated. Furthermore Caesar had later not supported Aristobulus' presumptuous and unreliable young son Antigonus but instead favored Antipater, who had more actively supported him and possessed scars all over his body. So one has to come to terms with the thought that Caesar had intervened in a biased manner with the Jews, as with all other peoples and nations, and as a result had aroused sympathies as well as antipathies—depending on one's point of view.

The one who must have been hated by all Jews, whether Caesareans or Anti-Caesareans, is Cassius Longinus. Because in 53/52, after Crassus' defeat against the Parthians, he had still been able to maintain control of the province Syria, then had turned against the rebelling province of Judaea, captured 30,000 Jews and in so doing had Pitholaus, who had defected and led the rebellion after Aristobulus, executed on Antipater's advice, whom he held in high regard (JOS. *AJ* 14.7.3, JOS. *BJ* 1.89). Flavius Josephus does not say how Pitholaus was executed. So it will have been the usual way of execution for rebels, in Judaea normally crucifixion. Not the least significant was the fact that it was Aristobulus' father Alexander Jannaeus, himself king of the Jews who had set standards in that respect. After he had killed umpteen thousands of Jews who were rebelling against him he had 800 of the captives nailed to the cross in the middle of Jerusalem and their wives and children slaughtered in front of their eyes, while he himself, boozing and lying with his concubines, was watching (JOS. *BJ* 1.4.5).

But now, nine years later, the same Cassius Longinus had made his mark for himself by murdering Caesar, and as a result the same Antipater joined him. Because of that, Caesar must have, for the Jews of Rome, inevitably become one of theirs, and the attempt on him an attempt on them too. They had suffered from the same deadly hand and naturally found themselves together in mourning, beyond all partiality. Caesar's death from the hand of Cassius Longinus must have carried more weight for them than the fact that it had occurred in front of Pompeius's statue. The exhibition of Caesar's body, tortured by all the wounds, at the tropaeum must have seemed a crucifixion to them particularly.

This being true all the more so in recollection, by the time when Suetonius, one and a half centuries later, writes and reports of the conspicuously long time that the Jews remained at Caesar's cremation site. For history had soon repeated itself among the children. The son of Aristobulus, Antigonus, who during an invasion of the Parthians in the year 40 as the last of the Hasmoneans, with their help had managed to become king instead of the captured Hyrcanus (in his hatred he had bitten off one of Hyrcanus' ears, so that he could no longer be high priest, since bodily integrity was a pre-condition for that). Soon afterwards, in 38, he is captured himself by the Romans and brought to Antonius in Antiochia, where Herod, the son of Antipater, bribed Antonius to have him killed (Jos. BJ 1.357; Jos. AJ 14.489-491; 15.9sq). Here too, Flavius Josephus does not say what kind of execution it was. Cassius Dio however (HR 49.22.6) speaks about a flagellation and crucifixion of Antigonus before his killing, a punishment that no other king had ever suffered under the Romans. One may ask oneself how much this flagellation and killing of Antigonus by Antonius may have affected the transformation of the exhibition of the tropaeum with the wax figure during Caesar's funeral, directed by the same Antonius.

But for the moment, Antonius' act of piety towards Caesar, preventing his body from being dragged like that of a tyrant through the streets of Rome and then thrown in the Tiber—as his murderers had planned—must have evoked, especially among the Jews, the memory of a previous act of piety by the same Antonius towards Aristobulus. This man had been brought captured to Rome by Pompeius in 63, and was able to flee together with his son Antigonus seven years later in order to take possession of Judaea again. But the rebellion failed and Aristobulus was brought to Rome a second time. However, in 49 Caesar freed him to fight the civil war for him against Pompeius in Judaea, for which he gave him two legions (Cass. Dio HR 41.18.1)—whereupon he was poisoned by Pompeians. His body, too, was denied a burial in home soil until Antonius finally sent it to the Jews, embalmed in honey, to be buried in the royal tombs (Jos. AJ 13.16.1-14.7.4; BJ 1.5.4-9.1).

Furthermore, it must be taken into consideration that Caesar did pay back, with high interest, all the money he had borrowed for 'his Gallic tarts to pay', as his soldiers had poked fun during the triumphal procession, and the amount was not negligible. But he was already about to go to war again, namely against the Parthians in order to grind out the defeat of Crassus. For that he had put 19 legions on stand by and sent them ahead. To finance the forthcoming greatest of all wars—after crushing the Parthians he wanted to attack the Germans from the rear in the East, marching around the Black Sea through the regions of the Scythes and the Sarmatians, and thus close the gap to Gaul—he had borrowed great sums of money again. We know about the hectic minting activity of those last months of his life. For it the financially strong Orientals will have been asked to pay up also, without exception—according to his well-known maxim: 'One needs money for the soldiers and one has soldiers for the money'. We thus have to assume that the Jewish financial circles took part one way or another. He will have particularly considered their inclusion for the reason alone that the Jews of the Adiabene were under Parthian sovereignity and a pro-Parthian party was active in Judaea. Therefore, after Caesar's assassination all was at stake for the Jews on Caesar's side as it was for all other Caesareans—not least the return of the temple treasure formerly purloined by Crassus, which could have been expected from a Caesar victorious against the Parthians.

For these reasons it can be concluded that Caesar's policy was not hostile towards the Jews, even if it was not conflict-free, and that it obligated as well as involved the Jews living in the City and the Empire. That is why Suetonius' remark that the Jews in Rome stayed and mourned at the site of Caesar's cremation for a long time can be regarded as certain and justified.

But is this sufficient to explain why they lingered there for a conspicuously long time?

Fortunately, as is often the case, the solution to the mystery is simpler than one might think. We have seen that the fifteenth of the Aramaic month Nisan (Hebrew

Abib), i. e. the first month of spring, beginning with the new moon, corresponds with the Ides of March. This is based on the calculation of the Jews for their Passover-feast 'after the cycle of the moon beginning from the spring equinox (= depending on calculation, between the 20th and 25th of March)' (Philo zu Ex. 12.2). But because all the other nations in principle did the same, as a rule they used the month of the civilian calendar of the respective areas wherein the spring equinox occurred—so in Syria it was regularly the *Xantikos,* in Alexandria the *Parmuthi* and in Rome just March. On the full moon of this month the Passover was celebrated (cf. G. GENTZ, *RE* s.v. 'Ostern' Sp. 1647-48). But now, one year earlier, 45 BC, Caesar had introduced the solar calendar, named the Julian calendar after him. Chance has it that on the Ides of March 44 BC it was full moon as can easily be calculated on the basis of Julian calendar which is still valid in the Eastern Church, as well as with the help of the Easter tables of Dionysius Exiguus. The month of March perfectly corresponded to Nizan.

So the Jews among the Caesareans, respectively the Caesareans among the Jews, celebrated their Passover in Rome in the year 44 BC on the same date as the Romans did the Ides, which also included the ritual offering of a lamb—*ovis Idulis*—to Jupiter. This happened at the end of the 14th and in the beginning of the 15th, because the day was reckoned as beginning at evening. But for the Jews, the feast of the unleavened bread (matzoth) followed from the 15th till the 21st of Nisan (Lv. 23.6). This means that they still had at least one holiday left until the end of the Matzoth festival after Caesar's funeral, which happened presumably on the 20th (cf. u.a. DRUMANN-GRÖBE 1.417). So, even if they did not have more reason to keep vigil at Caesar's funeral site than other denizens of Rome, they had more spare time.

It should be pointed out here that this fact—Matzoth festival following Passover in the Jewish religious calendar—later led to to continual arguments with the Christians, when they began to reckon Easter according to the solar/lunar system in order to prevent 'dark Easter' without a moon (which happened regularly during the use of the purely solar Julian calendar; that the Christians originally always celebrated Easter in March is substantiated by TERTULLIAN, *de jejun.* 14: *pascha celebramus annuo circulo in mense primo*). Because, whereas the Christians fasted until the resurrection of the Lord, the Jews terminated their fasting on the evening of the 14th, which led to the impression that they were scoffing at the death of Jesus or even that they were glad about it (cf. EPIPH. 70.10sq). But when the Christians joyfully celebrated the resurrection, the Jews still ate unleavened bread and bitter herbs for some days (namely the Matzoth is celebrated ἐν πικρίσιν, 'in bitterness', cf. Ex. 12:8), leading again to the assumption that they were mocking Christ's resurrection. This led to continuous irritations and finally to the determination of the Christian Easter so that it no longer coincided with the Jewish celebrations.

However, this later Easter dispute was pre-programmed because of the calendrical coincidences of Caesar's funeral. As it happens, the day on which Caesar's funeral took place, the 20th of March, was a Sunday. On the previous day, the Sabbath, there was a holiday for the Romans also: on that day fell the *Quinquatrus*, the fifth day after the Ides (according to Roman counting, cf. our phrase 'in eight days', 'in fifteen days'); for that reason the funeral was allowed to take place only the day after. This means that at that time already, while the Caesareans were mourning and, putting aside the Sabbath rest, preparing the funeral that was to be become the resurrection, the Anti-Caesareans however were celebrating the old-Roman holiday, respectively the Sabbath, ostensibly: in truth however they celebrated the successful murder of Caesar. Here the first connubium between the murderers of Caesar and the 'law-abiding' Jews took place, who not by chance will be allies in the soon rekindling civil war. Therefore, even later the celebrating of Easter with those still being Jews remained dubious and a bone of contention.

In order to realize the improbability of this coincidence that the moon phases as well as the week days correspond between Caesar's and Jesus' Passion one has to take into account that the Julian calendar has 365 days, ergo 52 weeks plus one day (52x7=364). Thus the week days should recur every seven years. However, because a leap day is inserted every four years the week days recur only after 28 years (7x4=28). The moon phases, however, recur every 19 years so that for both, week days and moon phases, to match one has to wait as many as 532 years (19x28=532). That is to say that since Caesar's death the same week days and moon phases have recurred only three times, the fourth concurrence would then fall in the year 2084. This alone suffices to completely rule out the possibility of a merely coincidental calendrical concurrence between the Passion of Caesar and Jesus.

Whereas the calendrical and astronomical dates of the Gospel Passion account coincide with those of Caesar—death on a full moon day, funeral with resurrection on the following Sunday—Jesus would have to have lost his life either simultaneously with Caesar or 532 years after him so that all dates fit again.

The fortunate coincidence in Dionysius Exiguus' Easter tables was that there was a year in them—563 AD—in which a full moon fell on the 24th of March and Easter Sunday on the 25th, wherein the basic data of the Gospel could be squeezed in, making it possible to declare the year 31 AD occurring 532 years earlier the 'historical' Easter.

But this fortunate coincidence, turned into an ingenious idea, can only reduce the statistical improbability but by no means nullify it, because thus the alleged historical Easter date occurs 76 years—i.e. one Easter cycle—after Caesar's calendar reform. A fortuitousness that, coupled with the fact that the Julian leap years occur on years of Jesus' age divisible by four and that Jesus's birth even occurs exactly 100 years after that of Caesar, adds up to a sheer probabilistic impossibility.

This apart from the inner inconsistency of that bold solution—that way in which Jesus could not have been crucified on Friday because in the evening he had to take his Passover meal—there was just not enough time—Jesus was captured, taken to court, on the way from Pontius to Caiphas, back to Pilatus, before the people, etc., flagellated, crucified, taken off the cross and buried—and then the legal difficulties—the capture, trial and crucifixion all on a Passover Sabbath.

For comparison: With Caesar a whole week passed from the death to the gathering of the ashes – incidentally, this was according to the established custom. Leaning on several places in Vergil, the commentator Cruquianus says to HORAT. *epod.* 17.47: *Apud antiquos moris fuit, ut triduo corpus defuncti iaceret domi [...] et post triduum in rogum ponebatur. [...] item post triduum cinis in urnam condebatur et tumulo mandabatur.*—'With the ancients it was the custom that the body of the deceased lay at home for three day [...] and after three days it was put on the pyre [...] also after three days, the ashes were gathered into the urn and buried in the tomb.' Two times three days plus the *Quinquatrus,* which came in between, made the week complete for Caesar. Interestingly enough, the Christian liturgy speaks of a *Triduum,* from Good Friday until Easter Sunday or Easter Monday, therein distancing itself from the alleged historical Easter of Dionysius, where everything should have happened in an even shorter time span. One sees what happened: By reinterpreting the exposition of Caesar's wax figure on the tropaeum at the cremation as his crucifixion, the first *triduum* was understood as the time of the court case between Jesus' capture and crucifixion and thus only the second triddum remained. The notion of the Passion Week, however, was preserved.

But back to Caesar and our question:

A clear indication of this associating by some of the Jews with the murderers of Caesar is given by Flavius Josephus himself.

Among the Roman benefactors of the Jews—who secured their cult which encountered resistance in the whole Empire and especially in the free towns or those allied with Rome in Asia minor—Josephus (Jos. *AJ* 14.10) counts, besides Caesar, who apparently made a start, and Augustus who confirmed it, a proconsul *Marcus Iunius Brutus, Son of Iunius,* of all people, who according to the predominant opinion of the commentators is the murderer of Caesar (*AJ* 14.10.25 [§262-264]; cf. Benedictus Niese, *Flavii Iosephi Opera,* Berlin 1892, vol. III, p 288, among other things the lection *Marcus Iunius Brutus, Son of Caepio,* as well as NOETHLICHS (1996), p. 85 and note 480). It is said that this Brutus had been requested by the Jews of the town of Ephesos that they might practice Sabbath and traditional customs without interference and he as the proconsul had conceded this to them. Hence the Ephesians decided: According to the Romans nobody shall prevent a Jew from celebrating the Sabbath or for this reason convict him to pay a fine, but the Jews may do everything according to their laws.

If Jews should have stayed particularly long at Caesar's cremation site out of gratitude to him, then other Jews should have abstained from it out of gratitude to Brutus. Even if one assumes that Brutus gave that permission to the Jews of Ephesos only later, e.g. 42 BC when he was in Asia, one would hardly want to suppose that Brutus had favored the Jews then, shortly before his Philippi, where the demon of the dead Caesar was to appear before him again, if they all had been with the mourners and so had been counted among those who had caused his flight from Rome. On the contrary: Just then, at the time of Caesar's funeral, the association between Brutus and likeminded Jews must have arisen and it must have had to do with the Sabbath celebration. Had they celebrated the *Quinquatrus* falling on the Sabbath of the week of Passover not only at the same time, but also together?

A coincidental similarity in the appearance and manner might have also contributed to the fusion of the image of the Jews with that of the murderers of Caesar. These, who posed as liberators, ostentatiously wore the *pilleus,* a felt hat or cap, the traditional Roman liberty cap. Brutus had it stamped on his coins, between two daggers and the inscription EID(ibus) MAR(tiis), 'on the Ides of march' (cf. ill. 30, p. 95), as a sign of the regained liberty of the Roman citizens from the alleged tyrant. Now, the same *pilleus* was also worn by freedmen as a sign of their personally won liberty (cf. MARQUARDT–MAU (1886) p. 355 u. Anm. 8: Nonius p. 528: *Plautus in Amphitruone* (462): *Ut ego hodie raso capite calvus capiam pilleum.*—'in order that I, with shaved head, receive the cap of liberty today'). It was far from uncommon that the Jews gained Roman citizenship by way of manumission, and so they presented exactly this habitus (which Jews, bound to tradition, interestingly maintain until today). It was a similarity that was even completed by the fact that Brutus wore a beard in order to emphasize the connection with the old Brutus, while those mourning over Caesar did not shave either anymore (according to custom). Since in times of tumults, in dangers, in war, and eminently during civil war, it was usual practice *servos ad pilleum vocare*—'to call the slaves to the liberty cap', which means promising them liberty so that they joined in the battle instead of running away or defecting. And since Brutus did call all to insurrection, it probably resulted in many a confusion with fatal consequences. Caesar's friend Helvius Cinna had indeed been lynched by the enraged crowd only because he was mistaken for the homonymous Cornelius Cinna, who had spoken against Caesar. So the uncanny situation arose that Caesar's freedmen, especially those named in the testament, who according to tradition walked alongside the relatives and heirs in front of or beside the bier out of gratitude, that they wore the same cap as the conspirators and all those to whom Brutus had given liberty in the heat of the battle. On that day all wearers of caps lived in danger, all the more so if they wore a beard also. And if the conspirators had left Rome even before the funeral reception (cf. NIC. DAM. 17, PLUT. *Brut.* 21), the same crowd that tore Helvius Cinna into pieces on the spot without listening to explanations, certainly caught many another man, whether he was the right one or not.

A reverberation of this ambivalent relationship, first of the Caesareans and then of the Christians, towards the Jews could also resonate in Suetonius' account. Writing between two Jewish wars, the secretary of Hadrian—who soon had to cope with the Bar-Kochba insurrection—at any rate, always reports on the negative attitude of the emperors towards the Jews and with a preference to issues connected with money or expulsions at that. (The famous passage that we already dealt with in the chapter 'Re-Orientation'—SUET. *Claud.* 25.4: *Iudaeos impulsore chresto assidue tumultuantis Roma expulit*—does not make an exception either, since we meanwhile know, how it is translated correctly: '...he banished from Rome the Jews, who were practicing usury and by that continually created unrest'). So that one finally is quite surprised to learn that Jews stayed particularly long at Caesar's cremation site, when he has not given a reason for it. What did he want to say? Look, all emperors after Caesar treated the Jews badly, only Caesar did not: for they mourned especially long over his murder? Does Suetonius here really want to praise their reverence—that the Jews had stood at his bustum out of attachment and adoration to Caesar and stood there longest of all, even longer than the Gauls themselves—or rather to report gossip—that they had stood there longest of all, at night, in order to hush up the fact that they together with Antipater, were already about to reach an agreement with the murderers of Caesar, or even, to have the opportunity to screen the ashes for gold. Or both?

Suetonius remains silent about why the Jews were so eager here. But by the sequence of his account he seems to suggest ironically to the reader what they might have been looking for in a place where such a lot of jewelry had come under the ashes—relics? Because staying longer than necessary at a *bustum,* a spent funeral pyre, was suspicious, for it was implied that one might search through the ashes for the remnants of the molten valuables that had been thrown into the fire by the mourners.

That even respected personalities were not immune to that suspicion is shown by Plutarchus who reports an accusation of Cato, who was above suspicion, a reproach which probably was raised by Caesar in his *Anticato* against the upholder of moral standards he was in conflict with. When Cato's brother died, Cato had arranged a splendid funeral, in which a lot of incense goods, many precious garments and much jewelry donated by cities and rulers had been burnt together with the dead. Cato pretended to not want to accept money and gifts, but had to put up with being reproached in writing of having sieved the ashes of the deceased in order to get hold of the melted gold (PLUT. *Cato Minor* 11). Since the reproach against Cato had been taken up by Caesar himself in his *Anticato* (cf. TSCHIEDEL (1981) p. 113 sqq), Caesar's followers will hardly for their part have sieved Caesar's ashes: ergo it remained a 'valuable' relic in that respect also. The oldest sacral law, recorded in the twelve tables, forbade giving the dead person gold into the grave (*«Neve aurum addito ... Cui auro dentes iuncti escunt, ast im cum illo sepelirei ureive se fraude esto.»*: cf. CIC., *leg.* 2.24.60. This was probably in order to not encourage desecration by plunderers). In Caesar's case, at any rate, it is said that only the bones which remained after the cremation were picked up for burying in the family tomb (cf. DIO CASS. HR 44.51.1-2: τὰ γὰρ ⟨ὀστᾶ⟩ αὐτοῦ οἱ ἐξελεύθεροι προανείλοντο καὶ ἐς τὸ πατρῷον μνημεῖον κατέθεντο—'for his freedmen had already picked up his bones and buried them in the family tomb'), so that the relics now would have been available for picking up by the mourners, i.e. in the case of Caesar by the whole people, because except for the murderers all were mourning.

This, however, was risqué. Because the robbing of dead people was punishable with the death penalty and for its imposition during the civil war, the suspicion was sufficient. After Philippi, Antonius spread his very precious purple robe across the body of Brutus and instructed a freedman to take care of the burial. When he later learned that the freeman had not burnt the purple robe together with the body and also had embezzled a big part of the money destined for the burial, he had him executed (PLUT. *Ant.* 22, *Brut.* 53) (Mark's lection—'...and when they had crucified him, they parted his garments casting lots upon them...'—could still retain a memory of that). And as burial gifts belonged to the dead person it is hardly conceivable that those, of all people, who had thrown the offerings on Caesar's funeral pyre—and everyone had thrown just what they had with them, the actors their triumphal garments (cf. SUET. *Jul.* 84), the veterans their gold and silver decorated splendor weapons (cf. SUET. *Jul.* 67), the family mothers their pieces of jewelry and even the golden breastplaques and purple-fringed tunics of their children—now went there again and fetched back remains of the melted things: A gift is a gift. But they must have been pikked up, those relics, because they were too valuable, in every respect. Since at first an altar was erected at the cremation site, where the people carried on bringing offerings, and later the temple of Divus Iulius was added, one could assume that those relics were kept in that temple, like exvotos. But did they all get there? Did they all still exist? That altar was first knocked over by the consuls, the initiators were killed, even crucified, and years passed until the temple of Divus Iulius could be consecrated. Had the same freedmen of Caesar, who had 'picked up his bones and buried them in the family tomb,' also saved the relics and did their status succor them in doing so, because being Romans and strangers at the same time, they were less affected by the religious taboos? And had they handed them over to the followers of Caesar from all the peoples of the earth whom Suetonius calls 'the many foreigners who lived in Rome', who 'had sung dirges in groups according to their respective customs' and who had thus now become the moving force of the cult of Divus Iulius? Had they distributed them among Caesar's followers and thereby scattered them over the whole Empire, where they were kept in all the *caesarea* resp. basilicas, which had already emerged everywhere in the Empire and continued to emerge? And did 'especially the Jews who even visited the cremation site for many nights in a row' distinguish themselves in that respect too? In any case, when centuries later St. Helena, the mother of Constantine, let the allegedly 'true cross' be searched for and wanted to find it in Jerusalem and found it, it is said that the place was revealed to her by an inspired Jew (Cyriacus: cf. Paulinus of Nola, *ep.* 31.5). Had the tradition about it already formed from the relics at Caesar's cremation site? Was it therefore regarded as a matter of course that 'particularly the Jews' knew where some, and not the unimportant ones, of 'His' relics were hiding? Did the traditional collecting of relics on the part of the Christians as well as the dealing in relics that inevitably went along with it, originate at Caesar's cremation site?

184 In Jerusalem the Greek patriarch lights the Easter fire in the Holy Sepulchre. As he leaves the tomb, he lights the torches of the believers who then run with them out of the church and announce the resurrection: *Christós anesti!* In the Eastern churches (Greece, Armenia, etc.) the Easter fire is enormous, and in some rural parishes there is still an effigy of 'Judas' on top, understood by the people as the burning of Judas. A comparable custom is seen in the West too, indeed not always at Easter, but in the week between the 15th and the 20th of March, presumably the ancient date of Easter. For example at the 'fallas' of Valencia and environs they also burn a huge fire with effigies of Judas in multifarious variations. Does 'Judas' here stand for 'Julas', i.e. 'Julius'? (Compare: *IVLIVS* > *IOYΛAC* > *IOYΔAC*). With this custom the people would be faithfully re-enacting the cremation of Caesar's body—which in the meantime had become incomprehensible to them—so they would have changed its meaning to the desired burning of Judas.

185 Cf. DIO CASS. *HR* 47.19.1.

186 STAUFFER (1957), p. 135, note 4, does just this, but does not specify the common archetypes.
187 Cf. GABBA (1956), as well the *Introduzione* van GABBA (1958).
188 That Appianus could have used novel-like sources has often been suggested, cf. i.a. SCHWARTZ (Ed.), *RE*, s.v. Appianus, Sp. 222-37, explicitly in reference to Antonius' funeral speech: Sp. 230; ANDRÉ (1949), p. 41 sqq.
189 WEINSTOCK (1971), p. 354. He points out that a praetexta *Cato* by Curiatius Maternus existed (TAC. *Dial.* 2.1; cf. TEUFFEL-KROLL 2.296, s.v. Vespasian), which leads us to assume a praetexta *Iulius Caesar*, in the same way that the *Cato* by Cicero was followed immediately by Caesar's *Anticato*—and they were read in counterpoise.
190 Even if this is not absolutely confirmed by CIC. *Att.* 14.10.1 and *Phil.* 2.90sq (cf. DRUMANN & GROEBE, 1899-1922², reprint Hildesheim 1964, 1 p. 74), yet the publication of the *oratio funebris* by Antonius in accordance with Roman tradition is probable (cf. BENGTSON (1977), p. 82 sqq). Hence the speech as rendered by Appianus can be regarded as authentic.
191 Cf. NICOLAUS DAMASCENUS, *Bios Kaisaros, FGrH*, ed. F. Jacoby, 26.82, i.a.
192 Suetonius does not mention the name Caesar at all in his report on the funeral (*Jul.* 84).
193 NICOLAUS DAMASCENUS, *Bios Kaisaros, FGrH*, ed. F. Jacoby, 26.97: οἰκέται δὲ δὴ τρεῖς, οἵπερ ἦσαν πλησίον, ὀλίγον ὕστερον ἐνθέμενοι τὸν νεκρὸν εἰς φορεῖον οἴκαδε ἐκόμιζον διὰ τῆς ἀγορᾶς. ὁρᾶν δ' ἐνῆν ἔνθεν καὶ ἔνθεν ἀπεσταλμένων τῶν παρακαλυμμάτων, αἰωρουμένας τὰς χεῖρας καί τὰς ἐπὶ τοῦ προσώπου πληγάς. ἔνθα οὐδεὶς ἀδάκρυς ἦν ὁρῶν τὸν πάλαι ἴσα καὶ θεὸν τιμώμενον· οἰμωγῆι τε πολλῆι καὶ στόνωι συμπαρεπέμπετο ἔνθεν καὶ ἔνθεν ὀλοφυρομένων ἀπό τε τῶν τεγῶν καθ' οὕς ἂν γένοιτο καὶ ἐν ταῖς ὁδοῖς καὶ προθύροις. καὶ ἐπειδὴ πλησίον τῆς οἰκίας ἐγένετο, πολὺ δὴ μείζων ὑπήντα κωκυτός· ἐξ<επ>επηδήκει γὰρ ἡ γυνὴ μετὰ πολλοῦ ὄχλου γυναικῶν τε καὶ οἰκετῶν, ἀνακαλουμένη τόν ἄνδρα καὶ ἑαυτὴν ὀδυρομένη, ὅτι μάτην προύλεγε μὴ ἐξιέναι τὴν ἡμέραν ἐκείνην. τῶι δ' ἤδη μοῖρα ἐφειστήκει πολὺ κρείττων ἢ κατὰ τὴν αὐτῆς ἐλπίδα.
194 PLUT. *Caes.* 1-2: εἶτ' ἀποπλέων, ἁλίσκεται περὶ τὴν Φαρμακοῦσσαν νῆσον ὑπὸ πειρατῶν, ἤδη τότε στόλοις μεγάλοις καὶ σκάφεσιν ἀπλέτοις κατεχόντων τὴν θάλατταν. Πρῶτον μὲν οὖν αἰτηθεὶς ὑπ' αὐτῶν λύτρα εἴκοσι τάλαντα, κατεγέλασεν ὡς οὐκ εἰδότων ὅν ἡρήκοιεν, αὐτὸς δ' ὡμολόγησε πεντήκοντα δώσειν· ἔπειτα τῶν περὶ αὐτὸν ἄλλον εἰς ἄλλην διαπέμψας πόλιν ἐπὶ τὸν τῶν χρημάτων πορισμόν, ἐν ἀνθρώποις φονικωτάτοις Κίλιξι μεθ' ἑνὸς φίλου καὶ δυοῖν ἀκολούθοιν ἀπολελειμμένος, οὕτω καταφρονητικῶς εἶχεν, ὥστε πέμπων ὁσάκις ἀναπαύοιτο προσέταττεν αὐτοῖς σιωπᾶν. ἡμέραις δὲ τεσσαράκοντα δυεῖν δεούσαις, ὥσπερ οὐ φρουρούμενος ἀλλὰ δορυφορούμενος ὑπ' αὐτῶν, ἐπὶ πολλῆς ἀδείας συνέπαιζε καὶ συνεγυμνάζετο, καὶ ποιήματα γράφων καὶ λόγους τινὰς ἀκροαταῖς ἐκείνοις ἐχρῆτο, καὶ τοὺς μὴ θαυμάζοντας ἄντικρυς ἀπαιδεύτους καὶ βαρβάρους ἀπεκάλει, καὶ σὺν γέλωτι πολλάκις ἠπείλησε κρεμᾶν αὐτούς· οἱ δ' ἔχαιρον, ἀφελείᾳ τινὶ καὶ παιδιᾷ τὴν παρρησίαν ταύτην νέμοντες. ὡς δ' ἧκον ἐκ Μιλήτου τὰ λύτρα καὶ δοὺς ἀφείθη, πλοῖα πληρώσας εὐθὺς ἐκ τοῦ Μιλησίων λιμένος ἐπὶ τοὺς λῃστὰς ἀνήγετο, καὶ καταλαβὼν ἔτι πρὸς τῇ νήσῳ ναυλοχοῦντας, ἐκράτησε τῶν πλείστων. καὶ τὰ μὲν χρήματα λείαν ἐποιήσατο, τοὺς δ' ἄνδρας ἐν Περγάμῳ καταθέμενος εἰς τὸ δεσμωτήριον, αὐτὸς ἐπορεύθη πρὸς τὸν διέποντα τὴν Ἀσίαν Ἴουγκον, ὡς ἐκείνῳ προσῆκον ὄντι στρατηγῷ κολάσαι τοὺς ἑαλωκότας. ἐκείνου δὲ καὶ τοῖς χρήμασιν ἐποφθαλμιῶντος (ἦν γὰρ οὐκ ὀλίγα), καὶ περὶ τῶν αἰχμαλώτων σκέψεσθαι φάσκοντος ἐπὶ σχολῆς, χαίρειν ἐάσας αὐτὸν ὁ Καῖσαρ εἰς Πέργαμον ᾤχετο, καὶ προαγαγὼν τοὺς λῃστὰς ἅπαντας ἀνεσταύρωσεν, ὥσπερ αὐτοῖς δοκῶν παίζειν ἐν τῇ νήσῳ προειρήκει πολλάκις.
SUET. *Jul.* 4: [...] *Rhodum secedere statuit, et ad declinandam inuidiam et ut per otium ac requiem Apollonio Moloni clarissimo tunc dicendi magistro operam daret.*

huc dum hibernis iam mensibus traicit, circa Pharmacussam insulam a praedonibus captus est mansitque apud eos non sine summa indignatione prope quadraginta dies cum uno medico et cubicularis duobus. nam comites seruosque ceteros initio statim ad expediendas pecunias, quibus redimeretur, dimiserat. numeratis deinde quinquaginta talentis expositus in litore non distulit quin e uestigio classe deducta persequeretur abeuntis ac redactos in potestatem supplicio, quod saepe illis minatus inter iocum fuerat, adficeret.
SUET. Jul. 74: sed et in ulciscendo natura lenissimus piratas, a quibus captus est, cum in dicionem redegisset, quoniam suffixurum se cruci ante iurauerat, iugulari prius iussit, deinde suffigi [...].

195 PLUT. Caes. 1-2: καὶ σὺν γέλωτι πολλάκις ἠπείλησε κρεμᾶν αὐτούς ... καὶ προαγαγὼν τοὺς λῃστὰς ἅπαντας ἀνεσταύρωσεν, ὥσπερ αὐτοῖς δοκῶν παίζειν ἐν τῇ νήσῳ προειρήκει πολλάκις. Appianus also uses the same verb kremô for 'to crucify', for example when he reports that Antonius had the slave followers of Amatius crucified. APP. BC 3.3.9: ἕως ἑτέρων ἐπιπεμφθέντων ἐξ Ἀντωνίου ἀμυνόμενοί τε ἀνῃρέθησαν ἔνιοι καὶ συλληφθέντες ἕτεροι ἐκρεμάσθησαν, ὅσοι θεράποντες ἦσαν, οἱ δὲ ἐλεύθεροι κατὰ τοῦ κρημνοῦ κατερρίφησαν. As the rebellion originated because Amatius had erected an altar on the site of Caesar's funeral pyre, the confusion of 'to cremate', cremo > kremô, 'to crucify', could have originated here. As statues of Caesar are also concerned here, called by Appianus—andriantes—similar to the word for the wax simulacrum on Caesar's cross—andreikelon—the confusion could have been executed backwards there as well. To make it more complete, we note here that during the slaughter of Amatius' followers, as well as during the cremation of Caesar, people were hurled from the Tarpeian rock—in the one instance the free citizens amongst the followers of Amatius and in the other the daring fellows who wanted to cremate Caesar's body on the Capitol. Appianus calls the Tarpeian rock krêmnos 'overhanging bank'—the root of which is the same as for kremô. Not by chance are both words found in the above cited quotation from Appianus—as if the one would demand the presence of the other: this could have given the last kick to the confusion.

196 Namely the fashion of crucifixion was not uniform: cf. MOMMSEN (1899), p. 918sqq.

197 Cf. PLUT. Rom. 16: τοῦ δὲ Ῥωμύλου τὰς εἰκόνας ὁρᾶν ἔστιν ἐν Ῥώμῃ τὰς τροπαιοφόρους πεζὰς ἁπάσας.

198 PLUT. Rom. 16: Ὁ δὲ Ῥωμύλος, ὡς ἂν μάλιστα τὴν εὐχὴν τῷ τε Διὶ κεχαρισμένην καὶ τοῖς πολίταις ἰδεῖν ἐπιτερπῆ παράσχοι σκεψάμενος, ἐπὶ στρατοπέδου δρῦν ἔτεμεν ὑπερμεγέθη καὶ διεμόρφωσεν ὥσπερ τρόπαιον, καὶ τῶν ὅπλων τοῦ Ἄκρωνος ἕκαστον ἐν τάξει περιήρμοσε καὶ κατήρτησεν, αὐτὸς δὲ τὴν μὲν ἐσθῆτα περιεζώσατο, δάφνῃ δ' ἐστέψατο τὴν κεφαλὴν κομῶσαν. ὑπολαβὼν δὲ τῷ δεξιῷ τὸ τρόπαιον ὤμῳ προσερειδόμενον ὀρθόν, ἐβάδιζεν ἐξάρχων ἐπινικίου παιᾶνος ἐν ὅπλοις ἑπομένῃ τῇ στρατιᾷ, δεχομένων τῶν πολιτῶν μετὰ χαρᾶς καὶ θαύματος. ἡ μὲν οὖν πομπὴ τῶν αὖθις θριάμβων ἀρχὴν καὶ ζῆλον παρέσχε, τὸ δὲ τρόπαιον ἀνάθημα Φερετρίου Διὸς ἐπωνομάσθη—τὸ γὰρ πλῆξαι φερῖρε Ῥωμαῖοι καλοῦσιν, εὔξατο δὲ πλῆξαι τὸν ἄνδρα καὶ καταβαλεῖν [...].

199 We are almost forced to answer the question in the affirmative. For if Simon stands for Antonius, then kêryx, 'herald', stands for Kyrene, and so Simon a Cyrenian reflects Antonius per praeconem, 'Antonius by the herald', who according to Suetonius, read out that decision of the Senate that awarded Caesar all the divine and human honors at the same time, and also the oath by which all the senators obliged themselves to protect him. SUET. Jul. 84: Laudationis loco Antonius per praeconem pronuntiauit senatus consultum, quo omnia simul ei diuina atque humana decreuerat, item ius iurandum, quo se cuncti pro salutem unius astrinxerat; quibus perpauca a se uerba addidit.

200 TAC. *Hist.* 4.11: *seruile supplicium*. Free non-Romans and citizens were threatened with crucifixion in the case of offences that were typical for slaves, such as incitement to rebellion, homicide, robbery, switching sides to the enemy, high treason etc.
201 PLUT. *Rom.* 12.4: τούτου μὲν οὖν οὐκ ἔστιν ὅ τι μᾶλλον ηὔξησε τὴν Ῥώμην, ἀεὶ προσποιοῦσαν ἑαυτῇ καὶ συννέμουσαν ὧν κρατήσειεν.
202 Cf. i.a. ROSSO FIORENTINO, *Deposizione dalla croce*, Volterra Pinacoteca, as well as generally Fra Angelico.
203 Cf. BATTENBERG (1980), p. 87 sqq.
204 Cf. ZANKER (1990), p. 61-63.
205 Well-known is a signet-ring of Mithradates VI with moon and star. Cf. O. Ja. NEVEROD, «Mitridat Evpator i perstii-pecati iz Pantikapeja», *Sovetskaja Archeologija 1*, 1968, p. 235 sqq. For the discussion about the symbolism of moon and star in the imperial coinage of Caesar cf. BATTENBERG (1980), p. 72 n. 1 and passim, but he cannot demonstrate any results (epilogue of l. c.: 'But this explanation is not satisfying either').
206 SUET. *Jul.* 79: *proximo autem senatu Lucium Cottam quindecimuirum sententiam dicturum, ut, quoniam fatalibus libris contineretur Parthos nisi a rege non posse uinci, Caesar rex appellaretur.* Following PLUT. *Caes.* 64.1 and APP. *BC* 2.110 Caesar had planned to continue being *dictator* in Rome and to accept the title 'king' in the Eastern provinces.
207 Tablet of stone from the middle of the ninth century BC. The sun-god Schamasch on the right on the throne beneath the tent receives a king, on the left accompanying two Godheads. The symbol of the sun is located in the middle on the altar. Beneath the tent on the right above are depicted the cosmic symbols moon, sun and the star of Astarte.
208 The plate made of gold plated silver is embossed and decorated with jewels. It has a diameter of 61 cm and it was found at the village Malaya Pereshchepina (near Poltava). On the basis of the inscription it is dated between 491 and 518 AD. At that time bishop Paternus lived in Constantiana, the former Milesian settlement Tomi on the Black Sea. It became famous as the town of Ovidius' banishment and it furnishes early evidence of Christianity (today the Romanian port and city Constanta). We have only depicted the isolated bottom of the plate.
209 Cf. ZANKER (1990), p. 43. FITTSCHEN (1976), p. 187, argues for the issuing of the coin in 17 BC or shortly after, because a comet appeared again during the secular games of that year, which was again connected with Caesar (cf. the source indicated in the study). In any case we find ourselves in the period after the consecration of the temple of Divus Iulius, which took place in 29 BC.
210 The cross in Jesus' aureole is mostly a cross of the Maltese type, which only appears to have four points. In reality it is a star with eight rays because it can be seen as both light on a dark background and vice versa. This is especially recognizable in the earlier reproductions. Hence we are led back to the *sidus Iulium*.
211 Cf. SIMON (1986), p. 51. Following the example of the cult-statue of Mars the author reconstructs (p. 56) the statue of Augustus of Prima Porta with a lance pointed down in the right hand and a laurel branch in the left. As Divus Iulius holds the 'lance' in the left on the Lentulus-denarius the tip did not necessarily point to the front.
212 This wreath was meant for the victorious Agrippa, who will not by chance soon sit next to his father-in-law Augustus on the *sella curulis* (à propos: wasn't there something like this? 'He shall sit on the right hand of the Father...'?)
213 Cf. ZANKER (1990), p. 89, ill. 64 and p. 265, ill. 208. As mentioned elsewhere, Capricorn was Augustus' sign of the zodiac. Hence the Victoria on the antefix with the Capricorns beside the globe is unambiguously Augustan.

214 This impression is a little softened in another coinage of the same edition by Lentulus, located in the Glasgow Hunter Coin Cabinet. There the little figure on the hand of Divus Iulius looks somewhat feminine, however the little wing in the right above does not hang from the body but from the extremity of the left 'arm' (which is the right one from the viewers standpoint), so that also here, if we were to think of a Victoria at all, we would think of one *en face* and with the tropaeum on the left arm.

215 FITTSCHEN (1976) speaks up for Divus Iulius, when he finds here the typical Augustan triad of gods—Mars Ultor-Venus-Divus Iulius. SIMON (1979) on the other hand, speaks up for Gaius Caesar, the grandson and adoptive child of Augustus, asserting that the patron was the exceptionally well educated Iuba, who accompanied Gaius Caesar on his Oriental travels and who had written books for him on, amongst other things, Arabia. His wife was Selene, daughter of Antonius and Cleopatra, who was educated for some time in the house of Augustus' sister Octavia. For the artists had the tendency to depict gods, heroes and even other contemporaries with the features of their patrons—compare the adaptation of the features of Caesar and Octavianus to those of Antonius on the coins of Antonius depicted in ill. 93 and 96, as well as those of Caesar on the coins of Octavianus in ill. 92 and 98. So if the sculptor of Cherchel had received an order for Divus Iulius, he would have given him the features of the contemporary Caesar, Gaius, and vice versa, he would have opted to give Gaius Caesar, in the presence of Venus and Mars, a heroic representation à la Divus Iulius. In whichever case we have to reckon with the features of Gaius Caesar in the appearance of Divus Iulius. Our matter—the use of the Cherchel-torso in the examination of the appearance of Divus Iulius on the coins of Lentulus—is justified by that.

216 FITTSCHEN (1976), p. 184. The armored statue was originally painted, so that the sculptor could have left the depiction of aspects in the background to the painter—in this case aspects of the Victoria that were not emphasized in the relief.

217 Moreover there is a possibility—in order to not exclude any from the outset—that neither the garment of Victoria nor the trunk of the palm-tree were depicted at the left foot of the tropaeum, but flames—which would reflect Caesar's funeral pyre.

218 The fact that the tropaeum on the Prima-Porta-breastplate was sculpted to the back, whereas in that of Cherchel it is situated in the middle front could hint that, although the armored statue of Cherchel, for stylistic reasons, is estimated to be younger than the other and dependent on it, the central motif is older. For the divine triad Mars Ultor-Venus-Divus Iulius on which it is based, or which it reflects, was designed immediately after Philippi and the avowal of a temple for Mars Ultor (42 BC), and it existed since the time of the dedication of the temple of Divus Iulius (29 BC) at the latest, which was also realized in the form of a statue.

219 SIMON (1986), p. 223-4.

220 PLUT. *Sulla* 9, 7-9. Cf. discussion by BATTENBERG (1980), p. 168-71. His epilogue to p. 171: '[...] würde ich mich für die Vergottungstheorie entscheiden—my decision would be for the theory of the deification.' The fact that the untenable hypothesis of 'Sulla's dream' was raised at all indicates how reluctant scholars are to discern religious, even primal Christian motifs in Caesar.

221 In order to give only one example: On a limestone from the Coptic cemetery of Armant in Egypt we see a dolphin bearing a cross ($4^{th}/5^{th}$ century, Paris, Musée du Louvre).

222 We can see a crab on the head of the personified Jordan on the mosaic in the Baptisterium of the Arians in Ravenna—a sea crab, not a freshwater one—hence it cannot be a crab from the Jordan but rather from the Ionian sea.

223 Cf. the denarius of Servilius for Cassius after the victory over the fleet of Rhodos at Cos in 42 BC, whereon a crab holds a galleon figurehead in his claws:

79. Denarius of Servilius for Cassius, 42 BC

224 Cf. PLUT. *Ant.* 15.

225 ALFÖLDI (1953), p. 10, had also at first interpreted the veil on Caesar's head as a symbol of mourning, but then, following the prevailing opinion (cf. i.a. R.A. CARSON, *Gnomon 28, 1956*, p. 183) that sees in the reproduction *capite velato* the holding of priesthood, or even the 'homo pius', he interpreted it as an attribute of the *pontifex maximus*. Accordingly the dates of the coins that show Caesar with a veil were corrected to before the Ides of March. This outcome is not compelling because the veil does not characterize Caesar generally as *pontifex maximus*, but in a special way. As we saw before, on his first coinage illustrating his office as *pontifex maximus*, all the insignia are present (cf. ill. 20). It is not clear why he should have suddenly depicted himself *capite velato* in February-March in the year 44. The veil could indicate the fact that Caesar was buried as *pontifex maximus*, through which he narrowly escaped the violation of his body and became the object of an apotheosis demanded by the people. Hence a simultaneous genesis of the coins that show Caesar and Antonius *capite velato* is conceivable. The fact that the same P. Sepullius Macer was involved in striking the coins could also support it. Moreover we can observe the especially accentuated inclination of the head of Venus on the rear of the illustrated Caesar-coin of Macer, as if the goddess were also mourning. Also the abstract arrangement of the cross on the rear of Maridianus' denarius as well as its unusual surplus weight—7.61 grams instead of the customary 4 or so—rendering it unsuitable as currency and branding it as 'not of this world'. The appearance of all the 'veil' coins after the Ides of March is absolutely conceivable. Only the title CAESAR DICT · PERPETVO instead CAESAR PARENS PATRIAE on two Macer-denarii (*Crawford 480.11* and *480.13* against *480.20*) seems not to support it. But if the last mentioned coin was struck after Caesar's death on the order of Antonius, possibly parallel to the inscription on Caesar's statue as mentioned by Cicero and Suetonius (PARENTI OPTIME MERITO and PARENS PATRIAE), then we could assume that the first release of the Macer coin with Caesar *capite velato* still displayed the last title of his lifetime. In any case we have to consider that at least the Macer-denarius *Crawford 480/20* had to be minted after Caesar's murder, because the rear side with desultor and horses alludes to the Parilia, which were celebrated on the 21st of April: And this denarius had the wreathed head of Caesar *capite velato* and the title CAESAR PARENS PATRIAE on its front side.

226 Cf. the depiction of the ascension on the rear side of the altar of Augustus as Pontifex Maximus, between 12 and 2 BC, Vatican, Museo Gregoriano Profano. HELBIG (1963-72, nr. 255), KRAUS (1967, table 180) and ZANKER (BullComm 82, 1970/71 (1975), 153) explain it as the apotheosis of Julius Caesar. Erika SIMON (1986) and H. Prückner interpret this ascension as that of Romulus-Quirinus. In any case the one ascending to heaven is not borne by an eagle as with the later emperor conse-

crations, but by horses—as if the desultor-motif on the coins struck immediately after the Ides of March had been obligatory.

In one of the most ancient of all depictions of Christ (circa 210 AD) in the Necropolis beneath the Basilica of Peter in Rome, we see the triumphant Christ also being borne to heaven by horses (cf. *Der triumphierende Christus* [Christus Helios]; R. REISER (1995), p. 187). Interestingly, there, he is not standing on the chariot but separately behind the horses like Romulus/Divus Iulius on the Augustus-altar. One could more aptly interpret him as Christ Romulus resp. Christ Divus Iulius.

89. Reiderian plate: Caesar's last dream

Other early Christian depictions of the Ascension originate from another tradition. In the famous Reiderian plate, created around 400 AD, today in the Bavarian National Museum in Munich, one sees Christ ascending to heaven on a stairway of clouds, grasping God the Father's hand jutting out from a cloud. On the left there is Jesus' tomb in the form of a round little temple; behind it a laurel protrudes on which birds are picking; beneath one sees soldiers and other persons sleeping or gazing up in awe. This could be an apt depiction of the dream Caesar had the very night before his murder (SUET. *Jul.* 81): He seemed to be floating above the clouds and grasping the right hand of Jupiter; the day before, birds had been observed tearing to pieces a wren carrying a sprig of laurel. The round shape of Jesus' 'tomb' fits in also: It corresponds to that of the round altar at the temple of Divus Iulius, (cf. ill. 91, p. 117) the canopy seeming to be borrowed from that of the temple of Vesta resp. the temple of Mars Ultor which was originally planned and at first probably built in a round shape also.

227 Instead, the temple of *Divus Iulius,* built later by Octavianus, was consecrated. In parallel to that, the temple of *Mars ultor,* the avenging Mars, was inaugurated. Octavianus, who proscribed and persecuted Caesar's murderers and like Sulla proscribed all his other opponents as well, no longer showed interest in a temple to *Clementia Caesaris* which was seen as the cause of Caesar's death (cf. APP. *BC* 3.4.8).

228 Because of the name AVG_VST(us) on the rear of the coin—some authors assume the child's face to be a self portrait of Augustus as the young Octavianus.

229 SUET. *Aug.* 5: *Natus est Augustus M. Tullio Cicerone C. Antonio conss. VIII Kal. Octob. paulo ante solis exortum, regione Palati ad Capita bubula, ubi nunc sacrarium habet, aliquando post quam excessit constitutum.*

230 SUET. *Aug.* 96.
231 It can be observed on various coins and cameos in particular:

100. Swimming Capricorn and fishing youth with the features of Augustus

Cf. SIMON (1986), p. 159.
232 An image adorning the *Codex aureus* from 870 AD in the Bayerische Staatsbibliothek of Munich (Clm 14000, fol. 6r) depicts the adoration of a 'lamb of God' that has distinctly elaborated testicles: Below it there is an eight pointed star. Cf. REISER (1995), p. 89.
233 ZANKER (1990), p. 179, ill. 136 sees Pax herself in it (who gave the Ara Pacis its name), brought into line by the symbols of fertility with Tellus, the goddess of earth, as well as the fertility-providing Venus.
234 Depictions of the Madonna and child and the boy John are not so rare—to name just one: Giuliano Bugiardini, Galleria dell'Accademia, Firenze.

Excursus—Re-Orientation

235 The only point that has occasionally been disputed in the research on the matter is whether Caesar's apotheosis took place during his lifetime or posthumously. Different opinions were represented by e.g. DOBESCH (1966) and GESCHE (1968). Stefan WEINSTOCK (1971) wrote a summa on this theme without rationalistic limitations. Some of the inaccuracies (the author died before the book was published) have been corrected in the review by A. ALFÖLDI, *Gnomon* 47, 1975, p. 154-79. We may assume the opinion of ALFÖLDI (1973), p.p. 99-128 (Pl. IV-XIII) to be the final point of the discussion: Deification during lifetime with posthumous, though not uncontested, confirmation. See also CLAUSS (1999), who thinks among other things that Caesar had already been addressed as a god at the crossing of the Rubicon.
236 APP. *BC* 2.106-8: ὁ δὲ Καῖσαρ ἐς Ῥώμην ἠπείγετο, τὰ ἐμφύλια πάντα καθελών, ἐπὶ φόβου καὶ δόξης, οἵας οὔ τις πρὸ τοῦ· ὅθεν αὐτῷ τιμαὶ πᾶσαι, ὅσαι ὑπὲρ ἄνθρωπον, ἀμέτρως ἐς χάριν ἐπενοοῦντο, θυσιῶν τε πέρι καὶ ἀγώνων καὶ ἀναθημάτων ἐν πᾶσιν ἱεροῖς καὶ δημοσίοις χωρίοις, ἀνὰ φυλὴν ἑκάστην καὶ ἐν ἔθνεσιν ἅπασι, καὶ ἐν βασιλεῦσιν, ὅσοι Ῥωμαίοις φίλοι. σχήματά τε ἐπεγράφετο ταῖς εἰκόσι ποικίλα, καὶ στέφανος ἐκ δρυὸς ἦν ἐπ' ἐνίαις ὡς σωτῆρι τῆς πατρίδος, ᾧ πάλαι τοὺς ὑπερασπίσαντας ἐγέραιρον οἱ περισωθέντες. ἀνερρήθη δὲ καὶ πατὴρ πατρίδος, καὶ δικτάτωρ ἐς τὸν ἑαυτοῦ βίον ᾑρέθη καὶ ὕπατος ἐς δέκα ἔτη, καὶ τὸ σῶμα ἱερὸς καὶ ἄσυλος εἶναι καὶ χρηματίζειν ἐπὶ θρόνων ἐλεφαντίνων τε καὶ χρυσέων, καὶ θύειν μὲν αὐτὸν αἰεὶ θριαμβικῶς ἠμφιεσμένον, τὴν δὲ πόλιν ἀνὰ ἔτος ἕκαστον, αἷς αὐτὸς ἡμέραις ἐν παρατάξεσιν ἐνίκα, ἱερέας δὲ καὶ ἱερείας ἀνὰ πενταετὲς εὐχὰς δημοσίας ὑπὲρ αὐτοῦ τίθεσθαι, καὶ τὰς ἀρχὰς εὐθὺς καθισταμένας ὀμνύναι μηδενὶ τῶν ὑπὸ Καίσαρος ὁριζομένων ἀντιπράξειν. ἔς τε τιμὴν τῆς γενέσεως αὐτοῦ τὸν Κυϊντίλιον μῆνα 'Ιούλιον ἀντὶ Κυϊντιλίου μετωνόμασαν εἶναι. καὶ νεὼς ἐψηφίσαντο πολλοὺς αὐτῷ γενέσθαι καθάπερ θεῷ καὶ κοινὸν αὐτοῦ καὶ 'Επιεικείας, ἀλλήλους δεξιουμένων· οὕτως ἐδεδοίκεσαν μὲν ὡς δεσπότην, εὔχοντο δὲ σφίσιν ἐπιεικῆ γε-

νέσθαι. Εἰσὶ δ' οἳ καὶ βασιλέα προσειπεῖν ἐπενόουν, μέχρι μαθὼν αὐτὸς ἀπηγόρευσε καὶ ἠπείλησεν ὡς ἀθέμιστον ὄνομα μετὰ τὴν τῶν προγόνων ἀράν. σπεῖραι δ' ὅσαι στρατηγίδες αὐτὸν ἐκ τῶν πολέμων ἔτι ἐσωματοφυλάκουν, ἀπέστησε τῆς φυλακῆς καὶ μετὰ τῆς δημοσίας ὑπηρεσίας ἐπεφαίνετο μόνης... καὶ τοῖς ἐχθροῖς διηλλάσσετο καὶ τῶν πεπολεμηκότων οἱ πολλοὺς προῆγεν ἀθρόως ἐς ἐτησίους ἀρχὰς ἢ ἐς ἐθνῶν ἢ στρατοπέδων ἡγεμονίας.

237 SUET. *Jul.* 85: cf. note 37.

238 The respective involvement of Antonius and Octavianus in the deification of Caesar naturally had its highs and lows, according to political opportunity: cf. ALFÖLDI (1973), p.99-128 (pl.IV-XIII).

239 WEINSTOCK (1971), p.403.

240 Cf. WEINSTOCK (1971), p.398-411.

241 Flavius JOSEPHUS *AJ* 17.8.3; *BJ* 1.33.9. Cf. OTTO W.: P.W., *RE*, Suppl.II, Sp.167, s.v. Herodes, Nr.22; SCHALIT (1969).

242 SUET. *Jul.* 88: [...] *in deorum numerum relatus est, non ore modo decernentium, sed et persuasione uolgi*. In the meantime it has become generally accepted that the cult of Divus Iulius was the precursor of the ensuing emperor cult and also that the latter represents the connection between the earlier Hellenistic ruler cult and later Christianity. Cf. TAYLOR (1931); DOBESCH (1966); GESCHE (1968); WEINSTOCK (1971); WLOSOK (1978); PRICE (1984); CLAUSS (1999). What is little accounted for however is the fact that the emperor cult does not begin with Caesar, but actually with Octavianus Augustus, who as Appianus reports, indeed followed the footsteps of his adoptive father—but it is precisely this that illustrates the difference between the two men—Caesar did not follow anyone's footsteps at all. He had become absolute ruler, but by himself and had himself founded no dynasty. That was the reason for Antonius' opposition to Octavianus, whose political claims to inheritance he did not want to acknowledge as they were incompatible with the Republican tradition. This resistance of Antonius led to repeated wars, wherein Antonius *incerta fortuna* held his ground for a long period till he finally perished. There are two things of interest: for a long period Antonius refused to be inaugurated as *flamen Divi Iulii*, as high priest of the new God, precisely because he wanted to prevent Octavianus ipso facto becoming *Divi Filius*—the son of God; and the fact that Octavianus ordered the son of Antonius, who had sought refuge at a statue of Divus Iulius, where qua the *lex templi* he should have enjoyed the right of asylum, to nevertheless be torn away and executed (SUET. *Aug.* 17.10). So Octavianus as Divi Filius had set himself higher than Divus Iulius, whose rights he restricted at the same time he claimed to be his only heir (it is no coincidence that in the same regard he had driven Antonius and Cleopatra to death, and even had Caesar's son Caesarion killed, cf. SUET. *Aug.* l.c.). For this reason an incurable cesura had developed between the emperor's cult—the dynastic claim of Octavianus Augustus and many of the following emperors to be the only legitimate heirs of Caesar in a political and religious respect—and all the people, who in contrast to the respective actual and all too human emperor emphasized the unequalled and insurmountable divinity of the Empire's founder Divus Iulius Caesar and hung on to him. Christianity originated to a lesser extent from the emperor's cult but far more from this loyal adoration of Divus Iulius by the people who defied the dynastic claims.

243 Euhemeros lived at the end of the 4th and the beginning of the 3rd century BC. His famous book, ἱερὰ ἀναγραφή, which named the conditions for the deification of a ruler—εὐεργεσία and σωτηρία, 'well-doing, benefaction, charity, welfare' and 'deliverance, salvation, preservation, security, safety, health, well-being'—and hence outlined the theoretical motivation for the ruler cult, became a matter of polemics: he was accused of diminishing the status of the gods to the level of mankind. But

the book was so important that it was translated by Ennius into Latin. Following Ennius' translation it is cited by the Church Fathers, notably Lactantius.

244 App. BC 2.146: πρῶτα μὲν ὡς θεὸν οὐράνιον ὕμνει καὶ ἐς πίστιν θεοῦ γενέσεως τὰς χεῖρας ἀνέτεινεν, ἐπιλέγων ὁμοῦ σὺν δρόμῳ φωνῆς πολέμους αὐτοῦ καὶ μάχας καὶ νίκας καὶ ἔθνη, ὅσα προσποιήσειε τῇ πατρίδι, καὶ λάφυρα, ὅσα πέμψειεν, ἐν θαύματι αὐτῶν ἕκαστα ποιούμενος [...].

245 ἱστορία περὶ τὰ πρόσωπα ἀνδρῶν ἐπιφανῶν (ἥρωος, θεοῦ)—cf. CANCIK (1984).

246 REISER (1984).

247 2. Εὐαγγέλιον κατὰ Μάρκον. ἐγράφη ῥωμαϊστὶ ἐν Ῥώμῃ μετὰ ιβ' ἔτη τῆς ἀναλήψεως κυ. Fam. 13 of the 'Datumsvermerke—Annotations about dates', cited by ZUNTZ (1984), p.60.

248 HARRIS (1893).

249 COUCHOUD (1926).

250 TAC. *Hist.* 4.81: *Per eos mensis quibus Vespasianus Alexandriae statos aestivis flatibus dies et certa maris opperiebatur, multa miracula evenere, quis caelestis favor et quaedam in Vespasianum inclinatio numinum ostenderetur. e plebe Alexandrina quidam oculorum tabe notus genua eius advolvitur, remedium caecitatis exposcens gemitu, monitu Serapidis dei, quem dedita superstitionibus gens ante alios colit; precabaturque principem ut genas et oculorum orbis dignaretur respergere oris excremento. alius manum aeger eodem deo auctore ut pede ac vestigio Caesaris calcaretur orabat. Vespasianus primo inridere, aspernari; atque illis instantibus modo famam vanitatis metuere, modo obsecratione ipsorum et vocibus adulantium in spem induci: postremo aestimari a medicis iubet an talis caecitas ac debilitas ope humana superabiles forent. medici varie disserere: huic non exesam vim luminis et redituram si pellerentur obstantia; illi elapsos in pravum artus, si salubris vis adhibeatur, posse integrari. id fortasse cordi deis et divino ministerio principem electum; denique patrati remedii gloriam penes Caesarem, inriti ludibrium penes miseros fore. igitur Vespasianus cuncta fortunae suae patere ratus nec quicquam ultra incredibile, laeto ipse vultu, erecta quae adstabat multitudine, iussa exequitur. statim conversa ad usum manus, ac caeco reluxit dies. utrumque qui interfuere nunc quoque memorant, postquam nullum mendacio pretium.*

251 PLUT. *Grac.* 9: τὰ μὲν θηρία τὰ τὴν Ἰταλίαν νεμόμενα καὶ φωλεὸν ἔχει, καὶ κοιταῖόν ἐστιν αὐτῶν ἑκάστῳ καὶ κατάδυσις, τοῖς δ' ὑπὲρ τῆς Ἰταλίας μαχομένοις καὶ ἀποθνῄσκουσιν ἀέρος καὶ φωτός, ἄλλου δ' οὐδενὸς μέτεστιν, ἀλλ' ἄοικοι καὶ ἀνίδρυτοι μετὰ τέκνων πλανῶνται καὶ γυναικῶν, οἱ δ' αὐτοκράτορες ψεύδονται τοὺς στρατιώτας ἐν ταῖς μάχαις παρακαλοῦντες ὑπὲρ τάφων καὶ ἱερῶν ἀμύνεσθαι τοὺς πολεμίους· οὐδενὶ γάρ ἐστιν οὐ βωμὸς πατρῷος, οὐκ ἠρίον προγονικὸν τῶν τοσούτων Ῥωμαίων, ἀλλ' ὑπὲρ ἀλλοτρίας τρυφῆς καὶ πλούτου πολεμοῦσι καὶ ἀποθνῄσκουσι, κύριοι τῆς οἰκουμένης εἶναι λεγόμενοι, μίαν δὲ βῶλον ἰδίαν οὐκ ἔχοντες.

252 Mt. 8:20: Αἱ ἀλώπεκες φωλεοὺς ἔχουσιν καὶ τὰ πετεινὰ τοῦ οὐρανοῦ κατασκηνώσεις, ὁ δὲ υἱὸς τοῦ ἀνθρώπου οὐκ ἔχει ποῦ τὴν κεφαλὴν κλίνῃ.

253 Cited after SCHWEITZER (1906/[9]1984), p.452 (see there for the source).

254 Cf. BLASS et al. ([17]1990), p.6-9 (with specification of the sources).

255 BLASS et al. ([17]1990), p.8, note 10; COUCHOUD (1926).

256 Cf. CANCIK (1975), p.120.

257 Cf. VITTINGHOFF (1952); OTTO, W.: P.W., *RE*, Suppl. II, Sp. 167 sqq., s.v. Herodes, n°22. See the glossary on further explanations about the Aramaic.

258 2 Tim. 4:13: τὸν φαιλόνην ὃν ἀπέλιπον ἐν Τρῳάδι παρὰ Κάρπῳ ἐρχόμενος φέρε, καὶ τὰ βιβλία, μάλιστα τὰς μεμβράνας.

259 Cf. ROBERTS & SKEAT (1983).

260 ROBERTS & SKEAT (1983), p.6 and p.15-29.

261 Suet. *Jul.* 56.6: *epistulae quoque eius ad senatum extant, quas primum uidetur ad paginas et formam memorialis libelli conuertisse, cum antea consules et duces non nisi transuersa charta scriptas mitterent.*
262 ROBERTS & SKEAT (1983), p.6 and p.35-37.
263 ROBERTS & SKEAT (1983), p.6 and p.39. The fact that the text of a Gospel was written on the rear side of a scroll with no text on the front is also interesting from another point of view: what should have been written on the front side? As if the copyist knew that there had to be another text and that the Gospel was a text of the reverse: namely the apostille to a text that was so well known that it was not necessary to write it down—it was enough to leave this place free—the *vita Divi Iulii?*
264 ROBERTS & SKEAT (1983), p.6 and p.45-53. They take apart all the reasons that were mentioned by earlier authors. Also the two alternative hypotheses they tried are inconclusive, as they themselves admit: *'[...] neither of the two hypotheses discussed above is capable of proof [...]'* (p.61).
265 In the following we seek to reflect the general consensus of researchers, or of the general controversy of the irreconcilable opponents in this minefield. Cf. DER KLEINE PAULY (1979), s.v. Jesus; WIKENHAUSER & SCHMID (^{6}1973); SCHWEITZER (1906/^{2}1913 and 1906/^{9}1984); HEILIGENTHAL (1997); MESSORI (1976/^{32}1986); MESSORI (1997), i.a.
266 ALBERT SCHWEITZER (1906/^{2}1913, chap.22, p.451sqq.) places in the category of first deniers of any historicity of Jesus i.a.: Charles François Dupuis (book printed by the Club des Cordeliers), Constantin François Volnay (counselor of Napoleon), Bruno Bauer (Hegelian), Albert Kalthoff, John M. Robertson, Peter Jensen, Andrzej Niemojewski, Christian Paul Fuhrmann, William Benjamin Smith, Arthur Drews, Thomas Whittaker, S. Hoekstra, Allard Pierson, Samuel Adrian Naber, G.J.P.J. Bolland, Samuel Lublinski, temporarily also Abraham Dirk Loman. It would be pointless to name all the others who joined the ranks after 1913. As a representative of all the others, see Paul-Louis Couchoud.
267 So also the modernist Alfred Loisy, although his positions were radical enough for him to be excommunicated. Symptomatic of the trench warfare between the two implacable positions is the biting polemic that Loisy first launched at Wrede, then against Couchoud.
268 Cf. COUCHOUD (1924).
269 RUDOLF BULTMANN: *so gut wie nichts*—'next to nothing' (in: *Die Erforschung der synoptischen Evangelien*—'Investigating the synoptic Gospels', Berlin ^{3}1960, p.12).
270 Cf. BORNKAMM (1956), p.11: 'Am Ende dieser Leben-Jesu-Forschung steht die Erkenntnis ihres eigenen Scheiterns—The conclusion of the Life of Jesus research is the discovery of its own failure', cited in HEILIGENTHAL (1997), p.8; cf. also SCHWEITZER (1906/^{2}1913), p.631.
[NB: As the good Augstein has passed on since then, we have considered whether we should leave out the following note for reasons of reverence: *de mortuis nihil nisi bene*. However, since his *Jesus Son of Man* is still haunting around, and nevertheless—or just because—*Der Spiegel* [a famous German news magazine] and its pseudo-enlightening counterparts all over the world have not been able to prevent the digital worst case scenario of the Mel Gibson movie with their positivistic critique of traditional ecclesiastical fabulation, and with this, apparent for all to see, they have completely failed, we still leave the note, or at least the core of it.]
A pompous victim of this impasse of the Life of Jesus research is Rudolf Augstein. For decades the editor of the news magazine *Der Spiegel* has been trying to adopt the results of scientific theology as weapons in his everlasting crusade to instruct and inform the public against the 'Wojtyla-Pope' who is holding on to 'sanctimonious legends'.

In doing so the theology journalist misses the realization that scientific theology is not scientific at all. Albert Schweitzer, whom he likes to quote, already had to state apropos David Friedrich Strauß: 'He fought a dogma of scientific theology which defends them more doggedly than the Church defends hers until today' (l.c. p.122). Augstein is seemingly the only person who has not yet noticed that it is not science that stands against the fostering of legends, but dogma standing against dogma, and that the dogmas of a wannabe-science of yesterday must inevitably succumb to those of the Church which are richer in tradition.

'Of yesterday' is not meant polemically here but temporally-factually. The same Albert Schweitzer, even in the sixth edition of his fundamental book in 1950, refused to update the second edition of 1913 opining that the historical investigation of the public appearance of Jesus which had begun in the last third of the eighteenth century 'has reached a certain completion during the first decade of the twentieth century' (l.c. p.29). Thus he had euphemistically dismissed all that had come later as futile elucubrations, including the teachings of the form-historical method and similar. Couchoud had namely demonstrated with Kantian inevitability in the twenties that anything trying to go beyond textual criticism runs into emptiness, so that the 'Life of Jesus research' was history, to be filed away. Albert Schweizer was spared the more or less esoteric and increasingly fanciful modern images of Jesus.

In spite of his profound insight into the Lacrima-Christi problem, he does not regard depicting Jesus as 'glutton and wine bibber' as insult, but as an attempt to 'present him with more popular touch'. The nation's philosopher of the Enlightenment untiringly rehashes his mulligan of myth and historiette again and again, and does not notice that the one hypothesis excludes the other: the derivation of the Gospels from myth excludes the historical existence of Jesus and vice versa. Augstein's eclectical combination of both neutralizes both ingredients and makes them appetizers for papal food in whose pot he tries to spit. So he must witness how the believers still prefer receiving Holy communion in church, rather than sipping from his stale soup.

271 See above note 40.
272 Amongst others, *OC (ὅς)*, 'he', was mistaken for *ΘC (θεός)*, 'God'.
273 Thus Mark, especially in the bi-lingual Bezae Cantabrigiensis.
274 Some facts: not even half the words in the Gospels are the same in all manuscripts. The vast majority of the worst changes were created before the start of the third century. Not one papyrus dates earlier than the 2nd century and no manuscript is regarded as coming from an archetype earlier than the same 2nd century. From the generally accepted date of the death of Christ a century of text tradition lies in darkness.

Of the different text types that the modern textual critics were able to establish, one is questionable (Caesarea-text); the value of the Byzantine and Egyptian ones is disputed; whereas on the Western and the so-called neutral text there is a debate about age and priority. Until today, no original text has been able to be established. The published Greek text, the foundation of all new translations, remains on the basis of the textus receptus, the 'generally accepted one', i.e. the Byzantine, i.e. from the viewpoint of textual-criticism: the worst.

If the reader wants to get a feeling for the frequent 'improving' changes and rechanges the scribes made while blaming one another, he or she may visit the following website where an amusing example is given concerning Heb. 1:3 in the *Codex Vaticanus Graece 1209, B/03*:

http://www-user.uni-bremen.de/~wie/Vaticanus/note1512.html

On page 1512, the beginning of Hebrews, a curious marginal note appears, where a later scribe complains about a change of the text of Heb. 1:3 made by an earlier hand: ἀμαθέστατε καὶ κακέ, ἄφες τὸν παλαιόν, μὴ μεταποίει—'Fool and knave, can't you leave the old lection untouched and not alter it!'

275 Cf. HEILIGENTHAL (1997), p. 108-119.
276 This cycle, like a game of Rock, Paper, Scissors between the historical-critical school, the mythological school and the traditionalists, is elucidated by MESSORI (1976/³²1986).
277 John and Jacobus only have a historical background if they are identical with the persons of the same names in Acts—which is purely hypothetical—and they also have to be the same persons who show up in Flavius Josephus. But then the father Zebedee is missing.
278 The nautical tow rope could be more original as the Evangelists were mocked for their miserable barbaric 'sailor language' (Celsus in ORIGENES, contra Celsum I 62), and not because of their 'Bedouin language'.
279 The same occurs mutatis mutandis with our contemporary scriptwriters: Why are there so many scripts about the world of scriptwriters? Why do so many directors make films about the movie-milieu? Because this is all they really know. The *cinéma vérité* becomes the *cinéma du cinéma*. The true novel is the novel about the writer.
280 Cf. SCHWEITZER (1906/²1913), p. 458 sq.
281 SUET. *Claud*. 25.4: *Iudaeos impulsore chresto assidue tumultuantis Roma expulit*.
282 It is still in use today in urban Rome: *far(ci) la cresta* means 'profiteer', 'to demand an extortionate price'.
283 TAC. *Ann*. 15.44: *sed non ope humana, non largitionibus principis aut deum placamentis decedebat infamia quin iussum incendium crederetur. ergo abolendo rumori Nero subdidit reos et quaesitissimis poenis adfecit quos per flagitia invisos vulgus chrestianos appellabat.* 'The form of the name *Christianos* was established in manuscripts by correction; it had previously been *chrestianos*. That this [...] form had been in use is attested to by, i.a., Lactantius IV 7 and Tertullianus *Apol.* 32 extr.' (TAC. *Ann*. 15.44, K. NIPPERDAY and G. ANDRESEN (Eds.), ¹¹1915, p. 264, note 4).
284 TAC. *Ann*. 15.44: *auctor nominis eius Christus Tiberio imperitante per procuratorem Pontium Pilatum supplicio adfectus erat; [...]*.
285 TAC. *Ann*. 15.38: *nec quisquam defendere audebat, crebris multorum minis restinguere prohibentium, et quia alii palam faces iaciebant atque esse sibi auctorem vociferabantur, sive ut raptus licentius exercerent seu iussu*.
286 TAC. *Ann*. 15.44: *igitur primum correpti qui fatebantur, deinde indicio eorum multitudo ingens haud proinde in crimine incendii quam odio humani generis convicti sunt. et pereuntibus addita ludibria, ut ferarum tergis contecti laniatu canum interirent, [aut crucibus adfixi aut flammandi,] atque ubi defecisset dies in usum nocturni luminis urerentur*. 'These words—*aut crucibus adfixi aut flammandi*, "nailed to the cross or destined for death in the flames"—are a foreign body, although a very old addition, because already Sulpicius Severus (4th century) read it here, inserted by someone who missed the typical punishments of Christians. But these words are inappropriate here because there is no *ludibrium* in these pains and they break the flow of the text.' (TAC. *Ann*. 15.44, K. NIPPERDAY and G. ANDRESEN (Eds.), ¹¹1915, p. 264, noot 13).
287 We are induced to the Roman (in this case the urban Roman) understanding of the word *chrestiani* by the fact that this word is a Latinism, like for example *herodiani* (Mk. 3:6).
288 TAC. *Ann*. 15.44: *repressaque in praesens exitiabilis superstitio rursum erumpebat, non modo per Iudaeam, originem eius mali, sed per urbem etiam quo cuncta undique atrocia aut pudenda confluunt celebranturque*.
289 SUET. *Nero* 16.2: *afflicti suppliciis christiani, genus hominum superstitionis nouae ac maleficae; [...]*.
290 1 Tes. 1:10: Ἰησοῦς ὁ ῥυόμενος. Cf. also Rom. 11:26 and Mt. 1:21: Ἰησοῦς· αὐτὸς γὰρ σώσει. Cf. Ecclesiasticus 46:1; PHILON *Nom. mutat.* § 21.

291 Flavius JOSEPHUS *Ant.J.* 20.200: ἅτε δὴ οὖν τοιοῦτος ὢν ὁ Ἄνανος, νομίσας ἔχειν καιρὸν ἐπιτήδειον διὰ τὸ τεθνάναι μὲν Φῆστον, Ἀλβῖνον δ' ἔτι κατὰ τὴν ὁδὸν ὑπάρχειν, καθίζει συνέδριον κριτῶν καὶ παραγαγὼν εἰς αὐτὸ τὸν ἀδελφὸν Ἰησοῦ τοῦ λεγομένου Χριστοῦ, Ἰάκωβος ὄνομα αὐτῷ, καί τινας ἑτέρους, ὡς παρανομησάντων κατηγορίαν ποιησάμενος παρέδωκε λευσθησομένους.
292 Mt. 13:55.
293 Act. 12:17; 15:13 sq; 21:18 sq.
294 Gal. 2:9; 1 Cor. 15:7.
295 Flavius JOSEPHUS *Ant.J.* 18.63 sq: [...] καὶ οὕτω παύεται ἡ στάσις. [Γίνεται δὲ κατὰ τοῦτον τὸν χρόνον Ἰησοῦς σοφὸς ἀνήρ, εἴγε ἄνδρα αὐτὸν λέγειν χρή· ἦν γὰρ παραδόξων ἔργων ποιητής, διδάσκαλος ἀνθρώπων τῶν ἡδονῇ τἀληθῆ δεχομένων, καὶ πολλοὺς μὲν Ἰουδαίους, πολλοὺς δὲ καὶ τοῦ Ἑλληνικοῦ ἐπηγάγετο· ὁ χριστὸς οὗτος ἦν. καὶ αὐτὸν ἐνδείξει τῶν πρώτων ἀνδρῶν παρ' ἡμῖν σταυρῷ ἐπιτετιμηκότος Πιλάτου οὐκ ἐπαύσαντο οἱ τὸ πρῶτον ἀγαπήσαντες· ἐφάνη γὰρ αὐτοῖς τρίτην ἔχων ἡμέραν πάλιν ζῶν τῶν θείων προφητῶν ταῦτά τε καὶ ἄλλα μυρία περὶ αὐτοῦ θαυμάσια εἰρηκότων. εἰς ἔτι τε νῦν τῶν Χριστιανῶν ἀπὸ τοῦδε ὠνομασμένον οὐκ ἐπέλιπε τὸ φῦλον.] Καὶ ὑπὸ τοὺς αὐτοὺς χρόνους ἕτερόν τι δεινὸν ἐθορύβει τοὺς Ἰουδαίους [...].
296 Cf. FLAVIUS JOSEPHUS *B.J.* 3.8.7 sq; 4.10. When Jotapata in Galilee was conquered by Vespasianus, Josephus fled with the last defenders into the subterranean canals. When they were found, his brothers-in-arms decided that they would rather face death than fall into the hands of the Romans. Josephus feigned to abide by the will of the majority, but then he presented a supposedly easier way for the collective suicide: the first to cast the lot was to be killed by the second, then he by the third and so on till only the last one would have the dreadful job of killing himself. The casting of the lots was organized by Josephus, who was trusted as the commander. And, as he himself says, 'only Josephus was left, maybe by good fortune or by divine providence' (sic!). So he could surrender to the Romans and save his life. He justified his betrayal of his brothers-in-arms and the violation of his duty as a general with the command of a divine mission: God had appeared to him so that he would proclaim to Vespasianus that the messiah awaited by the Jews, who was to arise at this time in Judaea, was not the leader of the rebels, but Vespasianus himself: He would become emperor, and so would his son Titus.
Cf. SUET. *Vesp.* 4: *Percrebuerat Oriente toto uetus et constans opinio esse in fatis ut eo tempore Iudaea profecti rerum potirentur. Id de imperatore Romano, quanto postea euentu paruit, praedictum Iudaei ad se trahentes rebellarunt [...]. Vesp.* 5: *et unus ex nobilibus captiuis Josephus, cum coniiceretur in uincula, constantissime asseuerauit, fore ut ab eodem breui solueretur, uerum iam imperatore.*
297 Presumably 50-60 AD.
298 1 Cor. 11:23-25.
299 Rom. 1:3 sq; 1. Cor. 15:3 sqq, i.a.
300 70/100 n.Chr., except Mark: mostly 40/60.
301 It is known that the so-called Western and probably most ancient order of arrangement, which e.g. the Codex Bezae Cantabrigiensis still has, was the following: Matthew, John, Luke, Mark. If we assume that the later Gospels were piled up on top of the earlier ones we would have—in the Western order read backwards—the chronological order of the origin of the Gospels, respectively their incorporation in the canon: Matthew coming last. But Matthew had to be made the first, so that he, thanks to his citations from the Jewish Bible, could establish the link to the 'Old Testament', which it became by a corresponding rearrangement of the order of the TaNaCh. Concerning the last matter cf. i.a. B. FEININGER, '"Schreib' dir alle Worte ... in ein Buch"—Das Alte Testament der Christen' ('"Write thee all the words ... in a book"—the Old Testament of the Christians') , Annemarie OHLER, 'Die jüdische

Bibel' ('The Jewish Bible'), W. A. LOHR, 'Fixierte Wahrheit?—Der neutestamentliche Kanon als "Heilige Schrift"' ('Fixed truth?—the canon of the New Testament as "Holy Scripture"'), in: 'Heilige Bücher' ('Holy Books'), *Freiburger Universitätsblätter*, Heft 121, September 1993, 32. Jahrgang, Freiburg i. Br.

302 This is confirmed by the fact that the Judeo-Christian apocryphal Gospels—of the Jews, the Ebionites and of the Twelve—are all based on Matthew.
303 Except perhaps Mark, but then from the Latin; cf. COUCHOUD (1926).
304 2. Εὐαγγέλιον κατὰ Μάρκον. ἐγράφη ῥωμαϊστὶ ἐν Ῥώμῃ μετὰ ιβ΄ ἔτη τῆς ἀναλήψεως κυ. Fam. 13 of the 'annotations about dates', cited by ZUNTZ (1984), p. 60. In other manuscripts it is rendered ι΄ ἔτη.
305 CANCIK (1984) p. 93, speaks in Hellenistic terminology of a ἱστορία περὶ τὰ πρόσωπα ἀνδρῶν ἐπιφανῶν (ἥρωος, θεοῦ)—a 'historical monograph about a famous man (a hero or a god)'.
306 This form historical method is borrowed from Gunkels' examination of Genesis and it in practice presupposes that the origin of the Old and New Testaments developed in the same way—which should be proved.
307 This seems to have been the case with the Septuagint. Cf. WUTZ (1925).
308 Dibelius and Bultmann take different types as a base and they can not even agree on terminology. Moreover Bultmann supposes a similar development for the pre-literary phase as for the later one of Mark through to Matthew and Luke—which is not at all self-evident. Then what if Couchoud (see above) were right that Mark was first written in Latin?
309 WIKENHAUSER & SCHMID (⁶1973), p. 293.
310 LOISY (1910), introduction.
311 COUCHOUD (1924), p. 84-5: *Dans plusieurs cantons de l'empire déifier un particulier était chose faisable. Mais dans une nation au moins la chose était impossible: c'est chez les Juifs. [...] Comment soutenir qu'un juif de Cilicie, pharisien d'éducation, parlant d'un juif de Galilée, son contemporain, ait pu employer sans frémir les textes sacrés où Jahvé est nommé? Il faudrait ne rien savoir d'un juif, ou tout oublier.*—'In several regions of the empire deifying a particular one was feasible. But in one nation at least the matter was impossible: with the Jews. [...] How could one assert that a Jew from Cilicia, educated as a Pharisee, when talking about a Jew from Galilaea, his contemporary, could have employed the sacred texts wherein Jahve is named without trembling? One would have to know nothing about a Jew anymore or forget everything.' [...] p. 113: *Il était frivole de s'opposer jusqu'au martyre à l'apothéose de l'empereur pour y substituer celle d'un de ses sujets. [...] En tout cas une déification, en milieu juif, même de la Dispersion, reste un fait sans exemple.*—'It was frivolous to oppose the apotheosis of the emperor to the point of martyrdom just to replace it with that of one of his subjects. [...] In any case, a deification in a Jewish milieu, even in the diaspora, remains an event without precedent.'
312 AUGSTEIN (1972), p. 56.
313 As is known, the metaphor was coined by Nietzsche: 'The founder of a religion can be unimportant—a match, nothing more!' (*Wille zur Macht*, Aphor. 232). The critics among the modern exegetes, especially Loisy, reproach the mythicists that without a historical residual-Jesus there would be no match. Couchoud answered that the picture of Jesus developed by the critics, that of a destitute Nabi from Galilee, would be a damp squib that could not at all have lit the enormous Christian brushfire, the glorious resurrected son of God: The match should be looked for with Paul, in his report of Peter's vision (1 Cor. 15:1-11). Cf. COUCHOUD (1924), p. 76-89.
314 LEIPOLDT (1923).
315 TORREY (1941), p. 37 sqq., regarded it as 'almost certain' that Paul in 2 Thes. 2 cited the Gospel of Mark. For an opposing view, see ZUNTZ (1984), p. 49.
316 Explicitly in Gal. 1:13-24, i.a.

317 Rom. 15:28; 1 Cor. 16:4; Gal. 2:10; i.a. He speaks of the *hagioi* from Jerusalem, which is translated in editions of the bible as 'Saints'. *Hagioi* does mean 'Saints' but when used in relation to people, it often had an ironic meaning, switching it completely to 'damned'. A similar phenomenon is seen in the Sicilian 'Honored Society', i.e. the Mafia, or also for 'brothers', which is ironically converted to 'What kind of brothers!' not just by the monks. As Paul distanced himself from the 'Saints' in Jerusalem (cf. Gal. 1:17; 1:19 i.a.) and because here it concerns the collection of money, which Paul himself sometimes calls robbery (2 Cor. 11:8: 'I robbed other churches, taking wages of them, to do you service.')—and hence is about competition between money collectors (2 Cor. 11:13, i.a.), the ironic sense would fit better. NB: Originally many evangelical expressions were meant ironically, but the deadly earnestness of the exegetes, copyists and translators extinguished it long ago: a serious problem.

318 'Judaists' and also 'Judeo-Christians' are word constructs of theologians.

319 The missionaries of the other parties mentioned in the first letter to the Corinthians (besides Paul's party, those of Apollos, Kephas and Christ) do not seem to have been Judaists either. From this split in the community of the Corinthians it can furthermore be seen that Paul was not the first missionary of the heathens because he declares expressly that he hardly baptized anybody (1. Cor. 1:14-5) and preached to already baptized ones (1. Cor. 1:17). Idem Col. 1:4 sqq.; 2:1, where Paul testifies that he did not found any of the neighboring communities (Colossae, Laodicea, Hierapolis); rather, according to Col. 1:7; 4:12 sq. the founder of the Colossians seems to have been *Epaphras*. This name is an abbreviated form of *Epaphroditos* (appears also in Phil 2.25), it means 'favorite of Aphrodite' (thus already unsuitable for a Jew), was considered a translation of the Latin *Felix* (proven as Greek form of Sulla's epithet, cf. PLUT. *Sull.* 34; APP. *BC* 1.97), is known as the name of the freedman whom Octavianus sent to Cleopatra in order to disperse her suicidal thoughts and provide for her joys (cf. PLUT. *Ant.* 79: since Cleopatra was regarded as Egyptian reincarnation of Venus it is hardly by chance that Octavianus' envoy was called *Epaphroditos:* Was he priest of Venus, the ancestral mother of the Iulii?) Now an *Epaphroditos* was a Christian parish founder, in fact not of one but of several. This one Paul calls *systratiôtês,* 'fellow-soldier', then *syndoulos,* 'fellow-slave', meaning 'slave of the same master': Were they 'fellow-prisoners of war'? Fellow-freedmen? Of the same Roman ruler—of Vespasianus? One may speculate. Anyway it can be concluded from the mentioned circumstances that not only the first Christians but also the first Christian missionaries were Gentiles. Then came Paul, and only after him came the Judaists with whom he can fight all the more easily as his communities consisted of Gentiles evangelized by Gentiles. The *communis opinio* that Christianity originates from Judaism seems hardly maintainable on the basis of Paul.

320 Apparently, concessions had to be made to Marcion, and it is due to his resistance that our canon is not more forged than it is. Cf. VON HARNACK (1924).

321 Amongst other things, the double ending of Romans.

322 AUFHAUSER (^{2}1925), p. 9.

323 AUFHAUSER (^{2}1925), p. 44-57.

324 The latest conspiracy theory, that nothing is said of Jesus in the published Qumran scrolls because the crucial scriptures are being held under lock and key by the Vatican, is nothing more than a cover up of the fact that Eisler & Co. have nothing up their sleeve. Amusingly enough, the road this excuse takes leads to Rome again!

325 Certainly the fact that Jews are willing to accept Jesus if he is regarded as a Jew could throw light on the motives that led to the Judaization of Divus Iulius in early Christianity.

326 Cf. GESCHE (1968); WEINSTOCK (1971); ALFÖLDI (1973), p. 99 sqq.

327 STAUFFER (1957), p. 21-23. STAUFFER (1952), passim.

328 For an overview of the research into Jesus from the point of view of the science of antiquity see Chr. BURCHARDT in *Der Kleine Pauly* (1979), s.v. 'Jesus', Sp. 1344 sqq.
329 Cf. SCHWEITZER (1906/⁹1984), p. 631; BORNKAMM (1956), p. 11; HEILIGENTHAL (1997), p. 8 and passim.
330 Cf. G. MORDILLAT / J. PRIEUR, *Corpus Christi*, archipel 33—La Sept ARTE, France 1998, broadcasted Easter 1998; video cassettes at La Sept Vidéo, Sainte Geneviève. Cf. also DAN BROWN, *The Da Vinci Code*, Doubleday, 2003.

IV. Words and Wonders

331 Near Dyrrhachium, in mountainous Epirus, today Durres (Durazzo) in Albania.
332 Mk. 4:35-5.20; CAES. *Civ.* 3.6: *Cerauniorum saxa.*
333 This is even more striking in view of the fact that the Gospel manuscripts differ at least as much among each other—*Gerasenes/Gergesenes/Gadarenes*—as they respectively do from the *Ceraunians* of Caesar, which really presents itself as the source for the variants.
334 Mk. 5:3 μνήμασιν, Vulgata: *monumentis.* VELL. 2.51.2: *mox etiam obsidione munimentisque eum complecteretur.* CAES. *Civ.* 3.43 sq and passim: *munitiones.*
335 VELL. 2.51.2: *Sed inopia obsidentibus quam obsessis erat grauior.*
336 CAES. *Civ.* 3.47: *pecus vero, cuius rei summa erat ex Epiro copia, magno in honore habebant.*
337 CAES. *Civ.* 3.48; PLUT. *Caes.* 39.
338 APP. BC 2.61: ὁ δὲ οὐχ ἥσθη, ἀλλ' εἶπεν, "οἵοις θηρίοις μαχόμεθα." PLUT. *Caes.* 39: ἠθύμουν γὰρ οἱ στρατιῶται, τὴν ἀγριότητα καὶ τὴν ἀπάθειαν τῶν πολεμίων ὥσπερ θηρίων ὀρρωδοῦντες.
339 Mk. 6:45-51.
340 PLUT. *Caes.* 38: τὴν μὲν ἑωθινὴν αὔραν, [...] πολὺς πνεύσας [...].
341 APP. BC 2.57.237-58.239: τὸ πνεῦμα δ' αὐτὴν καὶ τὸ κῦμα μετέωρον ἐς τὰς ὄχθας διερρίπτει, μέχρι πλησιαζούσης ἡμέρας οἱ μὲν ἐδεδοίκεσαν ὡς ἐν φωτὶ κατάδηλοι τοῖς πολεμίοις ἐσόμενοι, ὁ δὲ Καῖσαρ, τῷ δαιμονίῳ χαλεψάμενος ὡς φθονερῷ, ἐφῆκε τὴν ναῦν ἐπανιέναι. Ἡ μὲν δὴ πνεύματι ταχεῖ τὸν ποταμὸν ἀνέπλει, Καίσαρα δ' οἱ μὲν ἐθαύμαζον τῆς εὐτολμίας, οἱ δ' ἐπεμέμφοντο ὡς στρατιώτῃ πρέπον ἔργον εἰργασμένῳ, οὐ στρατηγῷ. ὁ δ' οὐκέτι λήσεσθαι προσδοκῶν Ποστούμιον ἀνθ' ἑαυτοῦ προσέταξε διαπλεῦσαί τε καὶ φράσαι Γαβινίῳ τὸν στρατὸν εὐθὺς ἄγειν διὰ θαλάσσης.
342 Antonius landed in the port of Nymphaeum at Lissos, then part of Dalmatia, today Lesh (Alessio) in Albania (APP. BC 2.59.245).
343 Mk. 8:10: Καὶ εὐθὺς ἐμβὰς εἰς τὸ πλοῖον μετὰ τῶν μαθητῶν αὐτοῦ ἦλθεν εἰς τὰ μέρη Δαλμανουθά.
344 Mk. 4:39: καὶ εἶπεν τῇ θαλάσσῃ, Mt. 8:24: ἐν τῇ θαλάσσῃ; only Luke 'improves' it to εἰς τὴν λίμνην (8:23). In the old Bible translations we correctly read 'sea', in modern editions it is of course 'corrected' to 'water', or 'waves', evidently in order to prepare the ground for the 'lake' of the last Gospel, Luke.
345 *Thalassa* for a *limnê* is otherwise only applied to the Caucasian (Caspian) Sea (ARIST. *Mete.* 1.13 p. 351a,8), but as a wilful naming by the local population because of the number and volume of the discharging rivers, and also because of the lack of a visible outlet: ἀλλ' ἥ γε ὑπὸ τὸν Καύκασον λίμνη, ἣν καλοῦσιν οἱ ἐκεῖ θάλατταν· αὕτη γὰρ ποταμῶν πολλῶν καὶ μεγάλων εἰσβαλλόντων οὐκ ἔχουσα ἔκρουν φανερὸν [...]. *Thalassa/thalatta* in Greek always indicates salt water only, for example a spring with salt water in the Erechtheion at Athens (cf. also Sicilian *la salata*, literally 'the salt water', for 'the sea').
346 Mt. 4:18, 8:24, 13:11, 14:24 sq, 15:29; Mk. 1:16, 2:13, 3:7, 7:31; Jn. 21:1; i.a.

347 Jn. 1:15: Ὁ ὀπίσω μου ἐρχόμενος ἔμπροσθέν μου γέγονεν, ὅτι πρῶτός μου ἦν.

348 Jn. 1:27: ὁ ὀπίσω μου ἐρχόμενος, οὗ οὐκ εἰμὶ [ἐγὼ] ἄξιος ἵνα λύσω αὐτοῦ τὸν ἱμάντα τοῦ ὑποδήματος.

349 Mk. 1:7: Ἔρχεται ὁ ἰσχυρότερός μου ὀπίσω μου, οὗ οὐκ εἰμὶ ἱκανὸς κύψας λῦσαι τὸν ἱμάντα τῶν ὑποδημάτων αὐτοῦ. Cf. also Mt. 3:11.

350 PLUT. Pomp. 73: ἐπεὶ δὲ καιρὸς ἦν δείπνου καὶ παρεσκεύασεν ὁ ναύκληρος ἐκ τῶν παρόντων, ἰδὼν ὁ Φαώνιος οἰκετῶν ἀπορίᾳ τὸν Πομπήϊον ἀρχόμενον αὐτὸν ὑπολύειν προσέδραμε καὶ ὑπέλυσε καὶ συνήλειψε. καὶ τὸ λοιπὸν ἐκ τούτου περιέπων καὶ ἐθεράπευων ὅσα δεσπότας δοῦλοι, μέχρι νίψεως ποδῶν καὶ δείπνου παρασκευῆς, διετέλεσεν, ὥστε τὴν ἐλευθεριότητα τῆς ὑπουργίας ἐκείνης θεασάμενον ἄν τινα καὶ τὸ ἀφελὲς καὶ ἄπλαστον εἰπεῖν· Φεῦ τοῖσι γενναίοισιν ὡς ἅπαν καλόν. The citation is from Euripides, fg. 961, from an unknown drama.

351 Jn. 13:4-6: ἐγείρεται ἐκ τοῦ δείπνου καὶ τίθησιν τὰ ἱμάτια καὶ λαβὼν λέντιον διέζωσεν ἑαυτόν· εἶτα βάλλει ὕδωρ εἰς τὸν νιπτῆρα καὶ ἤρξατο νίπτειν τοὺς πόδας τῶν μαθητῶν καὶ ἐκμάσσειν τῷ λεντίῳ ᾧ ἦν διεζωσμένος. ἔρχεται οὖν πρὸς Σίμωνα Πέτρον· λέγει αὐτῷ, Κύριε, σύ μου νίπτεις τοὺς πόδας;

352 It should be noted here, that behind the expression 'to girdle oneself'—'to gird oneself up' could be hidden. This was the typical course of action for men of antiquity when they wished to run, especially when taking flight, so as not to be hindered by the lengthy garment. A further indication of the origin of this situation: Pompeius was fleeing.

353 Jn. 1:20: καὶ ὡμολόγησεν καὶ οὐκ ἠρνήσατο, καὶ ὡμολόγησεν ὅτι Ἐγὼ οὐκ εἰμὶ ὁ Χριστός.

354 Jn. 3:25-28: Ἐγένετο οὖν ζήτησις ἐκ τῶν μαθητῶν Ἰωάννου μετὰ Ἰουδαίου περὶ καθαρισμοῦ. [...] ἀπεκρίθη Ἰωάννης καὶ εἶπεν, [...] αὐτοὶ ὑμεῖς μοι μαρτυρεῖτε ὅτι εἶπον [ὅτι] Οὐκ εἰμὶ ἐγὼ ὁ Χριστός [...]. The fact that the text here says metà Ioudaiou, 'with a Jew', and not, as we would expect 'with Jesus', has irritated many commentators. Accordingly there are numerous conjectures that suggest 'with Jesus', cf. ALAND & NESTLE ([18]1957): Ιησου Bentley cj : του Ιησου Baldensperger cj : των Ιησου Osc. Holtzmann cj. These conjectures would require fewer letters to be changed if one took as starting point, as in our hypothesis, that μετὰ Ἰουδαίου—metà Ioudaiou, was based on an original μετὰ Ἰουλίου—metà Iouliou, 'with Iulius'—which would not have been covered by the nomen-sacrum-abbreviation IC because of the genitive ending—and hence could not have been influenced by Iêsous but by Ioudaiou.

355 APP. BC 2.69.285: εἰσὶ δ' οἳ καὶ περὶ τῆς Καίσαρος ἀρχιερωσύνης ἐς ἀλλήλους ἤδη διήριζον. Cf. also PLUT. Caes. 42: ὥστε φιλονικεῖν ὑπὲρ τῆς Καίσαρος ἀρχιερωσύνης Δομίτιον καὶ Σπινθῆρα καὶ Σκιπίωνα διαμιλλωμένους ἀλλήλοις—'Domitius, Spinther and Scipio fought earnestly amongst each other for Caesar's office of Pontifex Maximus [...]'.

356 PLUT. Pomp. 74-5: "Ὁρῶ σε," εἶπεν, "ἄνερ, οὐ τῆς σῆς τύχης ἔργον, ἀλλὰ τῆς ἐμῆς, προσερριμμένον [...]. Ταῦτα εἰπεῖν τὴν Κορνηλίαν λέγουσι, τὸν δὲ Πομπήϊον ἀποκρίνασθαι· "Μίαν ἄρα, Κορνηλία, τύχην ᾔδεις τὴν ἀμείνονα, ἣ καὶ σὲ ἴσως ἐξηπάτησεν, ὅτι μοι χρόνον πλείονα τοῦ συνήθους παρέμεινεν. ἀλλὰ καὶ ταῦτα δεῖ φέρειν γενομένους ἀνθρώπους, καὶ τῆς τύχης ἔτι πειρατέον. οὐ γὰρ ἀνέλπιστον ἐκ τούτων ἀναλαβεῖν ἐκεῖνα τὸν ἐξ ἐκείνων ἐν τούτοις γενόμενον."

357 Jn. 3:29-31: ὁ ἔχων τὴν νύμφην νυμφίος ἐστίν· ὁ δὲ φίλος τοῦ νυμφίου ὁ ἑστηκὼς καὶ ἀκούων αὐτοῦ χαρᾷ χαίρει διὰ τὴν φωνὴν τοῦ νυμφίου. αὕτη οὖν ἡ χαρὰ ἡ ἐμὴ πεπλήρωται. ἐκεῖνον δεῖ αὐξάνειν, ἐμὲ δὲ ἐλαττοῦσθαι. Ὁ ἄνωθεν ἐρχόμενος ἐπάνω πάντων ἐστίν· ὁ ὢν ἐκ τῆς γῆς ἐκ τῆς γῆς ἐστιν [...].

358 Jn. 1:5: καὶ τὸ φῶς ἐν τῇ σκοτίᾳ φαίνει, καὶ ἡ σκοτία αὐτὸ οὐ κατέλαβεν.

359 App. BC 2.68.282: ὡς δὲ καὶ σέλας ἐξ οὐρανοῦ διαπτὰν ἀπὸ τοῦ Καίσαρος ἐς τὸ Πομπηίου στρατόπεδον ἐσβέσθη, οἱ μὲν ἀμφὶ τὸν Πομπήιον ἔσεσθαί τι λαμπρὸν αὐτοῖς ἔφασαν ἐκ τῶν πολεμίων, ὁ δὲ Καῖσαρ σβέσειν αὐτὸς ἐμπεσὼν τὰ Πομπηίου.

360 This would explain why Jn. 1:5 sqq has a doublet at Jn. 3:22 sqq.

361 Jn. 1:25: καὶ ἠρώτησαν αὐτὸν καὶ εἶπαν αὐτῷ, Τί οὖν βαπτίζεις εἰ σὺ οὐκ εἶ ὁ Χριστὸς οὐδὲ Ἠλίας οὐδὲ ὁ προφήτης;

362 Mk. 11:28-30: καὶ ἔλεγον αὐτῷ, Ἐν ποίᾳ ἐξουσίᾳ ταῦτα ποιεῖς; ἢ τίς σοι ἔδωκεν τὴν ἐξουσίαν ταύτην ἵνα ταῦτα ποιῇς; ὁ δὲ Ἰησοῦς εἶπεν αὐτοῖς, Ἐπερωτήσω ὑμᾶς ἕνα λόγον, καὶ ἀποκρίθητέ μοι καὶ ἐρῶ ὑμῖν ἐν ποίᾳ ἐξουσίᾳ ταῦτα ποιῶ· τὸ βάπτισμα τὸ Ἰωάννου ἐξ οὐρανοῦ ἦν ἢ ἐξ ἀνθρώπων; ἀποκρίθητέ μοι.

363 It is symptomatic here that in his commentaries Caesar always speaks only of *dilectus*, 'recruitment', but when his officers take up the pen they use the alternate word *lustratio*—as in the last book of *De Bello Gallico* or in the commentaries about the Alexandrian, African or Hispanic war (CAES. *Gal.* 8.52; *B. Afr.* 75.1; *B. Alex.* 56.5).

364 Mk. 1:4: καὶ κηρύσσων βάπτισμα μετανοίας εἰς ἄφεσιν ἁμαρτιῶν.

365 *Armilustrium* is translated by Lydos as καθαρμὸς ὅπλων, in the glossaries as ὁπλοκαθαρμός, ὁπλοκαθάρσια respectively ὅπλων κάθαρσις. Cf. MAGIE (1905), p. 33 and p. 150.

366 PLUT. *Caes.* 30.1-2: Οὐ μὴν ἀλλ' ἥ γε παρὰ Καίσαρος ἀξίωσις τὸ πρόσχημα τῆς δικαιολογίας λαμπρὸν εἶχεν· ἠξίου γὰρ αὐτός τε καταθέσθαι τὰ ὅπλα, καὶ Πομπηίου ταὐτὸ πράξαντος ἀμφοτέρους ἰδιώτας γενομένους εὑρίσκεσθαί τι παρὰ τῶν πολιτῶν ἀγαθόν, ὡς τοὺς αὐτὸν μὲν ἀφαιρουμένους, ἐκείνῳ δ' ἣν εἶχε βεβαιοῦντας δύναμιν, ἕτερον διαβάλλοντας ἕτερον κατασκευάζειν τύραννον. PLUT. *Caes.* 30.4: ἐν δὲ τῇ βουλῇ Σκιπίων μὲν ὁ Πομπηίου πενθερὸς εἰσηγήσατο γνώμην, ἂν ἐν ἡμέρᾳ ῥητῇ μὴ κατάθηται τὰ ὅπλα Καῖσαρ, ἀποδειχθῆναι πολέμιον αὐτόν.

Q. Caecilius Metellus Pius Scipio became Metellus by adoption. His former name was P. Cornelius Scipio Nasica. Consul for the year 52, he became father-in-law to Pompeius after the death of Caesar's daughter Julia and Pompeius' subsequent new marriage. The new father-in-law was a fierce opponent of the former one, Caesar, and he spoke on behalf of his son-in-law, who at first stayed in the city but later joined his troops outside the walls for formal juristic reasons. Cf. CAES. *Civ.* 1.2.1: *Haec Scipionis oratio, quod senatus in urbe habebatur Pompeiusque aderat, ex ipsius ore Pompei mitti uidebatur.*

CAES. *Civ.* 1.11.1: *Erat iniqua condicio postulare, [...] exercitum Caesaris uelle dimitti, dilectus habere.*

SUET. *Jul.* 29: *Cum adversariis autem pepigit, ut dimissis octo legionibus [...].*

VELL. 2.48.1: *[...] cum iustissimus quisque et a Caesare et a Pompeio uellet dimitti exercitus; quippe Pompeius in secundo consulatu Hispanias sibi decerni uoluerat easque per triennium absens ipse ac praesidens urbi per Afranium et Petreium, consularem ac praetorium, legatos suos, administrabat et iis, qui a Caesare dimittendos exercitus contendebant, adsentabatur, iis, qui ab ipso quoque, aduersabatur.*

VELL. 2.48.5: *Ad ultimum saluberrimas et coalescentes condiciones pacis, quas et Caesar iustissimo animo postulabat et Pompeius aequo recipiebat, discussit ac rupit, unice cauente Cicerone concordiae publicae.*

Cf. also SUET. *Jul.* 30: *Et praetextum quidem illi ciuilium armorum hoc fuit; [...]*—where *armorum* means 'civil war' rather than 'weapon', 'army'. Hence the εἰς ἄφεσιν ἁμαρτιῶν in Mark could theoretically also mean 'averting of the civil war' however ἄφεσις, 'dismissal', argues against it.

Also, because of this permanent demand for demobilization of the adversarial army and simultaneous recruiting of one's own, Mark could have had difficulties differentiating *dilectus*, 'recruitment', from *discessus*, 'departure, decampment' (cf. CAES. *Civ.* 1.26.4: *[...] ab armis sit discessum [...]*).

367 App. BC 2.32.133; 35.140.

368 Mk. 1:16: ἀμφιβάλλοντας [ἐν τῇ θαλάσσῃ]· ἦσαν γὰρ ἁλεεῖς. p) has βαλλοντας αμφιβληστρον. The nets, however, are mostly lacking in Mark (cf. ALAND & NESTLE ^{18}1957).

369 That the sentence in Mark does not necessarily originally refer to fishermen is indicated by the fact that in most of the Markan manuscripts, as in the papyri, no nets are mentioned. They only emerge later in the sequence of redaction—at first as *amphiblêstron*, casting-net in the singular, then gradually they become *diktya*, trawling nets in the plural, until in Luke they are no longer 'cast' at all, they are instead lowered down (the reference to 'cast' has now disappeared): χαλάσατε τὰ δίκτυα. Also that *(h)aleeis* had been a singular form like *alea* becomes believable through Luke, where Jesus speaks to Simon alone: εἶπεν πρὸς τὸν Σίμωνα (Lk. 5:4).

370 Politically north of the Rubicon, but geographically far south of it, which city names today—like for example Senigallia (near Ancona)—still testify to.

371 SUET. *Jul.* 75: *Denuntiante Pompeio pro hostibus se habiturum qui rei publicae defuissent, ipse medios et neutrius partis suorum sibi numero futuros pronuntiauit.* Cf. CAES. *Civ.* 1.33 u. 1.85. PLUT. *Caes.* 33; *Pomp.* 61. DIO CASS. *HR* 41.6.2. APP. *BC* 2.37.148.

372 Mk. 3, Mt. 12, Lk. 11.

373 Mk. 9:40. Variant: 'for he that is not against us is for us' (Lk. 9:50); see also Mt. 12:30 and Lk. 11:23.

374 PLUTARCHUS: ἦλθον, εἶδον, ἐνίκησα / DIO CASSIUS: καὶ ἦλθε πρὸς τὸν πολέμιον καὶ εἶδεν αὐτὸν καὶ ἐνίκησε / APPIANUS: ἐγὼ δὲ ἦλθον, εἶδον, ἐνίκησα / SUETONIUS: *veni, vidi, vici.*

375 Jn. 9:7: ἀπῆλθεν οὖν καὶ ἐνίψατο καὶ ἦλθεν βλέπων.

376 Jn. 9:11: ἀπελθὼν οὖν καὶ νιψάμενος ἀνέβλεψα.

377 Mk. 8:24: Βλέπω τοὺς ἀνθρώπους ὅτι ὡς δένδρα ὁρῶ περιπατοῦντας.

378 1st element, with Caesar: ἦλθον / ἦλθε, with Jesus: ἀπελθὼν / ἀπῆλθεν / περιπατοῦντας; 2nd element, with Caesar: εἶδον / εἶδεν, with Jesus: ἀνέβλεψα / βλέπων / βλέπω / ὁρῶ; 3rd element, with Caesar: ἐνίκησα / ἐνίκησε, with Jesus: νιψάμενος / ἐνίψατο / ἀνθρώπους ὡς δένδρα. The transition of ὁρῶ / εἶδον to βλέπω depends on the period and the linguistic register.

379 Here we document but a few of the innumerable Latin sources that show the regular appearance of *caesus* (and derivatives) with those fallen in battle. Amongst others VELL. 2.4.4 (on the killing of Tib. Gracchus): *iure caesum;* 2.52.3 (on the Pompeians fallen in the battle of Pharsalos): *caesos uiros;* or 2.55.1 (on the death of Curio in the battle in Africa): *occiso Curione;* 2.117.1 (on the Varus-battle): *caesi Vari;* SUET. *Jul.* 25.2 (on the ambush of the Germans on Caesar's winter quarters): *legatis per insidias caesis;* 30.4 (on Caesar viewing the soldiers killed in action at Pharsalos): *caesos profligatosque aduersarios prospicientem;* 76.1 (on the question, whether the killing of Caesar had been legitimate): *iure caesus;* LIV. *Periochae A.U.C.* 12.3 (on L. Caecilius, perished with his legions): *cum legionibus caesus est;* 22.8 (on the consul Flaminus, died in war against Hannibal): *cum exercitu caesus est;* 25.15 (on Centenius Paenula, also defeated by Hannibal): *cum exercitu caesus est;* 27.2 (idem): *cum exercitu [...] caesus est;* 27.19 (on Hasdrubal conquered on his part): *cum milibus hominum LVI caesus est;* 103.2 (on Catilina): *cum exercitu caesus est;* 110.18 (on Curio, killed in action against Juba, see above): *cum exercitu caesus est.* Cf. also the vocabulary of the *Periochae* 82.2 of LIVIUS, referring to Pharnaces' father Mithridates, defeated by his then opponent Sulla, in similar situation: *caesis hostium C et castris quoque expugnatis;* and 97.8, victory of Lucullus in Pontus: *caesis hostium amplius quam LX;* referring to murdered Roman citizens, *A.U.C. Perioch. ex P. Oxy.* 668.37.1: *[...] in Hispa]nia Romani caesi.*

Of course our argumentation presupposes that Latin sources were used, if not directly by the Evangelists nevertheless by their exemplars, the so-called Proto-Gospels.

The direct use of Latin exemplars is generally accepted for all of the three Greek writing historians and biographers who are often quoted here, Dio Cassius, Appianus and Plutarchus. (For Dio cf. i.a. Ed. SCHWARTZ, *RE* III 1684sqq; for Appianus cf. GABBA (1956), p.246; for Plutarchus ZIEGLER, K. & SONTHEIMER, W. (1979), s.v. Sp. 951.)

Dio Cassius certainly followed Livius for the part we are concerned with (from book 36 onwards), Appianus followed Asinius Pollio, likewise Plutarchus, albeit together with other sources.

Plutarchus himself admits to the insufficiency of his linguistic ability in Latin. Appianus' proficiency in Latin was such that his Greek is full of Latinisms (cf. *Demosth.* 2). Dio Cassius had the best knowledge, if for no other reason than that his father and he himself held high offices in the Empire (senator, praetor, consul suff.). However, translation errors of his are attested, too, or assumed (amongst others is his much discussed alleged 'Iupiter Iulius', *HP* 44,6,4: καὶ τέλος Δία τε αὐτὸν ἄντικρυς 'Ιούλιον προσηγόρευσαν, with it many authors assume that Dio only falsely reproduced the title *Divus* with his Δία. Cf. list of pros and cons in GESCHE, H. (1968), p.35-6, n.80: Both positions take a Latin exemplar as the starting point).

In our text of Pharnaces we have the possibility of ascertaining their recourse to a Latin exemplar by comparing a parallel text by Dio Cassius and Appianus. This is especially interesting for us because the Latin exemplar must have contained the word *caesus*.

In Livius' *Periochae* (A.U.C. 113.15) it is said of Pharnaces, that he is *victus*: *Pharnaces, Mithridatis filius, <r>ex Ponti, sine ulla belli mora victus est*. Referring to Pharnaces, unfortunately it cannot be seen directly that in the Latin Caesar sources there probably was also *caesus* to be found, because Suetonius and Velleius do not report in detail, just as little as the Periochae of Livius. However this can be deduced from the *Bellum Alexandrinum* (76)—where Pharnaces at first manages to flee, but where it is regretted that he could not be captured 'alive'—and more precisely from the Greek adaptations. In the more extensive Greek source of Dio Cassius it is written that Pharnaces fell, if not directly in the battle with Caesar then at least in the immediately following battle. (*HR* 42.47.5):

'Pharnaces escaped to the sea and later tried to force his way into Bosporus, but Asander repulsed and killed him.'

'Killed him'—ἀπέκτεινε. Here in the according Latin source from which Dio also scooped, *caesus est* must have occurred, accordant to established Latin usage.

This is confirmed by a comparison between Dio and Appianus who report in parallel that before Caesar's arrival, Pharnaces had looted the city of Amisos in the haughtiness of his victory over Domitius. Dio:

'[...] Pharnaces was greatly elated, and after acquiring all the rest of Pontus, captured Amisus also, though it long held out against him; and he plundered the city and killed all the men of military age there.'

Here also Dio says 'killed'—ἀπέκτεινε. However in the parallel place with Appianus it says 'made them eunuchs'—τομίας ἐπεποίητο: 'Being much elated by this affair he had subjugated the city of Amisus in Pontus, which was friendly to the Romans, sold their inhabitants into slavery, and made all male descendants eunuchs.'

The deviation becomes explicable only if one assumes a common Latin exemplar in which *excidi* was written, literally 'cut off', which in Latin means 'struck down, exterminated', in Greek however it can very well be misunderstood as 'castrated': ἐκτέμνω—*ek-temno*. This *ex-cidi*, verbal adjectiv *ex-cisus*, stems from *caedo*, whose verbal adjectiv is *caesus*. Probably in the source there was just the passive *caesi sunt*,

according to Latin style. Then Dio would have translated analogously 'cut down', Appianus literally 'cut, castrated'. The fact that both are right is shown by *Bellum Alexandrinum* (70), where Caesar blames Pharnaces of having committed an irreparable crime, namely 'killing' or 'castrating' Roman citizens who were out on business in Pontus—though for clear differentiation other, synonymous words are used here, *interfectis* and *exsectis*: «*itaque se magnas et graves iniurias civium Romanorum, qui in Ponto negotiati essent, quoniam in integrum restituere non posset, concedere Pharnaci: nam neque interfectis amissam vitam, neque exsectis virilitatem restituere posse; quod quidam supplicium gravius morte cives Romani subissent.*»
Since the examined place is part of the assumed model for John's healing of a blind man, that passage, uncertain even for the classical Greek historians—'struck (cut) down' versus 'castrated'—could have encouraged the Evangelist who was blinded by the word 'saw' to an even more creative translation: 'blind man'. A classical topos, by the way, that can already be found with King Oedipus, whose 'blinding' at the end of the tragedy is said to have stood euphemistically for his 'castration', the condign punishment for incest with the mother.

380 SUET. *Jul.* 79: *Neque ex eo infamiam affectati etiam regii nominis discutere ualuit, quanquam et plebei regem se salutanti «Caesarem se, non regem esse» responderit [...].* Cf. also PLUT. *Caes.* 60: καὶ καταβαίνοντος ἐξ Ἄλβης Καίσαρος εἰς τὴν πόλιν, ἐτόλμησαν αὐτὸν ἀσπάσασθαι βασιλέα· τοῦ δὲ δήμου διαταραχθέντος, ἀχθεσθεὶς ἐκεῖνος οὐκ ἔφη βασιλεύς, ἀλλὰ Καῖσαρ καλεῖσθαι καὶ γενομένης πρὸς τοῦτο πάντων σιωπῆς, οὐ πάνυ φαιδρὸς οὐδ' εὐμενὴς παρῆλθεν; [...]. APP. BC 2.108.450: ὁ δὲ τοῦτο μὲν ἤνεγκεν εὐσταθῶς, ἑτέρων δ' αὐτὸν ἀμφὶ τὰς πύλας ἰόντα ποθὲν βασιλέα προσειπόντων καὶ τοῦ δήμου στενάξαντος, εὐμηχάνως εἶπε τοῖς ἀσπασαμένοις· "οὐκ εἰμὶ Βασιλεύς, ἀλλὰ Καῖσαρ," ὡς δὴ περὶ τὸ ὄνομα ἐσφαλμένοις.

381 Caesar was proud of this, cf. his funeral speech about his father's sister Iulia, Marius' widow, SUET. *Jul.* 6: «*Amitae meae Iuliae maternum genus ab regibus ortum [...] est ergo in genere et sanctitas regum [...]*».

382 Cf. the preceding note. One suspects that it was at the *ovatio ex Monte Albano*. Cf. DEGRASSI (1947), p. 87, 567. WEINSTOCK (1971), p. 326-331.

383 Jn. 19:13-15: Ὁ οὖν Πιλᾶτος [...] ἤγαγεν ἔξω τὸν Ἰησοῦν καὶ ἐκάθισεν ἐπὶ βήματος εἰς τόπον λεγόμενον Λιθόστρωτον, [...] καὶ λέγει τοῖς Ἰουδαίοις, Ἴδε ὁ βασιλεὺς ὑμῶν [...] ἀπεκρίθησαν οἱ ἀρχιερεῖς, Οὐκ ἔχομεν βασιλέα εἰ μὴ Καίσαρα.

384 APP. BC 2.115.479-480: ὁ δὲ Καῖσαρ πρὸ μιᾶς τοῦδε τοῦ βουλευτηρίου χωρῶν ἐπὶ δεῖπνον ἐς Λέπιδον τὸν ἵππαρχον, ἐπήγετο Δέκμον Βροῦτον Ἀλβῖνον ἐς τὸν πότον καὶ λόγον ἐπὶ τῇ κύλικι προύθηκε, τίς ἄριστος ἀνθρώπῳ θάνατος· αἱρουμένων δὲ ἕτερα ἑτέρων αὐτὸς ἐκ πάντων ἐπῄνει τὸν αἰφνίδιον. καὶ ὁ μὲν ὧδε προυμαντεύετο ἑαυτῷ καὶ ἐλεσχήνευε περὶ τῶν ἐς τὴν αὔριον ἐσομένων. Cf. also PLUT. *Caes.* 63: ἐμπεσόντος δὲ λόγου, ποῖος ἄρα τῶν θανάτων ἄριστος, ἅπαντας φθάσας ἐξεβόησεν· "ὁ ἀπροσδόκητος."—'when the conversation turned to what sort of death was the best, before anyone else could answer Caesar exclaimed "The sudden one!"'

385 Mk. 14:12sqq; Mt. 26:17sqq; Lk. 22:7sqq; Jn. 13:21sqq.

386 Like for example the German *Regensburg* from *Castra Regina*—cf. note 80.

387 APP. BC 2.115.480: ἐπὶ δὲ τῷ πότῳ νυκτὸς αὐτῷ τὸ σῶμα νωθρὸν ἐγίγνετο, καὶ ἡ γυνὴ Καλπουρνία ἐνύπνιον αἵματι πολλῷ καταρρεόμενον ἰδοῦσα κατεκώλυε μὴ προελθεῖν. θυομένῳ τε πολλάκις ἦν τὰ σημεῖα φοβερά.

388 Jn. 13:21-27: λέγει οὖν αὐτῷ ὁ Ἰησοῦς, Ὃ ποιεῖς ποίησον τάχιον. Luther translated τάχιον as 'bald' ('soon'), which it can mean in a certain sense.

389 Cf. note 158.

390 APP. BC 2.146.611: καί που τῶν θρήνων αὐτὸς ὁ Καῖσαρ ἐδόκει λέγειν, ὅσους εὖ ποιήσειε τῶν ἐχθρῶν ἐξ ὀνόματος, καὶ περὶ τῶν σφαγέων αὐτῶν ἐπέλεγεν ὥσπερ ἐν θαύματι· "ἐμὲ δὲ καὶ τούσδε περισῶσαι τοὺς κτενοῦντάς με, [...]".

391 APP. BC 2.136.567: 'Then Piso yelled out as loud as he could and demanded that the consuls reconvene the senators, who were still present, which was done, and then he said "These men who talk of having killed a tyrant are now setting themselves up over us as a group of tyrants instead of one. They want to prevent me from burying the *Pontifex Maximus* [...]"'. Ἐκβοήσας οὖν ὁ Πείσων ὅτι μέγιστον καὶ τοὺς ὑπάτους ἔτι παροῦσάν οἱ τὴν βουλὴν ἀξιώσας συναγαγεῖν, εἶπεν· "οἱ τύραννον λέγοντες ἕνα ἀνῃρηκέναι τοσοίδε ἡμῶν ἀνθ' ἑνὸς ἤδη τυραννοῦσιν· οἳ θάπτειν με κωλύουσι τὸν ἀρχιερέα [...]. Note here that Appianus uses the same word *archierea* for *pontifex maximus* which in Mark stands for 'High priest' (cf. next note).

392 Mk. 15:31: ὁμοίως καὶ οἱ ἀρχιερεῖς ἐμπαίζοντες πρὸς ἀλλήλους μετὰ τῶν γραμματέων ἔλεγον, Ἄλλους ἔσωσεν, ἑαυτὸν οὐ δύναται σῶσαι [...].

393 CAES. Civ. 1.30: *Mittit [...] in Siciliam Curionem pro praetore cum legionibus III, eundem, cum Siciliam recepisset, protinus in Africam traducere exercitum iubet.* APP. BC 2.40.162: Ἀσίνιός τε Πολλίων ἐς Σικελίαν πεμφθείς, ἧς ἡγεῖτο Κάτων, πυνθανομένῳ τῷ Κάτωνι, πότερα τῆς βουλῆς ἢ τοῦ δήμου δόγμα φέρων ἐς ἀλλοτρίαν ἀρχὴν ἐμβάλλοι, ὧδε ἀπεκρίνατο· "ὁ τῆς Ἰταλίας κρατῶν ἐπὶ ταῦτά με ἔπεμψε." Καὶ Κάτων μὲν τοσόνδε ἀποκρινάμενος, ὅτι φειδοῖ τῶν ὑπηκόων οὐκ ἐνταῦθα αὐτὸν ἀμυνεῖται, διέπλευσεν ἐς Κέρκυραν καὶ ἐκ Κερκύρας ἐς Πομπήιον· ὁ δὲ Καῖσαρ ἐς Ῥώμην ἐπειχθεὶς [...]. Then, after a brief description of Caesar's entrance into Rome, Appianus continues with the nomination of Curio as governor of Sicily (2.41): Λέπιδον δὲ Αἰμίλιον ἐφίστη τῇ πόλει καὶ τὸν δήμαρχον Μᾶρκον Ἀντώνιον τῇ Ἰταλίᾳ καὶ τῷ περὶ αὐτὴν στρατῷ. ἔς τε τὰ ἔξω Κουρίωνα μὲν ἀντὶ Κάτωνος ᾑρεῖτο ἡγεῖσθαι Σικελίας [...]. We can conclude from these passages that Asinius had been an ordinary legate of Caesar with the special mission to take Sicily from the Pompeian governor Cato—in fact for the *legatus pro praetore*, the governor Curio, who would follow him and who had to cross the sea from Sicily to Africa. It seems that Asinius was sent directly from Brundisium whereas Curio did not advance with the army until he had been authorized in Rome (where Lepidus and Antonius received their orders too).

The fact that Caesar does not mention Asinius alongside Curio has raised the question of the status of Pollio in Sicily. But since Asinius Pollio is not mentioned at all in Caesar's *De bello civili*—for whatever reasons—neither here nor at the Rubicon nor at Pharsalos (with Appianus and Plutarchus he is not only present, but 'the' eyewitness), Asinius' not being named as legate in *De bello civili* cannot be considered as an *argumentum e silentio*.

394 Mk. 11:1-6: Καὶ ὅτε ἐγγίζουσιν εἰς Ἱεροσόλυμα εἰς Βηθφαγὴ καὶ Βηθανίαν πρὸς τὸ Ὄρος τῶν Ἐλαιῶν, ἀποστέλλει δύο τῶν μαθητῶν αὐτοῦ καὶ λέγει αὐτοῖς, Ὑπάγετε εἰς τὴν κώμην τὴν κατέναντι ὑμῶν, καὶ εὐθὺς εἰσπορευόμενοι εἰς αὐτὴν εὑρήσετε πῶλον δεδεμένον ἐφ' ὃν οὐδεὶς οὔπω ἀνθρώπων ἐκάθισεν· λύσατε αὐτὸν καὶ φέρετε. καὶ ἐάν τις ὑμῖν εἴπῃ, Τί ποιεῖτε τοῦτο; εἴπατε, Ὁ κύριος αὐτοῦ χρείαν ἔχει, καὶ εὐθὺς αὐτὸν ἀποστέλλει πάλιν ὧδε. καὶ ἀπῆλθον καὶ εὗρον πῶλον δεδεμένον πρὸς θύραν ἔξω ἐπὶ τοῦ ἀμφόδου καὶ λύουσιν αὐτόν. καί τινες τῶν ἐκεῖ ἑστηκότων ἔλεγον αὐτοῖς, Τί ποιεῖτε λύοντες τὸν πῶλον; οἱ δὲ εἶπαν αὐτοῖς καθὼς εἶπεν ὁ Ἰησοῦς, καὶ ἀφῆκαν αὐτούς. Mt. 21:1-6; Lk. 19:29-34; Jn. 12:12-15.

395 Lk. 19:30: Ὑπάγετε εἰς τὴν κατέναντι κώμην [...].

396 Theoretically Curio's moving on could also be expressed here.

397 Mk. 11:12-13: Καὶ τῇ ἐπαύριον ἐξελθόντων αὐτῶν ἀπὸ Βηθανίας ἐπείνασεν. καὶ ἰδὼν συκῆν ἀπὸ μακρόθεν ἔχουσαν φύλλα ἦλθεν, εἰ ἄρα τι εὑρήσει ἐν αὐτῇ, καὶ ἐλθὼν ἐπ' αὐτὴν οὐδὲν εὗρεν εἰ μὴ φύλλα· ὁ γὰρ καιρὸς οὐκ ἦν σύκων.

398 Mk. 11:12-14; Mk. 11:20-21.

399 APP. BC 2.40.162-41.165, see above Mk. 11:1-21.

400 Mk. 11:20: 'And in the morning, as they passed by, they saw the fig tree dried up from the roots.'—Καὶ παραπορευόμενοι πρωῒ εἶδον τὴν συκῆν ἐξηραμμένην ἐκ

ῥιζῶν. Here we not only have to compare *Curio(n)* with *xêron,* 'dried up', but perhaps also with *ek rizôn,* 'from the roots', then *Africam* with *aridam* (Lat. 'withered', cf. Vulgata) and *exêrammenên* (Greek 'withered') with *exercitum* (Lat. 'army'). Cf. CAES. *Civ.* 1.30: *in Africam traducere exercitum iubet.* This *iubet* of Caesar—the order to bring the army to Africa—would correspond to καὶ ἀποκριθεὶς εἶπεν αὐτῇ of Mk. 11:14—Jesus' command that the fig tree wither. Finally in the word 'wither' Curio's defeat in Africa could linger.

The picture of the fig tree with Jesus (standing for Sicily) could have been summoned from the figs of Tusculum, which Pompeius' comrades-in-arms were craving for and with which they incited him to wage the decisive battle at last: so that they finally could go home and taste the famous figs before the season was over (so sure were they that they would defeat Caesar, since after Dyrrhachium he already was virtually defeated; but it turned out differently at Pharsalos and they did not taste the figs of Tusculum ever again). Cf. PLUT. *Caes.* 41: Φαώνιος δὲ τὴν Κάτωνος παρρησίαν ὑποποιούμενος μανικῶς, ἐσχετλίαζεν εἰ μηδὲ τῆτες ἔσται τῶν περὶ Τουσκλάνον ἀπολαῦσαι σύκων διὰ τὴν Πομπηΐου φιλαρχίαν.—'Favonius, mimicking Cato's free way of speaking his mind, complained bitterly that he could eat no figs this year from his manor at Tusculum, because of Pompey's lust of power.'

401 The most well known: Q. *Caecilius* Metellus Celer, opposed Caesar's land legislation in 59 BC (he was unhappily married to Clodia, sister of Clodius); Q. *Caecilius* Metellus Pius Scipio Nasica, whose daughter Cornelia married Pompeius after the death of Julia, was co-consul in 52 BC (defeated at Pharsalos and again at Thapsos, he committed suicide); L. *Caecilius* Metellus, tribune of the people in 49 BC, unsuccessfully opposed Caesar's loan for armaments from the Aerarium (in the temple of Saturnus); Publius *Clodius* Pulcher, (changed his name from Claudius to the plebeian Clodius for political reasons in 59 BC), the infamous tribune of the people who in 62 BC intruded into Caesar's house during the feast of the *Bona Dea* in order to seduce Caesar's wife (he was accused of sacrilege, charged by his friend Cicero, but exonerated by Caesar and so was set free; from then on he opposed Cicero and supported Caesar); Appius *Claudius* Pulcher, brother of Clodius, father in law of Marcus Brutus, Censor 50 BC, then he was Proconsul in Greece as a follower of Pompeius (died before Pharsalos); M. *Claudius* Marcellus, Consul for 51 BC (accepted Caesar's mercy 46 BC, but was killed in Piraeus 45 BC); C. *Claudius* Marcellus, cousin of the previous, he was also an opponent of Caesar although he was married to his grand-niece Octavia, Consul 50 BC: he proclaimed the state of emergency against Caesar—without a decree from the Senate (changed sides to Caesar in 49 BC); C. *Claudius* Marcellus, cousin of both of the aforementioned, Consul 49 BC, together with L. *Lentulus* Crus: he declared Caesar's soldiers enemies of the state and drove the tribune of the people Antonius out of the Senate (in 48 he was still an admiral of Pompeius', died before Pharsalos); L. Cornelius *Lentulus* Crus (*Crus,* 'leg', was his nickname: *Lentulus Crus,* 'lame leg'), in 61 BC he was the chief prosecutor of *Clodius,* Consul in 49 BC, together with C. *Claudius* Marcellus (see above). After Pharsalos he fled to Egypt with Pompeius, where he was arrested and killed.

It is known that in their *fescennini,* the old-italic mocking and teasing verses which they sang during a triumphal procession and which often degenerated into coarse and unrestrained sprees, the legionaries did not even spare the triumphator, their imperator. By the way this tradition lives on in our carnival processions and carnival speeches. If Caesar was mocked like that as we know (cf. page 276 and note 599) it is easy to imagine how they will have sneered at the 'blind' *(Caecilii)* who did not get a look in, and the 'lame' (*Claudii, Lentuli, Crus,* etc.) who were made to get a move on! And since Caesar was looked upon as the therapist of the state (cf. PLUT.

Caes. 28.6) he thereby became the 'healer' of those 'lame' and 'blind' ones in the vernacular—like Jesus. It is a pity the biting irony got lost in the change.

402 The ceremony called *Damia* had to take place during the first week of December with the participation of the vestal virgins at the wife of a magistrate *cum imperio* who himself had to leave the house. At the time of the event Caesar already was *Praetor designatus* elected as praetor for the following year, as *Pontifex maximus* he lived in the time-honored *domus publica* at the Forum. The secret ceremonies of the female deity who was associated with Faunus/Lupercus resp. Dionysos/Liber were said to occur at night also, with wine, music and dancing as well as myrtle twigs playing an important role in them. PLUTARCHUS says about them (*Caes.* 9):
'Now the Romans have a goddess whom they call the Good one, the Greeks call her Gynaecia, i.e. the goddess of women; the Phrygians who draw on her for themselves say she had been the wife of king Midas whereas the Romans regard her as a nymph of the woods who united with Faunus and the Greeks take her for that mother of Dionysos whom they dare not name. When therefore the women hold the festivity they cover the tents with vine-twigs and lay a snake beside the goddess according to the myth. While the holy mysteries of the goddess are celebrated no man is allowed to attend not even to stay inside the house. Completely apart the women perform many actions during the divine service which are said to resemble those of the orphic mysteries. So when the time of the feast approaches which must be celebrated in the house of a consul or praetor, the same and with him all male persons go out. The wife takes over the house and prepares everything for the ceremony. The most important activities are celebrated at night. Frolic and much music accompany the nightly goings.'
The cult of the Bona Dea, mother of Dionysos, had survived the ban on the Bacchanals in Italy (resolution of the Senate of 186 BC: under penalty of death!), seemingly by perpetuation of the original form as an all women's cult. Clodius' creeping in had to be classified as an attempt to alter the feast of the Bona Dea into a Bacchanal. The active help given to Clodius by the lady's maids argues for the continuing popularity of this festive form. Probably he also felt encouraged by Caesar's attitude towards it, who lifted the ban on the cult of Bacchus *(Liber Pater)* again (cf. SERV. B. 5.29: «*hoc aperte ad Caesarem pertinet, quem constat primum sacra Liberi patris transtulisse Romam. ‹curru› pro ‹currui›. thiasos saltationes, choreas Liberi, id est Liberalia.*» Caesar's final victory in Munda was to come at just the right moment, on the Liberalia: on the 17th of March.).

403 Cf. APP. *BC* 2.14.52-4; PLUT. *Caes.* 9-10 and *Cic.* 28-30; SUET. *Jul.* 6 and 74. According to Plutarchus the beardless 'beauty' dressed up as a female harp player and sneaked into Caesar's house with the help of one of Pompeia's lady's maids, but his voice betrayed him.

404 It is reported that amongst them were also the wives of Sulpicius, of Gabinus, of Crassus and even of Pompeius and last but not least Servilia, sister of Cato and mother of Brutus, and also her daughter Tertia. Cf. SUET. *Jul.* 50.

405 As a serving magistrate—he was praetor in this year—Caesar was granted immunity. But if Clodius had been sentenced for sacrilege, Caesar—who had not persecuted him although he was *pontifex maximus* and *praetor*, making him a *praefectus morum*, 'arbiter of morals', twice over—would have found himself in a bad situation and certainly would have had to pay for his former dedication to the Catalinarians.

406 Lucullus.

407 Plutarchus reports that Cicero was forced into it by his wife Terentia. She was jealous of Clodius' sister Clodia, called *quadrantaria*, 'quarter-whore' (cheap whore). Cicero had a special relationship with her and had even promised to marry her.

408 This is less to be seen as a reprimand of Pompeia whom he backed with it but as a side blow at his own mother Aurelia and sister Julia who had accused Pompeia (cf. SUET. *Jul.* 74). This family quarrel could also explain the divorce. Differing from Suetonius—'Because members of my household [...]'—Plutarchus reports Caesar's answer as : 'Because my wife should not only be free of guilt but also of suspicion', but he adds that 'only some believed that Caesar spoke seriously'. Indeed the quick witted answer was taken to be an expression of the *ironia Caesaris*. Appianus and Dio Cassius do not mention this sentence.

409 In the case of a conviction Clodius could have been whipped to death and Pompeia could have been either buried alive or thrown from the Tarpeian rock.

410 Mk. 2:1-12; Mt. 9:1-8; Lk. 5:17-26.

411 Mk. 2:1-12: Καὶ εἰσελθὼν πάλιν εἰς Καφαρναοὺμ δι᾿ ἡμερῶν ἠκούσθη ὅτι ἐν οἴκῳ ἐστίν. καὶ συνήχθησαν πολλοὶ ὥστε μηκέτι χωρεῖν μηδὲ τὰ πρὸς τὴν θύραν, καὶ ἐλάλει αὐτοῖς τὸν λόγον. καὶ ἔρχονται φέροντες πρὸς αὐτὸν παραλυτικὸν αἰρόμενον ὑπὸ τεσσάρων. καὶ μὴ δυνάμενοι προσενέγκαι αὐτῷ διὰ τὸν ὄχλον ἀπεστέγασαν τὴν στέγην ὅπου ἦν, καὶ ἐξορύξαντες χαλῶσι τὸν κράβατον ὅπου ὁ παραλυτικὸς κατέκειτο. καὶ ἰδὼν ὁ Ἰησοῦς τὴν πίστιν αὐτῶν λέγει τῷ παραλυτικῷ, Τέκνον, ἀφίενταί σου αἱ ἁμαρτίαι. ἦσαν δέ τινες τῶν γραμματέων ἐκεῖ καθήμενοι καὶ διαλογιζόμενοι ἐν ταῖς καρδίαις αὐτῶν, Τί οὗτος οὕτως λαλεῖ; βλασφημεῖ· τίς δύναται ἀφιέναι ἁμαρτίας εἰ μὴ εἷς ὁ θεός; καὶ εὐθὺς ἐπιγνοὺς ὁ Ἰησοῦς τῷ πνεύματι αὐτοῦ ὅτι οὕτως διαλογίζονται ἐν ἑαυτοῖς λέγει αὐτοῖς, Τί ταῦτα διαλογίζεσθε ἐν ταῖς καρδίαις ὑμῶν; τί ἐστιν εὐκοπώτερον, εἰπεῖν τῷ παραλυτικῷ, Ἀφίενταί σου αἱ ἁμαρτίαι, ἢ εἰπεῖν, Ἔγειρε καὶ ἆρον τὸν κράβαττόν σου καὶ περιπάτει; ἵνα δὲ εἰδῆτε ὅτι ἐξουσίαν ἔχει ὁ υἱὸς τοῦ ἀνθρώπου ἀφιέναι ἁμαρτίας ἐπὶ τῆς γῆς— λέγει τῷ παραλυτικῷ, Σοὶ λέγω, ἔγειρε ἆρον τὸν κράβαττόν σου καὶ ὕπαγε εἰς τὸν οἶκόν σου. καὶ ἠγέρθη καὶ εὐθὺς ἄρας τὸν κράβατον ἐξῆλθεν ἔμπροσθεν πάντων, ὥστε ἐξίστασθαι πάντας καὶ δοξάζειν τὸν θεὸν λέγοντας ὅτι Οὕτως οὐδέποτε εἴδομεν.

412 Lk. 5:17: ἐκ πάσης κώμης [...].

413 Cf. 'comedy', from the Greek *kômôidia*, in fact 'singing of a *kômos*, i.e. a festive parade, a banquet, revel, carousal, merry-making', cf. also Latin *comis*, 'cheerful, affable, gracious, having good taste', as well as *comitas*, 'cheerful mood, brightness, graciousness, good taste'.

414 *Logos* in the sense of a testimony is substantiated here. Cf. PLUT. *Caes.* 10: μάρτυς δὲ πρὸς τὴν δίκην κληθείς, οὐδὲν ἔφη τῶν λεγομένων κατὰ τοῦ Κλωδίου γιγνώσκειν. ὡς δὲ τοῦ λόγου παραδόξου φανέντος ὁ κατήγορος ἠρώτησε "πῶς οὖν ἀπεπέμψω τὴν γυναῖκα". Because Caesar was praetor at this time, the presence of the term *legem dicere* in the Latin source used by Plutarchus has to be considered. This could have been used by Mark to change it to ἐλάλει αὐτοῖς τὸν λόγον: *logon* would then stand for *legem*.

415 Mk. 2:3: ὑπὸ τεσσάρων. PLUT. *Caes.* 10: ὑπὸ τῆς συνειδυίας θεραπαινίδος.

416 SUET. *Jul.* 74: «*in Publium Clodium, Pompeiae uxoris suae adulterum atque eadem de causa pollutarum caeremoniarum reum, testis citatus negavit se quicquam comperisse, quamuis et mater Aurelia et soror Iulia apud eosdem iudices omnia ex fide rettulissent; interrogatusque, cur igitur repudiasset uxorem: ‹Quoniam›, inquit, ‹meos tam suspicione quam crimine iudico carere oportere›*».

417 Whereas we believe that the Evangelist tells us how to enter an Oriental house with an inside court (respectively a Roman Atrium house), namely via the roof, he seems in reality to conceal Caesar's (respectively Jesus') adulterous wife: Not the woman, but the roof is ripped open.

418 APP. *BC* 2.14.52: ἕτεροι δὲ διὰ τὴν ἱερουργίαν ἐς ἀσέβειαν ἐδίωκον, καὶ συνηγόρευε τοῖς διώκουσι Κικέρων.

419 For 'accused' Plutarchus says *egrapsato*, cf. PLUT. *Cic.* 28: καὶ δίκην τις ⟨τῶν δημάρχων⟩ ἀσεβείας ἐγράψατο τῷ Κλωδίῳ.

420 Mk. 1:40-45; Mt. 8:1-4; Lk. 5:12-16.

421 One could object that a 'priest' is not a 'High priest'. Now it is true that the Greek Gospel text we have received uses 'priest' here, but the Vulgate has *principi sacerdotum*, 'High priests', as expected. One has been surprised that Hieronymus, in his emendation of the *Vetus Latina* on the basis of Greek manuscripts, did not change *principi sacerdotum* to *sacerdoti*. (HIERONYMUS *De vir. inl.* 235: '*Novum Testamentum graecae fidei reddidi*'; he changed the text of his schema in 3500 places); (cf. *Vulgata*, ALAND & NESTLE, [18]1957). Here again the reinterpretation of the Gospels as the Vita Caesaris gives us the solution to a heretofore unexplained peculiarity in the handing down of the texts: Hieronymus was not mistaken. He simply found 'High priest(s)' in the Greek manuscripts—at least in some of them—that were still available in his time.

422 Particularly over the *mos maiorum*, the 'custom of the ancestors'. Traditionalistic Romans regarded this as the constitution, and Caesar was repeatedly blamed for having broken it in order to introduce *novae res*, 'new (i.e. revolutionary) things'. As is known this opposition of the new to the old ('It has been said by those of old, but I say unto you…') is typical of Jesus' message—where we find the *terminus technicus* 'custom of the ancients', *mos maiorum*, as 'Mose and the prophets' (via *praefectus morum?*) and in the generalization as the opposition implied in 'New and Old Testament'. It is striking that in ancient manuscripts Μωσῆς (Greek transcription—*Môsês*) consistently appears whereas modern text critics in a know-all manner correct it to Μωϋσῆς (Greek transcription—*Môysês*), supposedly in order to standardize the orthography (according to ALAND & NESTLE, sic!), as if they knew better and as if the spelling were irrelevant in just those texts. So they themselves partly destroy the painstaking listing of the handwritten variations by straightening out the orthography. For example, it is only noticeable in the facsimile that in the Vulgate manuscripts the town corrected to and known as *Kapharnaum* respectively *Kapernaum/Capernaum* today was originally written *Cafarnaum*, which allows us to recognize it as a miswriting of *Corfinium*. It must be stated: With the slogan that Aland-Nestle & Co. adopted: *Te totum applica ad textum: rem totam applica ad te* (J.A. Bengel) text critics only sometimes find the old corrections that made things worse, because the *res tota* which they 'apply' on themselves is still the old—the Judaistic glasses through which they look are still the same and they fit even tighter thanks to the new feelings of guilt towards the Jews after World War II. Do they not see that they forge with the right what they correct with the left? They even feel they are merely fulfilling a belated duty. The political correctness to which we owe the metamorphosis of the *Vita Divi Iulii* into the Gospels still affects—under hardly changed conditions—modern textual criticism.

423 APP. *BC* 2.15.53: δημάρχους δὲ ᾑρεῖτο Οὐατίνιόν τε καὶ Κλώδιον τὸν Καλὸν ἐπίκλην, ὅν τινα αἰσχρὰν ἐν ἱερουργίᾳ γυναικῶν ποτε λαβόντα ὑπόνοιαν ἐπὶ Ἰουλίᾳ τῇ Καίσαρος αὐτοῦ γυναικὶ ὁ μὲν Καῖσαρ οὐκ ἔκρινεν, ὑπεραρέσκοντα τῷ δήμῳ, καίπερ ἀποπεμψάμενος τὴν γυναῖκα, ἕτεροι δὲ διὰ τὴν ἱερουργίαν ἐς ἀσέβειαν ἐδίωκον, καὶ συνηγόρευε τοῖς διώκουσι Κικέρων. καὶ κληθεὶς ἐς μαρτυρίαν ὁ Καῖσαρ οὐ κατεῖπεν, ἀλλὰ τότε καὶ δήμαρχον ἐς ἐπιβουλὴν τοῦ Κικέρωνος ἀπέφηνε, διαβάλλοντος ἤδη τὴν συμφροσύνην τῶν τριῶν ἀνδρῶν ἐς μοναρχίαν. οὕτω καὶ λύπης ἐκράτουν ὑπὸ χρείας καὶ τὸν ἐχθρὸν εὐηργέτουν ἐς ἄμυναν ἑτέρου.

424 APP. *BC* 2.13.49: ἐφ' οἷς αὐτὸν εἵλοντο Γαλατίας τῆς τε ἐντὸς Ἄλπεων καὶ ὑπὲρ Ἄλπεις ἐπὶ πενταετὲς ἄρχειν καὶ ἐς τὴν ἀρχὴν ἔδοσαν τέλη στρατοῦ τέσσαρα. And 14: δοκεῖ δὲ καὶ ὁ Κλώδιος ἀμείψασθαι πρότερος τὸν Καίσαρα καὶ συλλαβεῖν ἐς τὴν τῆς Γαλατίας ἀρχήν.

425 Cf. Jn.9:2: 'And his disciples asked him, saying, Master, who did sin, this man, or his parents, that he was born blind?'
The association with the *leper* might originally have been caused by the end of this story—'he was out there in desolate places' (Mk. 1:45)—or by the beginning of the next—where one is 'not in the room' or supposed to 'remain outside the door.' Also conceivable is a Latin source wherein Faunus as *Lupercus* and Dionysos as *Liber* were mentioned in connection with the Bona Dea. Two names that just would have to evoke the lection *lepros*. Or maybe another source in which the looks of the joking beauty *Pulcher* were characterized as *lepor, leporis*.

426 Mk. 2:14-17: καὶ παράγων εἶδεν Λευὶν τὸν τοῦ Ἀλφαίου καθήμενον ἐπὶ τὸ τελώνιον, καὶ λέγει αὐτῷ, Ἀκολούθει μοι. καὶ ἀναστὰς ἠκολούθησεν αὐτῷ. Καὶ γίνεται κατακεῖσθαι αὐτὸν ἐν τῇ οἰκίᾳ αὐτοῦ, καὶ πολλοὶ τελῶναι καὶ ἁμαρτωλοὶ συνανέκειντο τῷ Ἰησοῦ καὶ τοῖς μαθηταῖς αὐτοῦ· ἦσαν γὰρ πολλοὶ καὶ ἠκολούθουν αὐτῷ. καὶ οἱ γραμματεῖς τῶν Φαρισαίων ἰδόντες ὅτι ἐσθίει μετὰ τῶν ἁμαρτωλῶν καὶ τελωνῶν ἔλεγον τοῖς μαθηταῖς αὐτοῦ, Ὅτι μετὰ τῶν τελωνῶν καὶ ἁμαρτωλῶν ἐσθίει; καὶ ἀκούσας ὁ Ἰησοῦς λέγει αὐτοῖς [ὅτι] Οὐ χρείαν ἔχουσιν οἱ ἰσχύοντες ἰατροῦ ἀλλ' οἱ κακῶς ἔχοντες· οὐκ ἦλθον καλέσαι δικαίους ἀλλὰ ἁμαρτωλούς.

427 Cf. i.a. APP. *BC* 2.13.47-49.

428 Cf. the Greek play on words of Augustus—that in the house of Herodes a swine lived less dangerously than a son (Herodes, who according to the Jewish law would have been supposed to abstain from pork, had both sons of his Jewish wife Mariamme executed)—is only a play on words if a ὗς or ὕς or ὑύς for 'son'—but not a υἱός—corresponds to the 'swine' ὗς.

429 It was the Romans who were called 'porridge munchers' as today the Italians are called 'spaghetti munchers': cf. the jocular *pultiphagus* in Plautus. This is still preserved today in the slightly altered form of *polentone*, 'polenta muncher', an invective for northern Italians (*polenta* comes from *puls*, pl. *pultes,* presumably via the accusative *pultem,* and is possibly related to the German *Fladen*—flat cake; the English *poultice* demonstrates the same etymology).

430 *Alphaios* looks like a metathesis of *Pulcher* (via *Ulpher*—with aspiration dissimilation?).

431 An uncertainty that, by the way, we find again in the listing of names in the calling of the apostles: For example in Mt. 10:3 Matthew is the publican, but the son of Alpheus is Jacob, whereas Levi as the name of an apostle is not mentioned by any Evangelist.

432 AUGUSTINUS *De adult. coniug.* 2.6. The controversial passage that linguistically does not accord with John and appears in the wrong context was inserted there (7:53-8:11) in view of the verses 7:51 ('Doth our law judge [any] man, before it hear him, and know what he doeth?') and 8:15 ('I judge no man'). But in the manuscripts of the so-called Ferrar group the pericope about the adulteress is located after Lk. 21:38 (following the passage about the poor widow—which shows parallels to Cato's marriage to a widow: see below).

433 Jn.7:53-8:11: [[Καὶ ἐπορεύθησαν ἕκαστος εἰς τὸν οἶκον αὐτοῦ, Ἰησοῦς δὲ ἐπορεύθη εἰς τὸ Ὄρος τῶν Ἐλαιῶν. Ὄρθρου δὲ πάλιν παρεγένετο εἰς τὸ ἱερόν καὶ πᾶς ὁ λαὸς ἤρχετο πρὸς αὐτόν, καὶ καθίσας ἐδίδασκεν αὐτούς. ἄγουσιν δὲ οἱ γραμματεῖς καὶ οἱ Φαρισαῖοι γυναῖκα ἐπὶ μοιχείᾳ κατειλημμένην, καὶ στήσαντες αὐτὴν ἐν μέσῳ λέγουσιν αὐτῷ, Διδάσκαλε, αὕτη ἡ γυνὴ κατείληπται ἐπ' αὐτοφώρῳ μοιχευομένη· ἐν δὲ τῷ νόμῳ ἡμῖν Μωϋσῆς ἐνετείλατο τὰς τοιαύτας λιθάζειν. σὺ οὖν τί λέγεις; τοῦτο δὲ ἔλεγον πειράζοντες αὐτόν, ἵνα ἔχωσιν κατηγορεῖν αὐτοῦ. ὁ δὲ Ἰησοῦς κάτω κύψας τῷ δακτύλῳ κατέγραφεν εἰς τὴν γῆν. ὡς δὲ ἐπέμενον ἐρωτῶντες αὐτόν, ἀνέκυψεν καὶ εἶπεν αὐτοῖς, Ὁ ἀναμάρτητος ὑμῶν πρῶτος ἐπ' αὐτὴν βαλέτω λίθον. καὶ πάλιν κατακύψας ἔγραφεν εἰς τὴν γῆν. οἱ δὲ ἀκούσαντες ἐξήρχοντο εἷς καθ' εἷς ἀρξάμενοι ἀπὸ τῶν πρεσβυτέρων καὶ κατελείφθη μόνος καὶ ἡ

γυνὴ ἐν μέσῳ οὖσα. ἀνακύψας δὲ ὁ 'Ιησοῦς εἶπεν αὐτῇ, Γύναι, ποῦ εἰσιν; οὐδείς σε κατέκρινεν; ἡ δὲ εἶπεν, Οὐδείς, κύριε. εἶπεν δὲ ὁ 'Ιησοῦς, Οὐδὲ ἐγώ σε κατακρίνω· πορεύου, [καὶ] ἀπὸ τοῦ νῦν μηκέτι ἁμάρτανε.]]

434 Compare: 'voting stones (pebbles)' *psêphos*, pronounciation *psiphos* / *lithos* 'stone', ΨΗΦΟΣ / ΛΙΘΟΣ—respectively Lat. *tessera* / *lithos*, TESSERA / ΛΙΘΟΣ.

435 The condemning voting tablets bore a C (*condemno*), the absolving ones an A (*absolvo*).

436 Cf. PLUT. *Caes.* 10: ἀποφεύγει δ' οὖν τὸ ἔγκλημα, τῶν πλείστων δικαστῶν συγκεχυμένοις τοῖς γράμμασι τὰς γνώμας ἀποδόντων, ὅπως μήτε παρακινδυνεύσωσιν ἐν τοῖς πολλοῖς καταψηφισάμενοι, μήτ' ἀπολύσαντες ἀδοξήσωσι παρὰ τοῖς ἀρίστοις. Jn. 8:6: ὁ δὲ 'Ιησοῦς κάτω κύψας τῷ δακτύλῳ κατέγραφεν εἰς τὴν γῆν bzw. Joh 8.8: καὶ πάλιν κατακύψας ἔγραφεν εἰς τὴν γῆν. If the mispelling is in the Greek tradition we would have to compare ΚΑΤΑΨΗΦΙΣΑ(ΜΕΝΟΙ) on the one hand with ΚΑΤΩ-ΚΥΨΑΣ resp. ΚΑΤΑΚΥΨΑΣ on the other, further ΔΙΚΑΣΤΩΝ with ΔΑΚΤΥΛΩΙ—or in case of a direct misunderstanding of the Latin exemplar: ΚΑΤΩΚΥΨΑΣ with AC-CVSATORES (AC...TO > ΚΑΤΩ and CVSA...RES > ΚΥΨΑΣ) resp. IVDICIO with DIGITO (cf. SUET. *Jul.* 74).

437 SUET. *Jul.* 6: «In Corneliae autem locum Pompeiam duxit [...]; cum qua deinde diuortium fecit, adulteratam opinatus a Publio Clodio [...]»; ibidem 74: «[...] interrogatusque, cur igitur repudiasset uxorem [...]»; PLUT. *Caes.* 10: ὁ κατήγορος ἠρώτησε "πῶς οὖν ἀπεπέμψω τὴν γυναῖκα;"

438 Mt. 19:7-9; cf. also Mt. 5:31 sq; Mk. 10:4-12; Lk. 16:18.

439 Cf. SUET. *Jul.* 1: 'At the age of sixteen he lost his father. In the following year he was nominated priest of Jupiter, he broke an engagement made for him while he was still a boy, to marry one Cossutia, who came from an equestrian family but was very rich. Instead he married Cornelia, daughter of that Cinna who had been Consul four times, and later she bore him a daughter named Julia. And under no circumstances would he allow Sulla to force him to divorce her.' PLUT. *Caes.* 5: 'Now, in the case of elderly women, it was ancient Roman usage to pronounce funeral orations over them; but it was not customary in the case of young women, and Caesar was first to do so when his own wife died. This also brought him much favor, and earned him the sympathies of the multitude, who looked upon him as a man of great tenderness and kindness of heart. After the funeral of his wife, he went out to Spain as quaestor [...]. When he returned from the province, he married Pompeia as his third wife, already having by Cornelia a daughter who later became the wife of Pompeius the Great.'

440 Cf. Cicero's *Cato* and Caesar's *Anticato*. Cato's 'leasing out' of his wife to the elderly Hortensius—who bequeathed her all his possessions—only to remarry her as a wealthy widow, played a major role in this polemic. Cf. PLUT. *Cat. Mi.* 25; 52: εἰς ὃ δὴ μάλιστα λοιδορούμενος ὁ Καῖσαρ τῷ Κάτωνι φιλοπλουτίαν προφέρει καὶ μισθαρνίαν ἐπὶ τῷ γάμῳ. τί γὰρ ἔδει παραχωρεῖν δεόμενον γυναικός, ἢ τί μὴ δεόμενον αὖθις ἀναλαμβάνειν, εἰ μὴ δέλεαρ ἐξ ἀρχῆς ὑφείθη τὸ γύναιον Ὀρτησίῳ καὶ νέαν ἔχρησεν ἵνα πλουσίαν ἀπολάβῃ;—'Caesar castigated this deal in the sharpest tone and accused Cato of having debased marriage out of disdainful avarice to a money transaction: "If he needed a wife, why should he give her to somebody else? And if he did not need one, what caused him to take her back? Did not he use the poor woman from the beginning just as a bait for Hortensius? He lent her out while she was young that he might take her back as a rich widow."'

441 PLUT. *Cic.* 29: πολλὴ δ' ἦν δόξα καὶ ταῖς ἄλλαις δυσὶν ἀδελφαῖς πλησιάζειν τὸν Κλώδιον, ὧν Τερτίαν μὲν Μάρκιος ‹ὁ› Ῥήξ, Κλωδίαν δὲ Μέτελλος ὁ Κέλερ εἶχεν, ἣν Κουαδρανταρίαν ἐκάλουν, ὅτι τῶν ἐραστῶν τις αὐτῇ χαλκοῦς ἐμβαλὼν εἰς βαλάντιον ὡς ἀργύριον εἰσέπεμψε· τὸ δὲ λεπτότατον τοῦ χαλκοῦ νομίσματος κουα-

δράντην Ῥωμαῖοι καλοῦσιν. ἐπὶ ταύτῃ μάλιστα τῶν ἀδελφῶν κακῶς ἤκουσεν ὁ Κλώδιος.

442 Mk. 12:41-44: Καὶ καθίσας κατέναντι τοῦ γαζοφυλακίου ἐθεώρει πῶς ὁ ὄχλος βάλλει χαλκὸν εἰς τὸ γαζοφυλάκιον. καὶ πολλοὶ πλούσιοι ἔβαλλον πολλά· καὶ ἐλθοῦσα μία χήρα πτωχὴ ἔβαλεν λεπτὰ δύο, ὅ ἐστιν κοδράντης. καὶ προσκαλεσάμενος τοὺς μαθητὰς αὐτοῦ εἶπεν αὐτοῖς, Ἀμὴν λέγω ὑμῖν ὅτι ἡ χήρα αὕτη ἡ πτωχὴ πλεῖον πάντων ἔβαλεν τῶν βαλλόντων εἰς τὸ γαζοφυλάκιον· πάντες γὰρ ἐκ τοῦ περισσεύοντος αὐτοῖς ἔβαλον, αὕτη δὲ ἐκ τῆς ὑστερήσεως αὐτῆς πάντα ὅσα εἶχεν ἔβαλεν ὅλον τὸν βίον αὐτῆς.

443 Mk. 2:23-3:6 and parallel passages Mt. 12:1-14, Lk. 6:1-11.

444 Despite the explicit order of Pompeius. Cf. DIO CASS. HR 41.6.3-6.

445 Cf. DIO CASS. HR 41.17.1.

446 Cf. DIO CASS. HR 41.17.1-2: τοσούτου τε ἐδέησαν τὰ χρήματα ἃ ὑπέσχετό σφισι τότε γε λαβεῖν, ὥστε καὶ τἆλλά οἱ πάνθ' ὅσα ἐν τῷ δημοσίῳ ἦν πρὸς τὴν τῶν στρατιωτῶν, οὓς ἐφοβοῦντο, τροφὴν ἔδοσαν. καὶ ἐπὶ πᾶσιν τούτοις ὡς καὶ ἀγαθοῖς οὖσι τὴν ἐσθῆτα τὴν εἰρηνικὴν μετημπίσχοντο· οὐδέπω γὰρ αὐτὴν μετειλήφεσαν. ἀντεῖπε μὲν οὖν πρὸς τὴν περὶ τῶν χρημάτων ἐσήγησιν Λούκιός τις Μέτελλος δήμαρχος, καὶ ἐπειδὴ μηδὲν ἐπέρανε, πρός τε τοὺς θησαυροὺς ἦλθε καὶ τὰς θύρας αὐτῶν ἐν τηρήσει ἐποιήσατο· σμικρὸν δὲ δὴ καὶ τῆς φυλακῆς αὐτοῦ, ὥσπερ που καὶ τῆς παρρησίας, οἱ στρατιῶται φροντίσαντες τήν τε βαλανάγραν διέκοψαν (τὴν γὰρ κλεῖν οἱ ὕπατοι εἶχον, ὥσπερ οὐκ ἐξόν τισι πελέκεσιν ἀντ' αὐτῆς χρήσασθαι) καὶ πάντα τὰ χρήματα ἐξεφόρησαν.

PLUT. Caes. 35: Τοῦ δὲ δημάρχου Μετέλλου κωλύοντος αὐτὸν ἐκ τῶν ἀποθέτων χρήματα λαμβάνειν καὶ νόμους τινὰς προφέροντος, οὐκ ἔφη τὸν αὐτὸν ὅπλων καὶ νόμων καιρὸν εἶναι· "σὺ δ' εἰ τοῖς πραττομένοις δυσκολαίνεις, νῦν μὲν ἐκποδὼν ἄπιθι· παρρησίας γὰρ οὐ δεῖται πόλεμος· ὅταν δὲ κατάθωμαι τὰ ὅπλα συμβάσεων γενομένων, τότε παριὼν δημαγωγήσεις." "καὶ ταῦτ'" ἔφη "λέγω τῶν ἐμαυτοῦ δικαίων ὑφιέμενος· ἐμὸς γὰρ εἶ καὶ σὺ καὶ πάντες ὅσους εἴληφα τῶν πρὸς ἐμὲ στασιασάντων." ταῦτα πρὸς τὸν Μέτελλον εἰπών, ἐβάδιζε πρὸς τὰς θύρας τοῦ ταμιείου. μὴ φαινομένων δὲ τῶν κλειδῶν, χαλκεῖς μεταπεμψάμενος ἐκκόπτειν ἐκέλευεν. αὖθις δ' ἐνισταμένου τοῦ Μετέλλου καί τινων ἐπαινούντων, διατεινάμενος ἠπείλησεν ἀποκτενεῖν αὐτόν, εἰ μὴ παύσαιτο παρενοχλῶν· "καὶ τοῦτ'" ἔφη "μειράκιον οὐκ ἀγνοεῖς ὅτι μοι δυσκολώτερον ἦν εἰπεῖν ἢ πρᾶξαι." οὗτος ὁ λόγος τότε καὶ Μέτελλον ἀπελθεῖν ἐποίησε καταδείσαντα, καὶ τὰ ἄλλα ῥᾳδίως αὐτῷ καὶ ταχέως ὑπηρετεῖσθαι πρὸς τὸν πόλεμον. Ἐστράτευσε δ' εἰς Ἰβηρίαν, πρότερον ἐγνωκὼς τοὺς περὶ Ἀφράνιον καὶ Βάρρωνα Πομπηίου πρεσβευτὰς ἐκβαλεῖν [...].

APP. BC 2.41.164: ὁ δὲ Καῖσαρ ἐς Ῥώμην ἐπειχθεὶς τόν τε δῆμον, ἐκ μνήμης τῶν ἐπὶ Σύλλα καὶ Μαρίου κακῶν πεφρικότα, ἐλπίσι καὶ ὑποσχέσεσι πολλαῖς ἀνελάμβανε καὶ τοῖς ἐχθροῖς ἐνσημαινόμενος φιλανθρωπίαν εἶπεν, ὅτι καὶ Λεύκιον Δομίτιον ἑλὼν ἀπαθῆ μεθείη μετὰ τῶν χρημάτων. τὰ δὲ κλεῖθρα τῶν δημοσίων ταμιείων ἐξέκοπτε καὶ τῶν δημάρχων ἑνὶ Μετέλλῳ κωλύοντι θάνατον ἠπείλει. τῶν τε ἀψαύστων ἐκίνει χρημάτων, ἅ φασιν ἐπὶ Κελτοῖς πάλαι σὺν ἀρᾷ δημοσίᾳ τεθῆναι, μὴ σαλεύειν ἐς μηδέν, εἰ μὴ Κελτικὸς πόλεμος ἐπίοι. ὁ δὲ ἔφη Κελτοὺς αὐτὸς ἐς τὸ ἀσφαλέστατον ἑλὼν λελυκέναι τῇ πόλει τὴν ἀράν.

447 Cf. Mk. 2:18-3:6: Καὶ ἦσαν οἱ μαθηταὶ Ἰωάννου καὶ οἱ Φαρισαῖοι νηστεύοντες. καὶ ἔρχονται καὶ λέγουσιν αὐτῷ, Διὰ τί οἱ μαθηταὶ Ἰωάννου καὶ οἱ μαθηταὶ τῶν Φαρισαίων νηστεύουσιν, οἱ δὲ σοὶ μαθηταὶ οὐ νηστεύουσιν; καὶ εἶπεν αὐτοῖς ὁ Ἰησοῦς, Μὴ δύνανται οἱ υἱοὶ τοῦ νυμφῶνος ἐν ᾧ ὁ νυμφίος μετ' αὐτῶν ἐστιν νηστεύειν; ὅσον χρόνον ἔχουσιν τὸν νυμφίον μετ' αὐτῶν οὐ δύνανται νηστεύειν. ἐλεύσονται δὲ ἡμέραι ὅταν ἀπαρθῇ ἀπ' αὐτῶν ὁ νυμφίος, καὶ τότε νηστεύσουσιν ἐν ἐκείνῃ τῇ ἡμέρᾳ. οὐδεὶς ἐπίβλημα ῥάκους ἀγνάφου ἐπιράπτει ἐπὶ ἱμάτιον παλαιόν· εἰ δὲ μή, αἴρει τὸ πλήρωμα ἀπ' αὐτοῦ τὸ καινὸν τοῦ παλαιοῦ καὶ χεῖρον σχίσμα γίνεται. καὶ οὐδεὶς βάλλει οἶνον νέον εἰς ἀσκοὺς παλαιούς· εἰ δὲ μή, ῥήξει ὁ οἶνος τοὺς ἀσκοὺς

καὶ ὁ οἶνος ἀπόλλυται καὶ οἱ ἀσκοί· ἀλλὰ οἶνον νέον εἰς ἀσκοὺς καινούς. Καὶ ἐγένετο αὐτὸν ἐν τοῖς σάββασιν παραπορεύεσθαι διὰ τῶν σπορίμων, καὶ οἱ μαθηταὶ αὐτοῦ ἤρξαντο ὁδὸν ποιεῖν τίλλοντες τοὺς στάχυας. καὶ οἱ Φαρισαῖοι ἔλεγον αὐτῷ, Ἴδε τί ποιοῦσιν τοῖς σάββασιν ὃ οὐκ ἔξεστιν· καὶ λέγει αὐτοῖς, Οὐδέποτε ἀνέγνωτε τί ἐποίησεν Δαυίδ ὅτε χρείαν ἔσχεν καὶ ἐπείνασεν αὐτὸς καὶ οἱ μετ' αὐτοῦ, πῶς εἰσῆλθεν εἰς τὸν οἶκον τοῦ θεοῦ ἐπὶ Ἀβιαθὰρ ἀρχιερέως καὶ τοὺς ἄρτους τῆς προθέσεως ἔφαγεν, οὓς οὐκ ἔξεστιν φαγεῖν εἰ μὴ τοὺς ἱερεῖς, καὶ ἔδωκεν καὶ τοῖς σὺν αὐτῷ οὖσιν· καὶ ἔλεγεν αὐτοῖς, Τὸ σάββατον διὰ τὸν ἄνθρωπον ἐγένετο καὶ οὐχ ὁ ἄνθρωπος διὰ τὸ σάββατον· ὥστε κύριός ἐστιν ὁ υἱὸς τοῦ ἀνθρώπου καὶ τοῦ σαββάτου. Καὶ εἰσῆλθεν πάλιν εἰς τὴν συναγωγήν. καὶ ἦν ἐκεῖ ἄνθρωπος ἐξηραμμένην ἔχων τὴν χεῖρα· καὶ παρετήρουν αὐτὸν εἰ τοῖς σάββασιν θεραπεύσει αὐτόν, ἵνα κατηγορήσωσιν αὐτοῦ. καὶ λέγει τῷ ἀνθρώπῳ τῷ τὴν ξηρὰν χεῖρα ἔχοντι, Ἔγειρε εἰς τὸ μέσον. καὶ λέγει αὐτοῖς, Ἔξεστιν τοῖς σάββασιν ἀγαθὸν ποιῆσαι ἢ κακοποιῆσαι, ψυχὴν σῶσαι ἢ ἀποκτεῖναι; οἱ δὲ ἐσιώπων. καὶ περιβλεψάμενος αὐτοὺς μετ' ὀργῆς, συλλυπούμενος ἐπὶ τῇ πωρώσει τῆς καρδίας αὐτῶν λέγει τῷ ἀνθρώπῳ, Ἔκτεινον τὴν χεῖρα. καὶ ἐξέτεινεν καὶ ἀπεκατεστάθη ἡ χεὶρ αὐτοῦ. καὶ ἐξελθόντες οἱ Φαρισαῖοι εὐθὺς μετὰ τῶν Ἡρῳδιανῶν συμβούλιον ἐδίδουν κατ' αὐτοῦ ὅπως αὐτὸν ἀπολέσωσιν.

448 Diverse manuscripts have ἐξηραμμένην instead of ἐξηραμμένην. Cf. ALAND & NESTLE ([18]1957).

449 CAES. Civ. 3.70: His tantis malis haec subsidia succurrebant, quominus omnis deleretur exercitus, quod Pompeius insidias timens, credo quod haec praeter spem acciderant eius qui paulo ante ex castris fugientis suos conspexerat, munitionibus adpropinquare aliquamdiu non audebat, equitesque eius angustiis atque his a Caesaris militibus occupatis, ad insequendum tardabantur. ita parvae res magnum in utramque partem momentum habuerunt.

450 CAES. Civ. 3.105: Caesar cum in Asiam venisset, reperiebat T. Ampium conatum esse pecunias tollere Ephesо ex fano Dianae eiusque rei causa senatores omnes ex provincia evocavisse, ut his testibus in summam pecuniae uteretur, sed interpellatum adventu Caesaris profugisse. ita duobus temporibus Ephesiae pecuniae Caesar auxilium tulit. item constabat Elide in templo Minervae repetitis atque enumeratis diebus, quo die proelium secundum Caesar fecisset, simulacrum Victoriae, quod ante ipsam Minervam conlocatum esset et ante ad simulacrum Minervae spectavisset, ad valvas se templi limenque convertisse. eodemque die Antiochiae in Syria bis tantus exercitus clamor et signorum sonus exauditus est, ut in muris armata civitas discurreret. hoc idem Ptolomaide accidit. Pergamique in occultis ac reconditis templi, quo praeter sacerdotes adire fas non est—quae Graeci adyta appellant—tympana sonuerunt. item Trallibus in templo Victoriae, ubi Caesaris statuam consecraverant, palma per eos dies [in tecto] inter coagmenta lapidum ex pavimento exstitisse ostendebatur.

451 Padua was the hometown of Livius, who had a conspicuous inclination to omens and miraculous signs. Plutarchus bases the tradition of this anecdote on him.

452 PLUT. Caes. 47: Σημείων δὲ πολλῶν γενομένων τῆς νίκης ἐπιφανέστατον ἱστορεῖται τὸ περὶ Τράλλεις. ἐν γὰρ ἱερῷ Νίκης ἀνδριὰς εἱστήκει Καίσαρος, καὶ τὸ περὶ αὐτῷ χωρίον αὐτό τε στερεὸν φύσει καὶ λίθῳ σκληρῷ κατεστρωμένον ἦν ἄνωθεν· ἐκ τούτου λέγουσιν ἀνατεῖλαι φοίνικα παρὰ τὴν βάσιν τοῦ ἀνδριάντος. ἐν δὲ Παταβίῳ Γάϊος Κορνήλιος, ἀνὴρ εὐδόκιμος ἐπὶ μαντικῇ, Λιβίου τοῦ συγγραφέως πολίτης καὶ γνώριμος, ἐτύγχανεν ἐπ' οἰωνοῖς καθήμενος ἐκείνην τὴν ἡμέραν. καὶ πρῶτον μέν, ὡς Λίβιός φησι, τὸν καιρὸν ἔγνω τῆς μάχης, καὶ πρὸς τοὺς παρόντας εἶπεν ὅτι καὶ δὴ περαίνεται τὸ χρῆμα καὶ συνίασιν εἰς ἔργον οἱ ἄνδρες. αὖθις δὲ πρὸς τῇ θέᾳ γενόμενος καὶ τὰ σημεῖα κατιδών, ἀνήλατο μετ' ἐνθουσιασμοῦ βοῶν· "νικᾷς ὦ Καῖσαρ." ἐκπλαγέντων δὲ τῶν παρατυχόντων, περιελὼν τὸν στέφανον ἀπὸ τῆς κε-

φαλῆς ἐνώμοτος ἔφη μὴ πρὶν ἐπιθήσεσθαι πάλιν, ἢ τῇ τέχνῃ μαρτυρῆσαι τὸ ἔργον. ταῦτα μὲν οὖν ὁ Λίβιος οὕτως γενέσθαι καταβεβαιοῦται.
Dio Cass. HR 41.61.4-5: καὶ ἐν Τράλλεσι φοίνικά τε ἐν τῷ τῆς Νίκης ναῷ ἀναφῦναι καὶ τὴν θεὸν αὐτὴν πρὸς εἰκόνα τοῦ Καίσαρος ἐν πλαγίῳ που κειμένην μεταστραφῆναι, [...] καὶ ἐν Παταουίῳ τῆς νῦν Ἰταλίας τότε δὲ ἔτι Γαλατίας ὀρνιθάς τινας οὐχ ὅτι διαγγεῖλαι αὐτὴν ἀλλὰ καὶ δεῖξαι τρόπον τινά· Γάιος γάρ τις Κορνήλιος πάντα τὰ γενόμενα ἀκριβῶς τε ἐξ αὐτῶν ἐτεκμήρατο καὶ τοῖς παροῦσιν ἐξηγήσατο.

453 Mk.4:30-32: Καὶ ἔλεγεν, Πῶς ὁμοιώσωμεν τὴν βασιλείαν τοῦ θεοῦ ἢ ἐν τίνι αὐτὴν παραβολῇ θῶμεν; ὡς κόκκῳ σινάπεως, ὃς ὅταν σπαρῇ ἐπὶ τῆς γῆς, μικρότερον ὂν πάντων τῶν σπερμάτων τῶν ἐπὶ τῆς γῆς, καὶ ὅταν σπαρῇ, ἀναβαίνει καὶ γίνεται μεῖζον πάντων τῶν λαχάνων καὶ ποιεῖ κλάδους μεγάλους, ὥστε δύνασθαι ὑπὸ τὴν σκιὰν αὐτοῦ τὰ πετεινὰ τοῦ οὐρανοῦ κατασκηνοῦν.

454 The consonants carrying the sense are in inverted order: PhNK <|> SNP (here the K of ΦΟΙΝΙΚΑ tends to the sibilant because of the attraction of adjectives: cf. English Phoenician). Was the word ΦΟΙΝΙΚΑ, from a later Aramaic viewpoint, seen as a heterogram and hence inverted to CINAΠI? Or was the beginning of the word ΦΟ, respectively Φ, (ΦΙΝΙΚΑ could have stood perfectly in the exemplar) read as C, as sigma lunatum (with a metathesis of the last two vocals and the confusion of K and Π)?

455 But doves were nestling on the offshoot of the other palm tree that Caesar had found at Munda. Cf. SUET. Aug. 94.10, with an interpretation concerning Octavianus.

456 Mk.4:1: Καὶ πάλιν ἤρξατο διδάσκειν παρὰ τὴν θάλασσαν· καὶ συνάγεται πρὸς αὐτὸν ὄχλος πλεῖστος, ὥστε αὐτὸν εἰς πλοῖον ἐμβάντα καθῆσθαι ἐν τῇ θαλάσσῃ, καὶ πᾶς ὁ ὄχλος πρὸς τὴν θάλασσαν ἐπὶ τῆς γῆς ἦσαν.

457 Mk.4:2: καὶ ἐδίδασκεν αὐτοὺς ἐν παραβολαῖς πολλά καὶ ἔλεγεν αὐτοῖς ἐν τῇ διδαχῇ αὐτοῦ [...].

458 Mk.4:3-8: Ἀκούετε. ἰδοὺ ἐξῆλθεν ὁ σπείρων σπεῖραι. καὶ ἐγένετο ἐν τῷ σπείρειν ὃ μὲν ἔπεσεν παρὰ τὴν ὁδόν, καὶ ἦλθεν τὰ πετεινὰ καὶ κατέφαγεν αὐτό. καὶ ἄλλο ἔπεσεν ἐπὶ τὸ πετρῶδες ὅπου οὐκ εἶχεν γῆν πολλήν, καὶ εὐθὺς ἐξανέτειλεν διὰ τὸ μὴ ἔχειν βάθος γῆς· καὶ ὅτε ἀνέτειλεν ὁ ἥλιος ἐκαυματίσθη καὶ διὰ τὸ μὴ ἔχειν ῥίζαν ἐξηράνθη. καὶ ἄλλο ἔπεσεν εἰς τὰς ἀκάνθας, καὶ ἀνέβησαν αἱ ἄκανθαι καὶ συνέπνιξαν αὐτό, καὶ καρπὸν οὐκ ἔδωκεν. καὶ ἄλλα ἔπεσεν εἰς τὴν γῆν τὴν καλήν καὶ ἐδίδου καρπὸν ἀναβαίνοντα καὶ αὐξανόμενα καὶ ἔφερεν ἐν τριάκοντα καὶ ἐν ἑξήκοντα καὶ ἓν ἑκατόν.

459 Mk.4:9-11: καὶ ἔλεγεν, Ὃς ἔχει ὦτα ἀκούειν ἀκουέτω. Καὶ ὅτε ἐγένετο κατὰ μόνας, ἠρώτων αὐτὸν οἱ περὶ αὐτὸν σὺν τοῖς δώδεκα τὰς παραβολάς. καὶ ἔλεγεν αὐτοῖς, Ὑμῖν τὸ μυστήριον δέδοται τῆς βασιλείας τοῦ θεοῦ· ἐκείνοις δὲ τοῖς ἔξω ἐν παραβολαῖς τὰ πάντα γίνεται, [...].

460 Cf. i.a. LESCHHORN, p.211sqq.

461 Mk.4:12 (Jes.6:9-10): ἵνα / βλέποντες βλέπωσιν καὶ μὴ ἴδωσιν, / καὶ ἀκούοντες ἀκούωσιν καὶ μὴ συνιῶσιν, / μήποτε ἐπιστρέψωσιν καὶ ἀφεθῇ αὐτοῖς.

462 Mk.4:21-22: Καὶ ἔλεγεν αὐτοῖς, Μήτι ἔρχεται ὁ λύχνος ἵνα ὑπὸ τὸν μόδιον τεθῇ ἢ ὑπὸ τὴν κλίνην; οὐχ ἵνα ἐπὶ τὴν λυχνίαν τεθῇ; οὐ γάρ ἐστιν κρυπτὸν ἐὰν μὴ ἵνα φανερωθῇ, οὐδὲ ἐγένετο ἀπόκρυφον ἀλλ' ἵνα ἔλθῃ εἰς φανερόν.

463 Mk.4:26-29: Καὶ ἔλεγεν, Οὕτως ἐστὶν ἡ βασιλεία τοῦ θεοῦ ὡς ἄνθρωπος βάλῃ τὸν σπόρον ἐπὶ τῆς γῆς καὶ καθεύδῃ καὶ ἐγείρηται νύκτα καὶ ἡμέραν, καὶ ὁ σπόρος βλαστᾷ καὶ μηκύνηται ὡς οὐκ οἶδεν αὐτός. αὐτομάτη ἡ γῆ καρποφορεῖ, πρῶτον χόρτον εἶτα στάχυν εἶτα πλήρη[s] σῖτον ἐν τῷ στάχυϊ. ὅταν δὲ παραδοῖ ὁ καρπός, εὐθὺς ἀποστέλλει τὸ δρέπανον, ὅτι παρέστηκεν ὁ θερισμός.

464 Cf. for example WIKENHAUSER & SCHMID ([6]1973).

465 Cf. BLASS et al. ([17]1990), par. 5, especially footnote 10, p.7-8. Also the fact that in the bilingual manuscripts—like the Codex D, Bezae Cantabrigiensis—the Greek has

been corrected on the basis of Latin, it makes one ponder: why did the Latin text have a higher authority? Did one act on an older tradition that still knew that the Greek text was itself a translation of a Latin one?

V. Synoptic Comparison

466 PLUT. *Caes.* 68; SUET. *Jul.* 85; APP. *BC* 2.148; DIO CASS. *HR* 44.51.

467 As is known, the conclusion of Mark 16:9-20 is a later addition. This describes the appearance of the risen one, which was at first not believed (16:11); this corresponds to the appearance of Octavianus as the new Caesar, which was at first opposed. That just this is a later addition and alignment with the Gospel of John will give us a hint as to their respective authorship (see below).

468 DIO CASS. *HR* 44.51.1.

469 Caesar reports only on events up till the death of Pompeius and his arrival in Egypt, that is to say on the decisive years of the change of power in 49 and 48 BC. Even if we add the rest of the *Corpus Caesarianum—Bellum Alexandrinum, Africum* and *Hispaniense*—the report on Caesar's murder is still missing.

470 In both of Caesar's biographies that have come down to us—those by Plutarchus and Suetonius—the beginning is lost. But the childhood story of Caesar the selfmade man was surely not as elaborate as that of daddy's boy and heir, Octavianus.

471 Except for the war reports and a few letters, all of Caesar's writings are unfortunately lost. Amongst these were: *De analogia*, an *Anticato* and a poem *iter*, 'The journey' (SUET. *Jul.* 56). Also, none of the small works of his youth have been preserved: *Poems* and *Speeches* (PLUT. *Caes.* 2), *In Praise of Hecules*, a tragedy called *Oedipus* and *Collected Aphorisms*. Their nature was such that Augustus forbade their publication (SUET. ibid.). The beginning sections covering the childhood and youth of Caesar is also missing in our received biographies.

472 Cf. GABBA (1956).

473 The Gospel of John is so named because according to Jn. 24 it was written by the favorite disciple John, who in our hypothesis is Octavianus Augustus himself.

474 It is only in the Gospel of John that John the disciple is established as heir at the foot of the cross, he even takes the place of Jesus: '[...] he saith unto his mother, Woman, behold thy son!' (Jn. 19:26) (NB: Jesus does not address her with the expected 'Mother', but with 'Woman', Gr. *gynai,* which means 'Wife' too. This is correct: she was Calpurnia, his wife, becoming mother of the posthumously adopted son Octavianus, the new Caesar, the resurrected Jesus). This fits in with the ideology of Augustus, who saw himself as Caesar's heir, even as the new Caesar: *(h)o neos.* This passage is missing in Mark—it did not suit Marcus Antonius who had ambitions to assume the spiritual heritage as *flamen Divi Iulii.* Also this 'disciple, whom Jesus loved' was faster than Peter and 'did outrun Peter, and came first to the sepulchre' (Jn. 19:26, 20:2-4). This corresponds to the fact that Octavianus—through his fast actions and his overtaking of Antonius—came to possess the spoils of Caesar, i.e. the heritage and Caesar's succession. This is also missing in Mark, and it must be missing, because it was Octavianus' propaganda and it did not correspond to Marcus Antonius' point of view.

475 This could explain the false ending of Mark. It is possible that his original ending turned out so much philo-Petrine and anti-Johanine—i.e. pro Antonius and contra Octavianus—that it was later replaced by an ending favorable to John.

476 The lion on the coins of Marcus Antonius is linked by commentators not only with the sign of the zodiac of Antonius but also with the emblem of the Gallic city Lugdunum, where he is said to have had coins minted with the lion on the reverse (Massilia demonstrably had a lion on its municipal coat of arms) and with a passage in

Plinius (*Hist. Nat.* VIII 21), where it is reported that Antonius won acclaim by publicly appearing in a chariot drawn by a pair of lions. It is conspicuous however that, different from the coins minted in Lugdunum, on this one the lion holds a sword in his paw: according to Plutarchus (*Pomp.* 80) a lion with a sword was engraved in the signet ring of Pompeius, which Theodotos handed over to Caesar in Alexandria. As Caesar's *magister equitum*, Antonius, while Caesar was busy with war and with Cleopatra in Alexandria, had made off with the goods of Pompeius in Rome, especially his mansion which he had reconstructed to be even more luxurious than before (PLUT. *Caes.* 51). After Caesar's death Antonius got his treasure together with the files and documents from Caesar's wife Calpurnia (PLUT. *Ant.* 15). Amongst these there might have been the signet ring of Pompeius which Antonius might have used after he had obtained the East, i.e. the former sphere of control of Pompeius, during the division of the Empire with the other triumvirs Octavianus and Lepidus. If however, Caesar had given Pompeius' signet ring to Cleopatra, then Antonius should have received it from her.

In any case the lion, the heraldic animal of Marcus Antonius, is the symbol of the Evangelist Mark—as is demonstrated by the lion of Venice. Interestingly, the Venetians have the relics of Mark from Alexandria, the city where Marcus Antonius died and was buried.

477 In the case of Octavianus there was additionally the Capricorn as his birth sign, cf. note 231. The attributes of the other Evangelists also have their origin in the Caesar/Octavianus story: the bull of Luke is that of the founder of cities / respectively of Mars Ultor, the angel of Matthew is Victoria. The Tetramorph of Syrian origin was the relational framework (Ez. 1:4 sqq, Apk. 4:6 sqq).

478 SUET. *Jul.* 37-77, PLUT. *Caes.* 15-17.

479 APP. BC 2.14.52-53.

480 In EUSEBIUS, *Ekklêsiastikê historia* 3.39.15: "Μάρκος μὲν ἑρμηνευτὴς Πέτρου γενόμενος, ὅσα ἐμνημόνευσεν, ἀκριβῶς ἔγραψεν, οὐ μέντοι τάξει τὰ ὑπὸ τοῦ κυρίου ἢ λεχθέντα ἢ πραχθέντα. οὔτε γὰρ ἤκουσεν τοῦ κυρίου οὔτε παρηκολούθησεν αὐτῷ, ὕστερον δέ, ὡς ἔφην, Πέτρῳ· ὃς πρὸς τὰς χρείας ἐποιεῖτο τὰς διδασκαλίας, ἀλλ' οὐχ ὥσπερ σύνταξιν τῶν κυριακῶν ποιούμενος λογίων, ὥστε οὐδὲν ἥμαρτεν Μάρκος οὕτως ἔνια γράψας ὡς ἀπεμνημόνευσεν. ἑνὸς γὰρ ἐποιήσατο πρόνοιαν, τοῦ μηδὲν ὧν ἤκουσεν παραλιπεῖν ἢ ψεύσασθαί τι ἐν αὐτοῖς".

481 The later reconstruction of the 24 books of the Jews may serve as an illustration. They had been burned when the temple was destroyed, and were dictated by Ezra again, partly collected 'from the hearts of the people', partly obtained from a new revelation. Cf. 2 Ezr. 14:45 (also called 4 Esr.: apocryphon).

482 Cf. i.a. Chr. BURCHARD in *Der Kleine Pauly* (1979), s.v. 'Jesus', Sp. 1345.

483 Mk. 15:23-24: καὶ ἐδίδουν αὐτῷ ἐσμυρνισμένον οἶνον· ὃς δὲ οὐκ ἔλαβεν. καὶ σταυροῦσιν αὐτόν—'And they gave him to drink wine mingled with myrrh: but he received [it] not. And when they had crucified him...'

484 Lk. 23:56: ὑποστρέψασαι δὲ ἡτοίμασαν ἀρώματα καὶ μύρα.—'And they returned, and prepared spices and ointments.'

Jn. 19:39-40: ἦλθεν δὲ καὶ Νικόδημος, ὁ ἐλθὼν πρὸς αὐτὸν νυκτὸς τὸ πρῶτον, φέρων μίγμα σμύρνης καὶ ἀλόης ὡς λίτρας ἑκατόν. ἔλαβον οὖν τὸ σῶμα τοῦ Ἰησοῦ καὶ ἔδησαν αὐτὸ ὀθονίοις μετὰ τῶν ἀρωμάτων, καθὼς ἔθος ἐστὶν τοῖς Ἰουδαίοις ἐνταφιάζειν.—'And there came also Nicodemus, which at the first came to Jesus by night, and brought a mixture of myrrh and aloes, about an hundred pound [weight]. Then took they the body of Jesus, and wound it in linen clothes with the spices, as the manner of the Jews is to bury.'

485 Mt. 27:34-35: ἔδωκαν αὐτῷ πιεῖν οἶνον μετὰ χολῆς μεμιγμένον· καὶ γευσάμενος οὐκ ἠθέλησεν πιεῖν. σταυρώσαντες δὲ αὐτόν—'[...] They gave him vinegar to drink mingled with gall: and when he had tasted [thereof], he would not drink. And they

crucified him [...]'. In some manuscripts we see ὄξος, 'vinegar' instead of οἶνον, 'wine'.

486 As we saw in the case of Marcus Antonius, the name of his gens, Antonius, became Simon (Peter), who had—as Papias reports—Mark as 'interpreter'. This is very well understandable: Simon was the 'interpreted' name of Mark (Marcus Antonius).

487 APP. BC 2.1.1: ἕτερα ἐμφύλια Ῥωμαίοις τοιάδε ἐγίγνετο, μέχρι Γάιος Καῖσαρ καὶ Πομπήιος Μάγνος ἀλλήλοις ἐπολέμησαν [...], with a possible influence by APP. BC 2.72.299: Ἀλλὰ τάδε μὲν ᾠκονόμει θεὸς ἐς ἀρχὴν τῆσδε τῆς νῦν ἐπεχούσης τὰ πάντα ἡγεμονίας· VELL. 2.48: Intra breue deinde spatium, belli ciuilis exarserunt initia [...].

488 Mk. 1:1: Ἀρχὴ τοῦ εὐαγγελίου Ἰησοῦ Χριστοῦ [υἱοῦ θεοῦ].

489 Archê not only means 'commencement', 'beginning', but above all 'dominion', 'power', and as such is the translation of the Latin *imperium*. *Imperium* is translated with *archê* by, i.a., Nicolaus Damascenus (*Bios Kaisaros* 18.53), Dio Cassius (*HR* 45.2.7) and Appianus (*BC* 2.32.124): τῆς Καίσαρος ἀρχῆς τελευταία), but who also uses *êgemonia* (i.a. *BC* 3.18.66). Hence, via *euangelion tês archês*, 'message of victory of the (nascent) Empire', it could have become *archê tou evangeliou*, 'beginning of the Gospel'.

It is interesting to observe how in the respective first appearances of the name in Mark and in Appianus *Jesus Christus* corresponds to *Gaius Caesar* and not *Julius Caesar* as we might think. Caesar also speaks of himself as *Gaius Caesar* (PLUT. *Caes.* 46). On the occasion of the last redaction of Mark, *Gaius* was certainly near enough to *Jesus*, as was *Caesar* to *Christus*, to justify the substitution.

490 See above chapter WORDS AND WONDERS, *Baptism*. PLUT. *Caes.* 30.1-2 and 30.4. SUET. *Jul.* 29. VELL. 2.48.1 and 2.48.5. CAES. *Civ.* 1.11.1 and 1.26.4.
About Q. Caecilius Metellus Pius Scipio, a fierce opponent of Caesar see note 366. Cf. CAES. *Civ.* 1.2.1: *Haec Scipionis oratio, quod senatus in urbe habebatur Pompeiusque aderat, ex ipsius ore Pompei mitti uidebatur*.

491 Mk. 1:4: ἐγένετο Ἰωάννης [ὁ] βαπτίζων ἐν τῇ ἐρήμῳ καὶ κηρύσσων βάπτισμα μετανοίας εἰς ἄφεσιν ἁμαρτιῶν.

492 We have already also seen how the names Pompeius and Johannes (John) correspond to each other—via *(h)o Gnaios* > *Johannes*. But since Appianus calls both rivals *Gaius Caesar* and *Pompeius Magnus* at the beginning we have to think here as above with *Gaius Caesar* > *Jesus Christ* (see note 489) of a substitution of *Baptizôn Johannes* for *Pompeius Magnus*. Acoustically and in the writing they are not very far from each other but not overly close either. The transition could have occurred elsewhere so that it was clear to the Evangelist when editing that Magnus was to be replaced by John. Or we would have to give up our hypothesis that Johannes comes from *(h)o Gnaios* and rather determine a direct parentage from Magnus:
MAGNVS > ΙΩΑΝΝΗC; POMPEIVS MAGNVS > ΒΑΠΤΙΖΩΝ ΙΩΑΝΝΗC.
If however *Pompeius Magnus* was a unit in the exemplar then Mk. 1:1 and 1:4 would have belonged together originally: 'The beginning of the Gospel of Jesus Christ, [the Son of God]. John did baptize in the wilderness [...]' would have read: 'The beginning of the civil wars between Gaius Caesar and Pompeius Magnus. This one was in Rome [...]'. By inserting the Isaiah-citation Mk. 1:2-3, both components of *Pompeius Magnus* were separated: *Pompeius* got stuck with Jesus as *uiou theou*, 'Son of God', *Magnus* became independent as John and received as surrogate for *Pompeius (h)o baptizôn*, 'the baptist', which was borrowed from Metellus Scipio's *postulabat*, 'demanded'.
If we are seeing things correctly, then 'the baptist' would be the 'arming one' who demands 'disarmament' from his opponent. The sentence would originally have been built like that in order to accentuate the mendaciousness of Pompeius/John.

493 VELL. 2.49.4: *Cn. Pompeius consulesque et maior pars senatus, relicta Vrbe ac deinde Italia, transmisere Dyrrachium.*
SUET. *Jul.* 34: *[...] Brundisium tetendit, quo consules Pompeiusque confugerant quam primum transfretaturi.*
CAES. *Civ.* 1.6.3-7: *de reliquis rebus ad senatum refertur: tota Italia dilectus habeatur; [...] pecunia uti ex aerario Pompeio detur. [...] consules—quod ante id tempus accidit nunquam—[...] ex urbe proficiscuntur [...] totas Italia dilectus habentur, arma imperantur, pecunia a municipiis exiguntur, e fanis tolluntur, omnia diuina humanaque iura permiscentur.* CAES. *Civ.* 1.10.1: *Acceptis mandatis Roscius cum [L.] Caesare Capuam peruenit ibique consules Pompeiumque inuenit; postulata Caesaris renuntiat.*
DIO CASS. *HR* 41.6.1: φοβηθεὶς οὖν διὰ ταῦθ' ὁ Πομπήιος (καὶ γὰρ εὖ ἠπίστατο ὅτι πολὺ τοῦ Καίσαρος, ἄν γε ἐπὶ τῷ δήμῳ γένωνται, ἐλαττωθήσεται) αὐτός τε ἐς Καμπανίαν πρὶν τοὺς πρέσβεις ἐπανελθεῖν, ὡς καὶ ῥᾷον ἐκεῖ πολεμήσων, προαπῆρε, καὶ τὴν βουλὴν ἅπασαν μετὰ τῶν τὰς ἀρχὰς ἐχόντων ἀκολουθῆσαί οἱ ἐκέλευσεν, ἄδειάν τέ σφισι δόγματι τῆς ἐκδημίας δούς, καὶ προειπὼν ὅτι τὸν ὑπομείναντα ἔν τε τῷ ἴσῳ καὶ ἐν τῷ ὁμοίῳ τοῖς τὰ ἐναντία σφίσι πράττουσιν ἕξοι.
APP. *BC* 2.36.142: Ὧν οἱ ὕπατοι πυνθανόμενοι τὸν Πομπήιον οὐκ εἴων ἐπὶ τῆς ἑαυτοῦ γνώμης ἐμπειροπολέμως εὐσταθεῖν, ἀλλ' ἐξώτρυνον ἐκπηδᾶν ἐς τὴν Ἰταλίαν καὶ στρατολογεῖν ὡς τῆς πόλεως καταληφθησομένης αὐτίκα.
APP. *BC* 2.37.148: ἐξῄει τῆς τε βουλῆς καὶ τῆς πόλεως αὐτίκα ἐς τὴν ἐν Καπύῃ στρατιάν, καὶ οἱ ὕπατοι συνείποντο αὐτῷ· τοὺς ἄλλους δ' ἀπορία τε ἐς πολὺ κατεῖχε, καὶ διενυκτέρευον ἐν τῷ βουλευτηρίῳ μετ' ἀλλήλων. ἅμα δ' ἡμέρᾳ τὸ πλέον ὅμως ἐξῄει καὶ ἐδίωκε τὸν Πομπήιον.
APP. *BC* 2.39.152: Αὐτὸς δ' ὁ Πομπήιος τῶν ἀμφ' αὑτὸν ἤδη τελῶν τὰ μὲν ἔδωκε τοῖς ὑπάτοις προαπάγειν ἐς Ἤπειρον ἐκ Βρεντεσίου, καὶ διέπλευσαν οἵδε αὐτίκα ἀσφαλῶς ἐς Δυρράχιον· ἣν Ἐπίδαμνόν τινες εἶναι νομίζουσι διὰ τοιάνδε ἄγνοιαν.
PLUT. *Caes.* 34: Οἱ μὲν οὖν ὕπατοι μηδ' ἃ νόμος ἐστὶ πρὸ ἐξόδου θύσαντες ἔφυγον, ἔφευγον δὲ καὶ τῶν βουλευτῶν οἱ πλεῖστοι, τρόπον τινὰ δι' ἁρπαγῆς ἀπὸ τῶν ἰδίων ὅ τι τύχοιεν ὥσπερ ἀλλοτρίων λαμβάνοντες. εἰσὶ δ' οἳ καὶ σφόδρα τὰ Καίσαρος ᾑρημένοι πρότερον ἐξέπεσον ὑπὸ θάμβους τότε τῶν λογισμῶν, καὶ συμπαρηνέχθησαν οὐδὲν δεόμενοι τῷ ῥεύματι τῆς φορᾶς ἐκείνης.
PLUT. *Caes.* 35: Ὁ δὲ Καῖσαρ τήν τε τοῦ Δομιτίου στρατιὰν παρέλαβε, καὶ τοὺς ἄλλους, ὅσους ἐν ταῖς πόλεσι Πομπηίῳ στρατολογουμένους ἔφθασε καταλαβών. πολὺς δὲ γεγονὼς ἤδη καὶ φοβερός, ἐπ' αὐτὸν ἤλαυνε Πομπήιον. ὁ δ' οὐκ ἐδέξατο τὴν ἔφοδον, ἀλλ' εἰς Βρεντέσιον φυγών, τοὺς μὲν ὑπάτους πρότερον ἔστειλε μετὰ δυνάμεως εἰς Δυρράχιον, αὐτὸς δ' ὀλίγον ὕστερον ἐπελθόντος Καίσαρος ἐξέπλευσεν [...].

494 Mk. 1:5-6: καὶ ἐξεπορεύετο πρὸς αὐτὸν πᾶσα ἡ Ἰουδαία χώρα καὶ οἱ Ἱεροσολυμῖται πάντες, καὶ ἐβαπτίζοντο ὑπ' αὐτοῦ ἐν τῷ Ἰορδάνῃ ποταμῷ ἐξομολογούμενοι τὰς ἁμαρτίας αὐτῶν. καὶ ἦν ὁ Ἰωάννης ἐνδεδυμένος τρίχας καμήλου καὶ ζώνην δερματίνην περὶ τὴν ὀσφὺν αὐτοῦ [...]. The last sentence is a citation from the second Book of Kings (2 Kings 1:8, cf. Zach. 13:4) and it there signifies Elia; it is missing in the Bezae Cantabrigiensis and the Itala.

495 The region of Campania was decisive for the war in that the first colonies were settled there. The first settlers had been veterans of Pompeius, but the basis for the settlements was the *lex Iulia*, Caesar's land laws given during his consulate in the year 59 BC which made them possible. Accordingly Campania did not provide secure support to Pompeius (cf. CAES. *Civ.* 1.14: *Cn. Pompeius pridie eius diei ex urbe profectus iter ad legiones habebat, quas a Caesare acceptas in Apulia hibernorum causa disposuerat. dilectus circa urbem intermittuntur; nihil citra Capuam tutum esse omnibus uidetur. Capuae primumn sese confirmant et colligunt dilectumque colonorum, qui lege Iulia Capuam deducti erant, habere instituunt; gladiatoresque, quos*

ibi Caesar in ludo habebat, ad forum productos Lentulus ‹spe› libertatis confirmat atque iis equos attribuit et se sequi iussit; quos postea monitus ab suis, quod ea res omnium iudicio reprehendebatur, circum familiares conuentus Campaniae custodiae causa distribuit; DIO CASS. *HR* 41.6.4: see text below): He was forced to move on and go to the two legions in Apulia, which he had obtained from Caesar when he declared he had to wage war in Syria, then he had to withdraw via Brundisium to Dyrrhachium. The quotation in Mark taken from the second Book of the Kings (2 Kings 1:8) could in its part 'about his loins', *osphyn*, cover *asphalês*, 'secure', because Pompeius was not safe there—unless *Apulia* lingers on here.

Cf. CAES. *Civ.* 1.14, DIO CASS. *HR* 41.6.4.

496 CAES. *Civ.* 3.96.3: *Pompeius, iam cum intra uallum nostri uersarentur, equum nactus detractis insignibus imperatoriis decumana porta se ex castris eiecit protinusque equo citato Larisam contendit.*

PLUT. *Caes.* 45: ἀπεδύσατο μὲν τὴν ἐναγώνιον καὶ στρατηγικὴν ἐσθῆτα, φεύγοντι δὲ πρέπουσαν μεταλαβὼν ὑπεξῆλθεν.

APP. *BC* 2.81.343: καὶ εἰπὼν τήν τε στολὴν ἐνήλλαξε καὶ ἵππου ἐπιβὰς σὺν φίλοις τέσσαρσιν [...].

497 PLUT. *Caes.* 34: Οἱ μὲν οὖν ὕπατοι μηδ' ἃ νόμος ἐστὶ πρὸ ἐξόδου θύσαντες ἔφυγον, ἔφευγον δὲ καὶ τῶν βουλευτῶν οἱ πλεῖστοι, τρόπον τινὰ δι' ἁρπαγῆς ἀπὸ τῶν ἰδίων ὅ τι τύχοιεν ὥσπερ ἀλλοτρίων λαμβάνοντες. εἰσὶ δ' οἳ καὶ σφόδρα τὰ Καίσαρος ᾑρημένοι πρότερον ἐξέπεσον ὑπὸ θάμβους τότε τῶν λογισμῶν, καὶ συμπαρηνέχθησαν οὐδὲν δεόμενοι τῷ ῥεύματι τῆς φορᾶς ἐκείνης. οἰκτρότατον δὲ τὸ θέαμα τῆς πόλεως ἦν, ἐπιφερομένου τοσούτου χειμῶνος ὥσπερ νεὼς ὑπὸ κυβερνητῶν ἀπαγορευόντων πρὸς τὸ συντυχὸν ἐκπεσεῖν κομιζομένης.

DIO CASS. *HR* 41.7.1-3: κἀκ τούτου καὶ ἐς τὰ ἄλλα ὁμοίως πάντα θορυβώδης σφῶν καὶ ταραχώδης ἡ ἀνάστασις ἐγένετο. οἵ τε γὰρ ἐξιόντες (ἦσαν δὲ πάντες ὡς εἰπεῖν οἱ πρῶτοι καὶ τῆς βουλῆς καὶ τῆς ἱππάδος καὶ προσέτι καὶ τὸ τοῦ ὁμίλου) λόγῳ μὲν ἐπὶ πολέμῳ ἀφωρμῶντο, ἔργῳ δὲ τὰ τῶν ἑαλωκότων ἔπασχον· τήν τε γὰρ πατρίδα καὶ τὰς ἐν αὐτῇ διατριβὰς ἐκλιπεῖν καὶ τὰ ἀλλότρια τείχη οἰκειότερα τῶν σφετέρων νομίζειν ἀναγκαζόμενοι δεινῶς ἐλυποῦντο. οἵ τε γὰρ πανοικησίᾳ ἀνιστάμενοι τὰ ἱερὰ καὶ τοὺς οἴκους τό τε ἔδαφος τὸ πατρῷον ὡς καὶ τῶν ἀντιστασιωτῶν εὐθὺς ἐσόμενα ἀπέλιπον, καὶ αὐτοὶ οὕτω τὴν γνώμην, ἄν γε καὶ περισωθῶσιν, εἶχον ὡς κἂν τῇ Μακεδονίᾳ τῇ τε Θρᾴκῃ κατοικήσοντες [...].

498 One influence could have been carried on from the hastiness in leaving the city, a real 'flight', and could have hidden in the garment of camel's hair: *Triches* are 'hair' but *trechô* means 'run, race, hurry'; *kamêlos* is a 'camel', but also a 'caravan'; and a *kamilos* is a 'hawser': Did Mark here see Pompeius fleeing with all of his baggage or hastily hoisting the anchor and leading away his army, leaving the city behind him like a ship without a captain? The second influence might have been the 'ferrying over', *transfretare* in Latin: Simply perceived as *transferre*, and because *ferre* means 'to carry' and a camel is a 'pack-animal', Mark made 'to transcamel' out of it, a Latin-Aramaism typical for him. Then he applied the 'carrying' on the clothes (*endeduménos* means 'wore' in this sense), reinterpreted *trans* in *trichas*, 'hair', and thus transformed *transferre* into 'clothed with camel's hair'. Thirdly theoretically *trans fretum*, 'across the strait', could have become *trichas kamêlou* via *trans canalem* also. Nevertheless the 'camel' has more probably evolved from a misunderstood *Campania* resp. *Capua*.

499 APP. *BC* 2.36.144: τέρατά τε αὐτοῖς ἐπέπιπτε πολλὰ καὶ σημεῖα οὐράνια· αἷμά τε γὰρ ἔδοξεν ὁ θεὸς ὗσαι καὶ ξόανα ἱδρῶσαι καὶ κεραυνοὶ πεσεῖν ἐπὶ νεὼς πολλοὺς καὶ ἡμίονος τεκεῖν· ἄλλα τε πολλὰ δυσχερῆ προεσήμαινε τὴν ἐς ἀεὶ τῆς πολιτείας ἀναίρεσίν τε καὶ μεταβολήν.—'Many portents and signs in the sky took place. It seemed as if God let it rain blood, the statues of the gods issued sweat, lightning

struck several temples and a mule foaled. There were also many other prodigies that betokened the final abolition of the old order of the state and the revolution.'
500 App. BC 2.68.283: αὐτῷ δὲ τῷ Πομπηίῳ τῆς αὐτῆς νυκτός τινα τῶν ἱερείων ἐκφυγόντα οὐ συνελήφθη, καὶ μελισσῶν ἑσμὸς ἐπὶ τοῖς βωμοῖς ἐκάθισε, ζῴου νωχελοῦς.
501 Mk. 1:6: [...] καὶ ἐσθίων ἀκρίδας καὶ μέλι ἄγριον.
502 Plut. Pomp. 73: τοὺς δὲ θεράποντας ἀπιέναι πρὸς Καίσαρα κελεύσας καὶ μὴ δεδιέναι [...].
[...] ἐπεὶ δὲ καιρὸς ἦν δείπνου καὶ παρεσκεύασεν ὁ ναύκληρος ἐκ τῶν παρόντων, ἰδὼν ὁ Φαώνιος οἰκετῶν ἀπορίᾳ τὸν Πομπήϊον ἀρχόμενον αὑτὸν ὑπολύειν προσέδραμε καὶ ὑπέλυσε καὶ συνήλειψε. καὶ τὸ λοιπὸν ἐκ τούτου περιέπων καὶ θεραπεύων ὅσα δεσπότας δοῦλοι, μέχρι νίψεως ποδῶν καὶ δείπνου παρασκευῆς, διετέλεσεν, ὥστε τὴν ἐλευθεριότητα τῆς ὑπουργίας ἐκείνης θεασάμενον ἄν τινα καὶ τὸ ἀφελὲς καὶ ἄπλαστον εἰπεῖν· Φεῦ τοῖσι γενναίοισιν ὡς ἅπαν καλόν.
About the 'stronger' and about Caesar as *chrêstos* cf. Plut. Pomp. 75: τῶν δὲ Μιτυληναίων τὸν Πομπήϊον ἀσπασαμένων καὶ παρακαλούντων εἰσελθεῖν εἰς τὴν πόλιν, οὐκ ἠθέλησεν, ἀλλὰ κἀκείνους ἐκέλευσε τῷ κρατοῦντι πείθεσθαι καὶ θαρρεῖν· εὐγνώμονα γὰρ εἶναι Καίσαρα καὶ χρηστόν.
503 Mk. 1:7-8: καὶ ἐκήρυσσεν λέγων, Ἔρχεται ὁ ἰσχυρότερός μου ὀπίσω μου, οὗ οὐκ εἰμὶ ἱκανὸς κύψας λῦσαι τὸν ἱμάντα τῶν ὑποδημάτων αὐτοῦ. ἐγὼ ἐβάπτισα ὑμᾶς ὕδατι, αὐτὸς δὲ βαπτίσει ὑμᾶς ἐν πνεύματι ἁγίῳ.
504 Plut. Caes. 33: Φαώνιος δ' αὐτὸν ἐκέλευε τῷ ποδὶ κτυπεῖν τὴν γῆν, ἐπεὶ μεγαληγορῶν ποτε πρὸς τὴν σύγκλητον οὐδὲν εἴα πολυπραγμονεῖν οὐδὲ φροντίζειν ἐκείνους τῆς ἐπὶ τὸν πόλεμον παρασκευῆς· αὐτὸς γὰρ ὅταν ἐπίῃ κρούσας τὸ ἔδαφος τῷ ποδὶ στρατευμάτων ἐμπλήσειν τὴν Ἰταλίαν. οὐ μὴν ἀλλὰ καὶ τότε πλήθει δυνάμεως ὑπερέβαλλεν ὁ Πομπήϊος τὴν Καίσαρος· εἴασε δ' οὐδεὶς τὸν ἄνδρα χρήσασθαι τοῖς ἑαυτοῦ λογισμοῖς, ἀλλ' ὑπ' ἀγγελμάτων πολλῶν καὶ ψευδῶν καὶ φόβων, ὡς ἐφεστῶτος ἤδη τοῦ πολέμου καὶ πάντα κατέχοντος, εἴξας καὶ συνεκκρουσθεὶς τῇ πάντων φορᾷ ψηφίζεται ταραχὴν ὁρᾶν καὶ τὴν πόλιν ἐξέλιπε, κελεύσας ἕπεσθαι τὴν γερουσίαν καὶ μηδένα μένειν τῶν πρὸ τῆς τυραννίδος ᾑρημένων τὴν πατρίδα καὶ τὴν ἐλευθερίαν.
App. BC 2.37.146: Φαώνιος μὲν Πομπήϊον ἐπισκώπτων τοῦ ποτὲ λεχθέντος ὑπ' αὐτοῦ, παρεκάλει τὴν γῆν πατάξαι τῷ ποδὶ καὶ τὰ στρατόπεδα ἐξ αὐτῆς ἀναγαγεῖν· ὁ δὲ "ἕξετε," εἶπεν, "ἂν ἐπακολουθῆτέ μοι καὶ μὴ δεινὸν ἡγῆσθε τὴν Ῥώμην ἀπολιπεῖν, καὶ εἰ τὴν Ἰταλίαν ἐπὶ τῇ Ῥώμῃ δεήσειεν."
Dio Cass. HR 41.6.3-4: πρὸς δ' ἔτι καὶ τὰ χρήματα τὰ δημόσια τά τε ἀναθήματα τὰ ἐν τῇ πόλει πάντα ἀναιρεθῆναι προσέταξεν αὐτοῖς ψηφίσασθαι, ἐλπίζων παμπληθεῖς ἀπ' αὐτῶν στρατιώτας ἀθροίσειν. τοσαύτην γὰρ εὔνοιαν αὐτοῦ πᾶσαι ὡς εἰπεῖν αἱ ἐν τῇ Ἰταλίᾳ πόλεις εἶχον ὥστε, ἐπειδὴ ἤκουσαν αὐτὸν ὀλίγον ἔμπροσθεν ἐπικινδύνως νοσοῦντα, σωτήρια αὐτοῦ δημοσίᾳ θύσειν εὔξασθαι. καὶ ὅτι μὲν μέγα καὶ λαμπρὸν τοῦτ' αὐτῷ ἔδοσαν, οὐδ' ἄν εἷς ἀντιλέξειεν· οὐ γὰρ ἔστιν ὅτῳ ποτὲ ἄλλῳ, ἔξω τῶν μετὰ ταῦτα τὸ πᾶν κράτος λαβόντων, τοιοῦτόν τι ἐψηφίσθη· οὐ μὴν καὶ ἀκριβῆ πίστιν τοῦ μὴ οὐκ ἐγκαταλείψειν αὐτὸν πρὸς τὸν ἐκ τοῦ κρείττονος φόβον εἶχον.
505 Suet. Jul. 30: [...] transiit in citeriorem Galliam, conuentibusque peractis Rauennae substitit, bello uindicaturus si quid de tribunis plebis intercedentibus pro se grauius a senatu constitutum esset.
App. BC 2.32.124: Ὁ δ' ἄρτι τὸν ὠκεανὸν ἐκ Βρεττανῶν διεπεπλεύκει καὶ ἀπὸ Κελτῶν τῶν ἀμφὶ τὸν Ῥῆνον τὰ ὄρη τὰ Ἄλπεια διελθὼν σὺν πεντακισχιλίοις πεζοῖς καὶ ἱππεῦσι τριακοσίοις κατέβαινεν ἐπὶ Ῥαβέννης, ἣ συναφής τε ἦν τῇ Ἰταλίᾳ καὶ τῆς Καίσαρος ἀρχῆς τελευταία.
With respect to the correspondence about a disarmament between Caesar and Pompeius, compare Caes. Civ. 1.8-11 and the parallel tradition in Appianus, Plutarchus and Dio Cassius.

506 Mk. 1:9: Καὶ ἐγένετο ἐν ἐκείναις ταῖς ἡμέραις ἦλθεν Ἰησοῦς ἀπὸ Ναζαρὲτ τῆς Γαλιλαίας καὶ ἐβαπτίσθη εἰς τὸν Ἰορδάνην ὑπὸ Ἰωάννου.
507 PLUT. Caes. 32: λέγεται δὲ τῇ προτέρᾳ νυκτὶ τῆς διαβάσεως ὄναρ ἰδεῖν ἔκθεσμον· ἐδόκει γὰρ αὐτὸς τῇ ἑαυτοῦ μητρὶ μείγνυσθαι τὴν ἄρρητον μεῖξιν.
508 Mk. 1:10-11: καὶ εὐθὺς ἀναβαίνων ἐκ τοῦ ὕδατος εἶδεν σχιζομένους τοὺς οὐρανοὺς καὶ τὸ πνεῦμα ὡς περιστερὰν καταβαῖνον εἰς αὐτόν· καὶ φωνὴ ἐγένετο ἐκ τῶν οὐρανῶν, Σὺ εἶ ὁ υἱός μου ὁ ἀγαπητός, ἐν σοὶ εὐδόκησα.
509 Rufus Festus AVIENUS, Ora Maritima, vv 310-313: *ab arce qua diei occasus est, Veneri marinae consecrata est insula templumque in illa Veneris et penetral cavum oraculumque*.—'On the side of the fortress, where the day dies, there is an island consecrated to the Venus Marina and within is a temple with a deep crypt and an oracle site.' It is said that the crypt can still be seen today, but unfortunately it is situated in a restricted military area.
510 SUET. *Jul.* 7: *[...] Gadisque uenisset, animaduersa apud Herculis templum Magni Alexandri imagine ingemuit et quasi pertaesus ignauiam suam, quod nihil dum a se memorabile actum esset in aetate, qua iam Alexander orbem terrarum subegisset [...]. Etiam cofusum eum somnio proximae noctis (nam uisus erat per quietem stuprum matri intulisse) coiectores ad amplissimam spem incitauerunt, arbitrium terrarum orbis portendi interpretantes, quando mater, quam subiectam sibi uidisset, non alia esset quam terra, quae omnium parens haberetur*.
511 Many authors speak of the 'Republic' as being the time of the reign of the nobility, at first of the Patrician, then of the Senatorial oligarchy. This is wrong from the Roman perspective of the time insofar as *res publica* means only 'state' and does not refer to a special form of constitution. Not by chance did Caesar point this out when he called Sulla an illiterate, who claimed he had restored the *res publica* by laying down the dictatorship. Caesar made clear that the term *res publica* is an abstract and neutral one, referring neither to its form nor its content. SUET. *Jul.* 77: '*nihil esse rem publicam, appellationem modo sine corpore ac specie. Sullam nescisse litteras, qui dictaturam deposuerit.*' Cf. MORGAN (1997).
512 About the doves on Caesar's palm trees cf. note 455.
513 APP. *BC* 2.68.281-69.284: θυόμενός τε νυκτὸς μέσης τὸν Ἄρη κατεκάλει καὶ τὴν ἑαυτοῦ πρόγονον Ἀφροδίτην (ἐκ γὰρ Αἰνείου καὶ Ἴλου τοῦ Αἰνείου τὸ τῶν Ἰουλίων γένος παρενεχθέντος τοῦ ὀνόματος ἡγεῖτο εἶναι), νεών τε αὐτῇ νικηφόρῳ χαριστήριον ἐν Ῥώμῃ ποιήσειν εὔχετο κατορθώσας. [...] μικρόν τε πρὸ ἕω πανικὸν ἐνέπεσεν αὐτοῦ τῷ στρατῷ· καὶ τόδε περιδραμὼν αὐτὸς καὶ καταστήσας ἀνεπαύετο σὺν ὕπνῳ βαθεῖ· περιεγειράντων δ' αὐτὸν τῶν φίλων, ὄναρ ἔφασκεν ἄρτι νεὼν ἐν Ῥώμῃ καθιεροῦν Ἀφροδίτῃ νικηφόρῳ. Καὶ τόδε μὲν ἀγνοίᾳ τῆς Καίσαρος εὐχῆς οἵ τε φίλοι καὶ ὁ στρατὸς ἅπας πυθόμενοι ἥδοντο [...].
DIO CASS. HR 37.52.2: δόξης τε γὰρ ἐπιθυμῶν, καὶ τὸν Πομπήιον τούς τε ἄλλους τοὺς πρὸ αὐτοῦ μέγα ποτὲ δυνηθέντας ζηλῶν, οὐδὲν ὀλίγον ἐφρόνει, ἀλλ' ἤλπιζεν, ἄν τι τότε κατεργάσηται, ὕπατός τε εὐθὺς αἱρεθήσεσθαι καὶ ὑπερφυᾶ ἔργα ἀποδείξεσθαι, διά τε τἆλλα καὶ ὅτι ἐν τοῖς Γαδείροις, ὅτε ἐταμίευε, τῇ μητρὶ συγγίγνεσθαι ὄναρ ἔδοξε, καὶ παρὰ τῶν μάντεων ἔμαθεν ὅτι ἐν μεγάλῃ δυνάμει ἔσται. ὅθενπερ καὶ εἰκόνα Ἀλεξάνδρου ἐνταῦθα ἐν τῷ Ἡρακλέους ἀνακειμένην ἰδὼν ἀνεστέναξε, καὶ κατωδύρατο ὅτι μηδέν πω μέγα ἔργον ἐπεποιήκει.
514 What was said about Caesar's dream and Brutus' oracle explains why in antiquity there was no Oedipus but a King Oedipus.
515 APP. *BC* 2.33.133: Ἀντωνίου δὲ καὶ Κασσίου δημαρχούντοιν μετὰ Κουρίωνα καὶ τὴν Κουρίωνος γνώμην ἐπαινούντοιν, ἡ βουλὴ φιλονικότερον ἔτι τὴν Πομπηίου στρατιὰν φύλακα σφῶν ἡγοῦντο εἶναι, τὴν δὲ Καίσαρος πολεμίαν. καὶ οἱ ὕπατοι, Μάρκελλός τε καὶ Λέντλος, ἐκέλευον τοῖς ἀμφὶ τὸν Ἀντώνιον ἐκστῆναι τοῦ συνεδρίου, μή τι καὶ δημαρχοῦντες ὅμως πάθοιεν ἀτοπώτερον. ἔνθα δὴ μέγα βοήσας ὁ Ἀντώνιος ἀνά τε ἔδραμε τῆς ἕδρας σὺν ὀργῇ καὶ περὶ τῆς ἀρχῆς ἐπεθείαζεν

αὐτοῖς, ὡς ἱερὰ καὶ ἄσυλος οὖσα ὑβρίζοιτο, καὶ περὶ σφῶν, ὅτι γνώμην ἐσφέροντες, ἣν δοκοῦσι συνοίσειν, ἐξαλαύνοιντο σὺν ὕβρει, μήτε τινὰ σφαγὴν μήτε μύσος ἐργασάμενοι. ταῦτα δ' εἰπὼν ἐξέτρεχεν ὥσπερ ἔνθους, πολέμους καὶ σφαγὰς καὶ προγραφὰς καὶ φυγὰς καὶ δημεύσεις καὶ ὅσα ἄλλα αὐτοῖς ἔμελλεν ἔσεσθαι, προθεσπίζων ἀράς τε βαρείας τοῖς τούτων αἰτίοις ἐπαρώμενος. συνεξέθεον δ' αὐτῷ Κουρίων τε καὶ Κάσσιος· καὶ γάρ τις ἤδη στρατὸς ἑωρᾶτο ἐκ Πομπηίου περιιστάμενος τὸ βουλευτήριον. οἵδε μὲν δὴ τάχει πολλῷ πρὸς Καίσαρα, νυκτὸς αὐτίκα, λαθόντες ἐχώρουν ἐπὶ ὀχήματος μισθωτοῦ, θεραπόντων ἐσθῆτας ἐνδύντες. καὶ αὐτοὺς ἔτι ὧδε ἔχοντας ὁ Καῖσαρ ἐπεδείκνυ τῷ στρατῷ καὶ ἠρέθιζε λέγων, ὅτι καὶ σφᾶς τοσάδε ἐργασαμένους ἡγοῦνται πολεμίους καὶ τοιούσδε ἄνδρας ὑπὲρ αὐτῶν τι φθεγξαμένους οὕτως ἐξελαύνουσιν αἰσχρῶς. Ὁ μὲν δὴ πόλεμος ἑκατέρωθεν ἀνέῳκτο καὶ κεκήρυκτο ἤδη σαφῶς [...].

PLUT. Caes. 31: οἱ περὶ Λέντλον οὐκ εἴων ὑπατεύοντες, ἀλλὰ καὶ τῆς βουλῆς Ἀντώνιον καὶ Κουρίωνα προπηλακίσαντες ἐξήλασαν ἀτίμως, τὴν εὐπρεπεστάτην Καίσαρι τῶν προφάσεων αὐτοὶ μηχανησάμενοι καὶ δι' ἧς μάλιστα τοὺς στρατιώτας παρώξυνεν, ἐπιδεικνύμενος ἄνδρας ἐλλογίμους καὶ ἄρχοντας ἐπὶ μισθίων ζευγῶν πεφευγότας ἐν ἐσθῆσιν οἰκετικαῖς· οὕτω γὰρ ἀπὸ Ῥώμης σκευάσαντες ἑαυτοὺς διὰ φόβον ὑπεξῇεσαν.

CAES. Civ. 1.5.3-5: decurritur ad illum extremum atque ultimum senatus consultum [...] itaque [...] et de imperio Caesaris et de amplissimis uiris, tribunis plebis, grauissime acerbissimeque decernitur. profugiunt statim ex urbe tribunis plebis seseque ad Caesarem conferunt. is eo tempore erat Ravennae expectabatque suis lenissimis postulatis responsa [...]. CAES. Civ. 1.7.1-8.1: Quibus rebus cognitis Caesar apud milites contionatur [...]. conclamant legionis XIII, quae aderat, milites [...] sese paratos esse imperatoris sui tribunorumque plebis iniurias defendere. Cognita militum uoluntate Ariminum cum ea legione proficiscitur ibique tribunos plebis, qui ad eum confugerant, conuenit.

SUET. Jul. 33: Atque ita traiecto exercitu, adhibitis tribunis plebis, qui pulsi superuenerant, procontione fidem militum flens ac ueste a pectore discissa inuocauit.

516 Mk.1:12-13: Καὶ εὐθὺς τὸ πνεῦμα αὐτὸν ἐκβάλλει εἰς τὴν ἔρημον. καὶ ἦν ἐν τῇ ἐρήμῳ τεσσεράκοντα ἡμέρας [καὶ τεσσεράκοντα νύκτας] πειραζόμενος ὑπὸ τοῦ Σατανᾶ, καὶ ἦν μετὰ τῶν θηρίων, καὶ οἱ ἄγγελοι διηκόνουν αὐτῷ.

517 PLUT. Caes. 32: αὐτὸς δὲ τῶν μισθίων ζευγῶν ἐπιβὰς ἑνός, ἤλαυνεν ἑτέραν τινὰ πρῶτον ὁδόν· εἶτα πρὸς τὸ Ἀρίμινον ἐπιστρέψας, APP. BC 2.35.138: καὶ ζεύγους ἐπιβὰς ἤλαυνεν ἐς τὸ Ἀρίμινον, ἑπομένων οἱ τῶν ἱππέων ἐκ διαστήματος. SUET. Jul. 31: [...] Dein post solis occasum mulis e proximo pistrino ad uehiculum iunctis occultissimum iter modico comitatu ingressus est.

It can be reconstructed from the different sources that Caesar had displayed the tribunes of the people, those who hurried to him, to the soldiers in the same miserable condition in which they arrived at Ravenna: they were dressed like slaves and had used a rented cart. But possibly this happened in Ariminum (today Rimini). According to Caesar's account he seems to have delivered his speech to the soldiers in Ravenna on the tidings of the events in Rome (Civ. 1.7.1: quibus rebus cognitis Caesar apud milites contionatur), whereas he did not announce the arrival of the people's tribunes until in Ariminum (Civ. 1.8.1: Cognita militum uoluntate Ariminum cum ea legione proficiscitur ibique tribunos plebis, qui ad eum confugerant, conuenit). According to that he was brought tidings of the flight of the tribunes of the people before their arrival. He still had time to give the speech to the soldiers and march to Ariminum before they arrived there, where he showed them to the soldiers. This is not questioned by the accounts of Appianus and Plutarchus. It is different in Dio Cassius who has the speech take place only in Ariminum where Caesar prompted Curio and the others who had arrived together with him to report to the troop on the incidents while he further spurred on the people by adding words as they were required by the momentary situation (Dio Cass. *HR* 41.4.1: see text below).

It is conspicuous that in order to drive to Ariminum Caesar in turn, took a carriage and a harnessed team of mules from a mill. Allegedly he took a separate cart and went secretly for reasons of safety (cf. Plut. ibid.). However it looks as though Caesar had taken the mules in order to bring himself more in line with the tribunes— which might correspond to his style (cf. the anecdote about Oppius). Hence it would be possible to conclude that the draught animals of the carts of the people's tribunes were mules too. Which in turn would have suited the circumstances.

518 Caes. *Civ.* 1.7.1-8: *Quibus rebus cognitis Caesar apud milites contionatur. omnium temporum iniurias inimicorum in se commemorat; a quibus deductum ac deprauatum Pompeium queritur inuidia atque obtrectatione laudis suae, cuius ipse honori et dignitati semper fauerit adiutorque fuerit. nouum in re publica introductum exemplum queritur, ut tribunicia intercessio armis notaretur atque opprimeretur, quae superioribus annis <sine> armis esset restituta. [...] hortatur, cuius imperatoris ductu VIIII annis rem publicam felicissime gesserint plurimaque proelia secunda fecerint, omnem Galliam Germaniamque pacauerint, ut eius existimationem dignitatemque ab inimicis defandant. conclamant legionis* XIII, *quae aderat, milites [...] sese paratos esse imperatoris sui tribunorumque plebis iniurias defendere.*

519 Mk. 1:14-15: Μετὰ δὲ τὸ παραδοθῆναι τὸν Ἰωάννην ἦλθεν ὁ Ἰησοῦς εἰς τὴν Γαλιλαίαν κηρύσσων τὸ εὐαγγέλιον τοῦ θεοῦ καὶ λέγων ὅτι Πεπλήρωται ὁ καιρὸς καὶ ἤγγικεν ἡ βασιλεία τοῦ θεοῦ· μετανοεῖτε καὶ πιστεύετε ἐν τῷ εὐαγγελίῳ.

520 Caes. *Civ.* 1.9.2: *Sibi semper primam fuisse dignitatem uitaque potiorem. doluisse se, quod populi Romani beneficium sibi per contumeliam ab inimicis extorqueretur ereptoque semestri imperio in urbem retraheretur, cuius absenti rationem haberi proximis comitiis populus iussisset.*

521 Asinius Pollio was at the Rubicon, therefore he was an eye-witness. It is known that he had criticized Caesar's *commentarii*: They were imprecise and not very truthful, because Caesar in many cases may have believed what other individuals reported without scrutiny. And he might have sometimes reported his own acts erroneously, either deliberately or from forgetfulness. This is what led him to believe that Caesar planned to rewrite and correct it (Suet. *Jul.* 56). Here however Caesar reports of his own acts and the speech to the soldiers before the irreversible step which must have been so decisive that he could hardly have forgotten it. He could scarcely have changed it deliberately, because too many had heard it, not only the soldiers but also the people's tribunes and his officers. At the most he could have summarized the speech here (for example: *omnium temporum iniurias inimicorum in se commemorat*), and outlined it elaborately there (for example 1.7.2-6, the whole passage about the veto right of the tribunes from Sulla to Pompeius with an excursus about Saturninus and the Gracchi). Insofar it is justified to assume that the eye-witness Asinius Pollio has not reported a fundamentally different version of this speech of Caesar's. Since Mark is based on Asinius Pollio, as we have seen, in this case the direct comparison between Mark and Caesar is legitimate, even if other sources remain silent here or only report the theatrical part of the speech, namely the display of the people's tribunes who had fled in slave clothing.

522 Caes. *Civ.* 1.8.1: *Cognita militum uoluntate Ariminum cum ea legione proficiscitur [...].*

523 Caes. *Civ.*1.8.1: *[Cognita militum uoluntate Ariminum cum ea legione proficiscitur] ibique tribunos plebis, qui ad eum confugerant, conuenit.*
App. *BC* 2.35.138-141: καὶ ζεύγους ἐπιβὰς ἤλαυνεν ἐς τὸ Ἀρίμινον, ἑπομένων οἱ τῶν ἱππέων ἐκ διαστήματος. δρόμῳ δ' ἐλθὼν ἐπὶ τὸν Ῥουβίκωνα ποταμόν, ὃς ὁρίζει τὴν Ἰταλίαν, ἔστη τοῦ δρόμου καὶ ἐς τὸ ῥεῦμα ἀφορῶν περιεφέρετο τῇ γνώμῃ, λογιζόμενος ἕκαστα τῶν ἐσομένων κακῶν, εἰ τόνδε τὸν ποταμὸν σὺν ὅπλοις περά-

σειε. καὶ πρὸς τοὺς παρόντας εἶπεν ἀνενεγκών· "ἡ μὲν ἐπίσχεσις, ὦ φίλοι, τῆσδε τῆς διαβάσεως ἐμοὶ κακῶν ἄρξει, ἡ δὲ διάβασις πᾶσιν ἀνθρώποις." καὶ εἰπὼν οἷά τις ἔνθους ἐπέρα σὺν ὁρμῇ, τὸ κοινὸν τόδε ἐπειπών· "ὁ κύβος ἀνερρίφθω." δρόμῳ δ' ἐντεῦθεν ἐπιὼν Ἀρίμινόν τε αἱρεῖ περὶ ἕω καὶ ἐς τὸ πρόσθεν ἐχώρει [...].
PLUT. Caes. 32: αὐτὸς δὲ τῶν μισθίων ζευγῶν ἐπιβὰς ἑνός, ἤλαυνεν ἑτέραν τινὰ πρῶτον ὁδόν· εἶτα πρὸς τὸ Ἀρίμινον ἐπιστρέψας, ὡς ἦλθεν ἐπὶ τὸν διορίζοντα τὴν ἐντὸς Ἄλπεων Γαλατίαν ἀπὸ τῆς ἄλλης Ἰταλίας ποταμὸν (Ῥουβίκων καλεῖται), καὶ λογισμὸς αὐτὸν εἰσῄει, μᾶλλον ἐγγίζοντα τῷ δεινῷ καὶ περιφερόμενον τῷ μεγέθει τῶν τολμωμένων, ἔσχετο δρόμου, καὶ τὴν πορείαν ἐπιστήσας, πολλὰ μὲν αὐτὸς ἐν ἑαυτῷ διήνεγκε σιγῇ τὴν γνώμην ἐπ' ἀμφότερα μεταλαμβάνων, καὶ τροπὰς ἔσχεν αὐτῷ τότε ‹τὸ› βούλευμα πλείστας· πολλὰ δὲ καὶ τῶν φίλων τοῖς παροῦσιν, ὧν ἦν καὶ Πολλίων Ἀσίνιος, συνδιηπόρησεν, ἀναλογιζόμενος ἡλίκων κακῶν ἄρξει πᾶσιν ἀνθρώποις ἡ διάβασις, ὅσον τε λόγον αὐτῆς τοῖς αὖθις ἀπολείψουσι. τέλος δὲ μετὰ θυμοῦ τινος ὥσπερ ἀφεὶς ἑαυτὸν ἐκ τοῦ λογισμοῦ πρὸς τὸ μέλλον, καὶ τοῦτο δὴ τὸ κοινὸν τοῖς εἰς τύχας ἐμβαίνουσιν ἀπόρους καὶ τόλμας προοίμιον ὑπειπὼν "ἀνερρίφθω κύβος," ὥρμησε πρὸς τὴν διάβασιν, καὶ δρόμῳ τὸ λοιπὸν ἤδη χρώμενος, εἰσέπεσε πρὸ ἡμέρας εἰς τὸ Ἀρίμινον, καὶ κατέσχε.
DIO CASS. HR 41.4.1: πυθόμενος οὖν ταῦτα ἐκεῖνος ἔς τε Ἀρίμινον ἦλθεν, ἔξω τῆς ἑαυτοῦ ἀρχῆς τότε πρῶτον προχωρήσας, καὶ συναγαγὼν τοὺς στρατιώτας ἐκέλευσε τόν τε Κουρίωνα καὶ τοὺς ἄλλους τοὺς μετ' αὐτοῦ ἐλθόντας σφίσι τὰ πραχθέντα διηγήσασθαι. γενομένου δὲ τούτου προσπαρώξυνεν αὐτούς, ἐπειπὼν ὅσα ὁ καιρὸς ἀπῄτει.

524 Mk. 1:16: Καὶ παράγων παρὰ τὴν θάλασσαν τῆς Γαλιλαίας εἶδεν Σίμωνα καὶ Ἀνδρέαν τὸν ἀδελφὸν Σίμωνος ἀμφιβάλλοντας ἐν τῇ θαλάσσῃ· ἦσαν γὰρ ἁλεῖς.
525 APP. BC 2.41.165-42.7: Λέπιδον δὲ Αἰμίλιον ἐφίστη τῇ πόλει καὶ τὸν δήμαρχον Μάρκον Ἀντώνιον τῇ Ἰταλίᾳ καὶ τῷ περὶ αὐτὴν στρατῷ. ἔς τε τὰ ἔξω Κουρίωνα μὲν ἀντὶ Κάτωνος ᾑρεῖτο ἡγεῖσθαι Σικελίας, Κόιντον δὲ Σαρδοῦς, καὶ ἐς τὴν Ἰλλυρίδα Γάιον Ἀντώνιον ἔπεμπε καὶ τὴν ἐντὸς Ἄλπεων Γαλατίαν ἐπέτρεπε Λικινίῳ Κράσσῳ. ἐκέλευσε δὲ καὶ νεῶν στόλους δύο γίγνεσθαι κατὰ σπουδήν, ἀμφί τε τὸν Ἰόνιον καὶ περὶ τὴν Τυρρηνίαν· καὶ ναυάρχους αὐτοῖς ἔτι γιγνομένοις ἐπέστησεν Ὁρτήσιόν τε καὶ Δολοβέλλαν. Οὕτω κρατυνάμενος ὁ Καῖσαρ ἄβατον Πομπηίῳ γενέσθαι τὴν Ἰταλίαν ἐς Ἰβηρίαν ᾔει, ἔνθα Πετρηίῳ καὶ Ἀφρανίῳ τοῖς Πομπηίου στρατηγοῖς συμβαλὼν ἧττον αὐτῶν ἐφέρετο τά γε πρῶτα, μετὰ δὲ ἀγχωμάλως ἀλλήλοις ἐπολέμουν ἀμφὶ πόλιν Ἰλέρτην.
APP. BC 2.46.190-47.192: οὕτω μὲν δὴ τὰ σὺν Κουρίωνι ἐς Λιβύην ἐπιπλεύσαντα Ῥωμαίων δύο τέλη διώλετο ἅπαντα καὶ ὅσοι μετ' αὐτῶν ἦσαν ἱππέες τε καὶ ψιλοὶ καὶ ὑπηρέται τοῦ στρατοῦ· Ἰόβας δ' ἐς τὰ οἰκεῖα ἀνέστρεφε, μέγιστον ἔργον τόδε Πομπηίῳ καταλογιζόμενος. Καὶ τῶν αὐτῶν ἡμερῶν Ἀντώνιός τε περὶ τὴν Ἰλλυρίδα ἡττᾶτο ὑπὸ Ὀκταουίου κατὰ Δολοβέλλα Πομπηίῳ στρατηγοῦντος, καὶ στρατιὰ Καίσαρος ἄλλη περὶ Πλακεντίαν στασιάσασα τῶν ἀρχόντων κατεβόησεν, ὥς ἔν τε τῇ στρατείᾳ βραδύνοντες καὶ τὰς πέντε μνᾶς οὐ λαβόντες, ἥν τινα δωρεὰν αὐτοῖς ὁ Καῖσαρ ἔτι περὶ Βρεντέσιον ὑπέσχητο. ὧν ὁ Καῖσαρ πυθόμενος ἐκ Μασσαλίας ἐς Πλακεντίαν ἠπείγετο συντόμως καὶ ἐς ἔτι στασιάζοντας ἐπελθὼν ἔλεγεν ὧδε [...].
APP. BC 2.47.195-48.197: [...] χρήσομαι τῷ πατρίῳ νόμῳ καὶ τοῦ ἑνάτου τέλους, ἐπειδὴ μάλιστα τῆς στάσεως κατῆρξε, τὸ δέκατον διακληρώσω θανεῖν." θρήνου δὲ ἀθρόως ἐξ ἅπαντος τοῦ τέλους γενομένου, οἱ μὲν ἄρχοντες αὐτοῦ προσπεσόντες ἱκέτευον, ὁ δὲ Καῖσαρ μόλις τε καὶ κατ' ὀλίγον ἐνδιδοὺς ἐς τοσοῦτον ὅμως ὑφῆκεν, ὡς ἑκατὸν καὶ εἴκοσι μόνους, οἳ κατάρξαι μάλιστα ἐδόκουν, διακληρῶσαι καὶ δυώδεκα αὐτῶν τοὺς λαχόντας ἀνελεῖν. τῶν δὲ δυώδεκα τῶνδε ἐφάνη τις οὐδ' ἐπιδημῶν, ὅτε ἡ στάσις ἐγίγνετο· καὶ ὁ Καῖσαρ τὸν ἐμφήναντα λοχαγὸν ἔκτεινεν ἀντ' αὐτοῦ. Ἡ μὲν δὴ περὶ Πλακεντίαν στάσις οὕτως ἐλέλυτο, ὁ δὲ Καῖσαρ ἐς Ῥώμην παρῆλθε, καὶ αὐτὸν ὁ δῆμος πεφρικὼς ᾑρεῖτο δικτάτορα, οὔτε τι τῆς βουλῆς ψηφιζομένης οὔτε προχειροτονοῦντος ἄρχοντος. ὁ δέ, εἴτε παραιτησάμενος τὴν

ἀρχὴν ὥς ἐπίφθονον εἴτε οὐ χρῄζων, ἄρξας ἐπὶ ἕνδεκα μόνας ἡμέρας (ὧδε γάρ τισι δοκεῖ) ὑπάτους ἐς τὸ μέλλον ἀπέφηνεν ἑαυτόν τε καὶ Πούπλιον Ἰσαυρικόν. ἡγεμόνας τε ἐς τὰ ἔθνη περιέπεμπεν ἢ ἐνήλλαττεν, ἐφ' ἑαυτοῦ καταλέγων, ἐς μὲν Ἰβηρίαν Μᾶρκον Λέπιδον, ἐς δὲ Σικελίαν Αὖλον Ἀλβῖνον, ἐς δὲ Σαρδὼ Σέξστον Πεδουκαῖον, ἐς δὲ τὴν νεόληπτον Γαλατίαν Δέκμον Βροῦτον.

526 Mk. 3:13-19: Καὶ ἀναβαίνει εἰς τὸ ὄρος καὶ προσκαλεῖται οὓς ἤθελεν αὐτός, καὶ ἀπῆλθον πρὸς αὐτόν. καὶ ἐποίησεν δώδεκα [οὓς καὶ ἀποστόλους ὠνόμασεν] ἵνα ὦσιν μετ' αὐτοῦ καὶ ἵνα ἀποστέλλῃ αὐτοὺς κηρύσσειν καὶ ἔχειν ἐξουσίαν ἐκβάλλειν τὰ δαιμόνια· [καὶ ἐποίησεν τοὺς δώδεκα,] καὶ ἐπέθηκεν ὄνομα τῷ Σίμωνι Πέτρον, καὶ Ἰάκωβον τὸν τοῦ Ζεβεδαίου καὶ Ἰωάννην τὸν ἀδελφὸν τοῦ Ἰακώβου καὶ ἐπέθηκεν αὐτοῖς ὀνόμα[τα] Βοανηργές ὅ ἐστιν Υἱοὶ Βροντῆς· καὶ Ἀνδρέαν καὶ Φίλιππον καὶ Βαρθολομαῖον καὶ Μαθθαῖον καὶ Θωμᾶν καὶ Ἰάκωβον τὸν τοῦ Ἁλφαίου καὶ Θαδδαῖον καὶ Σίμωνα τὸν Καναναῖον καὶ Ἰούδαν Ἰσκαριώθ, ὃς καὶ παρέδωκεν αὐτόν.

527 Mk. 3:16: καὶ ἐπέθηκεν ὄνομα τῷ Σίμωνι Πέτρον. Mark could have read Appianus' *ephistê*, 'he placed him over someone' (he made him director), as *epethêken*, 'he placed before him', 'he imposed on him' (he gave him the name).

528 *Vulgata* (ALAND & NESTLE, [18]1957): *Et imposuit Simoni nomen Petrus: et Jacobum Zebedaei, et Ioannem fratri Iacobi, et imposuit eis nomina Boanerges, quod est Filii Tonitrui.*

529 Decimus Iunius Brutus had been adopted by a Postumius Albinus. An *Albinus Bruti f.* appears with C. Pansa on denarii of the year 43 BC (MOMMSEN RMW 652).

530 Metathesis: *Lepidus > Piledus > Philippus*. Also *Aemilius* could have helped here: AEMILIVM > ΦΙΛΙΠΠΟΝ.

531 CAES. *Civ.* 1.6.3-5: *Faustus Sulla pro praetore in Mauretaniam mittatur [...] de Fausto impedit Philippus tribunus plebis. [...] Philippus et Cotta priuato consilio praetereuntur, neque eorum sortes deiciuntur.*

532 DIO CASS. HR 41.18.1: τόν τε Ἀριστόβουλον οἴκαδε ἐς τὴν Παλαιστίνην, ὅπως τῷ Πομπηΐῳ τι ἀντιπράξῃ, ἔστειλε [...].

533 DIO CASS. HR 41.15.4-16.1: τὰ δ' αὐτὰ ταῦτα καὶ πρὸς τὸν δῆμον, καὶ αὐτὸν ἔξω τοῦ πωμηρίου συνελθόντα, εἰπὼν σῖτόν τε ἐκ τῶν νήσων μετεπέμψατο [...].

534 Mk. 3:20-21: Καὶ ἔρχεται εἰς οἶκον· καὶ συνέρχεται πάλιν [ὁ] ὄχλος, ὥστε μὴ δύνασθαι αὐτοὺς μηδὲ ἄρτον φαγεῖν. καὶ ἀκούσαντες οἱ παρ' αὐτοῦ ἐξῆλθον κρατῆσαι αὐτόν· ἔλεγον γὰρ ὅτι ἐξέστη.

535 DIO CASS. HR 41.15.2-4: πρός τε τὴν Ῥώμην ἦλθε, καὶ τῆς γερουσίας οἱ ἔξω τοῦ πωμηρίου ὑπό τε τοῦ Ἀντωνίου καὶ ὑπὸ τοῦ Λογγίνου παρασκευασθείσης [...] καὶ διὰ τοῦτ' οὔτ' ᾐτιάσατό τινα οὔτ' ἠπείλησέ τινι οὐδέν, ἀλλὰ καὶ καταδρομὴν κατὰ τῶν πολεμεῖν πολίταις ἐθελόντων οὐκ ἄνευ ἀρῶν ἐποιήσατο, καὶ τὸ τελευταῖον πρέσβεις ὑπέρ τε τῆς εἰρήνης καὶ ὑπὲρ τῆς ὁμονοίας σφῶν παραχρῆμα πρός τε τοὺς ὑπάτους καὶ πρὸς τὸν Πομπήϊον πεμφθῆναι ἐσηγήσατο.

CAES. *Civ.* 1.32.2-9: *ipse ad urbem proficiscitur. coacto senatu iniurias inimicorum commemorat [...] legatos ad Pompeium de compositione mitti oportere, neque se reformidare, quod in senatu Pompeius paulo ante dixisset, ad quos legati mitterentur, his auctoritatem attribui timoremque eorum qui mitterent significari. tenuis atque infirmi haec animi uideri. se uero, ut operibus anteire studuerit, sic iustitia et aequitate uelle superare.*

536 Mk. 3:22-28: καὶ οἱ γραμματεῖς οἱ ἀπὸ Ἱεροσολύμων καταβάντες ἔλεγον ὅτι Βεελζεβοὺλ ἔχει καὶ ὅτι ἐν τῷ ἄρχοντι τῶν δαιμονίων ἐκβάλλει τὰ δαιμόνια. καὶ προσκαλεσάμενος αὐτοὺς ἐν παραβολαῖς ἔλεγεν αὐτοῖς, Πῶς δύναται Σατανᾶς Σατανᾶν ἐκβάλλειν; καὶ ἐὰν βασιλεία ἐφ' ἑαυτὴν μερισθῇ, οὐ δύναται σταθῆναι ἡ βασιλεία ἐκείνη· καὶ ἐὰν οἰκία ἐφ' ἑαυτὴν μερισθῇ, οὐ δυνήσεται ἡ οἰκία ἐκείνη σταθῆναι. καὶ εἰ ὁ Σατανᾶς ἀνέστη ἐφ' ἑαυτὸν καὶ ἐμερίσθη, οὐ δύναται στῆναι ἀλλὰ τέλος ἔχει. ἀλλ' οὐ δύναται οὐδεὶς εἰς τὴν οἰκίαν τοῦ ἰσχυροῦ εἰσελθὼν τὰ σκεύη αὐτοῦ διαρπάσαι, ἐὰν μὴ πρῶτον τὸν ἰσχυρὸν δήσῃ, καὶ τότε τὴν οἰκίαν αὐτοῦ διαρπάσει.

Ἀμὴν λέγω ὑμῖν ὅτι πάντα ἀφεθήσεται τοῖς υἱοῖς τῶν ἀνθρώπων τὰ ἁμαρτήματα καὶ αἱ βλασφημίαι ὅσα ἐὰν βλασφημήσωσιν [...].

537 PLUT. Caes. 37: Ἐπανελθόντα δ' εἰς Ῥώμην Καίσαρα Πείσων μὲν ὁ πενθερὸς παρεκάλει πρὸς Πομπήϊον ἀποστέλλειν ἄνδρας ὑπὲρ διαλύσεως, Ἰσαυρικὸς δὲ Καίσαρι χαριζόμενος ἀντεῖπεν. DIO CASS. HR 41.16.4: καὶ μάλισθ' ὅτι οἱ πρέσβεις οἱ τὰς καταλλαγὰς δῆθεν πρυτανεύσοντες ᾑρέθησαν μέν, οὐκ ἐξῆλθον δέ, ἀλλ' ὅτι καὶ ἐμνήσθη ποτὲ περὶ αὐτῶν ὁ Πίσων ὁ πενθερὸς αὐτοῦ αἰτίαν ἔσχε.

538 CAES. Civ. 1.33.2-3: Probat rem senatus de mittendis legatis; sed qui mitterentur non reperiebantur, maximeque timoris causa pro se quisque id munus legationis recusabat. Pompeius enim discedens ab urbe in senatu dixerat eodem se habiturum loco, qui Romae remansissent, et qui in castris Caesaris fuissent. sic triduum disputationibus excusationibusque extrahitur. subicitur etiam L. Metellus tribunus plebis ab inimicis Caesaris, qui hanc rem distrahat, reliquasque res, quascumque agere instituerit, impediat. cuius cognito consilio Caesar frustra diebus aliquot consumptis, ne reliquum tempus amittat, infecti iis, quae agere destinauerat, ab urbe proficiscitur atque in ulteriorem Galliam peruenit.

539 SUET. Jul. 34: ire se ad exercitum sine duce et inde reuersurum ad ducem sine exercitu.

540 CAES. Civ. 2.21.5: eadem ratione priuate ac publice quibusdam ciuitatibus habitis honoribus Tarracone dicedit pedibusque Narbonem atque inde Massiliam peruenit. ibi legem de dictatore latam seseque dictatorem dictum a M. Lepido praetore cognoscit.

DIO CASS. HR 41.36.1: ἐν ὁδῷ δὲ ἔτ' ὄντος αὐτοῦ Μᾶρκος Αἰμίλιος Λέπιδος, οὗτος ὁ καὶ ἐν τῇ τριαρχίᾳ ὕστερον γενόμενος, τῷ τε δήμῳ συνεβούλευσε στρατηγῶν δικτάτορα τὸν Καίσαρα προχειρίσασθαι καὶ εὐθὺς εἶπεν αὐτὸν παρὰ τὰ πάτρια.

541 PLUT. Caes. 37: ἀλλ' ἐν ἡμέραις ἕνδεκα τὴν μὲν μοναρχίαν ἀπειπάμενος, ὕπατον δ' ἀναδείξας ἑαυτὸν καὶ Σερουΐλιον Ἰσαυρικόν [...]; DIO CASS. HR 41.36.4: ποιήσας δὲ ταῦτα καὶ τὸ ὄνομα τῆς δικτατορίας ἀπεῖπε [...].

542 Mk.8:27-30: Καὶ ἐξῆλθεν ὁ Ἰησοῦς καὶ οἱ μαθηταὶ αὐτοῦ εἰς τὰς κώμας Καισαρείας τῆς Φιλίππου· καὶ ἐν τῇ ὁδῷ ἐπηρώτα τοὺς μαθητὰς αὐτοῦ λέγων αὐτοῖς, Τίνα με λέγουσιν οἱ ἄνθρωποι εἶναι; οἱ δὲ εἶπαν αὐτῷ λέγοντες [ὅτι] Ἰωάννην τὸν βαπτιστήν, καὶ ἄλλοι, Ἠλίαν, ἄλλοι δὲ ὅτι εἷς τῶν προφητῶν. καὶ αὐτὸς ἐπηρώτα αὐτούς, Ὑμεῖς δὲ τίνα με λέγετε εἶναι; ἀποκριθεὶς ὁ Πέτρος λέγει αὐτῷ, Σὺ εἶ ὁ Χριστός. καὶ ἐπετίμησεν αὐτοῖς ἵνα μηδενὶ λέγωσιν περὶ αὐτοῦ.

543 See above, and also SUET. Jul. 69: et nonam quidem legionem apud Placentiam, quanquam in armis adhuc Pompeius esset, totam cum ignominia missam fecit aegreque post multas et supplicis preces, nec nisi exacta de sontibus poena, restituit [...].

544 Mk.6:6: Καὶ περιῆγεν τὰς κώμας κύκλῳ διδάσκων.

545 CAES. Civ. 3.6: Caesar ut Brundisium uenit, contionatus apud milites, quoniam prope ad finem laborum ac periculorum esset peruentum, aequo animo mancipia atque inpedimenta in Italia relinquerent, ipsi expediti naues conscenderent, quo maior numerus militum posset inponi, omniaque ex uictoria et ex sua liberalitate sperarent, conclamantibus omnibus, imperaret, quod uellet, quodcumque imperauisset, se aequo animo esset facturos, II. Nonas Ianuarias naues soluit. impositae, ut supra demonstratum est, legiones VII. postridie terram attigit.

APP. BC 2.53.217-20: "Οὔτε τῆς ὥρας τὸ χειμέριον, ὦ ἄνδρες, οἱ περὶ τῶν μεγίστων ἐμοὶ συναίρεσθε, οὔθ' ἡ τῶν ἄλλων βραδυτὴς ἢ ἔνδεια τῆς πρεπούσης παρασκευῆς ἐφέξει με τῆς ὁρμῆς· ἀντὶ γὰρ πάντων ἡγοῦμαί μοι συνοίσειν τὴν ταχυεργίαν. καὶ πρώτους ὑμᾶς, οἳ πρῶτοι συνεδράμομεν ἀλλήλοις, ἀξιῶ θεράποντας μὲν ἐνταῦθα καὶ ὑποζύγια καὶ παρασκευὴν καὶ πάνθ' ὑπολιπέσθαι, ἵνα ἡμᾶς αἱ παροῦσαι νῆες ὑποδέξωνται, μόνους δ' εὐθὺς ἐμβάντας περᾶν, ἵνα τοὺς ἐχθροὺς διαλάθοιμεν, τῷ μὲν χειμῶνι τύχην ἀγαθὴν ἀντιθέντες, τῇ δ' ὀλιγότητι τόλμαν, τῇ δ' ἀπορίᾳ τὴν τῶν ἐχθρῶν εὐπορίαν, ἧς ἔστιν ἡμῖν εὐθὺς ἐπιβαίνουσιν ἐπὶ τὴν γῆν κρατεῖν, ἢν εἰδῶμεν, ὅτι μὴ κρατήσασιν οὐδέν ἐστιν ἴδιον. ἴωμεν οὖν ἐπὶ θεράποντάς τε καὶ σκεύη καὶ ἀγορὰν τὴν ἐκείνων, ἕως χειμάζουσιν ἐν ὑποστέγοις. ἴωμεν, ἕως Πομπήιος ἡγεῖται κἀμὲ χειμάζειν ἢ περὶ πομπὰς καὶ θυσίας ὑπατικὰς εἶναι. εἰδόσι δ' ὑμῖν ἐκφέρω δυνατώτατον ἐν πολέμοις ἔργον εἶναι τὸ ἀδόκητον· φιλότιμον δὲ καὶ πρώτιστον δόξαν ἀπενέγκασθαι τῶν ἐσομένων καὶ τοῖς αὐτίκα διωξομένοις ἡμᾶς ἀσφαλῆ τὰ ἐκεῖ προετοιμάσαι. ἐγὼ μὲν δὴ καὶ τόνδε τὸν καιρὸν πλεῖν ἂν ἢ λέγειν μᾶλλον ἐβουλόμην, ἵνα με Πομπήιος ἴδῃ, νομίζων ἔτι τὴν ἀρχὴν ἐν Ῥώμῃ διατίθεσθαι· τὸ δὲ ὑμέτερον εὐπειθὲς εἰδὼς ὅμως ἀναμένω τὴν ἀπόκρισιν."

546 Mk. 6:7-13: καὶ προσκαλεῖται τοὺς δώδεκα καὶ ἤρξατο αὐτοὺς ἀποστέλλειν δύο δύο καὶ ἐδίδου αὐτοῖς ἐξουσίαν τῶν πνευμάτων τῶν ἀκαθάρτων, καὶ παρήγγειλεν αὐτοῖς ἵνα μηδὲν αἴρωσιν εἰς ὁδὸν εἰ μὴ ῥάβδον μόνον, μὴ ἄρτον, μὴ πήραν, μὴ εἰς τὴν ζώνην χαλκόν, ἀλλὰ ὑποδεδεμένους σανδάλια, καὶ μὴ ἐνδύσησθε δύο χιτῶνας. καὶ ἔλεγεν αὐτοῖς, Ὅπου ἐὰν εἰσέλθητε εἰς οἰκίαν, ἐκεῖ μένετε ἕως ἂν ἐξέλθητε ἐκεῖθεν. καὶ ὃς ἂν τόπος μὴ δέξηται ὑμᾶς μηδὲ ἀκούσωσιν ὑμῶν, ἐκπορευόμενοι ἐκεῖθεν ἐκτινάξατε τὸν χοῦν τὸν ὑποκάτω τῶν ποδῶν ὑμῶν εἰς μαρτύριον αὐτοῖς. Καὶ ἐξελθόντες ἐκήρυξαν ἵνα μετανοῶσιν, καὶ δαιμόνια πολλὰ ἐξέβαλλον, καὶ ἤλειφον ἐλαίῳ πολλοὺς ἀρρώστους καὶ ἐθεράπευον.

547 App. BC 2.64.267-8: Καὶ τάδε εἰπὼν ἐς Ἀπολλωνίαν εὐθὺς μετῄει καὶ ἀπ' αὐτῆς ἐς Θεσσαλίαν νυκτὸς ὑπεχώρει λανθάνων· Γόμφους τε πόλιν μικρὰν οὐ δεχομένην αὐτὸν ἐξεῖλεν ὑπὸ ὀργῆς καὶ ἐπέτρεψε τῷ στρατῷ διαρπάσαι. οἱ δ' ὡς ἐκ λιμοῦ πάντων ἐνεπίμπλαντο ἀθρόως καὶ ἐμεθύσκοντο ἀπρεπῶς, καὶ μάλιστα αὐτῶν οἱ Γερμανοὶ γελοιότατοι κατὰ τὴν μέθην ἦσαν [...].

Plut. Caes. 40-1: τότε δὲ καί τι νόσημα λοιμῶδες ἐλέχθη, τὴν ἀτοπίαν τῆς διαίτης ποιησάμενον ἀρχήν, ἐν τῇ στρατιᾷ περιφέρεσθαι τῇ Καίσαρος, [...] Ὁ δὲ τὴν μὲν ἄλλην πορείαν χαλεπῶς ἤνυσεν, οὐδενὸς παρέχοντος ἀγοράν, ἀλλὰ πάντων καταφρονούντων διὰ τὴν ἔναγχος ἧτταν· ὡς δ' εἷλε Γόμφους Θεσσαλικὴν πόλιν, οὐ μόνον ἔθρεψε τὴν στρατιάν, ἀλλὰ καὶ τοῦ νοσήματος ἀπήλλαξε παραλόγως. ἀφθόνῳ γὰρ ἐνέτυχον οἴνῳ, καὶ πιόντες ἀνέδην, εἶτα χρώμενοι κώμοις καὶ βακχεύοντες ἀνὰ τὴν ὁδὸν ἐκ μέθης, διεκρούσαντο καὶ παρήλλαξαν τὸ πάθος, εἰς ἕξιν ἑτέραν τοῖς σώμασι μεταπεσόντες.

Caes. Civ. 3.80: Coniuncto exercitu Caesar Gomphos peruenit, quod est oppidum primum uenientibus ab Epiro. [...] Pompeius nondum Thessaliae appropinquabat. Caesar castris munitis scalas musculosque ad repentinam oppugnationem fieri et crates parari iussit. quibus rebus effectis cohortatus milites docuit, quantum usum haberet ad subleuandam omnium rerum inopiam potiri oppiduo pleno atque opulento, simul reliquis ciuitatibus huius urbis exemplo inferri terrorem et id fieri celeriter, priusquam auxilia concurrerent. itaque usus singulari militum studio eodem quo uenerat die post horam nonam oppidum altissimis moenibus oppugnare adgressus ante solis occasum expugnauit et ad diripiendum militibus concessit statimque ab oppido castra mouit et Metropolim uenit, sic ut nuntios expugnati oppidi famamque antecederet.

548 App. BC 2.54.221-2: Ἀναβοήσαντος δὲ σὺν ὁρμῇ τοῦ στρατοῦ παντὸς ἄγειν σφᾶς, εὐθὺς ἐπὶ τὴν θάλασσαν ἦγεν ἀπὸ τοῦ βήματος, πέντε πεζῶν τέλη καὶ ἱππέας λογάδας ἑξακοσίους. καὶ ἐπ' ἀγκυρῶν ἀπεσάλευε κλυδωνίου διαταράσσοντος. χειμέριοι δ' ἦσαν τροπαί, καὶ τὸ πνεῦμα ἄκοντα καὶ ἀσχάλλοντα κατεκώλυε, μέχρι καὶ τὴν πρώτην τοῦ ἔτους ἡμέραν ἐν Βρεντεσίῳ διατρῖψαι. καὶ δύο τελῶν ἄλλων ἐπελθόντων, ὁ δὲ καὶ τάδε προσλαβὼν ἀνήγετο χειμῶνος ἐπὶ ὁλκάδων· [...] ὑπὸ δὲ χειμώνων ἐς τὰ Κεραύνια ὄρη περιαχθεὶς τὰ μὲν πλοῖα εὐθὺς ἐς Βρεντέσιον ἐπὶ τὴν ἄλλην στρατιὰν περιέπεμπε [...].

549 Mk. 4:35-5:2: Καὶ λέγει αὐτοῖς ἐν ἐκείνῃ τῇ ἡμέρᾳ ὀψίας γενομένης, Διέλθωμεν εἰς τὸ πέραν. καὶ ἀφέντες τὸν ὄχλον παραλαμβάνουσιν αὐτὸν ὡς ἦν ἐν τῷ πλοίῳ, καὶ ἄλλα πλοῖα ἦν μετ' αὐτοῦ. καὶ γίνεται λαῖλαψ μεγάλη ἀνέμου καὶ τὰ κύματα

ἐπέβαλλεν εἰς τὸ πλοῖον, ὥστε ἤδη γεμίζεσθαι τὸ πλοῖον. καὶ αὐτὸς ἦν ἐν τῇ πρύμνῃ ἐπὶ τὸ προσκεφάλαιον καθεύδων. καὶ ἐγείρουσιν αὐτὸν καὶ λέγουσιν αὐτῷ, Διδάσκαλε, οὐ μέλει σοι ὅτι ἀπολλύμεθα; καὶ διεγερθεὶς ἐπετίμησεν τῷ ἀνέμῳ καὶ εἶπεν τῇ θαλάσσῃ, Σιώπα, πεφίμωσο. καὶ ἐκόπασεν ὁ ἄνεμος καὶ ἐγένετο γαλήνη μεγάλη. καὶ εἶπεν αὐτοῖς, Τί δειλοί ἐστε; οὔπω ἔχετε πίστιν; καὶ ἐφοβήθησαν φόβον μέγαν καὶ ἔλεγον πρὸς ἀλλήλους, Τίς ἄρα οὗτός ἐστιν ὅτι καὶ ὁ ἄνεμος καὶ ἡ θάλασσα ὑπακούει αὐτῷ; Καὶ ἦλθον εἰς τὸ πέραν τῆς θαλάσσης εἰς τὴν χώραν τῶν Γερασηνῶν. καὶ ἐξελθόντος αὐτοῦ ἐκ τοῦ πλοίου εὐθὺς ὑπήντησεν αὐτῷ ἐκ τῶν μνημείων ἄνθρωπος ἐν πνεύματι ἀκαθάρτῳ [...].

550 CAES. Civ. 3.73: *Caesar ab superioribus consiliis depulsus omenm sibi commutandam beilli rationem existimauit. itaque uno tempore paesidiis omnibus deductis et oppugnatione dimissa coactoque in unum locum exercitu contionem apud milites habuit [...] 3.74: [...] simulque omnes arderent cupiditate pugnandi, cum superioris etiam ordinis nonnulli ratione permoti manendum eo loco et rem proelio committendam existimarent. contre ea Caesar neque satis militis perterritis confidebat spatiumque interponendum ad recreandos animos putabat, relictisque munitionibus magnopere rei frumentariae timebat. 3.75: Itaque nulla interposita mora sauciorum modo et aegrorum habita ratione impedimenta omnia silentio prima nocte ex castris Apollonia praemisit ac conquiescere ante iter confectum uetuit.*

APP. BC 2.63.264-64.267: ὡς δὲ ὁ Καῖσαρ οὐδὲ τοῦτ' ἀνασχόμενος ὀλίγους μόλις ἐκόλασεν, αὐτίκα πᾶσιν αὐτοῦ πρὸς τὴν μετριοπάθειαν ὁρμὴ τοσήδε ἐνέπιπτεν, ὡς εὐθὺς αὐτὸν ἄγειν ἀξιοῦν ἐπὶ τοὺς πολεμίους· καὶ ἐνέκειντο σφόδρα προθύμως, παρακαλοῦντές τε καὶ ὑπισχνούμενοι διορθώσεσθαι τὸ ἁμάρτημα νίκῃ καλῇ· κατά τε σφᾶς ἐπιστρεφόμενοι πρὸς ἀλλήλους ἰλαδὸν κατὰ μέρη συνώμνυντο, ἐφορῶντος αὐτοῦ Καίσαρος, μὴ ἐπανήξειν ἐκ τῆς μάχης, εἰ μὴ κρατοῖεν. Ὅθεν αὐτὸν οἱ μὲν φίλοι παρεκάλουν ἀποχρήσασθαι τοιᾷδε μετανοίᾳ καὶ προθυμίᾳ στρατοῦ· ὁ δ' ἐς μὲν τὸ πλῆθος εἶπεν, ὅτι μετὰ βελτιόνων καιρῶν αὐτοὺς ἐπὶ τοὺς πολεμίους ἄξει, καὶ μεμνῆσθαι τῆσδε τῆς προθυμίας διεκελεύσατο, τοὺς δὲ φίλους ἀνεδίδασκεν, ὅτι χρὴ καὶ τῶνδε προεξελεῖν τὸν φόβον τῆς ἥττης πολὺν αὐτοῖς ἐγγενόμενον καὶ τῶν πολεμίων τὸ φρόνημα ἀκμάζον προκαθελεῖν. ὡμολόγει τε μεταγιγνώσκειν πρὸς Δυρραχίῳ στρατοπεδεύσας. ἔνθα ἔστιν ἡ παρασκευὴ πᾶσα Πομπηΐῳ, δέον ἀποσπᾶν αὐτὸν ἑτέρωθι ἐς ὁμοίας ἀπορίας. Καὶ τάδε εἰπὼν ἐς Ἀπολλωνίαν εὐθὺς μετῄει καὶ ἀπ' αὐτῆς ἐς Θεσσαλίαν νυκτὸς ὑπεχώρει λανθάνων [...].

551 Mk. 5:12-13: καὶ παρεκάλεσαν αὐτὸν λέγοντες, Πέμψον ἡμᾶς εἰς τοὺς χοίρους, ἵνα εἰς αὐτοὺς εἰσέλθωμεν. καὶ ἐπέτρεψεν αὐτοῖς. καὶ ἐξελθόντα τὰ πνεύματα τὰ ἀκάθαρτα εἰσῆλθον εἰς τοὺς χοίρους, καὶ ὥρμησεν ἡ ἀγέλη κατὰ τοῦ κρημνοῦ εἰς τὴν θάλασσαν, ὡς δισχίλιοι, καὶ ἐπνίγοντο ἐν τῇ θαλάσσῃ.

552 In any case it should be clear that *thalassa* at the Gadarenes as well as the *swine* do not fit. The former because there is only a lake there and not a sea, and the latter because in the land of the Jews, swine were not bred. Both facts doubtlessly point, together with the name *Legion*, to an originally Roman story.

553 APP. BC 2.70.289: Στρατιὰ δ' ἦν, ὡς ἐμοὶ δοκεῖ, πολλῶν ἀμφίλογα εἰπόντων ἑπομένῳ μάλιστα Ῥωμαίων τοῖς τὰ πιθανώτατα γράφουσι περὶ τῶν ἐξ Ἰταλίας ἀνδρῶν, οἷς δὴ καὶ μάλιστα θαρροῦντες τὰ συμμαχικὰ οὐκ ἀκριβοῦσιν οὐδὲ ἀναγράφουσιν ὡς ἀλλότρια καὶ ὀλίγην ἐν αὐτοῖς εἰς προσθήκην χώραν ἔχοντα, Καίσαρι μὲν ἐς δισχιλίους ἐπὶ δισμυρίοις, καὶ τούτων ἱππέες ἦσαν ἀμφὶ τοὺς χιλίους, Πομπηΐῳ δὲ ὑπὲρ τὸ διπλάσιον, καὶ τούτων ἱππέες ἐς ἑπτακισχιλίους.

PLUT. Pomp. 69: ἦσαν δὲ οἱ μὲν μετὰ Καίσαρος δισχίλιοι πρὸς δισμυρίοις, οἱ δὲ μετὰ Πομπηΐου βραχεῖ πλείονες ἢ διπλάσιοι τούτων.

554 PLUT. Caes. 44: Πομπήϊος δ' ὡς κατεῖδεν ἀπὸ θατέρου τοὺς ἱππεῖς φυγῇ σκεδασθέντας, οὐκέτ' ἦν ὁ αὐτὸς οὐδ' ἐμέμνητο Πομπήϊος ὢν Μᾶγνος, ἀλλ' ὑπὸ θεοῦ μάλιστα βλαπτομένῳ τὴν γνώμην ἐοικώς [ἢ διὰ θείας ἥττης τεθαμβημένος], ἄφθογγος ᾤχετ' ἀπιὼν ἐπὶ σκηνήν, καὶ καθεζόμενος ἐκαραδόκει τὸ μέλλον, ἄχρι οὗ

τροπῆς ἁπάντων γενομένης ἐπέβαινον οἱ πολέμιοι τοῦ χάρακος καὶ διεμάχοντο πρὸς τοὺς φυλάττοντας. τότε δ' ὥσπερ ἔννους γενόμενος, καὶ ταύτην μόνην ὥς φασι φωνὴν ἀφεὶς "οὐκοῦν καὶ ἐπὶ τὴν παρεμβολήν," ἀπεδύσατο μὲν τὴν ἐναγώνιον καὶ στρατηγικὴν ἐσθῆτα, φεύγοντι δὲ πρέπουσαν μεταλαβὼν ὑπεξῆλθεν.

App. BC 2.81.339-343: Πομπήιος δ' ἐπεὶ τὴν τροπὴν εἶδεν, ἔκφρων αὑτοῦ γενόμενος ἀπῄει βάδην ἐς τὸ στρατόπεδον καὶ παρελθὼν ἐς τὴν σκηνὴν ἐκαθέζετο ἄναυδος, οἷόν τι καὶ τὸν Τελαμῶνος Αἴαντά φασιν ἐν Ἰλίῳ παθεῖν, ἐν μέσοις πολεμίοις ὑπὸ θεοβλαβείας. τῶν δ' ἄλλων ὀλίγοι πάνυ ἐσῄεσαν ἐς τὸ στρατόπεδον· τὸ γὰρ κήρυγμα τοῦ Καίσαρος ἑστάναι τε ἀκινδύνως ἐποίει, καὶ παραδραμόντων τῶν πολεμίων διεσκίδνη κατὰ μέρος. ληγούσης δὲ τῆς ἡμέρας ὁ Καῖσαρ τὸν στρατὸν ἀσχέτως που περιθέων ἱκέτευε προσπονῆσαι, μέχρι καὶ τὸν χάρακα τοῦ Πομπηίου λάβοιεν, ἐκδιδάσκων, ὅτι, εἰ συσταῖεν αὖθις οἱ πολέμιοι, μίαν ἡμέραν ἔσονται νενικηκότες, εἰ δὲ τὸ στρατόπεδον αὐτῶν ἕλοιεν, τὸν πόλεμον ἑνὶ τῷδε ἔργῳ κατωρθωκότες ἂν εἶεν. τάς τε οὖν χεῖρας αὐτοῖς ὤρεγε καὶ πρῶτος ἐξῆρχε δρόμου. τοῖς δὲ τὰ μὲν σώματα ἔκαμνε, τὴν δὲ ψυχὴν ὅ τε λογισμὸς καὶ ὁ αὐτοκράτωρ συντρέχων ἐκούφιζεν. ᾐώρει δὲ καὶ ἡ τῶν γεγονότων εὐπραξία καὶ ἐλπίς, ὅτι καὶ τὸν χάρακα αἱρήσουσι καὶ πολλὰ τὰ ἐν αὐτῷ· ἥκιστα δ' ἐν ἐλπίσιν ἢ εὐτυχίαις ἄνθρωποι καμάτων αἰσθάνονται. οἱ μὲν δὴ καὶ τῷδε προσπεσόντες ἐπεχείρουν σὺν πολλῇ πρὸς τοὺς ἀπομαχομένους καταφρονήσει, ὁ δὲ Πομπήιος μαθὼν ἐξ ἀλλοκότου σιωπῆς τοσοῦτον ἀπέρρηξεν· "οὐκοῦν καὶ ἐπὶ τὸν χάρακα ἡμῶν," καὶ εἰπὼν τήν τε στολὴν ἐνήλλαξε καὶ ἵππου ἐπιβὰς σὺν φίλοις τέσσαρσιν οὐκ ἀνέσχε δρόμου, πρὶν ἀρχομένης ἡμέρας ἐν Λαρίσσῃ γενέσθαι.

Caes. Civ. 3.96: Pompeius, iam cum intra uallum nostri uersarentur, equum nactus detractis insignibus imperatoriis decumana porta se ex castris eiecit protinusque equo citato Larisam contendit. neque ibi constitit, sed eadem celeritate paucos suos ex fuga nactus nocturno itinere non intermisso comitatu equitatum XXX ad mare peruenit nauemque frumentariam conscendit, saepe, ut dicebatur, querens tantum se opinionem fefellisse, ut a quo genere hominum uictoriam sperasset, ab eo initio fugae paene proditus uideretur.

555 Mk. 5:14-20: καὶ οἱ βόσκοντες αὐτοὺς ἔφυγον καὶ ἀπήγγειλαν εἰς τὴν πόλιν καὶ εἰς τοὺς ἀγρούς· καὶ ἦλθον ἰδεῖν τί ἐστιν τὸ γεγονός καὶ ἔρχονται πρὸς τὸν Ἰησοῦν καὶ θεωροῦσιν τὸν δαιμονιζόμενον καθήμενον ἱματισμένον καὶ σωφρονοῦντα, τὸν ἐσχηκότα τὸν λεγιῶνα, καὶ ἐφοβήθησαν. καὶ διηγήσαντο αὐτοῖς οἱ ἰδόντες πῶς ἐγένετο τῷ δαιμονιζομένῳ καὶ περὶ τῶν χοίρων. καὶ ἤρξαντο παρακαλεῖν αὐτὸν ἀπελθεῖν ἀπὸ τῶν ὁρίων αὐτῶν. καὶ ἐμβαίνοντος αὐτοῦ εἰς τὸ πλοῖον παρεκάλει αὐτὸν ὁ δαιμονισθεὶς ἵνα μετ' αὐτοῦ ᾖ. καὶ οὐκ ἀφῆκεν αὐτόν, ἀλλὰ λέγει αὐτῷ, Ὕπαγε εἰς τὸν οἶκόν σου πρὸς τοὺς σοὺς καὶ ἀπάγγειλον αὐτοῖς ὅσα ὁ κύριός σοι πεποίηκεν καὶ ἠλέησέν σε. καὶ ἀπῆλθεν καὶ ἤρξατο κηρύσσειν ἐν τῇ Δεκαπόλει ὅσα ἐποίησεν αὐτῷ ὁ Ἰησοῦς, καὶ πάντες ἐθαύμαζον.

556 Plut. Caes. 46: Ὁ δὲ Καῖσαρ ὡς ἐν τῷ χάρακι τοῦ Πομπηίου γενόμενος τούς τε κειμένους νεκροὺς ἤδη τῶν πολεμίων εἶδε καὶ τοὺς ἔτι κτεινομένους, εἶπεν ἄρα στενάξας· "τοῦτ' ἐβουλήθησαν, εἰς τοῦτό μ' ἀνάγκης ὑπηγάγοντο, ἵνα Γάιος Καῖσαρ ὁ μεγίστους πολέμους κατορθώσας, εἰ προηκάμην τὰ στρατεύματα, κἂν κατεδικάσθην." ταῦτά φησι Πολλίων Ἀσίνιος (HRR II 68) τὰ ῥήματα Ῥωμαϊστὶ μὲν ἀναφθέγξασθαι τὸν Καίσαρα παρὰ τὸν τότε καιρόν, Ἑλληνιστὶ δ' ὑφ' αὐτοῦ γεγράφθαι· τῶν δ' ἀποθανόντων τοὺς πλείστους οἰκέτας γενέσθαι, περὶ τὴν κατάληψιν τοῦ χάρακος ἀναιρεθέντας, στρατιώτας δὲ μὴ πλείους ἑξακισχιλίων πεσεῖν.

Whether Caesar had really spoken in Latin and Asinius wrote down his words in Greek, as Plutarchus remarks, is doubted by many commentators, because Asinius composed his *Historiae* in Latin. Hence it is assumed that it was vice-versa, that Caesar spoke Greek and Asinius reproduced his words in Latin. Then a copyist would have interchanged Latin and Greek because Plutarchus for his part has translated Asinius' quotation into the Greek.

557 Mk. 9:30-32: καὶ οὐκ ἤθελεν ἵνα τις γνοῖ· ἐδίδασκεν γὰρ τοὺς μαθητὰς αὐτοῦ καὶ ἔλεγεν αὐτοῖς ὅτι Ὁ υἱὸς τοῦ ἀνθρώπου παραδίδοται εἰς χεῖρας ἀνθρώπων, καὶ ἀποκτενοῦσιν αὐτόν, καὶ ἀποκτανθεὶς μετὰ τρεῖς ἡμέρας ἀναστήσεται. οἱ δὲ ἠγνόουν τὸ ῥῆμα, καὶ ἐφοβοῦντο αὐτὸν ἐπερωτῆσαι.

558 Mk. 9:30: Κἀκεῖθεν ἐξελθόντες παρεπορεύοντο διὰ τῆς Γαλιλαίας [...].

559 Mk. 8:31: Καὶ ἤρξατο διδάσκειν αὐτοὺς ὅτι δεῖ τὸν υἱὸν τοῦ ἀνθρώπου πολλὰ παθεῖν καὶ ἀποδοκιμασθῆναι ὑπὸ τῶν πρεσβυτέρων καὶ τῶν ἀρχιερέων καὶ τῶν γραμματέων καὶ ἀποκτανθῆναι καὶ μετὰ τρεῖς ἡμέρας ἀναστῆναι.

560 Mk. 8:32-33: καὶ παρρησίᾳ τὸν λόγον ἐλάλει. καὶ προσλαβόμενος ὁ Πέτρος αὐτὸν ἤρξατο ἐπιτιμᾶν αὐτῷ. ὁ δὲ ἐπιστραφεὶς καὶ ἰδὼν τοὺς μαθητὰς αὐτοῦ ἐπετίμησεν Πέτρῳ καὶ λέγει, Ὕπαγε ὀπίσω μου, Σατανᾶ, ὅτι οὐ φρονεῖς τὰ τοῦ θεοῦ ἀλλὰ τὰ τῶν ἀνθρώπων.

561 App. BC 2.33.131-2: καὶ οἱ ὕπατοι, Μάρκελλός τε καὶ Λέντλος, ἐκέλευον τοῖς ἀμφὶ τὸν Ἀντώνιον ἐκστῆναι τοῦ συνεδρίου, μή τι καὶ δημαρχοῦντες ὅμως πάθοιεν ἀτοπώτερον. ἔνθα δὴ μέγα βοήσας ὁ Ἀντώνιος ἀνά τε ἔδραμε τῆς ἕδρας σὺν ὀργῇ καὶ περὶ τῆς ἀρχῆς ἐπεθείαζεν αὐτοῖς, ὡς ἱερὰ καὶ ἄσυλος οὖσα ὑβρίζοιτο, καὶ περὶ σφῶν, ὅτι γνώμην ἐσφέροντες, ἣν δοκοῦσι συνοίσειν, ἐξελαύνοιντο σὺν ὕβρει, μήτε τινὰ σφαγὴν μήτε μύσος ἐργασάμενοι. ταῦτα δ' εἰπὼν ἐξέτρεχεν ὥσπερ ἔνθους, πολέμους καὶ σφαγὰς καὶ προγραφὰς καὶ φυγὰς καὶ δημεύσεις καὶ ὅσα ἄλλα αὐτοῖς ἔμελλεν ἔσεσθαι, προθεσπίζων ἀράς τε βαρείας τοῖς τούτων αἰτίοις ἐπαρώμενος.

562 Caes. Civ. 1.6.8: *omnia diuina humanaque iura permiscentur.*

563 App. BC 2.35.139-41: δρόμῳ δ' ἐλθὼν ἐπὶ τὸν Ῥουβίκωνα ποταμόν, ὃς ὁρίζει τὴν Ἰταλίαν, ἔστη τοῦ δρόμου καὶ ἐς τὸ ῥεῦμα ἀφορῶν περιεφέρετο τῇ γνώμῃ, λογιζόμενος ἕκαστα τῶν ἐσομένων κακῶν, εἰ τόνδε τὸν ποταμὸν σὺν ὅπλοις περάσειε. καὶ πρὸς τοὺς παρόντας εἶπεν ἀνενεγκών· "ἡ μὲν ἐπίσχεσις, ὦ φίλοι, τῆσδε τῆς διαβάσεως ἐμοὶ κακῶν ἄρξει, ἡ δὲ διάβασις πᾶσιν ἀνθρώποις." καὶ εἰπὼν οἷά τις ἔνθους ἐπέρα σὺν ὁρμῇ, τὸ κοινὸν τόδε ἐπειπών· "ὁ κύβος ἀνερρίφθω." δρόμῳ δ' ἐντεῦθεν ἐπιὼν Ἀρίμινόν τε αἱρεῖ περὶ ἕω καὶ ἐς τὸ πρόσθεν ἐχώρει [...].
Plut. Caes. 32: πολλὰ μὲν αὐτὸς ἐν ἑαυτῷ διήνεγκε σιγῇ τὴν γνώμην ἐπ' ἀμφότερα μεταλαμβάνων, καὶ τροπὰς ἔσχεν αὑτῷ τότε ⟨τὸ⟩ βούλευμα πλείστας· πολλὰ δὲ καὶ τῶν φίλων τοῖς παροῦσιν, ὧν ἦν καὶ Πολλίων Ἀσίνιος, συνδιηπόρησεν, ἀναλογιζόμενος ἡλίκων κακῶν ἄρξει πᾶσιν ἀνθρώποις ἡ διάβασις, ὅσον τε λόγον αὐτῆς τοῖς αὖθις ἀπολείψουσι. τέλος δὲ μετὰ θυμοῦ τινος ὥσπερ ἀφεὶς ἑαυτὸν ἐκ τοῦ λογισμοῦ πρὸς τὸ μέλλον, καὶ τοῦτο δὴ τὸ κοινὸν τοῖς εἰς τύχας ἐμβαίνουσιν ἀπόρους καὶ τόλμας προοίμιον ὑπειπὼν "ἀνερρίφθω κύβος," ὥρμησε πρὸς τὴν διάβασιν, καὶ δρόμῳ τὸ λοιπὸν ἤδη χρώμενος, εἰσέπεσε πρὸ ἡμέρας εἰς τὸ Ἀρίμινον, καὶ κατέσχε.
Suet. Jul. 31-2: *consecutusque cohortis ad Rubiconem flumen, qui prouinciae eius finis erat, paulum constitit, ac reputans quantum moliretur, conuersus ad proximos: «etiam nunc,» inquit, «regredi possumus; quod si ponticulum transierimus, omnia armis agenda erunt.» cunctanti ostentum tale factum est. quidam eximia magnitudine et forma in proximo sedens repente apparuit harundine canens; ad quem audiendum cum praeter pastores plurimi etiam ex stationibus milites concurrissent interque eos et aeneatores, rapta ab uno tuba prosiliuit ad flumen et ingenti spiritu classicum exorsus pertendit ad alteram ripam. tunc Caesar: «eatur,» inquit, «quo deorum ostenta et inimicorum iniquitas uocat. iacta alea est,» inquit. atque ita traiecto exercitu [...].*

564 Mk. 8:34-9:1: Καὶ προσκαλεσάμενος τὸν ὄχλον σὺν τοῖς μαθηταῖς αὐτοῦ εἶπεν αὐτοῖς, Εἴ τις θέλει ὀπίσω μου ἀκολουθεῖν, ἀπαρνησάσθω ἑαυτὸν καὶ ἀράτω τὸν σταυρὸν αὐτοῦ καὶ ἀκολουθείτω μοι. ὃς γὰρ ἐὰν θέλῃ τὴν ψυχὴν αὐτοῦ σῶσαι ἀπολέσει αὐτήν· ὃς δ' ἂν ἀπολέσει τὴν ψυχὴν αὐτοῦ ἕνεκεν ἐμοῦ καὶ τοῦ εὐαγγελίου σώσει αὐτήν. τί γὰρ ὠφελεῖ ἄνθρωπον κερδῆσαι τὸν κόσμον ὅλον καὶ ζημιωθῆναι τὴν

ψυχὴν αὐτοῦ; τί γὰρ δοῖ ἄνθρωπος ἀντάλλαγμα τῆς ψυχῆς αὐτοῦ; ὃς γὰρ ἐὰν ἐπαισχυνθῇ με καὶ τοὺς ἐμοὺς λόγους ἐν τῇ γενεᾷ ταύτῃ τῇ μοιχαλίδι καὶ ἁμαρτωλῷ, καὶ ὁ υἱὸς τοῦ ἀνθρώπου ἐπαισχυνθήσεται αὐτόν, ὅταν ἔλθῃ ἐν τῇ δόξῃ τοῦ πατρὸς αὐτοῦ μετὰ τῶν ἀγγέλων τῶν ἁγίων. Καὶ ἔλεγεν αὐτοῖς, Ἀμὴν λέγω ὑμῖν ὅτι εἰσίν τινες ὧδε τῶν ἑστηκότων οἵτινες οὐ μὴ γεύσωνται θανάτου ἕως ἂν ἴδωσιν τὴν βασιλείαν τοῦ θεοῦ ἐληλυθυῖαν ἐν δυνάμει.

565 App. BC 2.74.310: "[...] πρὸ δὲ πάντων, ὡς ἂν εἰδείην ὑμᾶς ἔγωγε ὧν συνετίθεσθε μεμνημένους τε καὶ νίκην πάντως ἢ θάνατον αἱρουμένους, καθέλετέ μοι προϊόντες ἐπὶ τὴν μάχην τὰ τείχη τὰ σφέτερα αὐτῶν καὶ τὴν τάφρον ἐγχώσατε, ἵνα μηδὲν ἔχωμεν, ἂν μὴ κρατῶμεν, ἴδωσι δ' ἡμᾶς ἀσταθμεύτους οἱ πολέμιοι καὶ συνῶσιν, ὅτι πρὸς ἀνάγκης ἐστὶν ἡμῖν ἐν τοῖς ἐκείνων σταθμεῦσαι."

App. BC 2.81.344: ὁ δὲ Καῖσαρ, ὡς ἐπηπείλησε παρατάσσων, ἐν τῷ Πομπηίου χάρακι ἐστάθμευσε, καὶ αὐτός τε τὴν ἐκείνου βρώμην καὶ ὁ στρατὸς ἅπας τὴν τῶν πολεμίων ἐδαίσαντο.

566 Caes. Civ. 3.96: In castris Pompei uidere licuit trichilas structas, magnum argenti pondus expositum, recentibus caespitibus tabernacula constrata, Luci etiam et Lentuli et nonnullorum tabernacula protecta hedera multaque praeterea, quae nimiam luxuriem et uictoriae fiduciam designarent, ut facile exixtimari posset nihil eos de euentu eius diei timuisse, qui non necessarias conquirerent uoluptates. at hi miserrimo ac patientissimo exercitu Caesaris luxuriem obiciebant, cui semper omnia ad necessarium usum defuissent.

Plut. Pomp. 72: Αἱροῦντες δὲ τὸ στρατόπεδον ἐθεῶντο τὴν ἄνοιαν καὶ κουφότητα τῶν πολεμίων. πᾶσα γὰρ σκηνὴ μυρσίναις κατέστεπτο καὶ στρωμναῖς ἀνθιναῖς ἤσκητο καὶ τραπέζαις ἐκπωμάτων μεσταῖς· καὶ κρατῆρες οἴνου προὔκειντο, καὶ παρασκευὴ καὶ κόσμος ἦν τεθυκότων καὶ πανηγυριζόντων μᾶλλον ἢ πρὸς μάχην ἐξοπλιζομένων. οὕτω ταῖς ἐλπίσι διεφθαρμένοι καὶ γέμοντες ἀνοήτου θράσους ἐπὶ τὸν πόλεμον ἐχώρουν.

567 Plut. Caes. 55: Μετὰ δὲ τοὺς θριάμβους ⟨τοῖς⟩ στρατιώταις τε μεγάλας δωρεὰς ἐδίδου, καὶ τὸν δῆμον ἀνελάμβανεν ἑστιάσεσι καὶ θέαις, ἑστιάσας μὲν ἐν δισμυρίοις καὶ δισχιλίοις τρικλίνοις ὁμοῦ σύμπαντας, θέας δὲ καὶ μονομάχων καὶ ναυμάχων ἀνδρῶν παρασχὼν ἐπὶ τῇ θυγατρὶ Ἰουλίᾳ πάλαι τεθνεώσῃ.

Plut. Caes. 57: αὖθις ἀνελάμβανε τὸν δῆμον ἑστιάσεσι καὶ σιτηρεσίοις, τὸ δὲ στρατιωτικὸν ἀποικίαις [...].

Suet. Jul. 38: populo praeter frumenti denos modios ac totidem olei libras trecenos quoque nummos, quos pollicitus olim erat, uiritim diuisit et hoc amplius centenos pro mora. annuam etiam habitationem Romae usque ad bina milia nummum, in Italia non ultra quingenos sestertios remisit. adiecit epulum ac uiscerationem et post Hispaniensem uictoriam duo prandia; nam cum prius parce neque pro liberalitate sua praebitum iudicaret, quinto post die aliud largissimum praebuit.

Vell. 2.56.2: Caesar omnium uictor regressus in urbem, quod humanam excedat fidem, omnibus qui contra se arma tulerant ignouit, magnificentissimisque gladiatorii muneris, naumachiae et equitum peditumque, simul elephantorum certaminis spectaculis epulique per multos dies dati celebratione repleuit eam.

Plin. NH IX 171: Murenarum uiuarium priuatim excogitauit ante alios C. Hirr<i>us, qui cenis triumphalibus Caesaris dictatoris sex milia numero murenarum mutua appendit. nam permutare quidem pretio noluit aliaue merce.

Plin. NH XIV 97: non et Caesar dictator triumphi sui cena uini Falerni amphoras, Chii cados in conuiuia distribuit? idem Hispaniensi triumpho Chium et Falernum dedit, epulo uero in tertio consulatu suo Falernum, Chium, Lesbium, Mamertinum, quo tempore primum quattuor genera uini adposita constat.

568 Mk 6:30-44: Καὶ συνάγονται οἱ ἀπόστολοι πρὸς τὸν Ἰησοῦν καὶ ἀπήγγειλαν αὐτῷ πάντα ὅσα ἐποίησαν καὶ ὅσα ἐδίδαξαν. καὶ λέγει αὐτοῖς, Δεῦτε ὑμεῖς αὐτοὶ κατ' ἰδίαν εἰς ἔρημον τόπον καὶ ἀναπαύσασθε ὀλίγον. ἦσαν γὰρ οἱ ἐρχόμενοι καὶ οἱ

ὑπάγοντες πολλοί, καὶ οὐδὲ φαγεῖν εὐκαίρουν. καὶ ἀπῆλθον ἐν τῷ πλοίῳ εἰς ἔρημον τόπον κατ᾽ ἰδίαν. καὶ εἶδον αὐτοὺς ὑπάγοντας καὶ ἐπέγνωσαν πολλοί καὶ πεζῇ ἀπὸ πασῶν τῶν πόλεων συνέδραμον ἐκεῖ καὶ προῆλθον αὐτούς. καὶ ἐξελθὼν εἶδεν πολὺν ὄχλον καὶ ἐσπλαγχνίσθη ἐπ᾽ αὐτούς, ὅτι ἦσαν ὡς πρόβατα μὴ ἔχοντα ποιμένα, καὶ ἤρξατο διδάσκειν αὐτοὺς πολλά. Καὶ ἤδη ὥρας πολλῆς γενομένης προσελθόντες αὐτῷ οἱ μαθηταὶ αὐτοῦ ἔλεγον ὅτι Ἔρημός ἐστιν ὁ τόπος καὶ ἤδη ὥρα πολλή· ἀπόλυσον αὐτούς, ἵνα ἀπελθόντες εἰς τοὺς κύκλῳ ἀγροὺς καὶ κώμας ἀγοράσωσιν ἑαυτοῖς τί φάγωσιν. ὁ δὲ ἀποκριθεὶς εἶπεν αὐτοῖς, Δότε αὐτοῖς ὑμεῖς φαγεῖν. καὶ λέγουσιν αὐτῷ, Ἀπελθόντες ἀγοράσωμεν δηναρίων διακοσίων ἄρτους καὶ δώσομεν αὐτοῖς φαγεῖν; ὁ δὲ λέγει αὐτοῖς, Πόσους ἄρτους ἔχετε; ὑπάγετε ἴδετε. καὶ γνόντες λέγουσιν, Πέντε, καὶ δύο ἰχθύας. καὶ ἐπέταξεν αὐτοῖς ἀνακλῖναι πάντας συμπόσια συμπόσια ἐπὶ τῷ χλωρῷ χόρτῳ. καὶ ἀνέπεσαν πρασιαὶ πρασιαὶ κατὰ ἑκατὸν καὶ κατὰ πεντήκοντα. καὶ λαβὼν τοὺς πέντε ἄρτους καὶ τοὺς δύο ἰχθύας ἀναβλέψας εἰς τὸν οὐρανὸν εὐλόγησεν καὶ κατέκλασεν τοὺς ἄρτους καὶ ἐδίδου τοῖς μαθηταῖς [αὐτοῦ] ἵνα παρατιθῶσιν αὐτοῖς, καὶ τοὺς δύο ἰχθύας ἐμέρισεν πᾶσιν. καὶ ἔφαγον πάντες καὶ ἐχορτάσθησαν, καὶ ἦραν κλάσματα δώδεκα κοφίνων πληρώματα καὶ ἀπὸ τῶν ἰχθύων. καὶ ἦσαν οἱ φαγόντες [τοὺς ἄρτους] πεντακισχίλιοι ἄνδρες.

Mk 8:1-9: Ἐν ἐκείναις ταῖς ἡμέραις πάλιν πολλοῦ ὄχλου ὄντος καὶ μὴ ἐχόντων τί φάγωσιν, προσκαλεσάμενος τοὺς μαθητὰς λέγει αὐτοῖς, Σπλαγχνίζομαι ἐπὶ τὸν ὄχλον, ὅτι ἤδη ἡμέραι τρεῖς προσμένουσίν μοι καὶ οὐκ ἔχουσιν τί φάγωσιν· καὶ ἐὰν ἀπολύσω αὐτοὺς νήστεις εἰς οἶκον αὐτῶν, ἐκλυθήσονται ἐν τῇ ὁδῷ· καί τινες αὐτῶν ἀπὸ μακρόθεν ἥκασιν. καὶ ἀπεκρίθησαν αὐτῷ οἱ μαθηταὶ αὐτοῦ ὅτι Πόθεν τούτους δυνήσεταί τις ὧδε χορτάσαι ἄρτων ἐπ᾽ ἐρημίας; καὶ ἠρώτα αὐτούς, Πόσους ἔχετε ἄρτους; οἱ δὲ εἶπαν, Ἑπτά. καὶ παραγγέλλει τῷ ὄχλῳ ἀναπεσεῖν ἐπὶ τῆς γῆς· καὶ λαβὼν τοὺς ἑπτὰ ἄρτους εὐχαριστήσας ἔκλασεν καὶ ἐδίδου τοῖς μαθηταῖς αὐτοῦ ἵνα παρατιθῶσιν, καὶ παρέθηκαν τῷ ὄχλῳ. καὶ εἶχον ἰχθύδια ὀλίγα· καὶ εὐλογήσας αὐτὰ εἶπεν καὶ ταῦτα παρατιθέναι. καὶ ἔφαγον καὶ ἐχορτάσθησαν, καὶ ἦραν περισσεύματα κλασμάτων ἑπτὰ σπυρίδας. ἦσαν δὲ ὡς τετρακισχίλιοι. καὶ ἀπέλυσεν αὐτούς.

Jn. 2:1-11: Καὶ τῇ ἡμέρᾳ τῇ τρίτῃ γάμος ἐγένετο ἐν Κανὰ τῆς Γαλιλαίας, καὶ ἦν ἡ μήτηρ τοῦ Ἰησοῦ ἐκεῖ· ἐκλήθη δὲ καὶ ὁ Ἰησοῦς καὶ οἱ μαθηταὶ αὐτοῦ εἰς τὸν γάμον. καὶ ὑστερήσαντος οἴνου λέγει ἡ μήτηρ τοῦ Ἰησοῦ πρὸς αὐτόν, Οἶνον οὐκ ἔχουσιν. [καὶ] λέγει αὐτῇ ὁ Ἰησοῦς, Τί ἐμοὶ καὶ σοί, γύναι; οὔπω ἥκει ἡ ὥρα μου. λέγει ἡ μήτηρ αὐτοῦ τοῖς διακόνοις, Ὅ τι ἂν λέγῃ ὑμῖν ποιήσατε. ἦσαν δὲ ἐκεῖ λίθιναι ὑδρίαι ἓξ κατὰ τὸν καθαρισμὸν τῶν Ἰουδαίων κείμεναι, χωροῦσαι ἀνὰ μετρητὰς δύο ἢ τρεῖς. λέγει αὐτοῖς ὁ Ἰησοῦς, Γεμίσατε τὰς ὑδρίας ὕδατος. καὶ ἐγέμισαν αὐτὰς ἕως ἄνω. καὶ λέγει αὐτοῖς, Ἀντλήσατε νῦν καὶ φέρετε τῷ ἀρχιτρικλίνῳ· οἱ δὲ ἤνεγκαν. ὡς δὲ ἐγεύσατο ὁ ἀρχιτρίκλινος τὸ ὕδωρ οἶνον γεγενημένον καὶ οὐκ ᾔδει πόθεν ἐστίν, οἱ δὲ διάκονοι ᾔδεισαν οἱ ἠντληκότες τὸ ὕδωρ, φωνεῖ τὸν νυμφίον ὁ ἀρχιτρίκλινος καὶ λέγει αὐτῷ, Πᾶς ἄνθρωπος πρῶτον τὸν καλὸν οἶνον τίθησιν καὶ ὅταν μεθυσθῶσιν τὸν ἐλάσσω· σὺ τετήρηκας τὸν καλὸν οἶνον ἕως ἄρτι. Ταύτην ἐποίησεν ἀρχὴν τῶν σημείων ὁ Ἰησοῦς ἐν Κανὰ τῆς Γαλιλαίας καὶ ἐφανέρωσεν τὴν δόξαν αὐτοῦ, καὶ ἐπίστευσαν εἰς αὐτὸν οἱ μαθηταὶ αὐτοῦ.

569 Compare the given citation from Plutarchus where the preparations for the feast in the camp of Pompeius are described, astonishingly for us, the luxury is called 'sacrifice': [...] καὶ παρασκευὴ καὶ κόσμος ἦν τεθυκότων καὶ πανηγυριζόντων μᾶλλον ἢ πρὸς μάχην ἐξοπλιζομένων—'[...] and everything prepared and put in array, in the manner rather of people who had offered sacrifice and wanted to celebrate a feast, than of soldiers who had armed themselves to go out to battle'. Besides one repeatedly finds the similarly sounding word θέας for 'spectacle' in the depiction of the triumphal feasts in Rome because they were accompanied by such. Back in Rome after the Spanish campaign one finds ἑστιάσες for feedings: αὖθις ἀνελάμβανε τὸν δῆμον

ἑστιάσεσι καὶ σιτηρεσίοις—'...and so he tried anew to win over the people by feedings and donations of grain'.

As so often in Mark, however, the 'fish' could be based on a mistaken perception of a Latin word, in this case *uiscus*, 'meat', from which 'distribution of meat', *uisceratio* is derived (cf. SUET. *Jul.* 38: *adiecit epulum ac uiscerationem*—see note 567). Did Mark read 'meat', *uiscus*, as *piscis*, 'fish', here?

570 CAES. *Civ.* 3.104, 106. APP. *BC* 2.84-6: Ὁ μὲν δὴ διὰ τάδε ἐς τὴν Αἴγυπτον ἔπλει· ἄρτι δ' ἐκπεσούσης ἀπ' Αἰγύπτου Κλεοπάτρας, ἣ τῷ ἀδελφῷ συνῆρχε, καὶ στρατὸν ἀμφὶ τὴν Συρίαν ἀγειρούσης, Πτολεμαῖος ὁ τῆς Κλεοπάτρας ἀδελφὸς ἀμφὶ τὸ Κάσσιον τῆς Αἰγύπτου ταῖς Κλεοπάτρας ἐσβολαῖς ἐφήδρευε, καί πως κατὰ δαίμονα ἐς τὸ Κάσσιον τὸ πνεῦμα τὸν Πομπήιον κατέφερε. θεασάμενος δὲ στρατὸν ἐπὶ τῆς γῆς πολὺν ἔστησε τὸν πλοῦν καὶ εἴκασεν, ὅπερ ἦν, παρεῖναι τὸν βασιλέα. πέμψας τε ἔφραζε περὶ ἑαυτοῦ καὶ τῆς τοῦ πατρὸς φιλίας. ὁ δὲ ἦν μὲν περὶ τρισκαίδεκα ἔτη μάλιστα γεγονώς, ἐπετρόπευον δ' αὐτῷ τὴν μὲν στρατιὰν Ἀχιλλᾶς, τὰ δὲ χρήματα Ποθεινὸς εὐνοῦχος· οἳ βουλὴν προυτίθεντο περὶ τοῦ Πομπηίου. καὶ παρὼν ὁ Σάμιος Θεόδοτος ὁ ῥήτωρ, διδάσκαλος ὢν τοῦ παιδός, ἀθέμιστον εἰσηγεῖτο ἔργον, ἐνεδρεῦσαι καὶ κτεῖναι Πομπήιον ὡς χαριουμένους Καίσαρι. κυρωθείσης δὲ τῆς γνώμης σκάφος εὐτελὲς ἐπ' αὐτὸν ἐπέμπετο, ὡς τῆς θαλάσσης οὔσης ἀλιτενοῦς καὶ μεγάλαις ναυσὶν οὐκ εὐχεροῦς, ὑπηρέται τέ τινες τῶν βασιλικῶν ἐνέβαινον ἐς τὸ σκάφος. καὶ Σεμπρώνιος, ἀνὴρ Ῥωμαῖος τότε μὲν τῷ βασιλεῖ, πάλαι δὲ αὐτῷ Πομπηίῳ στρατευσάμενος, δεξιὰν ἔφερε παρὰ τοῦ βασιλέως τῷ Πομπηίῳ καὶ ἐκέλευεν ὡς ἐς φίλον τὸν παῖδα διαπλεῦσαι. [...] καὶ ὃς αὐτίκα μὲν ἐπένευσεν, ἀποστραφέντα δ' εὐθὺς ἐπάταξε πρῶτος, εἶθ' ἕτεροι. καὶ τὸ μὲν γύναιον τοῦ Πομπηίου καὶ οἱ φίλοι ταῦτα μακρόθεν ὁρῶντες ἀνῴμωζόν τε καὶ χεῖρας ἐς θεοὺς ἐκδίκους σπονδῶν ἀνίσχοντες ἀπέπλεον τάχιστα ὡς ἐκ πολεμίας. Πομπηίου δὲ τὴν μὲν κεφαλὴν ἀποτεμόντες οἱ περὶ Ποθεινὸν ἐφύλασσον Καίσαρι ὡς ἐπὶ μεγίσταις ἀμοιβαῖς (ὁ δὲ αὐτοὺς ἠμύνατο ἀξίως τῆς ἀθεμιστίας), τὸ δὲ λοιπὸν σῶμά τις ἔθαψεν ἐπὶ τῆς ἠιόνος καὶ τάφον ἤγειρεν εὐτελῆ [...].

Plutarchus is consistent with Appianus to a large extent (PLUT. *Pomp.* 76-80), only the name of the murderer is *Septimius* instead of *Sempronius*, and he names a second one, the centurio *Salvius*. Cf. PLUT. *Pomp.* 78-80: Ταῦτα κυρώσαντες ἐπ' Ἀχιλλᾷ ποιοῦνται τὴν πρᾶξιν. ὁ δὲ Σεπτίμιόν τινα πάλαι γεγονότα Πομπηίου ταξίαρχον παραλαβών, καὶ Σάλβιον ἕτερον ἑκατοντάρχην καὶ τρεῖς ἢ τέτταρας ὑπηρέτας, ἀνήχθη πρὸς τὴν Πομπηίου ναῦν. [...] ἐν τούτῳ δὲ πελαζούσης τῆς ἁλιάδος φθάσας ὁ Σεπτίμιος ἐξανέστη καὶ Ῥωμαϊστὶ τὸν Πομπήιον αὐτοκράτορα προσηγόρευσεν. [...] ἀσπασάμενος οὖν τὴν Κορνηλίαν προαποθρηνοῦσαν αὐτοῦ τὸ τέλος, καὶ δύο ἑκατοντάρχας προεμβῆναι κελεύσας καὶ τῶν ἀπελευθέρων ἕνα Φίλιππον καὶ θεράποντα Σκύθην ὄνομα, [...] ἐν τούτῳ δὲ τὸν Πομπήιον τῆς τοῦ Φιλίππου λαμβανομένου χειρός, ὅπως ῥᾷον ἐξαναστάιη, Σεπτίμιος ὄπισθεν τῷ ξίφει διελαύνει πρῶτος, εἶτα Σάλβιος μετ' ἐκεῖνον, εἶτα Ἀχιλλᾶς ἐσπάσαντο τὰς μαχαίρας. [...] τοῦ δὲ Πομπηίου τὴν μὲν κεφαλὴν ἀποτέμνουσι, τὸ δὲ ἄλλο σῶμα γυμνὸν ἐκβαλόντες ἀπὸ τῆς ἁλιάδος τοῖς δεομένοις τοιούτου θεάματος ἀπέλιπον. παρέμεινε δὲ αὐτῷ Φίλιππος, ἕως ἐγένοντο μεστοὶ τῆς ὄψεως· εἶτα περιλούσας τῇ θαλάσσῃ τὸ σῶμα καὶ χιτωνίῳ τινὶ τῶν ἑαυτοῦ περιστείλας, ἄλλο δὲ οὐδὲν ἔχων, ἀλλὰ περισκοπῶν τὸν αἰγιαλὸν εὗρε μικρᾶς ἁλιάδος λείψανα, παλαιὰ μέν, ἀρκοῦντα δὲ νεκρῷ γυμνῷ καὶ οὐδὲ ὅλῳ πυρκαϊὰν ἀναγκαίαν παρασχεῖν. [...] Τοῦτο Πομπηίου τέλος. οὐ πολλῷ δὲ ὕστερον Καῖσαρ ἐλθὼν εἰς Αἴγυπτον ἄγους τοσούτου καταπεπλησμένην τὸν μὲν προσφέροντα τὴν κεφαλὴν ὡς παλαμναῖον ἀπεστράφη, τὴν δὲ σφραγῖδα τοῦ Πομπηίου δεξάμενος ἐδάκρυσεν· ἦν δὲ γλυφὴ λέων ξιφήρης. Ἀχιλλᾶν δὲ καὶ Ποθεινὸν ἀπέσφαξεν· αὐτὸς δὲ ὁ βασιλεὺς μάχῃ λειφθεὶς περὶ τὸν ποταμὸν ἠφανίσθη. Θεόδοτον δὲ τὸν σοφιστὴν ἡ μὲν ἐκ Καίσαρος δίκη παρῆλθε· φυγὼν γὰρ Αἴγυπτον ἐπλανᾶτο ταπεινὰ πράττων καὶ μισούμενος· Βροῦτος δὲ Μάρκος, ὅτε Καίσαρα κτείνας ἐκράτησεν, ἐξευρὼν αὐτὸν ἐν Ἀσίᾳ καὶ πᾶσαν αἰκίαν αἰκισάμε-

νος ἀπέκτεινεν. τὰ δὲ λείψανα τοῦ Πομπηΐου Κορνηλία δεξαμένη κομισθέντα, περὶ τὸν Ἀλβανὸν ἔθηκεν.
PLUT. Caes. 48: εἰς δ' Ἀλεξάνδρειαν ἐπὶ Πομπηΐῳ τεθνηκότι καταχθείς, Θεόδοτον μὲν ἀπεστράφη, τὴν Πομπηΐου κεφαλὴν προσφέροντα, τὴν δὲ σφραγῖδα δεξάμενος τοῦ ἀνδρὸς κατεδάκρυσεν.
DIO CASS. HR 42.5, 7, 8. LIV. Per. 112: *Cn. Pompeius cum Aegyptum petisset, iussu Ptolemaei regis, pupilli sui, auctore Theodoto praeceptore, cuius magna aput regem auctoritas erat, et Pothino occisus est ab Archelao, cui id facinus erat delegatum, in navicula antequam in terram exiret. Cornelia uxor et Sex. Pompei<us> filius Cypron refugerunt. Caesar post tertium diem insecutus, cum ei Theodotus caput Pompei et anulum obtulisset, infensus est et inlacrimavit.*

571 Mk. 6:14-29: Καὶ ἤκουσεν ὁ βασιλεὺς Ἡρῴδης, φανερὸν γὰρ ἐγένετο τὸ ὄνομα αὐτοῦ, καὶ ἔλεγον ὅτι Ἰωάννης ὁ βαπτίζων ἐγήγερται ἐκ νεκρῶν καὶ διὰ τοῦτο ἐνεργοῦσιν αἱ δυνάμεις ἐν αὐτῷ. ἄλλοι δὲ ἔλεγον ὅτι Ἠλίας ἐστίν· ἄλλοι δὲ ἔλεγον ὅτι προφήτης ὡς εἷς τῶν προφητῶν. ἀκούσας δὲ ὁ Ἡρῴδης ἔλεγεν, Ὃν ἐγὼ ἀπεκεφάλισα Ἰωάννην, οὗτος ἠγέρθη. Αὐτὸς γὰρ ὁ Ἡρῴδης ἀποστείλας ἐκράτησεν τὸν Ἰωάννην καὶ ἔδησεν αὐτὸν ἐν φυλακῇ διὰ Ἡρῳδιάδα τὴν γυναῖκα Φιλίππου τοῦ ἀδελφοῦ αὐτοῦ, ὅτι αὐτὴν ἐγάμησεν· ἔλεγεν γὰρ ὁ Ἰωάννης τῷ Ἡρῴδῃ ὅτι Οὐκ ἔξεστίν σοι ἔχειν τὴν γυναῖκα τοῦ ἀδελφοῦ σου. ἡ δὲ Ἡρῳδιὰς ἐνεῖχεν αὐτῷ καὶ ἤθελεν αὐτὸν ἀποκτεῖναι, καὶ οὐκ ἠδύνατο· ὁ γὰρ Ἡρῴδης ἐφοβεῖτο τὸν Ἰωάννην, εἰδὼς αὐτὸν ἄνδρα δίκαιον καὶ ἅγιον, καὶ συνετήρει αὐτόν, καὶ ἀκούσας αὐτοῦ πολλὰ ἠπόρει, καὶ ἡδέως αὐτοῦ ἤκουεν. Καὶ γενομένης ἡμέρας εὐκαίρου ὅτε Ἡρῴδης τοῖς γενεσίοις αὐτοῦ δεῖπνον ἐποίησεν τοῖς μεγιστᾶσιν αὐτοῦ καὶ τοῖς χιλιάρχοις καὶ τοῖς πρώτοις τῆς Γαλιλαίας, καὶ εἰσελθούσης τῆς θυγατρὸς αὐτοῦ Ἡρῳδιάδος καὶ ὀρχησαμένης ἤρεσεν τῷ Ἡρῴδῃ καὶ τοῖς συνανακειμένοις εἶπεν ὁ βασιλεὺς τῷ κορασίῳ, Αἴτησόν με ὃ ἐὰν θέλῃς, καὶ δώσω σοι· καὶ ὤμοσεν αὐτῇ [πολλά], Ὅ τι ἐάν με αἰτήσῃς δώσω σοι ἕως ἡμίσους τῆς βασιλείας μου. καὶ ἐξελθοῦσα εἶπεν τῇ μητρὶ αὐτῆς, Τί αἰτήσωμαι; ἡ δὲ εἶπεν, Τὴν κεφαλὴν Ἰωάννου τοῦ βαπτίζοντος. καὶ εἰσελθοῦσα εὐθὺς μετὰ σπουδῆς πρὸς τὸν βασιλέα ᾐτήσατο λέγουσα, Θέλω ἵνα ἐξαυτῆς δῷς μοι ἐπὶ πίνακι τὴν κεφαλὴν Ἰωάννου τοῦ βαπτιστοῦ. καὶ περίλυπος γενόμενος ὁ βασιλεὺς διὰ τοὺς ὅρκους καὶ τοὺς ἀνακειμένους οὐκ ἠθέλησεν ἀθετῆσαι αὐτήν· καὶ εὐθὺς ἀποστείλας ὁ βασιλεὺς σπεκουλάτορα ἐπέταξεν ἐνέγκαι τὴν κεφαλὴν αὐτοῦ. καὶ ἀπελθὼν ἀπεκεφάλισεν αὐτὸν ἐν τῇ φυλακῇ καὶ ἤνεγκεν τὴν κεφαλὴν αὐτοῦ ἐπὶ πίνακι καὶ ἔδωκεν αὐτὴν τῷ κορασίῳ, καὶ τὸ κοράσιον ἔδωκεν αὐτὴν τῇ μητρὶ αὐτῆς. καὶ ἀκούσαντες οἱ μαθηταὶ αὐτοῦ ἦλθον καὶ ἦραν τὸ πτῶμα αὐτοῦ καὶ ἔθηκαν αὐτὸ ἐν μνημείῳ.

572 DIO CASS. HR 42.7.2-3: καὶ ἐκεῖνον μὲν οὐκέτι περιόντα κατέλαβε, τῇ δ' Ἀλεξανδρείᾳ αὐτῇ μετ' ὀλίγων πολὺ πρὸ τῶν ἄλλων, πρὶν τὸν Πτολεμαῖον ἐκ τοῦ Πηλουσίου ἐλθεῖν, προσπλεύσας, καὶ τοὺς Ἀλεξανδρέας θορυβουμένους ἐπὶ τῷ τοῦ Πομπηΐου θανάτῳ εὑρών, οὐκ ἐθάρσησεν εὐθὺς ἐς τὴν γῆν ἐκβῆναι, ἀλλ' ἀνορμισάμενος ἀνεῖχε μέχρις οὗ τήν τε κεφαλὴν καὶ τὸν δακτύλιον αὐτοῦ πεμφθέντα οἱ ὑπὸ τοῦ Πτολεμαίου εἶδεν. οὕτω δὴ ἐς μὲν τὴν ἤπειρον θαρσούντως προσέσχεν, ἀγανακτήσεως δὲ ἐπὶ τοῖς ῥαβδούχοις αὐτοῦ παρὰ τοῦ πλήθους γενομένης αὐτὸς μὲν ἀγαπητῶς ἐς τὰ βασίλεια προκατέφυγε, τῶν δὲ δὴ στρατιωτῶν τινες τὰ ὅπλα ἀφῃρέθησαν, καὶ διὰ τοῦθ' οἱ λοιποὶ ἀνωρμίσαντο αὖθις, ἕως πᾶσαι αἱ νῆες ἐπικατήχθησαν.

CAES. Civ. 3.106-7: *Caesar paucos dies in Asia moratus cum audisset Pompeium Cypri visum, coniectans eum Aegyptum iter habere propter necessitudines regni reliquasque eius loci opportunitates cum legione una, quam se ex Thessalia sequi iusserat, et altera, quam ex Achaia a Q. Fufio legato evocaverat, equitibusque DCCC et navibus longis Rhodiis x et Asiaticis paucis Alexandriam pervenit. in his erant legionariorum milia tria CC; reliqui vulneribus ex proeliis et labore ac magnitudine itineris confecti consequi non potuerant. sed Caesar confisus fama rerum gestarum infirmis auxiliis proficisci non dubitaverat aeque omnem sibi locum tutum fore existimans. Alexandriae de Pompei morte cognoscit atque ibi primum e navi egrediens clamorem militum audit, quos rex in oppido praesidii causa reliquerat, et concursum ad se fieri videt, quod fasces anteferrentur. in hoc omnis multitudo maiestatem regiam minui praedicabat. hoc sedato tumultu crebrae continuis diebus ex concursu multitudinis concitationes fiebant conpluresque milites in viis urbis omnibus partibus interficiebantur. Quibus rebus animadversis legiones sibi alias ex Asia adduci iussit, quas ex Pompeianis militibus confecerat. ipse enim necessario etesiis tenebatur, qui navigantibus Alexandria flant adversissimi venti.*

573 Mk. 8:10-13: Καὶ εὐθὺς ἐμβὰς εἰς τὸ πλοῖον μετὰ τῶν μαθητῶν αὐτοῦ ἦλθεν εἰς τὰ μέρη Δαλμανουθά. Καὶ ἐξῆλθον οἱ Φαρισαῖοι καὶ ἤρξαντο συζητεῖν αὐτῷ, ζητοῦντες παρ' αὐτοῦ σημεῖον ἀπὸ τοῦ οὐρανοῦ, πειράζοντες αὐτόν. καὶ ἀναστενάξας τῷ πνεύματι αὐτοῦ λέγει, Τί ἡ γενεὰ αὕτη ζητεῖ σημεῖον; ἀμὴν λέγω ὑμῖν, εἰ δοθήσεται τῇ γενεᾷ ταύτῃ σημεῖον. καὶ ἀφεὶς αὐτοὺς πάλιν ἐμβὰς ἀπῆλθεν εἰς τὸ πέραν.

574 CAES. *Civ.* 3.107-112: *interim controversias regum ad populum Romanum et ad se, quod esset consul, pertinere existimans, atque eo magis officio suo convenire, quod superiore consulatu cum patre Ptolomaeo ex lege et senatus consulto societas erat facta, ostendit sibi placere regem Ptolomaeum atque eius sororem Cleopatram exercitus, quos haberent, dimittere et de controversiis iure apud se potius quam inter se armis disceptare. Erat in procuratione regni propter aetatem pueri nutricius eius, eunuchus nomine Pothinus. is primum inter suos queri atque indignari coepit regem ad causam dicendam evocari; deinde adiutores quosdam consilii sui nanctus ex regis amicis exercitum a Pelusio clam Alexandriam evocavit atque eundem Achillam, cuius supra meminimus, omnibus copiis praefecit. hunc incitatum suis et regis inflatum pollicitationibus, quae fieri vellet, litteris nuntiisque edocuit. in testamento Ptolomaei patris heredes erant scripti ex duobus filiis maior et ex duabus <filiabus> ea quae aetate antecedebat. haec uti fierent, per omnes deos perque foedera quae Romae fecisset, eodem testamento Ptolomaeus populum Romanum obtestabatur. tabulae testamenti unae per legatos eius Romam erant adlatae, ut in aerario ponerentur—hae cum propter publicas occupationes poni non potuissent, apud Pompeium sunt depositae—alterae eodem exemplo relictae atque obsignatae Alexandriae proferebantur. De his rebus cum ageretur apud Caesarem, isque maxime vellet pro communi amico atque arbitro controversias regum componere, subito exercitus regius equitatusque omnis venire Alexandriam nuntiatur. [...] interim filia minor Ptolomaei regis vacuam possessionem regni sperans ad Achillam sese ex regia traiecit unaque bellum administrare coepit. sed celeriter est inter eos de principatu controversia orta, quae res apud milites largitiones auxit; magnis enim iacturis sibi quisque eorum animos conciliabat. haec dum apud hostes geruntur, Pothinus, [nutricius pueri et procurator regni, in parte Caesaris,] cum ad Achillam nuntios mitteret hortareturque, ne negotio desisteret neve animo deficeret, indicatis deprehensisque internuntiis a Caesare est interfectus. haec initia belli Alexandrini fuerunt.*

PLUT. *Caes.* 48-9: Τὸν δ' αὐτόθι πόλεμον οἱ μὲν οὐκ ἀναγκαῖον, ἀλλ' ἔρωτι Κλεοπάτρας ἄδοξον αὐτῷ καὶ κινδυνώδη γενέσθαι λέγουσιν, οἱ δὲ τοὺς βασιλικοὺς αἰτιῶνται, καὶ μάλιστα τὸν εὐνοῦχον Ποθεινόν, ὃς πλεῖστον δυνάμενος, καὶ Πομπήϊον μὲν ἀνῃρηκὼς ἔναγχος, ἐκβεβληκὼς δὲ Κλεοπάτραν, κρύφα μὲν ἐπεβούλευε τῷ Καίσαρι—καὶ διὰ τοῦτό φασιν αὐτὸν ἀρξάμενον ἔκτοτε διανυκτερεύειν ἐν τοῖς πότοις ἕνεκα φυλακῆς τοῦ σώματος—φανερῶς δ' οὐκ ἦν ἀνεκτός, ἐπίφθονα πολλὰ καὶ πρὸς ὕβριν εἰς τὸν Καίσαρα λέγων καὶ πράττων. τοὺς μὲν γὰρ στρατιώτας τὸν κάκιστον μετρουμένους καὶ παλαιότατον σῖτον ἐκέλευσεν ἀνέχεσθαι καὶ στέργειν ἐσθίοντας τὰ ἀλλότρια, πρὸς δὲ τὰ δεῖπνα σκεύεσιν ἐχρῆτο ξυλίνοις καὶ κεραμεοῖς, ὡς τὰ χρυσᾶ καὶ ἀργυρᾶ πάντα Καίσαρος ἔχοντος εἴς τι χρέος. ὤφειλε γὰρ ὁ τοῦ βασιλεύοντος τότε πατὴρ Καίσαρι χιλίας ἑπτακοσίας πεντήκοντα μυριάδας, ὧν τὰς μὲν ἄλλας ἀνῆκε τοῖς παισὶν αὐτοῦ πρότερον ὁ Καῖσαρ, τὰς δὲ χιλίας ἠξίου τότε λαβὼν διαθρέψαι τὸ στράτευμα. τοῦ δὲ Ποθεινοῦ νῦν μὲν αὐτὸν ἀπιέναι καὶ τῶν μεγάλων ἔχεσθαι πραγμάτων κελεύοντος, ὕστερον δὲ κομιεῖσθαι μετὰ χάριτος, εἰπὼν ὡς Αἰγυπτίων ἐλάχιστα δέοιτο συμβούλων, κρύφα τὴν Κλεοπάτραν ἀπὸ τῆς χώρας μετεπέμπετο. Κἀκείνη παραλαβοῦσα τῶν φίλων Ἀπολλόδωρον τὸν Σικελιώτην μόνον, εἰς ἀκάτιον μικρὸν ἐμβᾶσα, τοῖς μὲν βασιλείοις προσέσχεν ἤδη συσκοτάζοντος· ἀπόρου δὲ τοῦ λαθεῖν ὄντος ἄλλως, ἡ μὲν εἰς στρωματόδεσμον ἐνδῦσα προτείνει μακρὰν ἑαυτήν, ὁ δ' Ἀπολλόδωρος ἱμάντι συνδήσας τὸν στρωματόδεσμον εἰσκομίζει διὰ θυρῶν πρὸς τὸν Καίσαρα. καὶ τούτῳ τε πρώτῳ λέγεται τῷ τεχνήματι τῆς Κλεοπάτρας ἁλῶναι λαμυρᾶς φανείσης, καὶ τῆς ἄλλης ὁμιλίας καὶ χάριτος ἥττων γενόμενος, διαλλάξαι πρὸς τὸν ἀδελφὸν ὡς συμβασιλεύσουσαν. ἔπειτα δ' ἐπὶ ταῖς διαλλαγαῖς ἑστιωμένων ἁπάντων, οἰκέτης Καίσαρος κουρεύς, διὰ δειλίαν ᾗ πάντας ἀνθρώπους ὑπερέβαλεν οὐδὲν ἐῶν ἀνεξέταστον, ἀλλ' ὠτακουστῶν καὶ πολυπραγμονῶν, συνῆκεν ἐπιβουλὴν Καίσαρι πραττομένην ὑπ' Ἀχιλλᾶ τοῦ στρατηγοῦ καὶ Ποθεινοῦ τοῦ εὐνούχου. φωράσας δ' ὁ Καῖσαρ, φρουρὰν μὲν περιέστησε τῷ ἀνδρῶνι, τὸν δὲ Ποθεινὸν ἀνεῖλεν· ὁ δ' Ἀχιλλᾶς φυγὼν εἰς τὸ στρατόπεδον περιίστησιν αὐτῷ βαρὺν καὶ δυσμεταχείριστον πόλεμον, ὀλιγοστῷ τοσαύτην ἀμυνομένῳ πόλιν καὶ δύναμιν. [...] τέλος δὲ τοῦ βασιλέως πρὸς τοὺς πολεμίους ἀποχωρήσαντος, ἐπελθὼν καὶ συνάψας μάχην ἐνίκησε, πολλῶν πεσόντων αὐτοῦ τε τοῦ βασιλέως ἀφανοῦς γενομένου. καταλιπὼν δὲ τὴν Κλεοπάτραν βασιλεύουσαν Αἰγύπτου καὶ μικρὸν ὕστερον ἐξ αὐτοῦ τεκοῦσαν υἱόν, ὃν Ἀλεξανδρεῖς Καισαρίωνα προσηγόρευον, ὥρμησεν ἐπὶ Συρίας.

VELL. 2.53: *Pompeius profugiens cum duobus Lentulis consularibus Sextoque filio et Fauonio praetorio quos comites ei fortuna adgregauerat, aliis, ut Parthos, aliis, ut Africam peteret, in qua fidelissimum partium suarum haberet regem Iubam, suadentibus, Aegyptum petere proposuit memor beneficiorum quae in patrem eius Ptolemaei, qui tum puero quam iuueni propior regnabat Alexandriae, contulerat. Sed quis in aduersis beneficiorum seruat memoriam? Aut quis ullam calamitosis deberi putat gratiam? Aut quando fortuna non mutat fidem? Missi itaque ab rege qui uenientem Cn. Pompeium—is iam a Mytilenis Corneliam uxorem receptam in nauem fugae comitem habere coeperat—consilio Theodoti et Achillae exciperent hortarenturque ut ex oneraria in eam nauem quae obuiam processerat transcenderet: quod cum fecisset, princeps Romani nominis imperio arbitrioque Aegyptii mancipii, C. Caesare P. Seruilio consulibus iugulatus est. Hic post tres consulatus et totidem triumphos domitumque terrarum orbem sanctissimi atque praestantissimi uiri, in id euecti super quod ascendi non potest, duodesexagesimum annum agentis, pridie natalem ipsius, uitae fuit exitus, in tantum in illo uiro a se discordante fortuna ut, cui modo ad uictoriam terra defuerat, deesset ad sepulturam. [...]* VELL. 2.54: *Non fuit maior in Caesarem quam in Pompeium fuerat regis eorumque, quorum is auctoritate regebatur, fides. Quippe cum uenientem eum temptassent insidiis ac deinde bello lacessere auderent, utrique summorum imperatorum, alteri superstiti, meritas poenas luere suppliciis.*

575 Mk.7:24-30: Ἐκεῖθεν δὲ ἀναστὰς ἀπῆλθεν εἰς τὰ ὅρια Τύρου. καὶ εἰσελθὼν εἰς οἰκίαν οὐδένα ἤθελεν γνῶναι, καὶ οὐκ ἠδυνήθη λαθεῖν· ἀλλ' εὐθὺς ἀκούσασα γυνὴ περὶ αὐτοῦ, ἧς εἶχεν τὸ θυγάτριον αὐτῆς πνεῦμα ἀκάθαρτον, ἐλθοῦσα προσέπεσεν πρὸς τοὺς πόδας αὐτοῦ· ἡ δὲ γυνὴ ἦν Ἑλληνίς, Συροφοινίκισσα τῷ γένει· καὶ ἠρώτα αὐτὸν ἵνα τὸ δαιμόνιον ἐκβάλῃ ἐκ τῆς θυγατρὸς αὐτῆς. καὶ ἔλεγεν αὐτῇ, Ἄφες πρῶτον χορτασθῆναι τὰ τέκνα, οὐ γάρ ἐστιν καλὸν λαβεῖν τὸν ἄρτον τῶν τέκνων καὶ τοῖς κυναρίοις βαλεῖν. ἡ δὲ ἀπεκρίθη καὶ λέγει αὐτῷ, Κύριε, καὶ τὰ κυνάρια ὑποκάτω τῆς τραπέζης ἐσθίουσιν ἀπὸ τῶν ψιχίων τῶν παιδίων. καὶ εἶπεν αὐτῇ, Διὰ τοῦτον τὸν λόγον ὕπαγε, ἐξελήλυθεν ἐκ τῆς θυγατρός σου τὸ δαιμόνιον. καὶ ἀπελθοῦσα εἰς τὸν οἶκον αὐτῆς εὗρεν τὸ παιδίον βεβλημένον ἐπὶ τὴν κλίνην καὶ τὸ δαιμόνιον ἐξεληλυθός.

576 Cf. *Bellum Alexandrinum*, incipit: «*Bello Alexandrino conflato, Caesar Rhodo, atque ex Suria Ciliciaque omnem classem accersit, ex Creta sagittarios, equites Nabataeorum Malcho evocat: tormenta undique conquiri, et frumentum mitti, auxiliaque adduci iubet.*» Indeed, Mithridates Pergamenus who was hurrying to his aid from Cilicia was supposed to come via Syria and he got further reinforcement there from the Nabatean Malchus who already supported Cleopatra. In the Alexandrian war Mithridates was able to intervene decisively in favor of Caesar. Caesar in turn goes from Egypt to Pontus, towards Pharnaces, again via Syria: cf. also *Bell. Alex.* 65: «*Quum in Suriam Caesar ex Aegypto venisset...*».
That *Tyros* can stand for *Syria* is substantiated by the variants of *Syrophoini(ki)ssa* which is sometimes also called *Tyrophoinissa* in other manuscripts. Theoretically the 'region of Tyrus', *ta (h)oria Tyrou*, could also be the lake *Mareotis*. Alexandria was situated between this lake and the open sea. Some Gospel manuscripts write in fact *methoria Tyrou*. But *methoria* could resolve into to *me ta horia*—and we would be again at the *cohortes*.

577 Mk. 8:14-21: Καὶ ἐπελάθοντο λαβεῖν ἄρτους καὶ εἰ μὴ ἕνα ἄρτον οὐκ εἶχον μεθ' ἑαυτῶν ἐν τῷ πλοίῳ. καὶ διεστέλλετο αὐτοῖς λέγων, Ὁρᾶτε, βλέπετε ἀπὸ τῆς ζύμης τῶν Φαρισαίων καὶ τῆς ζύμης Ἡρῴδου. καὶ διελογίζοντο πρὸς ἀλλήλους ὅτι Ἄρτους οὐκ ἔχουσιν. καὶ γνοὺς λέγει αὐτοῖς, Τί διαλογίζεσθε ὅτι ἄρτους οὐκ ἔχετε; οὔπω νοεῖτε οὐδὲ συνίετε; πεπωρωμένην ἔχετε τὴν καρδίαν ὑμῶν; ὀφθαλμοὺς ἔχοντες οὐ βλέπετε καὶ ὦτα ἔχοντες οὐκ ἀκούετε; καὶ οὐ μνημονεύετε, ὅτε τοὺς πέντε ἄρτους ἔκλασα εἰς τοὺς πεντακισχιλίους, πόσους κοφίνους κλασμάτων πλήρεις ἤρατε; λέγουσιν αὐτῷ, Δώδεκα. Ὅτε τοὺς ἑπτὰ εἰς τοὺς τετρακισχιλίους, πόσων σπυρίδων πληρώματα κλασμάτων ἤρατε; καὶ λέγουσιν [αὐτῷ], Ἑπτά. καὶ ἔλεγεν αὐτοῖς, Οὔπω συνίετε;

578 PLUT. Caes. 49-50: ὥρμησεν ἐπὶ Συρίας. Κἀκεῖθεν ἐπιὼν τὴν Ἀσίαν, ἐπυνθάνετο Δομίτιον μὲν ὑπὸ Φαρνάκου τοῦ Μιθριδάτου παιδὸς ἡττημένον ἐκ Πόντου πεφευγέναι σὺν ὀλίγοις, Φαρνάκην δὲ τῇ νίκῃ χρώμενον ἀπλήστως, καὶ Βιθυνίαν ἔχοντα καὶ Καππαδοκίαν, Ἀρμενίας ἐφίεσθαι τῆς μικρᾶς καλουμένης, καὶ πάντας ἀνιστάναι τοὺς ταύτῃ βασιλεῖς καὶ τετράρχας. εὐθὺς οὖν ἐπὶ τὸν ἄνδρα τρισὶν ἤλαυνε τάγμασι, καὶ περὶ πόλιν Ζῆλαν μάχην μεγάλην συνάψας αὐτὸν μὲν ἐξέβαλε τοῦ Πόντου φεύγοντα, τὴν δὲ στρατιὰν ἄρδην ἀνεῖλε· καὶ τῆς μάχης ταύτης τὴν ὀξύτητα καὶ τὸ τάχος ἀναγγέλλων εἰς Ῥώμην πρός τινα τῶν φίλων Μάτιον ἔγραψε τρεῖς λέξεις· "ἦλθον, εἶδον, ἐνίκησα." Ῥωμαϊστὶ δ' αἱ λέξεις, εἰς ὅμοιον ἀπολήγουσαι σχῆμα ῥήματος, οὐκ ἀπίθανον τὴν βραχυλογίαν ἔχουσιν.

APP. BC 2.91.381-4: Τοσάδε μὲν δὴ Καῖσαρ ἐργασάμενος ἐν Ἀλεξανδρείᾳ διὰ Συρίας ἐπὶ Φαρνάκην ἠπείγετο. ὁ δὲ ἤδη μὲν εἴργαστο πολλὰ καὶ περιεσπάκει τινὰ Ῥωμαίων χωρία καὶ Δομιτίῳ Καίσαρος στρατηγῷ συνενεχθεὶς ἐς μάχην ἐνενικήκει πάνυ λαμπρῶς, καὶ τῷδε μάλιστα ἐπαρθεὶς Ἀμισὸν πόλιν ἐν τῷ Πόντῳ ῥωμαΐζουσαν ἐξηνδραπόδιστο καὶ τοὺς παῖδας αὐτῶν τομίας ἐπεποίητο πάντας· προσιόντος δὲ τοῦ Καίσαρος ἐταράσσετο καὶ μετεγίγνωσκε καὶ ἀπὸ σταδίων διακοσίων γενομένῳ πρέσβεις ἔπεμπεν ὑπὲρ εἰρήνης, στέφανόν τε χρύσειον αὐτῷ φέροντας καὶ ἐς γάμον ὑπ' ἀνοίας ἐγγυῶντας Καίσαρι τὴν Φαρνάκους θυγατέρα. ὁ δ' αἰσθόμενος ὧν φέρουσι, προῆλθε μετὰ τοῦ στρατοῦ καὶ ἐς τὸ πρόσθεν ἐβάδιζε λεσχηνεύων τοῖς πρέσβεσι, μέχρι προσπελάσας τῷ χάρακι τοῦ Φαρνάκους καὶ τοσόνδε εἰπών· "οὐ γὰρ αὐτίκα δώσει δίκην ὁ πατροκτόνος;" ἐπὶ τὸν ἵππον ἀνεπήδησε καὶ εὐθὺς ἐκ πρώτης βοῆς τρέπεταί τε τὸν Φαρνάκην καὶ πολλοὺς ἔκτεινε, σὺν χιλίοις που μάλιστα ὧν ἱππεῦσιν τοῖς πρώτοις αὐτῷ συνδραμοῦσιν· ὅτε καί φασιν αὐτὸν εἰπεῖν· "ὦ μακάριε Πομπήιε, τοιούτοις ἄρα κατὰ Μιθριδάτην τὸν τοῦδε πατέρα πολεμῶν ἀνδράσι μέγας τε ἐνομίσθης καὶ μέγας ἐπεκλήθης." ἐς δὲ Ῥώμην περὶ τῆσδε τῆς μάχης ἐπέστειλεν· "ἐγὼ δὲ ἦλθον, εἶδον, ἐνίκησα." Μετὰ δὲ τοῦτο Φαρνάκης μὲν ἀγαπῶν ἐς τὴν ἀρχὴν Βοσπόρου, τὴν δεδομένην οἱ παρὰ Πομπηίου, συνέφυγεν [...].
DIO CASS. HR 42.45-8.

SUET. *Jul.* 35: *ab Alexandria in Syriam et inde Pontum transiit urgentibus de Pharnace nuntiis, quem Mithridatis Magni filium ac tunc occasione temporum bellantem iamque multiplici successu praeferocem, intra quintum quam adfuerat diem, quattuor quibus in conspectum uenit horis, una profligauit acie; crebro commemorans Pompei felicitatem, cui praecipua militiae laus de tam inbelli genere hostium contigisset.* SUET. *Jul.* 37: *Pontico triumpho inter pompae fercula trium uerborum praetulit titulum «veni vidi vici» non acta belli significantem sicut ceteris, sed celeriter confecti notam.*

VELL. 2.55: *[...] nam uictus ab eo Pharnaces uix quidquam gloriae eius adstruxit [...].*

579 Mk. 7:31-37: Καὶ πάλιν ἐξελθὼν ἐκ τῶν ὁρίων Τύρου ἦλθεν διὰ Σιδῶνος εἰς τὴν θάλασσαν τῆς Γαλιλαίας ἀνὰ μέσον τῶν ὁρίων Δεκαπόλεως. καὶ φέρουσιν αὐτῷ κωφὸν καὶ μογιλάλον καὶ παρακαλοῦσιν αὐτὸν ἵνα ἐπιθῇ αὐτῷ τὴν χεῖρα. καὶ ἀπολαβόμενος αὐτὸν ἀπὸ τοῦ ὄχλου κατ' ἰδίαν ἔβαλεν τοὺς δακτύλους αὐτοῦ εἰς τὰ ὦτα αὐτοῦ καὶ πτύσας ἥψατο τῆς γλώσσης αὐτοῦ, καὶ ἀναβλέψας εἰς τὸν οὐρανὸν ἐστέναξεν καὶ λέγει αὐτῷ, Εφφαθα, ὅ ἐστιν, Διανοίχθητι. καὶ [εὐθέως] ἠνοίγησαν αὐτοῦ αἱ ἀκοαί, καὶ ἐλύθη ὁ δεσμὸς τῆς γλώσσης αὐτοῦ καὶ ἐλάλει ὀρθῶς. καὶ διεστείλατο αὐτοῖς ἵνα μηδενὶ λέγωσιν· ὅσον δὲ αὐτοῖς διεστέλλετο, αὐτοὶ μᾶλλον περισσότερον ἐκήρυσσον. καὶ ὑπερπερισσῶς ἐξεπλήσσοντο λέγοντες, Καλῶς πάντα πεποίηκεν, καὶ τοὺς κωφοὺς ποιεῖ ἀκούειν καὶ [τοὺς] ἀλάλους λαλεῖν.

580 Mark's choice of words—'through the midst of the coasts of Decapolis'—leaves open the possibility that this 'midst', *meson*, stands for a more original *meros*, 'part', (cf. Mt. 2:22: *ta merê tês Galilaias*, 'the region of Galilee', actually 'the parts of Galilee'). These 'parts' could be something different than the 'coasts of Decapolis, the region', namely 'parts of legions', the 'units', the 'troops'. And in both cases: Here in Mark it could have been the units that Caesar received from Deiotaros, and in Matthew it could have been the troops that Caesar concentrated in the Cisalpina before the outbreak of the civil war. This strengthens the conjecture that we have to sense a *cohortium* behind the *tôn horiôn*.

581 SUET. *Jul.* 24: *Qua fiducia ad legiones, quas a re publica acceperat, alias priuato sumptu addidit, unam etiam ex Transalpinis conscriptam, uocabulo quoque Gallico (Alauda enim appellabatur), quam disciplina cultuque Romano institutam et ornatam postea uniuersam ciuitate donauit.*

TAC. *Ann.* 11.24: *tunc solida domi quies et adversus externa floruimus, cum Transpadani in civitatem recepti, cum specie deductarum per orbem terrae legionum additis provincialium validissimis fesso imperio subventum est.*

582 SUET. *Jul.* 41: *Senatum suppleuit [...].* SUET. *Jul.* 80: *Peregrinis in senatum allectis libellus propositus est: «Bonum factum! Ne quis senatori nouo curiam monstrare uelit», et illa vulgo canebantur:*
«*Gallos Caesar in triumphum ducit, idem in curiam;*
Galli bracas deposuerunt, latum clauum sumpserunt.»
SUET. *Jul.* 76: *Eadem licentia spreto patrio more magistratus in pluris annos ordinauit, decem praetoris uiris consularia ornamenta tribuit, ciuitate donatos et quosdam e semibarbaris Gallorum recepit in curiam.*

583 SUET. *Jul.* 58: *at idem obsessione castrorum in Germania nuntiata per stationes hostium Gallico habitu penetrauit ad suos.*

584 PLUT. *Caes.* 26: ἔδοξε δὲ κατ' ἀρχάς τι καὶ σφαλῆναι, καὶ δεικνύουσιν 'Αρβέρνοι ξιφίδιον πρὸς ἱερῷ κρεμάμενον, ὡς δὴ Καίσαρος λάφυρον· ὃ θεασάμενος αὐτὸς ὕστερον ἐμειδίασε, καὶ τῶν φίλων καθελεῖν κελευόντων οὐκ εἴασεν, ἱερὸν ἡγούμενος.

585 Mk. 8:26: καὶ ἀπέστειλεν αὐτὸν εἰς οἶκον αὐτοῦ λέγων, Μηδὲ εἰς τὴν κώμην εἰσέλθῃς.

586 Plut. Caes. 51: καὶ κακῶς ἤκουσεν, ὅτι τῶν στρατιωτῶν στασιασάντων καὶ δύο στρατηγικοὺς ἄνδρας ἀνελόντων, Κοσκώνιον καὶ Γάλβαν, ἐπετίμησε μὲν αὐτοῖς τοσοῦτον ὅσον ἀντὶ στρατιωτῶν πολίτας προσαγορεῦσαι, χιλίας δὲ διένειμεν ἑκάστῳ δραχμὰς καὶ χώραν τῆς Ἰταλίας ἀπεκλήρωσε πολλήν.
App. BC 2.92.386-94.396: πυθόμενος δ' ἐν Ῥώμῃ στάσιν εἶναι καὶ Ἀντώνιον τὸν ἵππαρχον αὐτοῦ τὴν ἀγορὰν στρατιᾷ φυλάσσειν, πάντα μεθεὶς ἐς Ῥώμην ἠπείγετο. ὡς δ' ἦλθεν, ἡ μὲν στάσις ἡ πολιτικὴ κατεπαύετο, ἑτέρα δ' ἐπ' αὐτὸν ἀνίστατο τοῦ στρατοῦ, ὡς οὔτε τὰ ἐπηγγελμένα σφίσιν ἐπὶ τῷ κατὰ Φάρσαλον ἔργῳ λαβόντες οὔτε ἐννόμως ἔτι βραδύνοντες ἐν τῇ στρατείᾳ· ἀφεθῆναί τε πάντες ἐπὶ τὰ αὑτῶν ἠξίουν. ὁ δ' ἐπηγγέλλετο μὲν αὐτοῖς ἀοριστά τινα ἐν Φαρσάλῳ, καὶ ἕτερα ἀόριστα, ὅταν ὁ ἐν Λιβύῃ πόλεμος ἐκτελεσθῇ· τότε δ' ἔπεμπεν ἄλλας ὁρίζων ἑκάστῳ χιλίας δραχμάς. οἱ δὲ αὐτὸν οὐχ ὑπισχνεῖσθαι μᾶλλον ἢ αὐτίκα διδόναι πάντα ἐκέλευον· καὶ περὶ τῶνδε Σαλούστιον Κρίσπον πεμφθέντα πρὸς αὐτοὺς ὀλίγου καὶ διέφθειραν, εἰ μὴ διέφυγε. πυθόμενος δ' ὁ Καῖσαρ τέλος μὲν ἄλλο στρατιωτῶν, οἳ τὴν πόλιν ἐξ Ἀντωνίου παρεφύλασσον, περιέστησε τῇ οἰκίᾳ καὶ ταῖς τῆς πόλεως ἐξόδοις, δείσας περὶ ἁρπαγῆς· αὐτὸς δέ, πάντων δεδιότων καὶ παραινούντων αὐτῷ τὴν ὁρμὴν τοῦ στρατοῦ φυλάξασθαι, μάλα θρασέως αὐτοῖς ἔτι στασιάζουσιν ἐς τὸ Ἄρειον πεδίον ἐπῆλθεν οὐ προμηνύσας καὶ ἐπὶ βήματος ὤφθη. Οἱ δὲ σὺν θορύβῳ τε ἄνοπλοι συνέτρεχον καί, ὡς ἔθος, ἄφνω φανέντα σφίσιν ἠσπάζοντο αὐτοκράτορα. κελεύσαντος δ' ὅ τι θέλοιεν εἰπεῖν, περὶ μὲν τῶν δωρεῶν ἐς ὄψιν εἰπεῖν αὐτοῦ παρόντος οὐδὲ ἐτόλμησαν ὑπὸ τῆς αὐτῆς ἐκπλήξεως, ὡς δὲ μετριώτερον, ἀφεθῆναι τῆς στρατείας ἀνεβόησαν, ἐλπίσαντες στρατοῦ δεόμενον ἐς τοὺς ὑπολοίπους πολέμους αὐτὸν ἐρεῖν τι καὶ περὶ τῶν δωρεῶν. ὁ δὲ παρὰ τὴν ἁπάντων δόξαν οὐδὲ μελλήσας ἀπεκρίνατο· "ἀφίημι." καταπλαγέντων δ' αὐτῶν ἔτι μᾶλλον καὶ σιωπῆς βαθυτάτης γενομένης ἐπεῖπε· "καὶ δώσω γε ὑμῖν τὰ ἐπηγγελμένα ἅπαντα, ὅταν θριαμβεύσω μεθ' ἑτέρων." ἀδοκήτου δ' αὐτοῖς ἅμα καὶ τοῦδε καὶ φιλανθρώπου φανέντος, αἰδὼς αὐτίκα πᾶσιν ἐνέπιπτεν καὶ λογισμὸς μετὰ ζήλου, εἰ δόξουσι μὲν αὐτοὶ καταλιπεῖν σφῶν τὸν αὐτοκράτορα ἐν μέσοις τοσοῖσδε πολεμίοις, θριαμβεύσουσι δ' ἀνθ' αὑτῶν ἕτεροι καὶ σφεῖς τῶν ἐν Λιβύῃ κερδῶν ἐκπεσοῦνται, μεγάλων ἔσεσθαι νομιζομένων, ἐχθροί τε ὁμοίως αὐτοῦ τε Καίσαρος ἔσονται καὶ τῶν πολεμίων. δείσαντες οὖν ἔτι μᾶλλον ἡσύχαζον ἐξ ἀπορίας, ἐλπίζοντες ἐνδώσειν τι καὶ τὸν Καίσαρα καὶ μεταγνώσεσθαι διὰ τὴν ἐν χερσὶ χρείαν. ὁ δ' ἀνθησύχαζε καὶ τῶν φίλων αὐτὸν παρακαλούντων ἐπιφθέγξασθαί τι πρὸς αὐτοὺς ἄλλο καὶ μὴ βραχεῖ καὶ αὐστηρῷ λόγῳ πολλὰ συνεστρατευμένους ἐγκαταλιπεῖν, ἀρχόμενος λέγειν πολίτας ἀντὶ στρατιωτῶν προσεῖπεν· ὅπερ ἐστὶ σύμβολον ἀφειμένων τῆς στρατείας καὶ ἰδιωτευόντων. Οἱ δ' οὐκ ἐνεγκόντες ἔτι ἀνέκραγον μετανοεῖν καὶ παρεκάλουν αὐτῷ συστρατεύεσθαι. ἀποστρεφομένου τε τοῦ Καίσαρος καὶ ἀπιόντος ἀπὸ τοῦ βήματος, οἱ δὲ σὺν ἐπείξει πλέονι βοῶντες ἐνέκειντο παραμεῖναί τε αὐτὸν καὶ κολάζειν σφῶν τοὺς ἁμαρτόντας. ὁ δ' ἔτι μέν τι διέτριψεν, οὔτε ἀπιὼν οὔτε ἐπανιών, ὑποκρινόμενος ἀπορεῖν· ἐπανελθὼν δ' ὅμως ἔφη κολάσειν μὲν αὐτῶν οὐδένα, ἄχθεσθαι δ', ὅτι καὶ τὸ δέκατον τέλος, ὃ προετίμησεν αἰεί, τοιαῦτα θορυβεῖ. "καὶ τόδε," ἔφη, "μόνον ἀφίημι τῆς στρατείας· δώσω δὲ καὶ τῷδε ὅμως τὰ ὑπεσχημένα ἅπαντα, ἐπανελθὼν ἐκ Λιβύης. δώσω δὲ καὶ γῆν ἅπασιν ἐκτελεσθέντων τῶν πολέμων, οὐ καθάπερ Σύλλας, ἀφαιρούμενος ἑτέρων ἣν ἔχουσι καὶ τοῖς ἀφαιρεθεῖσι τοὺς λαβόντας συνοικίζων καὶ ποιῶν ἀλλήλοις ἐς αἰεὶ πολεμίους, ἀλλὰ τὴν τοῦ δήμου γῆν ἐπινέμων καὶ τὴν ἐμαυτοῦ, καὶ τὰ δέοντα προσωνούμενος." κρότου δὲ καὶ εὐφημίας παρὰ πάντων γενομένης, τὸ δέκατον ὑπερήλγει τέλος, ἐς μόνον αὐτὸ τοῦ Καίσαρος ἀδιαλλάκτου φανέντος· καὶ σφᾶς αὐτὸν ἠξίουν διακληρῶσαί τε καὶ τὸ μέρος θανάτῳ ζημιῶσαι. ὁ δὲ οὐδεὶν αὐτοὺς ὑπερεθίζειν ἔτι δεόμενος ἀκριβῶς μετανοοῦντας, συνηλλάσσετο ἅπασι καὶ εὐθὺς ἐπὶ τὸν ἐν Λιβύῃ πόλεμον ἐξῄει.
Dio Cass. HR 42.52-5.
Suet. Jul. 67: nec milites eos pro contione, sed blandiore nomine commilitones appellabat [...].

SUET. Jul. 70: *decimanos autem Romae cum ingentibus minis summoque etiam urbis periculo missionem et praemia flagitantes, ardente tunc in Africa bello, neque adire cunctatus est, quanquam deterrentibus amicis, neque dimittere; sed una uoce, qua 'Quirites' eos pro militibus appellarat, tam facile circumegit et flexit, ut ei milites esse confestim responderint et quamuis recusantem ultro in Africam sint secuti; ac sic quoque seditiosissimum quemque et praedae et agri destinati tertia parte multauit.*

587 Mk. 12:1-12: Καὶ ἤρξατο αὐτοῖς ἐν παραβολαῖς λαλεῖν, Ἀμπελῶνα ἄνθρωπος ἐφύτευσεν καὶ περιέθηκεν φραγμὸν καὶ ὤρυξεν ὑπολήνιον καὶ ᾠκοδόμησεν πύργον καὶ ἐξέδετο αὐτὸν γεωργοῖς καὶ ἀπεδήμησεν. καὶ ἀπέστειλεν πρὸς τοὺς γεωργοὺς τῷ καιρῷ δοῦλον ἵνα παρὰ τῶν γεωργῶν λάβῃ ἀπὸ τῶν καρπῶν τοῦ ἀμπελῶνος· καὶ λαβόντες αὐτὸν ἔδειραν καὶ ἀπέστειλαν κενόν. καὶ πάλιν ἀπέστειλεν πρὸς αὐτοὺς ἄλλον δοῦλον· κἀκεῖνον ἐκεφαλίωσαν καὶ ἠτίμασαν. καὶ ἄλλον ἀπέστειλεν· κἀκεῖνον ἀπέκτειναν, καὶ πολλοὺς ἄλλους, οὓς μὲν δέροντες, οὓς δὲ ἀποκτέννοντες. ἔτι ἕνα εἶχεν υἱὸν ἀγαπητόν· ἀπέστειλεν αὐτὸν ἔσχατον πρὸς αὐτοὺς λέγων ὅτι Ἐντραπήσονται τὸν υἱόν μου. ἐκεῖνοι δὲ οἱ γεωργοὶ πρὸς ἑαυτοὺς εἶπαν ὅτι Οὗτός ἐστιν ὁ κληρονόμος· δεῦτε ἀποκτείνωμεν αὐτόν, καὶ ἡμῶν ἔσται ἡ κληρονομία. καὶ λαβόντες ἀπέκτειναν αὐτόν καὶ ἐξέβαλον αὐτὸν ἔξω τοῦ ἀμπελῶνος. τί [οὖν] ποιήσει ὁ κύριος τοῦ ἀμπελῶνος; ἐλεύσεται καὶ ἀπολέσει τοὺς γεωργούς, καὶ δώσει τὸν ἀμπελῶνα ἄλλοις. οὐδὲ τὴν γραφὴν ταύτην ἀνέγνωτε, / Λίθον ὃν ἀπεδοκίμασαν οἱ οἰκοδομοῦντες, / οὗτος ἐγενήθη εἰς κεφαλὴν γωνίας· / παρὰ κυρίου ἐγένετο αὕτη / καὶ ἔστιν θαυμαστὴ ἐν ὀφθαλμοῖς ἡμῶν; / Καὶ ἐζήτουν αὐτὸν κρατῆσαι, καὶ ἐφοβήθησαν τὸν ὄχλον, ἔγνωσαν γὰρ ὅτι πρὸς αὐτοὺς τὴν παραβολὴν εἶπεν. καὶ ἀφέντες αὐτὸν ἀπῆλθον.

588 SUET. Jul. 42: *de pecuniis mutuis disiecta nouarum tabularum expectatione, quae crebro mouebatur, decreuit tandem, ut debitores creditoribus satis facerent per aestimationem possessionum, quanti quasque ante ciuile bellum comparassent, deducto summae aeris alieni, si quid usurae nomine numeratum aut perscriptum fuisset; qua condicione quarta pars fere crediti deperibat.*

DIO CASS. HR 42.50.4: ὅθενπερ καὶ χρεῶν ἀποκοπὰς ἀξιοῦντος τοῦ πλήθους γενέσθαι οὐκ ἐποίησεν, εἰπὼν ὅτι καὶ αὐτὸς πολλὰ ὀφείλω· DIO CASS. HR 42.51.1-3: τοῖς τε γὰρ πολλοῖς ἐχαρίσατο τόν τε τόκον τὸν ἐποφειλόμενόν σφισιν ἐξ οὗ πρὸς τὸν Πομπήιον ἐξεπολεμώθη πάντα, καὶ τὸ ἐνοίκιον ὅσον ἐς πεντακοσίας δραχμὰς ἦν ἐνιαυτοῦ ἑνὸς ἀφείς, καὶ προσέτι καὶ τὰς τιμήσεις τῶν κτημάτων, ἐν οἷς τὴν ἀπόδοσιν τῶν δανεισμάτων κατὰ τοὺς νόμους γίγνεσθαι ἔδει, πρὸς τὴν ἐν τῷ χρόνῳ ἀξίαν ἐπαναγαγών, ἐπειδὴ τῷ πλήθει τῶν δεδημοσιωμένων πολὺ πάντα ἐπευώνιστο.

589 Mk. 12:13-17: Καὶ ἀποστέλλουσιν πρὸς αὐτόν τινας τῶν Φαρισαίων καὶ τῶν Ἡρῳδιανῶν ἵνα αὐτὸν ἀγρεύσωσιν λόγῳ. καὶ ἐλθόντες λέγουσιν αὐτῷ, Διδάσκαλε, οἴδαμεν ὅτι ἀληθὴς εἶ καὶ οὐ μέλει σοι περὶ οὐδενός· οὐ γὰρ βλέπεις εἰς πρόσωπον ἀνθρώπων, ἀλλ' ἐπ' ἀληθείας τὴν ὁδὸν τοῦ θεοῦ διδάσκεις· ἔξεστιν δοῦναι κῆνσον Καίσαρι ἢ οὔ; δῶμεν ἢ μὴ δῶμεν; ὁ δὲ εἰδὼς αὐτῶν τὴν ὑπόκρισιν εἶπεν αὐτοῖς, Τί με πειράζετε; φέρετέ μοι δηνάριον ἵνα ἴδω. οἱ δὲ ἤνεγκαν. καὶ λέγει αὐτοῖς, Τίνος ἡ εἰκὼν αὕτη καὶ ἡ ἐπιγραφή; οἱ δὲ εἶπαν αὐτῷ, Καίσαρος. ὁ δὲ Ἰησοῦς εἶπεν αὐτοῖς, Τὰ Καίσαρος ἀπόδοτε Καίσαρι καὶ τὰ τοῦ θεοῦ τῷ θεῷ. καὶ ἐξεθαύμαζον ἐπ' αὐτῷ.

590 DIO CASS. HR 42.51.4-5: τούτους τε οὖν ταῦτα πράξας ἀνηρτήσατο, καὶ τῶν προσεταιριστῶν τῶν τε συναγωνιστῶν τοὺς μὲν βουλευτὰς ἱερωσύναις τε καὶ ἀρχαῖς ταῖς τε ἐς τὸν λοιπὸν τοῦ ἔτους ἐκείνου χρόνον καὶ ταῖς ἐς νέωτα (ἵνα γὰρ πλείους αὐτῶν ἀμείψηται, στρατηγούς τε δέκα ἐς τὸ ἐπιὸν ἔτος ἀπέδειξε καὶ ἱερέας ὑπὲρ τὸ νενομισμένον· τοῖς τε γὰρ ποντίφιξι καὶ τοῖς οἰωνισταῖς, ὧν καὶ αὐτὸς ἦν, τοῖς τε πεντεκαίδεκα καλουμένοις ἕνα ἑκάστοις προσένειμε, καίπερ αὐτὸς βουληθεὶς πάσας τὰς ἱερωσύνας λαβεῖν ὥσπερ ἐψήφιστο), τοὺς δὲ ἱππέας τοῦ

τέλους τούς τε ἑκατοντάρχους καὶ τοὺς ὑπομείονας ἄλλοις τέ τισι καὶ τῷ καὶ ἐς τὸ συνέδριόν τινας ἀπ' αὐτῶν ἀντὶ τῶν ἀπολωλότων καταλέξαι.

SUET. *Jul.* 42: Cuncta collegia praeter antiquitus constituta distraxit.

591 SUET. *Jul.* 76: Tertium et quartum consulatum titulo tenus gessit, contentus dictaturae potestate decretae cum consulatibus simul [...].

DIO CASS. HR 42.55.4: ταῦτά ⟨τε⟩ ἐν ἐκείνῳ τῷ ἔτει, ἐν ᾧ δικτάτωρ μὲν ὄντως αὐτὸς τὸ δεύτερον ἦρξεν, ὕπατοι δὲ ἐπ' ἐξόδῳ αὐτοῦ ἀποδειχθέντες ὅ τε Καλῆνος καὶ ὁ Οὐατίνιος ἐλέγοντο εἶναι, ἐποίησε [...].

592 SUET. *Jul.* 35: Dehinc Scipionem ac Iubam reliquias partium in Africa refouentis deuicit.

VELL. 2.55: Nusquam erat Pompeius corpore, adhuc ubique uiuebat nomine. Quippe ingens partium eius fauor bellum excitauerat Africum quod ciebat rex Iuba et Scipio, uir consularis, ante biennium quam extingueretur Pompeius, lectus ab eo socer, eorumque copias auxerat M. Cato, ingenti cum difficultate itinerum locorumque inopia, perductis ad eos legionibus: qui uir, cum summum ei a militibus deferretur imperium, honoratiori parere maluit. Admonet promissae breuitatis fides quanto omnia transcursu dicenda sint. Sequens fortunam suam Caesar peruectus in Africam est, quam, occiso Curione, Iulianarum duce partium, Pompeiani obtinebant exercitus. Ibi primo uaria fortuna, mox pugnauit sua, inclinataeque hostium copiae; nec dissimilis ibi aduersus uictos quam in priores clementia Caesaris fuit.

DIO CASS. HR 42.56-43.13.

APP. BC 95-100.397: Διαβαλὼν δ' ἐκ Ῥηγίου τὸν πορθμὸν ἐπὶ Μεσσήνης ἐς Λιλύβαιον ἦλθε. καὶ πυθόμενος Κάτωνα μὲν τὴν παρασκευὴν τοῦ πολέμου ναυσὶ καὶ πεζῷν τινι μέρει φρουρεῖν ἐν Ἰτύκῃ μετὰ τῶν τριακοσίων, οὓς ἀπὸ σφῶν ἐκ πολλοῦ προβούλους ἐπεποίηντο τοῦ πολέμου καὶ σύγκλητον ἐκάλουν, τὸν δ' αὐτοκράτορα Λεύκιον Σκιπίωνα καὶ τοὺς ἀρίστους ἐν Ἀδρυμητῷ στρατοπεδεύειν, διέπλευσεν ἐπὶ τὸν Σκιπίωνα.; [409-412]: οὐ μὴν οὐδ' ἐς ὕπνον ἀπιὼν ἐνήλλαξέ τι τῶν συνήθων, πλὴν ὅτι υἱὸν ἠσπάσατο φιλοφρονέστερον. τὸ δὲ ξιφίδιον τῇ κλίνῃ τὸ σύνηθες οὐχ εὑρὼν παρακείμενον ἐξεβόησεν, ὅτι προδιδοῖτο ὑπὸ τῶν οἰκείων τοῖς πολεμίοις· τίνι γὰρ ἔφη χρήσεσθαι προσιόντων, ἂν νυκτὸς ἐπίωσι; τῶν δὲ αὐτὸν παρακαλούντων μηδὲν ἐφ' ἑαυτὸν βουλεύειν, ἀλλ' ἀναπαύεσθαι χωρὶς ξιφιδίου, ἀξιοπιστότερον ἔτι εἶπεν· "οὐ γὰρ ἔστι μοι θέλοντι καὶ δι' ἐσθῆτος ἐμαυτὸν ἀποπνῖξαι καὶ ἐς τὰ τείχη τὴν κεφαλὴν ἀπαράξαι καὶ ἐς τράχηλον κυβιστῆσαι καὶ τὸ πνεῦμα κατασχόντα ἐκτρῖψαι·" πολλά τε ὅμοια εἰπὼν παρήγαγεν αὐτοὺς παραθεῖναι τὸ ξιφίδιον. ὡς δὲ ἐτέθη, Πλάτωνος αἰτήσας τὴν περὶ ψυχῆς συγγραφὴν ἀνεγίνωσκε. Καὶ ἐπεὶ τέλος εἶχε τῷ Πλάτωνι ὁ λόγος, ἀναπαύεσθαι τοὺς περὶ θύρας ὑπολαβὼν ἔτρωσεν αὐτὸν ὑπὸ τὰ στέρνα· προπεσόντων δ' αὐτῷ τῶν σπλάγχνων καὶ στόνου τινὸς ἐξακουσθέντος ἐσέδραμον οἱ περὶ θύρας· καὶ οἱ ἰατροὶ τὰ σπλάγχνα ἔτι σῶα ὄντα ἐνέθηκαν ἔνδον καὶ τὰς πληγὰς ἐπιρράψαντες ἐπέδησαν. ὁ δὲ ἀνενεγκὼν αὖθις ὑπεκρίνετο καὶ κατεμέμφετο μὲν ἑαυτῷ πληγῆς ἀσθενοῦς, χάριν δ' ὡμολόγει τοῖς περισώσασι καὶ καταδαρθεῖν ἔφη δεῖσθαι. οἱ μὲν δὴ τὸ ξίφος ἔχοντες ᾤχοντο καὶ τὰς θύρας ὡς ἠρεμοῦντι ἐπέκλεισαν· ὁ δ' ὕπνου δόξαν αὐτοῖς παρασχὼν τὰ δεσμὰ ταῖς χερσὶ μετὰ σιγῆς ἀπερρήγνυ καὶ τὰς ῥαφὰς τοῦ τραύματος ἀνέπτυσσεν, οἷα θηρίον τό τε τραῦμα καὶ τὴν γαστέρα εὐρύνως ὄνυξι καὶ δακτύλοις ἐρευνῶν καὶ τὰ σπλάγχνα διαρρίπτων, μέχρι ἐτελεύτησεν, ἔτη μὲν ἀμφὶ πεντήκοντα γεγονώς, ὁμολογούμενος δὲ τήν τε γνώμην, ἐς ὅ τι κρίνειε, πάντων ἀνδρῶν ἐπιμονώτατος φῦναι καὶ τὸ δίκαιον ἢ πρέπον ἢ καλὸν οὐκ ἔθεσι μᾶλλον ἢ μεγαλοψύχοις λογισμοῖς ὁρίσαι. [...] τοιόσδε μὲν δὴ Κάτων ἦν, καὶ αὐτὸν οἱ Ἰτυκαῖοι λαμπρῶς ἔθαπτον· ὁ δὲ Καῖσαρ ἔφη μέν οἱ φθονῆσαι Κάτωνα καλῆς ἐπιδείξεως [...].

PLUT. *Caes.* 52-4: Τῶν δὲ περὶ Κάτωνα καὶ Σκιπίωνα μετὰ τὴν ἐν Φαρσάλῳ μάχην εἰς Λιβύην φυγόντων κἀκεῖ, τοῦ βασιλέως Ἰόβα βοηθοῦντος αὐτοῖς, ἠθροικότων δυνάμεις ἀξιολόγους, ἔγνω στρατεύειν ὁ Καῖσαρ ἐπ' αὐτούς· [...] οἱ γὰρ Νομάδες, ἐπιφαινόμενοι πολλοὶ καὶ ταχεῖς ἑκάστοτε, κατεῖχον τὴν χώραν· καί ποτε τῶν Καίσαρος ιππέων σχολήν αγόντων (έτυχε γάρ αυτοίς ανήρ Λίβυς επιδεικνύμενος όρχησιν άμα και μοναυλών θαύματος αξίως), οι μεν εκάθηντο τερπόμενοι, τοις παισί τους ίππους επιτρέψαντες, εξαίφνης δε περιελθόντες εμβάλλουσιν οι πολέμιοι, και τους μεν αυτού κτείνουσι, τοις δ' εις το στρατόπεδον προτροπάδην ελαυνομένοις συνεισέπεσον. ει δε μη Καίσαρ αυτός, άμα δε Καίσαρι Πολλίων Ασίνιος, βοηθούντες εκ του χάρακος έσχον την φυγήν, διεπέπρακτ' αν ο πόλεμος. [...] οι μεν ‹ουν› ταύτα περί της μάχης εκείνης αναγγέλλουσιν· οι δ' ου φασιν αυτόν εν τω έργω γενέσθαι, συντάττοντος δε την στρατιάν και διακοσμούντος άψασθαι το σύνηθες νόσημα· τον δ' ευθύς αισθόμενον αρχομένου, πριν εκταράττεσθαι και καταλαμβάνεσθαι παντάπασιν υπό του πάθους την αίσθησιν ήδη σειομένην, εις τινα των πλησίον πύργων κομισθήναι και διαγαγείν εν ησυχία. των δε πεφευγότων εκ της μάχης υπατικών και στρατηγικών ανδρών οι μεν εαυτούς διέφθειραν αλισκόμενοι, συχνούς δε Καίσαρ έκτεινεν αλόντας.

PLUT. Caes. 17: η δε των πόνων υπομονή παρά την του σώματος δύναμιν εγκαρτερείν δοκούντος εξέπληττεν, ότι και την έξιν ων ισχνός, και την σάρκα λευκός και απαλός, και την κεφαλήν νοσώδης, και τοις επιληπτικοίς ένοχος (εν Κορδύβη πρώτον αυτώ του πάθους ως λέγεται τούτου προσπεσόντος), ου μαλακίας εποιήσατο την αρρωστίαν πρόφασιν, αλλά θεραπείαν της αρρωστίας την στρατείαν, ταις ατρύτοις οδοιπορίαις και ταις ευτελέσι διαίταις και τω θυραυλείν ενδελεχώς και ταλαιπωρείν απομαχόμενος τω πάθει και το σώμα τηρών δυσάλωτον.

SUET. Jul. 45: Fuisse traditur excelsa statura, colore candido, teretibus membris, ore paulo pleniore, nigris uegetisque oculis, ualitudine prospera, nisi quod tempore extremo repente animo linqui atque etiam per somnum exterreri solebat. comitiali quoque morbo bis inter res agendas correptus est. SUET. Jul. 57: Armorum et equitandi peritissimus, laboris ultra fidem patiens erat. in agmine nonnumquam equo, saepius pedibus anteibat, capite detecto, seu sol seu imber esset [...].

Cf. also MAGGI & REGGI (1986).

593 Mk.9:14-29: Και ελθόντες προς τους μαθητάς είδον όχλον πολύν περί αυτούς και γραμματείς συζητούντας προς αυτούς. και ευθύς πας ο όχλος ιδόντες αυτόν εξεθαμβήθησαν και προστρέχοντες ησπάζοντο αυτόν. και επηρώτησεν αυτούς, Τί συζητείτε προς αυτούς; και απεκρίθη αυτώ εις εκ του όχλου, Διδάσκαλε, ήνεγκα τον υιόν μου προς σε, έχοντα πνεύμα άλαλον· και όπου εάν αυτόν καταλάβη ρήσσει αυτόν, και αφρίζει και τρίζει τους οδόντας και ξηραίνεται· και είπα τοις μαθηταίς σου ίνα αυτό εκβάλωσιν, και ουκ ίσχυσαν. ο δε αποκριθείς αυτοίς λέγει, Ω γενεά άπιστος, έως πότε προς υμάς έσομαι; έως πότε ανέξομαι υμών; φέρετε αυτόν πρός με. και ήνεγκαν αυτόν προς αυτόν. και ιδών αυτόν το πνεύμα ευθύς συνεσπάραξεν αυτόν, και πεσών επί της γης εκυλίετο αφρίζων. και επηρώτησεν τον πατέρα αυτού, Πόσος χρόνος εστίν ως τούτο γέγονεν αυτώ; ο δε είπεν, Εκ παιδιόθεν· και πολλάκις και εις πυρ αυτόν έβαλεν και εις ύδατα ίνα απολέση αυτόν· αλλ' ει τι δύνη, βοήθησον ημίν σπλαγχνισθείς εφ' ημάς. ο δε Ιησούς είπεν αυτώ, Το Ει δύνη, πάντα δυνατά τω πιστεύοντι. ευθύς κράξας ο πατήρ του παιδίου έλεγεν, Πιστεύω· βοήθει μου τη απιστία. ιδών δε ο Ιησούς ότι επισυντρέχει όχλος, επετίμησεν τω πνεύματι τω ακαθάρτω λέγων αυτώ, Το άλαλον και κωφόν πνεύμα, εγώ επιτάσσω σοι, έξελθε εξ αυτού και μηκέτι εισέλθης εις αυτόν. και κράξας και πολλά σπαράξας εξήλθεν· και εγένετο ωσεί νεκρός, ώστε τους πολλούς λέγειν ότι απέθανεν. ο δε Ιησούς κρατήσας της χειρός αυτού ήγειρεν αυτόν, και ανέστη. και εισελθόντος αυτού εις οίκον οι μαθηταί αυτού κατ' ιδίαν επηρώτων αυτόν, Ότι ημείς ουκ ηδυνήθημεν εκβαλείν αυτό; και είπεν αυτοίς, Τούτο το γένος εν ουδενί δύναται εξελθείν ει μη εν προσευχή.

594 Mk.14:33-35: και ήρξατο εκθαμβείσθαι και αδημονείν και λέγει αυτοίς, Περίλυπός εστιν η ψυχή μου έως θανάτου· μείνατε ώδε και γρηγορείτε. και προελθών μικρόν έπιπτεν επί της γης και προσηύχετο ίνα ει δυνατόν εστιν παρέλθη απ' αυτού η ώρα [...].

595 Plut. Cic. 39: ἐκ δὲ τούτου διετέλει τιμῶν καὶ φιλοφρονούμενος, ὥστε καὶ γράψαντι λόγον ἐγκώμιον Κάτωνος ἀντιγράφων τόν τε λόγον αὐτοῦ καὶ τὸν βίον ὡς μάλιστα τῷ Περικλέους ἐοικότα καὶ Θηραμένους ἐπαινεῖν. ὁ μὲν οὖν Κικέρωνος λόγος Κάτων, ὁ δὲ Καίσαρος Ἀντικάτων ἐπιγέγραπται.
Plut. Cat. Mi. 25; Cat. Mi. 52: ὁ μὲν οὖν Πομπήϊος οὔτε δύναμιν ἔχων ἑτοίμην, οὔθ' οὓς κατέλεγε τότε προθύμους ὁρῶν, ἐξέλιπε τὴν Ῥώμην, ὁ δὲ Κάτων ἔπεσθαι καὶ συμφεύγειν ἐγνωκώς, τὸν μὲν νεώτερον υἱὸν εἰς Βρεττίους ὑπεξέθετο πρὸς Μουνάτιον, τὸν δὲ πρεσβύτερον εἶχε σὺν ἑαυτῷ. τῆς δ' οἰκίας καὶ τῶν θυγατέρων κηδεμόνος δεομένων, ἀνέλαβε πάλιν τὴν Μαρκίαν, χηρεύουσαν ἐπὶ χρήμασι πολλοῖς· ὁ γὰρ Ὁρτήσιος θνήσκων ἐκείνην ἀπέλιπε κληρονόμον. εἰς ὃ δὴ μάλιστα λοιδορούμενος ὁ Καῖσαρ τῷ Κάτωνι φιλοπλουτίαν προφέρει καὶ μισθαρνίαν ἐπὶ τῷ γάμῳ. τί γὰρ ἔδει παραχωρεῖν δεόμενον γυναικός, ἢ τί μὴ δεόμενον αὖθις ἀναλαμβάνειν, εἰ μὴ δέλεαρ ἐξ ἀρχῆς ὑφείθη τὸ γύναιον Ὁρτησίῳ καὶ νέαν ἔχρησεν ἵνα πλουσίαν ἀπολάβῃ; [...] εἰ δ' ἄλλῃ πῃ μὴ καλῶς πέπρακται τὰ περὶ τὸν γάμον, ἐπισκεπτέον. ἐγγυησάμενος γοῦν τὴν Μαρκίαν ὁ Κάτων καὶ τὸν οἶκον ἐπιτρέψας ἐκείνῃ καὶ τὰς θυγατέρας, αὐτὸς ἐδίωκε Πομπήϊον. Ἀπ' ἐκείνης δὲ λέγεται τῆς ἡμέρας μήτε κεφαλὴν ἔτι κείρασθαι μήτε γένεια, μήτε στέφανον ἐπιθέσθαι, πένθους δὲ καὶ κατηφείας καὶ βαρύτητος ἐπὶ ταῖς συμφοραῖς τῆς πατρίδος ἓν σχῆμα νικώντων ὁμοίως καὶ νικωμένων ἄχρι τελευτῆς διαφυλάξαι.
App. BC 2.99.413-414: Μαρκίᾳ γέ τοι τῇ Φιλίππου συνὼν ἐκ παρθένου καὶ ἀρεσκόμενος αὐτῇ μάλιστα καὶ παῖδας ἔχων ἐξ ἐκείνης ἔδωκεν ὅμως αὐτὴν Ὁρτησίῳ τῶν φίλων τινί, παίδων τε ἐπιθυμοῦντι καὶ τεκνοποιοῦ γυναικὸς οὐ τυγχάνοντι, μέχρι κἀκείνῳ κυήσασαν ἐς τὸν οἶκον αὖθις ὡς χρήσας ἀνεδέξατο. [...] Κικέρωνος δὲ ποιήσαντος ἐγκώμιον ἐς αὐτὸν ἐπιγράψαντος Κάτων, ἀντέγραψε κατηγορίαν ὁ Καῖσαρ καὶ ἐπέραψεν Ἀντικάτων.
596 Mk. 12:38-40: Καὶ ἐν τῇ διδαχῇ αὐτοῦ ἔλεγεν, Βλέπετε ἀπὸ τῶν γραμματέων τῶν θελόντων ἐν στολαῖς περιπατεῖν καὶ ἀσπασμοὺς ἐν ταῖς ἀγοραῖς καὶ πρωτοκαθεδρίας ἐν ταῖς συναγωγαῖς καὶ πρωτοκλισίας ἐν τοῖς δείπνοις, οἱ κατεσθίοντες τὰς οἰκίας τῶν χηρῶν καὶ προφάσει μακρὰ προσευχόμενοι· οὗτοι λήμψονται περισσότερον κρίμα.
597 App. BC 2.101.418-102.425. Plut. Caes. 55. Suet. Jul. 37.
598 Mk. 11:7-11: καὶ φέρουσιν τὸν πῶλον πρὸς τὸν Ἰησοῦν καὶ ἐπιβάλλουσιν αὐτῷ τὰ ἱμάτια αὐτῶν, καὶ ἐκάθισεν ἐπ' αὐτόν. καὶ πολλοὶ τὰ ἱμάτια αὐτῶν ἔστρωσαν εἰς τὴν ὁδόν, ἄλλοι δὲ στιβάδας κόψαντες ἐκ τῶν ἀγρῶν. καὶ οἱ προάγοντες καὶ οἱ ἀκολουθοῦντες ἔκραζον, / Ὡσαννά· / Εὐλογημένος ὁ ἐρχόμενος ἐν ὀνόματι κυρίου· / Εὐλογημένη ἡ ἐρχομένη βασιλεία τοῦ πατρὸς ἡμῶν Δαυίδ· / Ὡσαννὰ ἐν τοῖς ὑψίστοις. Καὶ εἰσῆλθεν εἰς Ἱεροσόλυμα εἰς τὸ ἱερόν [...].
599 Suet. Jul. 51: Ne prouincialibus quidem matrimoniis abstinuisse uel hoc disticho apparet iactato aeque a militibus per Gallicum triumphum: / Vrbani seruate uxores: / moechum caluom adducimus; / Aurum in Gallia effutuisti, hic sumpsisti mutuum.
600 Hirt. Gal. 8.50-51: Ipse hibernis peractis contra consuetudinem in Italiam quam maximis itineribus est profectus, ut municipia et colonias appellaret, quibus M. Antonii, quaestoris sui, commendaverat sacerdotii petitionem. [...] Exceptus est Caesaris adventus ab omnibus municipiis et coloniis incredibili honore atque amore. tum primum enim veniebat ab illo universae Galliae bello. nihil relinquebatur, quod ad ornatum portarum, itinerum, locorum omnium, qua Caesar iturus erat, excogitari poterat. cum liberis omnis multitudo obviam procedebat, hostiae omnibus locis immolabantur, tricliniis stratis fora templaque occupabantur, ut vel spectatissimi triumphi laetitia praecipi posset. tanta erat magnificentia apud opulentiores, cupiditas apud humiliores.
601 Hirt. Gal. 8.52: Cum omnes regiones Galliae togatae Caesar percucurrisset, summa celeritate ad exercitum Nemetocennam rediit legionibusque ex omnibus hibernis ad fines Treverorum evocatis eo profectus est ibique exercitum lustravit.

Mk. 11:1: καὶ περιβλεψάμενος πάντα, ὀψίας ἤδη οὔσης τῆς ὥρας, ἐξῆλθεν εἰς Βηθανίαν μετὰ τῶν δώδεκα.

602 Suet. Jul. 35: *Dehinc Scipionem ac Iubam reliquias partium in Africa refouentis deuicit, Pompei liberos in Hispania.*

Vell. 2.55: *Victorem Africani belli Caesarem grauius excepit Hispaniense—nam uictus ab eo Pharnaces uix quidquam gloriae eius adstruxit,—quod Cn. Pompeius, Magni filius, adulescens impetus ad bella maximi, ingens ac terribile conflauerat, undique ad eum adhuc paterni nominis magnitudinem sequentium ex toto orbe terrarum auxiliis confluentibus. Sua Caesarem in Hispaniam comitata fortuna est, sed nullum umquam atrocius periculosiusque ab eo initum proelium adeo ut plus quam dubio Marte descenderet equo consistensque ante recedentem suorum aciem, increpita prius fortuna quod se in eum seruasset exitum, denuntiaret militibus uestigio se non recessurum: proinde uiderent quem et quo loco imperatorem deserturi forent. Verecundia magis quam uirtute acies restituta et a duce quam a milite fortius. Cn. Pompeius, grauis uulnere inuentus inter solitudines auias, interemptus est; Labienum Varumque acies abstulit.*

Plut. Caes. 56: Συντελεσθέντων δὲ τούτων ὕπατος ἀποδειχθεὶς τὸ τέταρτον, εἰς Ἰβηρίαν ἐστράτευσεν ἐπὶ τοὺς Πομπηΐου παῖδας, νέους μὲν ὄντας ἔτι, θαυμαστὴν δὲ τῷ πλήθει στρατιὰν συνειλοχότας καὶ τόλμαν ἀποδεικνυμένους ἀξιόχρεων πρὸς ἡγεμονίαν, ὥστε κίνδυνον τῷ Καίσαρι περιστῆσαι τὸν ἔσχατον. ἡ δὲ μεγάλη μάχη περὶ πόλιν συνέστη Μοῦνδαν, ἐν ᾗ Καῖσαρ ἐκθλιβομένους ὁρῶν τοὺς ἑαυτοῦ καὶ κακῶς ἀντέχοντας, ἐβόα διὰ τῶν ὅπλων καὶ τῶν τάξεων περιθέων, εἰ μηδὲν αἰδοῦνται, λαβόντας αὐτὸν ἐγχειρίσαι τοῖς παιδαρίοις. μόλις δὲ προθυμίᾳ πολλῇ τοὺς πολεμίους ὠσάμενος, ἐκείνων μὲν ὑπὲρ τρισμυρίους διέφθειρε, τῶν δ' ἑαυτοῦ χιλίους ἀπώλεσε τοὺς ἀρίστους. ἀπιὼν δὲ μετὰ τὴν μάχην πρὸς τοὺς φίλους εἶπεν, ὡς πολλάκις μὲν ἀγωνίσαιτο περὶ νίκης, νῦν δὲ πρῶτον περὶ ψυχῆς. ταύτην τὴν μάχην ἐνίκησε τῇ τῶν Διονυσίων ἑορτῇ, καθ' ἣν λέγεται καὶ Πομπήϊος Μάγνος ἐπὶ τὸν πόλεμον ἐξελθεῖν· διὰ μέσου δὲ χρόνος ἐνιαυτῶν τεσσάρων διῆλθε. τῶν δὲ Πομπηΐου παίδων ὁ μὲν νεώτερος διέφυγε, τοῦ δὲ πρεσβυτέρου μεθ' ἡμέρας ὀλίγας Δείδιος ἀνήνεγκε τὴν κεφαλήν. Τοῦτον ἔσχατον Καῖσαρ ἐπολέμησε τὸν πόλεμον· ὁ δ' ἀπ' αὐτοῦ καταχθεὶς θρίαμβος ὡς οὐδὲν ἄλλο Ῥωμαίους ἠνίασεν. οὐ γὰρ ἀλλοφύλους ἡγεμόνας οὐδὲ βαρβάρους βασιλεῖς κατηγωνισμένον, ἀνδρὸς δὲ Ῥωμαίων κρατίστου τύχαις κεχρημένου παῖδας καὶ γένος ἄρδην ἀνῃρηκότα ταῖς τῆς πατρίδος ἐπιπομπεύειν συμφοραῖς οὐ καλῶς εἶχεν, ἀγαλλόμενον ἐπὶ τούτοις ὧν μία καὶ πρὸς θεοὺς καὶ πρὸς ἀνθρώπους ἀπολογία τὸ μετ' ἀνάγκης πεπρᾶχθαι, καὶ ταῦτα πρότερον μήτ' ἄγγελον μήτε γράμματα δημοσίᾳ πέμψαντα περὶ νίκης ἀπὸ τῶν ἐμφυλίων πολέμων, ἀλλ' ἀπωσάμενον αἰσχύνῃ τὴν δόξαν.

App. BC 2.103.426-104.33: Αὐτὸς δὲ ἤδη τέταρτον ὑπατεύων ἐπὶ τὸν νέον Πομπήϊον ἐστράτευεν ἐς Ἰβηρίαν, ὅσπερ αὐτῷ λοιπὸς ἦν ἔτι πόλεμος ἐμφύλιος, οὐκ εὐκαταφρόνητος· τῶν τε γὰρ ἀρίστων ὅσοι διεπεφεύγεσαν ἐκ Λιβύης, ἐκεῖ συνέδραμον, καὶ στρατὸς ὁ μὲν ἐξ αὐτῆς Λιβύης τε καὶ Φαρσάλου τοῖς ἡγεμόσι συνῆλθεν, ὁ δὲ ἐξ Ἰβήρων τε καὶ Κελτιβήρων, ἔθνους ἀλκίμου καὶ χαίροντος ἀεὶ μάχαις. πολὺς δὲ καὶ δούλων ὅμιλος ἐστρατεύετο τῷ Πομπηίῳ· καὶ τέταρτον ἔτος εἶχον ἐν τοῖς γυμνασίοις καὶ γνώμην ἕτοιμον ἀγωνίσασθαι μετὰ ἀπογνώσεως. [...] Δι' ἃ καὶ ὁ Καῖσαρ αὐτὸς ἐβράδυνεν, ἔστε πού τι αὐτῷ κατασκεπτομένῳ προσπελάσας ὁ Πομπήϊος ὠνείδισεν ἐς δειλίαν. καὶ τὸ ὄνειδος οὐκ ἐνέγκων ὁ Καῖσαρ ἐξέτασσε παρὰ πόλιν Κορδύβην, σύνθημα καὶ τότε δοὺς Ἀφροδίτην· ἔδωκε δὲ καὶ ὁ Πομπήϊος Εὐσέβειαν. ὡς δὲ καὶ συνιόντων ἤδη τοῦ Καίσαρος στρατοῦ τὸ δέος ἥπτετο καὶ ὄκνος ἐπεγίγνετο τῷ φόβῳ, θεοὺς πάντας ὁ Καῖσαρ ἱκέτευε, τὰς χεῖρας ἐς τὸν οὐρανὸν ἀνίσχων, μὴ ἑνὶ πόνῳ τῷδε πολλὰ καὶ λαμπρὰ ἔργα μῆναι, καὶ τοὺς στρατιώτας ἐπιθέων παρεκάλει τό τε κράνος τῆς κεφαλῆς ἀφαιρῶν ἐς πρόσωπον ἐδυσώπει καὶ προὔτρεπεν. οἱ δὲ οὐδ' ὣς τι μετέβαλλον ἀπὸ τοῦ δέους, ἕως ὁ Καῖσαρ αὐτὸς ἁρπάσας τινὸς ἀσπίδα καὶ τοῖς ἀμφ' αὐτὸν ἡγεμόσιν εἰπών· "ἔσται

τοῦτο τέλος ἐμοί τε τοῦ βίου καὶ ὑμῖν τῶν στρατειῶν," προύδραμε τῆς τάξεως ἐς τοὺς πολεμίους ἐπὶ τοσοῦτον, ὡς μόνους αὐτῶν ἀποσχεῖν δέκα πόδας καὶ διακόσια αὐτῷ δόρατα ἐπιβληθῆναι καὶ τούτων τὰ μὲν αὐτὸν ἐκκλῖναι, τὰ δὲ ἐς τὴν ἀσπίδα ἀναδέξασθαι. τότε γὰρ δὴ τῶν τε ἡγεμόνων προθέων ἕκαστος ἵστατο παρ' αὐτόν, καὶ ὁ στρατὸς ἅπας ἐμπεσὼν μετὰ ὁρμῆς ὅλην ἠγωνίζετο τὴν ἡμέραν, προύχων τε καὶ ἡττώμενος αἰεὶ παρὰ μέρος, μέχρις ἐς ἑσπέραν μόλις ἐνίκησεν, ὅτε καὶ φασὶν αὐτὸν εἰπεῖν, ὅτι πολλάκις μὲν ἀγωνίσαιτο περὶ νίκης, νῦν δὲ καὶ περὶ ψυχῆς.
Dio Cass. HR 43.28-41.

603 Mk. 10:35-45: Καὶ προσπορεύονται αὐτῷ Ἰάκωβος καὶ Ἰωάννης οἱ υἱοὶ Ζεβεδαίου λέγοντες αὐτῷ, Διδάσκαλε, θέλομεν ἵνα ὃ ἐὰν αἰτήσωμέν σε ποιήσῃς ἡμῖν. ὁ δὲ εἶπεν αὐτοῖς, Τί θέλετέ [με] ποιήσω ὑμῖν; οἱ δὲ εἶπαν αὐτῷ, Δὸς ἡμῖν ἵνα εἷς σου ἐκ δεξιῶν καὶ εἷς ἐξ ἀριστερῶν καθίσωμεν ἐν τῇ δόξῃ σου. ὁ δὲ Ἰησοῦς εἶπεν αὐτοῖς, Οὐκ οἴδατε τί αἰτεῖσθε. δύνασθε πιεῖν τὸ ποτήριον ὃ ἐγὼ πίνω ἢ τὸ βάπτισμα ὃ ἐγὼ βαπτίζομαι βαπτισθῆναι; οἱ δὲ εἶπαν αὐτῷ, Δυνάμεθα. ὁ δὲ Ἰησοῦς εἶπεν αὐτοῖς, Τὸ ποτήριον ὃ ἐγὼ πίνω πίεσθε καὶ τὸ βάπτισμα ὃ ἐγὼ βαπτίζομαι βαπτισθήσεσθε, τὸ δὲ καθίσαι ἐκ δεξιῶν μου ἢ ἐξ εὐωνύμων οὐκ ἔστιν ἐμὸν δοῦναι, ἀλλ' οἷς ἡτοίμασται. Καὶ ἀκούσαντες οἱ δέκα ἤρξαντο ἀγανακτεῖν περὶ Ἰακώβου καὶ Ἰωάννου. καὶ προσκαλεσάμενος αὐτοὺς ὁ Ἰησοῦς λέγει αὐτοῖς, Οἴδατε ὅτι οἱ δοκοῦντες ἄρχειν τῶν ἐθνῶν κατακυριεύουσιν αὐτῶν καὶ οἱ μεγάλοι αὐτῶν κατεξουσιάζουσιν αὐτῶν. οὐχ οὕτως δέ ἐστιν ἐν ὑμῖν, ἀλλ' ὃς ἂν θέλῃ μέγας γενέσθαι ἐν ὑμῖν, ἔσται ὑμῶν διάκονος, καὶ ὃς ἂν θέλῃ ἐν ὑμῖν εἶναι πρῶτος ἔσται πάντων δοῦλος· καὶ γὰρ ὁ υἱὸς τοῦ ἀνθρώπου οὐκ ἦλθεν διακονηθῆναι ἀλλὰ διακονῆσαι καὶ δοῦναι τὴν ψυχὴν αὐτοῦ λύτρον ἀντὶ πολλῶν.

604 Cf. App. BC 2.104.430: σύνθημα καὶ τότε δοὺς Ἀφροδίτην· ἔδωκε δὲ καὶ ὁ Πομπήιος Εὐσέβειαν.

605 Vell. 2.56: *Caesar omnium uictor regressus in urbem, quod humanam excedat fidem, omnibus qui contra se arma tulerant ignouit [...].*
Suet. Jul. 76: *non enim honores modo nimios recepit: continuum consulatum, perpetuam dictaturam praefecturamque morum, insuper praenomen Imperatoris, cognomen Patris patriae, statuam inter reges, suggestum in orchestra; sed et ampliora etiam humano fastigio decerni sibi passus est: sedem auream in curia et pro tribunali, tensam et ferculum circensi pompa, templa, aras, simulacra iuxta deos, puluinar, flaminem, lupercos, appellationem mensis e suo nomine; ac nullos non honores ad libidinem cepit et dedit.*
Plut. Caes. 57: Οὐ μὴν ἀλλὰ καὶ πρὸς τὴν τύχην τοῦ ἀνδρὸς ἐγκεκλικότες, καὶ δεδεγμένοι τὸν χαλινόν, καὶ τῶν ἐμφυλίων πολέμων καὶ κακῶν ἀναπνοὴν ἡγούμενοι τὴν μοναρχίαν, δικτάτορα μὲν αὐτὸν ἀπέδειξαν διὰ βίου· τοῦτο δ' ἦν ὁμολογουμένη [μὲν] τυραννίς, τῷ ἀνυπευθύνῳ τῆς μοναρχίας τὸ ἀκατάπαυστον προσλαβούσης· τιμὰς δὲ τὰς πρώτας Κικέρωνος εἰς τὴν βουλὴν γράψαντος, ὧν ἀμῶς γέ πως ἀνθρώπινον ἦν τὸ μέγεθος, ἕτεροι προστιθέντες ὑπερβολὰς καὶ διαμιλλώμενοι πρὸς ἀλλήλους, ἐξειργάσαντο καὶ τοῖς πρᾳοτάτοις ἐπαχθῆ τὸν ἄνδρα καὶ λυπηρὸν γενέσθαι διὰ τὸν ὄγκον καὶ τὴν ἀτοπίαν τῶν ψηφιζομένων, οἷς οὐδὲν ἧττον οἴονται συναγωνίσασθαι τῶν κολακευόντων Καίσαρα τοὺς μισοῦντας, ὅπως ὅτι πλείστας κατ' αὐτοῦ προφάσεις ἔχωσι καὶ μετὰ μεγίστων ἐγκλημάτων ἐπιχειρεῖν δοκῶσιν. ἐπεὶ τά γ' ἄλλα, τῶν ἐμφυλίων αὐτῷ πολέμων πέρας ἐσχηκότων, ἀνέγκλητον ‹ἑαυτὸν› παρεῖχε· καὶ τό γε τῆς Ἐπιεικείας ἱερὸν οὐκ ἀπὸ τρόπου δοκοῦσι χαριστήριον ἐπὶ τῇ πρᾳότητι ψηφίσασθαι. καὶ γὰρ ἀφῆκε πολλοὺς τῶν πεπολεμηκότων πρὸς αὐτόν, ἐνίοις δὲ καὶ ἀρχὰς καὶ τιμάς, ὡς Βρούτῳ καὶ Κασσίῳ, προσέθηκεν· ἐστρατήγουν γὰρ ἀμφότεροι· καὶ τὰς Πομπηίου καταβεβλημένας εἰκόνας οὐ περιεῖδεν, ἀλλ' ἀνέστησεν, ἐφ' ᾧ καὶ Κικέρων εἶπεν, ὅτι Καῖσαρ τοὺς Πομπηίου στήσας ἀνδριάντας τοὺς ἰδίους ἔπηξε. τῶν δὲ φίλων ἀξιούντων αὐτὸν δορυφορεῖσθαι καὶ πολλῶν ἐπὶ τοῦτο παρεχόντων ἑαυτούς, οὐχ ὑπέμεινεν, εἰπὼν ὡς βέλτιόν ἐστιν ἅπαξ ἀποθανεῖν ἢ ἀεὶ προσδοκᾶν. τὴν δ' εὔνοιαν ὡς κάλλιστον ἅμα καὶ βεβαιότατον ἑαυτῷ

περιβαλλόμενος φυλακτήριον, αὖθις ἀνελάμβανε τὸν δῆμον ἑστιάσεσι καὶ σιτηρεσίοις, τὸ δὲ στρατιωτικὸν ἀποικίαις [...].

APP. BC 2.106.440-107.444: ὁ δὲ Καῖσαρ ἐς Ῥώμην ἠπείγετο, τὰ ἐμφύλια πάντα καθελών, ἐπὶ φόβου καὶ δόξης, οἵας οὔ τις πρὸ τοῦ· ὅθεν αὐτῷ τιμαὶ πᾶσαι, ὅσαι ὑπὲρ ἄνθρωπον, ἀμέτρως ἐς χάριν ἐπενοοῦντο, θυσιῶν τε πέρι καὶ ἀγώνων καὶ ἀναθημάτων ἐν πᾶσιν ἱεροῖς καὶ δημοσίοις χωρίοις, ἀνὰ φυλὴν ἑκάστην καὶ ἐν ἔθνεσιν ἅπασι, καὶ ἐν βασιλεῦσιν, ὅσοι Ῥωμαίοις φίλοι. σχήματά τε ἐπεγράφετο ταῖς εἰκόσι ποικίλα, καὶ στέφανος ἐκ δρυὸς ἦν ἐπ᾽ ἐνίαις ὡς σωτῆρι τῆς πατρίδος, ᾧ πάλαι τοὺς ὑπερασπίσαντας ἐγέραιρον οἱ περισωθέντες. ἀνερρήθη δὲ καὶ πατὴρ πατρίδος, καὶ δικτάτωρ ἐς τὸν ἑαυτοῦ βίον ᾑρέθη καὶ ὕπατος ἐς δέκα ἔτη, καὶ τὸ σῶμα ἱερὸς καὶ ἄσυλος εἶναι καὶ χρηματίζειν ἐπὶ θρόνων ἐλεφαντίνων τε καὶ χρυσέων, καὶ θύειν μὲν αὐτὸν αἰεὶ θριαμβικῶς ἠμφιεσμένον, τὴν δὲ πόλιν ἀνὰ ἔτος ἕκαστον, αἷς αὐτὸς ἡμέραις ἐν παρατάξεσιν ἐνίκα, ἱερέας δὲ καὶ ἱερείας ἀνὰ πενταετὲς εὐχὰς δημοσίας ὑπὲρ αὐτοῦ τίθεσθαι, καὶ τὰς ἀρχὰς εὐθὺς καθισταμένας ὀμνύναι μηδενὶ τῶν ὑπὸ Καίσαρος ὁριζομένων ἀντιπράξειν. ἔς τε τιμὴν τῆς γενέσεως αὐτοῦ τὸν Κυιντίλιον μῆνα Ἰούλιον ἀντὶ Κυιντιλίου μετωνόμασαν εἶναι. καὶ νεὼς ἐψηφίσαντο πολλοὺς αὐτῷ γενέσθαι καθάπερ θεῷ καὶ κοινὸν αὐτοῦ καὶ Ἐπιεικείας, ἀλλήλους δεξιουμένων· οὕτως ἐδεδοίκεσαν μὲν ὡς δεσπότην, εὔχοντο δὲ σφίσιν ἐπιεικῆ γενέσθαι. Εἰσὶ δ᾽ οἳ καὶ βασιλέα προσειπεῖν ἐπενόουν, μέχρι μαθὼν αὐτὸς ἀπηγόρευσε καὶ ἠπείλησεν ὡς ἀθέμιστον ὄνομα μετὰ τὴν τῶν προγόνων ἀράν. σπεῖραι δ᾽ ὅσαι στρατηγίδες αὐτὸν ἐκ τῶν πολέμων ἔτι ἐσωματοφυλάκουν, ἀπέστησε τῆς φυλακῆς καὶ μετὰ τῆς δημοσίας ὑπηρεσίας ἐπεφαίνετο μόνης.

DIO CASS. HR 44.4-7: ἐγένετο δὲ τὰ δοθέντα αὐτῷ μετ᾽ ἐκεῖνα ὅσα εἴρηται τοσάδε καὶ τοιάδε· καθ᾽ ἓν γάρ, εἰ καὶ μὴ πάντα ἅμα μήτε ἐσηνέχθη μήτε ἐκυρώθη, λελέξεται. τὰ μὲν γὰρ πρῶτα φαίνεσθαί τε αὐτὸν ἀεὶ καὶ ἐν αὐτῇ τῇ πόλει τὴν στολὴν τὴν ἐπινίκιον ἐνδεδυκότα, καὶ καθέζεσθαι ἐπὶ τοῦ ἀρχικοῦ δίφρου πανταχῇ πλὴν ἐν ταῖς πανηγύρεσιν, ἐψηφίσαντο· τότε γὰρ ἐπί τε τοῦ δημαρχικοῦ βάθρου καὶ μετὰ τῶν ἀεὶ δημαρχούντων θεᾶσθαι ἔλαβε. σκῦλά τέ τινα ὅπιμα ἐς τὸν τοῦ Διὸς τοῦ Φερετρίου νεὼν ἀναθεῖναί οἱ ὥσπερ τινὰ πολέμιον αὐτοστράτηγον αὐτοχειρίᾳ [ποῖ] πεφονευκότι, καὶ τοῖς ῥαβδούχοις δαφνηφορούσιν ἀεὶ χρῆσθαι, μετά τε τὰς ἀνοχὰς τὰς Λατίνας ἐπὶ κέλητος ἐς τὴν πόλιν ἐκ τοῦ Ἀλβανοῦ ἐσελαύνειν ἔδοσαν. πρός τε τούτοις τοιούτοις οὖσι πατέρα τε αὐτὸν τῆς πατρίδος ἐπωνόμασαν καὶ ἐς τὰ νομίσματα ἐνεχάραξαν, τά τε γενέθλια αὐτοῦ δημοσίᾳ θύειν ἐψηφίσαντο, καὶ ἐν ταῖς πόλεσι τοῖς τε ναοῖς τοῖς ἐν τῇ Ῥώμῃ πᾶσιν ἀνδριάντα τινὰ αὐτοῦ εἶναι ἐκέλευσαν, καὶ ἐπί γε τοῦ βήματος δύο, τὸν μὲν ὡς τοὺς πολίτας σεσωκότος τὸν δὲ ὡς τὴν πόλιν ἐκ πολιορκίας ἐξῃρημένου, μετὰ τῶν στεφάνων τῶν ἐπὶ τοῖς τοιούτοις νενομισμένων ἱδρύσαντο. νεών τε Ὁμονοίας καινῆς, ὡς καὶ δι᾽ αὐτοῦ εἰρηνούντες, οἰκοδομῆσαι, καὶ πανήγυριν αὐτῇ ἐτησίαν ἄγειν ἔγνωσαν. ὡς δὲ ταῦτα ἐδέξατο, τά τε ἕλη οἱ τὰ Πομπτῖνα χῶσαι καὶ τὸν ἰσθμὸν τὸν τῆς Πελοποννήσου διορύξαι βουλευτήριόν τε τι καινὸν ποιῆσαι προσέταξαν, ἐπειδὴ τὸ Ὁστίλιον καίπερ ἀνοικοδομηθὲν καθῃρέθη, πρόφασιν μὲν τοῦ ναὸν Εὐτυχίας ἐνταῦθ᾽ οἰκοδομηθῆναι, ὃν καὶ ὁ Λέπιδος ἱππαρχήσας ἐξεποίησεν, ἔργῳ δὲ ὅπως μήτε ἐν ἐκείνῳ τὸ τοῦ Σύλλου ὄνομα σῴζοιτο καὶ ἕτερον ἐκ καινῆς κατασκευασθὲν Ἰούλιον ὀνομασθείη, ὥσπερ που καὶ τόν τε μῆνα ἐν ᾧ ἐγεγέννητο Ἰούλιον κἀκ τῶν φυλῶν μίαν τὴν κλήρῳ λαχοῦσαν Ἰουλίαν ἐπεκάλεσαν. καὶ αὐτὸν μὲν τιμητὴν καὶ μόνον καὶ διὰ βίου εἶναι, τά τε τοῖς δημάρχοις δεδομένα καρποῦσθαι, ὅπως, ἄν τις ἢ ἔργῳ ἢ καὶ λόγῳ αὐτὸν ὑβρίσῃ, ἱερός τε ᾖ καὶ ἐν τῷ ἄγει ἐνέχηται, τὸν δὲ δὴ υἱόν, ἄν τινα γεννήσῃ ἢ καὶ ἐσποιήσηται, ἀρχιερέα ἀποδειχθῆναι ἐψηφίσαντο. ὡς δὲ καὶ τούτοις ἔχαιρε, δίφρος τέ οἱ ἐπίχρυσος, καὶ στολὴ ᾗ ποτε οἱ βασιλῆς ἐκέχρηντο, φρουρά τε ἐκ τῶν ἱππέων καὶ ἐκ τῶν βουλευτῶν ἐδόθη· καὶ προσέτι καὶ εὔχεσθαι ὑπὲρ αὐτοῦ δημοσίᾳ κατ᾽ ἔτος ἕκαστον, τήν τε τύχην αὐτοῦ ὀμνύναι, καὶ τὰ πραχθησόμενα αὐτῷ πάντα κύρια ἕξειν ἐνόμισαν. κἀκ τούτου καὶ πενταετηρίδα οἱ ὡς ἥρωι, ἱεροποιούς τε ἐς τὰς τοῦ Πανὸς γυμνοπαιδίας, τρίτην τινὰ ἑταιρίαν [ἣν]

Ἰουλίαν ὀνομάσαντες, κἂν ταῖς ὁπλομαχίαις μίαν τινὰ ἀεὶ ἡμέραν καὶ ἐν τῇ Ῥώμῃ καὶ ἐν τῇ ἄλλῃ Ἰταλίᾳ ἀνέθεσαν. καὶ ἐπειδὴ καὶ τούτοις ἠρέσκετο, οὕτω δὴ ἔς τε τὰ θέατρα τόν τε δίφρον αὐτοῦ τὸν ἐπίχρυσον καὶ τὸν στέφανον τὸν διάλιθον καὶ διάχρυσον, ἐξ ἴσου τοῖς τῶν θεῶν, ἐσκομίζεσθαι κἂν ταῖς ἱπποδρομίαις ὀχὸν ἐσάγεσθαι ἐψηφίσαντο. καὶ τέλος Δία τε αὐτὸν ἄντικρυς Ἰούλιον προσηγόρευσαν, καὶ ναὸν αὐτῷ τῇ ⟨τ᾽⟩ Ἐπιεικείᾳ αὐτοῦ τεμενισθῆναι ἔγνωσαν, ἱερέα σφίσι τὸν Ἀντώνιον ὥσπερ τινὰ Διάλιον προχειρισάμενοι. καὶ ἅ γε μάλιστα τὴν διάνοιαν αὐτῶν ἐξέφηνεν, ἅμα τε ταῦτα ἐψηφίζοντο καὶ τάφον αὐτῷ ἐντὸς τοῦ πωμηρίου ποιήσασθαι ἔδοσαν· τά τε δόγματα τὰ περὶ τούτων γιγνόμενα ἐς μὲν στήλας ἀργυρᾶς χρυσοῖς γράμμασιν ἐνέγραψαν, ὑπὸ δὲ δὴ τοὺς πόδας τοῦ Διὸς τοῦ Καπιτωλίου ὑπέθεσαν, δηλοῦντές οἱ καὶ μάλα ἐναργῶς ὅτι ἄνθρωπος εἴη.

606 Mk. 12:28-34: Καὶ προσελθὼν εἷς τῶν γραμματέων ἀκούσας αὐτῶν συζητούντων, ἰδὼν ὅτι καλῶς ἀπεκρίθη αὐτοῖς ἐπηρώτησεν αὐτόν, Ποία ἐστὶν ἐντολὴ πρώτη πάντων· ἀπεκρίθη ὁ Ἰησοῦς ὅτι Πρώτη ἐστίν, Ἄκουε, Ἰσραήλ, κύριος ὁ θεὸς ἡμῶν κύριος εἷς ἐστιν, καὶ ἀγαπήσεις κύριον τὸν θεόν σου ἐξ ὅλης τῆς καρδίας σου καὶ ἐξ ὅλης τῆς ψυχῆς σου καὶ ἐξ ὅλης τῆς διανοίας σου καὶ ἐξ ὅλης τῆς ἰσχύος σου. δευτέρα αὕτη, Ἀγαπήσεις τὸν πλησίον σου ὡς σεαυτόν. μείζων τούτων ἄλλη ἐντολὴ οὐκ ἔστιν. καὶ εἶπεν αὐτῷ ὁ γραμματεύς, Καλῶς, διδάσκαλε, ἐπ᾽ ἀληθείας εἶπες ὅτι εἷς ἐστιν καὶ οὐκ ἔστιν ἄλλος πλὴν αὐτοῦ· καὶ τὸ ἀγαπᾶν αὐτὸν ἐξ ὅλης τῆς καρδίας καὶ ἐξ ὅλης τῆς συνέσεως καὶ ἐξ ὅλης τῆς ἰσχύος καὶ τὸ ἀγαπᾶν τὸν πλησίον ὡς ἑαυτὸν περισσότερόν ἐστιν πάντων τῶν ὁλοκαυτωμάτων καὶ θυσιῶν. καὶ ὁ Ἰησοῦς ἰδὼν [αὐτὸν] ὅτι νουνεχῶς ἀπεκρίθη εἶπεν αὐτῷ, Οὐ μακρὰν εἶ ἀπὸ τῆς βασιλείας τοῦ θεοῦ. καὶ οὐδεὶς οὐκέτι ἐτόλμα αὐτὸν ἐπερωτῆσαι.

607 Mt. 5:43-45: Ἠκούσατε ὅτι ἐρρέθη, Ἀγαπήσεις τὸν πλησίον σου καὶ μισήσεις τὸν ἐχθρόν σου. ἐγὼ δὲ λέγω ὑμῖν, ἀγαπᾶτε τοὺς ἐχθροὺς ὑμῶν καὶ προσεύχεσθε ὑπὲρ τῶν διωκόντων ὑμᾶς, ὅπως γένησθε υἱοὶ τοῦ πατρὸς ὑμῶν τοῦ ἐν οὐρανοῖς, ὅτι τὸν ἥλιον αὐτοῦ ἀνατέλλει ἐπὶ πονηροὺς καὶ ἀγαθοὺς καὶ βρέχει ἐπὶ δικαίους καὶ ἀδίκους.

608 App. BC 1.4.15: στασιώτην τε μέγιστον, ᾧ διὰ μεγαλουργίαν πολεμικὴν Μέγας ἐπώνυμον ἦν, οὗτος δὴ μάλιστα πολέμου κράτει σαφῶς καθελών, οὐδενὸς αὐτῷ θαρροῦντος εἰς οὐδὲν ἔτι ἀντειπεῖν, δεύτερος ἐπὶ Σύλλᾳ δικτάτωρ ἐς τὸ διηνεκὲς ᾑρέθη· καὶ στάσεις αὖθις κατεπαύοντο πᾶσαι [...].

609 Mk. 13:1-2: Καὶ ἐκπορευομένου αὐτοῦ ἐκ τοῦ ἱεροῦ λέγει αὐτῷ εἷς τῶν μαθητῶν αὐτοῦ, Διδάσκαλε, ἴδε ποταποὶ λίθοι καὶ ποταπαὶ οἰκοδομαί. καὶ ὁ Ἰησοῦς εἶπεν αὐτῷ, Βλέπεις ταύτας τὰς μεγάλας οἰκοδομάς; οὐ μὴ ἀφεθῇ ὧδε λίθος ἐπὶ λίθον ὃς οὐ μὴ καταλυθῇ.

610 Mk. 13:7: [...] πολέμους καὶ ἀκοὰς πολέμων [...].

611 App. BC 1.5.18: [...] τοὺς ἐχθροὺς ἀλλήλοις τῶν στασιωτῶν ἀντιπαρεχόντων καὶ ἐς τοῦτο ἀμελούντων καὶ φίλων καὶ ἀδελφῶν· τοσοῦτον ἐκράτει τῆς ἐς τὰ οἰκεῖα εὐνοίας ἡ ἐς τὰ ἀντίπαλα φιλονικία.

612 Mk. 13:12: καὶ παραδώσει ἀδελφὸς ἀδελφὸν εἰς θάνατον καὶ πατὴρ τέκνον, καὶ ἐπαναστήσονται τέκνα ἐπὶ γονεῖς καὶ θανατώσουσιν αὐτούς [...].

613 Mk. 13:6: πολλοὶ ἐλεύσονται ἐπὶ τῷ ὀνόματί μου λέγοντες ὅτι Ἐγώ εἰμι, καὶ πολλοὺς πλανήσουσιν.

614 App. BC 1.5.19: προϊόντες τε τὴν Ῥωμαίων ἀρχὴν ὡς ἰδιωτικὸν σφῶν κτῆμα διενείμαντο ἐφ᾽ ἑαυτῶν τρεῖς οἵδε ἄνδρες, Ἀντώνιός τε καὶ Λέπιδος καὶ ὅτῳ πρότερον μὲν Ὀκτάουιος ὄνομα ἦν, Καίσαρι δὲ πρὸς γένους ὢν καὶ θετὸς ἐν διαθήκαις ὑπ᾽ αὐτοῦ γενόμενος Καῖσαρ ἐκ τοῦδε μετωνομάζετο.

615 Mk. 13:3: Καὶ καθημένου αὐτοῦ εἰς τὸ Ὄρος τῶν Ἐλαιῶν κατέναντι τοῦ ἱεροῦ ἐπηρώτα αὐτὸν κατ᾽ ἰδίαν Πέτρος καὶ Ἰάκωβος καὶ Ἰωάννης καὶ Ἀνδρέας, [...].

Antonius and *Lepidus* should have divided into 'Peter' *(Petrus)* and 'James' *(Jacobus)* here—we can leave open who is who for the moment—whereas 'John' *(Johannes)* stands for *Octavianus* as usual. 'Andrew' *(Andreas)* cannot possibly be *Cu-*

rio this time—as we assumed was the case with the disciples at the Rubicon/Jordan river—he having long since died. This time 'Andrew' could be *Asinius,* who intervened as peacemaker in the fight for succession between Antonius and Octavianus (he was consul in 40 BC; Vergilius celebrated him in verse in the 4th eclogue as restorer of the *Saturnia regna*). Both names have the same number of letters, the same word beginning, the same word ending and both contain a 'n' in the core: *ASINIVS > ANΔPEAC.* But then one would have to wonder whether the disciple, who forms a pair together with Simon at the Jordan, is not Asinius as well, who like Curio was at the Rubicon; we could at least ask if that was not the reason why Asinius became Andrew here. Other possibilities for Andrew are pseudo-Marius *Amatius* and *Ahenobarbus* who also played a role in the controversy over succession (for numismatical evidence of the latter cf. ALFÖLDI (1973) p. 111-112, pl. XIII, 1-4).

616 Mk. 13:8: ἀρχὴ ὠδίνων ταῦτα.
617 App. BC 2.72.299: 'Ἀλλὰ τάδε μὲν ᾠκονόμει θεὸς ἐς ἀρχὴν τῆσδε τῆς νῦν ἐπεχούσης τὰ πάντα ἡγεμονίας.
618 App. BC 4.8.31-12.48.
619 App. BC 4.12.48-13.51: ἅμα δὲ ταῖς προγραφαῖς αἵ τε πύλαι κατείχοντο καὶ ὅσαι ἄλλαι τῆς πόλεως ἔξοδοί τε καὶ λιμένες ἢ ἕλη καὶ τέλματα ἢ εἴ τι ἄλλο ἐς φυγὴν ὕποπτον ἦν ἢ ἐς λαθραίους καταφυγάς· τήν τε χώραν ἐπετέτραπτο τοῖς λοχαγοῖς ἐρευνᾶν περιθέουσι, καὶ ἐγίγνετο πάντα ὁμοῦ. Εὐθὺς οὖν ἦν ἀνά τε τὴν χώραν καὶ ἀνὰ τὴν πόλιν, ὡς ἕκαστός πῃ συνελαμβάνετο, ἀνδροληψία αἰφνίδια πολλὰ καὶ τρόποι τῶν φόνων ποικίλοι τῶν τε κεφαλῶν ἀποτομαὶ τοῦ μισθοῦ χάριν ἐς ἐπίδειξιν φυγαί τε ἀπρεπεῖς καὶ σχήματα ἄτοπα ἐκ τοῦ πρὶν περιφανοῦς. κατέδυνον γὰρ οἱ μὲν ἐς φρέατα, οἱ δὲ ἐς τὰς ὑπονόμους τάφρους ἐπὶ τὰ ἀκάθαρτα, οἱ δὲ ἐς καπνώδεις ὑπωροφίας ἢ τῶν τεγῶν ταῖς κεραμίσι βυομέναις ὑπεκάθηντο μετὰ σιγῆς βαθυτάτης. ἐδεδοίκεσαν γὰρ οὐχ ἧσσον τῶν σφαγέων οἱ μὲν γυναῖκας ἢ παῖδας οὐκ εὐμενῶς σφίσιν ἔχοντας, οἱ δὲ ἐξελευθέρους τε καὶ θεράποντας, οἱ δὲ καὶ δανεισμάτων χρήστας ἢ χωρίων γείτονας ἐπιθυμίᾳ τῶν χωρίων. Cf. also 4.13-51, passim.
620 Mk. 13:14-17: Ὅταν δὲ ἴδητε τὸ βδέλυγμα τῆς ἐρημώσεως ἑστηκότα ὅπου οὐ δεῖ, ὁ ἀναγινώσκων νοείτω, τότε οἱ ἐν τῇ Ἰουδαίᾳ φευγέτωσαν εἰς τὰ ὄρη, ὁ [δὲ] ἐπὶ τοῦ δώματος μὴ καταβάτω μηδὲ εἰσελθάτω ἆραί τι ἐκ τῆς οἰκίας αὐτοῦ, καὶ ὁ εἰς τὸν ἀγρὸν μὴ ἐπιστρεψάτω εἰς τὰ ὀπίσω ἆραι τὸ ἱμάτιον αὐτοῦ. οὐαὶ δὲ ταῖς ἐν γαστρὶ ἐχούσαις καὶ ταῖς θηλαζούσαις ἐν ἐκείναις ταῖς ἡμέραις.
621 App. BC 4.15.60: τῶν δὲ ἐκφυγόντων οἱ μὲν ὑπὸ ναυαγίων ἀπώλλυντο, ἐς πάντα σφίσι τῆς τύχης ἐπιβαρούσης, οἱ δὲ ἐπανήχθησαν ἐκ παραλόγων ἐπί τε ἀρχὰς τῆς πόλεως καὶ στρατηγίας πολέμων καὶ θριάμβους.
App. BC 4.16.63: (οὐ γὰρ ἀξιαφήγητον ἀναίρεσις ἁπλῆ καὶ φυγὴ ἢ τῶν τριῶν ἀνδρῶν τισι συγγνόντων ὕστερον ἐπάνοδος ἢ ἐπανελθόντων ἀφανὴς καταβίωσις) [...].
622 Mk. 13:20: καὶ εἰ μὴ ἐκολόβωσεν κύριος τὰς ἡμέρας, οὐκ ἂν ἐσώθη πᾶσα σάρξ· ἀλλὰ διὰ τοὺς ἐκλεκτοὺς οὓς ἐξελέξατο ἐκολόβωσεν τὰς ἡμέρας.
623 Mk. 13:22: καὶ τότε ἐάν τις ὑμῖν εἴπῃ, Ἴδε ὧδε ὁ Χριστός, Ἴδε ἐκεῖ, μὴ πιστεύετε· ἐγερθήσονται γὰρ ψευδόχριστοι καὶ ψευδοπροφῆται καὶ δώσουσιν σημεῖα καὶ τέρατα πρὸς τὸ ἀποπλανᾶν, εἰ δυνατόν, τοὺς ἐκλεκτούς.
624 Mk. 13:11: καὶ ὅταν ἄγωσιν ὑμᾶς παραδιδόντες, μὴ προμεριμνᾶτε τί λαλήσητε, ἀλλ' ὃ ἐὰν δοθῇ ὑμῖν ἐν ἐκείνῃ τῇ ὥρᾳ τοῦτο λαλεῖτε· [...].
625 SUET. *Jul.* 60: *Proelia non tantum destinato, sed ex occasione sumebat ac saepe ab itinere statim* [...].
626 Mk. 13:24-25: Ἀλλὰ ἐν ἐκείναις ταῖς ἡμέραις μετὰ τὴν θλῖψιν ἐκείνην / ὁ ἥλιος σκοτισθήσεται, / καὶ ἡ σελήνη οὐ δώσει τὸ φέγγος αὐτῆς, / καὶ οἱ ἀστέρες ἔσονται ἐκ τοῦ οὐρανοῦ πίπτοντες, / καὶ αἱ δυνάμεις αἱ ἐν τοῖς οὐρανοῖς σαλευθήσονται.
627 VERG. *Georg.* 1.466-8; 487-8: *ille etiam exstincto miseratus Caesare Romam, / cum caput obscura nitidum ferrugine texit, / impiaque aeternam timuerunt saecula*

noctem. [...] non alias caelo ceciderunt plura sereno / fulgura, nec diri totiens arsere cometae.

628 Cf. BOTERMANN, p. 204 and passim.
629 Mk. 14.
630 Mk. 16.
631 Mk. 10:17-27; 28-31.
632 PLUT. *Ant.* 16 and parallel traditions.
633 Mk. 10:35-45.
634 Mk. 12:18-27; SUET. *Aug.* 18.
635 Mk. 10:46-52.
636 PLUT. *Caes.* 65 and parallel tradition.
637 This enables one to draw a conclusion about the open question as to which person stands behind the apostle Bartholomew: if *Bartimaeus* comes from *Artemidoros*, then *Bartholomew* could be either a doublet of it, or it could have been derived from *Antonius* (respectively *Aristobulus*) with a corresponding generation of the initial *B* (see also below, note 649, *Bethania* from *Antonius*).
638 SUET. *Jul.* 68; Mk. 9:42-50.
639 PLUT. *Pomp.* 53 and parallel traditions.
640 Mk. 5:21-43.
641 Mk. 1:40-45; 2:1-12; 2:13-17.
642 PLUT. *Caes.* 45 and parallel tradition. The peg for inserting the excursus at this place, after the *healing of the possessed* (i.e. after Dyrrhachium and Pharsalos), would have been the new wife of Pompeius, Cornelia. She was a musician, and hence this could have been the reason for Caesar's ridicule of Pompeius' horsemen, who were from the young aristocracy, in his speech to his soldiers before the battle of Pharsalos as dancers. So the 'dancers' would have evoked Cornelia and Cornelia Julia.
643 Mk. 9:2-13.
644 PLUT. *Caes.* 14.
645 Mk. 14:1-2.
646 DIO CASS. *HR* 44.15.2.
647 Mk. 14:3-9.
648 PLUT. *Caes.* 61: γυμνοί; PLUT. *Ant.* 12: ἀληλιμμένοι λίπα.
649 *Antonius* (no doubt in the Greek accusative, as is often the case) should be compared with *Bêthania* here (in the dative, but the *iota subscriptum* is not necessarily written): ANTONIA > BHΘANIA; note the resemblance of the two decisive initial letters: AN > BH. Whether 'made of ivory', *eburneum*, should be compared with *myrou nardou*, 'spike oil', is one of the hypotheses.
650 Caesar was conscious of what the offer of the laurel-wreathed diadem meant for him, because he finally stood up angrily from the platform, tore the toga from his neck and shouted that he would offer his throat to everyone who demanded it. PLUT. *Ant.* 12: ἀνέστη μὲν οὖν ὁ Καῖσαρ ἀχθεσθεὶς ἀπὸ τοῦ βήματος, καὶ τὸ ἱμάτιον ἀπάγων ἀπὸ τοῦ τραχήλου τῷ βουλομένῳ παρέχειν τὴν σφαγὴν ἐβόα. A different description is given in PLUT. *Caes.* 60 where the same saying is put in Caesar's mouth in another occasion (during the reading of the honouring resolutions of the Senate in the Venus-temple): ὥστε κἀκεῖνον ἐννοήσαντα παραχρῆμα μὲν οἴκαδε τραπέσθαι καὶ βοᾶν πρὸς τοὺς φίλους ἀπαγαγόντα τοῦ τραχήλου τὸ ἱμάτιον, ὡς ἕτοιμος εἴη τῷ βουλομένῳ τὴν σφαγὴν παρέχειν [...]. Cf. also APP. *BC* 2.109.454.
651 Mk. 14:10-11; APP. *BC* 2.111.464-112.469 and parallel tradition.
652 APP. *BC* 2.120.503, 121.508, 141.591.
653 Mk. 14:12-26; PLUT. *Caes.* 63 and parallel tradition.
654 Mk. 14:30.
655 APP. *BC* 2.124.520; DIO CASS. *HR* 44.7.4.

656 App. *BC* 2.144.602.
657 App. *BC* 2.114.476.
658 Plut. *Caes.* 58.
659 Suet. *Jul.* 79.
660 Mk. 14:27.
661 Plut. *Caes.* 60, 61, the first sentence respectively, and parallel tradition; Mk. 14:27. The presence of the name *Galilaea* in this pericope, which as we have seen points to *Gallia*, could have produced an overdetermination of the name *Petrus*. In the accounts there repeatedly is talk about how both Bruti had already been particularly favored by Caesar earlier, the one, Decimus Brutus, being given his succession in Gallia Transalpina, the other, Marcus Brutus, that in Gallia Cisalpina (App. *BC* 2.111.465; 2.124.518). Thus, surprisingly, behind this 'Peter' could not only stand *Simon Petrus*, i.e. *Antonius* (with or without *Lepidus*) but also *Brutus*. This is not insurmountable in terms of the writing and the sound: BRVTVS > ΠΕΤΡΟC. This suspicion is substantiated by the presence of *Brutus* as *Petrus* in the next pericope.
662 Suet. *Jul.* 78; Plut. *Caes.* 60, *Ant.* 12; App. *BC* 2.107.446, 2.109.454-455; Dio Cass. *HR* 44.8.
663 Mk. 14:32-36: Καὶ ἔρχονται εἰς χωρίον οὗ τὸ ὄνομα Γεθσημανί καὶ λέγει τοῖς μαθηταῖς αὐτοῦ, Καθίσατε ὧδε ἕως προσεύξωμαι. καὶ παραλαμβάνει τὸν Πέτρον καὶ [τὸν] Ἰάκωβον καὶ [τὸν] Ἰωάννην μετ' αὐτοῦ καὶ ἤρξατο ἐκθαμβεῖσθαι καὶ ἀδημονεῖν καὶ λέγει αὐτοῖς, Περίλυπός ἐστιν ἡ ψυχή μου ἕως θανάτου· μείνατε ὧδε καὶ γρηγορεῖτε. καὶ προελθὼν μικρὸν ἔπιπτεν ἐπὶ τῆς γῆς καὶ προσηύχετο ἵνα εἰ δυνατόν ἐστιν παρέλθη ἀπ' αὐτοῦ ἡ ὥρα, καὶ ἔλεγεν, Αββα ὁ πατήρ, πάντα δυνατά σοι· παρένεγκε τὸ ποτήριον τοῦτο ἀπ' ἐμοῦ· ἀλλ' οὐ τί ἐγὼ θέλω ἀλλὰ τί σύ.
664 We have seen already the other possible bowdlerized translations of *CAPITOLIVM*—'place of skull' *(< ΚΡΑΝΙΟΥ ΤΟΠΟΝ < CAPI TOLIVM)* and 'oil-garden' *(< CAMPVS OLEI)*.
665 Mk. 14:32-36.
666 Plut. *Caes.* 62 and parallel tradition.
667 Dio Cass. *HR* 44.13; Plut. *Brut.* 13.
668 Mk. 14:35.
669 Plut. *Caes.* 63; Mk. 14:41-42.
670 Mk. 14:43-51; Plut. *Caes.* 66 and parallel tradition.
671 App. *BC* 2.117.491. Plut. *Caes.* 66: εἰσιόντος δὲ Καίσαρος ἡ βουλὴ μὲν ὑπεξανέστη θεραπεύουσα, τῶν δὲ περὶ Βροῦτον οἱ μὲν ἐξόπισθεν τὸν δίφρον αὐτοῦ περιέστησαν, οἱ δ' ἀπήντησαν ὡς δὴ Τιλλίῳ Κίμβρῳ περὶ ἀδελφοῦ φυγάδος ἐντυγχάνοντι συνδεησόμενοι, καὶ συνεδέοντο μέχρι τοῦ δίφρου παρακολουθοῦντες. ὡς δὲ καθίσας διεκρούετο τὰς δεήσεις καὶ προσκειμένων βιαιότερον ἠγανάκτει πρὸς ἕκαστον, ὁ μὲν Τίλλιος τὴν τήβεννον αὐτοῦ ταῖς χερσὶν ἀμφοτέραις συλλαβὼν ἀπὸ τοῦ τραχήλου κατῆγεν, ὅπερ ἦν σύνθημα τῆς ἐπιχειρήσεως. Plut. *Brut.* 17: Καίσαρι δ' εἰσιόντι μὲν ἡ σύγκλητος ὑπεξανέστη, καθεζόμενον δ' εὐθὺς ἐκεῖνοι περιέσχον ἀθρόοι, Τίλλιον Κίμβρον ἐξ ἑαυτῶν προβάλλοντες, ὑπὲρ ἀδελφοῦ φυγάδος δεόμενον, καὶ συνεδέοντο πάντες, ἁπτόμενοί τε χειρῶν καὶ στέρνα καὶ κεφαλὴν καταφιλοῦντες. ἀποτριβομένου δὲ τὰς δεήσεις τὸ πρῶτον, εἶθ' ὡς οὐκ ἀνίεσαν ἐξανισταμένου βίᾳ, Τίλλιος μὲν ἀμφοτέραις ταῖς χερσὶν ἐκ τῶν ὤμων κατέσπασε τὸ ἱμάτιον [...].
672 Mk. 14:44.
673 Mk. 14:51-52.
674 App. *BC* 2.117.492, 2.119.499. Moreover, the story about the foreign slave who hurried to Caesar in vain before the assault, could have contributed to the origin of the picture of a youth, which is reported by Plutarchus at the end of *Caes.* 64. Another cause could have been the report about the slaves, who carried Caesar's body home after the assault (cf. Nicolaus Damascenus).

675 PLUT. *Brut.* 14.
676 APP. *BC* 2.121.508-122.511.
677 PLUT. *Ant.* 13.
678 It is known that the Romans did not divide the night into hours, but into four *vigiliae,* 'night watches' or 'vigils', so that the time ἔτι πρὸ ἡμέρας, 'still before dawn', mentioned by Appianus, fell in one of the night watches, in the *quarta* or maybe even in the *tertia vigilia.* And his summons will have reached the senators in the *secunda vigilia* (nobody slept on this night anyway). So Mark's repeated hints to the 'second crowing' of the cock and also to the 'third denial' could be caused by Latin statements regarding time in his exemplar (which may have been more accurate than Appianus'). In his currently still unpublished manuscript *Taubenflug und Hahnenschrei—'Ornithologisches' zum Markusevangelium. II. Der Hahn* (Dove's flight and cock-crowing—'Ornithological issues' about the Mark-Gospel. II. The Cock) Gert Lüderitz, Tübingen, has not only demonstrated that there were no cocks in Jerusalem—keeping them was forbidden—and that Mark's 'cock-crowing', *alektorophônia* (13:35: there Mark gives the names of all the four nightwatches) corresponds to the Latin *gallicinium* and hence it is a time span—the *tertia vigilia,* the 'third nightwatch'—but he also proved, that the *secundis galliciniis,* 'at the second cock-crowing', was used as an equivalent for the *quarta vigilia,* 'in the third nightwatch'. So Mark's 'the second time the cock crew' (14:72) has to be understood as an utterance in respect of the time: 'before the fourth nightwatch'.
679 PLUT. *Caes.* 68; APP. *BC* 2.147.613; Mk. 14:66-72.
680 Mk. 14:53-65.
681 APP. *BC* 2.118.498.
682 The translation of *aulê* with 'palace' is inconsistent in so far as two pericopes further (15:16) Mark himself explains *aulê* as *praetorium.*
683 SUET. *Jul.* 83: *postulante ergo Lucio Pisone socero testamentum eius aperitur recitaturque in Antoni domo, quod Idibus Septembribus proximis in Lauicano suo fecerat demandaueratque uirgini Vestali maximae. Quintus Tubero tradit heredem ab eo scribi solitum ex consulatu ipsius primo usque ad initium ciuilis belli Cn. Pompeium, idque militibus pro contione recitatum. sed nouissimo testamento tres instituit heredes sororum nepotes, Gaium Octauium ex dodrante, et Lucium Pinarium et Quintum Pedium ex quadrante reliquo[s]; in ima cera Gaium Octauium etiam in familiam nomenque adoptauit; plerosque percussorum in tutoribus fili, si qui sibi nasceretur, nominauit, Decimum Brutum etiam in secundis heredibus.*
684 About this problem cf. SCHMITTHENNER (1973).
685 The *domô* in Mark's *oikodomô* probably comes from a *domus,* which may have stood in the original exemplar instead of *familia.*
686 CIC. *ad Att.* 16.15.3: *quamquam enim in praesentia belle iste puer retundit Antonium, tamen exitum expectare debemus. at quae contio! nam est missa mihi. iurat 'ita sibi parentis honores consequi liceat', et simul dextram intendit ad statuam.* μηδὲ σωθείην ὑπό γε τοιούτου!
687 Mk. 14:61-62: πάλιν ὁ ἀρχιερεὺς ἐπηρώτα αὐτὸν καὶ λέγει αὐτῷ, Σὺ εἶ ὁ Χριστὸς ὁ υἱὸς τοῦ εὐλογητοῦ; ὁ δὲ Ἰησοῦς εἶπεν, Ἐγώ εἰμι, / καὶ ὄψεσθε τὸν υἱὸν τοῦ ἀνθρώπου / ἐκ δεξιῶν καθήμενον τῆς δυνάμεως / καὶ ἐρχόμενον μετὰ τῶν νεφελῶν τοῦ οὐρανοῦ.
688 The addition ὁ Χριστὸς is missing in Φ pc k—cf. ALAND & NESTLE (^{18}1957).
689 CIC. 13.*Phil.* 11.24.
690 SUET. *Jul.* 82: *Fuerat animus coniuratis corpus occisi in Tiberim trahere, bona publicare, acta rescindere, sed metu Marci Antoni consulis et magistri equitum Lepidi destiterunt.*
APP. *BC* 2.128.535, 134.559; DIO CASS. *HR* 44.35.1.
691 Mk. 14:65.

692 Dio Cass. HR 44.5.3. This information about the inheritance of Caesar's position as *pontifex maximus* is only mentioned by Dio Cassius and so it is questionable; cf. Schmitthenner (1973), p. 9: '[...] the chapters of Cass. Dio 44.4-7 stand in a historiographic tradition that combines reality, plans, and—one must add—things foisted with libelous intention specifically to motivate the hatred which led to the murder.' Even if it was falsely rumored that Caesar wanted to make his heir *pontifex maximus*, the rumor was nevertheless still around in Dio Cassius' time (and nobody was wondering about it, because the later emperors were all *pontifex maximus* themselves). Because it is precisely about the hatred that led to the murder in the examined passage of Mark, the information could have stood in Mark's exemplar— but in this case as an addition by Octavianus, because the allusion '…or even only adopted ones?…' is all-too much in the interest of Octavianus to have been planned by Caesar.

693 App. BC 2.135.563-4: Τοιαῦτα εἰπόντος τοῦ Ἀντωνίου σὺν ἀνατάσει τε καὶ ὁρμῇ βαρυτέρᾳ, γίγνεται δόγμα, ἡσυχαζόντων ἤδη καὶ ἀγαπώντων ἁπάντων, φόνου μὲν οὐκ εἶναι δίκας ἐπὶ τῷ Καίσαρι, κύρια δὲ εἶναι τὰ πεπραγμένα αὐτῷ πάντα καὶ ἐγνωσμένα, "ἐπεὶ τῇ πόλει συμφέρει." ἐβιάσαντο γὰρ τόδε ἐς ἀσφάλειαν οἱ τῶν περισῳζομένων οἰκεῖοι προστεθῆναι μάλιστα, ὡς οὐ δικαίως φυλασσόμενα μᾶλλον ἢ διὰ χρείαν. καὶ ὁ Ἀντώνιος αὐτοῖς ἐς τοῦτο ἐνέδωκεν.

694 Mk. 15:1-5.

695 App. BC 2.130.542-131.547: Ὧδε δὲ ἔτι ἐχόντων, ὁ Ἀντώνιος καὶ ὁ Λέπιδος ἐκ τοῦ βουλευτηρίου προῆλθον· καὶ γάρ τινες αὐτοὺς ἐκ πολλοῦ συνδραμόντες ἐκάλουν. ὡς δὲ ὤφθησαν ἐκ μετεώρου καὶ σιγὴ κεκραγότων μόλις ἐγίγνετο, [...] ἐπιβοώντων δ' ἑτέρων τὸ πεπραγμένον ἐπεξιέναι καὶ τῶν πλεόνων περὶ τῆς εἰρήνης παρακαλούντων, τοῖς μὲν περὶ τῆς εἰρήνης ἔφη· "περὶ τούτου σκοποῦμεν, ὡς ἔσται τε καὶ γενομένη διαμενεῖ· δυσεύρετον γὰρ ἤδη τὸ ἀσφαλὲς αὐτῆς, ὅτι μηδὲ Καίσαρα ὤνησαν ὅρκοι τοσοίδε καὶ ἀραί." ἐς δὲ τοὺς ἐπεξιέναι παρακαλοῦντας ἐπιστραφεὶς ἐπῄνει μὲν ὡς εὐορκότερα καὶ εὐσεβέστερα αἱρουμένους καί "αὐτὸς ἄν," ἔφη, "συνετασσόμην ὑμῖν καὶ τὰ αὐτὰ πρῶτος ἐβόων, εἰ μὴ ὕπατος ἦν, ᾧ τοῦ λεγομένου συμφέρειν μᾶλλον ἢ τοῦ δικαίου μέλει· ὧδε γὰρ ἡμῖν οἱ ἔνδον παραινοῦσιν. οὕτω δέ που καὶ Καῖσαρ αὐτός, οὓς εἷλε πολέμῳ τῶν πολιτῶν, διὰ τὸ συμφέρον τῆς πόλεως περισώσας ὑπ' αὐτῶν ἀπέθανε." Τοιαῦτα τοῦ Ἀντωνίου παρὰ μέρος τεχνάζοντος [...].

Suet. Jul. 75: *Acie Pharsalica proclamauit, ut ciuibus parceretur, deincepsque nemini non suorum quem uellet unum partis aduersae seruare concessit. Nec ulli perisse nisi in proelio reperientur* [...].

696 Mk. 15:6-8: Κατὰ δὲ ἑορτὴν ἀπέλυεν αὐτοῖς ἕνα δέσμιον ὃν παρῃτοῦντο. ἦν δὲ ὁ λεγόμενος Βαραββᾶς μετὰ τῶν στασιαστῶν δεδεμένος οἵτινες ἐν τῇ στάσει φόνον πεποιήκεισαν. καὶ ἀναβὰς ὁ ὄχλος ἤρξατο αἰτεῖσθαι καθὼς ἐποίει αὐτοῖς.

697 Mk. 15:9-15: ὁ δὲ Πιλᾶτος ἀπεκρίθη αὐτοῖς λέγων, Θέλετε ἀπολύσω ὑμῖν τὸν βασιλέα τῶν Ἰουδαίων; ἐγίνωσκεν γὰρ ὅτι διὰ φθόνον παραδεδώκεισαν αὐτὸν οἱ ἀρχιερεῖς. οἱ δὲ ἀρχιερεῖς ἀνέσεισαν τὸν ὄχλον ἵνα μᾶλλον τὸν Βαραββᾶν ἀπολύσῃ αὐτοῖς. ὁ δὲ Πιλᾶτος πάλιν ἀποκριθεὶς ἔλεγεν αὐτοῖς, Τί οὖν [θέλετε] ποιήσω [ὃν λέγετε] τὸν βασιλέα τῶν Ἰουδαίων; οἱ δὲ πάλιν ἔκραξαν, Σταύρωσον αὐτόν. ὁ δὲ Πιλᾶτος ἔλεγεν αὐτοῖς, Τί γὰρ ἐποίησεν κακόν; οἱ δὲ περισσῶς ἔκραξαν, Σταύρωσον αὐτόν. ὁ δὲ Πιλᾶτος βουλόμενος τῷ ὄχλῳ τὸ ἱκανὸν ποιῆσαι ἀπέλυσεν αὐτοῖς τὸν Βαραββᾶν, καὶ παρέδωκεν τὸν Ἰησοῦν φραγελλώσας ἵνα σταυρωθῇ.

698 Cf. in connection with this the sense of *invidia* in Suetonius, where it does not mean 'envy', but 'jealousy, hatred'—Suet. Jul. 84: *Inter ludos cantata sunt quaedam ad miserationem et invidiam caedis eius accomodata, ex Pacuvi Armorum iudicio «Men servasse, ut essent qui me perderent?»*

699 Mk. 15:34: καὶ τῇ ἐνάτῃ ὥρᾳ ἐβόησεν ὁ Ἰησοῦς φωνῇ μεγάλῃ, Ελωι ελωι λεμα σαβαχθανι; ὅ ἐστιν μεθερμηνευόμενον Ὁ θεός μου ὁ θεός μου, εἰς τί ἐγκατέλιπές με;

700 The lection ελωι is borrowed from the Septuagint (Ps. 22:2); the variants that can be ascertained in the manuscripts—ηλι, λαμα, σαβαφθανι, ζαφθανι etc. (cf. ALAND & NESTLE [18]1957)—show on the one hand how unstable and how secondary the Aramaic reading is and on the other hand, how they revolve around the Latin text of Pacuvius (φ, (f), for v; z, (z), for s(e)r, etc.). Interestingly we can detect on the basis of the comparison between Mark and Pacuvius that the first word *mene* was fully written in Mark's exemplar and not abbreviated to *men*.

701 Mk. 15:40-41: ᾿Ησαν δὲ καὶ γυναῖκες ἀπὸ μακρόθεν θεωροῦσαι, ἐν αἷς καὶ Μαρία ἡ Μαγδαληνὴ καὶ Μαρία ἡ ᾿Ιακώβου τοῦ μικροῦ καὶ ᾿Ιωσῆτος μήτηρ καὶ Σαλώμη, αἳ ὅτε ἦν ἐν τῇ Γαλιλαίᾳ ἠκολούθουν αὐτῷ καὶ διηκόνουν αὐτῷ, καὶ ἄλλαι πολλαὶ αἱ συναναβᾶσαι αὐτῷ εἰς ῾Ιεροσόλυμα.

702 Mk. 15:39: ᾿Ιδὼν δὲ ὁ κεντυρίων ὁ παρεστηκὼς ἐξ ἐναντίας αὐτοῦ ὅτι οὕτως ἐξέπνευσεν εἶπεν, ᾿Αληθῶς οὗτος ὁ ἄνθρωπος υἱὸς θεοῦ ἦν.

703 CIC. Phil. 3.2.3-5, 3.4.8-9, 4.2.1, 5.16.43, 12.4.9: C. Caesar adulescens, paene potius puer, incredibili ac divina quadam mente atque virtute, cum maxime furor arderet Antoni, [...] nec postulantibus nec cogitantibus nobis, quia non posse fieri videbatur, firmissimum exercitum ex invicto genere veteranorum militum comparavit, patrimoniumque suum [...] in rei publicae salutis conlocavit [...] Cui quidem hodierno die, patres conscripti [...] tribuenda est auctoritas, ut rem publicam non modo a se susceptam sed etiam a nobis commendatam possit defendere. [...] Quod autem praesidium erat salutis libertatisque vestrae, si C. Caesaris fortissimorum sui patris militum exercitus non fuisset? Cuius de laudibus et honoribus qui ei pro divinis et immortalibus meritis divini immortalesque debentur. [...] Quis tum nobis, quis populo Romano optulit hunc divinum adulescentem deus? [...] C. Caesarem deorum beneficio natum ad haec tempora. Caesaris [...] incredibilis ac divina virtus. Cf. ALFÖLDI (1973), p. 120: 'C'est le ton solennel de la sotériologie hellénistique qu'on retrouve dans ces plaidoyers [...]. Par ces louanges, Cicéron se mettait malgré lui à l'unisson de la monarchie naissante.'

704 SUET. Jul. 52: Dilexit et reginas, [...] sed maxime Cleopatram, cum qua et conuiuia in primam lucem saepe protraxit et eadem naue thalamego paene Aethiopia tenus Aegytum penetrauit, nisi exercitus sequi recusasset, quam denique accitam in urbem non nisi maximis honoribus praemiisque auctam remisit filiumque natum appellare nomine suo passus est. SUET. Jul. 79: Quin etiam uaria fama percrebruit migraturum Alexandream uel Ilium, translatis simul opibus imperii exhaustaque Italia dilectibus et procuratione urbis amicis permissa [...]. About Cleopatra's frustrated hope for the nomination of her son Caesarion in Caesar's will cf. NICOLAUS DAMASCENUS 20.68.

705 With respect to Caesar's sexual dalliances in Gallia, about which his soldiers had sung at the Gallic triumph cf. note 599 and SUET. Jul. 51. The fact that a Gaius Julius Vindex could emerge later in Aquitania and call Gauls and Romans to a rebellion against the hated Nero, surely has to do with the seed Caesar had spread in Gallia (the first name-bearer had become a Roman citizen under Caesar). That Caesar's specialty was just such love affairs with married women is evident in the list in SUET. Jul. 50.

706 SUET. Jul. 52: Heluius Cinna Tr. Pl. plerisque confessus est habuisse se scriptam paratemque legem, quam Caesar ferre iussisset cum ipse abesset, ut ei uxores liberorum quaerendorum causa quas et quot uellet ducere licet.

707 SUET. Jul. 84: [...] matronae etiam pleraeque ornamenta sua, quae gerebant, et liberorum bullas atque praetextas.

708 DIO CASS. HR 44.51.1-2: [...] βωμὸν δέ τινα ἐν τῷ τῆς πυρᾶς χωρίῳ ἱδρυσάμενοι (τὰ γὰρ ⟨ὀστᾶ⟩ αὐτοῦ οἱ ἐξελεύθεροι προανείλοντο καὶ ἐς τὸ πατρῷον μνημεῖον κατέθεντο) θύειν τε ἐπ' αὐτῷ καὶ κατάρχεσθαι τῷ Καίσαρι ὡς καὶ θεῷ ἐπεχείρουν.

οἱ οὖν ὕπατοι ἐκεῖνόν τε ἀνέτρεψαν, καί τινας ἀγανακτήσαντας ἐπὶ τούτῳ ἐκόλασαν, [...].

App. BC 3.2.2-3.9: Ἀντώνιον μὲν ἡ βουλὴ δι' αἰτίας εἶχεν ἐπὶ τοῖς ἐπιταφίοις τοῦ Καίσαρος, ὑφ' ὧν δὴ μάλιστα ὁ δῆμος ἐρεθισθεὶς ὑπερεῖδε τῆς ἄρτι ἐπεψηφισμένης ἀμνηστίας καὶ ἐπὶ τὰς οἰκίας τῶν σφαγέων σὺν πυρὶ ἔδραμον· ὁ δὲ αὐτὴν χαλεπαίνουσαν ἑνὶ τοιῷδε πολιτεύματι ἐς εὔνοιαν ἑαυτοῦ μετέβαλεν. Ἀμάτιος ἦν ὁ Ψευδομάριος· Μαρίου γὰρ ὑπεκρίνετο υἱωνὸς εἶναι καὶ διὰ Μάριον ὑπερήρεσκε τῷ δήμῳ. γιγνόμενος οὖν κατὰ τήνδε τὴν ὑπόκρισιν συγγενὴς τῷ Καίσαρι, ὑπερήλγει μάλιστα αὐτοῦ τεθνεῶτος καὶ βωμὸν ἐπῳκοδόμει τῇ πυρᾷ καὶ χεῖρα θρασυτέρων ἀνδρῶν εἶχε καὶ φοβερὸς ἦν ἀεὶ τοῖς σφαγεῦσιν· ὧν οἱ μὲν ἄλλοι διεπεφεύγεσαν ἐκ τῆς πόλεως καὶ ὅσοι παρ' αὐτοῦ Καίσαρος εἰλήφεσαν ἡγεμονίας ἐθνῶν, ἀπεληλύθεσαν ἐπὶ τὰς ἡγεμονίας, Βροῦτος μὲν ὁ Δέκμος ἐς τὴν ὅμορον τῆς Ἰταλίας Κελτικήν, Τρεβώνιος δὲ ἐς τὴν Ἀσίαν τὴν περὶ Ἰωνίαν, Τίλλιος δὲ Κίμβερ ἐς Βιθυνίαν· Κάσσιος δὲ καὶ Βροῦτος ὁ Μᾶρκος, ὧν δὴ καὶ μάλιστα τῇ βουλῇ διέφερεν, ᾕρηντο μὲν καὶ οἵδε ὑπὸ τοῦ Καίσαρος ἐς τὸ μέλλον ἔτος ἡγεμονεύειν, Συρίας μὲν ὁ Κάσσιος καὶ Μακεδονίας ὁ Βροῦτος, ἔτι δὲ ὄντες ἀστικοὶ στρατηγοί ... ὑπ' ἀνάγκης καὶ διατάγμασιν οἷα στρατηγοὶ τοὺς κληρούχους ἐθεράπευον, ὅσοις τε ἄλλοις ἐπενόουν, καὶ τὰ κληρουχήματα συγχωροῦντες αὐτοῖς πιπράσκειν, τοῦ νόμου κωλύοντος ἐντὸς εἴκοσιν ἐτῶν ἀποδίδοσθαι. Τούτοις δὲ αὐτοῖς ὁ Ἀμάτιος, ὅτε συντύχοι, καὶ ἐνεδρεύσειν ἐλέγετο. τῷδε οὖν τῷ λόγῳ τῆς ἐνέδρας ὁ Ἀντώνιος ἐπιβαίνων οἷα ὕπατος συλλαμβάνει καὶ κτείνει τὸν Ἀμάτιον χωρὶς δίκης, μάλα θρασέως· καὶ ἡ βουλὴ τὸ μὲν ἔργον ἐθαύμαζεν ὡς μέγα καὶ παράνομον, τὴν δὲ χρείαν αὐτοῦ προσεποιοῦντο ἥδιστα· οὐ γὰρ αὐτοῖς ἐδόκει ποτὲ χωρὶς τοιᾶσδε τόλμης ἀσφαλῆ τὰ κατὰ Βροῦτον καὶ Κάσσιον ἔσεσθαι. οἱ δὲ τοῦ Ἀματίου στασιῶται καὶ ὁ ἄλλος δῆμος ἐπ' ἐκείνοις πόθῳ τε τοῦ Ἀματίου καὶ ἀγανακτήσει τοῦ γεγονότος, ὅτι μάλιστα αὐτὸ ὁ Ἀντώνιος ἐπεπράχει ὑπὸ τοῦ δήμου τιμώμενος, οὐκ ἠξίουν σφῶν καταφρονεῖν· τὴν ἀγορὰν οὖν καταλαβόντες ἐβόων καὶ τὸν Ἀντώνιον ἐβλασφήμουν καὶ τὰς ἀρχὰς ἐκέλευον ἀντὶ Ἀματίου τὸν βωμὸν ἐκθεοῦν καὶ θύειν ἐπ' αὐτοῦ Καίσαρι πρώτους. ἐξελαυνόμενοι δ' ἐκ τῆς ἀγορᾶς ὑπὸ στρατιωτῶν ἐπιπεμφθέντων ὑπὸ Ἀντωνίου μᾶλλον τε ἠγανάκτουν καὶ ἐκεκράγεσαν καὶ ἕδρας ἔνιοι τῶν Καίσαρος ἀνδριάντων ἐπεδείκνυον ἀνῃρημένων. ὡς δέ τις αὐτοῖς ἔφη καὶ τὸ ἐργαστήριον, ἔνθα οἱ ἀνδριάντες ἀνεσκευάζοντο, δείξειν, εὐθὺς εἵποντο καὶ ἰδόντες ἐνεπίμπρασαν, ἕως ἑτέρων ἐπιπεμφθέντων ἐξ Ἀντωνίου ἀμυνόμενοί τε ἀνῃρέθησαν ἔνιοι καὶ συλληφθέντες ἕτεροι ἐκρεμάσθησαν, ὅσοι θεράποντες ἦσαν, οἱ δὲ ἐλεύθεροι κατὰ τοῦ κρημνοῦ κατερρίφθησαν.

709 Dio Cass. HR 47.19.2: πρὸς δὲ τούτοις ἀπεῖπον μὲν μηδεμίαν εἰκόνα αὐτοῦ, καθάπερ θεοῦ τινος ὡς ἀληθῶς ὄντος, ἐν ταῖς τῶν συγγενῶν αὐτοῦ ἐκφοραῖς πέμπεσθαι, ὅπερ ἐκ τοῦ πάνυ ἀρχαίου καὶ τότε ἔτι ἐγίγνετο.

710 App. BC 2.148.616-617: ἔνθα βωμὸς πρῶτος ἐτέθη, νῦν δ' ἐστὶ νεὼς αὐτοῦ Καίσαρος, θείων τιμῶν ἀξιουμένου· ὁ γάρ τοι θετὸς αὐτῷ παῖς Ὀκτάουιος, τό τε ὄνομα ἐς τὸν Καίσαρα μεταβαλὼν καὶ κατ' ἴχνος ἐκείνου τῇ πολιτείᾳ προσιών, τήν τε ἀρχὴν τὴν ἐπικρατοῦσαν ἔτι νῦν, ἐρριζωμένην ὑπ' ἐκείνου, μειζόνως ἐκρατύνατο καὶ τὸν πατέρα τιμῶν ἰσοθέων ἠξίωσεν· [...].

711 Mk. 15:42-47; 16:1-8: Καὶ ἤδη ὀψίας γενομένης, ἐπεὶ ἦν παρασκευή ὅ ἐστιν προσάββατον, ἐλθὼν Ἰωσὴφ [ὁ] ἀπὸ Ἁριμαθαίας εὐσχήμων βουλευτής, ὃς καὶ αὐτὸς ἦν προσδεχόμενος τὴν βασιλείαν τοῦ θεοῦ, τολμήσας εἰσῆλθεν πρὸς τὸν Πιλᾶτον καὶ ᾐτήσατο τὸ σῶμα τοῦ Ἰησοῦ. ὁ δὲ Πιλᾶτος ἐθαύμασεν εἰ ἤδη τέθνηκεν καὶ προσκαλεσάμενος τὸν κεντυρίωνα ἐπηρώτησεν αὐτὸν εἰ πάλαι ἀπέθανεν· καὶ γνοὺς ἀπὸ τοῦ κεντυρίωνος ἐδωρήσατο τὸ πτῶμα τῷ Ἰωσήφ. καὶ ἀγοράσας σινδόνα καθελὼν αὐτὸν ἐνείλησεν τῇ σινδόνι καὶ ἔθηκεν αὐτὸν ἐν μνημείῳ ὃ ἦν λελατομημένον ἐκ πέτρας καὶ προσεκύλισεν λίθον ἐπὶ τὴν θύραν τοῦ μνημείου. ἡ δὲ Μαρία ἡ Μαγδαληνὴ καὶ Μαρία ἡ Ἰωσῆτος ἐθεώρουν ποῦ τέθειται.

Καὶ διαγενομένου τοῦ σαββάτου Μαρία ἡ Μαγδαληνὴ καὶ Μαρία ἡ [τοῦ] Ἰακώβου καὶ Σαλώμη ἠγόρασαν ἀρώματα ἵνα ἐλθοῦσαι ἀλείψωσιν αὐτόν. καὶ λίαν πρωῒ τῇ μιᾷ τῶν σαββάτων ἔρχονται ἐπὶ τὸ μνημεῖον ἀνατείλαντος τοῦ ἡλίου. καὶ ἔλεγον πρὸς ἑαυτάς, Τίς ἀποκυλίσει ἡμῖν τὸν λίθον ἐκ τῆς θύρας τοῦ μνημείου; καὶ ἀναβλέψασαι θεωροῦσιν ὅτι ἀποκεκύλισται ὁ λίθος· ἦν γὰρ μέγας σφόδρα. καὶ εἰσελθοῦσαι εἰς τὸ μνημεῖον εἶδον νεανίσκον καθήμενον ἐν τοῖς δεξιοῖς περιβεβλημένον στολὴν λευκήν, καὶ ἐξεθαμβήθησαν. ὁ δὲ λέγει αὐταῖς, Μὴ ἐκθαμβεῖσθε· Ἰησοῦν ζητεῖτε τὸν Ναζαρηνὸν τὸν ἐσταυρωμένον· ἠγέρθη, οὐκ ἔστιν ὧδε· ἴδε ὁ τόπος ὅπου ἔθηκαν αὐτόν. ἀλλὰ ὑπάγετε εἴπατε τοῖς μαθηταῖς αὐτοῦ καὶ τῷ Πέτρῳ ὅτι Προάγει ὑμᾶς εἰς τὴν Γαλιλαίαν· ἐκεῖ αὐτὸν ὄψεσθε, καθὼς εἶπεν ὑμῖν. καὶ ἐξελθοῦσαι ἔφυγον ἀπὸ τοῦ μνημείου, εἶχεν γὰρ αὐτὰς τρόμος καὶ ἔκστασις· καὶ οὐδενὶ οὐδὲν εἶπαν· ἐφοβοῦντο γάρ.

712 SUET. *Jul.* 85: cf. note 37.
713 Regarding Piso, Calpurnia's father, who was the real undertaker of Caesar, cf. the already quoted passages of Appianus; for Atia as the testamentary co-appointee cf. NICOLAUS DAMASCENUS 17.48: ἐπισκήψειε δὲ καὶ Ἀτίᾳ τῇ μητρὶ τοῦ παιδὸς τῆς ἑαυτοῦ ταφῆς ἐπιμεληθῆναι.
714 The short ending of Mark stands in the manuscripts, which place it directly after 16:8 and it reads: ΑΛΛΩΣ [[Πάντα δὲ τὰ παρηγγελμένα τοῖς περὶ τὸν Πέτρον συντόμως ἐξήγγειλαν. Μετὰ δὲ ταῦτα καὶ αὐτὸς ὁ Ἰησοῦς (εφανη) ἀπὸ ἀνατολῆς καὶ ἄχρι δύσεως ἐξαπέστειλεν δι' αὐτῶν τὸ ἱερὸν καὶ ἄφθαρτον κήρυγμα τῆς αἰωνίου σωτηρίας. ἀμήν.]]—Theologians translate it like this, e.g.: 'All that was ordered they reported briefly to those around Peter. Then Jesus himself also sent from the rise to the setting through them the holy and everlasting message of the eternal salvation.' This text design and this translation do not make much sense in respect of the language and the content, which could be the reason why this passage is often suppressed. They are based on the assumption that among others δύσεως means 'setting of the sun' and that it is not a form of δύω, 'to come up', (that εφανη after ὁ Ἰησοῦς is missing in most manuscripts and was still added sometimes should make one sit up and take notice). Or also the fact that τὸ ἱερὸν should be interpreted as an adjective, 'holy', and not rather as a substantive, 'holy area, temple'.
715 Cf. PLUT. *Ant.* 15; DIO CASS. *HR* 44.53.
716 Apollonia was an important point at the Via Egnatia, in the South of Illyria, today the village Poian in Albania.
717 Τὸ ἱερὸν could therefore, not only because of its spelling, simply stand for *Rome*.
718 Cf. ZANKER, p. 43, ill. 25 b; p. 64, ill. 44 b; p. 219, ill. 168 b.
719 Re-examining it, we find that very few details are missing—for example that 'Simon a Cyrenian' according to Mark was 'coming out of the country' and that he was 'the father of Alexander and Rufus' (Mk. 15:21: Καὶ ἀγγαρεύουσιν παράγοντά τινα Σίμωνα Κυρηναῖον ἐρχόμενον ἀπ' ἀγροῦ, τὸν πατέρα "Ἀλεξάνδρου καὶ Ῥούφου, ἵνα ἄρῃ τὸν σταυρὸν αὐτοῦ). We have seen in the chapter 'Crux', that *Simon a Cyrenian* stands for *Antonius per praeconem*, 'Antonius by the Herald'. Suetonius (*Jul.* 76) gives as one of the reasons which led to Caesar's murder that he no longer handed over important offices to top-ranking Romans but to his servants and freedmen, amongst which was the command of the three legions he had left in Alexandria: 'to Rufio, who grew up in his house, son of a freedman'. Was it written in Mark's exemplar that the father of Rufio, who was in command in Alexandria, served Antonius as a herald?
720 SUET. *Aug.* 6.
721 SUET. *Aug.* 2 and 4.
722 SUET. *Aug.* 21.4-5. Parthians on bended knee during the return of the *signa*, can be seen on coins, cf. i.a. *B.M.C. 4549*, *Imp. 40*, *R.I.C. 122*, also *B.M.C. 4525*, *Imp. 14*, *R.I.C. 99*; kneeling Armenian: *B.M.C. 4547*, *Imp. 43*, *R.I.C. 119*, as well

B.M.C. p. 62 note, Imp. p. 5 note, R.I.C. 103; kneeling Gaul, offering a standard: B.M.C. 4678, Imp. 127, R.I.C. 175.

723 SUET. Aug. 94.3.
724 SUET. Aug. 94.4.
725 SUET. Aug. 94.4-5; Lk. 2:22-35.
726 SUET. Aug. 94.6-7; Lk. 2:41-52.
727 SUET. Aug. 70.1-2; Mk. 16:14; Lk. 24:30.
728 SUET. Jul. 42.2: neue ii, qui pecuariam facerent, minus tertia parte puberum ingenuorum inter pastores haberent. Caesar's contempt for the shepherds is a noticeable guideline of his writings. In the civil war he repeatedly accuses Pompeius of recruiting even herdsmen. Since the slave insurgency the herdsmen-slaves did not only epitomize barbarism and all that was abhorred, but they were the enemy par excellence to the family farmers the Romans were and still wanted to be. From the populares' point of view, there was also the fact that the great land owners could only maintain their latifundia through the use of slaves, and by giving up agriculture and turning to pasture farming. But thereby grain became scarce, the cities were full of starving proletarians whereas recruits for the army were missing which could only be provided effectively by free, small farmers. The main device of the legionary was the spade and not the crook. Caesar's settlement of colonies was aimed at increasing the number of free farmers and disposing of the herdsman-slaves—and thus reducing the city proletariat. The regulation that the cattle-breeders had to have at least one third of their herdsman composed of freemen, made cattle-breeding less attractive and induced the free herdsmen to switch over to agriculture. For in the long term, pasturing could only be managed as a family business. But if the family grew, the scarce land had to be husbanded more intensively; thus pasturing was restricted to areas that were absolutely unsuitable for agriculture.
729 SUET. Jul. 43.4.
730 SUET. Jul. 42.3.
731 SUET. Jul. 6, Lk. 1:28. We have to compare *Amitae meae* and *Ave Maria, gratia plena* with *maternum genus* and also *dominus tecum* with *cum diis coniunctum*. N.B.: Luke is not as close to the original text as is Mark.

Final Observations—History

732 About Asinius Pollio cf. ANDRÉ (1949) and FELDMAN (1953), p. 73-80.
733 Φ Λ Α Ο Υ Ι Ο Σ
    Σ   Α Ο Υ Λ Ο Σ
    Π   Α Ο Υ Λ Ο Σ

It is conspicuous that *Flavius* in the scholarly Greek writing contains the complete graphism of *Saulus* and *Paulus*: $Φ + I = Σ + Π$—the other elements are identical, there is only a metathesis of the Liquida $Λ$.

This would explain why Paulus has two names, *Saulus/Paulus*, which would originate from two different lections in the manuscripts.

734 SUET. Vesp. 4.4: [...] ipse potissimum delectus est ut et industriae expertae nec metuendus ullo modo ob humilitatem generis ac nominis.
735 Cf. HAHN (1906).
736 For the poor writing occurring to somebody like Augustus, cf. SUET. Aug. 88.
737 Hieronymus about *herodiani* (Mt. 22:16, Mk. 3:6): [...] qui Herodem Christum esse credebant [...], cf. MIGNE PL XXIII.178; cf. PERS. 5.179 sqq.
738 Cf. note 183.

Chronology

100 BC	*July, 13th:* Gaius Iulius Caesar is born, in the sixth consulate of his uncle Marius.
88 BC	Outbreak of the Civil War between the party in the Senate (optimates) of L. Cornelius Sulla and the people's party (populares) of Gaius Marius, Caesar's uncle.
87 BC	Caesar is appointed flamen Dialis.
82-79	Dictatorship of Sulla.
75 BC	Pompeius battles Sertorius without success in Spain.
73 BC	Caesar becomes pontifex (priest).
73-71	Slaves' insurrection led by Spartacus. Pompeius and Crassus have many rebelling slaves crucified.
72 BC	Sertorius is murdered. Decisive victories of Pompeius over Sertorius' followers.
63 BC	Caesar becomes pontifex maximus.
62 BC	Bona Dea scandal. P. Clodius Pulcher is accused of sacrilege. Caesar as pontifex maximus testifies in favor of him.
60 BC	First triumvirate: collusion between Caesar, Pompeius and Crassus against the optimates.
59 BC	Caesar's first consulate. Increasing tensions between him and the Senate.
58-52	Caesar conquers Gaul. The Gauls under the leadership of Vercingetorix are decisively defeated at Alesia.
54 BC	Caesar's daughter Iulia, the wife of Pompeius, dies.
52 BC	Anarchy in Rome, Clodius murdered. The Senate and Pompeius move closer together. Increasing distance between Pompeius and Caesar.
49-45	Civil War between Caesar and the Pompeians.
49 BC	Liberation resp. Occupation of Italy; siege of Massilia; first Spanish campaign.
January	
1-7	Sittings of the Senate in Rome. Handling of the written compromise proposal of Caesar. The proposal is rejected.
7	Senatus consultum ultimum: emergency decree of the Senate. The people's tribunes flee from Rome to Caesar.
10	Caesar crosses the Rubicon: alea iacta esto.
12	Taking of Ariminum (Rimini).
17	Pompeius leaves Rome.
18	The consuls and the Senate leave Rome.
February	
15	Caesar besieges Corfinium.
21	Taking of Corfinium.

25	Pompeius in Brundisium (Brindisi).
March	
2	9 cohorts of Pompeius defect to Caesar.
4	The consuls evade with 30 cohorts to Dyrrachium (Durazzo/Durres).
9	Caesar before Brundisium.
17	Pompeius follows the consuls to Greece with 20 cohorts.
31	Caesar in Rome for the first time (since the beginning of the Civil War).
April	
beginning	Caesar seizes the treasury in the temple of Saturnus against the resistance of Metellus.
	Caesar sends his legates into the provinces.
7	Caesar leaves Rome.
19	Caesar before Massilia (Marseille).
22	Curio goes to Sicily.
June	
5	Caesar heads to Spain. Beginning of the first Spanish campaign.
22	Caesar before Ilerda.
26	Battle at Ilerda. Caesar beats Pompeius' legates.
27	First sea battle at Massilia.
28	Caesar cuts off the Pompeians from the Ebro.
July	
31	Second sea battle at Massilia.
August	
2	Afranius and Petreius capitulate.
8	Curio goes to Africa.
13	Curio before Utica.
16	Battle at Utica.
20	Battle at the Bagradas and death of Curio.
September	
7	Caesar in Spain before Corduba (Córdoba).
17	Caesar consults the oracle in the temple of Venus Marina in Gades (Cádiz).
22	The camp of Afranius is resolved.
October	
25	Caesar in Massilia. Message from Rome, that he has been appointed dictator by praetor M. Lepidus.
November	
middle	Mutiny in Placentia (Piacenza).
December	
2/12	Caesar in Rome for the 2nd time.
22	Caesar in Brundisium.
48 BC	Campaign against Pompeius: Epirus, Thessaly, Asia minor, Egypt.
January	
4	Caesar embarks from Brundisium.
5	Landing in Epirus.
6	Occupation of Oricum.
7	Occupation of Apollonia.
9	Pompeius before Dyrrachium.
March	
middle	Death of Bibulus.

27	Antonius lands in Dalmatia.
April	
3	Antonius unites with Caesar.
5	Pompeius encamps at the Genusus.
8	Destruction of Caesar's fleet at Oricum.
June	
middle	Caesar begins with the encirclement of Pompeius.
July	
6	Pompeius breaks through the blockade.
9	Caesar withdraws to Apollonia.
12	Caesar begins his march to Thessaly.
24	Unification with Domitius.
26	Storming of Gomphoi (Gomphi).
29	Caesar encamps on the plain of Thessaly.
August	
1	Unification of Pompeius with Scipio.
9	Battle at Pharsalus. Caesar prevails. Pompeius flees to Egypt.
10	Caesar in Lárisa (Larissa).
16	Pompeius in Mytilene.
September	
19	Caesar in Asia minor.
28	Pompeius lands in Egypt and is murdered. His body is decapitated.
October	
2	Caesar in Alexandria. The rhetor Theodotos offers Pompeius' head to Caesar.
November	
9	Beginning of the Alexandrine War.
11	Burning of the Egyptian fleet / Caesar beleaguered in the palace waits for reinforcement from Asia minor.
17	Execution of Pothinus.
December	
2	Achillas is killed by Ganymedes on Arsinoe's order.
28	Defeat of Domitius by Pharnaces in Nikopolis in Pontus.
47 BC	Egypt, Pontus, Rome, Departure for Africa.
January	
6	Caesar conquers the island of Pharos.
17	Caesar releases Ptolemy.
March	
6	Battle of Pelusium: Antipatros conquers the city.
15	Battle at the 'Castra Ioudaeorum'.
16	Sea battle at the island of Tauris.
27	Battle at the Nile. Exitus of Ptolemy. Cleopatra sole queen. Alexandria surrenders.
April–May	Caesar stays in Egypt. Visit to Alexanders' tomb. Consultation of the astronomers about the calendar problem. Cruise on the Nile with Cleopatra.
June	
28	Caesar departs for Syria.
July	
28	Deiotaros with Caesar.

August
2   Battle of Zela, defeat of Pharnaces: veni, vidi, vici.
29   Birth of Caesarion, the 'little Caesar'.
September
26   Caesar lands in Tarentum.
end   Mutiny of two legions in Campania.
October
4   Caesar in Rome for the 3rd time.
December
beginning   Caesar leaves Rome towards Sicily.
17   Arrival in Lilybaeum (Marsala).
25   Departure for Africa.
28   Landing in Hadrumetum (Sousse/Susah).
            Camp in Ruspina (Monastir).

46 BC   Africa, Rome, Departure for Spain.
January
1   Taking of Leptis.
4   Battle of Ruspina.
12   Scipio unites with Labienus and Petreius.
22   Arrival of two legions of Caesar.
February
17   Iuba combines his army with Scipio.
28   Arrival of two more legions of Caesar.
April
4   Caesar marches to Thapsos. Scipio follows him.
6   Battle of Thapsos. Rest of the Pompeians flee to Spain.
12   Suicide of Cato in Utica.
16   Caesar in Utica.
July
25   Caesar in Rome for the 4th time.
August   Celebration of the four triumphs: over Gallia (Vercingetorix); Egypt (Arsinoe); Pontus (Pharnaces); Africa (Iuba).
September Sanctification of the Forum Iulium and the temple of Venus Genetrix. Calendar reform.
November
beginning   Caesar departs for Spain.
December
beginning   Arrival in Obulco (Porcuna).

45 BC   Second Spanish campaign, Rome.
January   Operations around Corduba.
March
17   Battle of Munda.
            Gnaeus Pompeius, son of Pompeius Magnus, killed on the run.
April
12   Caesar in Gades (Cádiz).
21   Rome's Foundation Day. Parilia festival.
            First superhuman honors for Caesar decreed by the Senate.
30   Caesar in Hispalis (Sevilla).

CHRONOLOGY

October
beginning   Caesar in Rome for the 5th time.
           Fifth triumph – Ovatio – over the sons of Pompeius.

44 BC   Rome, preparation of the campaign against the Parthians, Caesar's assassination, outrage of the people, the struggle for his succession initiates.

January
14   Caesar imperator, consul and dictator for the fifth time.
26   After the *Feriae Latinae* in Alba Caesar moves into Rome on horseback.

February
14   Caesar *dictator perpetuo*, (for life).
15   Feast of the Lupercalia, with the new college of the *Luperci Iulii*.
       Caesar declines the 'king's diadem' which Antonius as a Lupercus offers him.

March
14   Caesar takes Decimus Iunius Brutus along to supper at the house of Lepidus, his *magister equitum*. While the chalice goes around Caesar praises the sudden death as the best.
15   Assassination of Caesar in the curia of Pompeius at the beginning of a Senate meeting. Caesar's medical attendant Antistius states 23 stab wounds, one of them lethal: the second which was inflicted on him in the chest.
19   Burial of Caesar. Speech of Antonius. Caesar's Will and Testament is read out. The enraged people burn his body at the Forum and hunt for his murderers.
25-28   Coming from Apollonia in Epirus Octavianus lands at Brundisium.

April
3-4   Law of Antonius to abolish dictatorship. Reorganization of the consular provinces.
9   Amatius puts on riots in Rome.
12-19   Ludi Cereales (festival of public games in Ceres' honor).
13   Amatius is executed.
middle   Antonius surrounds himself with body guards.
18   Caesar's bequest is published.
from 23   Octavianus marches to Rome.
27-28   Antonius and Dolabella have followers of Amatius executed.

May
6/7   Arrival of Octavianus in Rome.
21   Tribunes refuse to let Octavianus position Caesar's honorary armchair.
21-30   Octavianus visits Antonius in the gardens of Pompeius, where he reveals to him that he as testamentarily adopted son claims Caesar's inheritance. Antonius defies him.

June
2   Octavianus starts to pay off Caesar's heritage to the people.
    Law of Antonius reinforcing Caesar's official acts.

July
6-13   Ludi Apollinares (festival of public games in honor of Apollo).
13   Caesar's birthday.
20-30   Ludi victoriae Caesaris (festival of public games to celebrate Caesar's victory): Antonius prevents the positioning of a golden armchair in honor of Caesar. A comet appears at the sky, the Sidus Iulium.

end	Agitation of Octavianus against Antonius, then reconciliation.
August	
17	Brutus and Cassius leave Italy.
September	Octavian agitates amongst the soldiers of Antonius.
October	
5/6	Detentions amongst the body guards of Antonius. Octavianus is accused of an attempt on Antonius' life.
9	Antonius travels to Brundisium.
middle	Mutiny of the Macedonian legions in Brundisium.
end	Octavianus campaigns in Campania amongst the veterans settled by Caesar.
December	
beginning	Antonius occupies Gallia Cisalpina; Decimus Brutus resists, leaves for Rome, but is surrounded in Mutina (Modena).
43 BC	Cicero stirs up war against Antonius. Octavianus joins the belligerent consuls with his private army and receives propraetorial authority. Antonius allies with Lepidus. The second triumvirate is formed.
1 *jan.*	Cicero gives his 5th Philippic against Antonius in the Senate.
29 *may*	Agreement between Lepidus and Antonius.
19 *aug.*	Octavian and Pedius consuls.
ca. 20 *aug.*	Cancellation of the amnesty for the murderers of Caesar.
end *aug.*	Resolutions against Lepidus and Antonius are cancelled. Asinius Pollio joins Antonius.
september	Flight and death of Decimus Brutus.
11 *nov.*	Meeting of Antonius, Lepidus und Octavianus on a river island between Mutina and Bononia (Bologna): establishment of the 2nd triumvirate, which is acknowledged under constitutional law (*Lex Titia: Triumviri rei publicae constituendae* = three men for the reorganization of the state) and is restricted to five years.
middle nov.	Reign of terror in Rome. Proscriptions are decreed. More than 2000 knights and 200 senators, amongst them Cicero, are outlawed.
42 BC	
1 *jan.*	The triumviri and everybody else swear an oath to respect Caesar's acts. Caesar's consecration confirmed. The Lex templi prescribes the construction of the Temple of Divus Iulius on the Forum Romanum (and his worship in all cities in the empire and outside).
oct./nov.	Battles at Philippi. Antonius defeats Cassius. 20 days later Brutus is defeated also. Antonius goes to the East (Asia, Syria, Egypt).
41 BC	Merciless fight of Octavianus against the consul Lucius Antonius, brother of Antonius, and Antonius' ex-wife Fulvia in Perusia (Perugia).
40 BC	Agreement of Brundisium arranged by Maecenas. The empire is devided: Antonius who marries Octavia, the sister of Octavianus, obtains the East, Octavianus the West, Lepidus Africa. Italy becomes neutral territory.
39 BC	Treaty of Misenum: Sextus Pompeius promises crop supplies to Rome, in return he receives Sicily, Sardinia, Corsica and Achaia.
38 BC	Renewal of the triumvirate for another five years.
37 BC	Treaty of Tarent arranged by Asinius Pollio who becomes consul. Antonius lets Octavianus have his fleet for use against Sextus Pompeius.

36 BC	Octavianus' general Agrippa defeats S. Pompeius at Mylae and Naulochos. Lepidus is elected pontifex maximus and thus excluded. After divorcing Octavia Antonius marries Cleopatra.
34 BC	Antonius occupies Armenia. He tries to establish a hellenistic-oriental sultanate, expands Cleopatra's sphere of control and makes Caesarion co-regent.
32 BC	Octavianus publicizes Antonius' Will and Testament which is deposited at the vestals and thus fuels war. Officially this Ptolemaic War is directed against Cleopatra.
31 BC	*September 9th:* The Battle of Actium. In this sea battle Agrippa prevails over Cleopatra's fleet. She flees to Egypt, Antonius follows her.
30 BC	*August 3rd:* Octavianus takes Alexandria. Antonius and Cleopatra commit suicide. Octavianus has Caesarion murdered and is thus Caesar's sole remaining heir. Egypt becomes a Roman province.
27 BC	Reestablishment of the Republic. Octavianus is conferred the honorary name Augustus. Advent of the Principate which can be seen as the beginning of the emperor's era.
12 BC	After Lepidus' death Octavianus finally becomes pontifex maximus also.
14 AD	*August 19th:* Augustus dies quietly, something after him almost no other emperor is granted.
14-37	Emperor Tiberius.
37-41	Emperor Caligula.
41-54	Emperor Claudius.
54-68	Emperor Nero.
64 AD	Great Fire of Rome.
68 AD	Suicide of Nero. End of the Iulio-Claudian House.
69-79	Vespasianus becomes emperor and founder of the Flavian House.
79-81	Emperor Titus.
81-96	Emperor Domitianus.

Glossary

Aramaic Aramaic is a Semitic language with a strong Churritic substrate. Churritic was a non-Semitic, non-Indo-Germanic language. The Arameans who had developed from a mergence of north-western-Semitic nomads and remnants of the dispersed Churrites, forayed into Assyria at the end of the second millenium BC, further infiltrating afterwards until their language gradually replaced the Accadic/Assyric one. As a consequence their alphabetic script also replaced the old cuneiform writing. Aramaic became the official language of the New-Babylonian empire, its scope covered all of the Fertile Crescent and reached into Egypt. It remained the empire's language even after the Persian conquest. Under Hellenic rule, Aramaic lost its official status but kept its importance as the lingua franca of the Orient and was replaced only in the course of the first millenium AD by the Arabic language. For early Christianity Aramaic was mainly important in its Syrian variants. It is still spoken even today in some enclaves, amongst other places in three Syrian villages. A couple of texts of the Jewish bible (i.e. the Christian's Old Testament) are written in Aramaic. In the New Testament Aramaisms can be identified especially in Mark.
The Aramaic script, adopted from the Egyptian alphabetic hieroglyphs (possibly via Phoenician intermediation), replaced the cuneiform writing. It also provided in its classical form the basis for the Eastern Greek alphabet which first spread in Asia minor and Ionia, then with the reform of Eucleides spread in Attica and over all of Greece and is still valid today. (The prior so-called Western Greek alphabet which had come to Greece without an Aramaic detour has become the basis of the Latin script via Etruscan intermediation; cf. i.a. TAC. *Ann.* 11.14). Much later, around the 8th century AD the Aramaic script in its cursive form was adopted by the Jews and since then has been known as the so-called 'Hebrew' quadrata.

Ara Pacis (Augustae) – [Lat. 'Altar of Augustan Peace']. Splendid Altar of Victory, which the Senate resolved to erect in the year 13 BC to celebrate the return of Augustus from the victorious campaigns in Spain and Gaul. It stood on the via Flaminia, at today's via Lucina, but has been rebuilt in another place in the meantime (1937).

Artemis Greek goddess, Lat. *Diana*. She was the daugther of Zeus and Leto and twin sister of Apollo. The popular goddess' oldest function was being mistress of the open countryside, the trees and the animals. Depicted as huntress armed with bow and arrow. Protectress of the offspring, midwife and helper in child rearing. Being inaccessible for love she remained the virgin goddess to whom the girls devoted their clothes and toys. Famous but of a partly different nature were the goddesses of Asia minor called Artemis. Of one of them, the

	Artemis of Ephesos, Caesar twice saved the temple treasure (cf. CAES. *Civ.* 3.105).
As	Oldest Roman coin. The as, the standard of the monetary system, was made of copper and weighed one Roman pound (327 grams) in the time of the early republic. In the first century BC the as fell into desuetude but was reintroduced under Augustus with the much lower weight of about 10 grams.
Astarte	Palestine goddess of fertility, almost always depicted as a nude but not a chaste virgin. Her correspondent in Assyria-Babylonia is Ishtar.
Atargatis	Syrian goddess, similar to *Astarte.*
Augur	plural *augures* – member of a priest college in Rome. It was of Etruscan origin *(disciplina etrusca).* The *augures* had to interpret from the birds' flight, clamor or eating behavior whether the gods approved or disapproved of state-controlled actions. Beside them the *haruspices* (singular: *haruspex*) were active, who examined the viscera of sacrifical animals. See there.
Augustan	Adjective of *Augustus,* later honorary name of *Octavianus,* grandnephew and posthumously adopted son of Caesar.
Augusteum, plural *augustea* – Temple of Divus Augustus; following the example of the temples of Caesar (cf. *Caesareum*), Augustea were built in most of the Empire's cities and municipia, often together with temples of the goddess Roma.	
Aureus	plural *aurei* – [< Lat. *aureum*, 'gold']. Gold coin.
Baalbek	Location north of Damascus, at the foot of the Anti-Libanon mountains. In Hellenistic time it was called *Heliopolis,* 'City of the Sun God'; Caesar left behind legions as praesidium there, from the time of Augustus it was a Roman colony. During the first and second century AD the city was enriched with splendid temples amongst them the main temple consecrated to Jupiter Heliopolitanus (Baal, Helios) and a smaller one consecrated to Venus-Atargatis. In Christian time a basilica was built in the great yard. Today impressive ruins can be seen there.
Bezae Cantabrigiensis (ms) – The oldest bilingual codex *(D)* of the New Testament that has survived. For some time it was in the possession of Beza, now it is in Cambridge, hence the name – *ms* stands for 'manuscript'. The codex is dated between the 4th and 6th century and almost completely contains the Gospels in the Western order Mt, Jh, Lk, Mk (which very probably represents the reverse order of their inclusion into the canon) and parts of the Acts of the Apostles. The bilingualism argues for the manuscript's genesis in a place where both Greek and Latin were spoken and understood. To be considered are—in addition to the capitals where *utraque lingua,* 'both languages', were used: Southern Gaul, Southern Italy, Sicily, the Roman province Africa, Illyria or Egypt. Here and there the writer incorporated a Latin character in a Greek word. The Greek text is on the left side, which by some is considered to be the honorary one; however it is the back side of the writing material, at least in the first half of each signature. WIKENHAUSER, A. & SCHMID, J. (^{6}1973), p. 89, [our translation]: 'The Latin text is in no way a translation of the Greek parallel text, but it can be seen clearly [...], that on the one hand the Greek text has influenced the Latin one and on the other hand the Latin text has affected the Greek one. A number of special versions of the Greek text apparently are back-translations from Latin. This finding can be made understandable only thus: that the writer of this manuscript was not the first to create this bilingual text, but the Codex has a previous history within which the peculiar mutual dependency was formed, in fact by attentive read-	

ers. So there was at least one preceding codex which already was bilingual. The Codex Cantabrigiensis is the most important, until a few years ago also the only, Greek witness of the so-called "western" text which is otherwise attested to by the Old Latin and Old Syrian translation. In the meantime it has been proven by two papyri originating from Egypt that this text was prevalent in Egypt also.' In our respect it is one of the most important Gospel manuscripts. Cf. illustration pp. 144 and 145.

Caesareum plural *caesarea* – Temple of Divus Iulius (Caesar). Caesarea arose in all cities and municipia of the Empire and also beyond at the *socii et amici populi Romani*, the allies and friends of the Roman people. Many cities obtained the name Caesarea with or without an addition. One now finds them under a different name or as a ruin, among other places in Turkey, Lebanon, Palestine, Syria, Algeria and Spain.

Canon [Lat. 'rule, norm, guideline', < Gr. *kanôn,* actually 'staff of reed']. ~ of writings: 1) Index of exemplary authors of antiquity established by the Alexandrian grammarians. 2) Unalterable list of scriptures accepted by a denomination, e.g. the New Testament of the Christians. Those writings which are not included in the canon are called apocryphal writings or apocrypha.

Capitol Smallest of the seven hills of Rome to the west of the Forum. It has two hilltops; on the northern one stood the *arx,* the castle, and the temple of *Iuno Moneta,* on the southern one the temple of *Iupiter Capitolinus* was located, where *Minerva* was revered as well (Capitoline Trias); here also the temple of *Fides,* of fidelity, and the *Tabularium,* i.e. the city archive were situated. At the *asylum,* the saddle between the two hilltops, the aliens were taken in and traitors were thrown down from the Tarpeian Rock. In every respect Rome's most sacred hill.

Consul [Lat. actually 'counselor', < *consulere,* 'to consult, to take counsel, to take decisions, to take measures']. Designation of office of the two highest Roman magistrates during the time of the Republic. They were elected for a one-year term by the People's Assembly, called together the Senate as well as the People's Assembly, over which they both presided, and carried out the resolutions of the two bodies. In times of war they were commanders-in-chief of the Roman army. When the Principate was established the office lost much of its importance.

Curia [< Lat. *co-uiria,* actually 'men's meeting']. Originally the name of each of the 30 divisions in which according to tradition Romulus arranged the Roman people. Later the name of the assembly building of the Senate on the Forum. Today's name of the Papal administration and its seat is derived from it.

Dea Roma [Lat. 'Goddess Rome']. Personalization of Rome acknowledged with cultic worship following the model of Athena.

Denarius plural *denarii* – [Lat. < *deni,* 'per ten']. Ancient Roman silver coin, primarily worth ten asses, ten pounds of copper.

Diadoches [< Gr. *diadochoi,* 'successors']. The commanders with highest rank in the army of Alexander the Great who after his death (323 BC) divided his world empire amongst themselves: Antipater acquired Macedonia, Lysimachos Thracia, Antigonos Asia minor, Seleukos Babylonia, Ptolemaios Egypt.

Dictator [Lat. 'commander', < *dictare,* 'to dictate']. Extraordinary magistrate, who in case of a state emergency was appointed on the suggestion of the Senate for usually six months and received almost absolute power for a well-defined task. The last two dictatorships of the time of the Republic were those of Sulla (82-79) and Caesar (46-44). These were not time-bound or subject to a restricted task. *Dictator,* in the sense of somebody who dictates something, school master, reciter of texts, has resulted in the Dutch and German word *Dichter,* for poet. By the same ambiguity the *dictator* Caesar could become the *Master, Rabbi* Jesus in the Gospels.

Dupondius Coin with the value of 2 asses. The name stands for *duo asses pondo,* 'two-pounder'. The dupondius was made of bronze or brass.

Ecclesiasticus – Title of the oldest book of the Vulgate also known as 'Jesus Sirach'.

Epiphanes [Gr. 'appearing']. Cf. *Epiphania,* the revelation of the Lord, especially in the Adoration of the Three Wise Men (Kings) from the East (Feast of Epiphany, the 6th of January), the baptism in the Jordan river and the Wedding of Cana.

Erinyes Goddesses of revenge, furies. The Erinyes live in the underworld but they appear in order to avenge torts especially murder. They are imagined as frightening, hideous looking women carrying scourges with flames shooting from their eyes and their heads wreathed with serpents. They are fast because they have the wings of a bat and they are inexorable and omniscient. If necessary they torture the criminal and drive him to madness. After a confession of guilt they become benevolent, then they are called Eumenides. In Athens they had a sanctuary.

Eusebius Eusebius of Caesarea († 339), early Christian scholar, student of the presbyter Pamphilus hence his surname Pamphili. Around 313 Eusebius became bishop of Caesarea, the Roman capital of Palestine. Afterwards he was court theologian of Constantine the Great, whose life he pictured and aggrandized. Eusebius wrote the first Church History amply providing it with quotations from older writings.

Figurehead Ship's bow ornament graven of wood, often in form of a female figure.

Furies [< Lat. *Furiae*]. See *Erinyes.*

Genius [Lat. 'tutelary spirit', actually 'genitor']. In Roman antiquity divine embodiment of a human's essence. The genius was a personal tutelary spirit of the man whom he had originated and whom he accompanied through life; the tutelary spirit of women was called *Iuno.* Somebody's birthday was the festive day of his genius. Communities and places had their genius too.

Gens [Lat. 'a race, nation, people, clan, kin']. *Gens Iulia* – the gens to which Caesar's family of the *Iulii Caesares* belonged also.

Gergovia Capital of the mighty Gallic tribe of the Arvernians, who lived in the Auvergne. The fortress which lay near the Elaver river (department Allier) in Gallia was unavailingly besieged by Caesar in 52 BC.

Gracchi Name of two Roman brothers – *Tiberius* and *Gaius Sempronius Gracchus* – who made a stand for social reforms and were both murdered, Tiberius in 133 and Gaius in 121 BC.

Hadad God of tempest and thunderstorm with the western Semites especially the Arameans. Hadad is identical with the Babylonian Adad and the Hittitic Teshub. He is depicted with hammer and bolt. Thus equated with Zeus and Jupiter.

Haruspex plural *haruspices* – Member of a priest college in Rome. It was of Etruscan origin *(disciplina etrusca).* The haruspices inspected and interpreted the viscera, especially the liver of sacrificial animals in order to learn the will of the gods. A profession similar to that of the *augures* (singular *augur*), see there.

Herm [< Lat. *herma* < Gr. *Hermês,* actually '(statue of) Hermes']. Pillar or column which is crowned with a bust, originally one of the god Hermes.

Homily [< Eccl. Lat. *homilia,* 'sermon', actually 'speech to the people']. The Greek *homilía* means 'the being together, community, conversation'. A homily is a sermon which primarily comprises an edifying exegesis of a holy scripture.

Incubo [Lat. 'somebody who is sleeping on something', < *incubare,* 'to lie in or on, to be bedded']. Somebody who sleeps in a temple lying on the fur of a sacrificial animal in order to receive divine revelation by dreams while at the same time he guards the temple. Thus an incubo stands for a ghost who watches over the temple treasure. Besides he is the ghost who haunts the profaning person in his sleep and oppresses and chokes him.

Right of Intercession – The right of the people's tribunes to *inter-cedere,* actually 'to step between', i.e. to veto. The Right of Intercession provided the people's tribunes with the most important weapon for protecting the ordinary people, the plebs, against the great influence resp. misuse of power of officers, consuls and the Senate.

Itala (ms) A Latin bible translation recommended by Augustinus. To be distinguished from the Vulgate of Hieronymus (cf. *Vulgata*). The Itala is one of the Old Latin translations only preserved in fragments. Today the entirety of these fragments is mostly not denoted as Itala but as *Vetus Latina,* 'the old Latin one'.

Judaism [< Late Lat. *Iudaismus,* < Gr. *Ioudaismós* with the same meaning]. 1) Judeo-Christian law-abiding movement in early Christianity. 2) Jewish religion, Jewry. Derived from that, the adjective: *judaistic.*

Judaists Christians in early Christianity, who came to it from resp. via Jewry.

Judaize To conform to the Jewish religion; also make Jewish, bring under Jewish influence. Derived therefrom: *rejudaize, dejudaize.*

Jupiter Stator – ['Flight inhibitor', < Lat. *sistere,* 'to cause (a person or animal) to stand, to bring to a standstill, check, halt, stop (persons, etc., in motion)']. Epithet of Jupiter, who is assigned the power to bring a fleeing army to a standstill and thus to bring about a fortunate and unexpected turn in battle. On the *via sacra* in Rome stood a temple of Jupiter Stator at the place where the Latins fleeing from the Sabins came to a halt. According to tradition Romulus consecrated that temple.

Jupiter-herm – A herm which is crowned with a bust of Jupiter.

Lectisternium – [< Lat. *lectus,* 'bed', and *sternere,* 'to spread out']. A lectisternium was a meal of the gods whereat images of gods crowned with wreaths were set on pillows and served food.

Legate [< Lat. *lêgere,* 'to send (off)']. In ancient Rome: 1) A delegate of the Senate to foreign states. 2) Right-hand man of the commander, sub-commander. 3) Deputy governor.

Lictor plural *lictores* – [< Lat. *ligare,* 'to bind']. Lictores were civil servants who walked ahead of high Roman magistrates and carried the fasces. The *fasces,* a bundle of rods bound together around an ax with the blade projecting, was the symbol of authority of the magistrates and of their right to chastise and impose death penalty.

Limes [Lat. 'borderline, frontier rampart, patrolled and fortified line marking the frontier']. The word particularly stands for the boundary which was built by Domitianus in Germania between the Rhine and the Danube river in 83 AD. This limes extended 550 km and contained more than 100 watchtowers and over 100 castella.

Lituus [Lat.]. Crook of the augures.

Lupercal Grotto of the Roman she-wolf at the foot of the Palatine hill.

Lupercalia Festival of *Lupercus*, the Old-Roman god of shepherds [< *lupus*, 'wolf']. This feast of purification and fertility took place on the 15th of February (today St. Valentine's day). On that day after the sacrificial offering the priests called *Luperci*, mostly youths, ran round and round the Palatine hill clothed in an apron made of furs of the sacrificed bucks. The women would go to meet them with outstretched hands and let themselves be hit by whip-like strips of goat hide believing this would insure fertility and easy childbirth.

Mars Ultor [Lat. 'Avenging Mars']. The war god Mars in his capacity of avenger. Octavianus had a temple for Mars Ultor built on his forum. There he kept the standards which the Parthians had snatched from Crassus at the battle of Carrhae but later had given back.

Metathesis [Gr. 'transposition']. Transposition within a word of letters, sounds or syllables, also by borrowing to a different language (e. g. *weps > wasp, brid > bird, hros > horse, formaticus (Lat.) > fromage (French), Herakles > Hercules*, etc. It occurs especially frequently with liquidae, i.e. the consonants 'l' and 'r'. Often accompanied by folk etymologies, e. g. *truquer*, French for 'to bamboozle, fake', which resulted in the synonymous German *türken*, as if it had anything to do with Turks, or *Proserpina*, who was called *Persephone* in Greek, as if she were the 'Persian-speaking one' – *Perse-phone*.

Mitre [< Lat. *mitra* < Gr. *mítra*, 'bandage, turban']. 1) Cap-like headpiece of ancient Orient rulers (Babylonians, Assyrians, Persians); with Hellenics and Romans worn by women and effeminate men. 2) Headpiece of high catholic clergymen, bishop's mitre.

Munda Old city near Cordoba in Southern Spain, where Caesar defeated the sons of Pompeius in 45 BC.

Municipium, plural *municipia* – [Lat. actually 'companionship of *municipes*, fellow citizens', i.e. 'those who participate in civic duties' (< *munia capere*, 'take duties')]. Free city whose citizens had Roman citizenship and thus had the same duties *(munia)* as the *cives Romani*, 'the Roman citizens'.

Necropolis [< Gr. *nekrópolis*, 'city of the dead']. Large cemetery from ancient or prehistoric times.

Orchestra [Gr. actually 'dancing place']. Round room in old Grecian theater, in which the choir acted out. In Rome it was the Senator's place of honor in the front of the theater.

Palatine [< Lat. *Palatium*]. One of the seven hills of Rome south of the Forum, it is the oldest area of settlement in Rome: *Roma quadrata*. There the house of Romulus had stood and the imperial residences were built, thus the Palatine became the epitome of 'palace'. It began with Augustus, who was born at the foot of the Palatium, *ad capita bubula*, 'by the oxen's heads', and who had a temple of Apollo built there alongside his residence. At the foot of the Palatine the *Lupercal* was located also (see there).

Paludamentum – [Lat.]. War or, soldier's cloak, especially of the Roman commanders.

Pharsalos City in Thessaly, Greece. The decisive battle between Caesar and Pompeius took place near Pharsalos in 48 BC.

Pietà [Ital. 'piety, pity']. Depiction of Mary with Christ's body in her lap.

Pietas [Lat. 'filial love, grateful love, dutiful ethos, piety', < *pius* 'affectionate towards parents, dutiful, pious']. A very Roman virtue. There also existed a goddess named Pietas.

Plebs [Lat.]. The bulk of the citizens, the non-patricians in ancient Rome.

Pomerium [Lat. 'place left blank on both sides of the city wall', probably < *post murum*, 'behind the wall']. Sacred city limit outside and inside the city wall in ancient Rome. It was forbidden to enter it while armed, therefore the holders of military power *(imperium)* stayed outside the city. Triumphs are excepted, later an exception is made for Augustus also.

Pompeian(s) – Follower(s) of Pompeius.

Praesidium, plural *praesidia* – [Lat. actually 'protection, standby']. Securing, sentinel, garrison, post, castellum, bastion, entrenchment.

Praetor [Lat. actually *prae itor,* 'the one preceding (the army)']. In the early Republican period of Rome two praetors elected for a one year term were the highest magistrates. After the institution of the consulate they became the highest judicial officers. The *praetor urbanus* was responsible for lawsuits amongst Romans, the *praetor peregrinus* for lawsuits against or amongst foreigners staying in Rome.

Proscriptions – [< Lat. *proscribere,* 'to announce publicly in writing']. The public announcement of persons who were declared outlaws in ancient Rome, especially by Sulla, later by the triumviri Octavianus, Antonius and Lepidus.

Rhetor [< Gr. *rhêtôr,* 'orator']. Orator of antiquity.

Rostra Plural of *rostrum* (v.i.). Rostrum or speaking platform at the Forum Romanum which was adorned with captured ship's prows.

Rostrum [Lat. actually 'beak']. The beak of a ship, used for ramming.

Sestertius [Lat. *Ses-tertius (nummus),* < *sesquitertius,* 'half-third as = (2 $^1/_2$) two and a half as', i.e. ($^1/_4$) a quarter denarius]. The original value of a quarter denarius held till 217 BC. Later it amounted to four asses. The sestertius was the most current Roman silver coin. According to the original meaning of the word – two and a half – the sestertius was abbreviated as IIS (one+one+semi). From that developed HS. Curiously: IIS written on top of each other has in our time produced the symbol for Dollar: $ – actually with two bars.

Sidus Iulium – [Lat. 'Star of Iulius']. During the obsequies organized by Octavianus for his murdered adoptive father a comet appeared. The people believed it was the soul of Caesar ascended to heaven and named it *sidus Iulium*. In Christian imagery it turned into the Star of Bethlehem. Octavianus Augustus had metal models of the sidus affixed on all statues of Divus Iulius. From this developed the aureole, the gloriole of the Saints.

Sol [Lat. 'Sun']. The personalization of Sol is the Sun God, Gr. *Hêlios*, Pers. *Mithras*, brother of *Luna*, 'moon', later equated with Apollo. At all times the autocrats were identified with Sol. On December 25th, solstice according to the Roman calendar, the feast of *Sol Invictus*, the Undefeated Sun, was celebrated during the time of the emperors. On the same date the Christians celebrate Christmas.

Spolia [Lat. actually 'something stripped off', < *spoliare,* actually '(to take off (the killed enemy's) armor']. 1) In ancient Rome: captured weapons, booty. 2) In archeology: recycled components from other buildings, e.g. columns, friezes, etc.

Summus pontifex – [Lat. 'supreme priest'; *pontifex* < *pons, pontis,* 'bridge' and *facere,* 'to make']. As 'bridge builder' the *pontifex* forms the connection between heaven and earth. Honorary title of the pope as a variant of *pontifex maximus.*

Synnaos [Gr. from *syn-* 'together' and *naos* 'temple']: 'worshipped together (with another deity) in the same temple'.

Tiara	[Lat. 'cap' < Gr. *tiára*, borrowing from Persian origin]. 1) High, copped headdress of the old Persian and Armenian kings. 2) Papal headdress made of white silk with three golden crowns placed on top of each other and two hanging standards which he wears on celebratory occasions without liturgical character.
Tribunal	[< Lat. *tribunal*, 'stand of the tribunes, bench']. In ancient Rome the elevated place where the praetor administered justice.
Triskelis	[< Gr. *triskelês*, 'tripod']. Greek symbol for Sicily. A figure composed of three usually curved or bent branches (running legs) radiating from the center in 120° degree distance. The triskelis can be found on Greek coins in Sicily. The triangular island Sicily was a Greek colony for a long time.
Triumvir	plural *triumviri* – Each of the three men who held the highest authority in their hands in Rome. Together they were called the *Triumvirate*. See there.
Triumvirate	– team of three men, three men's rule. Form of government in which three men hold authority in their hands. This happened twice in Rome. The first triumvirate (60 BC) was a mutual agreement between Caesar, Pompeius and Crassus. The second triumvirate (43 BC) was a formal public alliance between Antonius, Lepidus and Octavianus.
Tropaeum	[Lat. < Gr. *tropaion*, actually 'turning point']. Victory monument consecrated to the gods at the site where the enemy was first put to flight. It was made up of a stump or a pole on which the captured weapons of the defeated enemy were hung. To facilitate that, a crossbeam was affixed sometimes so that the tropaeum in practice had the shape of a Latin cross.
Venus	[Lat. actually 'love, passion, love pleasure, grace, beauty']. Roman goddess of beauty and love equated with Aphrodite. She is the daughter of Jupiter resp. born from the foam of the sea. Wife of Vulcanus (god of the smiths) and Mars (war god), mother of Amor and Aeneas. Since the gens Iulia descended from Aeneas Venus is regarded the ancestral mother *(Venus Genetrix)* of that lineage and thus of Caesar. In 46 BC Caesar consecrated a temple to her on the Forum.
Vicar of Christ	– [< Lat. *vicarius*, 'deputy, successor']. Vicar is mostly used in the sense of a proxy of an ecclesiastic. The vicar of Christ is Christ's proxy on earth, i.e. the Pope.
Vindication war	– [< Lat. *vindicatio* 'protection from violence, self-defence', < *vindicare* 'to claim titles, to relieve, to protect, to intercede penalizingly against presumptious persons, to punish, to avenge']. In Caesar's understanding the civil war formally served the purpose of vindicating the damaged rights of the people's tribunes.
Vita	[Lat. 'life', Gr. *bios*.]. Life, course of life, life story, biography. Biography of characters from antiquity and of saints.
Vulgata	[< Eccl. Lat. *(versio) vulgata*, 'the generally used (version)', < *vulgare*, 'to bring amongst the people, to make common']. 1) The most prevalent version of a certain text from antiquity. 2) The revision of the Old-Latin bible translation *(Itala, Vetus Latina)* which was begun by St. Hieronymus in the 4th century and later declared authentic.

Literature

PRIMARY LITERATURE

The Corpus Caesarianum

CAESAR (Gaius Iulius Caesar; 100-44). Roman commander and statesman.
COMMENTARII DE BELLO GALLICO LIBRI I-VIII
GUTHARDT, A. (1995). *Bellum Gallicum*. Münster: Aschendorff. ISBN: 3-402-02018-1.
ZINK, N. (1988). *Caesar: Commentarii Rerum Gestarum Belli Galli, Libri* I-VIII. Frankfurt am Main: Diesterweg. ISBN: 3-425-04348-X.
SCHÖNBERGER, O. (1999). *Der Gallische Krieg* (Latin-German). Düsseldorf / Zürich: Artemis & Winkler. ISBN: 3-7608-1352-6 , 3-7608-1718-1.
DEISSMANN, M. (2000). *Der Gallische Krieg*. Stuttgart: Reclam. ISBN: 3-15-001012-8.
DEISSMANN, M. (1995). *De bello Gallico: lateinisch-deutsch = Der gallische Krieg*. Stuttgart: Reclam. ISBN: 3-15-009960-9.
SCHÖNBERGER, O. (1990). *Der Gallische Krieg* (Latin-German). München: Artemis-Verlag. ISBN: 3-7608-1658-4.
DORMINGER, G. (1986). *Der Gallische Krieg* (Latin-German). Darmstadt: Wissenschaftliche Buchgesellschaft / München: Artemis-Verlag. ISBN: 3-7608-1513-8.
HIRTIUS, & HAMMOND, C. (1999). *Seven commentaries on the Gallic war; with an eight commentary by Aulus Hirtius* (Latin-English). Oxford: Oxford University Press. ISBN: 0-19-283582-3 , 0-19-283120-8 .
EDWARDS, H.J. (1917, 18th rep.). *The Gallic War* (Latin-English). Cambridge, Mass.: Harvard University Press. ISBN: 0-674-99080-3.
EDWARDS, H.J. (1986). *The Gallic war, books* I-VIII (Latin-English). London: Heinemann. ISBN: 0-434-99072-8.
CONSTANS, L.-A. & BALLAND, A. (1996). *Guerre des Gaules. T.I: Livres I-IV* (Latin-French). Paris: Les Belles Lettres. ISBN: 2-251-01031-9.
CONSTANS, L.-A. & BALLAND, A. (1995). *Guerre des Gaules. T.II: Livres V-VIII* (Latin-French). Paris: Les Belles Lettres. ISBN: 2-251-01032-7.
BRINDESI, F. (1999). *La guerra gallica*. Milano: Biblioteca universale Rizzoli. ISBN: 88-17-15094-0.
MARINONI, E. (1997). *La guerra gallica*. Milano: Rusconi. ISBN: 88-18-16013-3.
PENNACINI, A. (1996). *La guerra gallica* (Latin-Italian). Torino: Enaudi. ISBN: 88-06-13942-8.
LIPPARINI, G. (1992). *La guerra gallica* (Latin-Italian). Bologna: Zanichelli. ISBN: 88-08-00982-3.
GOYA Y MUNIAÍN, J. (1997). *Guerra de la Galias*. Barcelona: Circulo de Lectores. ISBN: 84-226-6694-4.
HUNINK, V. (2000). *Oorlog in Gallië*. Amsterdam: Athenaenum–Polak & Van Gennep. ISBN: 90-253-0647-0 , 90-253-0631-4.

VAN KATWIJK-KNAPP, F.H. (1990). *De Gallische oorlog*. Amsterdam: Wereldbibliotheek. ISBN: 90-284-0032-X , 90-289-0609-6.

COMMENTARII DE BELLO CIVILI LIBRI I-III

KRANER, F. (1999). C. *Iulii Caesaris Commentarii de bello civili*. Zürich: Weidmann. ISBN: 3-615-11000-5.

KLOTZ, A. (1992). *Commentarii bellis civilis*. Stuttgardiae: Teubner. ISBN: 3-8154-1125-4.

SCHÖNBERGER, O. (1999). *Der Bürgerkrieg* (Latin-German). Düsseldorf / Zürich: Artemis & Winkler. ISBN: 3-7608-1512-X.

DEISSMANN-MERTEN, M. (1996). *Der Bürgerkrieg*. Stuttgart: Reclam. ISBN: 3-15-001090-X.

DORMINGER, G. (1979). *Der Bürgerkrieg* (Latin-German). München: Heimeran-Verlag. ISBN: 3-7765-2014-0.

CARTER, J.M. (1998). *The civil war* (Latin-English). Oxford: Oxford University Press. ISBN: 0-19-283923-3.

CARTER, J.M. (1997). *The civil war, with the anonymous Alexandrian, African, and Spanish wars*. Oxford: Oxford University Press. ISBN: 0-19-283151-8.

CARTER, J.M. & WILLCOCK, M.M. (1993). *The Civil War Book III* (Latin-English). Warminster: Aris & Philips. ISBN: 0-85668-582-8, 0-85668-583-6.

CARTER, J.M. & WILLCOCK, M.M. (1991). *The Civil War Books I & II* (Latin-English). Warminster: Aris & Philips. ISBN: 0-85668-461-9 , 0-85668-462-7.

PESKETT, A.G. (1914, 11th rep.). *The Civil Wars* (Latin-English). Cambridge, Mass.: Harvard University Press. ISBN: 0-674-99043-9.

PESKETT, A.G. (1979). *The Civil Wars, books I-III* (Latin-English). London: Heinemann. ISBN: 0-434-99039-6.

FABRE, P. (1997). *Guerre civile. T.I: Livres I-II* (Latin-French). Paris: Les Belles Lettres. ISBN: 2-251-01028-9.

FABRE, P. (1997). *Guerre civile. T.II: Livre III* (Latin-French). Paris: Les Belles Lettres. ISBN: 2-251-01029-7.

LA PENNA, A. (1999). *La guerra civile*. Venezia: Marsilio. ISBN: 88-317-7248-1.

ZAFFAGNO, E. (1996). *La guerra civile* (Latin-Italian). Milano: Garzanti. ISBN: 88-11-58728-X.

LIPPARINI, G. (1993). *La guerra civile*. Bologna: Zanichelli. ISBN: 88-08-00984-x.

BRUNO, M. (1989). *La guerra civile* (Latin-Italian). Milano: Rizzoli. ISBN: 88-17-12463-X.

LÓPEZ SOTO, V. (1986). *La guerra civil; la guerra Alejandría; la guerra de África; la guerra de España*. Barcelona: Juventud. ISBN: 84-261-1119-X.

VAN ROOIJEN-DIJKMAN, H.W.A. (2003). *Burgeroorlog*. Amsterdam: Athenaenum–Polak & Van Gennep. ISBN: 90-253-0657-8.

BELLVM ALEXANDRINVM / BELLVM AFRICANVM / BELLVM HISPANIENSE

KLOTZ, A. & HIRTIUS, A. (1993). C. *Iuli Caesaris Commentarii. Vol. III, Commentarii Belli Alexandrini, Belli Africi, Belli Hispaniensis: Accedunt C. Iuli Caesaris et A. Hirti fragmenta*. Stutgardiae: in aedibus B.G. Teubneri. ISBN: 3-519-11126-8.

SCHNEIDER, R. (1962). *Bellum Alexandrinum*. Berlin: Weidmann.

SCHNEIDER, R. (1962). *Bellum Africanum*. Berlin: Weidmann.

PASCUCCI, G. (1965). C. *Iulii Caesaris Bellum hispaniense*. Firenze: le Monnier.

WAY, A.G. (1955, 5th rep.). *Alexandrian, African and Spanish Wars* (Latin-English). Cambridge, Mass.: Harvard University Press. ISBN: 0-674-99443-4.

ANDRIEU, J. (1983). *Guerre d'Alexandrie* (Latin-French). Paris: Les Belles Lettres. ISBN: 2-251-01026-2.

BOUVET, A. & RICHARD, J.-CL. (1997). *Guerre d'Afrique* (Latin-French). Paris: Les Belles Lettres. ISBN: 2-251-01399-7.
DIOURON, N. (1999). *Guerre d'Espagne* (Latin-French). Paris: Les Belles Lettres. ISBN: 2-251-01413-6.
LORETO, L. (2001). *La lunga guerra civile: Alessandria-Africa-Spagna / Pseudo-Cesare* (Latin-Italian). Milano: Biblioteca universale Rizzoli. ISBN: 88-17-86626-1.
ICART, J. & DOLÇ, M. (1987). *Guerra d'Alexandria*. Barcelona: Fundació Bernat Metge. ISBN: 84-7225-384-4, 84-7225-382-6.
ICART, J. & DOLÇ, M. (1988). *Guerra d'Àfrica; Guerra d'Hispània* (Latin-Catalan). Barcelona: Fundació Bernat Metge. ISBN: 84-7225-401-1, 84-7225-400-3.
CASTRO SÁNCHEZ, J. (1992). *La guerra de Hispania* (Latin-Spanish). Madrid: Ediciones clásicas. ISBN: 84-7882-043-4.

Literature dependent on Asinius Pollio

APPIANUS (before 110–after 165). Greek historian.
HISTORIA ROMANA LIBRI XIII-XVII = BELLA CIVILIA LIBRI I-V
VEH, O. & WILL, W. (1989). *Römische Geschichte. Tl. 2: Die Bürgerkriege*. Stuttgart: A. Hiersemann. ISBN: 3-7772-8915-9.
CARTER, J.M. (1996). *The civil wars*. Harmondsworth: Penguin Books. ISBN: 0-14-044509-9.
WHITE, H. (1913, 8th rep.). *Roman History. Vol. III. The civil wars, Books I-III.26* (Greek-English). Cambridge, Mass.: Harvard University Press. ISBN:0-674-99005-6.
WHITE, H. (1913, 7th rep.). *Roman History. Vol. IV. The civil wars, Books III.27-V* (Greek-English). Cambridge, Mass.: Harvard University Press. ISBN:0-674-99006-4.
WHITE, H. (1979). *Appian's Roman History, Vol. III: The civil wars, Books I-III.3* (Greek-English). London: Heinemann. ISBN 0-434-99004-3.
WHITE, H. (1979). *Appian's Roman History, Vol. IV: The civil wars, Books III.4-V* (Greek-English). London: Heinemann. ISBN 0-434-99005-1.
TORRENS, P. (2000). *Les guerres civiles à Rome. Livre III*. Paris: Les Belles Lettres. ISBN: 2-251-33939-6.
COMBES-DOUNOUS, J.-I. & TORRENS, P. (1994). *Les guerres civiles à Rome. Livre II*. Paris: Les Belles Lettres. ISBN: 2-251-33923-X.
COMBES-DOUNOUS, J.-I., VOISIN, C. & TORRENS, P. (1993). *Les guerres civiles à Rome. Livre I*. Paris: Les Belles Lettres. ISBN: 2-251-33921-3.
GABBA, E. (1958-1970). *Appiani bellorum civilium liber I-V* (Greek-Italian). Firenze: La Nuova Italia.

PLUTARCHUS (ca. 46-120). Greek author.
VITAE PARALLELAE – {ROMVLVS; TIBERIVS (?-133) & CAIVS (153-121) GRACCHVS; SVLLA (138-78); POMPEIVS (106-48); CICERO (106-43); CAESAR (100-44); BRVTVS (85-42); ANTONIVS (82-30); CATO MINOR VTICENSIS (95-46)}
LINDSKOG, C., ZIEGLER, K.J.F. & GÄRTNER, H. (2000). *Plutarchi Vitae parallelae I-1 (i.a. Romulus)* (Greek). München/Leipzig: In aedibus K.G. Sauer. ISBN: 3-598-71672-9 / 3-519-01672-9.
LINDSKOG, C., ZIEGLER, K.J.F. & GÄRTNER, H. (1994). *Plutarchi Vitae parallelae I-2 (i.a. Cicero)* (Greek). München: K.G. Saur. ISBN: 3-598-71671-0 , 3-598-71691-5.
LINDSKOG, C., ZIEGLER, K.J.F. & GÄRTNER, H. (1993). *Plutarchi Vitae parallelae II-1* (Greek). München: K.G. Sauer. ISBN: 3-598-71673-7.
LINDSKOG, C., ZIEGLER, K.J.F. & GÄRTNER, H. (1994). *Plutarchi Vitae parallelae II-2 (i.a. Caesar)* (Greek). München: K.G. Saur. ISBN: 3-598-71674-5 , 3-598-71692-3.

LINDSKOG, C., ZIEGLER, K.J.F. & GÄRTNER, H. (1996). *Plutarchi Vitae parallelae III-1 (i.a. Antonius et Gracchi)* (Greek). München: K.G. Sauer. ISBN: 3-598-71675-3.
LINDSKOG, C. & ZIEGLER, K.J.F. (1973). *Plutarchi Vitae parallelae III-2 (i.a. Sulla et Pompeius)* (Greek). München: K.G. Sauer. ISBN: 3-598-71676-1.
AX, W. (1996). *Griechische und römische Heldenleben. 2. Teil: Coriolan, die Gracchen, Sulla, Pompeius, Cäsar, Cicero, Brutus.* Wiesbaden: VMA-Verlag. ISBN: 3-928127-30-6.
ZIEGLER, K., WUHRMANN, W. & FUHRMANN, M. (1994). *Fünf Doppelbiographien : griechisch und deutsch. Tl. 1: Alexandros und Caesar. Aristeides und Marcus Cato. Perikles und Fabius Maximus. Tl. 2: Gaius Marcius und Alkibiades. Demosthenes und Cicero.* Zürich: Artemis und Winkler. ISBN: 3-7608-1683-5.
ZIEGLER, K. & WUHRMANN, W. (1991). *Von große Griechen und Römern: 5 Doppelbiographien.* München: Deutscher Taschenbuch Verlag. ISBN: 3-423-02259-0.
ZIEGLER, K. & WUHRMANN, W. (1955-1980). *Grosse Griechen und Römer. Vol. 1-6.* Zürich: Artemis-Verlag. ISBN: Vol. 1, 1979: 3-7608-3606-2; Vol. 2, 1979: 3-7608-3607-X; Vol. 3, 1955: — *(u.a. Sulla und Pompeius)*; Vol. 4, 1980: 3-7608-3609-7; Vol. 5, 1980: 3-7608-3610-X, 3-423-020725 *(u.a. Caesar und Antonius)*; Vol. 6, 1965: — *(u.a. Tiberius und Gaius Gracchus)*.
Waterfield, R. & Stadter, P.A. (1999). Roman Lives (i.a.: Antony, Caesar, the Gracchi, Pompey, Sulla). Oxford: Oxford University Press. ISBN: 0-19-282502-X.
MOSSMAN, J. (1998). *Lives of the noble Grecians and Romans.* Ware: Wordsworth Editions Ltd. ISBN: 1-853-26794-5.
CLOUGH, A.H. & DRYDEN, J. (1992). *The lives of the noble Grecians and Romans (2 Volumes).* New York: The Modern Library. ISBN: 0-394-60407-5 / 0-679-60008-6 (Vol. 1); 0-679-60009-4 (Vol. 2).
CLOUGH, A.H. (2001). *Plutarch's Lives : the Dryden Translation.* Vol. 1. New York: the Modern Library. ISBN: 0-375-75676-0.
EDWARDS, M.J.E. (1991). *The lives of Pompey, Caesar and Cicero: a companion to the Penguin translation from "Fall of the Roman Republic".* Bristol: Bristol Classical Press. ISBN: 1-85399-128-7.
PERRIN, B. (1968-1986). *Plutarch's Lives* (Greek-English). Vol. 1-11 [(a.o.: *Antony* (Vol. 9. ISBN: 0-674-99112-5), *Brutus* (Vol. 6: 0-674-99109-5), *Caesar and Cicero* (Vol. 7: 0-674-9910-9), *Cato the Younger* (Vol. 8: 0-674-99111-7), *Tiberius and Gaius Gracchus* (Vol. 10: 0-674-99113-3), *Pompey* (Vol. 5: 0-674-99097-8), *Romulus* (Vol. 1: 0-674-99052-8) and *Sulla* (Vol. 4: 0-674-99089-7)]. Cambridge, Mass.: Harvard University Press / London: Heinemann.
FLACELIÈRE, R., CHAMBRY, E., JUNEAUX, M. & SIMON, E. (1957-1993). *Vies* (Greek-French). Tomes I-XVI. [e.a.: *Antoine* (T.XIII, 1977. ISBN: 2-251-00261-8), *Brutus* (T.XIV, 1978: 2-251-00262-6), *Caton le Jeune* (T.X, 1976: 2-251-00258-8), *César* (T.IX), *Cicéron* (T.XII), *Les Gracques* (T.XI, 1976: 2-251-00259-6), *Pompée* (T.VIII, 1973: 2-251-00256-1), *Romulus* (T.I, 1993: 2-251-00249-9) et *Sylla* (T.VI, 1971: 2-251-00254-5)]. Paris: Les Belles Lettres.
TRAGLIA, A. (1996). *Vite / di Plutarco. Vol. 1 (i.a. Romolo)* (Greek-Italian). Torino: Unione Tipografico-Editrice Torinese. ISBN: 88-02-04602-6.
MAGNINO, D. (1992). *Vite / di Plutarco. Vol. 2 (i.a. Cicerone)* (Greek-Italian). Torino: Unione Tipografico-Editrice Torinese. ISBN: 88-02-04602-6 [sic].
AMERIO, M.L. & ORSI, D.P. (1998). *Vite di / Plutarco. Vol. 3 (i.a. Bruto, Catone Uticense)* (Greek-Italian). Torino: Unione Tipografico-Editrice Torinese. ISBN: 88-02-05334-0.
MAGNINO, D. (1996). *Vite / di Plutarco. Vol. 4 (i.a. Cesare)* (Greek-Italian). Torino: Unione Tipografico-Editrice Torinese. ISBN: 88-02-04941-6.
MARASCO, G. (1994). *Vite / di Plutarco. Vol. 5 (i.a. Antonio e Tiberio-Gaio Gracco)* (Greek-Italian). Torino: Unione Tipografico-Editrice Torinese. ISBN: 88-02-04725-1.

MERIANI, A. & ANDRIA, R.G. (1998). *Vite / di Plutarco. Vol. 6 (i.a. Silla, Pompeio)* (Greek-Italian). Torino: Unione Tipografico-Editrice Torinese. ISBN: 88-02-05316-2.
MAGNINO, D. & LA PENNA, A. (2000). *Vite parallele. Vol. 1: Alessandro; Cesare* (Greek-Italian). Milano: Biblioteca universale Rizzoli. ISBN: 88-17-11881-8.
ANDREI, O & SCUDERI, R. (1994). *Vite parallele. Vol. 4: Demetrio; Antonio* (Greek-Italian). Milano: Biblioteca universale Rizzoli. ISBN: 88-17-16709-6.
MAGNINO, D., SCARDIGLI, B. & MANFREDINI, M. (1991). *Vite parallele.Vol. 6: Agide e Cleomene; Tiberio e Caio Gracco* (Greek-Italian). Milano: Biblioteca universale Rizzoli. ISBN: 88-17-16795-9.
BEARZOT, C., GEIGER, J. & GHILLI, L. (1993). *Vite parallele. Vol. 8: Focione; Catone Uticense* (Greek-Italian). Milano: Biblioteca universale Rizzoli. ISBN: 88-17-16908-0.
LONGO, C.P., GEIGER, J. & GHILLI, L. (1999). *Vite parallele. Vol. 10: Demostene; Cicerone* (Greek-Italian). Milano: Biblioteca universale Rizzoli. ISBN: 88-17-17052-6.
FABRINI, P., SCARDIGLI, B. & DREHER, M. (2000). *Vite parallele: Dione; Bruto* (Greek-Italian). Milano: Biblioteca universale Rizzoli. ISBN: 88-17-17326-0.
AMPOLO, C. & MANFREDINI, M. (1993). *Vite parallele. Le vite di Teseo e di Romolo* (Greek-Italian). Milano: Fondazione Lorenzo Valla: A. Mondadori. ISBN: 88-04-31070-7.
SANTI AMANTINI, L., CARENA, C. & MANFREDINI, M. (1995). *Vite parallele. Le vite di Demetrio e di Antonio* (Greek-Italian). Milano: Fondazione Lorenzo Valla: A. Mondadori. ISBN: 88-04-37301-6.
ANGELI BERTINELLI, M.G. ET AL. (1997). *Vite parallele. Le vite di Lisandro e di Silla* (Greek-Italian). Milano: Fondazione Lorenzo Valla: A. Mondadori. ISBN: 88-04-41784-6.
RADT, S.L. (1967). *Hij kwam, zag en overwon (Julius Caesar)*. Hilversum: De Haan / Antwerpen: Standaard.

SUETONIUS (Gaius Suetonius Tranquillus; 75-150). Roman scholar and author.
DE VITA CAESARVM LIBRI I-VIII

MARTINET, H. (2000). *Die Kaiserviten / Berühmte Männer – De vita Caesarum / De viris illustribus* (Latin-German). Düsseldorf: Artemis & Winkler. ISBN: 3-7608-1698-3.
WITTSTOCK, O. (1993). *Kaiserbiographien* (Latin-German). Berlin: Akademie-Verlag. ISBN: 3-05-001844-5.
HEINEMANN, M. HÄUSSLER, R. (1986). *Cäsarenleben*. Stuttgart: Kröner. ISBN: 3-520-13007-6.
SCHMITZ, D. (1999). *Caesar* (Latin-German). Stuttgart: Reclam. ISBN: 3-15-006695.
EDWARDS, C. (2001). *Suetonius' Lives of the Caesars*. Oxford: Oxford University Press. ISBN: 0-19-283271-9.
GRAVES, R. (2001). *The Lives of the twelve Caesars*. New York: Welcome Rain Publishers. ISBN: 1-566-49210-6.
BARTON, T. (1997). *Lives of the Twelve Caesars*. Ware: Wordsworth Editions Ltd. ISBN: 1-853-26475-X.
ROLFE, J.C., BRADLEY, K.R. & HURLEY, D.W. (1998). *Suetonius. Vol. I (Lives of the Caesars: book I-IV)* (Latin-English). Cambridge, Mass.: Harvard University Press. ISBN: 0-674-99570-8.
ROLFE, J.C., HURLEY, D.W. & GOOLD, G.P. (1997). *Suetonius. Vol. II (Lives of the Caesars: book V-VIII)* (Latin-English). Cambridge, Mass.: Harvard University Press. ISBN: 0-674-99565-1.
AILLOUD, H. (1989). *Vie des douze Césars. T.I: César. - Auguste.* (Latin-French). Paris: Les Belles Lettres. ISBN: 2-251-01258-3.
AILLOUD, H. (2000). *Vie des douze Césars. T.II: Tibère. - Caligula. - Claude. - Néron.* (Latin-French). Paris: Les Belles Lettres. ISBN: 2-251-01257-5.

AILLOUD, H. (1993). *Vie des douze Césars. T.III: Galba. - Othon. - Vitellius. - Vespasien. - Titus. - Domitien.* (Latin-French). Paris: Les Belles Lettres. ISBN: 2-251-01259-1.
DESSI, F. & LANCIOTTI, S. (1998). *Vite dei Cesari, Vol. 1-2* (Latin-Italian). Milano: Biblioteca universale Rizzoli. ISBN: 88-17-17124-7 (Vol. 1); 88-17-17125-5 (Vol. 2).
GAGGERO, G. (1994). *Vite de dodici Cesari.* Milano: Rusconi libri. ISBN: 88-18-70081-2.
NOSEDA, E. (1991). *Vita dei Cesari.* Milano: Garzanti. ISBN: 88-11-58187-7.
PICÓN, V. (1998). *Vidas de los Cesares.* Madrid: Cátedra. ISBN: 84-376-1636-0.
DEN HENGST, D. (2000). *Keizers van Rome.* Amsterdam: Athenaenum–Polak & Van Gennep. ISBN: 90-253-4969-2.

Other important primary literature

NICOLAUS DAMASCENUS (ca. 64–after 4). Greek historian and philosopher.
BIOS KAISAROS (VITA CAESARIS)
JACOBY, F. (1996). *Die Fragmente der Griechischen Historiker. Zweiter Teil: Zeitgeschichte. A. Universalgeschichte und Hellenika. (u.a. Fragment Nr. 90)* (Greek). Leiden: Brill. ISBN: 90-040-8179-8.
JACOBY, F. (1993). *Die Fragmente der Griechischen Historiker. Zweiter Teil: Zeitgeschichte. C. Kommentar zu Nr. 64-105.* Leiden: Brill. ISBN: 90-040-1106-4.
BELLEMORE, J. (1984). *The life of Augustus* (Greek-English). Bristol: Bristol Classical Press. ISBN: 0-86292-142-2.
HALL, C.M. (1923). *Nicolaus of Damascus' Life of Augustus (Smith College Classical Studies nr. IV)* (Greek-English). Northampton, Massachusetts.
SCARDIGLI, B. & DELBIANCO, P. (1983). *Vita di Augusto.* Firenze: Nardini-Centro internazionale del libro. ISBN: 88-404-4223-5.
TURTURRO, G. (1945). *Vita di Augusto* (Greek-Italian). Bari: Città di Castello.

VELLEIUS (Gaius Velleius Paterculus; 1st half of the 1st cent. AD). Latin historian.
AD M. VINICIVM CONSVLEM LIBRI DVO (= HISTORIA ROMANA)
ELEFANTE, M. (1997). *Ad M. Vinicium consulem libri duo.* Hildesheim: G. Olms. ISBN: 3-487-10257-9.
WATT, W.S. (1998). *Vellei Paterculi historiarum ad M. Vinicium consulem libri duo.* Stuttgart / Leipzig: In aedibus B.G.Teubneri. ISBN: 3-8154-1873-9 / 3-322-00451-1.
STEGMANN, C., BLUME, H.D. & VON HALM, K.F. (1968). *C. Vellei Paterculi Ex Historiae Romanae libris duobus quae supersunt.* Stutgardiae: Teubner.
GIEBEL, M. (1998). *Historia Romana. Römische Geschichte* (Latin-German). Stuttgart: Reclam. ISBN: 3-15-008566-7.
SHIPLEY, F.W. & AUGUSTUS. (1924, 7th rep.). *Velleius Paterculus' Compendium of Roman History, books I-II* (Latin-English). *Res Gestae Divi Augusti, books I-VI* (Latin-Greek-English). Cambridge, Mass.: Harvard University Press. ISBN: 0-674-99168-0.
HELLEGOUARC'H, J. (1982). *Histoire romaine. T.1: Livre I* (Latin-French). Paris: Les Belles Lettres. ISBN: 2-251-01298-2.
HELLEGOUARC'H, J. (1982). *Histoire romaine. T.2: Livre II* (Latin-French). Paris: Les Belles Lettres. ISBN: 2-251-01316-4.
ELEFANTE, M. (2000). *I due libri a console Marco Vinicio* (Latin-Italian). Napoli: Loffredo. ISBN: 88-8096-710-X.
NUTTI, R. (1997). *Storia Romana* (Latin-Italian). Milano: Biblioteca universale Rizzoli. ISBN: 88-17-17189-1.
AGNES, L., FLORO, L.A. & DEANGELI, J.C. (1991). *Le storie. Epitome e frammenti.* Torino: Unione Tipografico-Editrice Torinese. ISBN: 88-02-04291-8.

DIO CASSIUS (Dio Cassius Cocceianus; ca. 155-235). Greek historian.
HISTORIA ROMANA LIBRI XXXVII- L

BOISSEVAIN, U.P. (1955). *Historiarum Romanorum quae supersunt, Vol. I: libri 1-40*. G. Olms. ISBN: 3-296-11401-7.

BOISSEVAIN, U.P. (1955). *Historiarum Romanorum Quae Supersunt, Vol. II: libri 41-60*. G. Olms. ISBN: 3-296-11402-5.

VEH, O. (1985). *Römische Geschichte. Bd. II: Bücher 36-43*. Zürich: Artemis. ISBN: 3-7608-3671-2.

VEH, O. (1986). *Römische Geschichte. Bd. III: Bücher 44-50*. Zürich: Artemis. ISBN: 3-7608-3672-0.

CARY, E. & FOSTER, H.B. (1914, 5th rep.). *Dio's Roman history. III: Books XXXVI-XL* (Greek-English). Cambridge, Mass.: Harvard University Press / London: Heinemann. ISBN: 0-674-99059-5 / 0-434-99053-1.

CARY, E. & FOSTER, H.B. (1916, 5th rep.). *Dio's Roman history. IV: Books XLI-XLV* (Greek-English). Cambridge, Mass.: Harvard University Press / London: Heinemann. ISBN: 0-674-99073-0 / 0-434-99066-3.

CARY, E. & FOSTER, H.B. (1917, 5th rep.). *Dio's Roman history. V: Books XLVI-L* (Greek-English). Cambridge, Mass.: Harvard University Press / London: Heinemann. ISBN: 0-674-99091-9.

FREYBURGER, M.-L. & RODDAZ, J.-M. (1991). *Histoire romaine. Livres 50 et 51* (Greek-French). Paris: Les Belles Lettres. ISBN: 2-251-00416-5.

FREYBURGER, M.-L. & RODDAZ, J.-M. (1994). *Histoire romaine. Livres 48 et 49* (Greek-French). Paris: Les Belles Lettres. ISBN: 2-251-00441-6.

FREYBURGER, M.-L. & RODDAZ, J.-M. (1996). *Histoire romaine. Livres 40 et 41* (Greek-French). Paris: Les Belles Lettres. ISBN: 2-251-33928-0.

NORCIO, G. (2000). *Storia romana. Vol. 4 (Libri XLVIII-LI)* (Greek-Italian). Milano: Biblioteca Universale Rizzoli. ISBN: 88-17-17099-2.

NORCIO, G. (2000). *Storia romana. Vol. 3 (Libri XLIV-XLVII)* (Greek-Italian). Milano: Biblioteca Universale Rizzoli. ISBN: 88-17-17098-4.

NORCIO, G. (2000). *Storia romana. Vol. 2 (Libri XXXIX-XLIII)* (Greek-Italian). Milano: Biblioteca Universale Rizzoli. ISBN: 88-17-17033-X.

NORCIO, G. (1997). *Storia romana. Vol. 1 (Libri XXXVI-XXXVIII)* (Greek-Italian). Milano: Biblioteca Universale Rizzoli. ISBN: 88-17-17032-1.

DE VRIES, G.H. (2000). *Vier keizers: Rome onder Tiberius, Caligula, Claudius en Nero*. Amsterdam: Athenaenum–Polak & Van Gennep. ISBN: 90-253-0871-6.

DE VRIES, G.H. (2003). *Augustus - Keizer van Rome*. Amsterdam: Athenaenum–Polak & Van Gennep. ISBN: 90-253-0662-4.

CICERO (Marcus Tullius Cicero; 106-43). Latin author.
EPISTVLAE:
AD ATTICVM; AD FAMILIARES; AD QVINTVM FRATREM; AD BRVTVM

WATT, W.S. (1978). *Epistulae. Vol. II. Part I (ad Att. 1-8)* Oxford: Oxford University Press. ISBN: 0-19-814645-0.

SHACKLETON BAILEY, D.R. (1963). *Epistulae. Vol. II. Part II (ad Att. 9-16)*. Oxford: Oxford University Press. ISBN: 0-19-814641-8.

WATT, W.S. (1982). *Epistulae. Vol. I. (ad Fam.)*. Oxford: Oxford University Press. ISBN: 0-19-814660-4.

WATT, W.S. (1994). *Epistulae. Vol. III. (ad Q.F., ad Brut., Fragm.)*. Oxford: Oxford University Press. ISBN: 0-19-814614-0.

SALVATORE, A. (1989). *M. Tulli Ciceronis Epistulae ad Quintum fratrem*. Milano: Sumptibus A. Mondadori. ISBN: 88-04-28349-1.

KASTEN, H. (1998). *Atticus-Briefe. Epistulae ad Atticum* (Latin-German). München: Artemis & Winkler ISBN: 3-7608-1518-9.
KASTEN, H. (1997). *An seine Freunde. Epistolae ad familiares* (Latin-German). Düsseldorf: Artemis & Winkler. ISBN: 3-7608-1517-0.
KASTEN, H. (1980). *M. Tulli Ciceronis Epistularum ad familiares libri XVI / Marcus Tullius Cicero an seine Freunde* (Latin-German). München: Heimeran. ISBN: 3-7765-2019-1.
M.J. & Kasten, H. (1976). *M. Tulli Ciceronis epistulae ad Quintum fratrem, epistulae ad Brutum, fragmenta epistularum / Cicero, Q.T., Brutus* (Latin-German). München: Heimeran. ISBN: 3-7765-2022-1.
BLANK-SANGMEISTER, U. (1993). *Epistulae ad Quintum fratrem* (Latin-German). Stuttgart: Reclam. ISBN: 3-15-007095-3.
SHACKLETON BAILEY, D.R. (1999). *Cicero. Volume XXII. Letters to Atticus. Letters 1-89* (Latin-English). Cambridge, Mass.: Harvard University Press. ISBN: 0-674-99571-6.
SHACKLETON BAILEY, D.R. (1999). *Cicero. Volume XXIII. Letters to Atticus. Letters 90-165A* (Latin-English). Cambridge, Mass.: Harvard University Press. ISBN: 0-674-99572-4.
SHACKLETON BAILEY, D.R. (1999). *Cicero. Volume XXIV. Letters to Atticus. Letters 166-281* (Latin-English). Cambridge, Mass.: Harvard University Press. ISBN: 0-674-99573-2.
SHACKLETON BAILEY, D.R. (1999). *Cicero. Volume XXIX. Letters to Atticus. Letters 282-426. Index* (Latin-English). Cambridge, Mass.: Harvard University Press. ISBN: 0-674-99540-6.
SHACKLETON BAILEY, D.R. (2001). *Cicero. Volume XXV. Letters to friends. Letters 1-113* (Latin-English). Cambridge, Mass.: Harvard University Press. ISBN: 0-674-99588-0.
SHACKLETON BAILEY, D.R. (2001). *Cicero. Volume XXVI. Letters to friends. Letters 114-280* (Latin-English). Cambridge, Mass.: Harvard University Press. ISBN: 0-674-99589-9.
SHACKLETON BAILEY, D.R. (2001). *Cicero. Volume XXVII. Letters to friends. Letters 281-435. Index* (Latin-English). Cambridge, Mass.: Harvard University Press. ISBN: 0-674-99590-2.
GLYNN WILLIAMS, W. & CARY, M. (1965-1979). *The letters to his friends (3 volumes)* (Latin-English). Cambridge, Mass.: University Press. ISBN: 0-674-99225-3; 0-674-99238-5; 0-674-99253-9 / London: Heinemann. ISBN: 0-434-99205-4; 0-434-99216-X; 0-434-99230-5.
GLYNN WILLIAMS, W., CARY, M. & HENDERSON, M.I. (1989/1972). *Cicero. Volume XVIII. Letters to his brother Quintus; Letters to Brutus; Handbook of electioneering; Letter to Octavian* (Latin-English). Cambridge, Mass.: Harvard University Press. ISBN: 0-674-99509-0 / London: Heinemann. ISBN: 0-434-99462-6.
CONSTANS, L.-A. (1969). *Correspondance. T.I: Lettres I-LV. (68-59 av. J.-C.)* (Latin-French). Paris: Les Belles Lettres. ISBN: 2-251-01037-8.
CONSTANS, L.-A. (1978). *Correspondance. T.II: Lettres LVI-CXXI. (58-56 av. J.-C.)* (Latin-French). Paris: Les Belles Lettres. ISBN: 2-251-01038-6.
CONSTANS, L.-A. (1971). *Correspondance. T.III: Lettres CXXII-CCIV. (55-51 av. J.-C.)* (Latin-French). Paris: Les Belles Lettres. ISBN: 2-251-01039-4.
CONSTANS, L.-A. & BAYET, J. (1967). *Correspondance. T.IV: Lettres CCV-CCLXXVIII. (51-50 av. J.-C.)* (Latin-French). Paris: Les Belles Lettres. ISBN: 2-251-01040-8.
BAYET, J., BEAUJEU, J. & JAL, P. (1983). *Correspondance. T.V: Lettres CCLXXIX-CCCLXXXIX. (50-49 av. J.-C.)* (Latin-French). Paris: Les Belles Lettres. ISBN: 2-251-01041-6.

BEAUJEU, J. (1993). *Correspondance. T. VI: Lettres CCCLXXXX-CCCCLXXVII. (mars 49-avril 46 av. J.-C.)* (Latin-French). Paris: Les Belles Lettres. ISBN: 2-251-01372-5.
BEAUJEU, J. (1991). *Correspondance. T. VII: Lettres CCCCLXXVIII-DLXXXVI. (avril 46-février 45 av. J.-C.)* (Latin-French). Paris: Les Belles Lettres. ISBN: 2-251-01043-2, 2-251-11043-7.
BEAUJEU, J. (1983). *Correspondance. T. VIII: Lettres DCLXXXVII-DCCVI. (mars-août 45 av. J.-C.)* (Latin-French). Paris: Les Belles Lettres. ISBN: 2-251-01322-9.
BEAUJEU, J. (1988). *Correspondance. T. IX: Lettres DCCVII-DCCCIII. (septembre 45-août 44 av. J.-C.)* (Latin-French). Paris: Les Belles Lettres. ISBN: 2-251-01339-3.
BEAUJEU, J. (1991). *Correspondance. T. X: Lettres DCCCIV-DCCCLXVI. (août 44-avril 43 av. J.-C.)* (Latin-French). Paris: Les Belles Lettres. ISBN: 2-251-01360-1.
BEAUJEU, J. & JAL, P. (1996). *Correspondance. T. XI: Lettres DCCCLXVII-DCCCCXXXV. (avril-juillet 43 av. J.-C.)* (Latin-French). Paris: Les Belles Lettres. ISBN: 2-251-01397-0.
DI SPIGNO, C. (1998). *Epistole ad Attico. Vol. 1: libri I-VIII* (Latin-Italian). Torino: Unione Tipografico-Editrice Torinese. ISBN: 88-02-05205-0.
RIZZO, S. (1991). *Tutte le opere di Cicerone. Vol. 20: Lettere ad Attico I-V* (Latin-Italian). Milano: Mondadori. ISBN: 88-04-35000-8.
GIANELLI, G. (1966). *Tutte le opere di Cicerone. Vol. 23: Lettere ai familiari I-IV* (Latin-Italian). Milano: Mondadori.
PERINI, G.B. ET AL. (1989). *Tutte le opere di Cicerone. Vol. 24, t. 2: Lettere ai familiari IX-XII* (Latin-Italian). Milano: Mondadori. ISBN: 88-04-33056-2.
BUFANO, A., AGNES, L. & LAMACCHIA, R. (1979). *Tutte le opere di Cicerone. Vol. 25, t. 2: Epistole a Bruto; Epistole al fratello Quinto; Framenti delle epistole; Epistola ad Ottaviano* (Latin-Italian). Milano: Mondadori.

PHILIPPICAE

CLARK, A. CURTIS (1992). *Orationes. Vol. 2. Pro Milone. Pro Marcello. Pro Ligario. Pro rege Deiotaro. Philippicae I-XIV*. Oxford: Oxford University Press. ISBN: 0-19-814616-X.
FUHRMANN, M. (2000). *Sämtliche Reden. Bd. 7: Für Marcellus. Für Ligarius. Für den König Deiotarus. Die Philippische Reden*. Zürich: Artemis & Winkler. ISBN: 3-7808-3518-X, 3-7608-3549-X.
KER, W.C.A. (1995). *Cicero. Volume XV. Philippics* (Latin-English). Cambridge, Mass.: Harvard University Press. ISBN: 0-674-99208-3.
SHACKLETON BAILEY, D.R. (1986). *Philippics* (Latin-English). Chapel Hill: University of North Carolina Press. ISBN: 0-8078-1657-4.
WUILLEUMIER, P. & BOULANGER, A. (1959). *Discours. Tome 19: Philippiques I à IV* (Latin-French). Paris: Les Belles Lettres. ISBN: 2-251-01072-6.
WUILLEUMIER, P. (1973). *Discours. Tome 20: Philippiques V à XIV* (Latin-French). Paris: Les Belles Lettres. ISBN: 2-251-01073-4.
MOSCA, B. (1996). *Le Filippiche (2 Vol)* (Latin-Italian). Milano: A. Mondadori. ISBN: 88-04-41801-X.
MOSCA, B. (1972). *Tutte le opere di Cicerone. Vol. 12: Le Filippiche* (Latin-Italian). Milano: Mondadori.

FLAVIUS JOSEPHUS (37/38-na 100). Jewish historian, wrote in Greek.

BELLVM IVDAICVM LIBRI I-VII

CLEMENTZ, H. (1997). *Geschichte des Jüdischen Krieges*. Wiesbaden: Fourier Verlag. ISBN: 3-921695-00-7.
CLEMENTZ, H. (1994). *Geschichte des Jüdischen Krieges*. Leipzig: Reclam. ISBN: 3-379-01519-9.

MICHEL, O. & BAUERNFEIND, O.G.H. (1962-1969). *De bello Judaico: griechisch und deutsch: der Jüdische Krieg*. Bd. I: Buch I-III (1962). Bd. II,1: Buch IV-V (1963, ISBN: 3-466-20027-X); Bd. II,2: Buch VI-VII (1969, 3-466-20028-8); Bd. III: Ergänzungen und Register (1969, 3-466-20132-2). München: Kösel-Verlag.

WILLIAMSON, G.A. & SMALLWOOD, E.M. (1996). *The Jewish War*. Harmondsworth: Penguin Books. ISBN: 0-14-044420-3.

THACKERAY, H.ST.J. (1997). *Josephus. Volume II. The Jewish War, books I-II* (Greek-English). Cambridge, Mass.: Harvard University Press. ISBN: 0-674-99568-6.

THACKERAY, H.ST.J. (1997). *Josephus. Volume III. The Jewish War, books III-IV* (Greek-English). Cambridge, Mass.: Harvard University Press. ISBN:0-674-99536-8.

THACKERAY, H.ST.J. (1997). *Josephus. Volume IV. The Jewish War, books V-VII. Index* (Greek-English). Cambridge, Mass.: Harvard University Press. ISBN:0-674-99569-4.

D'ANDILLY, A. (1979). *La guerre des juifs contre les Romains*. Paris: Lidis Éditions. ISBN: 2-85032-043-9.

SAVINEL, P. (1977). *La guerre des juifs*. Paris: Éditions de minuit. ISBN: 2-7073-0135-3.

PELLETIER, A. (1975). *Guerre des juifs. T.I: Livres I* (Greek-French). Paris: Les Belles Lettres.

PELLETIER, A. (1980). *Guerre des juifs. T.II: Livres II et III* (Greek-French). Paris: Les Belles Lettres. ISBN: 2-251-00181-6 , 2-251-10181-0.

PELLETIER, A. (1982). *Guerre des juifs. T.III: Livres IV et V* (Greek-French). Paris: Les Belles Lettres. ISBN: 2-251-00182-4.

VITUCCI, G. (1997). *La guerra giudaica. Vol. 1: libri I-III. Vol. 2: libri IV-VII* (Greek-Italian). Roma: Fondazione Lorenzo Valla. ISBN: 88-04-11823-7 (Vol. 1); 88-04-11824-5 (Vol. 2).

VITUCCI, G. (1996). *Guerra giudaica*. Milano: Mondadori. ISBN: 88-04-40688-7.

MEIJER, F.J.A.M. & WES, M.A. (1992). *De Joodse Oorlog & Uit mijn leven*. Baarn: Ambo. ISBN: 90-263-1152-4.

ANTIQVITATES, LIBRI XIV, XVII-XX

CLEMENTZ, H. (1998). *Des Flavius Josephus jüdische Altertümer (Bücher I-XX)*. Wiesbaden: Fourier. ISBN: 3-921695-19-8.

MARCUS, R. & WIKGREN, A. (1998). *Josephus. Volume X. Jewish Antiquities, books XIV-XV* (Greek-English). Cambridge, Mass.: Harvard University Press. ISBN: 0-674-99538-4.

MARCUS, R. & WIKGREN, A. (1998). *Josephus. Volume XI. Jewish Antiquities, books XVI-XVII* (Greek-English). Cambridge, Mass.: Harvard University Press. ISBN: 0-674-99578-3.

FELDMAN, L.H. (1998). *Josephus. Volume XII. Jewish Antiquities, books XVIII-XIX* (Greek-English). Cambridge, Mass.: Harvard University Press. ISBN:0-674-99477-9.

FELDMAN, L.H. (1998). *Josephus. Volume XIII. Jewish Antiquities, book XX* (Greek-English). *Index*. Cambridge, Mass.: Harvard University Press. ISBN: 0-674-99502-3.

D'ANDILLY, A. & BUCHON, J.A.C. (1997). *Histoire ancienne des Juifs; et La guerre des Juifs contre les Romains: 66-70 ap. J.-C.* Paris: Lidis Éditions. ISBN: 2-85032-063-3.

MORALDI, L. (1998). *Antichità Giudaiche (2 Vol.)*. Torino: Unione Tipografico-Editrice Torinese. ISBN: 88-02-05252-2.

MEIJER, F.J.A.M. & WES, M.A. (1998; 2002). *De Oude Geschiedenis van de Joden (Antiquitates Judaicae). Dl. 3: Boek XIV-XX*. Amsterdam: Ambo. ISBN: 90-263-1456-6, 90-6303-771-6 ; 90-263-1762-X.

TACITUS (P. Cornelius Tacitus; ca. 55-117). Latin historian.

ANNALES, LIBER XI; XV

FISHER, C.D. (1993). *Cornelii Taciti annalium: ab excessu divi Augusti libri*. Oxford: Oxford University Press. ISBN: 0-19-814633-7.
HEUBNER, H. (1993). *P. Cornelii Taciti libri qui supersunt. T.I: Ab excessu Divi Augusti* (Annales). Stuttgart: Teubner. ISBN: 3-519-11833-5.
RÖMER, F. (1976). *P. Corneli Taciti Annalium, libri 15-16*. Wien: Böhlau. ISBN: 3-205-07024-0.
HELLER, E. (1997). *Annalen: lateinisch und deutsch*. München: Artemis & Winkler. ISBN: 3-7608-1645-2 / Darmstadt: Wissenschaftliche Buchgesellschaft. ISBN: 3-534-05330-3.
JACKSON, J. (1937, rep.). *Tacitus. Volume IV. Annals 4-6, 9-11* (Latin-English). Cambridge, Mass.: Harvard University Press. ISBN: 0-674-99345-4.
JACKSON, J. (1937, rep.). *Tacitus. Volume V. Annals 13-16* (Latin-English). Cambridge, Mass.: Harvard University Press. ISBN: 0-674-99355-1.
GRANT, M. (1996). *The annals of imperial Rome*. London: Penguin Books. ISBN: 0-14-044060-7.
GRANT, M., WRIGHT, F.G. & GIFT, W.T. (1984). *The annals of imperial Rome*. New York: Dorset Press. ISBN: 0-88-029024-2.
WUILLEUMIER, P. & HELLEGOUARC'H, J. (1994). *Annales. T.III: Livres XI-XII* (Latin-French). Paris: Les Belles Lettres. ISBN: 2-251-01266-4.
WUILLEUMIER, P. & HELLEGOUARC'H, J. (1996). *Annales. T.IV: Livres XIII-XVI* (Latin-French). Paris: Les Belles Lettres. ISBN: 2-251-01267-2.
ARICI, A. (1998). *Annali* (Latin-Italian). Torino: Unione Tipografico-Editrice Torinese. ISBN: 88-02-02665-3.
CEVA, B. (1996/2000). *Annali (2 Vol.)* (Latin-Italian). Milano: Biblioteca universale Rizzoli. ISBN: 88-17-12309-9 (Vol. 1), 88-17-17146-8 (Vol. 1) / 88-17-17147-6 (Vol. 2).
STEFANONI, M. (1990). *Annali. Vol. 22: Libri 11-16* (Latin-Italian). Milano: Garzanti. ISBN: 88-11-51945-5.
WES, M.A. (1999). *Annalen (2 dl.)*. 's-Hertogenbosch: Voltaire. ISBN: 90-584-8001-1 / 90-584-8005-4.
MEIJER, J.W. (1990). *Jaarboeken (= Ab excessu divi Augusti annales)*. Baarn: Ambo. ISBN: 90-263-1065-X.

HISTORIAE LIBER IV

VRETSKA, H. (1999). *Tacitus: Historien,* lateinisch-deutsch. Stuttgart: Reclam. ISBN: 3-15-002721-7 , 3-15-022721-6.
BORST, J., HROSS, H. & BORST, H. (1984). *Historiae = Historien:* lateinisch-deutsch. München: Artemis-Verlag. ISBN: 3-7608-1633-9.
FISHER, C.D. (1963). *Historiae*. Oxford: Oxford University Press. ISBN: 0-19-814634-5.
MOORE, C.H. & JACKSON, J.C. (1931, rep.). *Tacitus. Volume III. Histories 4-5. Annals 1-3* (Latin-English). Cambridge, Mass.: Harvard University Press. ISBN: 0-674-99274-1.
LEVENE, D.S. & FYFE, W.H. (1999). *The Histories*. Oxford: Oxford University Press. ISBN: 0-19-283958-6 , 0-19-283158-5.
WELLESLEY, K. (1996). *The Histories*. London: Penguin Books. ISBN: 0-14-044150-6.
LE BONNIEC, H. & HELLEGOUARC'H, J. (1992). *Histoires. T.III: Livres 4 et 5* (Latin-French). Paris: Les Belles Lettres. ISBN: 2-251-01358-9.
ARICI, A. (1970). *Storie* (Latin-Italian). Torino: Unione Tipografico-Editrice Torinese. ISBN: 88-02-01848-0.
DESSI, F. (1998). *Storie. Vol. 2: libri III-V* (Latin-Italian). Milano: Rizzoli. ISBN: 88-17-16907-2.
MEIJER, J.W. (1995). *Historiën*. Amsterdam: Pandora. ISBN: 90-254-5582-4.

Secondary literature

ALAND, K. & NESTLE, E. (¹⁸1957). *Novum Testamentum graece et latine*, Stuttgart.
ALFÖLDI, A. (1953). *Studien über Caesars Monarchie*, Lund.
ALFÖLDI, A. (1959). 'Das wahre Gesicht Caesars', *Antike Kunst 2*, p. 27 sqq.
ALFÖLDI, A. (1969). 'Der früheste Denartypus des L. Buca mit CAESAR DICTATOR PERPETUO', *Schweizer Münzblätter 73*, 1-7.
ALFÖLDI, A. (1973). 'La divinisation de César dans la politique d'Antoine et d'Octavien entre 44 et 40 av. J.-C.' *Revue Numismatique Série 6, 15*, 99-128.
ANDRÉ, J. (1949). *La vie et l'oeuvre d'Asinius Pollion*, Paris.
ANSELMINO, A. (1977). *Terrecotte architettoniche dell'Antiquarium di Roma, I: Antefisse*, Roma.
AUFHAUSER, J. (²1925). 'Antike Jesus-Zeugnisse', In K. ALAND (Ed.), *Kleine Texte für theologischen und philologischen Vorlesungen und Übungen, 126*.
AUGSTEIN, R. (1972). *Jesus Menschensohn*, München/Gütersloh/Wien.
AULOK, H. VON (1957-68). *Sylloge Nummorum Graecorum Deutschland, Sammlung von Aulok*, Berlin.
BATTENBERG, C. (1980). *Pompeius und Caesar – Persönlichkeit und Programm in ihrer Münzpropaganda*, Dissertation, Marburg/Lahn.
BAUER, B. (1877). *Christus und die Caesaren. Der Ursprung des Christenthums aus dem römischen Griechenthum*, Berlin.
BAUER, W. (⁶1988). *Griechisch-deutsches Wörterbuch zu den Schriften des Neuen Testaments und der übrigen urchristlichen Literatur*, Berlin.
BENGTSON, H. (1977). *Marcus Antonius*, München.
BLASS, F., DEBRUNNER, A. & REHKOPF, F. (¹⁷1990). *Grammatik des neutestamentlichen Griechisch*, Göttingen.
BORDA, M., FUNAIOLI, G., PARETI, L. & VALORI, A. (1957). *Caio Giulio Cesare*, Istituto di Studi Romani editore, Roma.
BORNKAMM, G. (1956). *Jesus von Nazareth*, Stuttgart.
BOTERMANN, H. (1968). *Die Soldaten und die römische Politik in der Zeit von Caesars Tod bis zur Begründung des Zweiten Triumvirats*, München.
BOYCE, K. (1937). 'Corpus of the Lararia of Pompei', *MemAmAcRome 14*.
BROUGHTON, T. (1951-52). *The Magistrates of the Roman Republic*, 2 vols. New York.
BRUCKBERGER, R.-L. (1965). *L'histoire de Jésus-Christ*, Paris.
BULTMANN, R. (³1960). *Die Erforschung der synoptischen Evangelien*, Berlin.
CANCIK, H. (1975). 'Christus Imperator'. In H. v. STIETENCRON (Ed.), *Der Name Gottes*, Düsseldorf.
CANCIK, H. (1984). 'Die Gattung Evangelium'. In H. CANCIK (Ed.), *Markus-Philologie*, Tübingen.
CANCIK, H. / KONRAD HITZL (Ed.) (2003): *Die Praxis der Herrscherverehrung in Rom und seinen Provinzen*, Tübingen.
CANFORA, L. (1999). *Giulio Cesare – Il dittatore democratico*, Bari.
CANFORA, L. (2001). *Caesar – Der demokratische Diktator. Eine Biographie*, München.
CAROTTA, F. (CAM) (1988). 'Madonna mia', *BellaMadonna/Memoria 2089*, Cam Ed.: Almanac of the Kore Verlag, Freiburg i. Br., p. 9-15. ISBN 3-926023-75-9.
CAROTTA, F. (CAM) & BLUMENTEIG (1989). 'Jesses! Madonnenerscheinung in der Wiehre' (Jesus, my goodness! Apparition of the Madonna in the Wiehre), *Stadtzeitung* (City Newspaper) of Freiburg i. Br. n 4, April 1989, p. 22-24.
CAROTTA, F. (CAM) (1989). 'Caesars Kreuzigung – Das Evangelium nach Kleopatra' (Caesar's crucifixion—The Gospel according to Cleopatra), *BellaMadonna/Memoria 2090*, Cam Ed.: Almanac of the Kore Verlag, Freiburg i. Br., p. I–IX. ISBN 3-926023-76-7.

CAROTTA, F. (CAM) (1991). 'Jesus Christus, Caesar incognito' (Jesus Christ, Caesar incognito)', *die tageszeitung*, Berlin, Monday, December 23, 'die Wahrheit' (the Truth): p. 20.
CAROTTA, F. (1999). *War Jesus Caesar?* München.
CAROTTA, F. (2002). *Was Jezus Caesar?* Soesterberg.
CAROTTA, F. (2003). 'Il Cesare incognito – da Divo Giulio a Gesù', *Quaderni di Storia*, Edizioni Dedalo, Bari, 57, gennaio-giugno 2003, 357-375. ISSN 0391-6936 88-220-2557-1.
CARSON, R. (1978-81). *Principal Coins of the Romans, I-III*, London.
CHANTRAINE, P. (1933). *La formation des noms en grec ancien*, Paris
CHARALAMBAKIS, C. (1984). Ἱστορία τῆς μετακλασικῆς ἑλληνικῆς γλώσσας, Α.Ἡ ἑλληνιστική κοινή, Rethymno.
CLAUSS, M. (1999). *Kaisar und Gott*, Stuttgart.
COUCHOUD, P.-L. (1924). *Le Mystère de Jésus*, Paris.
COUCHOUD, P.-L. (1924). *The Enigma of Jesus*, London.
COUCHOUD, P.-L. (1926). 'L'évangile de Marc a-t-il été écrit en Latin?', *Revue de l'Histoire de Religions*, 94.
COURTNEY, G. (1992). *Et tu, Judas? Then fall Jesus!*. Lane Cove, Australia. ISBN: 0-646-08733-9.
CRAWFORD, M. (1974). *Roman Republican Coinage, I-II*, Cambridge.
DAHLMANN, H. (1934). 'Clementia Caesaris.' In D. RASMUSSEN (Ed.) (1976), *Caesar. Wege der Forschung*. Bd. XLIII (pp. 32-47). Darmstadt.
DEGRASSI, A. (1947). *Fasti consulares et triumphales*, Roma.
DER KLEINE PAULY (1979). *Lexikon der Antike in fünf Bänden*, München. Cf. ZIEGLER/ SONTHEIMER.
Die Inschriften von Ephesos, Teil II, (1979). WANKEL, H. et alii (Eds.), Bonn.
DOBESCH, G. (1966). *Caesars Apotheose zu Lebzeiten und sein Ringen um den Königstitel*, Wien.
DORMEYER, D. (2000). 'Plutarchs Cäsar und die erste Evangeliumsbiographie des Markus'. In R. VON HAELING (Ed.), *Rom und das himmlische Jerusalem. Die frühen Christen zwischen Anpassung und Ablehnung*. (pp. 29-52). Darmstadt.
DRUMANN, W. & GROEBE, P. (1899-1922²). *Geschichte Roms in seinem Übergange von der republikanischen zur monarchischen Verfassung oder Pompeius, Caesar, Cicero und ihre Zeitgenossen nach Geschlechtern und mit genealogischen Tabellen, I-VI*, Berlin-Leipzig; Nachdruck Hildesheim 1964.
FELDMAN, L.H. (1953). 'Asinius Pollio and his Jewish Interests', *Transactions and Proceedings of the American Philological Association, vol. 84*.
FITTSCHEN, K. (1976). 'Zur Panzerstatue in Cherchel'. In: *Jahrbuch des Deutschen Archäologischen Instituts 91*, 175-210.
GABBA, E. (1956). *Appiano e la storia delle guerre civili*, Firenze.
GABBA, E. (1958). *Appiani bellorum civilium liber primus*, Firenze.
GEHRIG, U., GREIFENHAGEN, A. & KUNISCH, N. (1968). *Führer durch die Antikenabteilung*. Berlin-Charlottenburg, Staatliche Museen Preußischer Kulturbesitz.
GELZER, M. (³1941). *Caesar der Politiker und Staatsmann*, München.
GESCHE, H. (1968). *Die Vergottung Caesars*, Kallmünz.
GLARE, P. (Ed.) (1996). *Oxford Latin Dictionary*, Oxford.
HAHN, L. (1906). *Rom und Romanismus im griechischen-römischen Osten*, Leipzig.
HARRIS, R. (1893). *A study of Codex Bezae (Text and Studies II 1)*, Cambridge.
HEILIGENTHAL, R. (1997). *Der verfälschte Jesus. Eine Kritik moderner Jesusbilder*, Darmstadt.
HELBIG, W. (1963-72). *Führer durch die öffentlichen Sammlungen klassischer Altertümer in Rom, I*, Tübingen.

HERBIG, R. (1967). 'Neue Studien zur Ikonographie des Gaius Iulius Caesar'. In D. RASMUSSEN (Ed.), *Caesar. Wege der Forschung.* Bd. XLIII (pp. 69-88). Darmstadt.
HERBIG, R. (^{4}1959). 'Neue Studien zur Ikonographie des Gaius Iulius Caesar', *Kölner Jahrbuch für Früh- und Vorgeschichte*, p. 7 sqq.
HINZ, P. (1973-81). *Deus homo – Das Christusbild von seinen Ursprüngen bis zur Gegenwart*, Berlin.
HUNGER, H., STEGMÜLLER, O., ERBSE, H., IMHOF, M., BÜCHNER, K., BECK, H.-G. & RÜDIGER, H. (1975). *Die Textüberlieferung der antiken Literatur und der Bibel*, München.
KAERST, J. (1917). *Geschichte des Hellenismus*, I, Berlin/Leipzig.
KAHN, A. (1986). *The education of Julius Caesar – a biography, a reconstruction*, New York.
KINDER, H. & HILGEMANN, W. (1966). *dtv-Atlas zur Weltgeschichte – Karten und chronologischer Abriß*, vol. 1.
KLUGE, F. (^{21}1975). *Etymologisches Wörterbuch der deutschen Sprache*, Berlin.
KRAFT, K. (1969). *Der goldene Kranz Caesars und der Kampf um die Entlarvung des 'Tyrannen'*, Darmstadt.
KRAUS, T. (Ed.) (1967). *Das römische Weltreich*, Berlin.
LANGE, K. (1938). *Herrscherköpfe des Altertums im Münzbild ihrer Zeit*, Berlin/Zürich.
LATTE, K. (1960). *Römische Religionsgeschichte*, München.
LEIDBUNDGUT, A. (1977). *Die römischen Tonlampen in der Schweiz*, Bern.
LEIPOLDT, J. (1923). *War Jesus Jude?* Leipzig/Erlangen.
LESCHHORN, W. (1993). *Antike Ären*, Stuttgart.
LIDDELL, H. & SCOTT, R. (Eds.) (1996). *Greek-English Dictionary*, Oxford.
LÜDERITZ, G. (1994). 'What is the Politeuma?'. In J. W. VAN HENTEN & P. W. VAN DER HORST (Eds.), *Studies in early Jewish Epigraphy*. Leiden/New York/Köln.
LÜDERITZ, G. (unpublished manuscript). *Taubenflug und Hahnenschrei – 'Ornithologisches' zum Markusevangelium. II. Der Hahn.* Tübingen.
LÜLING, G. (1992). *Der christliche Kult an der vorislamischen Kaaba als problem der Islamwissenschaft und christliche Theologie*, Erlangen. ISBN: 3-922317-16-2.
LUXEMBERG, C. (2000). *Dis syro-aramäische Lesart des Koran. Ein Beitrag zur Entschlüsselung der Koransprache*, Berlin. ISBN: 3-86093-274-8.
MAGGI, S. & REGGI, G. (1986). *Le condizioni di salute di Cesare nel 44 a. C.*, Lugano.
MAGIE, D. (1905/ MCMV). *De Romanorum iuris publici sacrique vocabulis sollemnibus in graecum sermonem conversis*, Leipzig/Lipsiae.
MARQUARDT, J. (1886: 2. Auflage von MAU, A.). *Das Privatleben der Römer*, Leipzig; Nachdruck Darmstadt 1964.
MESSORI, V. (1976/^{3}^{2}1986). *Ipotesi su Gesù*, Torino.
MESSORI, V. (1997). *Gelitten unter Pontius Pilatus?*, Köln.
MOMMSEN, T. (1899). *Römisches Strafrecht*, Leipzig.
MORGAN, L. (1997). '"levi quidem de re..." – Julius Caesar as Tyrant and Pedant', *JRS* 87.
NEVEROD, O. (1968). 'Mitridat Evpator i perstii-pecati iz Pantikapeja', *Sovetskaja Archeologija* 1.
NOETHLICHS, K. L. (1996). *Das Judentum und der römische Staat: Minderheitenpolitik im antiken Rom*, Darmstadt.
OBERLEITNER, W. (1985). *Geschnittene Steine*, Wien.
POPE, M. (1934). *From Latin to Modern French with special consideration of Anglo-Norman*, Manchester.
PRICE, S.R.F. (1984), *Rituals and Power. The Roman imperial cult in Asia Minor*, Cambridge.
PUTZGER, F. (1954). *Historischer Schulatlas – von der Altsteinzeit bis zur Gegenwart*, Bielefeld/Berlin/Hannover.

RASMUSSEN, D. (Ed.) (1967). *Caesar,* Darmstadt.
RAUBITSCHEK, A. (1954). 'Epigraphical Notes on Julius Caesar', *Journal of Roman Studies,* 44.
RE, PAULY, A. & WISSOWA, G. (1894 sqq), *Realencyclopädie der classischen Altertumswissenschaft.* Neubearbeitung, 83 Bände, Stuttgart. Also called 'Pauly-Wissowa' or 'Der Große Pauly', cf. DER KLEINE PAULY.
REISER, M. (1984). 'Der Alexanderroman und das Markusevangelium'. In H. CANCIK (Ed.), *Markus-Philologie,* Tübingen.
REISER, R. (1995). *Götter und Kaiser – Antike Vorbilder Jesu,* München.
RIZZO, G. (1929). *La pittura ellenistico-romana,* Milano.
ROBERTS, C. & SKEAT, T. (1983). *The Birth of the Codex,* London.
SCHALIT, A. (1969). *König Herodes – der Mann und sein Werk,* Berlin.
SCHEFOLD, K. (1957). *Die Wände Pompejis,* Berlin.
SCHMITTHENNER, W. (1973). *Oktavian und das Testament Caesars,* München.
SCHNEEMELCHER, W. (Ed.) (1990). *Neutestamentliche Apokryphen, I. Band,* Tübingen.
SCHWEITZER, A. (1906/²1913). *Geschichte der Leben-Jesu-Forschung,* Tübingen.
SCHWEITZER, A. (1906/⁹1984). *Geschichte der Leben-Jesu-Forschung,* Tübingen.
SCHWEITZER, A. & BOWDEN, J. (2000). *The quest of the historical Jesus.* London.
SCHWEITZER, A. & COPPELLOTTI, F. (1986). *Storia della ricerca sulla vita di Gesù,* Brescia.
SEGERT, S. (⁴1990). *Altaramäische Grammatik,* Leipzig.
SIMON, E. (1979). 'Sterngottheiten auf zwei augusteischen Panzerstatuen', *Würzburger Jahrbücher N.F. 5,* 263-272.
SIMON, E. (1986). *Augustus: Kunst und Leben in Rom um die Zeitwende,* München.
STAUFFER, E. (1952). *Christus und die Caesaren,* Hamburg.
STAUFFER, E. (1955), *Christ and the Caesars. Historical sketches.* Translated by Kaethe Gregor Smith and Ronald Gregor Smith. London: SCM-Press.
STAUFFER, E. (1957). *Jerusalem und Rom im Zeitalter Jesu Christi,* Bern.
STIETENCRON, H. v. (1975). *Der Name Gottes,* Düsseldorf.
STRACK, P. (1937). *Untersuchungen zur römischen Reichsprägung des zweiten Jahrhundert, Teil III. Die Reichsprägung zur Zeit des Antoninus Pius,* Stuttgart
TAYLOR, L. (1931). *The Divinity of the Roman Emperor,* Middeletown.
TORREY, C. (1941). *Documents of the Primitive Church,* New York/London.
TSCHIEDEL, H.-J. (1981). *Caesars 'Anticato – Eine Untersuchung der Testimonien und Fragmente',* Darmstadt.
VANDENBERG, P. (1986). *Cäsar und Kleopatra – Die letzeten Tage der römischen Republik,* München.
VESSBERG, O. (1941). *Studien zur Kunstgeschichte der römischen Republik,* Lund/Leipzig.
VITTINGHOFF, F. (1952). *Römische Kolonisation und Bürgerrechtspolitik unter Caesar und Augustus,* Mainz/Wiesbaden.
VOGELS, H. J. (Ed.) (1929). *Codicum novi testamenti specimina: paginas 51 ex codicibus manuscriptis et 3 ex libris impressis collegit ac phototypice repraesentatas,* Bonn/Bonnae.
VOLLENWEIDER, M.-L. (1966). *Die Steinschneidekunst und ihre Künstler in spätrepublikanischer und augusteischer Zeit,* Baden-Baden.
VON AULOK, H. (1957-68). *Sylloge Nummorum Graecorum Deutschland, Sammlung von Aulok,* Berlin.
VON DER DUNK, T. (2002). 'Bom onder het christendom. De overeenkomst tussen Brutus en Judas'. *Vrij Nederland, 6-4-2002,* 66-69, Amsterdam.
VON HARNACK, A. (1924). *Marcion: das Evangelium vom fremden Gott. Eine Monographie zur Geschichte der Grundlegung der katholischen Kirche. Neue Studien zu Marcion.* Leipzig.

WANKEL, H. et alii (1979). *Die Inschriften von Ephesos, Teil II*, Bonn.
WEINSTOCK, S. (1971). *Divus Julius*, Oxford.
WIKENHAUSER, A. & SCHMID, J. (^{6}1973). *Einleitung in das Neue Testament*, Freiburg/Basel/Wien.
WILLIAMS, M. F. (2003). 'The Sidus Iulium, the divinity of men, and the Golden Age in Virgil's Aeneid'. *Leeds International Classical Studies* 2.1, 1-29.
WISSOWA, G. (^{2}1912). *Religion und Kultus der Römer*, München.
WLOSOK, A. (Ed.) (1978). *Römischer Kaiserkult*, Darmstadt.
WUTZ, F. (1925). *Die Transkriptionen von der Septuaginta bis zu Hieronymus*, Berlin/Stuttgart/Leipzig.
ZANKER, P. (1990). *Augustus und die Macht der Bilder*, München.
ZANKER, P. & CUNIBERTO, F. (1989). *Augusto e il potero delle immagini*, Torino.
ZANKER, P. & SHAPIRO, A. (1988). *The power of images in the age of Augustus*, Ann Arbor.
ZIEGLER, K. & SONTHEIMER, W. (1979). *Der Kleine Pauly. Lexikon der Antike auf der Grundlage von Pauly's Realencyclopädie der classischen Altertumswissenschaft*. 5 Bde. München.
ZUNTZ, G. (1984). 'Wann wurde das Evangelium Marci geschrieben?' In H. CANCIK (Ed.), *Markus-Philologie*, Tübingen.
ZWIERLEIN-DIEHL, E. (1979). *Die antiken Gemmen des Kunsthistorischen Museums Wien, 2* , Wien.

Illustrations

1. Silver denarius of L. Aemilius Buca. Ø 1.9 cm. Sammlung Mamroth, Berlin-Pankow. – LANGE (1938), p. 92-93.
2. Caesar Tusculum, in the Castello Agliè. Torino, Museo d'Antichità.
3. Idem as 2
4. Idem as 2
5. Idem as 2
6. Caesar Farnese, Colossal Head. Napoli, Museo Nazionale.
7. Idem as 2
8. Caesar Torlonia. Roma, Museo Torlonia.
9. Caesar Vatican. Museo Vaticano, Sala dei busti.
10. Idem as 8
11. Head with oak wreath. Thasos, Archaeological Museum.
12. Idem as 8
13. B.M.C. R 3955 (Crawford 452/2).
14. B.M.C. R 3960 (Crawford 452/5).
15. Aureus of Costa, Brutus' legate. 8.15 gr. 42 BC, Imperatorial Coinage of Brutus. B.M.C. East 58.
16. Wreath, isolated – idem as 15
17. Montage – idem as 8
18. Caesar Uffizi. Firenze, Galleria degli Uffizi. Photo: Margarete Burghalter.
19. Caesar Camposanto. Pisa, Campo Santo.
20. B.M.C. Gaul 27 (Crawford 443).
21. B.M.C. Sp 87 (Crawford 468/2).
22. B.M.C. R 3837 (Crawford 437/2a).
23. Sestertius of Antoninus Pius. Cited according to STRACK (1937), Taf. XI Nr. 891. Cf. also the denarius of Hadrianus, Rev. ROMVLO CONDITORI. B.M.C. 710.
24. Pompeii, IX 13,5 – G.E. RIZZO, La pittura ellenistico-romana, Milano 1929, tav. 194.
25. Antoninianus of Elagabalus, Rev. MARS VICTOR. B.M.C. 19.
26. B.M.C. Af 6 (Crawford 460/3).
27. B.M.C. R 3911 A (Crawford 426/3).
28. B.M.C. East 42 (Crawford 506/2).
29. B.M.C. East 52 (Crawford 503/1).
30. B.M.C. East 68 (Crawford 508/3).
31. Idem as 21
32. B.M.C. East 52 (Crawford 503/1).
33. B.M.C. R 3955 (Crawford 452/2).
34. B.M.C. R 3960 (Crawford 452/5).
35. B.M.C. R 4159 (Crawford 480/6).
36. B.M.C. R 4169 (Crawford 480/19).
37. Plaster casts from the denarii in the Bibliothèque Nationale, Paris.

ILLUSTRATIONS 507

38. *B.M.C. R 4349, Imp. 633.* Sammlung Niggeler, Nr. 1015 *(Giard Nr. 68).* Fotoarchiv Antiker Münzen an der Universität Frankfurt/M.
39. *B.M.C. R 4360, Imp. 628;* Paris, Bibliothèque Nationale *(Giard Nr. 49).*
40. *B.M.C. R 4362, Imp. 637;* Paris, Bibliothèque Nationale *(Giard Nr. 43).*
41. *B.M.C. R 4152 (Crawford 480/4).*
42. *B.M.C. R 4167 (Crawford 480/5a).*
43. *B.M.C. 4532, Imp. 32 (R.I.C. 115).*
44. Louvre, Paris.
45. British Museum, London.
46. *B.M.C. Gaul 140, Imp. 328 (R.I.C. 253).*
47. *B.M.C. Gaul 138, Imp. 326 (R.I.C. 253).*
48. *B.M.C. 4584* and *Imp. 70 (R.I.C. Augustus 141);* cf. also *B.M.C. 4585* and *Imp. 71 (R.I.C. Augustus 142).* Sammlung Niggeler, Nr. 1039 *(Giard Nr. 273).* Fotoarchiv Antiker Münzen an der Universität Frankfurt/M.
49. Denarius of Lentulus. Sammlung Niggeler, Nr. 1055 *(Giard Nr. 555).* Fotoarchiv Antiker Münzen an der Universität Frankfurt/M.
50. Extrapolation from 46, 47, 48 and 49: Cam.
51. *R.I.C. 34, Cohen 30, Sear 4017.*
52. *Catalogue of West European Painting in the Hermitage,* Saint Petersburg. Detail: the bottom of the plate.
53. Idem as 49.
54. a) *La Resurrezione* by Raffaellino del Garbo, Galleria dell'Accademia, Firenze; b) *Salvator Mundi* by Pedro Berrugete, museum of the Cathedral of Palencia, Spain.
55. Idem as 49.
56. Idem as 40.
57. Antefix. Rome, Conservatory palace. – A. ANSELMINO, *Terrecotte architettoniche dell'Antiquarium comunale di Roma, I: Antefisse,* Roma 1977, Tab. XII. 52.
58. Clay lamp. Brugg, Vindonissa Museum. – A. LEIBUNDGUT, *Die römischen Tonlampen in der Schweiz,* Bern 1977, Tab. 23.3.
59. Museum of Cherchel. Photos G. Fittschen-Badura. – FITTSCHEN (1976), p. 175-210.
60. Musei Vaticani.
61. Berlin-Charlottenburg, Staatliche Museen Preußischer Kulturbesitz. – GEHRIG et alii (1968) p. 222 Tafel 27; VIERNEISEL, *RAB* 70 sq., ill. 53.
62. Double-Centenionalis of Decentius, Caesar 351-353 AD, *R.I.C. 293.*
63. Solidus of Anthemius, 467-472 AD, *Cohen 7.*
64. Solidus of Eudocia, wife of Theodosius II, 421-41 (†460) AD, *Goodacre 3, Tolstoi 90.*
65. Solidus of Olybrius, 472 AD, *Cohen 3.*
66. Tremissis of Romulus Augustus (Augustulus), 475-6 AD, *Cohen 10.*
67. *B.M.C. R 4161 (Crawford 480/1).*
68. Idem as 67
69. Good Friday procession figures from a village church in Campania.
70. The Pietà of Michelangelo, Saint Peter, Vatican.
71. *B.M.C. East 32 (Crawford 458).*
72. *B.M.C. Sic 3 (Crawford 445/1a).*
73. *B.M.C. Sic 5 (Crawford 457/1).*
74. *B.M.C. Sic 21 (Crawford 483/2).*
75. *B.M.C. Sic 15 (Crawford 511/2b).*
76. Left: Detail of Sextus' coin, ill. 75 and Nassidius' coin, ill. 74; right: Detail of Andrea Verrocchio, *The Baptism of Christ,* Uffizi. Graphical processing: Cam.
77. Wien, Kunsthistorisches Museum. – ZWIERLEIN-DIEHL (1979), p. 65, Nr. 805, Taf. 36. Museum's photograph.
78. *B.M.C. East 155 (Sydenham 1267).*

79. B.M.C. East 84 (Crawford 505/3).
80. B.M.C. East 141 (Crawford 533/2).
81. B.M.C. East 172 (Crawford 539/1).
82. Papal emblems: Der große Brockhaus, Wiesbaden 1955, s.v.
83. Idem as 36: B.M.C. R 4169 (Crawford 480/19).
84. B.M.C. R 4173 (Crawford 480/13).
85. B.M.C. R 4179 (Crawford 480/22).
86. B.M.C. R 4176 (Crawford 480/21).
87. Vaticano, Museo Gregoriano Profano.
88. Vaticano. Necropoli. Mausoleum M: Iulii.
89. Reiderian plate. München, Bayerisches Nationalmuseum.
90. B.M.C. Gaul 116 (Crawford 538/1).
91. B.M.C. Africa 33 (Crawford 540/2).
92. B.M.C. Gaul 75 (Crawford 490/2).
93. B.M.C. Gaul 54 (Crawford 488/1).
94. B.M.C. Gaul 31 (Crawford 489/2).
95. B.M.C. Gaul 46 (Crawford 492/2).
96. B.M.C. Gaul 47 (Crawford 493/1b).
97. B.M.C. East 180 (Crawford 543/1).
98. B.M.C. Gaul 106 (Crawford 535/1).
99. B.M.C. 684, (R.I.C. Augustus 540).
100. Cameo of Sardonyx. Detail. Collection Beverley. – VOLLENWEIDER (1966), p. 60, Taf. 61, 1.2.
101. Ara Pacis, Rome. Detail.
102. Marmoreal relief of Mars from Carthago. Algiers, museum.
103. Armor statue of Cherchel, detail. Idem as 59
104. Armor statue of Prima Porta, detail. Idem as 60
105. Lararium Pompei VIII 5.37 in the 'casa delle pareti rosse'. – BOYCE (1937), Nr. 371 tab. 31; SCHEFOLD (1957), p. 227.
106. Samos, Archaeological Museum. – IGR, IV, 1715; Ath. Mitt., XLIV, 1919, p. 34, n° 20; SEG, I, 382. – RAUBITSCHEK (1954), p. 69.
107. Vienna, Kunsthist. Museum Inv. IX A 26. Ø 22 cm. – OBERLEITNER (1985), p. 38. Museum's photograph.
108. Lost, formerly in the Bibliothèque Nationale, Paris. – Grueber, vol. II, p. 506.
109. B.M.C. R 4146 (Crawford 480/3).
110. B.M.C. Gaul 76 (Crawford 497/2a). – Tübingen, Archaeological Institute. Photo: D. Mannsperger.
111. Idem as 40
112. B.M.C. 4659, Imp. 117 (Giard Nr. 537). – Bank Leu 265, 1966 Nr. 44.
113. Graphical processing: Hubert Walter. – For detailed maps cf. i.a. VITTINGHOFF (1952); SCHALIT (1969); for a general outline: PUTZGER (1954); KINDER & HILGEMANN (1966).
114. Creu dels Improperis (croix des Outrages) in Pesillà la Ribera (Pézilla-la-Rivière).
115. Reconstruction drawing: Pol du Closeau, © 2002 Pol Corten, Zuilenstraat 52, 3512 ND Utrecht, The Netherlands.
116. Column or Passion Sarcophagus, Rome, Vatican, ex Lat. 171, Repertorim I nr. 49.
117. Second plate from a Passion cycle of an ivory box, North-Italic 420/430, London, British Museum.
118. Lid of a relic box from Palestine, late 6th cent., Vatican, Chapel Sancta Sanctorum.
119. Rabula Codex, miniature, Syrian Evangeliarium from the year 586, Florence, Bibl. Laur. Plut. I 56 fol. 13a.
120. Ivory relief, Narbonne, St-Just, treasury of the Church, early 9th cent., court school of Charlemagne.

ILLUSTRATIONS

121. Ivory triptychon (middle part), 10th cent., Berlin, Staatliche Museen.
122. Miniature from the year 975, in the commentary to the revelation of John by Beatus de Liébana, written ca. 785 abbey of San Salvador de Tábara (near Zamora).
123. Crucifix from San Damiano, revered by Francis of Assisi (1181-1226).
124. Giotto, fresco, Padua, Arena Chapel, ca. 1305.
125. P.P. Rubens, 1620, Royal Museum of Fine Arts, Antwerpen.
126. Signet stone emanated from Orphic-Christian syncretism, with the likeness of the Crucified One, 2nd half of the 3rd century. Inscription on this exemplar: *ΟΡΦΕΟC BAKKIKOC* (on others: *ΟΡΦΕΟC BAKXIKOC*).
127. Magic gem with the likeness of the Crucified One, 3rd cent., now in the collection Péreire in Paris. (N.B.: In the Greek text of the inscription there appears the name Christ.)

(B.M.C.) British Museum Catalog of Coins of the Roman Republic, London.
(B.M.C.) (Imp.) Coins of the Roman Empire in the British Museum, London.
(R.I.C.) Roman Imperial Coinage, Vol. I–X, London 1923-92.
(Carson) R.A.G. CARSON, *Principal Coins of the Romans,* vol. I, *The Republic c. 290-31 B.C.* 1978; vol. II, *The Principate 31 B.C.–A.D. 296.* 1979; vol. III, *The Dominate.* 1981. London.
(Cohen) H. COHEN, *Description historique des monnaies frappées sous l'empire romain,* 2e édition, 8 vol., Paris 1880-92.
(Crawford) M.H. CRAWFORD, *Roman Republican Coinage,* vols 1-2, Cambridge 1975.
(Goodacre) H. GOODACRE, *A Handbook of the Coinage of the Byzantine Empire,* 2nd edition, London 1957.
(Grueber) H.A. GRUEBER, *Coins of the Roman Republic in the British Museum,* vols 1-3, London 1910 (reprint 1970).
(Seaby) H.A. SEABY, *Roman Silver Coins,* Vol. I. The Republic–Augustus. 3rd edition, London 1978.
(Sear) D.R. SEAR, *Roman Coins and their Values,* 4th revised edition, London 1988.
(Sydenham) E.A. SYDENHAM, *The coinage of the Roman Republic,* London 1952.
(Tolstoi) J. TOLSTOI, *Vizantijskije monety – monnaies byzantines,* 9 parts. Petrograd 1912-14.

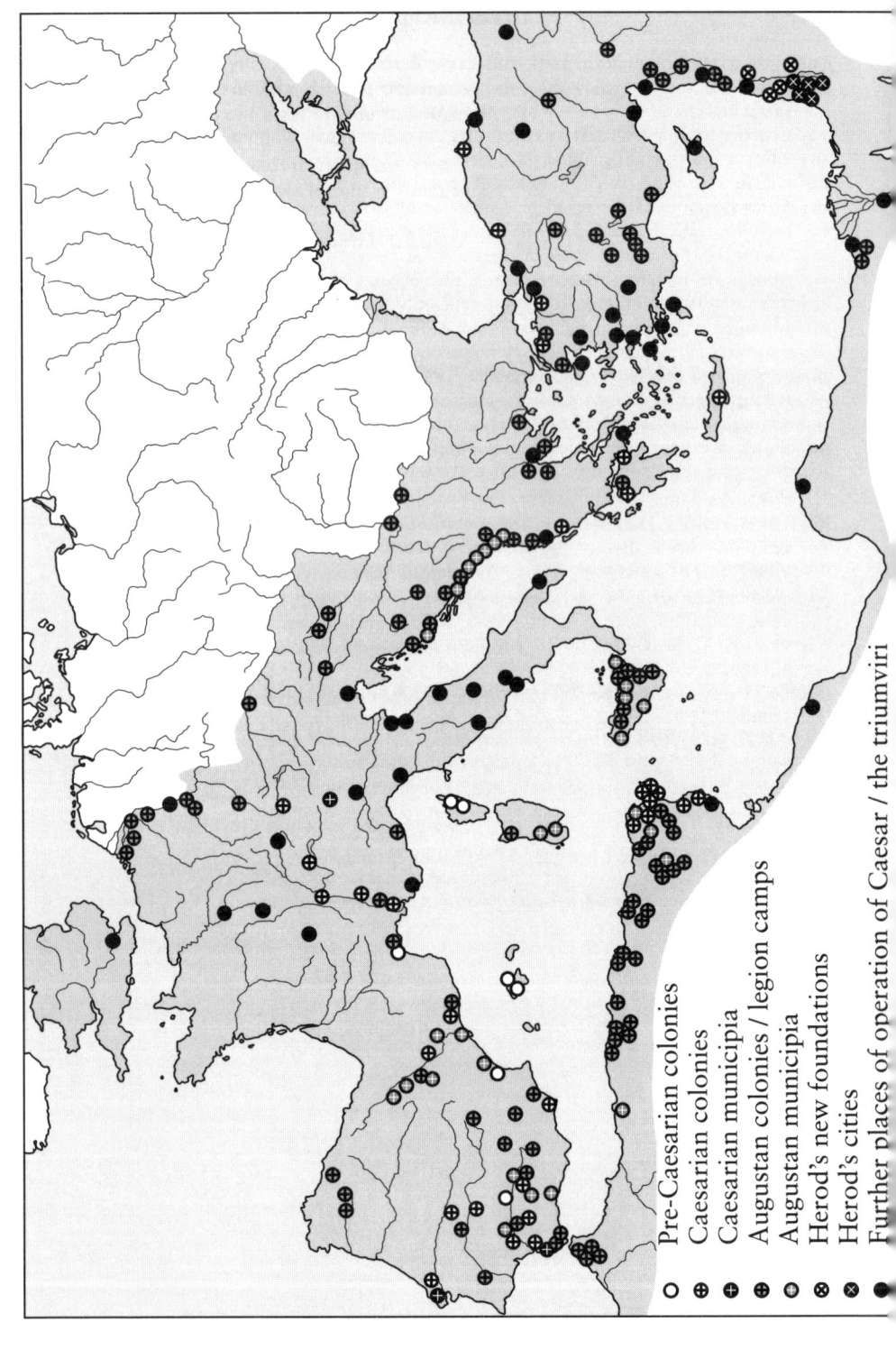

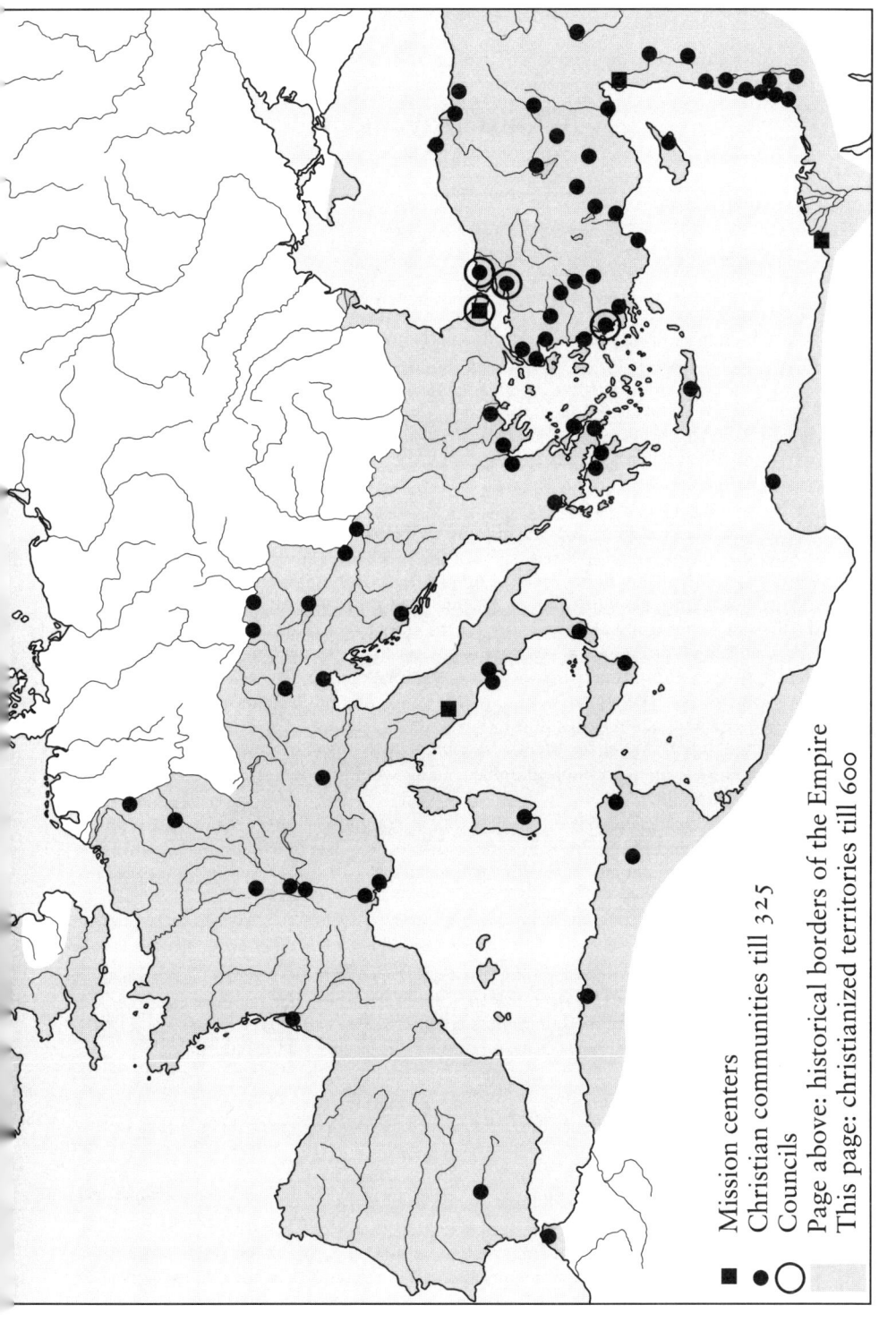

Acknowledgements

All those who have assisted me in these years with suggestions, criticism, patience, active help or effective advice putting forward new elements, I hereby express my most cordial thanks: to the friends from Tübingen, Berlin, Frankfurt/M, Munich, Zürich, Karlsruhe and Freiburg as well as those from Athens, Oxford, Saint Petersburg, Verona and Utrecht. Furthermore I am grateful for the latest help from Waren/Müritz, Sydney, Toledo (USA), Konstanz, Honolulu and Madrid.

I would like to emphatically thank:

Erika Simon, who had the kindness and courage to write the afterword; even more for her writing those lines about the Torlonia Head, which provoked its perception as Caesar's Pietà and with it gave the impulse to this work. Her informations and tips in the questions concerning archaeology and the proofreading of the chapter Crux were very adjuvant. Fotis Kavoukopoulos in Athens, previously at the University of Crete, and today at the Pedagogical Institute of Athens (Ministry of Education), for the foreword, the linguistic counseling and especially for the clues to the dramatic development of the Greek language during the 1st century AD. Gert Lüderitz, theologian and epigraphist from Tübingen, for the many tips and the specialist expertise from the profession's point of view. Bernhard Drinnenberg for support with the first outline concept and proofreading. Rainer Kimmig, indologist at the Univeristy of Tübingen, for orientating references ex oriente. Hubert Walter for friendly assistance with image processing.

I thank Margarete without whom this book would never have come about and to whom I dedicate it.

I thank Rodolfo, who passed away before its completion, who provided me with the spark of social and liberal ethos for life; and Rita, who has followed him by now, who instilled in me faith but also suspiciousness: the desire to know everything and to believe nothing.

Francesco Carotta

P.S. A special thanks for proofreading the English rough translation to Gary Courtney, author of an autonomous book on this topic (see Literature). Furthermore I thank in advance all those who want to communicate their criticism and suggestions to me – I shall answer to the best of my ability. You can contact me, besides via the publishing house, at:

jesus.caesar@carotta.de
www.carotta.de/forum.html

—where you will also learn about current issues on the progress of this work as well as further background information.

On the preceding two pages—Maps:

113. The comparison between the Roman colonization (top) and Christianity (bottom) illustrates that the latter spread from the East, however across the territory of the colonies founded by Caesar and Octavianus and within the borders of the Empire defined by them.